Selected Works

Also by Terrence McNally

Corpus Christi

Some Men and Deuce

Dedication or The Stuff of Dreams

The Stendhal Syndrome

What Every Catholic Should Know

Kiss of the Spider Woman

Three Plays by Terrence McNally

Selected Works

A Memoir in Plays

TERRENCE McNALLY

Grove Press
New York

Published simultaneously in Canada
Printed in the United States of America

FIRST EDITION

ISBN 978-0-8021-2357-2

Grove Press
an imprint of Grove Atlantic
154 West 14th Street
New York, NY 10011

Distributed by Publishers Group West

groveatlantic.com

15 16 17 18   10 9 8 7 6 5 4 3 2 1

For my husband, Tom Kirdahy

CONTENTS

AT RISE

This is how my plays begin. So shall these few words about *Terrence McNally: A Memoir in Plays.*

A memoir is selective memory. It's how the writer wants to be remembered. It's the whole truth and nothing but the truth—all from one unchallenged point of view. There is no prosecutor, no judge, no moral referee even. A good liar can write a good memoir: "It's my life; I'll describe and define it as I wish." A great liar will write an even better one. The truth needs massaging. That's what artists do: improve the truth and find meaning in "all our yesterdays (that) have lighted fools the way to dusty death."

Critics and scholars write biographies, sometimes lasting ones; artists write memoirs, their side of their own story, at least as they choose to tell it. More importantly, they leave behind a body of work. The real truth about an artist is in the work and there is no getting away from the work. It all begins and ends with it. It tells more about an artist than any amount of biographical research or autobiographical self-recrimination ever will.

In that spirit, I offer these eight plays, written over the past quarter of a century. Some of them are generally considered my "best" plays, a designation no parent likes, but they are each representative of who I am, both as a playwright and a fellow traveler on this planet. These plays, and the many others not included in this volume, are my truth. I cannot put a spin on them. They are what they are. They are my last, my only, appeal to the jury.

I'd been asked before to write a perhaps more conventional memoir. Perhaps I will one day. I arrived in New York at the end of the Golden Age of Broadway and participated firsthand in the exhilarating birth of Off-Broadway and a whole new generation of American playwrights. I've grown up and grown old with a lot of famous men and women. I've worked hard. I still do. I am a lucky man.

But for the moment, this anthology of plays and informal recollections of how and why some of them were written, is how I choose to tell my story, some of my colleagues' stories, and how we lived and worked together in a common pursuit: to tell the truth. It's a theatrical truth, to be sure, but something very close to the one that we all experience yet find so difficult to articulate.

It can't be Googled, that's for certain. The American Theatre just may be the last mom-and-pop business in America. The movies aren't; television isn't. If you see a play tonight, you can be certain one person, not a corporation or a board of directors, wrote it. That is theatre's primal truth.

The day this is no longer true must never come.

So once more unto the breach, dear friends, once more.

At rise:

Terrence McNally, January 2015

FRANKIE AND JOHNNY
IN THE CLAIR DE LUNE (1987)

I distinctly remember the inspiration for *Frankie and Johnny in the Clair de Lune*. It was a bitterly cold Saturday night in New York and I was standing in line at my corner Blockbuster in Chelsea waiting to check out the videos I had so carefully chosen to spend the rest of my weekend watching alone.

I don't remember the titles, not a one of them. What remains vivid is how many of us were in that line. Each of us, male and female, gay and straight, had decided to spend the next thirty-six hours in front of our VCRs watching movies instead of talking or laughing or making love with someone else.

None of us was very young but none of us was very old either. I was single again and approaching fifty myself. We were all at that age when most people want to be partnered with someone they love but have grown weary of the search and wary of who was still out there. The ritual of dating is best enjoyed by people in high school. It is no fun for people approaching fifty.

Positioned cannily next to the checkout station was a freezer filled with ice cream of every flavor imaginable. Next to that was an abundance of popcorn, potato chips and pretzels. Excellent. No need to shop for food now either. Häagen-Dazs and Pringles were all any of us needed to make it to Monday morning.

Frankie and Johnny is about a man who gets off that line to look for something more. It's about a woman with no expectations for just about anything. It's a play about a couple taking the first tentative step towards eyes-wide-open intimacy. Brushing your teeth together as they do at the play's end can be a beautiful thing.

I didn't start writing the play when I got back to my apartment or even the morning after. Inspiration is a shock of recognition. You still have to write the play and writing is writing, it always will be. Inspiration becomes intuition as you try to find the way to tell the story you want to tell. It was a couple of years until I found my way to this one: just how many of us were out there not even trying to connect with one another anymore.

It was a bleak time in New York for people like Frankie and Johnny. The economy was bad. People who could afford to were leaving the city. AIDS had made the most basic expressions of affection and desire an occasion for fear and distrust as well. There was no time less romantic in Manhattan than the late 1980s when I began to write the play, nor an apartment less comforting than Frankie's where I set it. If love were going to conquer all, it would have a good fight on its hands.

Frankie and Johnny is the first play of my second act as a playwright. In the 60s, 70s and 80s I was everywhere learning my craft: Broadway, Off-Broadway, Off-Off-Broadway, regional theatres. Many of those plays were successful and are still done and one of them, my very first, . . .*And Things That Go Bump in the Night* in 1965, was a Broadway fiasco of legendary proportions. (I remembered that experience when I wrote *Broadway, Broadway,* which closed out of town during its pre-Broadway tryout in Philadelphia in 1978. Thirty-six years later it made it successfully to Broadway as *It's Only a Play*).

These plays—*Next, The Ritz, Bad Habits* and *Where Has Tommy Flowers Gone?* the most notable of them—now seem to be the first act for the plays that were to come. None of them are included in this collection. Because of length, it was a Hobson's choice. Fortunately, it was not a Sophie's. They are all available in acting editions.

What most characterizes my earlier plays is how much I figure in them. My own voice is too often louder than the voices of my characters. I am so eager to let the audience know how I feel about everything and everyone that I can fall into either preaching or caricature, two cardinal sins if you aim to be a good and honest playwright. My two gods are Shakespeare and Chekhov and they committed neither.

You can look in vain through Shakespeare's play for his philosophy or his opinion of his characters. The man is nowhere to be found in them, only the playwright. He allows his characters their full range of humanity and consequent complexity without revealing his own hand. Chekhov is equally invisible in his assessment of the human situation and the people in it. In-stead, he lets the audience decide who is "good," who is "bad," and who is merely human. I have never tired of seeing their plays performed, of study-ing them, or simply reveling in their craft and artistry. You cannot over-read or over-study or over-know *King Lear* or *The Seagull*. It would be a foolish playwright who did not know his or her Shakespeare and Chekhov. It's the best piece of advice I give when I speak with young playwrights. That, and to read Moss Hart's *Act One* and to decide for yourself if you want to spend the rest of your life collaborating with actors, directors, designers and producers. A novelist works with his or her editor; a playwright works with legions.

It is not a career for the arrogant or the thin-skinned. A novelist never has to stand shoulder to shoulder at a urinal during intermission while men to either side of him say uncomplimentary things about his work. Of course a novelist is not present for a standing ovation either, so I suppose it's a trade-off.

I don't take it on good faith that people like a play of mine; I know if they, or don't, simply by standing at the back of the theatre and being one of them. There is no hiding from an audience, even a rave from the *New York Times* won't protect you from an unhappy one.

I began the actual work on *Frankie and Johnny* during the summer of 1986 when I was invited to participate in the playwright's conference at the Sundance Institute in Utah. Robert Redford and Sundance have done more for the performing arts in this country than has ever been appropriately recognized. I hadn't been out of the city in years when I was invited there and I flourished in the mountain air and clear light.

I was writing the part of Johnny for F. Murray Abraham, an actor who had been so wonderful in so many of my plays, especially *Tommy Flowers* and *Bad Habits*. Frankie would be Liza Minnelli. I had met Liza on *The Rink,* an original musical I wrote with John Kander and Fred Ebb. They had begun the project with another playwright and had already written the score. That was the first and last time I will write a libretto to a preexisting score. I was writing to connect the dots instead of inspiring my collaborators to make new music where there had only been dialogue.

I had a crush on Liza Minnelli. Everyone did. Mine was a talent crush. I thought she could do anything. She taught me a lot about generosity in the theatre. She gave 100% of herself every performance. Why shouldn't a playwright? Her costar, Chita Rivera, taught me about technique. Without technique, an actor only hits the bull's-eye on occasion. With solid technique, a performer hits it every performance. I still had a lot to learn from both women.

So when Liza asked me to write her a *real* play, a *serious* play, I agreed without hesitation. My play would reveal to the world the fine dramatic actress that Liza and I knew she could be.

To the best of my knowledge, and to make a long story short, Liza has never read *Frankie and Johnny*. I don't remember to how many addresses in how many exotic locations I Fed-Exed her the script. Somehow it always got lost or left behind in her nomadic life. After a year of waiting for her, I asked an actress I had met at Sundance when I was just beginning the play if she would like to play Frankie. In fact, she had inspired me with her honest acting as much as Liza had with her one-of-a-kind charisma.

Her name was Kathy Bates and the truth was I would develop an even deeper talent crush on her than I did on Liza. I had seen her in Marsha Norman's *'Night Mother* and been devastated by the raw force and bold truth of her performance. She made me want to write deeper and better for *myself,* not for someone else. I had found a muse. The truth is I was imagining her as Frankie even as I was writing the part for Liza. I never told Kathy the play had been intended for someone else. I didn't have to—she made it indelibly her own.

With F. Murray Abraham as Johnny, we inaugurated Manhattan Theatre Club's Stage II in the spring of 1987. From the first preview, the play was successful and Lynne Meadow, MTC's artistic director, asked us to put off the critics until the beginning of the new season when she would officially open the play at Stage I, which was considerably larger and more prestigious. Everyone agreed and after a month of sold-out preview performances, we parted company for the summer.

In early September, when we reassembled, Murray was no longer part of the company. He had "gotten a movie." We were all understandably devastated. He was a star. He'd won the Best Actor Oscar for *Amadeus*. No one I'd written the play for would be in it. First Liza, now Murray.

The same thing happened several years later when Kathy "got a movie" and was unable to appear in *Lips Together, Teeth Apart*. This time it was a part I had written only for Kathy. By then, she had already won *her* Oscar for *Misery*. Again, I was devastated but I would soon learn these were occupational hazards. Actors are always "getting movies" or television pilots. The sooner a disillusioned playwright accepts that, the better. Hollywood's seduction of the theatre's steadily shrinking talent pool of actors, writers and directors is not going to stop. In retrospect, I'm lucky Hollywood's attempts at wooing me were so infrequent and halfhearted.

Fortunately, Kenneth Welsh was an amazing Johnny, albeit a very different one than Murray's. The play still "worked" and Kathy was happy as a clam—just as Nathan Lane, Christine Baranski and Anthony Heald took a collective sigh of relief when Swoosie Kurtz came to our rescue in Kathy's absence. Like it or not, everyone is replaceable. I don't like it, I never will, but watching actors like Kennie and Swoosie in rehearsal and in performance, I have come to admit it's true.

A lot of great actresses have played Frankie but it will always be Kathy Bates's play. She inspired it as much as those people on line with me in Chelsea or Liza Minnelli, for whom I had made it my mission to write the greatest female role since Cleopatra.

There is an enormous difference writing a part *for* an actor and writing a part *about* them. I have written many plays for Nathan Lane but I have never written a character for him to play that even remotely resembles the Nathan I know offstage. If I did write parts *about* certain actors, no one else would be very good in them and the plays would have a very short performance life. *Frankie and Johnny* is one of my most-performed plays because the parts are rich enough for actors as different as Kathy Bates and Edie Falco, who revived the play on Broadway and Michelle Pfeiffer, who did the movie, to play them effectively. Nathan Lane has a small part in the film and at that stage in his career I thought I was (we both thought, actually) doing him a favor. Unfortunately, my attempt to "open up" a two-character play as a film with a part for a talented friend—while understandable—was ineffectual. *Frankie and Johnny* stubbornly remained a film about just them.

The film also reveals how "unnatural" a play *Frankie and Johnny* is. The original production was reviewed as if I had finally discovered naturalism after my satiric, more overtly comic earlier work. Audiences are too easily fooled by someone making a Western omelet or peeling an onion. The smells of cooking permeated the theatre when the play premiered *but Frankie and Johnny* remains a poetic experience, not a realistic one. Real. That word has gotten more people into trouble in the theatre than any other. Actors try to be real and forget how to act. Audiences always know they are in a theatre waiting to be entertained; actors should remember that. They do most of the time. Great actors do all of the time.

The theatre is an illusion of reality, never reality itself. Plays are a re-enactment of something that has already happened: either in history or in the playwright's imagination. A play is a staging of what has already happened as if it were happening for the very first time. It's called a play because an actress is pretending to be Frankie. The actor pretending to be Johnny is pretending she's Frankie. The audience is pretending the actress and actor are Frankie and Johnny. It's called theatre and for a couple of hours we pretend we're somewhere else. Sometimes those hours are golden and deeply moving or hilarious and take our mind off things. They can also make us think. They can disturb and challenge us with intellectual points of view that are not our own. When they achieve that, the hours of theatre are real and precious, but that is not often, no matter how hard we try. Playwriting and theatre are hard; so is changing people's hearts and minds. I have always wanted to do both. Preaching to the choir has never been my style.

I dedicated *Frankie and Johnny* to my high school English teacher, Maurine McElroy. Mrs. Mac taught me to love the English language and not be afraid of Shakespeare. I wanted to dedicate a play to her that she might have heard about all the way down in Austin, where she was teaching at the University of Texas. I feared word about some of my earlier efforts had not spread to my adopted home state.

When I was able to bring her up to New York for the Broadway 2002 revival of the play and put her up in the Dorothy Parker suite at the Algonquin Hotel on West 44th St., it was one of the proudest nights of my life. I mention "Mrs. Mac" in many of my plays. I don't believe we can ever thank our teachers enough. My grandparents and parents took me to my first Broadway shows on trips to the city but it was Mrs. McElroy who made me understand that someone had written *Julius Caesar* and *Macbeth* and that his name was William Shakespeare and he would be my friend for life.

My only advice to actors and directors who are doing *Frankie and Johnny in the Clair de Lune* is to remember that the omelets and onions and the actors are real but Frankie and Johnny are characters in a play by Terrence McNally. The feelings they bring to it and evoke from the audience are also real. Everything else is *poetic* realism, which is easier said than achieved. It means *realer* than real. It means finding the essence of the words, the gestures we use to communicate with one another. I think we go to the theatre to learn how to be better, fuller human beings. Or at least be reminded that we can be.

Frankie and Johnny
in the Clair de Lune

for Maurine McElroy

FRANKIE AND JOHNNY IN THE CLAIR DE LUNE was first produced by the Manhattan Theatre Club Stage II at City Center in New York City on June 2nd, 1987, with the following cast:

FRANKIE   Kathy Bates

JOHNNY   F. Murray Abraham

VOICE OF RADIO ANNOUNCER   Dominic Cuskern

It transferred to Manhattan Theatre Club Stage I at City Center on October 14th, 1987, with the following cast:

FRANKIE   Kathy Bates

JOHNNY   Kenneth Welsh

VOICE OF RADIO ANNOUNCER   Dominic Cuskern

Both productions were directed by Paul Benedict. Sets by James Noone. Costumes by David Woolard. Lighting by David Noling. Sound by John Gromada. The Production Stage Manager was Pamela Singer.

This production transferred to the Westside Arts Theatre in New York City on December 4th, 1987. It was produced by Steven Baruch, Thomas Viertel, Richard Frankel and Jujamcyn Theatres/Margo Lion.

The present.

New York City

SETTING

Frankie's one-room apartment in a walk-up tenement in the West 50s. The fourth wall looks onto the backyard and the apartments behind. When the sofa bed is down, as it is for much of the play, the room is quite cramped.

CHARACTERS

FRANKIE

Striking but not conventional good looks. She has a sense of humor and fairly tough exterior. She is also frightened and can be very hard to reach.

JOHNNY

Johnny's best feature is his personality. He works at it. He is in good physical condition.

ACT ONE

AT RISE: Darkness. We hear the sounds of a man and a woman making love. They are getting ready to climax. The sounds they are making are noisy, ecstatic and familiar. Above all, they must be graphic. The intention is a portrait in sound of a passionate man and woman making love and reaching climax together.

The real thing.

They came.

Silence. Heavy breathing. We become aware that the radio has been playing Bach's Goldberg Variations in the piano version.

By this point, the curtain has been up for at least two minutes. No light, no dialogue, just the sounds of lovemaking and now the Bach.

FRANKIE   God, I wish I still smoked. Life used to be so much more fun. (*Johnny laughs softly.*)

What?

JOHNNY   Nothing. (*He laughs again, a little louder.*) Oh, God!

FRANKIE   Well it must be something!

JOHNNY   It's dumb, it's gross, it's stupid . . . (*He howls with laughter.*) I'm sorry. Jesus, this is terrible. I don't know what's gotten into me. I'll be all right. (*He catches his breath. Frankie turns on a bedside lamp.*) Really, I'm sorry. It has nothing to do with you.

FRANKIE   Are you okay now?

JOHNNY   Yes. No! (*He bursts into laughter again. And now Frankie bursts into laughter: a wild, uncontrollable, infectious sound.*) What are you laughing at?

FRANKIE   I don't know! (*Now they are both laughing hilariously. It is the kind of laughter that gets out of control and people have trouble breathing. Frankie rolls off the bed and lands on the floor with a slight thud.*)

JOHNNY   Are you okay?

FRANKIE   No! (*Now it is Frankie who is laughing solo. It is a wonderfully joyful sound: a lot of stored-up feeling is being released.*)

JOHNNY   Should I get you something?

FRANKIE   Yes! My mother!

JOHNNY   A beer, a Coke, anything?

FRANKIE   A bag to put over my head!

JOHNNY   You really want your mother?

FRANKIE   Are you crazy?

JOHNNY   You have the most . . . the most wonderful breasts.

FRANKIE   Thank you. (*She bursts into new laughter. This time Johnny doesn't join in at all. Eventually they are both still. They listen to the Bach in silence without moving.*)

That's nice music. Very . . . I want to say "chaste."

JOHNNY   I'll tell you why I was laughing. All of a sudden—just like that!—I remembered this time back in high school when I was making out with this really beautiful girl and was feeling incredibly suave and sophisticated and wondering if anybody would believe my good fortune and worrying if she was going to let me go all the way—I think it would have been her first time too—when all of a sudden I let out this incredibly loud fart. Like that. Only louder. It was awful. (*He laughs again.*) And there was no pretending it wasn't me. You couldn't say something like "Boy, did you hear that thunder?" or "Jesus, Peggy was that you?" The best I could come up with was "May I use your bathroom?" which only made it worse. And there in the bathroom was her mother taking a bath at ten o'clock at night. She has one arm up, washing her armpit. I said something real cool like, "Hello, Mrs. Roberts." She screamed and I ran out of the house. I tripped over the garbage cans and tore my pants climbing over the backyard fence. I must've run twenty blocks, most of them with dogs chasing me. I thought my life was over. We never mentioned what happened and I never dated her again and I lost my virginity with someone else. But why that fart banged back into my consciousness just then . . . !

FRANKIE   Could we change the subject?

JOHNNY   What's the matter?

FRANKIE   I'm not a prude . . .

JOHNNY   I know that! Any woman who . . .

FRANKIE   I just . . . we all draw the line somewhere.

JOHNNY   And with you it's farts?

FRANKIE   Is that going to be a problem?

JOHNNY   You don't think any kind of farting is funny?

FRANKIE   Not off the top of my head I don't.

JOHNNY   Hunh! I always have. I don't know why I find a lot of things funny. Like Corgis.

FRANKIE   Corgis?

JOHNNY   You know the dogs the Queen of England has?

FRANKIE   No.

JOHNNY   Sure you do. They're about this big, tan, and look like walking heads. Every time I see one, I get hysterical. Show me a Corgi and I'm yours.

FRANKIE   I guess a farting Corgi would really lay you out!

JOHNNY   See? You do have a sense of humor about it! (*They both laugh. Then silence. The Bach plays on.*)

FRANKIE   You know what I mean? About the music? It's pure.

JOHNNY   Did you come?

FRANKIE   No one's that good at faking it.

JOHNNY   I thought so. Good. I'm glad.

FRANKIE   There! Hear that? It makes me think of . . . grace.

JOHNNY   You mean, the thing it's good to be in the state of?

FRANKIE   The movement kind. You know . . . (*She moves her arm in a flowing gesture and sways her shoulders to the music.*) Flowing.

JOHNNY   So why were you laughing?

FRANKIE   I don't know. Because you were, I guess. You sounded so happy. Little did I know!

JOHNNY   I *was* happy. I'm still happy. Where are you going?

FRANKIE   Nowhere.

JOHNNY   You're going somewhere.

FRANKIE   The closet.

JOHNNY   Why?

FRANKIE   A robe.

JOHNNY   You don't need a—

FRANKIE   I'm cold.

JOHNNY   I want to bask in your nakedness.

FRANKIE   Sure you do. (*Frankie turns on the overhead room light.*)

JOHNNY   Ow!

FRANKIE   I'm sorry, I'm sorry! (*She turns off the overhead light. The first quick impression we have of the room is that it is modest and not especially tidy.*)

JOHNNY   Warn somebody when you're going to do that! I hate bright lights but especially right after making love. Talk about a mood changer! Besides, I think you see the other person better in the light of the afterglow. (*Pause.*) Did you hear what I just said?

FRANKIE   Yes.

JOHNNY   Just checking. (*While Frankie gets a robe out of the closet, Johnny goes through her purse on the bed table until he finds a pair of sunglasses.*)

FRANKIE   Remember when everybody used to light up the second it seemed they were through making love? "I'm coming, I'm coming, I came. You got a match?"

JOHNNY   I didn't smoke.

FRANKIE   Never?

JOHNNY   Ever.

FRANKIE   You've got a smoker's personality.

JOHNNY   That's what they tell me.

FRANKIE   I just made that up.

JOHNNY   So did I. And I didn't like the women who did.

FRANKIE   Did what? Smoked? Then you would have hated me. Marla the Human Furnace.

JOHNNY   Marla? I thought your name was Frances.

FRANKIE   It is, it is! Don't panic. I just made that up, too. I don't know where it came from. From what Freudian depth it sprung.

JOHNNY   Marla! Ecchh!

FRANKIE   You put too much stock in this name business, John. (*She comes back wearing a bathrobe. Johnny looks fairly ridiculous in her sunglasses.*)

JOHNNY   It's Johnny, please.

FRANKIE   Are those mine? I wish you'd stay out of my—

JOHNNY   I hate John.

FRANKIE   Did you hear me?

JOHNNY   I heard you.

FRANKIE   I wish you'd act like you heard me.

JOHNNY   May I wear your sunglasses?

FRANKIE   Yes.

JOHNNY   Thank you. God, you're beautiful. Are you coming back to bed?

FRANKIE   I don't know.

JOHNNY   John sounds like a toilet or a profession. And Jack only works if you're a Kennedy or a Nicholson.

FRANKIE   I read somewhere there are millions of young people, a whole generation, who don't have a clue who John Kennedy was. Do you believe it? To me, he was only yesterday. I love Jack Nicholson. Did you see *Prizzi's Honor*?

JOHNNY   Six times.

FRANKIE   Six times?

JOHNNY   The first time I popped for it, six bucks, the good old days, remember them? Seven bucks to get my goat, don't get me started! Then five on VCR, you know, a rental, when I was getting over my hernia and I couldn't get out of bed so hot.

FRANKIE   You've got a VCR?

JOHNNY   Oh sure. Stereo, TV, VCR. I'm working on a dish.

FRANKIE   And you've got a hernia?

JOHNNY   Had, had. Here, I'll show you.

FRANKIE   Wow. That's big. Did it hurt?

JOHNNY   *Comme ci, comme ça.* You got any scars?

FRANKIE   Everybody has scars.

JOHNNY   Where? I'll just look.

FRANKIE   No.

JOHNNY   Okay, okay. You know, they filmed it right near where I live.

FRANKIE   *Prizzi's Honor?*

JOHNNY   Oh sure.

FRANKIE   In Brooklyn?

JOHNNY   Brooklyn Heights. Please, don't get us confused with the rest of the borough. Would you like it if I referred to your neighborhood as Chinatown?

FRANKIE   Fifty-third and Tenth?

JOHNNY   Anyway! You know the house that guy lived in, the one with the funny voice? Hinley or something. He got nominated for an Oscar or something but I don't think he won. Or maybe he did.

FRANKIE   The one who played the Don?

JOHNNY   That's the one. Headley, Henkley, Hinley.

FRANKIE   You live in that house?

JOHNNY   No, but I can see their roof from my bathroom window.

FRANKIE   Oh.

JOHNNY   You know what those movie stars get when they're on location like that? Their own trailers with their name on the door. Big long trailers. Not like the kind you see in Montauk, those ugly little Airstream jobbies. At least I think they're ugly. No, these are the big long kind like you see sitting up on blocks in a trailer park that people live in full time, people who aren't going anywhere in 'em they're so big! I'm talking trailers with bedrooms and bathtubs. I'm talking major mobile homes.

FRANKIE   I hate trailers.

JOHNNY   So do I. That's not the point.

FRANKIE   I'd rather die than live in a trailer. The very words "mobile home" strike me with such terror.

JOHNNY   I believe I had the floor.

FRANKIE   Who the hell wants a living room that moves for Christ's sake? Ecch! Sorry.

JOHNNY   Anyway, they each have their own trailer. I mean, Jack Nicholson is on one side of the street in his block-long trailer and Kathleen Turner is on the other in hers.

FRANKIE   I'm sorry but I don't get her message.

JOHNNY   Will you let me finish?

FRANKIE   Do you?

JOHNNY   Yes, but that's not the point either. They also give these trailers to people you never even heard of, like this Hinley, Headley, Hinckley, what's-his-face character.

FRANKIE   Is that the point?

JOHNNY   I'm not saying he's not a good actor but his own trailer? I'm in the wrong business.

FRANKIE   We both are.

JOHNNY   Do you think I talk too much?

FRANKIE   I don't think you always give the other person a chance to—

JOHNNY   That's what my best friend says. "I talk because I got a lot to say, Ernie," I tell him but he doesn't seem to understand that. Talking to you comes real easy. I appreciate that. And I won't pretend I wasn't looking forward to this evening.

FRANKIE   Well, it's been very—

JOHNNY   What do you mean, "been"? It still is. "The night is young, the stars are clear and if you care to go walking, dear." I admit I love the sound of my own voice. So shoot me, give me the electric chair, it ain't over till the fat lady sings. Can I have a beer?

FRANKIE   I'm sorry.

JOHNNY   You say that too much. (*He goes to refrigerator as Frankie crosses to floor lamp by easy chair and turns it on.*)

FRANKIE   Is this okay? I hate gloom.

JOHNNY   Light like this is fine. It's the harsh blinding kind I can't stand. Now where are you going?

FRANKIE   Just in here. (*She goes to bathroom door, opens it, turns on light, goes in, leaving door open so that more light spills into the room.*) Keep talking. I can hear you.

JOHNNY   You mean about the light? There are some delicatessens I just won't go into, they're so bright. There's one over on Madison Avenue and 28th St. that is so bright from the overhead fluorescents that you wouldn't believe it. I complained. I don't even like to shop there and I complained. "What are you trying to do? Get an airplane to land in here?" They just looked at me like I was an idiot. Of course, I doubt if they even spoke English. Most Koreans don't. It's getting to the point where you can count on one hand the number of people who speak English in this city. (*He goes to bathroom door and stands watching Frankie within.*) Look, I know I talk too much. It's just that certain things get my goat. Things like ninety-foot trailers for people I never heard of . . . (*Frankie comes out of the bathroom. She has changed into a brightly colored kimono. She has a hairbrush in her hand and will brush her hair during the following.*) Hi there.

FRANKIE   Hello.

JOHNNY   . . . waste, especially water—you got a leaky faucet around here? Lady, I'm your plumber—and the fact this is supposed to be an English-speaking nation only nobody speaks English anymore. Other than that, I'm cool and I'll shut up now and won't say another word. I'm locking my mouth and throwing away the key. (*He watches Frankie brush her hair.*)

FRANKIE   Did you get Easter off? (*Johnny shakes his head.*) Neither did I. And watch us twiddle our thumbs. Last Easter you could've shot a moose in there. Forget tips. I've already decided, I'm gonna call in sick. Life's too short, you know? You want some juice? It's homemade. I mean, I squeezed it myself. That's right, you're working on a beer. I'd offer you a joint but I don't do that anymore. Not that I think other people shouldn't. It's just that I can't personally handle it anymore. I mean, I didn't like what it was doing to me. I mean, the bottom line is: it isn't good for you. For me, I mean. It isn't good for me. Hey, come on, don't!

JOHNNY   Can I say one more thing?

FRANKIE   I wish you would.

JOHNNY   I could watch you do that for maybe the rest of my life.

FRANKIE   Get real.

JOHNNY   I think a woman brushing and fixing her hair is one of the supremely great sights of life. I'd put it up there with the Grand Canyon and a mother nursing her child. Triumphant facts of nature. That's all. Now I'm locking my eyes shut and throwing away the key. (*He closes his eyes.*)

FRANKIE   What am I supposed to do?

JOHNNY   Sshh, pretend you can't hear. Next thing she'll want is your ears.

FRANKIE   Oh my God, it's three o'clock! Look, I'd ask you to stay over but . . . I don't know about you but I'm kind of drained, you know? I mean, that was pretty intense back there. Harrowing. No, not harrowing, that doesn't sound right. I'm too pooped to pop, all right? Oh come on, you know what I mean. (*Johnny inhales very slowly and very deeply.*)

JOHNNY   She's wearing something new. This part is called Scent Torture. I love it. I love it!

FRANKIE   You know, you're a very intense person. One minute you're making love like somebody just let you out of jail and the next you're telling me watching me brush my hair is like the Grand Canyon. Very intense or very crazy. Look, I'm glad what happened happened. If we both play our cards right, maybe it will happen again . . . Hello?

JOHNNY   I hear you.

FRANKIE   I wish you'd open your eyes. (*Johnny very slowly opens his eyes and turns his face to Frankie. He reacts as if blinded.*)

JOHNNY   Aaaagggg! It's worse than the delicatessen! Such blinding beauty!

FRANKIE   I'm serious. (*Johnny stops screaming and looks at her again.*)

JOHNNY (*Quietly.*)   So am I.

FRANKIE   That's exactly what I mean. One minute you're kidding and the next you're looking at me like that.

JOHNNY   Like what?

FRANKIE   Like that! People don't go around looking at one another like that. It's too intense. You don't look, you stare. It gives me the creeps. I suppose it's very flattering but it's not something I feel real comfortable with. It's like if you would send me a million roses, I'd be impressed but I wouldn't know where to put them. I don't need a million roses. One would be just fine. So if you just looked at me *occasionally* in the future like that. Look, obviously I like you. I like you a lot. What's the matter?

JOHNNY   I'm just drinking all this in.

FRANKIE   You're not the easiest person to talk to anybody ever met.

JOHNNY   I certainly hope not. How old are you?

FRANKIE   None of your business. How old are you?

JOHNNY   What do you think?

FRANKIE   Mid-forties.

JOHNNY   Ouch!

FRANKIE   Maybe late-thirties.

JOHNNY   I can live with that.

FRANKIE   Come on, how old are you?

JOHNNY   I don't know.

FRANKIE   Everybody knows how old they are.

JOHNNY   I used to, then I forgot.

FRANKIE   That's a great answer. Can I borrow it?

JOHNNY   I did.

FRANKIE   Who from?

JOHNNY   Some old lady on the Carson show? I don't remember. Half the things I got up here, I don't remember where they came from. It doesn't seem fair. People ought to get credit for all the things they give and teach us. You're fabulous.

FRANKIE   I feel like I'm supposed to say "thank you."

JOHNNY   It's not necessary.

FRANKIE   Instead, I want to ask you to quit sneaking up on me like that. We're talking about one thing, people who teach, and wham! you slip in there with some kind of intimate, personal remark. I like being told I'm fabulous. Who wouldn't? I'd like some warning first, that's all. This is not a spontaneous person you have before you.

JOHNNY   You're telling me that wasn't spontaneous?

FRANKIE   That was different. I'm talking about the larger framework of things. What people are doing in your life. What they're doing in your bed is easy or at least it used to be back before we had to start checking each other out. I don't know about you but I get so sick and tired of living this way, that we're gonna die from one another, that every so often I just want to act like Saturday night really is a Saturday night, the way it used to be.

JOHNNY   I'm very glad we had this Saturday night.

FRANKIE   I never would have said that if I knew you better.

JOHNNY   How well do you want to know me?

FRANKIE   I'll let you know Monday between orders. "I got a BLT down working!" "Tell me about your childhood." "Take the moo out of two!" "Were you toilet trained?"

JOHNNY   Come here.

FRANKIE   Are you sure you don't want something before you go?

JOHNNY Come here.

FRANKIE I've got some meat loaf in the fridge.

JOHNNY Come here. (*Frankie moves a few steps towards Johnny, who is sitting on the edge of the bed.*)

FRANKIE What?

JOHNNY Closer. (*Frankie moves closer to Johnny, who pulls her all the way towards him and buries his face in her middle.*)

FRANKIE I can toast some bread. Butter and catsup. A cold meat loaf sandwich. All the way back to Brooklyn . . .

JOHNNY Heights.

FRANKIE Heights! This time of night. Aren't you hungry?

JOHNNY I'm starving.

FRANKIE No!

JOHNNY Why not?

FRANKIE We just did.

JOHNNY So?

FRANKIE I can't.

JOHNNY What do you mean, you can't?

FRANKIE I don't want to. (*Johnny immediately stops nuzzling Frankie. Both hands fly up with palms outward.*)

You don't have to take it like that. I'm sorry. Just not right now. You know, you're right: I do say "I'm sorry" a lot around you. There's something about you that makes me feel like I'm letting you down all the time. Like you have all these expectations of me that I can't fulfill. I'm sorry—there I go again!—but what you see here is what you get. I am someone who likes to eat after making love and right now I feel like a cold meat loaf sandwich on white toast with butter and catsup with a large glass of very cold milk and I wish you would stop looking at me like that.

JOHNNY Open your robe.

FRANKIE No. Why?

JOHNNY   I want to look at your pussy.

FRANKIE   No. Why?

JOHNNY   It's beautiful.

FRANKIE   It is not. You're just saying that.

JOHNNY   I think it is. I'm telling you, you have a beautiful pussy—!

FRANKIE   I hate that word, Johnny!

JOHNNY   —all right, thing! and I'm asking you to open your robe so I can look at it. Just look. Fifteen seconds. You can time me. Then you can make *two* cold meat loaf sandwiches and *two* big glasses of milk. Just hold the catsup on one.

FRANKIE   I don't know if you're playing games or being serious.

JOHNNY   Both. Serious games. Do you have to name everything? If I had said "You have a beautiful parakeet" you'd have let me see it and we'd be eating those sandwiches already.

FRANKIE   I had a parakeet. I hated it. I was glad when it died. (*She opens her robe.*) Okay?

JOHNNY   Oh! Yes!

FRANKIE (*Continuing to hold her robe open as Johnny sits on the edge of the bed and looks.*)   I'm timing this! I told my cousin I didn't want a bird. I hate birds. She swore I'd love a parakeet. What's to love? (*She almost drops the robe.*) They don't do anything except not sing when you want them to, sing when you don't and make those awful scratching noises on that awful sandpaper on the floor of their cell. I mean cage! If I ever have another pet it'll be a dog. A Golden Lab. Something that shows a little enthusiasm when you walk through the door. Something you can hold. The only time I got my hands on that goddamn parakeet was the day it dropped dead and I had to pick it up to throw it in the garbage can. Hey, come on! This has gotta be fifteen seconds. (*Frankie closes her robe. Johnny takes her hand, kisses it, rubs his cheek against it. Frankie stands awkwardly.*) You really would like a sandwich?

JOHNNY   But no catsup.

FRANKIE   Catsup's what makes a cold meat loaf sandwich good.

JOHNNY   I'm allergic. Catsup and peaches.

FRANKIE   Ugh!

JOHNNY   Well not in the same dish! (*He is still nuzzling her fingers.*)

FRANKIE   Can I have my hand back?

JOHNNY   Do you want it back?

FRANKIE   Well you want a sandwich, don't you?

JOHNNY   I want you to notice how we're connecting. My hand is flowing into yours. My eyes are trying to see inside yours.

FRANKIE   That's not connecting. That's holding and staring. Connecting is when the other person isn't even around and you could die from just thinking of them.

JOHNNY   That's missing. This is connecting.

FRANKIE   Yeah, well it ain't how a sandwich gets made. (*She takes her hand from Johnny and goes to kitchen area of the apartment where she takes out all the makings of her meat loaf sandwich and begins to prepare them. Johnny will just watch her from his place on the bed.*) My father used to say a good meat loaf and gravy with mashed potatoes was food fit for the gods.

JOHNNY   You're kidding! That's exactly what my old man used to say.

FRANKIE   Of course, considering our family budget we didn't have too many other options. Guess what, pop? I still don't. (*She laughs. Johnny laughs with her.*) You want to turn on the television?

JOHNNY   Why?

FRANKIE   We don't have to watch it. You know, just sound. I do it all the time. Company. It beats a parakeet.

JOHNNY   I'd rather watch you.

FRANKIE   Do you ever watch the Channel 5 Movie Club on Saturday night? That's right, you got a VCR. They have this thing called the Movie Club. Talk about dumb gimmicks. You put your name and address on a postcard. If they draw it, you go on the air and tell everybody what your favorite movie is and they show it, along with intermission breaks where they tell you certain little-known facts about the movie I just as soon wouldn't have known, such as "Susan Hayward was already stricken with fatal cancer when she made this sparkling comedy." Kind of puts a pall on things, you know?

JOHNNY   I was on that program.

FRANKIE   You were not.

JOHNNY   Sure I was.

FRANKIE   What was your favorite movie?

JOHNNY   I forget.

FRANKIE   You probably don't even have one. (*Johnny has gotten up off the bed and come over to where Frankie is working. He finds a place to sit very close to where she stands making the sandwiches.*)

JOHNNY   You know what I was thinking while I was looking at you over there?

FRANKIE   I should have guessed this was coming.

JOHNNY   I was thinking "There's got to be more to life than this," but at times like this I'll be goddamned if I know what it is.

FRANKIE   You don't give up, do you?

JOHNNY   I want to drown in this woman. I want to die here. So why is she talking about parakeets and meat loaf? The inequity of human relationships! I actually thought that word: "inequity." I didn't even know it was in my vocabulary. And what's that other one? Disparity! Yeah, that's it. The disparity between us at that moment. I mean, there I was, celebrating you, feasting on your loveliness, and you were talking about a fucking, pardon my French, parakeet!

FRANKIE   Maybe it's because I was ill at ease.

JOHNNY   Because of me?

FRANKIE   Maybe I don't like being looked at down there that way how the hell should I know!

JOHNNY   Bullshit! You don't like being looked at, period.

FRANKIE   Ow!

JOHNNY   What happened?

FRANKIE   I cut myself.

JOHNNY   Let me see.

FRANKIE   It's all right.

JOHNNY   Let me see. (*He sucks the blood from her finger.*)

FRANKIE   Look, I don't think this is going to work out. It was very nice while it lasted but like I said . . .

JOHNNY   You'll live. (*He releases her hand.*)

FRANKIE   . . . I'm a BLT down sort of person and I think you're looking for someone a little more pheasant under glass. Where are you going?

JOHNNY   I'll get a bandage.

FRANKIE   That's okay.

JOHNNY   No problem.

FRANKIE   Really. What are you doing? (*Johnny has gone into the bathroom. We hear him going through the medicine cabinet looking for a bandage as he continues to speak through the open door.*)

JOHNNY   I don't remember you saying you were a BLT down sort of person.

FRANKIE   I thought I implied it when I was talking about the meat loaf. (*Johnny comes out of the bathroom with a box of Band-Aids and a bottle of iodine.*)

JOHNNY   It's because I said you had a beautiful pussy, isn't it? Give me your finger. (*Frankie holds out her finger while Johnny disinfects and dresses it.*)

FRANKIE   It's because you said a lot of things. Ow!

JOHNNY   A man compliments a woman. All right, maybe he uses street talk but it's nice street talk, affectionate. It's not one of them ugly words, like the one I'm sure we're both familiar with, the one that begins with "c." I didn't even say you had a beautiful "c." I was saying something loving and you took offense.

FRANKIE   I told you I wasn't very spontaneous!

JOHNNY   Boy, if you had said to me, "Johnny, you have the most terrific dick on you" I would be so happy. (*He finishes with the Band-Aids.*) There you go.

FRANKIE   Thank you.

JOHNNY   You want to see scarred fingers! (*He holds up his hands to Frankie.*)

FRANKIE (*Wincing at the sight.*)   Please!

JOHNNY   They don't hurt.

FRANKIE   I don't want to look.

JOHNNY (*Looking at them.*)   It's hard to connect them. I mean, I'm not the type who should have scarry hands.

FRANKIE   You're so good with knives. I've watched you.

JOHNNY   She admits it. The haughty waitress has cast a lustful gaze on the Knight of the Grill.

FRANKIE   "Can that new guy chop and dice," Dena tells me. "Look at him go."

JOHNNY   Now, sure! It's a breeze. I can dice an onion blindfolded. These scars were then. On my way up the culinary ladder. I knew you were looking at me.

FRANKIE   It's human curiosity. A new face in the kitchen. Male. Look, I never said I was a nun.

JOHNNY   Hey, it's okay. It was mutual. I was looking at you.

FRANKIE   Besides, there aren't that many short-order cooks who have a dictionary and a copy of Shakespeare in their locker.

JOHNNY   You'd be surprised. We're an inquiring breed. We have our own quiz show: *Cooks Want to Know.*

FRANKIE   The one before you, Pluto, I'm not kidding, he said his name was Pluto, I swear to God! you know what he would have done with your books? Cooked 'em!

JOHNNY   So you noticed what I was reading, too?

FRANKIE   Call me the Bionic Eye. I don't miss a trick.

JOHNNY   You know what I liked about you? The way you take the time to talk to that old guy who comes in every day about 3:30.

FRANKIE   Mr. Leon.

JOHNNY   With the cane and a copy of the *Post* and always has a flower in his lapel. You really are nice with him.

FRANKIE   He's really nice with me.

JOHNNY   You really talk to him. I also like the way you fluff up that thing you wear on your uniform. It looks like a big napkin.

FRANKIE   It's supposed to be a handkerchief.

JOHNNY   I like the way you're always fluffing it.

FRANKIE   What are you? Spying on me from the kitchen?

JOHNNY   No spying. Watching.

FRANKIE   I'm going to be very self-conscious from now on.

JOHNNY   Watching and liking what I see.

FRANKIE   You in night school or something?

JOHNNY   This is my kind of night school.

FRANKIE   I meant the Shakespeare and the big words.

JOHNNY   I'm doing that on my own.

FRANKIE   Why?

JOHNNY   You don't want be going out with a semi-illiterate, subcretinous, proto-moronic asshole do you?

FRANKIE   Listen, it's easy to use words I don't know.

JOHNNY   What? Asshole? God, I like you.

FRANKIE   You still want a sandwich before you go?

JOHNNY   I still want a sandwich.

FRANKIE   Then you're going. You're not staying over.

JOHNNY   We'll cross that bridge when we get to it.

FRANKIE   There's no bridge to cross.

JOHNNY   What are you scared of?

FRANKIE   I'm not scared. (*She has resumed making sandwiches. Johnny watches her intently.*) I'm not scared. I'm . . .

JOHNNY   Yes, you are.

FRANKIE   Well not like in a horror movie. I don't think you're going to pull out a knife and stab me, if that's what you mean. Could we change the subject?

JOHNNY   What do you mean?

FRANKIE   Oh come on! You're gonna stand there and tell me you're not weird?

JOHNNY   Of course I'm weird.

FRANKIE   There's a whole other side of you I never saw at work.

JOHNNY   You thought all I did was cook?

FRANKIE   There's a whole other side of you I never saw when we were doing it either.

JOHNNY   It was probably your first experience with a passionate, imaginative lover.

FRANKIE   My first experience with an animal is more like it.

JOHNNY   Did you ever see an animal do to another animal's toes what I did to yours?

FRANKIE   Will you keep your voice down?

JOHNNY   You got this place bugged?

FRANKIE   I'm sure the whole building heard you. Ooooo! Ooooo! Ooooo!

JOHNNY   What do expect, the way you kept twirling your fingers around inside my ears?

FRANKIE   Nobody ever put their fingers in your ears before?

JOHNNY   Maybe for a second but not the way you did, like you were drilling for something. I thought to myself "Maybe she gets off on putting her fingers in guys' ears." But did I say anything? Did I call you weird?

FRANKIE   You should have said something.

JOHNNY   Why?

FRANKIE   I would have stopped.

JOHNNY   Are you crazy? I loved it. I'll try anything once, especially in that department. You got any new ideas? Keep 'em coming, keep 'em coming. I'll tell you when to stop.

FRANKIE   I can just hear you now at work: "Hey, guys, that Frankie puts her fingers in your ears!"

JOHNNY   That is probably just about the last thing in the entire world I would ever do about tonight: talk about it to anyone, especially those animals at work. You really don't know me.

FRANKIE   It wouldn't be the first time one of the guys had yak-yak-yakked about it.

JOHNNY   Women yak, too. Hey, no catsup!

FRANKIE   Yeah, but about dumb things.

JOHNNY   All yakking is dumb. "I slept with Frankie." "Oh yeah, well I slept with Nancy Reagan." "Big effing pardon-my-French deal, the two of youse. I slept with Mother Teresa." So it goes. This wall of disparity between us, Frankie, we gotta break it down. So the only space left between us is just us.

FRANKIE   Here's your sandwich.

JOHNNY   Here's my guts.

FRANKIE   I'm sorry. I'm not good at small talk.

JOHNNY   This isn't small talk. This is enormous talk.

FRANKIE   Whatever you call it. I'm not good at it.

JOHNNY   Sure you are. You just have to want to be.

FRANKIE   Maybe that's it. I forgot the milk.

JOHNNY   Something's going on in this room, something important. You don't feel it?

FRANKIE   I told you what I felt.

JOHNNY   You don't want to feel it. Two people coming together: sure it's a little scary but it's pardon-my-French again fucking wonderful, too. My heart is so full right now. Put your hand here. I swear to God, you can feel the lump. Go on, touch it.

FRANKIE   You're too needy. You want too much. I can't.

JOHNNY   That's where you're wrong.

FRANKIE   You had the whole thing. There's no more where it came from. I'm empty.

JOHNNY   I know that feeling. It's terrible. The wonderful thing is, it doesn't have to last.

FRANKIE   Turn the light off! I want to show you something. (*Johnny turns off the light.*) Down one floor, over two buildings, the window with the kind of gauzy curtains. You see? (*Johnny has joined her at the window.*)

JOHNNY   Where?

FRANKIE   There!

JOHNNY   The old couple in the bathrobes? What about 'em?

FRANKIE   I've been watching them ever since I moved in. Almost eight years now. I have never seen them speak to one another, not once. He'll sit there reading the paper and she'll cook an entire meal without him looking up. They'll eat it in total silence. He'll help her wash up sometimes but they still won't say a word. After a while the lights go out and I guess they've gone to bed. (*Johnny has seen something else out the window.*)

JOHNNY   Jesus!

FRANKIE   Those two! The Raging Bull I call him. She's Mary the Masochist. They moved in about eighteen months ago.

JOHNNY   Hey!

FRANKIE   It's their thing.

JOHNNY   He's beating the shit out of her.

FRANKIE   She loves it.

JOHNNY   Nobody could love getting hit like that. We ought to do something.

FRANKIE   I saw her in the A&P. She was wearing a nurse's uniform. Living with him, that was a smart career choice. She had on sunglasses, you know, to hide the bruises. I went up to her, I figured it was now or never, and I said "I live in the building behind you. I've seen how he hits you. Is there anything I can do?" and she just looked at me and said, "I don't know what you're talking about."

JOHNNY   Jesus, Jesus, Jesus.

FRANKIE   Some nights when there's nothing on television I sit here in the dark and watch them. Once I ate a whole bunch of grapes watching them. One night she ended up on the floor and didn't move until the next morning. I hate being used to them.

JOHNNY   I would never hit you. I would never hit a woman.

FRANKIE   I think you had better finish that and go.

JOHNNY   You are missing one hell of an opportunity to feel with your own hand the human heart. It's right here.

FRANKIE   Maybe next time. (*Johnny looks at her and then downs the glass of milk in one long mighty gulp.*) Thank you.

JOHNNY   Your meat loaf is directly from Mount Olympus. Your father was a very lucky guy.

FRANKIE   It's his recipe. He taught me.

JOHNNY   Yeah? My old man was a great cook, too.

FRANKIE   Mine didn't have much choice.

JOHNNY   How do you mean?

FRANKIE   My mother left us when I was seven.

JOHNNY   I don't believe it! My mother left us when I was seven.

FRANKIE   Oh come on!

JOHNNY   Boy, you really, really, really and truly don't know me. Just about the last thing in the entire world I would joke about is a mother who wasn't there. I don't think mothers are sacred. I just don't think they're especially funny.

FRANKIE   Me and my big mouth! I don't think you realize how serious I am about wanting you to leave now.

JOHNNY   I don't think you realize how serious I am about us.

FRANKIE   What us? There is no us.

JOHNNY   I'm working on it. Frankie and Johnny! We're already a couple.

FRANKIE   Going out with someone just because his name is Johnny and yours is Frankie is not enough of a reason.

JOHNNY   I think it's an extraordinary one. It's fate. You also said you thought I had sexy wrists.

FRANKIE   One of the biggest mistakes in my entire life!

JOHNNY   It's gotta begin somewhere. A name, a wrist, a toe.

FRANKIE   Didn't they end up killing each other?

JOHNNY   She killed him. They odds are in your favor. Besides, we're not talking about ending up. I'm just trying to continue what's been begun.

FRANKIE   If he was anything like you, no wonder she shot him.

JOHNNY   It was a crime of passion. They were the last of the red-hot lovers. We're the next.

FRANKIE   You're not from Brooklyn.

JOHNNY   Brooklyn Heights.

FRANKIE   I knew you were gonna say that! You're from outer space.

JOHNNY   Allentown, Pennsylvania, actually.

FRANKIE   Very funny, very funny.

JOHNNY   You've never been to Allentown.

FRANKIE   Who told you? Viv? Martin? I know, Molly the Mouth.

JOHNNY   Now who's from outer space? What the pardon-my-French fuck are you talking about?

FRANKIE   One of them told you I was from Allentown so now you're pretending you are so you can continue with this coincidence theory.

JOHNNY   You're from Allentown? I was born in Allentown.

FRANKIE   Very funny. Very funny.

JOHNNY   St. Stephen's Hospital. We lived on Martell St.

FRANKIE   I suppose you went to Moody High School, too.

JOHNNY   No, we moved when I was eight. I started out at Park Lane Elementary though. Did you go to Park Lane? That is incredible! This is better than anything in Shirley MacLaine.

FRANKIE   It's a small world and Allentown's a big city.

JOHNNY   Not that small and not that big.

FRANKIE   I still don't believe you.

JOHNNY   Of course you don't. It's one big pardon-my-French again fucking miracle and you don't believe in them.

FRANKIE   I'll tell you one thing: I could never, not in a million years, be seriously involved with a man who said "Pardon my French" all the time.

JOHNNY   Done. Finished. You got it.

FRANKIE   I mean, where do you pick up an expression like that?

JOHNNY   Out of respect for a person. A woman in this case.

FRANKIE   The first time you said it tonight I practically told you I had a headache and had to go home.

JOHNNY   That's so scary to me! That three little words, "Pardon my French," could separate two people from saying three little words that make them connect.

FRANKIE   What three little words?

JOHNNY   I love you.

FRANKIE   Oh. Them. I should've guessed.

JOHNNY   Did you ever say them to anyone?

FRANKIE   Say them and mean them? My father, my first true love and a couple thousand men since. That's about it.

JOHNNY   I'm not counting.

FRANKIE   You're really from Allentown? (*Johnny nods, takes a bite out of his sandwich and makes a "Cross My Heart" sign over his chest. Then he pushes his empty milk glass towards Frankie meaning he would like a refill, which she will get.*) How did you get so lucky to get out of there at eight?

JOHNNY   (*Talking and eating.*)   My mother. She ran off with somebody she'd met at an A.A. meeting. My father took us to Baltimore. He had a sister. She couldn't cope with us. We ended up in foster homes. Could I have a little salt? I bounced all over the place. Washington, D.C. was the best. You go through that Smithsonian Institute they got there and there ain't nothing they're gonna teach you in college! That place is a gold mine. Portland, Maine, is nice, too. Cold though.

FRANKIE   You didn't miss much not staying in Allentown . . . My big highlight was . . .

JOHNNY   What?

FRANKIE   Nothing. It's stupid.

JOHNNY   I've told you stupid things.

FRANKIE   Not this stupid.

JOHNNY   No fair.

FRANKIE   All right! I played Fiona in our high school production of *Brigadoon*.

JOHNNY   What's stupid about that? I bet you were wonderful.

FRANKIE   It's hardly like winning a scholarship to Harvard or being the class valedictorian. It's an event; it shouldn't be a highlight.

JOHNNY   So you're an actress!

FRANKIE   You mean at this very moment in time?

JOHNNY   I said to myself "She's not just a waitress."

FRANKIE   Yeah, she's an unsuccessful actress! What are you really?

JOHNNY   I'm really a cook.

FRANKIE   Oh. When you put it like that, I'm really a waitress. I haven't tried to get an acting job since the day I decided I was never going to get one. Somebody told me you gotta have balls to be a great actress. I got balls, I told 'em. No, Frankie you got a big mouth!

JOHNNY   Would you . . . ? You know . . .?

FRANKIE   What?

JOHNNY   Act something for me.

FRANKIE   What are you? Nuts? You think actors go around acting for people just like that? Like we do requests?

JOHNNY   I'm sorry. I didn't know.

FRANKIE   Acting is an art. It's a responsibility. It's a privilege.

JOHNNY   And I bet you're good at it.

FRANKIE   And it looks like I'll die with my secret. Anyway, what happened to your mother?

JOHNNY   I tracked her down when I was eighteen. They were still together, living in Philadelphia and both drinking again. They say Philadelphia will do that to you.

FRANKIE   So you saw her again? You see, I never did.

JOHNNY   But how this potbellied, balding, gin-breathed stranger could have been the object of anyone's desire but especially my mother's! She was still so beautiful, even through the booze, but he was one hundred percent turkey.

FRANKIE   Mine was killed in a car wreck about three, no, four years ago. She was with her turkey. He got it, too. I didn't hear about it for almost a month.

JOHNNY   What people see in one another! It's a total mystery. Shakespeare said it best: "There are more things in heaven and on earth than are dreamt of in your philosophy, Horatio." Something like that. I'm pretty close. Did you ever read *Hamlet*?

FRANKIE   Probably.

JOHNNY   I like him. I've only read of a couple of his things. They're not easy. Lots of old words. Archaic, you know? Then all of a sudden he puts it all together and comes up with something clear and simple and it's real nice and you feel you've learned something. This Horatio was Hamlet's best friend. He thought he had it all figured out, so Hamlet set him straight. Do you have a best friend?

FRANKIE   Not really.

JOHNNY   That's okay. I'll be your best friend.

FRANKIE   You think a lot of yourself, don't you?

JOHNNY   Look, I'm going all over the place with you. I might as well come right out with it: I love you. I'm in love with you. I personally think we should get married and I definitely want us to have kids, three or four. There! That wasn't so difficult. You don't have to say anything. I just wanted to get it out on the table. Talk about a load off!

FRANKIE   Talk about a load off? Talk about a crock of shit.

JOHNNY   Hey, come on, don't. One of the things I like about you, Frankie, is that you talk nice. Don't start that stuff now.

FRANKIE   Well fuck you how I talk! I'll talk any fucking way I fucking feel like it! It's my fucking apartment in the fucking first place and who the fuck are you to come in here and start telling me I talk nice. (*She has started to cry.*)

JOHNNY   I'm sorry.

FRANKIE   Out of the blue, just like that, you've decided we're going to get involved?

JOHNNY   If you want to understate it like that.

FRANKIE   Whatever happened to a second date?

JOHNNY   We were beyond that two hours ago.

FRANKIE   Maybe you were.

JOHNNY   I like your apartment. That's a nice robe. You're a very pretty woman but I guess all the guys tell you that. Is that what you want?

FRANKIE   I don't want this.

JOHNNY   That has occurred to me. Dumb, I am not. Nervy and persistent, those I plead guilty to. I'm also something else people aren't too accustomed to these days: courageous. I want you and I'm coming after you.

FRANKIE   Has it occurred to you that maybe I don't want you?

JOHNNY   Only a couple hundred times. I got my work cut out for me.

FRANKIE   Just because you take me out to dinner—!

JOHNNY   That wasn't my fault!

FRANKIE   Then the movies—!

JOHNNY   It got four stars!

FRANKIE   And end up making love—!

JOHNNY   Great love.

FRANKIE   Okay love.

JOHNNY   Great love. The dinner and the movie were lousy. We were dynamite.

FRANKIE   Okay, good love. So why do you have to go spoil everything?

JOHNNY   I told you I loved you! That makes me unlovable?

FRANKIE   It makes you a creep!

JOHNNY   Oh.

FRANKIE   No, I take that back. You're not a creep. You're sincere. That's what's so awful. Well, I'm sincere, too. I sincerely do not want to continue this.

JOHNNY   Pretend that we're the only two people in the entire world, that's what I'm doing, and it all falls into place.

FRANKIE   And I was looking forward to seeing you again.

JOHNNY   I'm right here.

FRANKIE   "God," I was thinking, "make him want to see me again without him knowing that's what I want."

JOHNNY   I already did know. God had nothing to do with it.

FRANKIE   I said "see you again," not the stuff you're talking about. Kids for Christ's sake!

JOHNNY   What's wrong with kids?

FRANKIE   I hate kids.

JOHNNY   I don't believe that.

FRANKIE   I'm too old to have kids.

JOHNNY   No, you're not.

FRANKIE   I can't have any. Now are you happy?

JOHNNY   We'll adopt.

FRANKIE   You just don't decide to fall in love with people out of the blue.

JOHNNY   Why not?

FRANKIE   They don't like it. How would you like it if Helen came up to you and said, "I'm in love with you. I want to have your baby."?

JOHNNY   Who's Helen?

FRANKIE   At work.

JOHNNY   That Helen?

FRANKIE   You'd run like hell.

JOHNNY   She's close to seventy.

FRANKIE   I thought love was blind.

JOHNNY   It's the exact opposite. Besides, I'd tell her I was in love with you.

FRANKIE   You don't know me.

JOHNNY   Is that what this is all about? Of course I don't know you. You don't know me either. We got off to a great start. Why do you want to stop?

FRANKIE   Does it have to be tonight?

JOHNNY   Yes!

FRANKIE   Who says?

JOHNNY   We may not make it tomorrow. I might get knifed if you make me go home. You might choke on a chicken bone. Unknown poison gases could kill us both in our sleep. When it comes to love, life's cheap and it's short. So don't fuck with it and don't pardon my French.

FRANKIE   This is worse than *Looking for Mr. Goodbar.*

JOHNNY   Look, Frankie. I might see someone on the BMT tonight, get lucky and get laid, and think I was in love with her. This is the only chance we have to really come together, I'm convinced of it. People are given one moment to connect. Not two, not three, one! They don't take it, it's gone forever and they end up not only pardon-my-French-for-the-very-last-time screwing that person on the BMT but marrying her.

FRANKIE   Boy, are you barking up the wrong tree.

JOHNNY   I never thought I could be in love with a woman who said "barking up the wrong tree."

FRANKIE   You've driven me to it. I never used that expression in my entire life.

JOHNNY   You sure you don't want to feel this lump?

FRANKIE   Why won't you go?

JOHNNY   The only difference between us right now is I know how this is going to end—happily—and you don't. I need a best friend, too. Could I trouble you for another glass of milk?

FRANKIE   Okay, milk, but then I really want you to go. Promise?

JOHNNY   You drive a hard bargain. Milk for exile from the Magic Kingdom.

FRANKIE   Promise?

JOHNNY   Promise.

FRANKIE   Say it like you mean it.

JOHNNY   I promise.

FRANKIE   It's a good thing you're not an actor.

JOHNNY   All right, I don't promise.

FRANKIE   Now I believe you. (*She goes to the refrigerator and pours a glass of milk.*)

JOHNNY   It's just words. It's all words. Words, words, words. He said that, too, I think. I read somewhere Shakespeare said just about everything. I'll tell you one thing he didn't say: I love you, Frankie. (*Frankie brings him a glass of milk.*)

FRANKIE   Drink your milk.

JOHNNY   I bet that's something else he never said: "Drink your milk," *The Merry Wives of Windsor*, Act III, scene ii. I don't think so. The Swan of Avon ain't got nothing on us.

FRANKIE   Did anybody ever tell you you talk too much?

JOHNNY   Yeah, I told you about half an hour ago. There's no virtue in being mute.

FRANKIE   I'm not a mute.

JOHNNY   Did I say you were?

FRANKIE   I talk when I have something to say.

JOHNNY   Did I say she was a mute?

FRANKIE   You know, not everybody thinks life is a picnic. Some of us have problems. Some of us have sorrows. But people like you are so busy telling us what you want, how you feel, you don't even notice the rest of us who aren't exactly jumping up and down for joy.

JOHNNY   I haven't done anything but notice you.

FRANKIE   Shut up!

JOHNNY   Who's jumping up and down?

FRANKIE   I said, shut up! Just drink your milk and go. I don't want to hear your voice again tonight.

JOHNNY   What do you want?

FRANKIE   I want to be alone. I want to watch television. I want to eat ice cream. I want to sleep. I want to stop worrying. I'm trapped in my own apartment with a fucking maniac.

JOHNNY   We all have problems, you know.

FRANKIE   Right now, mine begin and end with you. You said you'd go.

JOHNNY   I lied.

FRANKIE   All I have to do is open that window and start screaming.

JOHNNY   In this city? Lots of luck.

FRANKIE   I have neighbors upstairs, friends . . .

JOHNNY   No one's gonna want to get involved in us. They'll just tell you to call the police.

FRANKIE   Don't think it hasn't crossed my mind.

JOHNNY   They'll come, give or take an hour or two. They'll make me leave but I'll be right back. That's a very handy fire escape. If not tonight, then tomorrow or the day after that. Sooner or later, you're gonna have to deal with me. Why don't we just get it over with? Besides, tomorrow's Sunday. We can sleep in. (*At some point before this, the music on the radio has changed to Scriabin's Second Symphony. Neither Frankie nor Johnny heard the announcement. Ideally, the audience didn't either.*)

FRANKIE   I *am* trapped in my own apartment with a fucking maniac!

JOHNNY   You don't mean that. I'm trying to improve my life and I'm running out of time. I'm still going around in circles with you. There's gotta be that one thing I say that makes you listen. That makes us connect. What station are you on?

FRANKIE   What?

JOHNNY   It looks like it's about ninety. You got a paper? (*He starts rummaging about for a newspaper.*)

FRANKIE   What do you think you're doing?

JOHNNY   I want to get the name of that piece of music you liked for you.

FRANKIE   I don't care anymore.

JOHNNY   Well, I do. When you come across something beautiful, you gotta go for it. It doesn't grow on trees, beautiful things. (*Johnny has found the radio station call letters in the newspaper.*) WKCC. (*As he dials the information.*) I owe you a quarter.

FRANKIE   He's nuts. Out and out loco!

JOHNNY (*Into the phone.*)   Give me the number for WKCC. Thank you. (*To Frankie.*) Without the name, we'll lose that music and I'll never find it on my own. You let something like that slip through your fingers and you deserve rock and roll! (*He hangs up and immediately redials.*) I hate these recordings that give you the number now. One less human contact. (*To Frankie.*) Where are you going?

FRANKIE   Out, and you better not be here when I get back.

JOHNNY   You want to pick up some Häagen-Dazs Vanilla Swiss Almond while you're out?

FRANKIE   I said get out! (*She starts throwing things.*) You're a maniac! You're a creep! You're a . . . Oh!

JOHNNY (*Into the phone.*)   May I speak to your disc jockey? . . . Well excuse me! (*He covers the phone. To Frankie.*) They don't have a disc jockey. They have someone called Midnight with Marlon. (*Into phone.*) Hello, Marlon? My name is Johnny. My friend and I were making love and in the afterglow, which I sometimes think is the most beautiful part of making love, she noticed that you were playing some really beautiful music, piano. She was right. I don't know much about quality music, which I could gather that was, so I would like to know the name of that particular piece and the artist performing it so I can buy the record and present it to my lady love, whose name is Frankie and is that a beautiful coincidence or is it not? (*Short pause.*) Bach. Johann Sebastian, right? I heard of him. The Goldberg Variations. Glenn Gould. Columbia Records. (*To Frankie.*) You gonna remember this? (*Frankie smacks him hard across the cheek. Johnny takes the phone from his ear and holds it against his chest. He just looks at her. She smacks him again. This time he catches her hand while it is still against his cheek, holds it a beat, then brings it to his lips and kisses it. Then, into the phone, he continues but what he says is really for Frankie, his eyes never leaving her.*) Do you take requests, Marlon? Then make an exception! There's a man and a woman. Not young, not old. No great beauties, either one. They meet where they work: a restaurant and it's not the Ritz. She's a waitress. He's a cook. They meet but they don't connect. "I got two medium burgers working" and "Pick up, side of fries" is pretty much the extent of it. But she's noticed him, he can feel it. And he's noticed her. Right off. They both knew tonight was going to happen. So why did it take him six weeks for him to ask her if she wanted to see a movie that neither of them could tell you the name of right now? Why did they eat ice cream sundaes before she asked him if he wanted to come up since they were in the neighborhood? And then they were making love and for maybe an hour they forgot the ten million things that made them think "I don't love this person. I don't even like them" and instead all they knew was that they were together and it was perfect and they were perfect and that's all there was to know about it and as they lay there, they both began the million reasons not to love one another like a familiar rosary. Only this time he stopped himself. Maybe it was the music you were playing. They both heard it. Only now they're both beginning to forget they did. So would you play something for Frankie and Johnny on the eve of something that ought to last, not self-destruct. I guess I want you to play the most beautiful music ever written and dedicate it to us. (*He hangs up.*) Don't go.

FRANKIE   Why are you doing this?

JOHNNY   I'm tired of looking. Everything I want is in this room. (*He kisses her. Frankie responds. It quickly gets passionate. Frankie starts to undress.*)

JOHNNY   Let me.

FRANKIE   Hunh?

JOHNNY   Let me do it. (*He helps her out of her raincoat. Then he takes it and hangs it up. Frankie stands a little awkwardly in the center of the room waiting for him to come back to her.*) Make yourself at home. That was a little joke. No, that was a little bad joke. (*He turns off the lamp.*)

FRANKIE   What's the matter?

JOHNNY   Nothing.

FRANKIE   Leave the lights on.

JOHNNY   It's better off.

FRANKIE   I want to see you this time. (*Johnny has started unbuttoning her blouse.*)

JOHNNY   I don't like to make love with the lights on.

FRANKIE   Why not?

JOHNNY   I can't.

FRANKIE   That's a good reason. (*Johnny is having a little difficulty undressing her.*)

JOHNNY   It's because of Archie.

FRANKIE   Okay, I'll bite. Who's Archie?

JOHNNY   A huge Great Dane at one of my foster families. I mean, massive. Whenever I'd jack off, he'd just stare at me. At it. Talk about serious castration anxiety! So I got in the habit of doing it with the lights off.

FRANKIE   Sometimes I am so glad I'm a girl.

JOHNNY   I'm also a romantic. I think everything looks better in half-light and shadows.

FRANKIE   That's not romance, that's hiding something. Romance is seeing somebody for what they really are and still wanting them warts and all.

JOHNNY   I got plenty of them. (*He stops undressing her.*) I'm forty-five.

FRANKIE   You look younger. I'm thirty-seven.

JOHNNY   So do you. I'm forty-six.

FRANKIE   Honest?

JOHNNY   I'll be forty-eight the tenth of next month.

FRANKIE   What do you want for your birthday?

JOHNNY   To be able to stop bullshitting about things like my age.

FRANKIE   I'll be thirty-nine on the eleventh.

JOHNNY   We're both what-do-you-ma-call-its!

FRANKIE   Figures! Gimme a hand with the bed. I hate it when the sheets get like that. (*Frankie starts straightening up the bed. Johnny turns off another light in the room before helping her to smooth the sheets and blankets.*) I'm the one who ought to be hiding from the light. Me and my goddamn inverted nipples. I hate the way they look.

JOHNNY   Don't be silly.

FRANKIE   Yeah? You be a woman and have someone invert your nipples and see how you like it.

JOHNNY   I love your nipples.

FRANKIE   Well I hate 'em.

JOHNNY   What do you know? (*They stand on opposite sides of the bed shaking out the sheets.*) Listen, I wish I was circumcised.

FRANKIE   Sounds like you had your chance and blew it.

JOHNNY   Hunh?

FRANKIE   The dog. Skip it, skip it. ! I'll be forty-one on the eleventh.

JOHNNY   Big deal. So what do you want?

FRANKIE   The same thing you do and a new pair of tits.

JOHNNY   Hey, it means a lot to me you talk nice. (*Johnny crosses to the window to close the shade. Frankie goes to bed and lies down on it.*) Jesus. (*He points to something outside the window and above it.*)

FRANKIE   Come away from there. It's not good for you.

JOHNNY   Come here. Quick. (*He stands at the window. Moonlight covers his body.*)

FRANKIE   I mean it. I've looked too long.

JOHNNY   There's a full moon! You can just see it between the buildings. Will you look at that! Now that's what I call beautiful!

FRANKIE   I ordered it just for you. Macy's. Twenty-five bucks an hour.

JOHNNY   Look at it!

FRANKIE   Later.

JOHNNY   It won't be there later. (*Frankie joins him at the window.*) You can almost see it move.

FRANKIE (*Lowering her gaze.*)   All quiet on the Western Front. For now. Come on. (*She moves to bed.*) Come on. I want you to make love to me. (*Johnny turns from window.*)

JOHNNY   I want to make love to you.

FRANKIE   Woof! Woof! (*Nothing.*) It was a joke, I'm sorry.

RADIO ANNOUNCER   This young man was very persuasive . . .

JOHNNY   Sshh! Listen! (*He moves quickly to the bedside radio and turns up the volume.*)

RADIO ANNOUNCER   So although it's against my policy to play requests, there's an exception to every rule. I don't know if this is the most beautiful music ever written, Frankie and Johnny—and how I wish that really were your names but I know when my leg is being pulled—but whoever you are, wherever you are, whatever you're doing, I hope this is something like what you had in mind. (*Debussy's "Clair de Lune" is heard. Johnny switches off the bedside lamp and kisses Frankie. Then he gets up quickly and goes to window and reaches for the shade. He sees the two couples in the apartments across the courtyard. He looks up at the moon. There is moonlight spilling onto his face and body. He decides not to pull the shade, allowing the moonlight to spill into the room. He moves away from the window and disappears in the shadows of the bed. We hear a distant siren. We hear the Debussy. We hear the sounds of Frankie and Johnny starting to make love. Fifteen seconds of this. Abrupt silence. Total blackout.*)

END OF ACT ONE

ACT TWO

AT RISE: *The only illumination in the room comes from the television set. In its gray light, we can see Frankie and Johnny in the bed, under the covers. They both stare at it. The only sound is coming from the radio: now it is playing "The Ride of the Valkyries." Thirty seconds of the Wagner.*

JOHNNY Is that Charles Bronson? (*Johnny turns down radio.*) Is that Charles Bronson?

FRANKIE Or that other one. I always get people in those kinds of movies confused.

JOHNNY James Coburn?

FRANKIE I think that's his name.

JOHNNY Whoever he is, I hate him. It's not Clint Eastwood?

FRANKIE No, I know what Clint Eastwood looks like. Look, you don't have to make such a big deal about it.

JOHNNY I'm not making a big deal about it.

FRANKIE Then how come we stopped?

JOHNNY I haven't stopped. We're taking a little break. Will you look at that! I am appalled at the violence in the world today.

FRANKIE It's okay if we don't.

JOHNNY I know.

FRANKIE Really.

JOHNNY I said I know. Jesus, he drove a fucking nail through his head!

FRANKIE I had my eyes shut.

JOHNNY And when did that asshole go from playing our song to those screaming meemies? I thought he liked us. That kind of music is bad enough during normal hours. But when you're trying to make love to someone . . . ! Talk about not knowing how to segue from one mood to the next! I ought to call that station and complain. (*We hear him trip over something.*) Goddamnit! (*Frankie turns on the bedside lamp.*)

FRANKIE   Are you all right?

JOHNNY   I wish you wouldn't leave—. Yeah. Since I'm up, you want something?

FRANKIE   Johnny.

JOHNNY   You're the one who's making a big deal about it. I'm fine. I'm not upset. Look, I'm dancing. Now yes or no? What do you want?

FRANKIE   A Western on white down and a glass of milk.

JOHNNY   Very funny. What do you want? A beer? (*We can see him in the light of the open refrigerator as he searches for food and drink.*)

FRANKIE   I want a Western and a glass of milk.

JOHNNY   We're in the middle of something. This is a little rest, not a major food break. Besides, you just ate.

FRANKIE   I'm still hungry.

JOHNNY   I'm opening you a beer.

FRANKIE   I want a Western and a glass of milk.

JOHNNY   I never know when you're kidding me or not. I think that's one of those things I like about you but I'm not sure.

FRANKIE   I'm not kidding you. I'm starving and what I would like is one of your Westerns and a glass of milk. Everyone says you make a great Western.

JOHNNY   They do?

FRANKIE   So come on, Johnny, Johnny . . . ravish me with your cooking.

JOHNNY   You mean, since I couldn't ravish you with my body?

FRANKIE   No, that's not what I mean.

JOHNNY   Look, this is a temporary hiatus. I would like to keep it that way.

FRANKIE   So would I. I'll eat fast.

JOHNNY   All I'm saying is that if we get into real food now and I start cooking you a Western and chopping onions and peppers, it's going to be very hard to get back into the mood for what we were doing and which, contrary to your impression perhaps, I was enjoying enormously. All I asked for was a little breather for Christ's sake!

FRANKIE   I only asked for a sandwich.

JOHNNY   You asked for a Western. Westerns mean chopping and dicing and sautéing and . . . you know what goes into a Western! Come on, Frankie, it's not like you asked for a peanut butter and jelly on a Ritz cracker. You want food food.

FRANKIE   I suppose I could call it that.

JOHNNY   All right, all right! (*He starts getting ingredients out of the refrigerator and slamming onto work counter.*) I just wish somebody would tell me how we got from a mini-sex problem to a major pig-out.

FRANKIE   I don't think there's a connection.

JOHNNY   I wasn't going to tell you this but since you're not sparing my feelings, I'm not going to go on sparing yours: this is the first time anything like this ever happened to me.

FRANKIE   So?

JOHNNY   Well if you can't make the connection . . . !

FRANKIE   Between what and what?

JOHNNY   It takes two to tango.

FRANKIE   You mean it's my fault you conked out?

JOHNNY   I didn't say it was anybody's fault. And I didn't conk out. I'm resting.

FRANKIE   Oh, the old And-On-The-Seventh-Day Syndrome!

JOHNNY   There's no need to be sarcastic.

FRANKIE   Then don't blame me your dancing dog didn't dance when you told it to. That sounds terrible. Don't blame me for your limp dick. Now what about my Western?

JOHNNY   You expect me to make you a sandwich after that?

FRANKIE   After what?

JOHNNY   Insulting my manhood.

FRANKIE   I didn't insult your manhood. I merely described a phase it was going through. Everything has phases. To talk about the new moon doesn't insult the old one. You have a lovely manhood. It's just in eclipse right now so you can make me one of your terrific Westerns.

JOHNNY   This is the first time this has ever happened to me. I swear to God.

FRANKIE   I believe you.

JOHNNY   I hate it. I hate it a lot.

FRANKIE   Just be glad you have someone as sympathetic as me to share it with.

JOHNNY   Don't make fun.

FRANKIE   I'm not. (*She goes to him and comforts him.*) It's okay.

JOHNNY   You're lucky women don't have problems like this.

FRANKIE   We've got enough of our own in that department.

JOHNNY   It's male menopause. I've been dreading this.

FRANKIE   You know what I think it was? The moonlight. You were standing in it. It was bathing your body. I've always been very suspicious of what moonlight does to people.

JOHNNY   It's supposed to make them romantic.

FRANKIE   Or turn you into a werewolf. That's what I was raised on. My grandmother was always coming into my bedroom to make sure the blinds were down. She was convinced sleeping in the moonlight would turn you into the wolfman. I thought if I slept in the moonlight I'd wake up a beautiful fairy princess, so I kept falling asleep with the blinds open and she kept coming in and closing them. She always denied it was her. "Wasn't me, precious. Must have been your Guardian Angel." Remember them?

JOHNNY   What do you mean "remember"?

FRANKIE   One night I decided to stay awake and catch her in the act. It seemed like forever. When you're at that age, you don't have anything to stay awake *about*. So you're failing geography, so what? Finally my grandmother came into the room. She had to lean across my bed to close the blinds. Her bosom was so close to my face. She smelled so nice. I pretended I was still sleeping and took the deepest breath of her I could. In that one moment, I think I knew what it was like to be loved. Really loved. I was so safe, so protected! That's better than being pretty. I'll never forget it. The next thing I knew it was morning and I still didn't look like Audrey Hepburn. Now when I lie in bed with the blinds up and the moonlight spilling in, I'm not thinking I want to be someone else, I just want my Nana back.

JOHNNY   Nana? You called your grandmother Nana? That's what I called mine.

FRANKIE   It's not that unusual.

JOHNNY   It's incredible! I don't know anybody else who called their grandmother Nana. I always thought it was very unusual of me and more than anything else I wanted to be like everyone else.

FRANKIE   You, like everyone else?

JOHNNY   It was a disaster. "Why do we call her Nana?" I used to ask my mother—this was before Philadelphia—"Everyone else says grandma." "We just do," she told me. My mother was not one for great answers. Sort of a Sphinx in that department. Anyway, I for one am very glad you didn't wake up Audrey Hepburn. She's too thin. People should have meat on their bones. "Beware yon Cassius. He hath a lean and hungry look."

FRANKIE   Who's Cassius?

JOHNNY   I don't know. But obviously he was thin and Shakespeare thinks we should be wary of skinny people.

FRANKIE   Why?

JOHNNY   Well you know how they are. Grim. Kind of waiting and watching you all the time.

FRANKIE   Like Connie?

JOHNNY   Who?

FRANKIE   Connie Cantwell. She works weekends. Red hair, wears a hairnet?

JOHNNY   Exactly! Wouldn't you beware her?

FRANKIE I've actually seen her steal tips.

JOHNNY There you go! He's filled with little tips like that. "Neither a borrower nor a lender be."

FRANKIE That's just common sense. You don't have to be a genius to figure that one out.

JOHNNY Of course not. But he put it in poetry so that people would know up here what they already knew in here and so they would remember it. "To be or not to be."

FRANKIE Everyone knows that. Do I want to kill myself?

JOHNNY Well?

FRANKIE Well what?

JOHNNY Do you want to kill yourself?

FRANKIE Of course not. Well not right now. Everybody wants to kill themselves some of the time.

JOHNNY They shouldn't.

FRANKIE Well they do! That doesn't mean they're gonna do it. Can we get off this?

JOHNNY The list just gets longer and longer.

FRANKIE What list?

JOHNNY The us list, things we got in common.

FRANKIE What do you want to kill yourself about sometimes?

JOHNNY Right now? My limp dick. I'm kidding, I'm kidding. I'm going to start warning you before I say something funny.

FRANKIE You don't have to warn me. Just say something funny.

JOHNNY I want to kill myself sometimes when I think I'm the only person in the world and the part of me that feels that way is trapped inside this body that only bumps into other bodies without ever connecting with the only other person in the world trapped inside of them. We gotta connect. We just have to. Or we die.

FRANKIE We're connecting.

JOHNNY Are we?

FRANKIE   I am. I feel very . . .

JOHNNY   Say it.

FRANKIE   I don't know what it is.

JOHNNY   Say it anyway.

FRANKIE   Protective, but that's crazy!

JOHNNY   It's nice.

FRANKIE   I'm looking for somebody to take care of me this time.

JOHNNY   We all are.

FRANKIE   Why do we keep going from one subject I don't like to another?

JOHNNY   We're like an FM station when you're out driving in a car. We keep drifting and we gotta tune ourselves back in.

FRANKIE   Who says?

JOHNNY   Hey, I'm being nice.

FRANKIE   May I say something without you biting my head off?

JOHNNY   Aw, c'mon!

FRANKIE   I mean it!

JOHNNY   You are the woman I've been looking for all my adult life. You can say anything you want. Speak, queen of my heart, speak!

FRANKIE   That's just what I was talking about.

JOHNNY   What? Queen of my heart?

FRANKIE   I'm not the queen of anybody's heart.

JOHNNY   Fine. So what is it?

FRANKIE   This is going to sound awfully small potatoes now.

JOHNNY   You couldn't speak in small potatoes if you wanted to.

FRANKIE   I still want a Western.

JOHNNY   You don't give up. You're like a rat terrier with a bone.

FRANKIE   I'm sorry.

JOHNNY   I didn't hear that.

FRANKIE   All right, I'm *not* sorry. I'm a very simple person. I get hungry and I want to eat.

JOHNNY   I'm also a very simple person.

FRANKIE   Sure you are!

JOHNNY   I see something I want, I don't take no. I used to but not anymore.

FRANKIE   What is that supposed to mean?

JOHNNY   My life was happening to me. Now I'm making it happen. Same as with you and this sandwich. You wanted it, went for it and won. (*He turns and opens the refrigerator.*) You can tell a lot about someone from what they keep in their icebox. That and their medicine chest. I would've made a terrific detective.

FRANKIE   Just stay out of my medicine chest. And I didn't appreciate you going through my purse either.

JOHNNY   Someone is clearly not prepared for the eruption into her what-she-thinks-is-humdrum life of an extraordinary man, chef and fellow worker. Why don't you try our friend on the radio again? (*Frankie will go to radio and turn it on.*) Personally, I think it was all his fault. When it comes to music, I'm a mellow sort of guy. That last thing he played was for people playing with themselves, not one another. "If music be the food of love, play on." You-Know-Who.

FRANKIE   (*At the radio.*)   I would love a cigarette.

JOHNNY   Over my dead body.

FRANKIE   That doesn't mean I'm going to smoke one. (*She turns up the volume. We hear the César Franck Sonata for Violin and Piano.*) How's that?

JOHNNY   *Comme ci, comme ça.*

FRANKIE   It's pretty.

JOHNNY   Let's put it this way: he's not Bach. The first thing in the morning I'm going to buy you those Goldberg Variations.

FRANKIE   It's Sunday. Everything'll be closed.

JOHNNY   Monday then.

FRANKIE   I guess Bach was Jewish. The Goldberg Variations.

JOHNNY   I read somewhere a lot of great composers were.

FRANKIE   I thought you were Jewish.

JOHNNY   In New York, that's a good assumption.

FRANKIE   I just realized I don't know your last name.

JOHNNY   I don't know yours.

FRANKIE   Mine's right on the bell. It's all over this place.

JOHNNY   We don't need last names. We're Frankie and Johnny. (*Closing the refrigerator door.*) Boy, you just shot my icebox theory all to hell. You should be an Irish longshoreman from what you've got in there.

FRANKIE   I am. Had you fooled for a while there, didn't I? (*Johnny is getting ready to make the Western.*)

JOHNNY   Now watch how I do this. After this, you're on your own! (*Johnny begins to work with the food and the utensils. He works swiftly, precisely and with great élan. He is a virtuoso in the kitchen. Frankie will pull up a stool and watch him work.*)

FRANKIE   I know I'm going to regret saying this but I thought I was the only person I knew who referred to one of those things as an icebox.

JOHNNY   Now who's pulling whose leg?

FRANKIE   And I don't say things like phonograph or record player. Just "icebox" and I only dimly remember us having one when I was about that big.

JOHNNY   Do you know what the population of New York City is?

FRANKIE   Eight million?

JOHNNY   Nine million, six hundred eighty-four thousand, four hundred eleven. Exactly two of them refer to those things as iceboxes. Those two, after you-know-what-ing their brains out, are now engaged in making a Western sandwich somewhere in Hell's Kitchen.

FRANKIE   It's Clinton actually.

JOHNNY   You still gonna call that a coincidence? Boy, I bet the Swan of Avon would have had something to say about that.

FRANKIE   I believe there's a reason for everything and I like to know what it is. One and one are two.

JOHNNY   That's mathematics. We're talking people.

FRANKIE   One and one should be two with them, too. Too many people throw you a curve nowadays and you end up with a three.

JOHNNY   Do I hear the voice of bitter experience?

FRANKIE   I wasn't born yesterday, if that's what you're talking about. (*She has watched Johnny intently during this as he has continued to prepare the Western.*) That's something I've never seen anyone do.

JOHNNY   What?

FRANKIE   Chop the pepper that fine.

JOHNNY   'Cause they're looking for shortcuts.

FRANKIE   You're incredible with that knife.

JOHNNY   Thank you.

FRANKIE   And don't say it's all in the wrists.

JOHNNY   It is.

FRANKIE   I hate that expression. It's such a "fuck you." What people really mean is "I know how to do it and you don't. Ha ha ha!"

JOHNNY   What brought that on? We're talking nice and Bingo! the armor goes up.

FRANKIE   What about your armor?

JOHNNY   I don't have any?

FRANKIE   Everybody has armor. They'd be dead if they didn't.

JOHNNY   Bloody but unbowed.

FRANKIE   Besides, I wasn't talking about you.

JOHNNY   Where's your cayenne?

FRANKIE   I don't have any. I don't even know what it is. What's that you just put in?

JOHNNY   Wouldn't you like to know? (*He does a good imitation of Frankie.*) "Ha ha ha!"

FRANKIE   C'mon!

JOHNNY   Salt, just salt!

FRANKIE   Is that all?

JOHNNY   Cooking's no big deal.

FRANKIE   It is if you can't.

JOHNNY   You just never had anyone to cook for. The way I feel about you I feel a Duck à l'Orange Flambé with a puree of water chestnuts coming on!

FRANKIE   I like food. I just never saw the joy in cooking it. My mother hated cooking. Her primary utensil was a can opener. I even think she resented serving us on plates. She used to eat right out the pots and pans. "One less thing to clean. Who's to know? We ain't got company."

JOHNNY   This isn't the right kind of bread.

FRANKIE   Gee, I'll run right now!

JOHNNY   There you go again! You want a good Western down, you need the right bread.

FRANKIE   Did you always want to be a cook?

JOHNNY   About as much as you wanted to be a waitress.

FRANKIE   That bad, hunh?

JOHNNY   When I look at some of the choices I made with my life, it seems almost inevitable I would end up slinging hash.

FRANKIE   Same with me and waitressing. I was supposed to graduate high school and work for a second cousin who had a dental laboratory.

JOHNNY   That place down by the old train station?

FRANKIE   Yeah, that's the one.

JOHNNY   His son was in my class. Arnold, right?

FRANKIE   You knew my cousin Arnold?

JOHNNY   Enough to say hello. Finish your story.

FRANKIE   Anyway, they made bridges, plates, retainers, stuff like that there. A dentist would take a paraffin impression of the patient's mouth and make plaster of paris molds for the technicians to work from.

JOHNNY   No wonder the acting bug bit.

FRANKIE   I never had what it takes. I hope I have what it takes to be something but I know it's not an actress. You know what I'm thinking about?

JOHNNY   What?

FRANKIE   You won't laugh?

JOHNNY   Of course not.

FRANKIE   I can't. It's too . . . I'll tell you later. I can't now.

JOHNNY   Okay. I'll tell you one thing. You didn't miss much not graduating high school. I had almost two years of college. We both ended up working for a couple of crazed Greeks. (*He imitates their boss.*) "Cheeseburger, cheeseburger" is right.

FRANKIE   That was very good.

JOHNNY   Thank you.

FRANKIE   A teacher.

JOHNNY   Hunh?

FRANKIE   What I'm thinking of becoming.

JOHNNY   Why would I laugh at that?

FRANKIE   I don't know. It just seems funny. Someone who can't spell "cat" teaching little kids to. I'll have to go back to school and learn before I can teach them but . . . I don't know, it sounds nice. (*She hasn't stopped watching Johnny work with the eggs.*) Aren't you going to scramble them?

JOHNNY   It's better if you just let them set.

FRANKIE   In the restaurant, I've seen you beat 'em. That's when I noticed you had sexy wrists.

JOHNNY   That's in the restaurant: I'm in a hurry. These are my special eggs for you. (*He starts cleaning up while the eggs set in a skillet on the stove top.*)

FRANKIE   You don't have to do that.

JOHNNY   I know.

FRANKIE   Suit yourself.

JOHNNY   I bet I know what you're thinking: "He's too good to be true."

FRANKIE   Is that what you want me to think?

JOHNNY   Face it, Frankie, men like me do not grow on trees. Hell, *people* like me don't. (*He holds his wet hands out to her.*) Towel? (*Frankie picks up a dish towel on the counter and begins to dry his hands for him.*) So you think I have sexy wrists?

FRANKIE   I don't think you're gonna break into movies on 'em.

JOHNNY   What do you think is sexy about them?

FRANKIE   I don't know. The shape. The hairs. That vein there. What's that?

JOHNNY   A mole.

FRANKIE   I could live without that.

JOHNNY   First thing Monday morning, it comes off. (*He is kissing her hands. Frankie lets him but keeps a certain distance, too.*)

FRANKIE   Are you keeping some big secret from me?

JOHNNY   It's more like I'm keeping several thousand little ones.

FRANKIE   I'd appreciate a straight answer.

JOHNNY   No, I'm not married.

FRANKIE   Men always think that's the only question women want to ask.

JOHNNY   So fire away.

FRANKIE   Well were you?

JOHNNY   I was.

FRANKIE   How many times?

JOHNNY   Once. Is that it?

FRANKIE   Men have other secrets than being married. You could be a mass murderer or an ex-convict.

JOHNNY   I am. I spent two years in the slammer. Forgery.

FRANKIE   That's okay.

JOHNNY   The state of New Jersey didn't seem to think so.

FRANKIE   It's no skin off my nose.

JOHNNY   Anything else?

FRANKIE   You could be gay.

JOHNNY   Get real, Frankie.

FRANKIE   Well you could!

JOHNNY   Does this look like a gay face?

FRANKIE   You could have a drug problem or a drinking problem.

JOHNNY   All right, I did.

FRANKIE   Which one?

JOHNNY   Booze.

FRANKIE   There, you see?

JOHNNY   It's under control now.

FRANKIE   You could still be a real shit underneath all that.

JOHNNY   But I'm not.

FRANKIE   That's your opinion.

JOHNNY   You just want a guarantee we're going to live happily ever after.

FRANKIE   Jesus, God knows, I want something. If I was put on this planet to haul hamburgers and French fries to pay the rent on an apartment I don't even like in the vague hope that some stranger will not find me wanting enough not to want to marry me then I think my being born is an experience that is going to be equaled in meaninglessness only by my being dead. I got a whole life ahead of me to feel like this? Excuse me, who do I thank for all this? I think the eggs are ready.

JOHNNY   Everything you said, anybody could say. I could give it back to you in spades. You didn't invent negativity.

FRANKIE   I didn't have to.

JOHNNY   And you didn't discover despair. I was there a long time before you ever heard of it.

FRANKIE   The eggs are burning.

JOHNNY   Fuck the eggs! This is more important!

FRANKIE   I'm hungry! (*Frankie has gone to the stove to take the eggs off. Johnny grabs her from behind and pulls her towards him.*)

JOHNNY   What's the matter with you?

FRANKIE   Let go of me!

JOHNNY   Look at me! (*They struggle briefly. Frankie shoves Johnny who backs into the hot skillet and burns his back.*) Aaaaaaaaaaaaaaa!

FRANKIE   What's the matter—?

JOHNNY   Oooooooooooooo!

FRANKIE   What happened—?

JOHNNY   Ow! Ow! Ow! Ow! Ow! Ow! Ow!

FRANKIE   Oh my God!

JOHNNY   Oooo! Oooo! Oooo! Ooooo! Oooo! Oooooo!

FRANKIE   I'm sorry, I didn't mean to—!

JOHNNY   Jesus, Frankie, Jesus Christ!

FRANKIE   Tell me what to do!

JOHNNY   Get something!

FRANKIE   What?

JOHNNY   Ice.

FRANKIE   Ice for burns? Don't move. (*Frankie puts the entire tray of ice cubes on Johnny's back. The scream that ensues is greater than the first one.*)

JOHNNY   AAAAAAAAAAAAAAAAAAAAAAAAA!!!!!!!!!!

FRANKIE   You said to—! (*Johnny nods vigorously.*) Should I keep it on? (*Johnny nods again, only this time he bites his fingers to keep from crying out.*) We'd be a terrific couple. One of us would be dead by the end of the first week. One date practically did it. All I asked you to do was turn off the eggs but no! everything has to be a big deal with you! I would have made the world's worst nurse.

JOHNNY (*Between gasps of pain.*)   Butter.

FRANKIE   What?

JOHNNY   Put some butter on it.

FRANKIE   Butter's bad on burns.

JOHNNY   I don't care.

FRANKIE   I may have some . . . oh what–do–you–call–it–when–you–have–a–sunburn, it comes in a squat blue bottle?

JOHNNY   Noxzema!

FRANKIE   That's it!

JOHNNY   It breaks me out. Get the butter.

FRANKIE   It's margarine.

JOHNNY   I don't care. (*Frankie gets the margarine out of the refrigerator.*)

FRANKIE   It sounds like you got a lot of allergies.

JOHNNY   Just those three.

FRANKIE   Catsup, Noxzema and . . . What was the other one?

JOHNNY   Fresh peaches. Canned are okay. (*Frankie puts the margarine on Johnny's back.*) Ooooooooooooo!

FRANKIE   Does that feel good?

JOHNNY   You have no idea.

FRANKIE   More?

JOHNNY   Yes, more. Don't stop.

FRANKIE   You're gonna smell like a . . . whatever a person covered in margarine smells like.

JOHNNY   I don't care.

FRANKIE   To tell the truth, it doesn't look all that bad.

JOHNNY   You think I'm faking this?

FRANKIE   I didn't say that.

JOHNNY   What do you want? Permanent scars? (*Pause. Frankie puts more margarine on Johnny's back.*)

FRANKIE   Did your first wife do this for you?

JOHNNY   Only wife. I told you that.

FRANKIE   Okay, so I was fishing.

JOHNNY   No, checking. Were you married?

FRANKIE   No, never.

JOHNNY   Anyone serious?

FRANKIE   Try "terminal."

JOHNNY   What happened?

FRANKIE   He got more serious with who I thought was my best friend.

JOHNNY   The same thing happened to me.

FRANKIE   You know what the main thing I felt was? Dumb.

JOHNNY   I know, I know!

FRANKIE   I even introduced them. I lent them money. Money from my credit union. I gave her my old television. A perfectly good Zenith. They're probably watching Charles Bronson together at this very moment. I hope it explodes and blows their faces off. No, I don't. I hope it blows up and the fumes kill them. Aren't there supposed to be poison gases in a television set?

JOHNNY   I wouldn't be surprised.

FRANKIE   That or he's telling her she looks like shit, who told her she could change her hair or where's his car keys or shut the fuck up, he's had a rough day. I didn't know how exhausting unemployment could be. God, why do we get involved with people it turns out hate us?

JOHNNY   Because . . . .

FRANKIE   . . . we hate ourselves. I know. I read the same book.

JOHNNY   How long has it been?

FRANKIE   Seven years. (*Johnny lets out a long stream of air.*) What? You, too? (*Johnny nods.*) Any kids?

JOHNNY   Two.

FRANKIE   You see them?

JOHNNY   Not as much as I'd like. She's remarried. They live in Maine in a beautiful house overlooking the sea.

FRANKIE   I bet it's not so beautiful.

JOHNNY   It's beautiful. I could never have provided them with anything like that. The first time I saw it, I couldn't get out of the car. I felt so ashamed. So forgotten. The kids came running out of the house. They looked so happy to see me but I couldn't feel happy back. All of a sudden, they looked like somebody else's kids. I couldn't even roll down the window. "What's the matter, daddy?" I started crying. I couldn't stop. Sheila and her husband had to come out of the house to get me to come in. You know what I wanted to do? Run that crewcut asshole insurance salesman over and drive off with the three of them. I don't know where we would've gone. We'd probably still be driving.

FRANKIE   That would've been a dumb thing to do.

JOHNNY   I never said I was smart.

FRANKIE   I'll tell you a secret: you are.

JOHNNY   I said I was passionate. I don't let go of old things easy and I grab new things hard.

FRANKIE   Too hard.

JOHNNY   There's no such thing as too hard when you want something.

FRANKIE   Yes, there is, Johnny. The other person. (*There is a pause. Frankie has stopped working on Johnny's back. Instead she just stares at it. Johnny looks straight ahead. The music has changed to the Shostakovich Second String Quartet.*)

JOHNNY   What are you doing back there?

FRANKIE   Nothing. You want more butter or ice or something? (*Johnny shakes his head.*)

JOHNNY   It's funny how you can talk to people better sometimes when you're not looking at them. You're right there. (*He points straight ahead.*) Clear as day.

FRANKIE   I bet no one ever said this was the most beautiful music ever written.

JOHNNY   I don't mind.

FRANKIE   I don't know what the radio was doing on that station in the first place. That's not my kind of music. But I could tell you were enjoying it and I guess I wanted you to think I had higher taste than I really do.

JOHNNY   So did I.

FRANKIE   I liked what he played for us though, but he didn't say its name.

JOHNNY   Maybe it doesn't need one. You just walk into a fancy record shop and ask for the most beautiful music ever written and that's what they hand you.

FRANKIE   Not if I was the salesperson. You'd get "Michelle" or "Eleanor Rigby" or "Lucy in the Sky with Diamonds." Something by the Beatles. I sort of lost interest in pop music when they stopped singing.

JOHNNY   The last record I bought was the Simon and Garfunkel Reunion in Central Park. It wasn't the same. You could tell they'd been separated.

FRANKIE   Sometimes I feel like it's still the sixties. Or that they were ten or fifteen years ago, not twenty or twenty-five. I lost ten years of my life somewhere. I went to Bruce Springsteen last year and I was the oldest one there.

JOHNNY   Put yours arms around me. (*Frankie puts her arms Johnny's shoulders.*) Tighter. (*Frankie's hands begin to stroke Johnny's chest and stomach.*) Do you like doing that?

FRANKIE   I don't mind.

JOHNNY   We touch our own bodies there and nothing happens. Something to do with electrons. We short-circuit ourselves. Stroke my tits. There! (*He tilts his head back until he is looking up at her.*) Give me your mouth. (*Frankie bends over and kisses him. It is a long one.*) That tongue. Those lips. (*He pulls her down towards him for another long kiss.*) I want to die like this. Drown.

FRANKIE   What do you want from me?

JOHNNY   Everything. Your heart. Your soul. Your tits. Your mouth. Your fucking guts. I want it all. I want to be inside you. Don't hold back.

FRANKIE   I'm not holding back.

JOHNNY   Let go. I'll catch you.

FRANKIE   I'm right here.

JOHNNY   I want more. I need more.

FRANKIE   If I'd known what playing with your tit was gonna turn into—

JOHNNY   Quit screwing with me, Frankie.

FRANKIE   You got a pretty weird notion of who's screwing with who. I said I liked you. I told you that. I'm perfectly ready to make love to you. Why do you have to start a big discussion about it. It's not like I'm saying "no."

JOHNNY   I want you to do something.

FRANKIE   What?

JOHNNY   I want you to go down on me.

FRANKIE   No.

JOHNNY   I went down on you.

FRANKIE   That was different.

JOHNNY   How?

FRANKIE   That was then.

JOHNNY   Please.

FRANKIE   I'm not good at it.

JOHNNY   Hey, this isn't a contest. We're talking about making love.

FRANKIE   I don't want to right now.

JOHNNY   You want me to go down on you again?

FRANKIE   If I do it will you shut up about all this other stuff?

JOHNNY   You know I won't.

FRANKIE   Then go down on yourself.

JOHNNY   What happened? You were gonna do it.

FRANKIE   Anything to get you to quit picking at me. Go on, get out of here. Get somebody else to go down on you.

JOHNNY   I don't want somebody else to go down on me.

FRANKIE   Jesus! I just had a vision of what it's going to be like at work Monday after this! I'm not quitting my job. I was there first.

JOHNNY   What are you talking about?

FRANKIE   I don't think we're looking for the same thing.

JOHNNY   We are. Only I've found it and you've given up.

FRANKIE   Yes! Long before the sun ever rose on your ugly face.

JOHNNY   What scares you more? Marriage or kids?

FRANKIE   I'm not scared. And I told you: I can't have any.

JOHNNY   I told you: we can adopt.

FRANKIE   I don't love you.

JOHNNY   That wasn't the question.

FRANKIE   You hear what *you* want to hear.

JOHNNY   Do you know anybody who doesn't?

FRANKIE   Not all the time.

JOHNNY   You're only telling me you don't love me so you don't have to find out if you could. Just because you've given up on the possibility. I'm not going to let you drag me down with you. You're coming up to my level if I have to pull you by the hair.

FRANKIE   I'm not going anywhere with a man who for all his bullshit about marriage and kids and Shakespeare . . .

JOHNNY   It's not bullshit!

FRANKIE   . . . Just wants me to go down on him.

JOHNNY   Pretend it was a metaphor.

FRANKIE   Fuck you it was a metaphor! It was a blow job. What's a metaphor?

JOHNNY   Something that stands for something else.

FRANKIE   I was right the first time. A blow job.

JOHNNY   A sensual metaphor for mutual acceptance.

FRANKIE   Fuck you. Besides, what's mutual about a blow job?

JOHNNY   I made that up. I'm sorry. It wasn't a metaphor. It was just something I wanted us to do.

FRANKIE   And I didn't.

JOHNNY   Let it go, will you? One lousy little peccadillo and it's off with his head!

FRANKIE   Stop using words I don't know. What's a peccadillo?

JOHNNY   A blow job! Notice I haven't died you didn't do it—

FRANKIE   I noticed.

JOHNNY   And let me notice something for you: you wouldn't have died if you had. Thanks for making me feel about this big. (*He gets up and starts gathering and putting on his clothes.*) I'm sorry, I mistook you for a kindred spirit. Kindred: two of a kind, sharing a great affinity.

FRANKIE   I know what kindred means!

JOHNNY   Shall we go for affinity!

FRANKIE   That's the first really rotten thing you've said all night. Somebody who would make fun of somebody else's intelligence, no worse, their education or lack of—that is somebody I would be very glad not to know. I thought you were weird, Johnny. I thought you were sad. I didn't think you were cruel.

JOHNNY   I'm sorry.

FRANKIE   It's a cruelty just waiting to happen again and I don't want to be there when it does.

JOHNNY   Please! (*There is an urgency in his voice that startles Frankie.*) I'm not good with people. I want to be. I can get away with it for long stretches but I always hang myself in the end.

FRANKIE   Hey, c'mon, don't cry. Please, don't cry.

JOHNNY   It's not cruelty. It's a feeling I don't matter. That nobody hears me. I'm drowning. I'm trying to swim back to shore but there's this tremendous undertow and I'm not getting anywhere. My arms and legs are going a mile a minute but they aren't taking me any closer to where I want to be.

FRANKIE   Where's that?

JOHNNY   With you.

FRANKIE   You don't know me.

JOHNNY   Yes, I do. It scares people how much we really know one another, so we pretend we don't. You know me. You've known me all your life. Only now I'm here. Take me. Use me. Try me. There's a reason we're called Frankie and Johnny.

FRANKIE   There's a million other Frankies out there and a billion other Johnnys. The world is filled with Frankies and Johnnys and Jacks and Jills.

JOHNNY   But only one this Johnny, one this Frankie.

FRANKIE   We're too different.

JOHNNY   You say po-tah-toes? All right, I'll say po-tah-toes! I don't care. I love you. I want to marry you.

FRANKIE   I don't say po-tah-toes. Who the hell says po-tah-toes?

JOHNNY   Are you listening to me?

FRANKIE   I'm trying very hard not to!

JOHNNY   That's your trouble. You don't want to hear anything you don't think you already know. Well I'll tell you something, Cinderella: Your Prince Charming has come. Wake up before another thousand years go by! Don't throw me away like a gum wrapper because you think there's something about me you may not like. I have what it takes to give you anything and everything you want. Maybe not up here . . . (*He taps his head.*) . . . or here . . . (*He slaps his hip where he wears his wallet.*) . . . but here. And that would please me enormously. All I ask back is that you use your capacity to be everyone and everything for me. It's within you. If we could do that for each other we'd give our kids the universe. They'd be Shakespeare and the most beautiful music ever written and a saint maybe or a champion athlete or president all rolled into one. Terrific kids! How could they not be? We have a chance to make everything turn out all right again. Turn our back on everything that went wrong. We can begin right now and all over again but only if we begin right now, this minute, this room and us. I know this thing, Frankie.

FRANKIE   I want to show you something, Johnny. (*She pushes her hair back.*) He did that. The man I told you about. With a belt buckle. (*Johnny kisses the scar.*)

JOHNNY   It's gone now.

FRANKIE   It'll never go.

JOHNNY   It's gone. I made it go.

FRANKIE   What are you? My guardian angel?

JOHNNY   It seems to me the right people are our guardian angels.

FRANKIE   I wanted things, too, you know.

JOHNNY   I know.

FRANKIE   A man, a family, kids . . . He's the reason I can't have any.

JOHNNY   He's gone. Choose me. Hurry up. It's getting light out. I turn into a pumpkin.

FRANKIE (*Looking towards the window.*)   It's getting light out! (*Frankie goes to the window.*)

JOHNNY   You are so beautiful standing there.

FRANKIE   The only time I saw the sun come up with a guy was my senior prom. (*Johnny has joined her at the window. As they stand there looking out, we will be aware of the rising sun.*) His name was Johnny Di Corso but everyone called him Skunk. (*She takes Johnny's hand and clasps it to her but her eyes stay looking out the window at the dawn.*) He was a head shorter than me and wasn't much to look at but nobody else had asked me. It was him or else. I was dreading it. But guess what? That boy could dance! You should have seen us. We were the stars of the prom. We did Lindys, the mambo, the Twist. The Monkey, the Frug. All the fast dances. Everybody's mouth was down to here. Afterwards we went out to the lake to watch the sun come up. He told me he was going to be on *American Bandstand* one day. I wonder if he ever made it. (*Johnny puts his arm around her and begins to move her in a slow dance step.*)

JOHNNY   There must be something about you and sunrises and men called Johnny.

FRANKIE   You got a nickname?

JOHNNY   No. You got to be really popular or really unpopular to have a nickname.

FRANKIE   I'll give you a nickname. (*They dance in silence awhile. Silence, that is, except for the Shostakovich which they pay no attention to.*) You're not going to like me saying this but you're a terrible dancer.

JOHNNY   Show me.

FRANKIE   Like that.

JOHNNY   There?

FRANKIE   That's better.

JOHNNY   You're going to make a wonderful teacher. (*He starts to hum.*)

FRANKIE   What's that supposed to be?

JOHNNY   Something from *Brigadoon.*

FRANKIE   That isn't from *Brigadoon.* That isn't even remotely from *Brigadoon.* That isn't even remotely something from anything. (*They dance. Frankie begins to hum.*) That's something from *Brigadoon.* You can't have kids in a place this size.

JOHNNY   Who says?

FRANKIE   How big is your place?

JOHNNY   Even smaller. We'll be a nice snug family. It'll be wonderful.

FRANKIE   Does it always get light so fast this time of year?

JOHNNY   Unh-unh. The sun's in a hurry to shine on us.

FRANKIE   Pardon my French, but that's bullshit.

JOHNNY   You can sleep all day today.

FRANKIE   What are you planning to do?

JOHNNY   Watch you.

FRANKIE   You're just weird enough to do it, too. Well forget it. I can't sleep with people watching me.

JOHNNY   How do you know?

FRANKIE   I was in the hospital for my gall bladder and I had a roommate who just stared at me all the time. I made them move me. I got a private room for the price of a semi. Is this the sort of stuff you look forward to finding out about me?

JOHNNY   Unh-hunh!

FRANKIE   You're nuts.

JOHNNY   I'm happy!

FRANKIE   Where are you taking me?

JOHNNY   The moon.

FRANKIE   That old place again?

JOHNNY   The other side this time. (*Johnny has slow-danced Frankie to the bed. The room is being quickly flooded with sunlight.*)

FRANKIE   If you don't turn into a pumpkin, what do you turn into?

JOHNNY   You tell me? (*He kisses her very gently.*)

FRANKIE   Just a minute. (*She gets up and moves quickly to the bathroom. Johnny turns off all the room lights. He starts to close the blinds but instead raises them even higher. Sunlight pours across him. The Shostakovich ends. Johnny moves quickly to the radio and turns up the volume as the announcer's voice is heard.*)

RADIO ANNOUNCER   . . . that just about winds up my stint in the control room. This has been *Music Till Dawn with Marlon.* I'm still thinking about Frankie and Johnny. God, how I wish you two really existed. Maybe I'm crazy but I'd still like to believe in love. Why the hell do you think I work these hours? Anyway, you two moonbeams, whoever, wherever you are, here's an encore. (*Debussy's "Clair de Lune" is heard again. Johnny sits, listening. He starts to cry he is so happy. He turns as Frankie comes out of the bathroom. She is brushing her teeth.*)

JOHNNY   They're playing our song again.

FRANKIE   Did they say what it was this time?

JOHNNY   I told you! You just walk into a record shop and ask for the most beautiful music . . .

FRANKIE   Watch us end up with something from *The Sound of Music*, you'll see! You want to brush? (*She motions with her thumb to the bathroom. She steps aside as Johnny passes her to go in.*) Don't worry. It's never been used. (*Still brushing her teeth she goes to the window and looks out.*) Did you see the robins? (*She listens to the music.*) This I can see why people call pretty. (*She sits on the bed, listens and continues to brush her teeth. A little gasp of pleasure escapes her.*) Mmmmm! (*Johnny comes out of the bathroom. He is brushing his teeth.*)

JOHNNY   I'm not going to ask whose robe that is.

FRANKIE   Sshh! (*She is really listening to the music.*)

JOHNNY   We should get something with fluoride.

FRANKIE   Sshh!

JOHNNY   Anti-tartar buildup, too.

FRANKIE   Johnny! (*Johnny sits next to her on the bed. They are both brushing their teeth and listening to the music. They continue to brush their teeth and listen to the Debussy. The lights are fading.*)

END OF PLAY.

THE LISBON TRAVIATA (1989)

The reasons I chose to become a playwright are Ethel Merman and Ger-trude Lawrence of Broadway, Sister Mary Margaret of the Ursuline Order of Roman Catholic nuns in Dallas, Texas, and Zoe Caldwell of the Royal Shakespeare Company Stratford-on-Avon *via* Melbourne, Australia.

Here's why.

I had a very strong desire to make myself heard. I would become a writer to accomplish this. If there were alternatives, they never occurred to me.

I just didn't know which kind of writer to be. Becoming a Time-Life writer was my parents' ambition for me. Those two magazines had shown up in our mailbox every week since I had begun to read. Before that, there were all those big and colorful *Life* magazine photos to marvel at.

A Time-Life career would be an exciting one with a regular paycheck. My father was a self-employed salesman, so financial security was an iffy situa-tion in our house. At times, I used to think my father wished he worked for someone but secretly I was very proud of him that he didn't. He didn't root for my writing aspirations but he didn't discourage them, either. A Time-Life son would suit him just fine.

My high school journalism teacher, Miss Van Meter, would have steered me towards investigative reporting and writing for the *New York Times*. Our English teacher, Mrs. McElroy, was waiting for the next Great American Novel to be written but none of us turned out to be its author. Through four years of college, when I worked in the summers as a reporter for the *Corpus Christi Times-Caller*, journalism seemed to be the inevitable career choice for me. I loved being a newspaper man: the camaraderie of the newsroom, the freedom to roam around town collecting a story (even if it was only Corpus Christi, Texas), and my editor's deadline that had to be met regard-less of anything—or else. My almost primal love of being the first with the news quickly evaporated with the advent of television reporters and their cameras and "live," on-the-scene news gathering. Their stories aired on the late news; mine weren't available until the next morning. If I couldn't be first with news, I would do something else.

Ethel Merman is the first person I can remember seeing on a stage. The occasion was Irving Berlin's *Annie Get Your Gun* when she created the role of

Annie Oakley. It was 1946 and I was eight years old. She embedded herself into my DNA with her strong, clear, dominating performance. Every word and gesture was clean and powerful and, yes, loud. She wanted to make herself heard as much as I did. The year before, I'd been taken by my mother's German-descendant parents to my very first show, a performance of *The Red Mill*. I don't remember anything about Victor Herbert's American operetta. I've read there was a real mill on the stage and the vanes moved. Even then, Merman in a spotlight was more vivid.

No fear of my Merman memories fading. I still see her on the stage of the Imperial Theatre. She defies me not to see and listen to her, in fact. There is no need to be subtle because she's putting it all out there. Subtle performers are more withholding than the supergenerous performing talents like Merman's. She doesn't whimper, "Please, love me." Rather she demands, "Love me, damnit." No wonder there were and still are people who can't stand her. They will not, they cannot submit to the force of her personality and artistry. As a performer, she was the kind of writer I wanted to be.

She also had perfect diction, a total commitment to reaching the audience all the way to the last rows of the balcony and the awareness that she was on a *stage* in a *show* performing for an *audience*. She never forgot that she was Ethel Merman and that we had come to see her. If I were going to write plays, it would be for someone like that: an actor, through and through.

Gertrude Lawrence was the muse of Noël Coward and just about every great American composer. She wasn't a distinguished singer and her few movies reveal an acting talent of nongargantuan proportions. She wasn't beautiful but she wore clothes well and had a look, which I think means good posture and a savvy stylist. None of this particularly mattered when she walked onto the stage of the St. James Theatre. She was radiant with her own special light. She was the most beautiful person I had ever seen. It was a Wednesday matinee of Rodgers and Hammerstein's *The King and I*. My father's father, who had seen and loved Gertrude Lawrence in *everything*, including a performance of *The King and I* the month before, wanted to share the experience with his thirteen-year-old grandson when he traveled up from Texas.

When the curtain rose, she was on a ship with her young son, who was about my age, and they were both very frightened. They were in a strange land, Siam, where she had been summoned from England to tutor the king's children. Anna was a widow and her son was half an orphan. There was no Mr. Owens to protect them. She was pretending she wasn't terrified so her little boy wouldn't be afraid. She did this by singing a song in a wobbly, frail, plaintive voice while looking out into the darkened theatre at the audience. She was singing to us, of course, but to me in particular. She knew I was there and how much I had looked forward to this performance. I had practically worn out the cast recording in anticipation of this matinee.

She looked frightened, resolute, and absolutely beautiful. Immediately I wanted Gertrude Lawrence to be my mother and I hated the child actor who was taking my rightful place at her side while she taught him to whistle a happy tune. My mother disappointed me for not being Gertrude Lawrence and taking me away from Dallas, where we were living for the time, and straight to Bangkok, if not Broadway.

My grandfather had told me Miss Lawrence was going to take a much deserved vacation after the Saturday evening performance that week. She never came back from it. She died three and a half weeks later on September 6, 1952. I cried. When I read they buried her in her "Shall We Dance" ball gown, I cried some more. For three hours she had been my mother.

Sister Mary Margaret was a terrifying teacher. No one could rap a 6th grader's knuckles with a ruler harder and with more self-satisfaction than she. She loved her calling. Ordinarily, I would leave her to the likes of Christopher Durang, except that she changed my life more decisively than any of my illustrious professors at Columbia.

One day, she came into our classroom lugging a phonograph and some 78 rpm records. "We're going to listen to some opera," she said and proceeded to put on the Love Duet from Puccini's *Madama Butterfly*. That was the extent of her introduction to this art form that has figured so prominently in my work. No "This is beautiful music, children" or "This is the scene where Pinkerton and Cio-Cio San pledge their love." She simply put the records on and began to correct papers while her students were meant to listen to the passionate, almost erotic melodies filling our parochial school classroom.

I was the only one who did. The rest were soon busy pulling pigtails, aiming spitballs or falling asleep while the music played to its ecstatic finish. I was in Heaven. I was certain it was the most beautiful thing I'd ever heard. I was drawn into this world of melody and feeling without a moment's hesitation. I wanted to live there forever and in that moment I think I knew I would. There was no barrier between reality and art. One could lead me to the other and then back again. I lived fully in one; I lived more fully in the other. I wanted both. That hot Dallas classroom vibrating with the voices of Licia Albanese and James Melton singing the music of Giacomo Puccini was my own conduit to other people whose hearts were as big as mine, whose feelings were as urgent. I knew if I couldn't express my own feelings in my life and work, I would explode. Art wasn't an escape from reality, it was a *heightened* reality all its own, perhaps a more truthful one. Art was an escape *to* the truth, not a turning away from it.

I was about to begin my senior year at Columbia when I went to Europe for the first time. I had three goals: to see Laurence Olivier in *Coriolanus* at Stratford, to experience firsthand the *David* in Florence and to run with the bulls in Pamplona. I accomplished the last two and eventually wrote a play about experiencing the Michelangelo for the first time. The wet-your-pants terror I experienced running *from*, definitely not *with,* the bulls is not likely to make it to the stage.

I missed *Coriolanus* because of a lost passport and an implacable emigration official at Le Havre who would not let me cross the English Channel without the proper credentials, even when I cried real tears as I told her I would miss both Sir Laurence as Coriolanus and Charles Laughton as King Lear. The importance, the necessity of art is not apparent to all mortals. She was as impatient with my pleading as I was uncomprehending of a person who would not bend the rules to save a desperate student from a suicidal frenzy of disappointment. Sir Laurence Olivier as Coriolanus, the greatest triumph of his illustrious career at that point in a play that is seldom done, and he falls from a platform fifteen feet above the stage and is caught by his ankles every performance. One slip and there would be no more Laurence Olivier in *anything.* You must let me pass!

Non, monsieur.

I got Zoe Caldwell instead. When I finally made it to England, I had one day left before the Columbia charter flight home. Stratford was offering *All's Well That Ends Well*, a play performed even less frequently than *Coriolanus*. It was directed by Sir Tyrone Guthrie and it featured the legendary Dame Edith Evans as the Countess of Roussillon. The role of her ward, Helena, was played by Zoe Caldwell, a young actress Guthrie had discovered in her native Australia.

From the moment I heard that profound, richly-ripened voice and felt her incredible, urgent presence I knew what kind of writer I wanted to be: a playwright. If I wanted to make myself heard, I needed to put my words into the mouths and bodies of *actors*, especially actors like this one. Everything this young woman said, even in iambic pentameter, was heard and understood. She made words important. When she spoke, it mattered. Shakespeare could not have wanted a finer interpreter.

Even from my usual place in the theatre—in Stratford, just as it was in New York, somewhere in the last rows of the farthest balcony—there was no distance between us. This actress playing Helena was in close-up from curtain up to curtain down. All notions of being a journalist had vanished by the first interval.

It would be a couple of years before I actually wrote a real play (I don't count the Columbia Varsity Show, *A Little Bit Different,* a spoof of current events and celebrities I wrote with Ed Kleban who would go on to write the lyrics for *A Chorus Line*), but I always knew what I wanted it to *be* when I did: a play with words and action that were clear and deeply felt, a play in which everything mattered. I was more determined than ever to be heard. And if Zoe Caldwell wasn't going to be in that play, I would settle for Laurence Olivier or Gertrude Lawrence or Ethel Merman. Instead, I ended up with Nathan Lane, Chita Rivera, Kathy Bates, Christine Baranski, Audra McDonald, Liza Minnelli, Tyne Daly, F. Murray Abraham, Angela Lansbury, Richard Thomas, Marian Seldes, John Glover, and even Zoe Caldwell, truly a dream come true.

I always write for a voice. I always write for a presence.

Maria Callas had been a voice I heard and a presence I felt ever since I first experienced them both on a long-playing record of Donizetti's *Lucia di Lammermoor* in Corpus Christi, Texas. My high school friend Rand Carter was a year older but we shared a passion for opera. He was eager to share his discovery of this unfamiliar voice with me.

It didn't take much persuasion to become a fan of this unknown Greek soprano with the unlikely middle name of Meneghini. Her voice was dark and mysterious with flashes of brilliance. It was a voice unlike any other. I immediately thought it was beautiful: odd, yes, but beautiful. My father adored Edith Piaf. I had my recordings of *Annie Get Your Gun* and *The King and I.* Unconventional voices were no stranger to me. Callas's hypnotized me. It made me listen. It had something to say. She was singing but she was speaking as well. The music she made with her voice was spontaneous, as if no soprano had ever sung those familiar notes of Lucia's Mad Scene before her. With centuries of performing tradition behind a piece of music or a play, it becomes harder and harder to be that kind of performer. Yet only recently, Simon Russell Beale managed to make Hamlet's "To be or not to be" sound like a speech I had never heard before. Listening to him, I was standing in the pit with the other groundlings at the Globe Theatre in 1601 and *Hamlet* was a new play. Great interpreters are the equals of the creators they interpret. It is a divine collaboration—not a contest—and when it happens, rejoice.

Fifty years after they were made, Maria Callas's recordings still astonish me for her discovery of what all those notes opera singers sing really mean.

The Lisbon *Traviata* is an acknowledgment of what she has meant to me. Mendy's passion for her is mine. Stephen's passions are those that art, even great art, cannot satisfy. Those have been my passions, too.

The play is about the demands of the flesh as much as it is about the needs of the heart. In an ideal world, Stephen and Mendy would be partners. In the real world, even friendship is difficult when sexual desire is not reciprocated. Stephen loses Mike to Paul and even Maria's Lisbon *Traviata* cannot heal that wound of the flesh and spirit.

The most controversial part of the play has always been the final scene. Written when the AIDS crisis was threatening to engulf even the most cocooned gay men, I wanted to tear that cocoon off and see what acts of passion a gay man was capable of. Not any gay man, *this* gay man.

Most operas end in violent death because a great love has been betrayed. If the classic love-tragedies were about men and women, it was time to test Stephen and Mike's passions against those of Carmen and Don José. *The Lisbon Traviata* is about opera lovers and the people who fall out of love with them. I was surprised when people were shocked or offended that I had written a "politically incorrect" play about a gay man who murders another gay man. AIDS was decimating our community. I thought it was time to write operatically about the darker impulses that control all men, gay as well as straight, and what happens when our self-defenses against the encroaching terror of abandonment and loneliness can no longer defend us. Opera and Maria Callas aren't enough to save Stephen, just as Judy Garland and disco weren't enough to save so many of my peers.

When it premiered in 1989, it was a "gay" play and many actors were reluctant to be in it. They blamed their agents. "I love the play but ICM won't let me do it," became the steady tattoo of refusals. Nevertheless, when we finally assembled the cast, it was a wonderful one. John Slattery, buck naked, made his New York debut in it, something I never get tired of reminding him. Nathan Lane, Anthony Heald, and Dan Butler were the other fearless actors who disregarded the consequences of being in so "gay" a play as this one.

The play is no more or no less autobiographical than any of my work. All my plays are emotionally autobiographical but very seldom literally so. They are not about what I've done but what I've felt. I hadn't thought of Rand Carter and his recording of *Lucia di Lammermoor* those many years ago in Corpus Christi until I sat down to write this piece. *The Lisbon Traviata* is not about us. It's about unrequited passion, which is a theme more people than two adolescents of burgeoning sexuality listening to LPs in South Texas can relate to.

Nathan Lane created the role of Mendy at the Manhattan Theatre Club. It is one of the few parts I did not write for him. Talk about a presence, a voice and a determination to be heard. He is arguably the best stage actor of his generation in the American theatre. If he is underappreciated it is by those who mistake effortlessness for seriousness and confuse huffing and puffing and heavy lifting with great acting.

The only actor who might have been better as Mendy than Nathan is Zoe Caldwell but then I have often thought Nathan would be a definitive Callas in *Master Class*. The truth is, I write almost everything for either one of them, even when there isn't the remotest chance either one of them will play it. I am happily the servant of two muses. My indenture to them began at the Imperial and St. James theatres in New York City, flourished in Sister Mary Margaret's classroom in Texas and was finalized in the last rows of the Royal Shakespeare Company, Stratford on Avon, in the summer of 1959.

The Lisbon Traviata

for Dominic Cuskern

THE LISBON TRAVIATA was revised and produced at the Mark Taper Forum (Gordon Davidson, Artistic Director), in Los Angeles, California, on November 16, 1990. It was directed by John Tillinger; the set design was by Philipp Jung; the costume design was by Jane Greenwood; the lighting design was by Ken Billington; the sound design was by Gary and Timmy Harris; the production stage manager was James T. McDermott and the stage manager was Craig Palanker. The cast was as follows:

STEPHEN   Richard Thomas

MENDY   Nathan Lane

MIKE   Dan Butler

PAUL   Sean O'Bryan

THE LISBON TRAVIATA was originally produced Off-Broadway by the Manhattan Theatre Club (Lynne Meadow, Artistic Director; Barry Grove, Managing Director), in New York City, on May 19, 1989. The production was transferred to the Promenade Theatre in New York City, on October 31, 1989. It was directed by John Tillinger; the set design was by Philipp Jung; the costume design was by Jane Greenwood; the lighting design was by Ken Billington; the sound design was by Gary and Timmy Harris and the production stage manager was Pamela Singer. The cast was as follows:

STEPHEN   Anthony Heald

MENDY   Nathan Lane

MIKE   Dan Butler

PAUL   John Slattery

An earlier version of THE LISBON TRAVIATA was produced by Sherwin M. Goldman, Westport Productions and Theatre Off Park Inc. at Theatre Off Park in New York City, on June 4, 1985. It was directed by John Tillinger; the set design was by Philipp Jung; the costume design was by C.L. Hundley; the lighting design was by Michael Orriss Watson; the sound design was by Gary Harris; the production stage manager was John M. Atherlay and the stage manager was Charlie Eisenberg. The cast was as follows:

STEPHEN   Benjamin Hendrickson

MENDY   Seth Allen

MIKE   Stephen Schnetzer

PAUL   Steven Culp

THE CHARACTERS

MENDY
Middle-aged, appealing, somewhat out of shape. Wears good clothes well.
Intelligent. His manner can be excessive (it often is) and may take some
getting used to.

STEPHEN
Ten years younger than Mendy but looks even younger. Good-looking. Fair.
In trim. Somewhat closed and guarded in his manner.

MIKE
Several years younger than Stephen. Handsome, sexual. Dark clothing. Moves
well. Direct manner.

PAUL
Mid-twenties. Good-looking. Appealing, friendly, open manner. Likes himself.

SETTING

The time of the play is now.

The place of the play is New York City.

A word about the settings:

Mendy's apartment is warm, romantic, crowded with good antiques. It is
a floor-through in a brownstone in the West Village. One would be hard-
pressed to imagine a lovelier cocoon. The windows are heavily draped. There
is a fire in the fireplace.

Stephen and Mike's apartment, by comparison, is lean and modern. It is a
one-bedroom in a newish high-rise in the same neighborhood. There is at
least one abstract painting on the wall. A large leather sofa dominates the
living room.

The one thing both apartments have in common are lots and lots of phonograph records, cassettes and reel-to-reel tapes and the elaborate equipment for
playing them. Mendy's records and tapes are strewn all over the place. Those
in Stephen and Mike's place are alphabetically arranged in a large, hi-tech
cabinet and many built-in shelves. Mendy's hi-fi equipment is probably out
of date. Stephen and Mike's is the latest thing.

ACT ONE

Mendy's. After dinner. There are dessert plates and coffee cups about. Phonograph records are strewn everywhere. A general but genial clutter. Stephen is seated on the end of a chaise, not lying back in it. His shoes are off. Mendy is at the hi-fi, trying to find a certain groove on a well-worn record. He has the volume up quite high, so that that the noise of the needle scratching against the record is quite loud and painful.

STEPHEN   Jesus, Mendy!

MENDY   Damnit!

STEPHEN   Be careful!

MENDY   I can't wait for you to hear this.

STEPHEN   Just put it on at the beginning.

MENDY   She's not at the beginning.

STEPHEN   I can wait for her. Anything but that.

MENDY   I've been playing it all day.

STEPHEN   I'm sure you have. Mendy, please!

MENDY   Here we are!

STEPHEN   I don't—

MENDY   Sshh!

STEPHEN   I—

MENDY   Sshh! (*The needle has found the groove Mendy was looking for and begun to track the record. Unfortunately, and almost at once, we hear a steady clunk, clunk, clunk. Not only is the record badly scratched, but the needle is stuck.*)

STEPHEN   I don't believe you.

MENDY   I just bought it!

STEPHEN   All it takes you is one playing to ruin a brand-new record.

MENDY   Sshh! Listen. (*He gives the tone arm a push.*)

STEPHEN   I told you to put everything on tape.

MENDY   You're not listening. Sshh!

STEPHEN   Though God knows you'd probably find a way to scratch a tape, too.

MENDY   Will you listen?

STEPHEN   I'm sure even a CD wouldn't survive you.

MENDY   *Ascolta!* (*The needle is tracking now. What we are listening to is a "pirated" recording of Maria Callas. The sound is appropriately dim and distant and decidedly low-fidelity. The music is Violetta's recitative "È strano . . . è strano" preceding the aria "Ah fors'è lui" from the first act of Verdi's* La Traviata.) It's to die.

STEPHEN   *La Traviata.*

MENDY   I can just see her. Jet-black hair parted in the middle, a chignon in the back, flashing eyes, that white dress with the red carnation, the use of the fan.

STEPHEN   (*Eyes closed, concentrating.*)   Just a minute.

MENDY   And the gloves. Long white kid gloves over the elbow. God, she was so beautiful. The glory, the glory.

STEPHEN   Okay! I think I've got it. *Traviata*, London, June 20, 1958 with Cesare Valletti and Mario Zanasi. The conductor was Nicola Rescigno. Am I right?

MENDY   You've heard it?

STEPHEN   Of course I've heard it. I have it. Just turn it off. Those scratches are worse than chalk on a blackboard. I thought you were going to put on something I hadn't heard.

MENDY   When did you buy it?

STEPHEN   I don't know. A month ago, six weeks. May I see the album cover, please?

MENDY   They told me it just came out.

STEPHEN   Where was that? The album, Mendy.

MENDY   Music Masters. (*He hands Stephen the album.*)

STEPHEN (*Looking at the album.*)   Music Masters! Well no wonder. They haven't even gotten in the Lisbon *Traviata* yet. I told you to go to Discophile.

MENDY   What Lisbon *Traviata*?

STEPHEN   The *Traviata* she sang in Lisbon, March 27, 1958. What do you mean, "What Lisbon *Traviata*?"

MENDY   Stephen!

STEPHEN   "June 21." I could have sworn it was June 20. I think this is a mistake. (*He will find a book among a pile on the floor and start looking for the information he requires.*)

MENDY   Stephen!

STEPHEN   What?

MENDY   There's a Lisbon *Traviata*?

STEPHEN   Kraus is the Alfredo.

MENDY   Alfredo Kraus is the Alfredo?

STEPHEN   No, his sister, Lily Kraus. What do you care? You don't like Alfredo Kraus.

MENDY   I do if he sings with Maria.

STEPHEN (*Finding the date.*)   "June 20." When I'm wrong, I'm wrong. But when I'm right, I'm right. Have you heard Nilsson's *Frau Ohne Schatten* from Munich?

MENDY   Stephen, this isn't funny. How is she?

STEPHEN   Loud, louder, and loudest. She runs the gamut. But Rysanek is spectacular.

MENDY   Stephen, how is she?

STEPHEN   Who she? What she? I don't even know what you're talking about.

MENDY   Maria!

STEPHEN   Oh, that she!

MENDY   On the Lisbon *Traviata*!

STEPHEN   She's fantastic. Did you get the new *Masked Ball* on Phillips?

MENDY   I can't believe you didn't bring it.

STEPHEN   I assumed you had it. Save your money. Caballé and Carreras have their moments but Colin Davis's conducting is so non-echt Italian, you know?

MENDY   Stephen, I'm talking about the Lisbon *Traviata*.

STEPHEN   So was I. Then I changed the subject to the new *Masked Ball*.

MENDY   Fuck the new *Masked Ball*.

STEPHEN   I don't know why you hate Caballé so much.

MENDY   She can't sing.

STEPHEN   Oh, come on, Mendy. She has a beautiful voice.

MENDY   It's not enough.

STEPHEN   You've got to admit she's trying. I mean, she has improved.

MENDY   Not enough. She'll never catch up to Callas. To Tebaldi, maybe. To Maria, never. Is Discophile still open?

STEPHEN   What do I look like? Information Please?

MENDY   What's their number?

STEPHEN   What am I supposed to do while you run over there?

MENDY   You haven't heard Sutherland's *Merry Widow*, I bet.

STEPHEN   I hate Sutherland. So do you. You'd buy anything.

MENDY   What's their number?

STEPHEN   It's after nine.

MENDY   What's their number, will you?

STEPHEN   How should I know?

MENDY   Be that way! (*Mendy has gone to the phone and punch-dialed the number for information.*)

STEPHEN   It's not that good a performance. The London is better.

MENDY   You just said it was fantastic.

STEPHEN   It is, but not that fantastic.

MENDY (*Into the phone.*)   Information?

STEPHEN   You know they charge a quarter for that?

MENDY (*Into the phone.*)   Do you have the number for a Discophile on West 8th Street in the Village?

STEPHEN   Michael does the same thing.

MENDY (*Into phone.*)   Yes, it's in Manhattan. (*Covers the phone, groans.*) Oy! All this talk about the Third World. New York is the Third World.

STEPHEN   If you think I'm going to sit here all by myself listening to scratchy records while you go over to—

MENDY (*Into the phone.*)   Discophile! It's a record shop. That's "D" as in . . . as in what? . . . you've got me so rattled . . . !

STEPHEN   "D" as in David.

MENDY (*Into the phone.*)   As in de los Ángeles. Not the town. The singer. Victoria de los Ángeles. All right, Information, have it your way: "D" as in David then. (*Covers phone.*) Do you believe this?

STEPHEN   Watkins 9-8818.

MENDY   What?

STEPHEN   Watkins 9-8818.

MENDY   Are you sure?

STEPHEN (*Pointing.*)   It's right on their shopping bag.

MENDY (*Into the phone.*)   Never mind, Information, and never was an organization less-aptly named. And don't charge me for this! I'm going to check next month's statement to see if you did. (*He hangs up.*)

STEPHEN   You're incredible.

MENDY   In this day and age in this particular "ville," one can't afford not to be. (*He punch-dials another number.*) Watkins 9-8818, was it?

STEPHEN   Have you heard Sill's last *Thaïs*? I was with my mother. It's what killed her.

MENDY   Unfortunately, I heard her first *Thaïs*.

STEPHEN   Anyone who never heard her early Manons never heard Sills.

MENDY   I heard her Manon.

STEPHEN   You heard her middle and late Manons. I said her first Manons.

MENDY   I heard her Manon in 1971 at the New York State Theatre and it was one big wobble.

STEPHEN   1971 was already her middle Manons. I'm talking about 68/69.

MENDY   (*Into the phone.*)   Hello? Discophile? You don't sound familiar. Are you new? (*Covers the phone.*) He's new. Be still my beating heart. (*Into phone.*) Do you have a copy of the Callas Lisbon *Traviata*? The Callas Lisbon *Traviata*. The Callas Big "C," little "a," double "l-a-s," Lisbon *Traviata*. It's a pirate. Thank you. (*Covers phone.*) No wonder he didn't sound familiar. They're playing Dame Janet Baker.

STEPHEN   Who else?

MENDY   (*Listening.*)   She's singing the *Nuits d'été*.

STEPHEN   They'll never beat Eleanor Steber's recording of that. Mike turned me on to that.

MENDY   (*Still listening.*)   No, wait. It's not Baker. It's too fruity . . . it's Crespin! Or is it? (*He listens hard.*)

STEPHEN   (*Trying to take the phone.*)   Here, let me.

MENDY   (*Pulling away with phone.*)   Just a minute. Did Crista Ludwig ever record it?

STEPHEN   I hope not. Will you let me?

MENDY   Don't grab! (*Stephen takes the phone from Mendy and listens.*) Suzanne Danco? Hildegard Behrens? Josephine Veasey? This is driving me crazy.

STEPHEN   (*Listening.*)   Number one, it's not *Nuits d'été*. It's *L'Invitation au Voyage*. Number two, it's Jessye Norman.

MENDY   Number three, fuck you.

STEPHEN (*Into phone.*)   Hello? (*He covers phone.*) They're out of the Lisbon *Traviata*. They have Dallas and London and he thinks La Scala if you want him to check.

MENDY   Give me that! (*He takes the phone.*) You're sure you don't have the Lisbon? Did you try the shelf under the Angel and RCA cutouts? Sometimes Franz puts them there. He isn't around by any chance? When do you expect it back in again? How many have you sold so far? Thirty? You've sold thirty Lisbon *Traviata*s? (*To Stephen.*) They've sold thirty Lisbon *Traviata*s! (*Back into phone.*) You wouldn't by any chance know offhand who you might have sold some of them to? Couldn't you look? I mean, you must keep receipts, some sort of record. I'm calling for Mme. Scotto. I'm her secretary and she asked me to track down a copy before she leaves town in the morning. Renata Scotto, who else?

STEPHEN   Absolutely incredible!

MENDY   She's doing her first Violetta in years and everybody's told her to listen to the Lisbon *Traviata* first. Mme Scotto never sings anything without listening to Callas first. I know she'd really appreciate it if you could make some effort to track one down. Yes, tonight. I told you, she's leaving in the morning, first thing. But couldn't you at least—! We've tried Music Masters. They're the ones who stuck me with this London *Traviata* everybody else seems to have already heard. Besides, they're closed. They don't work their staff like coolies. I don't think I've communicated the urgency of this call to you. Thank you for nothing. (*He hangs up. Stephen is glancing at his watch.*) Stephen?

STEPHEN   No. I'd love to hear some Flagstad.

MENDY   What do you mean, no? You don't even know what I was going to say.

STEPHEN   Mendy, I always know what you're going to say.

MENDY   Please.

STEPHEN   I said no.

MENDY   It's only eight blocks.

STEPHEN   I'm not going eight blocks and back in this weather for a record album.

MENDY   Who said anything about coming back? We'll go there and stay. This was a dinner invitation, not a slumber party. I'll pay for the cab.

STEPHEN   No!

MENDY   You're going to have to go home eventually. We'll just do it now.

STEPHEN   I'm not going home tonight.

MENDY   Where are you going?

STEPHEN   None of your business.

MENDY   Are you tricking with that guy I saw you with at *Parsifal*?

STEPHEN   Don't be ridiculous.

MENDY   You are!

STEPHEN   I am not.

MENDY   I can see it in your face!

STEPHEN   You think everyone's a trick.

MENDY   He lives just down the street. I've seen him walking his dog. He's cute. Larry Daimlett had him at the Pines last summer.

STEPHEN   So?

MENDY   He's very into drugs.

STEPHEN   He is not.

MENDY   Larry thinks he took cash from his wallet. Close to a hundred dollars. He knows he took his lime green cashmere cable-knit sweater from Paul Stuart.

STEPHEN   I don't believe you.

MENDY   The question is: do you believe Larry Daimlett?

STEPHEN   I believe Larry Daimlett would have liked to sleep with Hal at the Pines last summer.

MENDY   Hal? Is that his name? Hal what?

STEPHEN   Never mind. Koerner. Hal Koerner.

MENDY   That's the one. He's a writer and he waits tables at The Front Porch.

STEPHEN   Just three nights a week.

MENDY   But not enough to keep him in cashmere sweaters and out of other people's wallets.

STEPHEN   That's a really vicious story.

MENDY   Don't say I didn't warn you.

STEPHEN   We've had drinks a couple times. That's it. He likes to talk about literature.

MENDY   He looks like a real highbrow.

STEPHEN   He writes extremely well, as a matter of fact.

MENDY   What does he write?

STEPHEN   What do you mean, what does he write?

MENDY   What genre?

STEPHEN   Poetry.

MENDY   I'm biting my tongue.

STEPHEN   It's not what you're thinking.

MENDY   I don't suppose he knows you're an editor with a lot of influence at a major publishing house? No, he couldn't possibly.

STEPHEN   He's not like that. I'm not dating the guy. We may have a drink together after he gets off work tonight. I thought you had some new things to play for me.

MENDY   I thought I did, too. But it seems you've already heard them. Listen, why don't you put Mme Flagstad on the phonograph, make yourself comfortable and let me run over to your place and get it?

STEPHEN   Mike's there.

MENDY   I'll just be a second. All he has to do is hand it to me. I don't want to neck with him.

STEPHEN   He's got someone there with him.

MENDY   A trick?

STEPHEN   I didn't ask.

MENDY   Well, if it's not a trick I'm sure he wouldn't mind if I popped over and got it.

STEPHEN   I'll bring it over tomorrow.

MENDY   I'd like to hear it tonight.

STEPHEN   I'm sorry. How's this new *Tosca*?

MENDY   Terrible.

STEPHEN   Why did you buy it then?

MENDY   Because I didn't know it was terrible until I had listened to it. Couldn't you just call Mike and ask him if it would be okay for me to pop over?

STEPHEN   I can tell you it wouldn't be. (*Looking at the back of a record album.*) I wish Maria had recorded some of these arias. Maria should have recorded everything.

MENDY   If it was worth recording, she did.

STEPHEN   Callas sings Mussorgsky. Callas sings the Beatles. Callas sings "I'm Bad"!

MENDY   Maybe I could call Mike, even though I'm not officially speaking to him this week.

STEPHEN   Why not?

MENDY   I don't remember.

STEPHEN   I'm sure Michael does.

MENDY   I'm sure it was something I said or did. It usually is. I'm too much for most people. I can't help it. It's genetic. Stephen, please, please, please!

STEPHEN   It's just a record.

MENDY   That's easy for you to say. You've already heard it. Is it good?

STEPHEN   I told you, it's fantastic.

MENDY   I'll give you a thousand dollars.

STEPHEN   It's not that fantastic. The London is better. Lisbon is just another *Traviata*.

MENDY   Maria never sang "just another *Traviata*" in her life. She wasn't capable of "just another *Traviata*." The whole point of Maria is that she never sang "just another" anything. It's what killed her.

STEPHEN   What about those last *La Scala Medea*s?

MENDY   They were different. She was sick. She had a temperature, her blood pressure had fallen alarmingly. Her doctor told her not to appear. And if you'd listen to those recordings carefully, you'd hear that she brought a lot of new insights to the role.

STEPHEN   New insights but no voice.

MENDY   What about the way she does *Lontan! Lontan! Serpenti, via da me!?*

STEPHEN   You're going to hurt your voice doing that.

MENDY   I bet those little kids playing her children shit in their diapers when she said to them, *Lontan! Lontan! Serpenti, via da me!*

STEPHEN   All right, certain phrases were better, I grant you.

MENDY   And what about that high C at the end of the second act? Don't worry, I'm not going to attempt it.

STEPHEN   It's not a high C. It's a B flat and it's a fluke. She only took the high C in the Dallas performances.

MENDY   Are you sure it's not a C?

STEPHEN   Have you got it?

MENDY   Somewhere. I always thought she took the C in the La Scala performances with Schippers, too.

STEPHEN   The last time she took the C at the end of the second act of *Medea* was in Epidaurus.

MENDY   There's no recording of those two *Medea*s in Epidaurus.

STEPHEN   I was there.

MENDY   You never told me that.

STEPHEN   Well, I was.

MENDY   You heard Maria sing *Medea* in the ancient Greek theatre of Dionysus at Epidaurus.

STEPHEN   And the *Norma*s there, two years later.

MENDY   I don't believe you.

STEPHEN   Why not?

MENDY   Well how come you never mentioned it?

STEPHEN   I just did. It's not exactly the kind of thing you go around mentioning all the time. "Hi, I'm Steve. I heard Maria Callas sing *Medea* is Epidaurus, Greece. You live around here?"

MENDY   You think you would have mentioned it to me at least.

STEPHEN   You heard her concert at the Acropolis.

MENDY   August 5th! There was a full moon, as if she needed one!

STEPHEN   Well, if you heard her in Athens why can't I have heard her in Epidaurus?

MENDY   Who was Pollione?

STEPHEN   Jon Vickers.

MENDY   Vickers never sang *Norma* with her. It was the tragedy of his career and hers.

STEPHEN   Well, it was someone like Jon Vickers.

MENDY   The day Flaviano Labo is anything like Jon Vickers is the day Joan Sutherland does her first *Lulu*.

STEPHEN   Flaviano Labo, my God, that's right.

MENDY   The Adalgisa was what's-her-name . . . ? You know!

STEPHEN   That Greek mezzo with hair on her chest. What's-her-name? Paleo-something.

MENDY   Irene Paleolithic. All right, your final question, who sang the Clotilde?

STEPHEN   I don't remember. Nobody ever remembers who sang Clotilde. I doubt if even Maria would remember who sang Clotilde with her in Epidaurus.

MENDY   I bet she remembered who sang Clotilde with her in London on November 8, 1952.

STEPHEN   The whole world remembers who sang Clotilde with her in London in 1952: Big Joan Sutherland herself, The Beast from Down Under.

MENDY   Maria said Sutherland didn't have the legato to sing a good Clotilde.

STEPHEN   The rhythm to sing it is what Maria said.

MENDY   I read "legato."

STEPHEN   Well, you read wrong. Besides, Sutherland has legato. Even I would grant her that. But she always sings behind the beat. That's why Maria said Sutherland didn't have the rhythm to sing even a decent Clotilde. God knows what she thought of her *Norma*.

MENDY   You're too butch to know so much about opera.

STEPHEN   I'm not butch. Rise Stevens is butch. Are you still looking for that *Medea*?

MENDY   Here's Dallas, the first La Scala with Lenny, Covent Garden, the night she met Onassis, *O Notte Tremenda, Notte D'Orrore*, but where's the last La Scala?

STEPHEN   Mendy, I don't want to hear *Medea*. Any of them. I hate *Medea*. I loathe *Medea*. I despise *Medea*.

MENDY   Even with Maria?

STEPHEN   Even with Ethel Merman. It's boring music.

MENDY   Maria is never boring.

STEPHEN   She was in *Medea*.

MENDY   You're going to hell for that.

STEPHEN   I already have. I'm just here on a pass.

MENDY   I just can't believe you were there.

STEPHEN   I had a life before you, Mendy.

MENDY   I divide my life into two periods: Before Maria Callas, BMC, and After Maria Callas, AMC.

STEPHEN   I divided mine into before Michael and after him.

MENDY   It wasn't fair. I saw the divine Dr. Deller before you did. I took him to a *Bohème* with Gabriella Tucci and his beeper went off. He never knew how lucky he was. It was the Mimi from hell. Before I could take him to a decent performance, he'd met you.

STEPHEN   You had your revenge.

MENDY   Did I? I don't remember. What did I do? Poison your food?

STEPHEN   You took Peter Wingate to a performance of *Tristan* I could have given my right nut to see, just because I met Michael at your annual Callas birthday party.

MENDY   You didn't just meet Michael here, you left with him.

STEPHEN   Mendy, Michael wasn't interested in you.

MENDY   That's no excuse. He should have been. And so should you. Not inviting you to *Tristan* was my only revenge.

STEPHEN   I could have killed you. Nilsson and Vickers never sang *Tristan* together again. They were calling it the coupling of the century.

MENDY   I thought that was you and Mike.

STEPHEN   I guess we were sort of the Liz and Dick of Sheridan Square. I didn't know he was married. He didn't know I was still involved with Jimmy Marks. What a mess.

MENDY   I was so in love with you.

STEPHEN   You just thought you were in love with me.

MENDY   That's not true. When you two left together—I remember I was standing right over there listening to Bobby Staub hold forth about his dinner with Susan Sontag (thank God they never made a movie out of that)—and when I saw that door close on you two, I wanted to die. I knew you'd be making love within the hour.

STEPHEN   It was more like ten minutes. I kissed him in your hallway.

MENDY   Thanks a lot.

STEPHEN   I've never been that way with anyone. Usually I wait for them to make the first move. "Does it have to be tonight?" he asked. "If you ever want to see me again, it does." I couldn't believe myself.

MENDY   And here I was on the other side of the door feeling like a combination of the Marschallin—all gentle resignation, *ja, ja, ja* age deferring to beauty and all that shit—and the second act of *Tosca*—stab the son of a bitch in the heart. (*Mendy seizes a knife from the fruit bowl, and raises it dramatically.*)

STEPHEN   Careful, Mendy.

MENDY   *Questo è il baccio di Tosca!* (*He "stabs" Stephen who reacts melodramatically.*)

STEPHEN   *Aiuto . . . aiuto . . . muoio . . .*

MENDY   *È ucciso da una donna . . .* Killed by a woman! *Guardami! . . . Son Tosca, a Scarpia!*

STEPHEN   *Soccorso!*

MENDY   *Tu suffoco il sangue? . . . Muori! muori! muori!!! Ah è morto! . . . Or gli perdono!* (*Stephen starts to get up.*) Just a minute! I'm not finished. *È avanti a lui tremava tutta Roma.* (*He lets the knife drop and waits for the proper ovation. Instead.*)

STEPHEN   You want to hear something funny?

MENDY   I thought I just had. I don't know why I bother!

STEPHEN   The first time I saw Mike, I wasn't even sure he was gay.

MENDY   On these premises? Darling, I've been raided.

STEPHEN   He was so . . . I want to say masculine but that's not the word. There's something beyond masculine.

MENDY   I know. Me.

STEPHEN   The moment I saw him, even before he'd seen me, before we were introduced, I knew he was going to be the one. He was my destiny and I was his. I saw my future flash before me and it was all with him. It was like the first act of *Carmen*, Don José sees her, she throws him the acacia flower and his fate is sealed.

MENDY   Carmen isn't gay.

STEPHEN   She is when a certain mezzo's singing her.

MENDY   What did Mike throw you?

STEPHEN   Wouldn't you like to know?

MENDY   I love your choice of role models. Carmen and Don José. They were a fun couple.

STEPHEN   We're turning into . . . who? . . . I can't think of anyone who ends happily in opera.

MENDY   Hansel and Gretel.

STEPHEN   There you go! That's us. You know what I feel like? The Rosa Ponselle *Vestale* arias.

MENDY   The way you feel about *Medea* is the way I feel about *Vestale*. A whole opera about a fucking vestal virgin, besides they're in the country.

STEPHEN   What do you want to hear then?

MENDY   The Lisbon *Traviata*.

STEPHEN   You're obsessed with the Lisbon *Traviata*.

MENDY   You knew I would be.

STEPHEN   I thought you had it.

MENDY   I don't care what they're doing over there. I just want them to give me the record. Tell them I'll wear a ski mask. I'll go blindfolded. They can throw it down to me in the street out the window.

STEPHEN   Call them yourself. I'm not doing it.

MENDY   I should have told that cretin with attitude at Discophile I worked for Birgit Nilsson. I'm sure she has much more clout than Renata Scotto. (*Into phone.*) Hello, Mike? Who is this? (*Covers phone.*) "A friend of his." I bet. (*Into phone.*) Would you ask him to call Stephen when he gets back?

STEPHEN (*Sharply.*)   Mendy!

MENDY   Tell him I'm at Mendy's. He has the number. Thank you. (*He hangs up.*)

STEPHEN   Why did you do that, Mendy? He's going to think I was calling to check up on him.

MENDY   Mike's out getting pizza. They're listening to *Sweeney Todd*.

STEPHEN   I'm going to tell him it was you. And then *you're* going to tell him it was you.

MENDY   The trick sounded cute.

STEPHEN   You reduce everything to tricks.

MENDY   Maybe that's because I haven't had one since 1901.

STEPHEN   All great beauties are finally alone. Look at Maria. That apartment in Paris became her tomb.

MENDY   (*Begins to sing.*)   *In quelle trine morbide.*

STEPHEN   I should have known!

MENDY   *Sola, abbandonata in questo popoloso deserto che appellano Parigi.*

STEPHEN   I'm going to leave if you keep that up. Couldn't we just talk?

MENDY   Stephen, tell me something: why can't I find someone to love?

STEPHEN   Don't start, Mendy. Please!

MENDY   Is he?

STEPHEN   Is who what?

MENDY   The trick cute?

STEPHEN   He's all right.

MENDY   I thought you didn't know him.

STEPHEN   I said I didn't know if he was a trick.

MENDY   You just said he was.

STEPHEN   Maybe he is. Why don't you call him and ask him? You would, too!

MENDY   All I asked was, is he cute?

STEPHEN   I said he was all right.

MENDY   You've met him?

STEPHEN   No. I saw him. In our lobby. He was going up. I was coming down.

MENDY   Then how did you know it was him?

STEPHEN   He was completely naked except for this big sign around his neck: Mike's trick. I just did! What is this? The riddle scene from *Turandot*? Could we put something on?

MENDY   What's his name?

STEPHEN   I don't know. Paul.

MENDY   Paul? Just Paul?

STEPHEN   Paul Della Rovere.

MENDY   Paul Della Rovere! If that's not a trick's name, I'd like to know what is.

STEPHEN   He's a social worker, so I doubt it. You know what they're like: serious and looking for a real commitment.

MENDY   So am I, so am I! Why can't I meet someone like that? Do you want to give him my number? I've got an extra seat for *Daughter of the Regiment*.

STEPHEN   Has anyone ever said anything to you about your scotch?

MENDY   No, why?

STEPHEN   It's terrible.

MENDY   I don't drink.

STEPHEN   Well, your guests do and it's terrible.

MENDY   So tell me a good brand and I'll buy it. So what's going to happen?

STEPHEN   With Mike and I? Nothing.

MENDY   Mike and me. I can't believe you edit for a living.

STEPHEN   For content. I have an assistant for the grammar. That's who I should fix you up with.

MENDY   Does he like opera?

STEPHEN   He's getting there. He's into crossover albums. He just bought Teresa Stratas in *Funny Girl*.

MENDY   I think I'll pass. So what if Mike and this number get serious?

STEPHEN   They won't.

MENDY   Why not?

STEPHEN   They just won't. We have an agreement about that sort of thing. No involvement.

MENDY   So did you and Jimmy Marks when you met Mike.

STEPHEN   Jimmy and I weren't that serious about each other in the first place. We were each other's Pinkerton just pretending to be each other's Butterfly until the real thing came along. No one got hurt.

MENDY   That's not how I remember it.

STEPHEN   He got over it.

MENDY   Sometimes I think he's still in love with you.

STEPHEN   I hope not. I see Jimmy and Donald together and I can't believe we were ever lovers. There's this void. It's like it never happened.

MENDY   As if it never happened.

STEPHEN   Shut up, Mendy.

MENDY   Bad grammar is a knife in my heart, right here.

STEPHEN   You just need to get laid.

MENDY   Lots of luck in the Fabulous 80s!

STEPHEN   Some people are managing.

MENDY   I don't even care about sex anymore. I'd settle for a hug. Well, maybe not a hug.

STEPHEN   What ever happened to you and that curator at the Modern anyway?

MENDY   I took him to *Pelléas et Mélisande* and he fell asleep in the first scene. I had to wake him for intermission.

STEPHEN   *Pelléas?* Give the guy a break. Take him to *Tosca*, *Trovatore*. Something with balls.

MENDY   Debussy has balls. He just doesn't wear them on his sleeve.

STEPHEN   You're going to die with your secret, Mendy.

MENDY   I don't even know what it is.

STEPHEN   That's why it's your secret. I think you'd rather listen to opera than fuck.

MENDY   Opera doesn't reject me. The real world does. I don't understand love. *Non capisco amore.*

STEPHEN   I don't think I understand anything but; *Vissi d'arte, vissi d'amore.* I live for art, I live for love.

MENDY   I don't understand agreements either. I never thought the two of you would last. And when it did, I was a little envious. No, a lot envious. And now that it's sort of over . . .

STEPHEN   It's not over.

MENDY   I feel a little sad.

STEPHEN   I said, it's not over.

MENDY   The part I was jealous of is: the passion.

STEPHEN   Our passion is just fine. Thank you. It's just a little different.

MENDY   That's for sure. If he's with someone else, it sounds like the first act of *Carmen* is turning into the last. The final duet. Only in your production, who's Carmen and who's Don José?

STEPHEN   Wouldn't you like to know? (*Spoken.*) *Frappe-moi donc, ou laisse-moi passer!*

MENDY   You need more chest. Maria does it with more chest. Frappe-moi donc, ou laisse-moi passer! (*Stephen "stabs" him and Mendy falls dramatically. "Death" convulsions.*) Can I ask you a personal question?

STEPHEN   No.

MENDY   Do you and Mike still have sex?

STEPHEN   None of your business.

MENDY   So you don't. Do you think he'll move out?

STEPHEN   No. Besides, where would he go? Now *basta*, Mendy. I didn't come over here for this.

MENDY   What did you come over for?

STEPHEN   You invited me. For music, for conversation, for . . . not for this. What about Marilyn Horne's *Tancredi* from Dallas last year?

MENDY   It's in the country.

STEPHEN   Everything good you have is in the country.

MENDY   Everything good you have, like the Lisbon *Traviata*, is only eight blocks from here.

STEPHEN   What's the *Tancredi* like?

MENDY   Terrible. She's sharp.

STEPHEN   Marilyn Horne doesn't sharp. She flats.

MENDY   Well she sure as shit sharped November 5th in Dallas, Texas.

STEPHEN   Really? I'll have to hear it sometime.

MENDY   You'll have to come to Connecticut.

STEPHEN   I wouldn't cross the street to hear Marilyn Horne sing on pitch. She sings like a truck driver.

MENDY   What do you expect? Marilyn Horne was a truck driver. She was discovered singing the "Habanera" while operating a fork lift in a Los Angeles gravel pit.

STEPHEN   Now that's vicious.

MENDY   What's vicious is you not getting the goddamn Lisbon *Traviata*. How long does it take to get pizza anyway?

STEPHEN   Maria flats on the Lisbon *Traviata*.

MENDY   Where?

STEPHEN   Twice in *Ah, fors'è lui*, once in *Sempre Libera* and practically the entire *Dite alla giovine* is a quarter tone down.

MENDY   I don't believe you.

STEPHEN   It's on the record.

MENDY   Maria never flatted in her entire life. Sharped, yes; flatted, never.

STEPHEN   Maybe it was something she ate, a rancid paella or something. I don't know, Mendy, but she flatted in Lisbon just like Marilyn Horne sharped in Dallas.

MENDY   Fuck Marilyn Horne.

STEPHEN   I can't help it if I was born with perfect pitch.

MENDY   And fuck your perfect pitch. It's Maria's pitch that you're impugning.

STEPHEN   Who's impugning? I'm stating fact. On the night of March 27, 1958, Maria Callas sang flat in a performance of *La Traviata* at the Teatro San Marco in Lisbon, Portugal. Nobody's perfect.

MENDY   Maria is.

STEPHEN   Was.

MENDY   And always will be. (*He is dialing a number.*)

STEPHEN   Mendy, leave them alone!

MENDY   I may not have your ear but I have a pitch pipe I bought in Salzburg at that music shop three doors down from the house Mozart was born in. Herbert von Karajan was there buying batons.

STEPHEN   What does that have to do with anything?

MENDY   Herbert von Karajan would hardly be seen buying batons in a music shop that didn't sell excellent pitch pipes. We'll see how flat Maria was. (*Into phone.*) Is he back yet? What's-his-name! Your friend whose apartment you're at who's out buying pizza. They've got me so rattled over here I can't even remember his name.

STEPHEN   It's Michael.

MENDY   Thank you. (*Covers phone.*) I love this one's voice. Della—what was it?

STEPHEN   Della Rovere.

MENDY   He could be the first Italian hump tenor with that name.

STEPHEN   I thought you thought Franco Corelli was a hump.

MENDY   I never said I thought Franco Corelli was a hump. I said I like his legs in *Turandot*. He sang like a beast.

STEPHEN   Mike is going to kill you for this.

MENDY   They're playing *Sweeney Todd* so loud over there I don't know how they can think. I'll never understand what people see in musicals. I mean, why settle for *The Sound of Music* when you can have *Dialogues of the Carmelites*? (*Into phone.*) Mike? This is Mendy.

STEPHEN   Tell him it wasn't me who called before.

MENDY   I wonder if I could ask a favor.

STEPHEN   Tell him it wasn't me.

MENDY   Stephen's telling me to tell you it wasn't him, whatever that means. Listen—

STEPHEN   Let me talk to him when you're finished.

MENDY   You've got a record over there, it's Stephen's actually, the Lisbon *Traviata*.

STEPHEN   He won't have a clue what you're talking about.

MENDY   The Lisbon *Traviata*! If you could perhaps turn Mme. Lansbury down for just a moment . . . ? Thank you. (*Covers phone.*) He called him "Babe." What's-his-name? The Italian Hump. Mike called him "Babe."

STEPHEN   Mike calls everyone "Babe."

MENDY   I bet *Sweeney Todd*'s not all they're playing.

STEPHEN   Anyway, he's Portuguese.

MENDY   The Italian Hump is Portuguese? Maybe he was there.

STEPHEN   Maybe he was where?

MENDY (*Covers phone.*)   The Lisbon *Traviata*! (*Back into phone.*) Can you hear me now? Yes, perfectly. Listen, Mike, there's a favor I'd like to ask you. Well, it's two favors actually. (*To Stephen.*) Would you stop snooping at my desk?

STEPHEN   I'm not snooping. I was looking for *Opera News*.

MENDY (*Into phone.*)   Stephen left a record album there I specifically asked him to bring over with him tonight. I was wondering if I stopped by I might pick it up.

STEPHEN   Are these your tickets for *Elektra*? I got fourth row on the aisle.

MENDY   How soon? I could come right now. Couldn't you wait a couple of minutes until I got there? It's only a couple of blocks.

STEPHEN   Eight blocks, Mendy, and it's raining.

MENDY   What if I took a cab? You'll be passing right by here. I could meet you halfway.

STEPHEN   Who's the postcard from?

MENDY   I don't want to be a pest about it, Michael, but really, it's terribly important.

STEPHEN   It looks like Rio.

MENDY   If you just got back with pizza, I don't understand why you have to go rushing out again to the movies. If you'd returned my call when I asked you to call, just as soon as you got back with it, I could have been over there and gone by now. This is all really very inconsiderate of you, Michael. As a matter of fact, to me it *is* a matter of life and death. I'm sorry I feel this way about it, too.

STEPHEN   Why didn't you tell me Lester was sick?

MENDY   Never mind the second favor. I'm sorry I asked you the first.

STEPHEN   Don't hang up.

MENDY   The next time you're offered a pair of free tickets to the Met, they won't be from me. That's not the point. I offered them. Whether or not you wanted them is immaterial.

STEPHEN   Don't hang up.

MENDY   You're a selfish, self-centered, stereotypical, aging, immature queen. No wonder you don't have any friends. Yes, all that just because you won't bring a goddamn record album over here or let me come over there and get it! Besides, the Maria Callas Lisbon *Traviata* is not just another goddamn record album of Stephen's. Right now, at this particular moment in my not-so-terrific life, it's probably the most goddamn important thing in the world to me, but I wouldn't expect an insensitive faggot whose idea of a good time is sitting around listening to Angela Lansbury shrieking about "The Worst Pies in London," like yourself, to understand what I'm talking about. I'm not surprised you don't like opera. People like you don't like life.

STEPHEN   I want to talk to him when you're through.

MENDY   Not a moment too soon! (*Back into the phone.*) Your lover would like a word with you, Michael, though for the life of me, I can't imagine why. Although after tonight I can understand why he's well on his way to being your ex. There's not one person in this entire city who thought it would last, including David Minton.

STEPHEN   Who is David Minton?

MENDY (*Into phone.*)   I will simply never, never understand how Stephen got that way with you in the first place. (*Hands phone to Stephen.*) Here.

STEPHEN   You could've been over there by now. (*Into the phone.*) Mike? Hi.

MENDY   Tell him his friend Mr. Della Rovere used to work standing room at the old Met.

STEPHEN   I don't know. Some Callas record.

MENDY   I had him halfway through Flagstad's farewell *Isolde.*

STEPHEN   That's okay.

MENDY   I know some people who had him during her first.

STEPHEN   Did you know Lester Cantwell has been in the hospital in Rio de Janeiro for the past five weeks with a ruptured spleen?

MENDY   I refuse not to be taken seriously like this!

STEPHEN   Mendy got a postcard from him.

MENDY   Doesn't he think I meant any of it?

STEPHEN   I don't know. (*To Mendy.*) How long ago did you get it?

MENDY   After what I just said to him and he has the nerve to ask me about Lester Cantwell's ruptured spleen?

STEPHEN   Mendy, he's one of our best friends and we'd like to know.

MENDY   If he's one of your best friends then why don't you just call him? He's been back for at least three weeks.

STEPHEN (*Into phone.*)   Did you hear that? (*To Mendy.*) How is he?

MENDY   Like he always is: hysterical. Now he thinks he has AIDS. From what? I asked him. Watching *Dynasty* reruns? The spleen business was months ago if you'd just looked at the postmark and I thought I asked you not to snoop around my desk in the first place anyway.

STEPHEN (*Into phone.*)   I guess it has been a while since we spoke to him. What are you two up to anyway?

MENDY   Would you mind not monopolizing that thing? I'm expecting a call.

STEPHEN   It's a dumb movie but the special effects are fantastic. Where are you seeing it? The Greenwich? With their sound system? Lots of luck.

MENDY   I thought they were in such a hurry.

STEPHEN   We're just listening to records. Veal piccata. (*To Mendy.*) He loves your veal piccata.

MENDY   He's had his last helping.

STEPHEN (*Into phone.*)   I don't know. I might have something on later. I'm expecting a call.

MENDY   What am I? Stage door canteen? Some pit stop? Some place to kill time while you wait for a late date to call? Fuck you, too, Stephen.

STEPHEN   The guy I told you about. The writer.

MENDY   What writer? He's a waiter at a second-rate, over-priced gay hamburger stand.

STEPHEN   He wasn't sure if he'd be free after work.

MENDY   His kind never is. Stephen, I told you I was expecting a call.

STEPHEN   You want to hear something funny? I was going to ask you to walk Sammy. Sometimes I completely forget. Two years and sometimes I think he's still with us. Oh, listen, I think we might be low on milk.

MENDY   Listen to you two. You'd think you were married and had kids at Montessori.

STEPHEN   Why can't the two of you go to his place? I told you it wasn't definite. Why does he have to stay over? Forget it. I took a change with me. As long as he's out of there by eight. All right, I'll call when I know. But don't change your plans because of me. Maybe you better tell him about that loose floorboard on my side of the bed. We don't want a lawsuit on our hands. (*He laughs at something Mike says, then extends phone to Mendy.*) He wants to talk to you.

MENDY   Well, I don't want to talk to him.

STEPHEN   He wants to know what the other favor was, just in case.

MENDY   In case of what?

STEPHEN   In case he might be able to do it.

MENDY   You really don't take me seriously, either one of you!

STEPHEN   Oh, come on.

MENDY   I was only going to ask him, not that it matters now and I certainly wouldn't want to put him out or anything, even if he did spend three summers with me on Fire Island as a permanent, non-paying, non-dishwashing, non-anything but hanging-around-on-the-meat-rack guest, if his little Portuguese friend had maybe heard Maria's *Traviata* in Lisbon, but if he's so heavily into Stephen Sondheim, I would seriously doubt it!

STEPHEN   (*Into phone.*)   Did you hear that? (*To Mendy.*) He's asking him.

MENDY   He's just wasting his time. Six times over and back I could've been.

STEPHEN   Why don't you put on the Berlin *Lucia*?

MENDY   I'm sick of it. Besides, I lent it to Elaine.

STEPHEN   I thought Elaine hated opera.

MENDY   She does but she likes the Berlin *Lucia*. She was over the other night and loved it.

STEPHEN   That's amazing. I mean, wasn't Callas named in your divorce for alienation of affections?

MENDY   I don't know who I thought I was kidding. Certainly not Elaine.

STEPHEN   You still see her?

MENDY   Of course I do. She's one of my best friends. We had more than a kid together.

STEPHEN   Is she seeing anyone?

MENDY   Some stockbroker but Jason can't stand him. Neither can I.

STEPHEN   He must be ten by now.

MENDY   Thirteen. What's happening?

STEPHEN   I guess he's still asking. Thirteen! He's one thing I envy you. Remember the time we—?

MENDY   What loose board?

STEPHEN   —took him to *Rigoletto?*—Hunh?

MENDY   You said something about a loose floorboard on your side?

STEPHEN   Oh. There's a loose floorboard on my side of the bed and if you don't know about it, you could step on it wrong and it could pop up and you could hurt yourself. I should have let Mr. Della Rovere find out for himself.

MENDY   Then they are sleeping together?

STEPHEN   It would seem so.

MENDY   And in your bed?

STEPHEN   This is the first time he's ever asked that.

MENDY   I knew it. And you're sleeping with Ezra Pound *manqué.*

STEPHEN   Well, we'll see tonight. So far it's my brain he's interested in.

MENDY   The minute I saw you two at *Parsifal* I said to myself, "He's with a trick."

STEPHEN   Knowing you, you probably said it to the people you were with.

MENDY   Well, Stephen, it was kind of obvious: two grown men at a performance of *Parsifal.*

STEPHEN   What's so obvious about two men going to *Parsifal* together?

MENDY   Face it, Stephen, ice hockey at the Garden it's not. (*Indicating phone.*) What are they doing over there? Making love?

STEPHEN   Is there anyone or anything you don't reduce to sex?

MENDY   My son, Jason, my Volvo station wagon, and Maria Callas.

STEPHEN   You wonder why you don't have a lover but have you ever listened to yourself?

MENDY   I have an analyst for that.

STEPHEN   What does he say?

MENDY   She can't find a thing wrong with me.

STEPHEN   Another one! How many have you had?

MENDY   Ten years, six analysts. Elaine says I go through them like Kleenex.

STEPHEN   She should—(*Into phone.*) Hello?

MENDY   Know or talk?

STEPHEN   It's Paul.

MENDY   For me?

STEPHEN   He doesn't have all night.

MENDY (*Into phone.*)   Paul? This is Mendy. Did Mike tell you what I—? Well, that's what I was wondering but if you're not sure then I'm sure you weren't. Well of course someone sang it. Someone usually does. Otherwise there's no performance or they call it a play. (*Makes a face at Stephen.*)

STEPHEN   You're wasting your time.

MENDY (*Covers phone.*)   Pick up the extension! (*Back into phone.*)This would have been '56 or '57.

STEPHEN   It was 1958. March 25th and 27th.

MENDY   Stephen says it was 1958.

STEPHEN   March 25th and 27th.

MENDY   You were how old then? (*Covers phone.*) Don't pick up! You don't want to know. (*Back into phone.*) But you remember your grandfather taking you to an opera? This is encouraging. Tell me everything you remember about it. No, the one with bulls in it is *Carmen.* Very inappropriate for a child. *Traviata's* about a courtesan dying of consumption. A courtesan: what Stephen was before he became the youngest senior editor at Knopf and an avocation to which he will soon be returning if he doesn't come up with another bestseller.

STEPHEN   Mendy! He doesn't have to know that.

MENDY   No, horses and camels are *Aida.* I wish you could remember the singers as well as you do the animals. *Traviata* begins at a party. Everyone is drinking champagne and being very gay. I'll ignore that! And then the tenor's father, the baritone, comes in and ruins everything, as fathers will. And then there's a gambling scene and in the last act she reads a letter, *Teneste la promessa*, and dies. You remember that much? Then you definitely remember *Traviata*. Now try to describe the soprano who was singing Violetta. Violetta is the heroine. You're making me feel like Milton Cross. Skip it. Just tell me about the soprano. Other than the fact that you didn't like her, what can you tell me about her? "Lousy" is a strong word, Paul. So is "stunk." I don't care about your opinion as a matter of fact! I think you heard Maria Callas. That's a good question. I loved her so much. I still do. Everything about her. Anything. I'll take crumbs when it comes to Maria. Her time was so brief. That's why I was hoping maybe you could tell me something about her I didn't know. She's given me so much pleasure, ecstasy, a certain solace, I suppose; memories that don't stop. This doesn't seem to be such a terrible existence with people like her to illuminate it. We'll never see her like again. How do you describe a miracle? Do yourself a favor. Put on one of her records. *Puritani* or *Sonnambula* or *Norma*. If what you hear doesn't get to you, really speak to you, touch your heart, Paul, the truth of it, the intensity of feeling . . . well, I can't imagine such a thing. I don't think we could be friends. I know we couldn't. There's a reason we called her La Divina but if you don't even remember who sang *Traviata* that night, there's no point in going on with this even if you did hear Callas. For people like you, it might as well have been Zinka Milanov. Skip that one, too. Listen, thank you for your trouble. Enjoy the movie. No, I don't care what your grandfather thought of her either. The two of you heard the greatest singer who ever lived and you don't even remember it. Yes, she's dead, thanks to people like you! Murderer! I hope you hate the movie. (*He hangs up.*) God, I loathe the Portuguese.

STEPHEN   Half an hour ago you were in love with the sound of his voice.

MENDY   Half an hour ago I didn't know he was at the Lisbon *Traviata* and doesn't even remember her.

STEPHEN   He remembers the *Traviata*. It's Callas he doesn't remember.

MENDY   They're the same thing. And stop calling her that! Callas! It makes her sound faraway, formidable.

STEPHEN   She was and is. Now what do you want to hear?

MENDY   I don't care anymore! *Einstein on the Beach*.

STEPHEN   The whole thing?

MENDY   Oh, that's right: you're in a rush.

STEPHEN   I'm not in a rush right now. He doesn't get off until after midnight. It's a tentative date anyway. What about this *Andrea Chénier*?

MENDY   I'm not in the mood for Verismo.

STEPHEN   I just want to hear what Marton does with it.

MENDY   She does what she does with everything: screams her way through it.

STEPHEN   I like her *Tosca*.

MENDY   There is only one *Tosca*.

STEPHEN   That's ridiculous. You can't listen to Maria all the time.

MENDY   Why not?

STEPHEN   I was going to say it's not normal.

MENDY   You? Normal? Your whole life is a mockery of the word.

STEPHEN   What you said about her, just now, on the phone, it was touching.

MENDY   Oh please!

STEPHEN   I mean it. It's true, too. Sometimes I forget how much we owe her. There's my Maria and then there's the woman who changed the face of opera.

MENDY   Maria Callas *is* opera.

STEPHEN   You don't have to convert me, Mendy. If you'll remember, I was into her several years before you.

MENDY   It wasn't a contest.

STEPHEN   No, but it's a fact.

MENDY   Have it your way. You usually do.

STEPHEN   What is that supposed to mean?

MENDY   Nothing. I thought you were going to put something on.

STEPHEN   Everything means something.

MENDY   Well, don't you?

STEPHEN   You know I don't.

MENDY   I wasn't talking about Mike.

STEPHEN   Well, then don't make a remark like that.

MENDY   I was talking about . . . I don't know what I was talking about.

STEPHEN   You usually don't.

MENDY   Thanks a lot. What I meant was, you've always had someone.

STEPHEN   I've always wanted someone.

MENDY   You think I don't want someone?

STEPHEN   You're always looking too hard. It doesn't happen that way.

MENDY   How does it happen?

STEPHEN   I don't know. It just happens. But if you try making it happen, somehow it never does.

MENDY   In other words, I frighten people off with my needs?

STEPHEN   I didn't say that.

MENDY   That's what Elaine thinks.

STEPHEN   Everybody has needs, Mendy.

MENDY   And I guess your needs are more attractive than mine.

STEPHEN   I don't find any needs attractive, especially my own.

MENDY   That sounds ominous.

STEPHEN   It is.

MENDY   What are your needs?

STEPHEN   Mike, Mike, and more Mike. But we're going to be fine. We're going through a phase. I hate phases. I hate change. We were perfect.

MENDY   You and Mike aren't on the verge of breaking up?

STEPHEN   Michael and I are just on the verge of what to do with the rest of our lives. After eight years, it's inevitable.

MENDY   I'm sorry.

STEPHEN   I'm a big boy. So is Michael. We'll handle it. What about this *Nabucco*?

MENDY   The last thing I'm in the mood for tonight is a chorus of wailing Hebrews.

STEPHEN   I've spent the whole evening looking for a record I haven't heard and you say no!

MENDY   I've got the new *Adriana* with Caballé and Carreras.

STEPHEN   So do I. It's atrocious.

MENDY   Well, what do you expect from those two? The Spanish Frick and Frack.

STEPHEN   Nine thousand records and we can't find one!

MENDY   There's always Maria.

STEPHEN   I'm sick of Maria. I'm sick of opera. I'm sick of life.

MENDY   I'd hate to be your date tonight.

STEPHEN   You are my date tonight.

MENDY   I meant after.

STEPHEN   He's probably going to break it.

MENDY   Why would you say that?

STEPHEN   Just a hunch.

MENDY   I worry about you, Stephen.

STEPHEN   So do I. May I have some more scotch?

MENDY   I thought you didn't like it.

STEPHEN   When did that stop me? Could we put on some Leyla Gencer? She's good for when you're really fucked.

MENDY   I wish you'd tell me what's really going on.

STEPHEN   I'll be fine. The only thing I care about right now is that phone ringing.

MENDY   I don't believe that.

STEPHEN   You'd better. My self-esteem for the next couple of hours is in the hands of a mildly attractive young man I'm not even sure I approve of. I certainly don't his poetry. If you hear we're publishing him, call the Art Police and have me locked up.

MENDY   What are we going to do about you?

STEPHEN   I just want to feel somebody's arms around me for the next couple of hours. I want to make wild, hot, passionate love all night long. I want our mouths to ache from kissing. I want our bodies to stick together from our sweat; and then I want to start all over again.

MENDY   I suppose if you like that sort of thing . . . ! Aren't you worried about—?

STEPHEN   I'm terrified. Okay? There isn't a moment I'm out there that I'm not.

MENDY   Thank God I'm not eighteen. I don't know how they cope. At least we have Maria.

STEPHEN   What about this new *Wozzeck*?

MENDY   No. Absolutely not! I hate twentieth-century opera. So do you.

STEPHEN   Why did you buy it then?

MENDY   I was being pretentious. Give me *bel canto* or give me death.

STEPHEN   You hate the twentieth century.

MENDY   With increasingly good reason.

STEPHEN (*He has picked up a magazine.*)   Where did you get this?

MENDY   What?

STEPHEN   The new *Blueboy*?

MENDY   I don't know. I think Tom Ewing must have left it here.

STEPHEN   I still only have last month's.

MENDY   You actually read those things?

STEPHEN   No one reads them, Mendy. Are you sure you're gay?

MENDY   Ha, ha, ha!

STEPHEN (*Turning the pages in the magazine.*)   God, he's gorgeous. (*Mendy joins him and looks.*)

MENDY   He's all right.

STEPHEN   You wouldn't kick him out of bed.

MENDY   He's too beefy.

STEPHEN   They're called muscles. Good boys who go to the gym get them for Christmas.

MENDY   I would rather be tortured on a rack than exercise. I don't know how you stay so trim.

STEPHEN   Is this more your liking?

MENDY   He looks like Carlo Bergonzi as Radamès.

STEPHEN   Will you look at those legs?

MENDY   My needs are different.

STEPHEN   They're perfect.

MENDY   They're urgent.

STEPHEN   I love legs like that.

MENDY   If I don't get back in a relationship soon, I don't know what I'm going to do.

STEPHEN   I told you: don't fret it. Just lay back and let it happen.

MENDY   You make it sound like something obscene.

STEPHEN   With a little luck, it is. Don't worry, Mendy, one day he'll come along.

MENDY   Who?

STEPHEN   The right one for you. He'll be tall, dark and handsome and he'll ask you to recommend a recording of *Così Fan Tutte*.

MENDY   Yeah, and after I die just a little bit, I'll find out he's a gentle policeman with a wonderful dental program who just wants to be loved.

STEPHEN   He won't be anything like your fantasy of him.

MENDY   As long as he likes Maria.

STEPHEN   He'll probably hate her. I don't think we really know what our fantasies are until we meet them. We have fantasies *of* fantasies and run around in circles. Oh, my God!

MENDY   What's the matter?

STEPHEN   For a minute there I thought it was Hal.

MENDY   Your waiter friend.

STEPHEN   I wish you'd stop calling him that. He's a writer.

MENDY   Yeah! He looks like that?

STEPHEN   A little.

MENDY   No wonder you're hoping he'll call.

STEPHEN   I thought you'd seen him walking his dog.

MENDY   I have, but if he'd been dressed like that, believe me, I would never have noticed the dog. If this is what you go for, no wonder you never saw anything in me.

STEPHEN   I'm going to turn the page, all right?

MENDY   Why is that whenever I say anything serious, you let it pass?

STEPHEN   The only thing we ever saw in one another was Maria Callas.

MENDY   That's not true.

STEPHEN   Think about it. I'm going to turn the page, all right?

MENDY   Like I said: have it your way.

STEPHEN   Like you said: I usually do.

MENDY   That was a very hurtful thing you just said.

STEPHEN   It's true. (*He turns the page.*) If it weren't for Maria, I doubt we'd even be friends. (*He turns the page.*) Well, maybe we'd be friends but we wouldn't be—(*He turns the page.*)

MENDY   Wouldn't be what?

STEPHEN   Friends like this.

MENDY   I always thought we should have been lovers.

STEPHEN   I know, that's occurred to me too.

MENDY   So what happened? Mike doesn't even especially like opera. I don't know how you've stood it. He barely tolerates Maria.

STEPHEN   He doesn't have a choice, living with me. That one has a sexy neck.

MENDY   What do you do with a neck? We could have been lovers, too, if . . .

STEPHEN   Nice and thick.

MENDY   . . . if this had been the best of all possible worlds.

STEPHEN   Well it isn't. Michael has a wonderful neck. You know whose neck I've always loved? Alan Bates.

MENDY   You were so cute then.

STEPHEN   Thanks a lot.

MENDY   I had my good points, too.

STEPHEN   You still do.

MENDY   Well then?

STEPHEN   Can you see the two of us in bed together? First we'd get the giggles and then we'd quarrel over which *Puritani* to play.

MENDY   There is only one *Puritani* to play.

STEPHEN   The Mexico City, May 11, 1952 one.

MENDY   Over her 1954 Chicago performances?

STEPHEN   You see? Besides, they were in 1955. We would have killed one another by now.

MENDY   Sometimes I think we're the same person.

STEPHEN   Us?

MENDY   The only difference between us in that we're not. You know what I mean, we're like sisters. What are those? They look like want ads.

STEPHEN   They're the personals. Men looking for other men. "Gay white male, 40, nonsmoker, seeks same for safe and sane good times."

MENDY   I could never do that.

STEPHEN   Sure you could. Look, here's one for you. He's a 5'10," hairy weight-lifter who's into rare Renata Tebaldi tapes.

MENDY   Let me see that. Oh my God, he is! Did you put this in?

STEPHEN   It's a big world we live in. Someone for everyone. Why don't you call him? Maybe he's nice.

MENDY   If he likes Tebaldi, I doubt it. They're a mean little bunch. It was a Tebaldi fan who threw those radishes at Maria at the first Saturday matinee *Norma*. Tebaldi fans belong in a soccer stadium.

STEPHEN   You never seem to run into them anymore.

MENDY   It's true. After Renata stopped singing, it was as if they had vanished from the face of the earth. We, on the other hand, are still everywhere. I sometimes think we're increasing. Maria lives through us. We've kept her alive or maybe it's vice versa. We're some kind of survivors.

STEPHEN   She's the only one who didn't.

MENDY   You didn't tell me: how does she read the letter on it?

STEPHEN   What letter?

MENDY   Maria on the Lisbon *Traviata*.

STEPHEN   It's beautiful.

MENDY   Better than Dallas?

STEPHEN   Different. It's more like Covent Garden.

MENDY   It couldn't be better than Dallas. Nothing will ever be better than Dallas. (*And he's off!*) *Teneste la promessa. La disfida ebbe luogo, il Barone fu ferito, però migliora. Alfredo è in stranio suolo; il vostro sacrificio io stesso gli ho svelato. Egli a voi tornerà pel suo perdono; io pur verrò.* (*The telephone has begun to ring. Stephen looks at his watch.*)

STEPHEN   This won't be him. It's too early. (*Mendy has picked up the phone.*)

MENDY   *Curatevi: meritate un avvenir migliore. Giorgio Germont. È tardi!* You've reached Heartbreak House. This is Cio-Cio San speaking. Just a moment. (*Covers phone.*) You're going to kill me. It's your waiter friend.

STEPHEN   So soon?

MENDY   Ask him to drop by if he'd like.

STEPHEN (*Into phone.*)   Hi. How's it going? Mendy. He was just camping.

MENDY   That's not true. I was doing Maria. I wasn't camping. I never camp.

STEPHEN   We're just sitting around, playing a few records.

MENDY   And looking at his picture in *Blueboy*!

STEPHEN (*Covers phone.*)   Mendy!

MENDY   Ask him over.

STEPHEN (*Into phone.*)   So listen, are we going to be able to get together tonight, or what?

MENDY   He can come here first. There's food, tell him.

STEPHEN   Oh. I understand.

MENDY   He's standing you up? How dare he? Let me speak to that hussy—!

STEPHEN (*Covers phone.*)   If you don't shut up, I am going to break your face open! (*Into phone.*) Sorry, I could meet you after if it wouldn't be too late. I guess you're right. I was just hoping to see you tonight. I know it wasn't definite. I'm sorry, too. What about tomorrow night?

MENDY   You're supposed to be going to *Meistersinger* with me.

STEPHEN   That's right. I forgot. You know I got seats for Bruce Springsteen next Friday.

MENDY   You're not going to the Albanese recital in Newark?

STEPHEN   Do you think you'll have any time before then?

MENDY   She's doing two arias from *Rondine*!

STEPHEN   Like I said, I just want to see you sometime. You'd better get back there then. That's one mean maître d'. That's okay. I'll probably just head home. I've got the new Muriel Spark. I like her, too. Did you read—? Okay, okay! Go! Goodbye. Call when you can. (*He hangs up.*)

MENDY   What's the problem?

STEPHEN   Something came up.

MENDY   I'm sorry.

STEPHEN   It wasn't definite. He said this might happen.

MENDY   Join the club. I loathe the younger generation. They have no respect for old farts like us. What do you want me to put on?

STEPHEN   I knew this would happen.

MENDY   I know! Eileen Farrell, *I've Got a Right to Sing the Blues.*

STEPHEN   Shit. (*Doorbell rings.*)

MENDY   *Quelle bonne surprise!* Who can this be? Discophile! It's a new policy. They deliver.

STEPHEN   Mendy, I don't want to see any of your friends tonight.

MENDY   What's wrong with my friends? Pete and Timmy said they might stop by. (*He goes to window and looks out.*)

STEPHEN   I think I'm going to take off.

MENDY   There's a cab down there. (*The doorbell rings again, he goes to intercom.*) Hello?

MIKE'S VOICE   Hello? Mendy?

MENDY   Mike?

MIKE'S VOICE   Mendy? Can I come up?

MENDY   Sure. Second floor. (*Mendy presses the buzzer.*) It's Mike. What do you think he wants?

STEPHEN   He's probably locked himself out. I don't know what he'd do without me. Is he alone? (*Mendy goes to window and looks out.*)

MENDY   I can't tell. (*Knock on the door.*) You want to get it?

STEPHEN   It's not my apartment. (*Mendy goes to door and admits Mike who is casually dressed underneath an oilskin jacket. He has a record album in a plastic shopping bag with him.*)

MIKE   Here.

MENDY   What's that?

MIKE   What do you think?

MENDY   You didn't have to do that.

MIKE   It was on the way. No big deal.

MENDY   I was only kidding. Come in, come in. Stephen's still here.

MIKE   I'm dripping.

MENDY   Darling, these rugs were in the original production of *Kismet* with Otis Skinner.

MIKE   I've got a cab waiting. We're running late.

MENDY   Bring your friend up. A little dessert, coffee.

MIKE   Some other time.

MENDY   He probably thinks I'm a raving lunatic.

MIKE   Stephen?

MENDY   Excuse me.

MIKE   That's okay.

MENDY   My advice is needed in the kitchen. Stephen? It's the Lisbon *Traviata*. (*He sets the shopping bag down and goes.*)

STEPHEN   That was nice of you. He's been on me all evening.

MIKE   So what's happening?

STEPHEN   So what's happening?

MIKE   Do you know your plans yet?

STEPHEN   No.

MIKE   How soon will you know?

STEPHEN   I don't know! He's a working boy. He doesn't have a nice doctor to bundle him up in a warm taxi to see a movie I told you wasn't that good. Jesus, the new Almodóvar is right at the Quad. It's fabulous.

MIKE   He wants to see this one. (*Taxi begins honking impatiently off.*)

STEPHEN   There's a Chuck Norris retrospective on 42nd Street. Maybe you can make it.

MIKE   I've had a rough day, Stephen. The hospital was a nightmare. Billy Todd died, okay?

STEPHEN   I'm sorry.

MIKE   I'd like to know as soon as possible.

STEPHEN   Does it have to be tonight?

MIKE   You know my schedule. It could be weeks before I'm off again. His sister from Boston is at his place. I don't think she's ready for two men in one bed.

STEPHEN   Okay, okay, I hear you.

MIKE   It's sort of an anniversary. We met six months ago.

STEPHEN   I thought it was three.

MIKE   He's very sentimental about things like this.

STEPHEN   So are you. I'll try to arrange it.

MIKE   I'd really appreciate it.

STEPHEN   That jacket is not warm enough in this.

MIKE   I'll check the machine when we get out of the movie. (*Awkward moment. Mike hesitates about going to Stephen, decides to just wave.*)

STEPHEN   Aren't you even wearing a scarf?

MIKE   I'll see you, Mendy! (*He goes. Stephen crosses to window and looks out. Sounds of taxi door opening and closing. Mendy returns.*)

MENDY   That was very sweet of him. Every time I swear I'm never going to speak to him, he does something like this. Did you get a look at the chippy?

STEPHEN   No.

MENDY   I can't wait to hear this. (*He begins to open Mike's shopping bag. At the same time, Stephen goes to phone and dials a number.*) Who are you calling?

STEPHEN   Our machine.

MENDY (*Taking out album.*)   I don't believe this! He brought the London *Traviata*! It's the same one I have. Do you believe this? I don't. Stephen, it's the wrong *Traviata*.

STEPHEN   London, Lisbon, they're all the same to him.

MENDY   His heart was in the right place. He's basically a wonderful man. I hate him.

STEPHEN   (*Into phone.*)   Mike? My date just called. We're on. Have fun. We sure plan to. Bye. (*He hangs up.*)

MENDY   What was that all about? None of my business?

STEPHEN   I think I really will shove off. (*He will start getting ready to go.*)

MENDY   It's early. You just got here. I bet you haven't heard the tapes of the television documentary. It just came out.

STEPHEN   We've got *Meistersinger* tomorrow.

MENDY   Don't you want to hear it? They're all on it. Scotto, Caballé, Tebaldi, Gobbi, all of them. They all talk about how much she meant to them and how she changed the face of opera. Zeffirelli narrates.

STEPHEN   Some other time.

MENDY   It's very moving.

STEPHEN   I saw the program.

MENDY   You know you don't want to go.

STEPHEN   I don't know what I want to do.

MENDY   Then stay. You want some ice cream?

STEPHEN   I'll get the Lisbon *Traviata* to you.

MENDY   Why don't you want to hear the documentary? It brings her all back. It's as if she were in the room with you. You'll cry when you hear parts of it. I do every time.

STEPHEN   I already have it. Thanks for dinner.

MENDY   You already have it? We can listen to it together. Compare things. Where are you going?

STEPHEN   I'll probably go to a bar.

MENDY   You want me to come with you?

STEPHEN   We tried that, remember?

MENDY   It wasn't my fault.

STEPHEN   Mendy, I was doing fine with that one guy until you came over and burst into the second act of *Tosca*.

MENDY   No one has a sense of humor in those places.

STEPHEN   Including me.

MENDY   I thought he looked like Richard Tucker in *Pagliacci* anyway. I'll be good. Take me. Please.

STEPHEN   I do better on my own. So would you.

MENDY   Then where are you going? Not home with some stranger? Even you're not that self-destructive.

STEPHEN   There's a couch in my office.

MENDY   That's crazy.

STEPHEN   I can always go to a hotel.

MENDY   That's even crazier. Why don't you stay here? I'll make a bed up, I'll fix us some Sleepytime tea, we'll put on our pajamas, we'll listen to the documentary, we'll giggle, we'll dish, it'll be wonderful.

STEPHEN   I don't think so.

MENDY   Don't worry. I'm not going to make a pass at you. Now take your coat off. Sit.

STEPHEN   I'd like to but I've just got to get out of here and go someplace. (*Mendy exits.*) Where are you going? Mendy! What are you doing? (*Mendy quickly returns with bedding, pajamas and a robe for Stephen.*) You don't have to do that.

MENDY   It's no trouble.

STEPHEN   I haven't decided yet.

MENDY   Take your time. I can't wait for you to hear this.

STEPHEN   It's too late for the documentary.

MENDY   I'll just play the last side.

STEPHEN   I have a deadline tomorrow.

MENDY   Just the last side, I promise.

STEPHEN   All right, but as soon as it's finished—

MENDY   I know. Just sit down.

STEPHEN (*Sitting.*)   I mean it, too.

MENDY   Okay, okay. (*Stephen sits and starts idly flipping through the issue of Blueboy.*) You're not listening.

STEPHEN   I will, I will! (*He will continue to flip through the pages as the documentary begins to play. It is the PBS television documentary on the life of Maria Callas. Franco Zeffirelli is telling us about the life and legend of Maria Callas.*)

ZEFFIRELLI   On the morning of September 16, 1977, shortly after awakening, Maria Callas died of a heart attack in her Paris apartment. She was 54 years old.

MENDY   You're not listening.

STEPHEN   Yes, I am. (*He turns another page. He kicks off his shoes.*)

ZEFFIRELLI   There has been perhaps only one faithful companion to Maria throughout her life, her loneliness. The price sometimes one has to pay for the glory and success. It's also the price for being God's instrument. It really seems to me that God used Maria's talent to communicate to us his planet of beauty. To enrich our souls, to make us better men. Maria Callas, the glory of opera. (*Callas begins to sing "Ah, non credea mirarti" from* La Sonnambula.)

MENDY   Stephen!

STEPHEN   I'm listening, I'm listening. (*The voice of Maria Callas on the soundtrack is beginning to fade. Stephen continues to turn more pages. Mendy is silent.*)

END OF ACT ONE

ACT TWO

Stephen and Mike's apartment. Early morning. Pale, gray light from the windows. The room is in much disarray. We notice a box of pizza. There is a pair of pants on the floor. The needle on the phonograph is endlessly tracking the runoff groove at the end of the record side. The red light on the telephone answering machine is blinking, indicating that a message has been received. The door to the bedroom is closed.

A key is heard in the door. Stephen enters. He is in the same clothes as the evening before, only now he is wearing his coat over them. He carries a small duffel bag, a copy of the New York Times *and a brown paper bag that contains coffee and Danishes.*

STEPHEN   Good morning! It's me! (*He is no sooner through the door than he is aware of the phonograph needle tracking the end of the record. He puts down his things and goes to the phonograph. He takes the arm off the record, stops the turntable and removes the record, being careful to hold it by the edges and perhaps blowing off any dust that might have collected.*) George Michael. Who the hell is George Michael? Where did they leave the goddamn jacket? (*He is clearly looking for the record's protective inner sleeve and outer album cover.*) Goddamnit! (*He has seen them on the coffee table under the box of pizza. Some of the pizza has gotten onto them. He returns the record to its sleeve and jacket, then looks at the album cover a moment. He returns the album to the collection, filing it away alphabetically. Then he goes back to the stereo unit and switches it to an FM station. Rock music is heard. It is unbearably loud. Clearly, whoever was playing the stereo was running it at full volume. Stephen quickly lowers the volume and carefully tunes in a classical musical station.* Schubert's Wanderer Fantasie *is being played. Stephen satisfies himself with the volume and the reception. Next, he kicks off his shoes and takes off his coat. At the same time, he moves to the answering machine and rewinds the messages. As the following messages are played back, he will hang his coat up in the hall closet.*)

STEPHEN'S VOICE   Mike? My date just called. We're on. Have fun. We sure plan to. Bye.

MENDY'S VOICE   Mike? It's Mendy? You want to pick up? Hello? Don't tell me you're not back yet? What did you two go see? *Berlin Alexanderplatz?* All right, I guess you're not there. You brought me the wrong one. It's the Lisbon *Traviata* I'm after. Call me just as soon as you come in. I'll be up all night. Really. 4, 5 AM. How could I sleep knowing there's a new Maria. (*He sings.*) *"Nessun dorma, nessun dorma!"* (*He stops.*) Hello? Mike? I thought I heard someone pick up. Hello? I guess not. Please, Mike, just as soon as you come in. I really would appreciate it. How are you anyway? No one ever sees you anymore. It was lovely seeing you tonight and I appreciated the gesture, as futile as it was. Call sometime. I mean, call as soon as you get this message but call some other time, too. You know what I mean! (*To Stephen.*) Do you want to talk to him? (*To Mike.*) Okay. Ciao, Babe!

WOMAN'S VOICE (*Somewhat slurred.*)   Hello, Stephen. It's your mother. Nothing important. Just calling to say hi. You don't have to call back, if you don't want to. I love you. (*Short pause.*) It's your mother. Say hello to Mike. Hello, Mike. I hate these things.

MAN'S VOICE   This is a message for Stephen Riddick. Hi, it's Larry Newman. I'd really like to get together with you to go over the revisions on my manuscript. It's been weeks. I hate to bother you at home but I'm getting kind of edgy. I don't even know if you've gotten my other messages. Thank you.

MAN'S VOICE 2   Mike? Uh, Michael Deller? It's Allan Weeks from Baltimore. I was in your neighborhood for the evening. Sorry I missed you. I'll try you next trip. (*There are no more messages. Stephen goes to the machine and turns it off. The bedroom door opens. Paul starts into the living room. He is naked.*)

PAUL   Oh!

STEPHEN   Good morning.

PAUL   Good morning. Excuse me. (*He goes back into the bedroom and closes the door. Stephen sits with the coffee and Danish and opens the* Times. *He reads for a few moments, then lowers the paper and looks toward the bedroom. Then he raises the paper and reads again. The bedroom door opens and Mike comes out. He holds the bedclothes around his middle. He will begin to pick up the clothes scattered around the room.*)

MIKE   We didn't hear you come in. Sorry.

STEPHEN   It's all right.

MIKE   Have you been here long?

STEPHEN   I just got here.

MIKE   What time is it?

STEPHEN   I'm early. It's my fault. Tell your friend I'm sorry.

MIKE   We'll be out of your way.

STEPHEN   You're not in it. Take your time, both of you. We're all adults. If you've seen one, you've seen them all. I shouldn't have to tell a doctor that.

MIKE   I called our machine after the movie and got your message that it was all right for him to stay over.

STEPHEN   Happy to accommodate. Anything for a sister from Boston. How was the movie?

MIKE   You were right. We left halfway through. How was your evening?

STEPHEN   Great. You left the stereo on all night.

MIKE   Not again!

STEPHEN   That clunk, clunk, would drive me crazy.

MIKE   I guess we were in the bedroom and didn't hear it.

STEPHEN   He's attractive.

MIKE   I was better off with my old record player. Maybe it wasn't high fidelity but at least it turned itself off. From now on, I'll stick to the radio.

STEPHEN   That's not what I said. I said he's attractive.

MIKE   I heard you. You're right, he is.

STEPHEN   What are you looking for?

MIKE   It's all right.

STEPHEN   I think he left something over there. (*He motions with his head.*)

MIKE   Where? (*Stephen repeats the motion. Mike crosses and picks up a jockstrap.*) Thank you.

STEPHEN   Is that what they're wearing nowadays?

MIKE   So what did you and your friend do after he got off work?

STEPHEN   We had a couple of drinks at Uncle Charlie's.

MIKE   I haven't been to a bar in years. Was anybody there?

STEPHEN   Are you speaking society or numbers? On the slow side, on both fronts.

MIKE   What a fucked-up time we picked to live in.

STEPHEN   Then we went to his place and discussed Joyce Carol Oates to the wee hours of the morning. He's very intense.

MIKE   I hope that's not all you did.

STEPHEN   It's not. I brought coffee.

MIKE   He's got to get to work.

STEPHEN   At this hour? What is he? A milkman?

MIKE   They gave you three.

STEPHEN   I asked for three. I was trying to be nice. The Danish are just from Smiler's. Jon Vie wasn't open yet.

MIKE   That's okay. Thanks. (*He goes into the bedroom. The door closes. Stephen resumes reading the* Times *but a moment later he lets the paper fall and stares in front of him.*)

STEPHEN   They like the new Stoppard. (*Paul enters from bedroom, smiles at Stephen and exits into bathroom. Stephen resumes reading the* Times. *Now Mike comes out of the bedroom. He has put a bathrobe on.*)

MIKE   What's it like out?

STEPHEN   Sort of raw.

MIKE   They said more rain. (*He has gone to the closet and taken out a clean towel.*)

STEPHEN   What are you doing?

MIKE   He asked to take a shower.

STEPHEN   I thought he was . . . !

MIKE   What?

STEPHEN Nothing.

MIKE What?

STEPHEN Nothing. Do you have to use that towel? Use one of the old ones. I thought he was so late for work!

MIKE (*Evenly.*) He has time for a shower.

STEPHEN Those are our best towels. They're a set. I'm sorry, but I see no reason to take one of them when you have a whole closetful of old, perfectly good, unmatched ones to choose from.

MIKE Yes, Mother. (*He exchanges the towel he took for another one.*)

STEPHEN I'm just being practical. Only you would take a brand new towel from a brand new set instead of a single one.

MIKE Only you would care if I did.

STEPHEN It's common sense for Christ's sake! (*Mike goes back into the bedroom and closes the door. Stephen is clearly upset with himself.*) Shit, shit, shit! (*Almost to himself.*) I'm sorry. (*He's goes to bedroom door, starts to knock, then thinks better of it.*) I'll make more coffee! Okay? (*No response from the bedroom. Stephen starts for the kitchen but stops. The recording of Schubert's* Fantasie *being played by the FM station has gotten stuck. The same phrase is being repeated over and over and over. Stephen shakes his head. Mike comes out of the bedroom again. This time we can hear the sound of the shower running in the bathroom adjacent to the bedroom.*)

MIKE Did you say something?

STEPHEN NCN is fucking up. Listen to that. You'd think they'd care enough to listen to what they're broadcasting. Hello? (*Someone at the station bumps the needle and the record resumes playing properly.*) If I ran a station, heads would roll if that ever happened. I said I'd make more coffee.

MIKE Not for us. (*He sits and beings to eat his Danish.*)

STEPHEN (*Moving to kitchen area and beginning to prepare coffee.*) You know, with compact discs, stuck records, scratches, that sort of thing are going to be a thing of the past. The Brahms *Fourth* will be safe from people like you and Mendy.

MIKE I said not for us, thank you.

STEPHEN   I heard you. Though actually I was in Tower Records the other day and there was this man returning a CD he was complaining was defective. The Beethoven *Third*. The new Bernstein performance on Deutsche Grammophone. "What's the matter with it?" the salesman sort of sniffed. "I can't get access to the third movement," the man said. Do you believe it? "I can't get access to the third movement." Welcome to the future. We who have lived so long and borne so much, salute you. You sure he doesn't have time for coffee?

MIKE   He doesn't drink it.

STEPHEN   Another health nut! I can understand not smoking but all this other shit! Will he take decaf?

MIKE   We're fine.

STEPHEN   What time does he have to be at work anyway?

MIKE   We're going by his place first.

STEPHEN   The two of you? With his sister there? That's saucy of you.

MIKE   I said I'd drive him.

STEPHEN   Where does he live?

MIKE   106th Street and Amsterdam Avenue.

STEPHEN   In our car? So long hubcaps. So long tape deck. So long motor.

MIKE   It's Columbia.

STEPHEN   Fuck you, it's Columbia. It's Harlem. I ought to know. I went there.

MIKE   The neighborhood has changed.

STEPHEN   They were saying that when Lou Gehrig went there and look what happened to him.

MIKE   The car will be fine.

STEPHEN   What does he have to go home for anyway?

MIKE   To change.

STEPHEN   Into what? Another jockstrap?

MIKE   I said I'd drive him.

STEPHEN   The subway is faster. I just want to know what you have against the Seventh Avenue–Broadway IRT all of a sudden? It was good enough for us.

MIKE   I want to drive him. I like him.

STEPHEN   Why didn't you say so? That's all you had to say. Like I understand. I can relate to like. Like is lovely. Like is nice. Like is human. Like is likeable. I respect like. (*Mike goes to the stereo and changes radio stations. He finds a mellow-rock-type music and lowers the volume.*)

MIKE   Do you mind? That stuff is making me nuts.

STEPHEN   Schubert never made anyone nuts. Bruckner, maybe.

MIKE   His name is Paul.

STEPHEN   I know.

MIKE   He's a graduate student at Columbia.

STEPHEN   Social Work.

MIKE   You know all this.

STEPHEN   So why are you telling me?

MIKE   I really like him.

STEPHEN   He looks like a . . .

MIKE   I'm not interested.

STEPHEN   . . . something in the rodent family.

MIKE   That's your opinion. (*Calls off.*) Paul! Hurry up!

STEPHEN   Did you get your messages?

MIKE   I'm not on call for twenty-four hours. I'd like to enjoy them.

STEPHEN   It looks like you're off and running. So who's Allan Weeks? (*He changes his voice.*) He was in the neighborhood last night and he's sorry he missed you but he'll try you next trip. (*It's a deadly accurate imitation.*)

MIKE   He's a pathologist at Johns Hopkins. We met at a C.M.V. seminar for Christ's sake.

STEPHEN   What's keeping you? Dr. Al sounds like a real firecracker.

MIKE   He's married.

STEPHEN   Maybe his wife is disposable, too. I'm sorry. I'm sorry. I'm sorry, I'm sorry! I'm sorry about the towels, I'm sorry about what I just said, I'm sorry about this whole mess.

PAUL (*Off.*)   Mike!

MIKE   This has got to stop, Stephen.

STEPHEN   I know.

PAUL (*Off.*)   I'm out.

MIKE   I mean it.

PAUL (*Off.*)   She's all yours.

STEPHEN   Go on, take your shower. I'll be nice.

MIKE   I'd settle for civil.

STEPHEN   It's hard sometimes, okay?

MIKE   For me, too. (*Paul opens bathroom door.*)

PAUL   Did you hear me? I'm out.

MIKE   Thanks. (*Paul exits into bedroom. Then Mike turns and exits into the bathroom. The door closes. Stephen looks at the door a beat. We hear the shower being turned on again. This time Stephen crosses quickly to the bedroom door, knocks and opens it at the same time.*)

PAUL   Hello.

STEPHEN   Hello.

PAUL   I'm sorry about . . . ! We didn't hear you come in.

STEPHEN   In the movies. I think it's called "meeting cute." We're destined to be more than very good friends.

PAUL   We just didn't hear you.

STEPHEN   I'm not your sister from Boston. I think I can handle it. Don't tell anybody, but it's not exactly the first time.

PAUL   It's nice to finally meet you.

STEPHEN   Please! It's Jim, right?

PAUL No, it's Paul.

STEPHEN Paul, of course! Jim's fairer. Coffee?

PAUL I don't drink it.

STEPHEN Good thinking. Decaf?

PAUL (*Shaking his head.*) That's all right.

STEPHEN I'm Stephen.

PAUL I know. We spoke on the phone last night.

STEPHEN You broke my friend Mendy's heart. Cleft it in twain. And that's without even seeing you.

PAUL I didn't even know what he was talking about.

STEPHEN The Lisbon *Traviata*.

PAUL It sounds like a murder mystery. *The Lisbon Traviata.*

STEPHEN You think so?

PAUL Well, a mystery anyway. Something with criminals. *The Lisbon Traviata. The Maltese Falcon. The . . .*

STEPHEN You have a vivid imagination.

PAUL I'm afraid it just ran out.

STEPHEN Those are nice pants.

PAUL Thank you. They're from Barney's.

STEPHEN I wish you'd put something on.

PAUL I'm sorry. I am.

STEPHEN The stereo. I get nervous when something's not playing. Go ahead, I'll get your coffee.

PAUL I told you, I don't drink it.

STEPHEN It's decaf, cross my heart. If you have a caffeine attack, you can ring me at Knopf and call me a liar. Go ahead, put something on.

PAUL I wouldn't know where to begin.

STEPHEN They're all in alphabetical order by composer, title, or performer. If they're not, we know who to blame.

PAUL   I didn't know they made this many records.

STEPHEN   One of my many obsessions. It keeps me off the streets. My father always wondered why I wanted yet another *Aida*. "Because it's different from the other ones, Dad. You go to the Army-Navy game every year. Same game, different players. Same opera, different singers." He didn't see my logic. I thought it was brilliant for a toddler. How are you doing?

PAUL   It's hopeless.

STEPHEN   What would you say to a little Lisbon *Traviata*?

PAUL   I'd say, "Hello, little Lisbon *Traviata*." (*He laughs.*) I don't think so. Opera's kind of not my thing.

STEPHEN   I like the fit.

PAUL   I guess if I understood what they were singing about . . . !

STEPHEN   Love and death. That's all they're ever singing about. There's an occasional Anvil Chorus but it's basically boy meets girl, boy gets girl, boy and girl croak. That's all you need to know, from *Aida* to *Zaide*. I'll take you sometime.

PAUL   I'd be over my head.

STEPHEN   Nonsense. That's what you all think. Michael was the same way. Opera is about us, our life and death passions—we all love, we're all going to die. Maria understood that. That's where that voice came from, the heart, the soul, I'm tempted to say from some even more intimate place.

PAUL   Maria?

STEPHEN   Maria Callas, Greek-American soprano, 1923-1977, famous for the musical and dramatic intensity she brought to her characterizations. When did you two meet?

PAUL   Me and Mike?

STEPHEN   Ouch—Mike and I. Mendy introduced us. He insisted he was madly in love with me and then he introduced me to Michael. I believe that's called self-destructive.

PAUL   I met Mike where I used to work.

STEPHEN   Let me guess. His gym.

PAUL   No, I never worked in a gym.

STEPHEN   You have a beautiful body.

PAUL   Thank you. We met in a restaurant. Claudia's. In the Village.

STEPHEN   I know Claudia's. It used to be wonderful. Still, it's very pricey. I'm impressed.

PAUL   No, I was a waiter there, part-time.

STEPHEN   Another waiter. Somebody should write a book about men like us and their propensity for waiters.

PAUL   I couldn't afford to eat at Claudia's. I doubt I ever will.

STEPHEN   Let me guess, he slipped you his number on a matchbook.

PAUL   No. I said, "I get off at eleven. I could meet you at the bar across the street."

STEPHEN   Pretty cheeky!

PAUL   He was alone. He wasn't wearing a wedding ring. They're always telling us to go for it, so I went for it.

STEPHEN   Tell me about your intentions. Are they honorable?

PAUL   I think so.

STEPHEN   Dr. Deller is a good man.

PAUL   I know.

STEPHEN   And you know what they say about good men!

PAUL   Hard to find. Easy to lose. Smart to keep. Now I'm working part-time in a light gallery on the Upper East Side. I'm a graduate student at Columbia working for an M.S.W.

STEPHEN   Master of Social Work.

PAUL   Right.

STEPHEN   What's a light gallery?

PAUL   A gallery for lights. Lighting fixtures. One of these.

STEPHEN   What kind of social work?

PAUL   Medical. Eventually I'd like to end up in a hospital.

STEPHEN   Most of us usually do. I thought about being a priest—

PAUL   Me, too.

STEPHEN   —for about exactly five minutes. I think it was the wardrobe. Then I thought about joining the Peace Corps for exactly one. So much for my crush on Bobby Kennedy. Remember him?

PAUL   I spent two years in Zaire with the Peace Corps.

STEPHEN   Good for you!

PAUL   It was no picnic.

STEPHEN   I bet. I admire people who devote themselves to public service.

PAUL   That's probably why we do it.

STEPHEN   Are they twill?

PAUL   I'm sorry?

STEPHEN   You're very sweet when you smile like that. I can see what Michael sees in you. Now I'm sorry. We're even.

PAUL   I can see what you saw in Mike.

STEPHEN   What's that?

PAUL   I beg your pardon?

STEPHEN   What did I see in him?

PAUL   I shouldn't have to tell you. He's a wonderful man. He's warm. He's generous. He's funny.

STEPHEN   He's not that funny.

PAUL   You're right!

STEPHEN   I was hoping you could see what Michael sees in me.

PAUL   I can see what he saw in you but I don't think we ought to pursue this.

STEPHEN   Has Michael told you we're going skiing next month?

PAUL   No.

STEPHEN   We try to get to Aspen every year. Do you ski?

PAUL   Not really.

STEPHEN   What does that mean?

PAUL   No.

STEPHEN   We're both good skiers. Michael's terrific, in fact. (*I love calling him Michael when everyone else calls him Mike. I don't know why.*) Michael's been under a lot of strain. We need to get away a couple times each year to get back in synch with each other. Every August we try to sail off Maine for two weeks. Do you sail?

PAUL   No. I'm strictly handball.

STEPHEN   You should try it sometime. It's very liberating. Couples need time alone together. I think especially two men. I can't wait for Aspen.

PAUL   I hope you have a good time.

STEPHEN   Thank you. I'm sure we will. I went to Columbia.

PAUL   I know. Mike told me. He says you're an editor. A very good one.

STEPHEN   He's right. I make talented writers almost very good ones.

PAUL   You're famous.

STEPHEN   Poo!

PAUL   That's what Mike says.

STEPHEN   I can get seats for *Phantom of the Opera*.

PAUL   I'm not much of a theatregoer either. I'd like to go more but on my budget . . . ! I just saw *Cats*.

STEPHEN   You can die a happy man.

PAUL   Am I nuts, but I hated it? I'd rather see *Bambi*.

STEPHEN   I like your taste in theatre, men, and extremely sexy pants. We're going to get along famously. (*The sound of the shower has stopped.*)

MIKE (*Off.*)   Paul!

STEPHEN   We're in here!

MIKE (*Off.*)   Paul!

PAUL   Here I am.

STEPHEN   Am I anything like you expected?

PAUL   From Mike's description of you? Not in the least. (*The tea kettle has started to whistle.*)

STEPHEN   Your water's boiling. (*Mike opens the bathroom door.*)

MIKE   Stephen!

STEPHEN (*On his way to the bedroom.*)   Well, it's about time. (*He opens the door and goes in. The tea kettle continues to whistle. Mike crosses quickly, a towel around him, still wet from the shower.*)

MIKE   I'm sorry about all this. It's his fault. He's early.

PAUL   Early on purpose.

MIKE   Are you all right?

PAUL   I'm fine. I'd just like to get out of here.

MIKE   He didn't say anything to . . . ?

PAUL   I can handle him. Hurry up.

MIKE   Shit! He did! I knew it.

PAUL   I thought he knew.

MIKE   He does know.

PAUL   He sure hasn't accepted it.

MIKE   He's going to have to.

PAUL   That was practically the first thing I asked you. No strings, you said.

MIKE   I didn't want you to meet him like this.

PAUL   You think I did?

MIKE   He's really a very nice man.

PAUL   He spoke highly of you, too.

MIKE   I'm sorry.

PAUL   It's not anybody's fault. But you've got to tell him, Michael. Now go on, get dressed.

MIKE   You called me Michael.

PAUL   Do you mind?

MIKE   No . . . I liked it. I've got the whole day off. I can meet you for lunch. (*He hugs Paul.*) What I said last night . . . I meant it. I really do. (*Stephen comes out of the bedroom in time to see them.*)

STEPHEN   What are you trying to do? Burn the place down? (*He goes to the whistling kettle and turns the flame down.*) How big a spoonful? I'm afraid it's instant.

PAUL   Really, nothing for me.

MIKE   Why don't you come in while I dress?

PAUL   I'm fine right here.

MIKE   I wish you would.

PAUL   Really! Hurry up. (*Mike goes into the bedroom, leaving door ajar. Stephen is preparing a cup of decaffeinated coffee for Paul.*)

STEPHEN   Come and get it! (*Paul goes to Stephen and takes a cup from him.*) Milk? Sugar?

PAUL   No, thanks.

STEPHEN   I found something I think you might get a kick out of. (*He crosses to bedroom door and sticks his head in.*) Excuse us. We're going to put on a little music, loud. (*He closes the door.*) Mike basically hates opera. That should've clued me in years ago we weren't fated to last. After eight years, it gets pretty hard coming home night after night to a man who doesn't like *Idomeneo.* (*He hands Paul an envelope, which Paul will open while Stephen goes to stereo unit and puts on a CD. Inside the envelope is a collection of Polaroid photos.*) Those were taken our first year together. We were insatiable. Having each other for real wasn't enough. We wanted tangible proof of our priapic good fortune. They got me through a lot of nights when he was working late. He went crazy when he couldn't find them. I told him I'd destroyed them. I think he's forgotten all about them.

PAUL   Why did you give me these?

STEPHEN   Because I'm a shit. (*He presses the Play button. The music is quite loud. It is Alan Berg's* Wozzeck. *Mike comes out of the bedroom. He is in his socks and underwear.*)

MIKE   Stephen!

STEPHEN   He requested it. I swear to God. Just a second. What are you doing? The big hit tune's coming up. (*Mike presses the Stop button.*) Why no one's made a rap version of that!

MIKE   Stop it, Stephen!

STEPHEN   Now what would you say to a little Mad Scene with Maria herself? The high E alone is guaranteed to clear your sinuses.

MIKE   I said, cut it out.

STEPHEN   Okay, we'll stick with *Wozzeck*. (*He presses the Play button again. The music seems even louder. Mike hits him. Stephen goes down.*)

MIKE   Stop! Do it again and I'll break your fucking head open.

PAUL   Hey, come on you two, don't. I'm going. (*Stephen is getting to his feet.*)

STEPHEN   Your friend is talking to you.

MIKE   I mean it, Stephen. (*He presses the Stop button.*)

STEPHEN   Maybe you want him to see this side of you.

MIKE   Don't you dare turn that on. Don't make me do this, Stephen.

STEPHEN   The only thing that makes you do anything is your dick and your sick deluded idea that if you stick it in enough places maybe you'll forget what a miserable, fucked-up faggot you've become. (*He pushes the Play button. Mike hits him again. Again Stephen goes down. This time there is blood.*)

PAUL   Jesus, Mike!

MIKE   I haven't hit anyone since the fifth grade! What are you doing to me? (*To Paul.*) I told you to come in there with me!

PAUL   That's it. I'm going.

MIKE   I'm sorry! I—! (*To Stephen.*) Get up!

STEPHEN   If this is your idea of safe sex, I don't like it.

PAUL   I'll call you.

MIKE   Wait, I'm talking to you.

PAUL   I'm late. Here, I don't want these. (*Hands photos to Mike.*)

MIKE   What are they?

PAUL   I don't care.

MIKE   Where did you get these?

PAUL   I said I don't care.

MIKE   This was years ago.

PAUL   It's okay. Call. I'm late.

MIKE   What about lunch?

PAUL   I don't know. Make sure he's okay.

MIKE   I can be ready in a minute.

PAUL   I can't! (*Mike kisses Paul, who pulls away after a few moments.*) I'll call you. (*Mike kisses him again, this time more forcefully. Paul never really responds or relaxes into it. Finally, he pulls away.*) I gotta go. (*He goes to the door where he has some trouble with the different locks.*) Making a graceful exit from a New York City apartment—! (*He opens the apartment door. Mendy is standing there. His arm is poised to knock.*)

MENDY   Have I come at a bad time?

MIKE   Jesus, Mendy!

MENDY   I just wanted to return this. You brought the London *Traviata*. It's the Lisbon *Traviata* I'm after. It's all right. I'm a little dyslexic myself. The other night I wanted to listen to *Adriana Lecouvreur* and I put on *Ariadne Auf Naxos* instead. The music started and I got very confused. All that *schreing* in German! (*To Paul.*) Hi, I'm Mendy. Don't tell me: you're the young man who loves animals: Paul Della Rovere. That's not a name. It's a Portuguese love sonnet. I have two tickets for *Butterfly* Thursday. Vishnevskaya's singing. You'll cry like a baby. I'll hold your hand when she stabs herself and I'll have lots and lots of Kleenex handy. It's to die. We'll dine *aux deux* afterwards and I'll tell you everything you want to know about my checkered past.

MIKE   How did you get past our doorman?

MENDY   Darling, I am beyond doormen. I am a legend in my lifetime. I gave him two tickets to *Falstaff.*

PAUL I'll see you, Mike.

MIKE Wait, I'll come with you.

MENDY Thursday, the fountain at Lincoln Center, Paul, 7:45. I'll be in mauve. (*Mike and Paul go.*) I guess that was a no. Well, I still know how to clear a room. Stephen, what are you doing down there?

STEPHEN I thought you'd never ask.

MENDY Oh my God, Stephen, you're bleeding. What happened?

STEPHEN Michael hit me.

MENDY Why?

STEPHEN He didn't want to listen to *Wozzeck*.

MENDY No one wants to listen to *Wozzeck* but that's no excuse. Are you all right?

STEPHEN I'm fine. Dr. Deller's the one with problems. I showed his friend a few family photos and he went crazy. I don't know what's gotten into him. (*Mendy has seen the photographs on the coffee table and takes them up.*) It's ridiculous. He's got a crush on the guy, that's all. I don't blame him. He's cute. Mendy, are you listening to me?

MENDY You could sell these.

STEPHEN I haven't looked at them in years.

MENDY What were you thinking when you showed him these?

STEPHEN I wasn't thinking. I wanted him to know it was *two* lives he was fucking with.

MENDY You didn't need to do this.

STEPHEN Too late now.

MENDY How can I help you?

STEPHEN You can't. (*Mike returns.*)

MIKE I'd like you to leave, Mendy.

MENDY Not before you tell me what's going on here.

MIKE It's pretty obvious.

MENDY I'd like to be helpful.

MIKE   Then go.

MENDY   Stephen's my best friend.

STEPHEN   We're okay, Mendy. Go.

MENDY   If I had a lover . . .

MIKE   It's no wonder you don't.

MENDY   I'm sorry, but when I see my best friend on the floor . . .

MIKE   Get up, Stephen!

MENDY   . . . with blood streaming out of his mouth because you hit him . . . !

MIKE   It's not streaming, Mendy, but I'm sure it will be by the time you get through with it. It'll be a torrent. You'll have him dead. You'll make it an opera. You make everything an opera. Go home and put on a record. I'll take care of Stephen.

STEPHEN   Go, I'll call you.

MENDY   When?

STEPHEN   Soon, I promise.

MENDY   I hate what's happening. (*He goes to door and turns.*) I suppose the Lisbon *Traviata* is completely out of the question? I'm going. I'm going. I'm gone. (*He goes.*)

MIKE   (*He looks at Stephen who is still on the floor.*)   Get up, Stephen.

STEPHEN   You want to fuck me?

MIKE   This is pathetic.

STEPHEN   You want me to fuck you?

MIKE   You just did.

STEPHEN   I hope you know what you're doing.

MIKE   I wouldn't be surprised if he never wanted to see me again. I wouldn't walk into this mess.

STEPHEN   I worry about you. Has he been tested?

MIKE   Yes. We both have. Have you? (*He is trying to rip up the Polaroids.*) I asked you to destroy these.

STEPHEN   You'll need scissors to do that.

MIKE   You said you had.

STEPHEN   I lied.

MIKE   Where were they?

STEPHEN   The last place anybody would look. On the bookshelf behind *The Story of Civilization* by Will and Ariel Durant. (*Mike gives up trying to destroy the Polaroids.*) I told you. I'd forgotten how funny blood tastes.

MIKE   Get up, will you?

STEPHEN   Sort of like metal.

MIKE   At least . . . here! (*He tosses Stephen a kitchen towel.*) Wipe your mouth.

STEPHEN   It's us. We're tasting ourselves.

MIKE   You're still bleeding! (*He goes to Stephen, takes towel and wipes the blood off his chin.*)

STEPHEN   Why don't you want to fuck me? Ow! You used to love my ass. Ow, I said!

MIKE   Shut up. Hold it there until it stops. (*He holds towel to Stephen's chin.*) Put your head back. Here. Against me. Jesus, Stephen, what are you doing to me? What are we doing to each other?

STEPHEN   You know you're the only person I ever let fuck me. A lot of guys wanted to but I wouldn't let them. I guess I was saving myself for you.

MIKE   Let me look. (*He takes towel from Stephen's chin, then looks and dabs at it.*)

STEPHEN   I never really liked fucking you. You said "ouch" too much. Well, not "ouch" exactly. It was more like a whining moan of discomfort. "Are you okay, Mike?" "Unh-hunh." That "unh-hunh" was a real turn-off. (*Mike stops dabbing Stephen's chin, gets up and goes to the bathroom.*) Where are you going? That was nice. You want to hit me again? (*No response from the other room. We hear Mike going through the medicine chest in the bathroom.*) What are you doing in there? Don't get carried away, doctor. I'm fine. (*Mike returns. He has a small bottle of medicine in his hand.*) What's that?

MIKE   Never mind.

STEPHEN   I said I'm fine.

MIKE   Hold still.

STEPHEN   Hasn't he ever asked you about your ring?

MIKE   No.

STEPHEN   I would have.

MIKE   It's not a wedding ring.

STEPHEN   It's hardly costume jewelry either.

MIKE   Do you want it back?

STEPHEN   That's not what I'm saying.

MIKE   Hold still.

STEPHEN   What is it? Do I get a lollipop? (*Mike puts medicine on Stephen's lip.*) Is that it? Thank you. (*A delayed reaction.*) Ow!

MIKE   It makes me sick to think that I did that to you. Get up.

STEPHEN   I like it down here.

MIKE   Suit yourself.

STEPHEN   Mendy says I usually do.

MIKE   I told you I liked him, Stephen.

STEPHEN   I saw what you two are all about. K-Y and poppers.

MIKE   It's the best sex I've had in three years.

STEPHEN   That's not just my fault.

MIKE   Of course it's not.

STEPHEN   People go through phases.

MIKE   The pity is they stay there. I didn't deserve that. Neither did he. (*Mike moves away from him and retrieves the Polaroids.*) Anybody who would show these to someone else . . . !

STEPHEN   Is what? Is sick? Is crazy?

MIKE   I trusted you. These weren't for other people.

STEPHEN   The real tragedy is neither one of us is ever going to look that good again. (*Mike sits and looks at the Polaroids.*) Do you remember where we took those?

MIKE   No.

STEPHEN   Take a look.

MIKE   That weekend on the Cape?

STEPHEN   We thought those woods were so green and lush. Two days later we found out it was mostly poison ivy. You had to stand most of the way on the bus coming back. I had it all over my balls. It's the only time in my life I would have happily exchanged a pair of pants for a simple skirt. It's your last chance, I'm getting up. (*Stephen goes to the stereo.*) I'm going to put something on. Don't worry, something nice. I can't stand it without music. I'll put on something you'll like. Trust me. I'm not going to tell you what it is. You should be able to guess. We saw it together in Paris. It was Oscar Wilde's birthday and we were staying in the hotel he died in on the Seine. (*The music begins. It is the "Prelude" to Wagner's* Lohengrin. *Stephen sets it at a low easy-listening level.*) I'll give you three guesses and one hint: it's not *La Bohème.* Isn't that coffee cold? I'll make some fresh. (*He takes Mike's cup, moves to kitchen area, empties it and begins making coffee.*) I wasn't planning on going in today. Maybe we can catch that Diebenkorn show at the Modern I was telling you about. And we could pick up your watch. It's ready. They sent you a card. I don't know why they don't just call. (*Mike gets up, takes scissors from the desk and begins to methodically cut the Polaroids into little pieces. Stephen has come out of the kitchen area.*) Before you do that, did you see Sammy in one of them?

MIKE   No. Where?

STEPHEN   The one where we're . . . Here. (*He quickly dries his hands, comes to Mike, takes Polaroids, finds the one he is looking for and shows it to him.*) It's just the top of his head but still! Whatever we were doing that dog wanted to be doing it, too. Remember, there was that whole period whenever we were making love, he'd jump on the bed and bark. Arf arf arf!

MIKE   He thought you were attacking me.

STEPHEN   He was right, I was.

MIKE   God, I miss him.

STEPHEN   Me, too. I still think we should get another one. Not the same breed maybe but . . . I was thinking maybe a——. (*Mike resumes cutting the Polaroids.*) You sure you want to do that? There's no more where those came from.

MIKE   I know what we looked like eight years ago and it's not the way I care to remember either one of us.

STEPHEN   You could always send one to Knopf with an anonymous letter. "Stephen R. sucks cock" and sign it William F. Buckley.

MIKE   I think they know.

STEPHEN   The sadness? They couldn't possibly.

MIKE   Stephen, we'd better talk.

STEPHEN   We are talking. I've done nothing but. You're the silent one. (*He gestures toward the stereo.*) You give up? The "Prelude" to *Lohengrin.* Remember? You used to love it when I tried to teach you things.

MIKE   No, I didn't, Stephen.

STEPHEN   You were a pretty good pretender.

MIKE   I used to love a lot of things I don't anymore.

STEPHEN   Including me. (*He has turned on the radio to a rock and roll station. He dances to it.*) You liked to dance. We were good. I'll let you lead. (*He abruptly stops.*) You're not in the mood for this. Neither am I. (*He turns off the radio and starts searching for another CD.*)

MIKE   Could we have no music for a change?

STEPHEN   I'll keep it low.

MIKE   What's wrong with quiet?

STEPHEN   You have to listen to yourself think. I dare you not to like this. (Villa-Lobos's *Bachianas Brasileiras No. 5 is heard.*)

MIKE   Stephen, we have to talk.

STEPHEN   I am talking. You're not listening. (*He means the music.*) I can't say it any better than this. (*He crosses to Mike and stands behind him looking down at one last Polaroid Mike is about to destroy.*) Is that the last one? Wait. (*Mike stops.*) I still find the man in that picture very attractive.

MIKE   I don't recognize him.

STEPHEN   Look at those proportions. They're perfect.

MIKE   They're not perfect.

STEPHEN   To me they're perfect. My kind of perfect. The only kind I care about. (*They are both looking at this last Polaroid, Stephen leaning over Mike's shoulder, perhaps his hand on his shoulder.*) Wonderful full lips on a generous mouth. I like that enormously. Wonderful thick neck. I like that, too. Or did I already tell you that? I told someone I did. Deep, burning really nail-you eyes. Right at the camera, right through it and into mine. There's strength in that look but such a gentleness, too.

MIKE   Stephen.

STEPHEN   Where am I going to find that again?

MIKE   He wants to live with me, Stephen.

STEPHEN   Of course he wants to live with you. You're a catch, doctor. You have lousy hours but you're a catch. And see that line there? Defining the pelvis. I could trace it for hours. There's some wonderful name for it, somebody's girdle. Achilles' or Hercules' or Atlas' or . . . you took anatomy, help me out here.

MIKE   I don't remember.

STEPHEN   His is perfection. The thighs. Everything. He's everything I ever wanted. I can look at that picture and get hard. I used to look at them and masturbate when you were doing your residency and it seemed like you were never around. Even when you were sometimes. Once, I remember this so clearly, you were out here reading a new Updike, one of the Rabbits, and I was looking at those and jacking off. The last time you spent the night with Paul I did. The next time you spend the night with him I will.

MIKE   Jesus.

STEPHEN   Don't give me Jesus, give me the picture.

MIKE   No.

STEPHEN   This isn't easy for me to say. I want the picture, Mike. Let me have that much of you. Something. (*Mike starts to cut up the final Polaroid.*) All those years of analysis and I still say exactly what's on my mind. Do you want to live with him?

MIKE   I don't know. Maybe I should live alone.

STEPHEN   I have and believe me, it's not all it's cracked up to be. Before you know it, you're eating nothing but TV dinners and not bothering to flush. Little children start calling you Miss Havisham. (*Mike gets up and disposes of the pieces of Polaroid. Stephen stays where he was. Mike turns off stereo. There is a long silence.*)

MIKE   Why aren't you going in today?

STEPHEN   I think I should spend it with you.

MIKE   This will be the third time this month.

STEPHEN   What are you doing, spying on me?

MIKE   Brian McLaughlin called me at the hospital and asked me what the hell is going on. They're all worried you're sick. I told him it wasn't that. I told him I didn't know what it was.

STEPHEN   Middle-aged gay man blues turning into midlife crisis.

MIKE   People lose jobs this way.

STEPHEN   I'm thinking of joining a modern dance company.

MIKE   It's killing me. Watching you let it all slip away.

STEPHEN   Do you love him?

MIKE   I don't know.

STEPHEN   Ask a straight question, expect an evasive answer.

MIKE   I said I don't know.

STEPHEN   Let me rephrase that. Love is what *we're* supposed to have. Are you *in* love with him?

MIKE   Sometimes I think I am. That's about as straight an answer as I can give you.

STEPHEN   Was it like us?

MIKE   No.

STEPHEN   No whirlwind courtship?

MIKE   We didn't have a courtship.

STEPHEN   We didn't need one. One look and we knew. We both did. (*There is a silence between them.*) What you said to him, what you reminded him you said, what was that word?

MIKE   How fond I am of him.

STEPHEN   How "fond?" Did you say "fond," madam? Nay, you love. I know not "fond."

MIKE   Stephen, it's easy for you to play with words. Too easy. You can either hear what I want to say—it's pretty simple—or not. I don't have the time for anything else. This arrangement isn't working for either one of us.

STEPHEN   The arrangement is fine. It's me. I saw those records, the mess, and just went crazy. I'm sorry.

MIKE   That's how I am, Stephen. I always was. You just didn't notice. I scratch records, I eat pizza, I use the wrong towel.

STEPHEN   I said I was sorry.

MIKE   You can't have it both ways.

STEPHEN   I don't want it both ways. I want it this way. Just try to be careful next time.

MIKE   There will be a next time.

STEPHEN   I know.

MIKE   I like him.

STEPHEN   Fine.

MIKE   I really like him.

STEPHEN   Don't touch the stereo and you can bring a Boy Scout troop up here.

MIKE   I don't think you hear me anymore. You hear the words, but you don't hear what I'm saying.

STEPHEN   Try me.

MIKE   I have been.

STEPHEN   Try me!

MIKE   I'm tired, Stephen. I'm tired of tiptoeing through my life because it might interfere with yours. I'm tired of being told what opera to like, what book to read. I'm tired of being your father, your mother, your big brother, your best friend, your analyst, your cheerleader.

STEPHEN   You left out lover.

MIKE   I haven't been your lover since the first night I said to myself, "Who is this person lying at my side, this stranger, who hasn't heard or held me since the last time it pleased him?" That's the night I should have grabbed you by the shoulders and screamed, "I don't want this, Stephen. I don't need just another warm body next to mine. I'm much too needy myself to settle for so little." You weren't even sleeping. You were reading. Your friend was on the cassette player on your side of the bed. Maria Callas. You had your back to me. I had my arm around you. I was stroking one of your tits. I asked you how you thought I should handle Sarah—she was coming up to New York and wanted to see me. It was the first time since the divorce and I was scared. I'd hurt her in a way I was ashamed of. I really needed you and you just shrugged and said "You'll do the right thing" and turned the page. I kept my arm around you but you weren't the same person anymore. I was suddenly so scared. I was as alone as I must have made Sarah feel. I was holding on for dear life.

STEPHEN   Why didn't you tell me?

MIKE   You wouldn't have heard me.

STEPHEN   I'm listening now.

MIKE   I love you, Stephen. I'll always love you, but I haven't been your lover for a long time.

STEPHEN   People change, Michael. I can change.

MIKE   I think you're a good man, a decent and caring man, a deserving one. You'll find someone else.

STEPHEN   I don't want someone else.

MIKE   You don't deserve this. Neither of us do. (*Mike goes to phone and dials a number.*)

STEPHEN   I'll kill you before I let you run off and the two of you laugh at me.

MIKE   I'm sorry for the pain you're in.

STEPHEN   Then stop causing it. (*Stephen breaks the phone connection.*)

MIKE   Stephen, you can't want this relationship either.

STEPHEN I don't want a relationship. I want a lover.

MIKE So do I. (*Mike dials the number again.*)

STEPHEN Relationship! If I hear that asshole word one more time!

MIKE Shit! (*He hangs up and begins to dial another number.*)

STEPHEN I doubt if he's home yet, Michael. It takes at least—

MIKE I wasn't calling him.

STEPHEN You want the truth, Michael. I had a lousy night. My waiter friend stood me up. I spent the night at Mendy's sleeping on a lumpy chaise listening to Maria Callas.

MIKE I'm sorry.

STEPHEN Why? She was in fabulous voice. Don't cry for me, Argentina.

MIKE What happened? You were looking forward to seeing him.

STEPHEN I guess he decided he'd rather get some sleep or write another poem or be with someone else more than he wanted to get published. Youth has its priorities. People our age aren't one of them.

MIKE You should have told me. We could have gone somewhere else. A hotel, something.

STEPHEN Then why the hell didn't you? This is our home, Michael. (*He puts on Beverly Sills singing an aria from Mozart's* Zaide.)

MIKE (*Into phone.*) May I speak to Mr. Deller, please? His brother, Mike. Thank you, I'll hold.

STEPHEN You want to take a guess at this? Anyone would know this is Mozart. But you'll never guess the music. It's an aria from *Zaide*. He wrote it when he was two weeks old or something. It's hardly ever done. *Ruhe sanft, mein holdes leben* which I would translate roughly as: "Rest softly, my dearest life."

MIKE (*Into phone.*) Bob, Mike! Hi. Listen, can I stay with you two for a couple of nights? It's really gotten impossible here.

STEPHEN He knows? You told him?

MIKE I hope Ginny won't mind. I tried to call her first but there was no answer. Thanks. I don't know how he is. I haven't talked to

Mom since Sunday. I'm sure she'd call if there were any change. Okay. Thanks. Who? He's fine. Yeah. Bye. (*He hangs up.*)

STEPHEN   You told them?

MIKE   It was pretty obvious.

STEPHEN   I wish you'd made things more obvious to me. How is your father, anyway? I've been meaning to ask.

MIKE   The same I guess. One of us would have heard.

STEPHEN   Who's "fine"?

MIKE   Paul. Do you know where that overnight bag is?

STEPHEN   We left it in St. Bart's, it was falling apart.

MIKE   The blue one?

STEPHEN   Oh, you mean the tote! If it's not here, it's out in Sag. (*Mike goes into the bedroom, leaving the door open.*) How does he know Paul?

MIKE   We all had dinner and went to the theatre.

STEPHEN   On his budget? What did you see? *Cats*?

MIKE   How did you know?

STEPHEN   Just a wild guess. (*Mike gets a dark suit on a hanger out of the closet.*) I know it's none of my business as of thirty seconds ago but why are you taking your black wool suit to sleep on your brother's sofa?

MIKE   It's for Billy Todd's funeral tomorrow.

STEPHEN   From your description of him, you'll be the only one there not in full drag.

MIKE   I'm speaking. I didn't think it would be quite appropriate.

STEPHEN   A church full of queens lusting after the humpy doctor delivering his standard eulogy. Who asked you to speak? His lover?

MIKE   His family. He didn't have a lover.

STEPHEN   Of course not, he was madly in love with you. If I were you, I'd shake everybody up. People are sick and tired of hearing the same old dreary things at these affairs. He was wonderful. He had so much life to give. He was brave. Say, instead, aren't you sick and tired of these people depressing us just because they were unable to maintain a stable relationship? How many tears are we supposed to shed? Wouldn't we all rather be at a nice restaurant than sitting here moping over someone who probably, if the truth could be faced up to, even just a little bit, got what was coming to him?

MIKE Jesus, Stephen.

STEPHEN (*He bursts into tears.*)   I'm sorry but ever since you started telling me about him, I've been so jealous of him. That you were caring for him? Isn't that crazy?

MIKE Stephen, he was dying.

STEPHEN So am I. And then when you said he'd died last night, my first thought was he's free. No one can hurt him anymore. No one can leave him.

MIKE I didn't want this either, Stephen.

STEPHEN I was a good lover, Michael. I made you happy. We can try. At least try. We owe ourselves that.

MIKE It's not just about sex.

STEPHEN Yes it is. Right now it is. He's ten years younger than you. Of course it's about sex. Most of the time it is. We were wonderful that way. (*Mike exits to bedroom.*)

STEPHEN Do you think people like us read too many books about people like us? (*Meaning the music.*) Nice try, Bubbles. The good doctor has a heart of stone this morning. (*Calling off to Mike.*) It's on the top shelf in my closet. The blue tote. Behind the tennis balls. What do you want to hear? What about Tebaldi? You always liked her more than Maria. That should have been a tip off! How about the Lisbon *Traviata*? That seems to be the record du jour. (*Mike will continue to cross in and out of the bedroom and the bathroom packing certain items to take with him. Stephen will seem superfluous to his activities.*) What about the house anyway? What about Aspen? What do we tell George and Kenneth? That we're not coming? Just like that?

MIKE This is difficult enough. Let's not make it worse.

STEPHEN What am I supposed to tell my lawyer? I left everything to you. I'm not changing my will again.

MIKE   Tell him you want to leave everything to build a memorial statue to Maria Callas.

STEPHEN   You know, that's not a bad idea.

MIKE   Why not? She's dead. It's the living you have trouble with. (*He goes again. Stephen begins to play* La Traviata *and stands listening to the "Prelude" which begins to fill the room.*)

STEPHEN   I'll never forget the night she did this at the old Met. The excitement in the air. Everybody was there. Jackie Kennedy was in a box with Leonard Bernstein. No, that was for the return as Tosca seven years later and she was Jackie Onassis and she was with Adlai Stevenson. I'd been in love with the sound of her voice since the first records. That strange, sad siren song I knew she was singing just for me. I could play those records for hours. I had them memorized. Every nuance, the slightest intake of breath, the fiercest tones, the hushed, still pianissimo. Hers was the only voice who heard what I heard, said what I wanted to hear. This would be the first time I'd seen her. I'd waited on line for days for standing room. The curtain rose. I didn't see her at first. She was to one side. I'd thought she'd be center. But then she sang those first phrases—"*Flora, amici*"—and I saw her. She took my breath away. She wasn't just a voice on a record. She was there, she was real. I was on the same planet at the same moment in time as Maria Callas. The rest of the evening passed like a dream, a dream I remember more clearly than the color of my lover's eyes. I miss you, Mme Callas. (*He goes to the window and looks out. He stands with his back to us. Mike comes out of the bedroom with a small tote bag and some final articles he will pack in the suitcase.*)

MIKE   You have my brother's number?

STEPHEN   Don't go. Please, don't go.

MIKE   Will you be going out to the house this weekend?

STEPHEN   What do you care?

MIKE   I think it will be easier to get my things out if you aren't here.

STEPHEN   So soon? I don't see the hurry.

MIKE   Yes or no?

STEPHEN   If Caballé cancels her recital, yes. If she deigns to put in an appearance, no.

MIKE   When will you know?

STEPHEN   With Caballé it's right down to the wire. Why don't you call her? She's staying at Burger King. (*The phone begins to ring. They both look at the answering machine, waiting for it to pick up.*) That could be him. He could be home by now. I'm not going near it all day. The House of Knopf can think I'm dead. This is like waiting for water to boil. Don't give up on me, Michael. (*The answering machine finally picks up on the fourth ring.*)

STEPHEN   Hi. This is Stephen.

MIKE   And this is Mike. Neither of us is here.

STEPHEN   Or if we're here, we're not picking up.

MIKE   Leave a message and we'll get back to you.

STEPHEN   Thanks!

PAUL'S VOICE   Mike? It's Paul. Are you there? Do you want to pick up? (*Mike picks up the phone.*)

MIKE   Paul, where are you? What happened? I think we should, too. What did you tell them at work? The whole day? Great. How soon will you be here? See you. (*He hangs up.*)

STEPHEN   Let me guess. He said "I think we should talk" and you said "I think we should too." Now he's calling in sick. You see the effect you have on people. (*Mike is dialing another number.*)

MIKE   Go to hell.

STEPHEN   Now who are you calling?

MIKE (*Into phone.*)   This is Dr. Deller. Number 52. The blue BMW. That's me, Hector, you got it. How soon? (*He hangs up.*)

STEPHEN   What did they tell you? Ten minutes? That should be the name of that garage. It's the only English they speak. "Ten minutes." I don't want him in our car.

MIKE   Fine. We'll go to Avis.

STEPHEN   Why does it have to be this morning?

MIKE   He's on his way here.

STEPHEN   I love you.

MIKE   You can't love what we've become.

STEPHEN   Sleep with him, I don't care anymore. I'll pretend I don't care anymore. He's a trick. You don't walk away from us for a trick.

MIKE   This wouldn't be happening if he were.

STEPHEN   You can't leave. No one else will want me.

MIKE   That's not true. The moment I saw you, I thought you were the most terrific looking, acting, everything man I'd ever met.

STEPHEN   I look in the mirror and I no longer see a young, attractive man.

MIKE   You are attractive.

STEPHEN   I said young, attractive. I could castrate myself or I could castrate you or we could get heavily into saltpeter and just pretend that none of this mattered—none of it—and get another dog and gracefully grow old together.

MIKE   You'll be fine without me.

STEPHEN   Sometimes I think this is the most beautiful music ever written. Other times it's the Good Friday Music from *Parsifal* or *The Magic Flute*, Panima's aria, or *Fidelio*, the entire second act.

MIKE   I can't hold your hand anymore, Stephen.

STEPHEN   I'll die if you leave me.

MIKE   You just think you will.

STEPHEN   Don't tell me what I think, Michael. I know what I think. I think you are leaving me at a terrific moment in our long happy history of queerness to find a new mate to snuggle up with right at the height of our very own Bubonic Plague. Those are dark, mean and extremely dangerous streets right now. You can say all you want against Maria, no one's ever accused her of causing AIDS. Renata Scotto, yes; Maria, no.

MIKE   Why can't you be serious?

STEPHEN   It hurts too much, okay?

MIKE   You'll find someone.

STEPHEN   Asshole. Self-centered, smug, shit-kicking, got-himself-a-new-lover asshole. (*Maria Callas is heard singing on the stereo from The*

Lisbon Traviata.) "Sempre libera", "Always free"; that's you, Michael. Maria does this phrase better than anyone.

MIKE   I've spent the past half hour trying to get through to you. I've spent eight years. You live in *Tosca*. You live in *Turandot*. You live in some opera no one's ever heard of. It's hard loving someone like that. (*The house intercom buzzer is heard. Mike goes quickly to it.*)

MIKE   Hello?

PAUL'S VOICE   Mike? It's Paul. I'm in your lobby. Should I come up?

MIKE   I'll be right down. (*He hangs up and makes final preparations to leave.*)

STEPHEN   You really love him?

MIKE   Let me by.

STEPHEN   I told you, I'll kill you first. (*Stephen has the pair of scissors.*)

MIKE   Put those down, Stephen.

STEPHEN   Then tell me you don't love him. That you're not going down to him. Tell me you still love me.

MIKE   I love him, Stephen.

STEPHEN   Then you don't love me anymore? Then you don't love me anymore?

MIKE   No, I don't love you anymore. (*Stephen raises the scissors above his head, ready to strike.*) Do it or let me by, Stephen. Kill me or let me pass. (*The house intercom buzzer is heard again.*)

STEPHEN   This is the last time I'm going to warn you.

MIKE   You gave me this ring. I don't want it anymore. (*Mike takes off the ring and hands it to Stephen, who lets it drop to the floor. Mike starts to go. Stephen stabs him.*) Jesus! Jesus, Stephen, Jesus! I'm hurt. I'm really hurt!

STEPHEN   This isn't the right music. (*Stephen turns off the Lisbon Traviata and puts on the "Humming Chorus" from Madama Butterfly.*)

MIKE   Help me, Stephen. You've got to help me.

STEPHEN   I'm right here. (*He cradles Mike in his arms.*) Listen to the music, let it soothe you.

MIKE This is real, Stephen.

STEPHEN I know. Ssshh, listen. (*Mike is in shock. Blood is beginning to spill from his midsection. His life is oozing from him.*) Sometimes I think this is the most beautiful music ever written. Christ knows, it's the most banal. (*The intercom buzzer is heard again.*)

MIKE Paul! I'm hurt, Stephen, I'm really hurt. I'm scared to look. Stephen, please, you've got to call somebody. We can't handle this.

STEPHEN Yes, we can. Let me hold you.

MIKE You killed me, Stephen.

STEPHEN We killed each other. People don't just die from this. They die from what you were doing to me. They die from loss. (*The phone rings; answering machine picks up.*)

STEPHEN Hi. This is Stephen.

MIKE And this is Mike. Neither of us is here.

STEPHEN Or if we're here we're not picking up.

MIKE Leave a message and we'll get back to you.

STEPHEN Thanks!

MENDY'S VOICE Hello, Stephen? It's me. Albert Benedetti has just come by with a copy of the Lisbon *Traviata* and we've just put it on, and already it's to die.

MIKE (*Weakly.*) Mendy.

MENDY'S VOICE He also brought over Sutherland's first *Adriana* from San Diego if you really want to laugh. Vickers has canceled all his *Parsifal*s. Such is life. I hope you two are all right. Sometimes I don't know how Mike puts up with you. It's begun! She just sang "*Flora, amici.*" Divine woman! What would we do without her? Remember, we have *Meistersinger* tonight. (*He hangs up.*)

STEPHEN I'm sorry.

MIKE Please, call someone, before it's too late. (*There is knocking on the apartment door.*) Paul!

STEPHEN Sshh. When the music's over. Listen, it will soothe you.

MIKE   Hurry.

STEPHEN   When the music's over. (*The life continues to ebb from Mike. Their eyes have met and held. Slow fade to blackout.*)

END OF PLAY.

LIPS TOGETHER, TEETH APART (1991)

In 1985 Lynne Meadow, the artistic director of the Manhattan Theatre Club, said she would produce the next play I wrote, sight unseen. Those few words changed my career. MTC became my artistic home for more than a decade.

We were standing in the costume shop of their theatre at New York City Center during previews of a play of mine that had flopped ignominiously during its pre-Broadway engagement at the Forrest Theatre in Philadelphia eight years earlier. Thoroughly rewritten and retitled *It's Only a Play*, Lynne was giving me and *Broadway, Broadway* another chance. More significantly, she was offering me a place to work and develop as a playwright—and this was before the reviews of my first venture with them had come out. She was taking a big chance on me, the kind of chance every theatre artist needs.

I was liberated. After more than twenty years of shopping my plays to commercial producers, I could write the plays I wanted to write, not the plays I thought producers wanted me to write. It was one of the best days of my life.

I had taken the failure of the original production badly. James Coco, Geraldine Page and Lenny Baker were the stars. The director was my lover, Robert Drivas (in 1977 there was no other word for the man you were in a relationship with—even then it seemed inadequate and trite), an actor I had met during the travails of my first play, . . . *And Things That Go Bump in the Night*. *Bump* was the first play I'd written and it opened on Broadway at the Royale Theatre on April 26, 1965. I made a lot of mistakes with *Bump* but falling in love with my leading man wasn't one of them. Bobby was very talented, very handsome and very funny. I take the theatre very seriously, so did he, but as Emma Goldman said, "If I can't dance I don't want to be a part of your revolution." Bobby was an excellent dancer.

By the time I met him, my relationship with Edward Albee, who also took the theatre very seriously, was pretty much over. We were still living together, had been since I was a junior at Columbia, but I don't think Edward was any happier about the present status of our relationship than I was. Edward and I both drank too much (everyone we knew and ran with drank too much) and were unfaithful to each other too often and too casually to give maturing love a chance. Bobby was the breakup in the Albee-McNally cohabitation that was waiting to happen. I beat Edward to it.

The mistakes I made on *Bump* can be attributed to my youth and inexperience. I was terrified out of my wits but I pretended I knew what I was doing, the first sign of an in-over-his-head beginner.

Everything that was wrong about the production was somebody else's fault, not mine: the set was all wrong, the actors didn't "hear" me, and as for the director. . . . English wasn't even his first language, for God's sake! It never occurred to me that the fault might lie in my script.

I played the innocent victim of my colleagues' limitations pretty shamelessly. First-time playwrights are usually not known for their ability to examine their own responsibility when a play doesn't work. It's seldom, if ever, their fault. Consequently, I learned very little from the debacle of my first play. Instead, I nursed bad feelings and resentments but I didn't look hard enough at my script. It all begins and ends on the page. No actor, no director, no designer—no one—can help you if you haven't done your work properly. They can camouflage your mistakes for a time, they can distract the audience for half an act but eventually the play itself comes home to roost and if it isn't right, God help you. It can take a playwright an entire career before realizing the buck stops with them. I'm still working on this. Just last week at a rehearsal I was cursing an actor under my breath for his delivery until I finally admitted to myself it was the line, not him, that was the problem. It felt good when I fixed it. Did anyone congratulate or thank me? Not a peep. Playwriting is a job as much as it is self-expression.

Since breaking up with Edward and all through the rehearsals and previews of *Bump*, I had continued to drink too much. After all, it was my birthright as an American playwright with an Irish surname to be an alcoholic as well. Inebriation came with the territory. It never occurred to me that sobriety might be a useful state-of-mind for creativity. Dull, flavorless playwrights, I thought, got that way because they didn't join us at Sam's or Theatre Bar for up-until-closing-time drinking marathons while we talked about our craft. Alcohol, nicotine and creativity were our Holy Trinity. A mind either dulled or inflamed by Dewar's scotch (How I soon graduated to gin martinis!) was not the best judge of what was happening on the stage of the Royale Theatre.

What I was thinking from my standing place at the back of the orchestra was that *Bump* was a flawed, ambitious first play by a talented young playwright. I was optimistic enough to think anyone would see that, even the critics. (Fifty years later, I still do.)

The reviews were scathing and homophobic. Among other things, the critics were outraged by homosexual men who actually had sex. Comic-relief hairdressers and suicidal alcoholics knew their place as venerable comic/dramatic stereotypes. But sexually active men who locked lips and had orgasms and lived in the same real world as the audience were not suitable people to write plays about, especially on Broadway. In 1965, that sort of nonsense belonged downtown.

In those days I could still play the "They hate us because we're gay" card. On opening night I remember Jean Kerr, the humorist and my fellow playwright, saying to her husband, Walter, who was reviewing my play for the *New York Herald Tribune* (all the critics came on opening night in those days), as the marquee lights flashed, signaling the curtain going up (in those days everyone stood outside the theatre and smoked until the last possible moment), "Let's go see what his boyfriend has come up with." Clearly, they were going to see a play by a well-known writer's unknown bedmate. Little did they know Edward and I were kaput and the play's leading man was my bedfellow now. "At least get your facts right, lady," I wanted to yell after her as they brushed by me, an anonymous young playwright awaiting his fate at her husband's hands.

The reviews with a single exception—Michael Smith writing for *The Village Voice*—were annihilating. I did not expect the curtain to rise for a second performance. One-night stands were not infrequent in those days. The morning after *Bump* opened I was already making plans to return to my abandoned career as a journalist when two of the show's producers, Ted Mann and Paul Libin, called to tell me that since the production had come in under budget, they were going to keep the show open for two weeks at greatly reduced prices: one dollar for weekdays and matinees, two dollars for Friday and Saturday evenings. Even at those prices, I thought no one would come.

Instead, we sold out every performance to vocal, if divided, audiences. Some people loved the play; others detested it. Both groups made their voices heard at the curtain calls, which were tumultuous to say the least. At Columbia we had studied the riotous first night in Paris of Victor Hugo's *Hernani* in 1830. I felt part of the grand tradition of controversial theatre. I felt proud. Spontaneous pickets carrying placards appeared in front of the theatre by the fourth performance. They were demonstrating *for* the play, not against it. Yet the *New York Times* refused to believe it was anything but a publicity stunt, paid for by the producers. In our case, "All the news that's fit to print" went unreported.

I think if we had closed after that one opening night performance, I would never have written for the theatre again. My sense of shame alone would have prevented it. But thanks to my two forward-thinking producers, I felt like a playwright: an unsuccessful one, to be sure, but a playwright all the same. For sixteen more performances I was being heard. I owe my career to many people but none deserve my gratitude more than Ted Mann and Paul Libin.

Between *Bump* and my next Broadway play, *Broadway, Broadway*, I spent most of my time off-Broadway and at various regional theatres. I wrote a lot

of one-acts, which were very popular in those days thanks to the Beckett/
Albee pairing of *Krapp's Last Tape* and *The Zoo Story*. There was scarcely a
season when I was not in production below 14th St. My first success was
with *Next*, which starred my friend James Coco and was directed by Elaine
May and seemed to run forever. *Bad Habits* and *The Ritz* both transferred to
Broadway from their Off-Broadway birthplaces (in the case of *Bad Habits*,
Off-Off-Broadway, and *The Ritz*, Yale Repertory Theatre).

I was earning a living as a playwright and quit my job at *Columbia College
Today*, my *alma mater's* alumni magazine, after *Next* opened in 1969. I had
written the play while on a Guggenheim Fellowship but had held on to my
day job in Morningside Heights. Playwrights shouldn't have to starve for a
living and working a 40-hour week doing anything else other *than* playwriting is not going to hasten the completion of the next Great American Play
either. Tennessee Williams wrote his early plays at night while holding down
a day job at a shoe factory in St. Louis. I don't think I had that kind of will-
power. I was "too tired to write" after a day at the magazine. A grant from
the Guggenheim Foundation saved my ass and rescued me from self-pity. I
have been fortunate enough to earn my living (and sometimes it has been a
very modest one) as a playwright ever since.

With all this experience and acquired theatre wisdom behind me, by
the time we traveled to Philadelphia for the pre-Broadway engagement of
Broadway, Broadway in the late summer of 1977 I thought I finally knew what
I was doing. It turned out I didn't. The mistakes we made this time were
the mistakes of seasoned professionals, the kind we are all capable of in the
business of theatre, time after time after time. Unfortunately they weren't so
different from the mistakes we'd made twelve years earlier with *Bump*, only
this time I was a little more willing to look at my part in the dysfunctional
process we were calling rehearsals. I was still drinking to excess. So were the
director and the producer.

For those who work in it, the theatre doesn't get any easier. Over the
years, a playwright usually gets better at typing but the same playwright does
not necessarily get better at writing a play, no matter how long he or she
struggles with this difficult, imperfect form of self-expression. With luck, a
playwright learns to collaborate and rewrite as she or he matures. First drafts
are easy. The genius is in what happens after that first draft goes into rehearsal.

Broadway, Broadway in Philadelphia was my comic distillation of the
humiliation of . . . *And Things That Go Bump in the Night,* some twelve
years earlier on Broadway. In fact, it proved to be an equally dire experience. The critics were not patient with our embryo of a comedy about the
vicissitudes of a Broadway opening night, and offered little in the way of

encouragement. I began a furious series of rewrites but before the week had ended, the producer told us he was closing the show that Saturday night. The company bus ride back to New York on Sunday morning was a wake on wheels, without the booze. I remember standing around the fountain outside the Plaza Hotel (our arrival point back in the city for some unfathomable reason), waiting for our luggage to come off the bus. The goodbyes were brief and listless. I don't think any of us wanted to see any of the others ever again, at least not in this lifetime. Flops are *that* pulverizing to the body and the soul. It's ridiculous but true. I wouldn't wish a flop on anyone. Well, maybe one or two people.

The colorful, witty marquee for my play at the Eugene O'Neill Theatre on West 49th St., where *Broadway, Broadway* had been scheduled to open, stayed in place for what seemed like an eternity before another show booked the theatre. My humiliation was up in lights.

Five years later, Manhattan Punch Line Theatre presented a spirited revival of the play, now rewritten and retitled *It's Only a Play*. The reviews were very good but Off-Off-Broadway runs are limited. I figured this production was probably the last of the only play of mine I have ever called a comedy. Comedy is the word producers want to use to describe almost any play but *Death of a Salesman*. I insist on the word "play." Let the audience decide if it's a comedy.

John Tillinger, who seemed to have directed every play in New York in the 1980s, approached me about doing a revival of this new version at MTC with James Coco repeating his *tour de force* performance as James Wicker, a part I had written for him, just as I had the hapless Marion Cheever in *Next*.

All this is a very long preamble to that pivotal moment when Lynne told me she would present my next play, no matter what the critics said about the one in previews at her theatre. It is the kind of commitment very few artists get but every artist deserves: a pledge of support for a body of work, not a reward for coming up with a hit.

Lynne gave me the free pass I needed to write *Frankie and Johnny in the Clair de Lune*, which I figured would be a love story of interest only to people who were approaching fifty and not in a relationship, i.e., *me*. It took me twenty-plus years of shopping my plays all over town before I realized I needed a home more than a hit.

In those heady and exhilarating years at MTC, we all worked with the freedom and spontaneity of the best of that time when it seemed Off-Broadway was where almost everything exciting was happening. It *felt* like we began our plays on Monday, finished them on Friday and went into rehearsal the next Monday. I exaggerate, to be sure, but I can promise you that's how it *felt* to all of us. Productions happened easily, quickly, and joyfully. This was before the high cost of production made everyone nervous and the competition for subscribers became paramount. The goal became to keep old subscribers, rather than harvesting new ones. Once-bold theatre companies suddenly found reasons not to produce our plays. Before anyone realized what was happening, pre-production workshops and dramaturged-to-eternity development schedules took the place of getting a play up on its feet in rehearsal. The immediate contact of script, director and actor became a pedantic morass of tracing the "arc" of a character or dissecting the "themes" of a play. Such processing would have destroyed Shakespeare or Chekhov. There is no "arc" to Hamlet, that's why we're still fascinated with him. A dramaturg would have had a heart attack faced with the unprecedented structure of *The Seagull*.

Lips Together, Teeth Apart was the result of MTC announcing a new play by Terrence McNally in their subscription brochure before Terrence McNally had even the notion of an idea for one. I just knew I wanted to write a play for four of my favorite actors, the best of their generation: Nathan Lane, Christine Baranski, Anthony Heald and Kathy Bates. As it turned out, Kathy was unavailable and another actress I revered, Swoosie Kurtz, took her place in the company.

Lips is a play written for actors, first and foremost. But I also wanted to challenge the technical departments at MTC after the relatively simple demands *Frankie and Johnny* and *Lisbon* had made on them. I wanted great actors but this time I wanted flying kites and grilling burgers and hot dogs, too, not to mention a swimming pool. With *Lips*, I got it all. I experienced the exhilaration of being in the rehearsal room with great actors, a smart director and a trusting producer.

My greatest fear as a playwright is repeating myself. Fortunately, I love playing with form and the possibilities form offers a playwright are infinite. This time I wanted to write a three-act play. The form itself had been deemed nonviable. In choosing it, I knew I had to find a contained situation but I did not want to force an arbitrary "plot" on my four characters who find themselves on Fire Island on a Fourth of July weekend at the height of the AIDS catastrophe. The play's three-act structure is simplicity itself: morning, noon and night of the same "uneventful" day. The situation is their fear of intimacy. Their fear of mortality lurks in the swimming pool. Those are my fears as well.

The truth is, I don't believe much in conventional "plot." I got that from working with Elaine May when she directed my second play, *Next*. Behavior is everything. What I believe in are characters responding to a strong situation. My "stories" are their reactions. It was good enough for Chekhov.

The influence of music, especially opera, is everywhere in *Lips*. It is a play filled with arias, duets, trios and quartets. The actors complained about the difficulty of picking up cues in a quartet when two of the characters are off-stage but I was determined they would understand and truly hear my music before we left the rehearsal room. The technical department soon learned the sounds coming from the unseen houses next door are as important as anything said in the dialogue. *Lips* was my chance to show off as a playwright: everything I love about being a playwright in the theatre is there.

And I was responding to the AIDS crisis that engulfed all of us by talking about it as honestly as I knew how. This is not a play about homophobes. It's a play about homophobia. I can trace the first impulses to writing it to a lunch with a sophisticated woman who included me among her many and dearest friends. She asked me which glass I had taken a sip of water from. I was positive it was my own but she insisted on having the waiter bring her a fresh glass "just in case" and she didn't bat an eyelash while she did it. Not much later, a producer wanted to commission me to write a play for her theatre. She added one "tiny" caveat: "Just don't make it too gay. It can be a little gay, of course, Terrence, just not *too* gay." No wonder AIDS was being allowed to happen. Its victims were too marginalized to count as human beings who were dying. It was inevitable that *Lips* was a play I would write.

It has since turned out that in taking up the mantle of responsibility of producing new American plays in the face of Broadway's timidity, the not-for-profit companies have become more conservative in choosing their plays and playwrights. Fear of failure and caution about experimentation permeate the atmosphere in a way they never did. It's understandable and regrettable, but the more Off-Broadway behaves like Broadway, the less nurturing to the next generations of playwrights it will be. Theatres like MTC were the pay-offs for the boldness of the '60s. Of course that boldness still exists but it is finding it more difficult to make itself heard.

In retrospect, writing *Lips* was easy. Rounding up an extraordinary cast was easy. Getting it produced was easy. I realize I was one of the lucky ones, but there were a lot of us back then. Everything about making theatre was easier. It was in the city's very identity it seemed.

Anything was possible then. It still is, of course, but it's so much harder for a playwright to find a home. I advise young theatre artists to start their own theatre companies, which is what Lynne and her associate, Barry Grove, had done before they came to me with an offer I could not refuse. There are fewer Lucky Ones now because there are fewer opportunities for emerging play-wrights. The smart ones are creating their own opportunities. Good for them.

Our marriage began to sour when they initially canceled the production of *Corpus Christi* because of the furor created by the Catholic League who insisted I defamed Jesus Christ and the disciples by suggesting they may have been a collective of socially progressive gay men. Until then, I hadn't realized that Bill Donohue and his Catholic League (of one?) claimed Him as their own. I thought I was writing about some nice Jewish boys.

The cancellation caused an even greater furor in the theatrical community—Athol Fugard withdrew his play, which was to follow mine in the season—and I was not surprised when the MTC production was reinstated. Their own demonstrating against them was more powerful to MTC than the threats of intolerant religious hypocrites.

When I was invited to write a play to open their new theatre on West 47th St. I was both flattered and intimidated. The play, *Dedication or the Stuff of Dreams*, is the only play I have written for an *occasion*, in this case the dedication of the first new theatre on Broadway in many years. We had a small, private reading of the first act and Lynne declared herself well-pleased and it was announced in the *New York Times* that my play would open their new theatre on West 47th St., just as *Frankie and Johnny* had opened Stage II at City Center ten years earlier. When the script was finished, there was another "informal" reading, this time attended by a large crowd of people, most of whom I did not recognize. Lynne's initial enthusiasm for the play was cooled by the response to this unrehearsed, cold reading. The production was abruptly canceled and a new play was put in its place, Richard Greenberg's *The Violet Hour*, which was enjoying a successful run in Chicago. When Lynne called me with this abrupt change of plans, I asked her to sleep on it and call me in the morning. Not five minutes later my agent called me to tell me that the Greenberg was replacing the McNally.

A sad end to a successful decade of mutual trust and spontaneous, joyful creativity.

I have since returned to MTC with the first New York revival of *Master Class* and a new play, *Golden Age*, which was a disappointing, dispiriting experience for all of us.

You can go home again. What you can't go back to is the sense of "We can do anything. Just watch our dust!"

I will always think of *Lips Together, Teeth Apart* as the love child of Lynne's unconditional pledge of support in a cluttered costume shop on West 55th St. in 1991. Ten plays in as many years, most of them successful. Manhattan Theatre Club and I had a mutual Golden Age together.

Lips Together,
Teeth Apart

for Wendy Wasserstein

LIPS TOGETHER, TEETH APART was first presented by the Manhattan Theatre Club (Lynne Meadow, Artistic Director; Barry Grove, Managing Director) in New York City on May 28, 1991. It was directed by John Tillinger; the set design was by John Lee Beatty; the costume design was by Jane Greenwood; the lighting design was by Ken Billington; the sound design was by Stewart Werner; the fight staging was by Jerry Mitchell and the production stage manager was Pamela Singer. The cast was as follows:

CHLOE HADDOCK   Christine Baranski

SAM TRUMAN   Nathan Lane

JOHN HADDOCK   Anthony Heald

SALLY TRUMAN   Swoosie Kurtz

SAM TRUMAN
a self-employed businessman

SALLY TRUMAN
his wife

JOHN HADDOCK
head of admissions at a boys' prep school

CHLOE HADDOCK
his wife, Sam's older sister

The wooden deck of a summer beach house on Long Island.

At the rear of the stage and well behind our principal playing area, sliding glass/ screen doors in the center of the house open onto the cooking/dining area. People inside the house can be seen as they prepare a meal, eat, make a phone call, etc., even though the parts of the play we can actually hear and participate in all take place on the wooden deck outside the house itself. The same goes for the bedrooms. There are bedrooms to each side of this central kitchen/dining wing which can be reached from either inside the house or through sliding glass/screen doors that open onto the deck. As with the cooking/dining area, the people may also be seen, if not heard, when they are in their bedrooms, unless their blinds are specifically drawn. The master bedroom is Stage Right. Another, smaller bedroom is Stage Left. There is a locked door next to the Stage Left bedroom. We cannot see into the room behind it.

The deck itself is furnished with chairs, a picnic table and benches, chaises for sunning and a charcoal grill. There is also a swimming pool, though perhaps we see only a corner of it. The pool is lit for the last scene. There is an outdoor shower with a half-door for privacy. Finally, there are steps leading down from the deck to the dunes on which the house is built. Throughout the play, except in the last scene, there is a steady sea breeze. Things will blow in it. A Japanese silk fish will be inflated by it. Paper napkins will blow away. The roar of the ocean is steady. Sooner or later, we will get used to it.

The time of the play is now. It is Fourth of July weekend.

ACT ONE

AT RISE: *Tableau—Sally painting at easel, Chloe standing at the kitchen sink; within, John reading a newspaper, Sam testing the chlorine level in the pool.*

No one moves. Silence.

Music begins. The Farewell Trio from Mozart's Così *Fan* Tutte.

As the trio progresses, the stage and the actors will slowly come to "life."

The first movement will be the gentle stirrings of an ornamental flag in the early morning breeze.

Then Sally will begin to paint, Chloe to drink coffee in the kitchen, John to turn the pages of his New York Times, *Sam to retrieve the chlorine indicator—but all in time to the music, not reaching naturalistic behavior until the end of the piece.*

By the time the Trio ends, we will be in "real" time.

CHLOE   Is anyone still hungry? Does anyone want more? I've got eggs, bacon, bagels, Sara Lee, Entenmann's, fresh-squeezed orange juice, coffee, decaf (Colombian water processed), Special K, English muffins, French muffins, Dutch muffins, German muffins. Hello?

SAM   It looks clean. It looks immaculate. I can see right to the bottom. Somebody's been around. His friend must have kept up the pool service. I'm very impressed.

JOHN   It says here that eleven percent of this country is black. That's amazing. I would have thought it was more like fifty.

SALLY   I can see why people do still lifes. The light keeps changing. Every time I look up it's different. I'd be better off making the whole thing up. I think that's what the really great artists did anyway. I mean, whoever saw wheat fields like yellow ropes until van Gogh did? Well not "ropes" maybe; big fat squiggles of yellow paint he just squirted out of the tube.

CHLOE   Sometimes I wonder who we're really talking to.

JOHN   Whom we're really talking to, Petal.

CHLOE   They all heard me say "Is anyone still hungry? Does anyone want more?" Then why don't they answer? Apathy? Actual dislike? It was a simple question. I mean, I didn't ask "Does anybody know what the meaning of life is?" or "Are you sleeping with my husband, Sally?" or "Does anybody remember how late that little grocery store down by the ferry stays open?" All I asked was "Is anyone still hungry? Does anyone want more?" There's times like this, if I had a small hand gun, I'd use it. Tiny little pops. Pop! pop! pop! All fall down. (*Sally has stopped painting. She is watching someone on the beach in front of the house. None of the other three pays her any attention.*)

JOHN   Doesn't this country seem more than eleven percent black to you?

SAM   Not where you live. I'd say it seems more like zero percent, which is probably why you live there. (*To Sally.*) Where do you think they might have kept the chlorine, Sal, in case we need any?

SALLY   I don't know.

JOHN   Try the utility shed.

SAM   What's a utility shed?

JOHN   A shed for utilities.

SAM   I'm sorry. You're talking to a humble Trenton, New Jersey homeowner here. I keep everything in the garage. So where would I find this famous utility shed?

JOHN   They're usually under the house.

SAM   I bet I know where that is: under the house! Okay, okay, so I'm not Henny Youngman but you all thought I was pretty funny last night when I fell off that boardwalk hauling all those groceries in that little red wagon. What do these people have against cars and sidewalks?

CHLOE   It's an island.

SAM   So's Manhattan. They drive and walk all over the place.

CHLOE   And look at Manhattan. I don't care what anyone says. This is paradise. They want to keep it that way. Sally, it's heaven. The house, the setting. I am green. (*She comes over to Sally and squints at her painting.*) What is it or should I be able to tell?

SALLY   That. (*She nods towards the ocean.*)

CHLOE   That is that? Oh, I see. Very clever. What do you call that? Abstract expressionism? Pop Cubism? What?

SALLY   It's nothing, right now. I'll tell you when it's finished.

CHLOE (*To Sam and John.*)   Sshh, genius at work. Have we seen our neighbors yet?

SAM   You mean the boys from Ipanema next door? No. They're still getting their beauty sleep.

CHLOE   I'm sure they'll be very nice. I did a little research: it's strictly *crème de la crème* here. We should all have a wonderful brother like David to leave us something like this. (*Sam pulls something on a string out of the pool.*)

SAM   According to this gauge, the water is perfect. The question is: do we trust a gauge? I'm sorry but I'm very sensitive about pools. Our mother was very big on polio. And this was after they'd come up with a cure for it. She was ready for it to a make a big comeback. Grow up like that and you view a pool or a public toilet seat as a natural enemy.

CHLOE   Can we not talk about toilet seats right after breakfast? Thank you. I just hope you're all going to get into that pool—that includes you, too, Sally!—and stay there all weekend. If I weren't allergic to chlorine, you'd never get me out of that thing. Is that a kick in the ass or what?

SAM   So what are we going to do today? What's the agenda?

CHLOE   No agenda. Swim, take a walk, read, volleyball, paint, barbeque, nap, doze, eat, drink, laze, nothing.

SAM   That's a lot, sis. I'm exhausted.

JOHN   What time is it, Chloe?

CHLOE   What do you care what time it is? We're at the beach.

JOHN   What time is it, Sally?

CHLOE   Don't tell him, Sally.

JOHN   Sally?

SAM   It's a little after nine.

JOHN   Thank you. Petal? (*He holds up his empty coffee mug. Chloe takes it from him.*)

CHLOE   Oui, mon amour. One cup of java coming up! Sam? Sally?

SALLY   No, thank you.

CHLOE   Are you sure?

SALLY   Not now, thanks.

CHLOE   It's from Nussbaum's and Claverstock's, their special, special blend.

JOHN   Honey, they don't know about Nussbaum's and Claverstock's.

CHLOE   Well excuse me! I thought everyone knew about Nussbaum's and Claverstock's. It's only been written up in the every newspaper and magazine in America. Sam? *Encore du café?*

SAM   You're an angel of mercy! I thought you'd never ask. Of course I could have gotten it myself but I'm the kind of guy who likes to see a woman toil on his behalf.

CHLOE   Did you hear that, Mrs. Truman?

SAM   I'm old-fashioned. So sue me. God, if you weren't my sister I'd jump all over you. You are married to a winner, John, a winner.

CHLOE   Did you tell Dad we were getting together this weekend?

SAM   He wouldn't remember if I did. When are you going down again?

CHLOE   I'm trying for the weekend after Labor Day. I hate that place. The children and John won't go with me anymore. (*Sam and Chloe look out to sea.*)

SAM   Remind you of something?

CHLOE   What do you think? The 29th St. beach. So where's the roller coastère and the salt water taffy stand?

SAM   Those were the days! Fresh Air Camp.

CHLOE   Oh come on, it wasn't a Fresh Air Camp.

SAM   It was a Fresh Air Camp.

CHLOE   From Asbury Park to this. You've come a long way, baby.

SAM   We both have.

CHLOE   Nussbaum's and Claverstock's is this fabulous gourmet food shop in New Canaan. John hates me to shop there but if you want quality, you have to pay for it, right?

SAM   Sis, this is your kid brother you're talking to. Gourmet to me is a baked potato with sour cream.

CHLOE   Well, married to a woman who doesn't cook.

SAM   Sally cooks.

CHLOE   My lips are sealed. Relax. For the next three days you're in very good hands. (*She pats his stomach.*) When she telephoned, I told Sally I'd take care of everything this weekend. Most women would resent another woman taking over their kitchen.

SAM   It's not really her kitchen yet.

CHLOE   It's the Fourth of July. I'm going to celebrate if it kills me. They've predicted perfect weather for this weekend; I'm going to keep it that way. Gray skies are going to clear up, put on a happy face.

JOHN   Chloe, I thought you were bringing us fresh coffee.

CHLOE   I'm going, I'm going. *J'y vais à la cuisine.* And when I come back I'm going to blow my whistle and I expect everyone to jump in that pool. That goes for you, too, Sally. For the next three days I want you to think of me as your charming capable pool girl. Oops, oops, oops! Pool *person.* Sorry, Sally.

JOHN   Chloe.

CHLOE   *Je suis dehors d'ici.* I'm outta here! *Fermez la porte!*

SAM   What?

CHLOE   Close the door! (*Chloe goes through the sliding glass doors into the kitchen, which is just off the deck. We will be able to see her preparing coffee, even though she is clearly out of earshot. She sings to herself as she works.*)

SAM   What's with my sister? She seems unusually hyper, even for her.

JOHN   Really?

SAM   You haven't noticed a change?

JOHN   No, but then I'm married to her.

SAM   It's not the kids?

JOHN   The kids are fine. They're with their grandmother.

CHLOE (*From the kitchen.*)   How does everyone want their coffee?

JOHN   If you don't know after all these years—!

CHLOE (*Off.*)   I was being polite, John.

JOHN   Well don't. This group is beyond polite.

CHLOE (*At the door.*)   Besides, I was speaking to our hosts.

SAM   Oh, come on, Chloe. We're not your hosts. You're family.

CHLOE   Milk, Sam?

SAM   I don't suppose you have any half and half?

CHLOE   I do. Just for you. I know that's how you take it. Sugar?

SAM   Sweet 'n Low?

CHLOE   Half a packet?

SAM   More like a third.

CHLOE   Coming up. (*To John.*) See how simple that was, darling? (*She goes back into kitchen.*)

SAM   You two are okay?

JOHN   We're terrific. We have New England's longest-running, happiest, most fecund shotgun marriage.

SAM   Is that supposed to be funny?

JOHN   Not especially.

SAM   Because it's not.

JOHN   There was no major in comedy at Williams. There should be.

SAM   That's a very annoying habit of yours. Reading while someone is talking to you.

JOHN   I'm not really reading. I'm more like skimming. Besides, I can do both. You think your sister seems a little extra hyper, even by her own high standards, and I'm being told by that book reviewer whose name I can never pronounce that we should all be home reading a new biography of Melville this weekend. Apparently, the whale isn't a metaphor, it's a whale. You have my complete attention, Sam. (*He turns a page.*)

SAM   It's very unpolite.

JOHN   Impolite. I'm sorry.

SAM   I'd like you to stop it.

JOHN   Why?

SAM   I don't like it. (*He pulls the paper away from John.*) Look at me when I speak to you.

JOHN   All right.

SAM   That's more like it.

JOHN   What do you want to say?

SAM   It's very rude to read while people are speaking to you.

JOHN   I can see that.

SAM   It makes them feel unimportant.

JOHN   That was not my intention.

SAM   Well, that's how it comes across. (*He hands paper back to John.*) Don't let me interrupt you. I've made my point. (*John resumes reading. Sam crosses to Sally's painting.*) Did you hear all that? I guess that's telling him. Asshole. This is their last weekend. Quick, what's "fecund?" What's the matter?

SALLY   There's someone out there.

SAM   So?

SALLY   Way, way out there. Too far. I don't like it.

SAM   Where?

SALLY   Way, way out there. You can just see his head. There he is! See?

SAM   No.

SALLY   Now the waves are in the way. There!

SAM   I don't see anyone.

SALLY   Just before he swam out, he turned and waved but I don't think it was to me. I thought maybe he was—there! See him?—waving to David, that he hadn't heard, so I waved back, just in case, but it was more like he was waving to the house than to someone in it. It was like a salute or a farewell. Then he walked right into the surf and started swimming straight out, like he was going somewhere. You know, with a purpose. Strong, steady, powerful strokes.

SAM   If he's that kind of swimmer, I don't know what you're worrying about. We'll give him a big hand when he swims in.

SALLY   I've been watching him all morning. I got up early to paint and he was already down there on the beach, as if he'd been there all night. He was sitting with his knees pulled up to his chest, looking out to sea. At one point, he turned and looked up to the house here for a long, long time. Just stared.

SAM   Sure, he heard about your brother and was checking this place out to rob it. Let's make sure people know somebody's here.

SALLY   It was like that scene in that movie.

SAM   What scene, what movie?

SALLY   You know the one.

SAM   There are a million movies, Sally.

SALLY   Help me.

SAM   How should I know? You mangle the name of every one of them. Last Saturday you wanted to rent *Zorro the Greek*.

SALLY   The man swims out.

SAM   What man?

SALLY   I don't know. Gregory Peck!

SAM   Gregory Peck swims out into something? You sure you don't mean Johnny Weissmuller?

SALLY   No! *A Star Was Born*.

SAM   *A Star Was Born* with Gregory Peck?

SALLY   And Judy Garland.

SAM   Jesus, Sally!

SALLY   What did I say?

SAM   You know how this drives me crazy.

SALLY   It wasn't Judy Garland?

SAM   Yes, it was Judy Garland. But it was *A Star Is Born. A Star Is Born.* You are the only person on this entire planet who would say *A Star Was Born.* And it was James Mason.

SALLY   Well whoever he was—

SAM   He was James Mason, for Christ's sake!

SALLY   Well he never came back.

SAM   Of course he never came back. It was a sad movie.

SALLY   I thought it was a musical.

SAM   It was a sad musical. You're pushing all my buttons.

SALLY   There, you can see his robe on the beach where he dropped it.

SAM   We'll keep an eye out for him.

SALLY   He wasn't wearing anything.

SAM   You mean, he was naked? On a public beach? That's outrageous. Did you hear that, John? There's a guy out there skinny-dipping with women and children around.

JOHN   Very few women and even fewer children.

SAM   Anybody could see him. Sally did. It's against the law. Suppose I wanted to whip my dick out?

JOHN   This is Fire Island, Sam. I would strenuously argue against it.

SAM   That's not funny.

SALLY   He had a beautiful body.

SAM   I'm sure he did. Most of them do. It's one of their requirements. If I had nothing to all day but work out in a gym I would, too. Unfortunately, I own a construction company that has a funny way of going under every three months. And we all thought you were painting. (*He nuzzles Sally from behind.*) You're waiting for some strange guy to come out of the water so you can get a look at his whose-y. I'll show him a real whopper the next time he looks up here. Are you going to let me fly you to the moon this weekend? I'm all yours. Now what about this fecund? What does it mean when you say something is fecund?

SALLY   That it's fertile, abundant.

SAM   Oh. That's what I thought it meant.

SALLY   There he is! See him? Way, way, way out. No one should be out that far alone. (*Chloe is at the sliding glass door carrying a large tray with the coffee and lots of breakfast cakes and goodies. She has changed outfits.*)

CHLOE   Yoo-hoo! Come and get it!

SALLY   What if something happens to him?

SAM   Nothing's going to happen to him.

CHLOE   Does somebody want to give me a hand with this door? (*Sam goes to Chloe's aid. John lowers his newspaper and looks across the deck to Sally who continues to stand looking out to sea.*) I wasn't going to tempt anyone with more *délices du A&P* but with this salt air, nothing keeps. My buns are positively soggy. Don't look now, but there are signs of life next door. A young man in a red bikini. *Très, très* fetching. I said, don't look now, Sam!

SAM   I'm not looking. Jesus Christ!

CHLOE   Sam!

SAM   Did you see that guy, John?

JOHN   I used to look like that.

CHLOE   In your dreams.

JOHN   Does anybody mind if I do the puzzle?

CHLOE   They'd be too polite to say if they did. Sally, you need a microwave in the kitchen.

SAM   Sally doesn't like microwaves.

CHLOE   How can anyone live without a microwave! Well I guess if you don't have children . . . ! I brought out some more of those chocolate donuts you like.

SAM   Chloe, you are the devil in a . . . whatever that is you're wearing. (*He takes several donuts and muffins from the tray.*)

CHLOE You like it?

SAM (*To Sally.*) Honey, you should have something like this.

CHLOE It wouldn't suit her. (*To John.*) What can I get you, John?

JOHN I don't want anything. We just ate.

CHLOE A bran muffin at least. Just one. I'll toast and butter it for you.

JOHN I won't eat it.

CHLOE No one's going to make you, little boy. You can just look at it. (*To Sam.*) You want me to toast that for you, too?

SAM This is fine.

CHLOE It's not trouble. (*She takes a muffin from Sam's plate and heads back into the house.*) I'm toasting a muffin for you, John. (*No response.*) De rien, monsieur. (*She stands in front of the sliding glass door.*) Does somebody want to get this door for me? (*Sam opens it for her.*) Merci, mon frère. (*She goes into the house.*) Now if you'll be kind enough to close it for me before the beach gnats, sand flies and other uglies swarm in . . . ! (*Sam closes the sliding door.*) Merci encore. (*Again we will watch Chloe working in the kitchen and again we will be able to hear her singing to herself. Chloe is almost never silent. She also almost never stops working.*)

SAM You don't call that hyper?

JOHN I barely listen anymore, Sam.

SAM She hasn't shut up since we got here.

JOHN She's happy to see you.

SAM Shit!

JOHN What's the matter?

SAM That guy in the red bikini is looking down here.

JOHN Ignore him.

SAM I'm trying to. He waved at me.

JOHN So wave back.

SAM You wave back. Imagine if they thought we were queer. I'm gonna sit with my legs apart and smoke a cigar all weekend. Why do these houses have to be so close together?

JOHN Beach property is expensive.

SAM The first thing we're going to do if we keep this place is build a deck higher than theirs. I don't want people looking down on me. Right, honey? (*He joins Sally at her easel. John lowers his paper and looks at Sally.*)

SALLY I don't see him, Sam.

SAM He probably swam in while we were talking.

SALLY His robe's still there.

SAM I don't know what you're so worried about. Good swimmers like that know what they're doing. Besides, I don't know how you can see anything in this glare. I bet there's a good pair of binoculars around here somewhere. I'm gonna look around.

SALLY Sam? Why did you ask me about fecund?

SAM I don't know. I just did. I'll be right back. I bet I find something.

JOHN Look at me, Sally, I'm right here.

SAM I'll be right back. I bet I find something.

JOHN Look at me Sally, I'm right here. (*Sam and John continue this refrain in low, almost inaudible voices.*)

CHLOE (*From inside the kitchen.*) Did somebody say something?

SALLY I don't know whether to tell you I'm pregnant. I've disappointed you so many times. The last one would have been a boy. No, was a boy. He was a boy. You think I'm crazy to find out their sexes. You think it just makes losing them more painful. It probably does for you but I want to know what they would have been. It helps me to believe there's some reason we're having this trouble.

CHLOE (*From inside.*) Did somebody say something?

SAM I bet I find something. (*Goes to bedroom.*)

JOHN I'm right here.

SALLY (*Calling off.*) I will have a muffin, Chloe.

CHLOE (*From the kitchen.*) Coming right up!

SALLY No, I'm having this trouble—all by myself. Sam is the fecund one. I can reproduce but I'm unable to deliver them. We only go so far together. I wouldn't want me for a mother either. Too frightened, too sad, too late.

SAM (*From within.*)   Sally! Come here! Look what I found!

SALLY   Sam!

SAM   Can I have another coffee, sis?

CHLOE (*From within.*)   I just poured it. I read your mind.

SALLY   "That's crazy, Sal. Embryos don't think," Sam tells me, stroking my arm, proving he knows something about reproduction but completely missing my point. "It's comforting, Sam. It's a story. It has a beginning, a middle and an end. It has cause and effect, unborn heroes and a villain." I like it. The truth is just too formless to grasp.

SAM   Can I have another coffee, sis?

CHLOE (*From within.*)   I just poured it. I read your mind.

JOHN   I hope to God she can't read mine. (*He retreats behind his newspaper. Sam enters with a large carton of items from the closet. He gives a pair of binoculars to Sally. He starts rummaging through the carton, taking things out.*)

SAM   I hit the jackpot. There's a closet in there filled with all sorts of things.

SALLY   I don't think we should be doing this. I think we should ask Aaron first. (*During the following exchange, Sam will continue to remove various items from the carton.*)

SAM   It's our house now. Everything left is ours. I'm sure all the really good stuff is gone.

SALLY   Aaron wouldn't take anything that wasn't his.

SAM   Don't be so naïve.

SALLY   He was my brother's friend.

SAM   He was your brother's boyfriend. I'm sure he took what he wanted. Wake up and smell the coffee.

SALLY   I hate it when you talk like that. (*He's found the safety deposit box at the bottom of the carton.*)

SAM   Double Bingo! Talk like what?

SALLY   I don't want to know any more of my brother's secrets.

SAM   I think you found out the big one a long time ago. I'm going to need something to get in this: a file or a hammer. I'm going to look in that utility shed for a tool box.

SALLY   Why are you doing this?

SAM   Someone has to.

SALLY   Where are you going?

JOHN   It's under the house.

SALLY   Why are you doing this?

SAM   I know they talk about me. I've never left a room without knowing people talk about me. It's a terrible feeling, I've always had it, it had no beginning, it just was—but I've made my peace with it and I have my revenge. I talk about them. To myself. And I can really tell the truth to myself. Put two people together and truth doesn't stand a chance.

SALLY   Where are you going?

SAM   I'm going to look in that utility shed.

JOHN   I have cancer, Sally.

SAM   I'm going to look in that utility shed.

JOHN   We'll be right here.

SALLY   Just be careful.

SAM   Of what? "Be careful!" (*He goes.*)

SALLY (*Looking at her work.*)   How did they do it, the Masters? What did they know I don't?

JOHN   I have cancer, Sally.

SALLY   Oops, I'm sorry. You're trying to read.

JOHN   I have cancer, Sally. It's only a little speck now, a microscopic dot of pain and terror but they tell me it will soon grow and ripen and flower in this fertile bed of malignancy that has somehow become my body. I never meant it to. When it blossoms and when and if they cut it from me, all will marvel at its size, dark beauty and malevolence. They will then take this enormous cancer and give it to a medical university—Johns Hopkins or Cornell—and it will be displayed there in a Cancer Hall of Fame for generations of young doctors, to study and marvel at. No cancer will be worse than mine, Sally, nor none more virulent, more horrendous, more agonizing. I am scared, Sally. I am very, very scared.

SALLY (*Looking out to sea.*)   Whoever you are, my strong, silent, beautiful swimmer, come back safely. Look after him, God. Don't let him drown, even if that was his intention. Don't let him haunt my dreams. Amen.

CHLOE (*At the sliding glass door with a tray in hand.*)   *Me voilà!* I thought you'd all be in that pool by now.

JOHN   We will, Chloe, we will.

CHLOE   Does somebody want to give me a hand—? (*No one responds.*) Sometimes I feel like the Invisible Woman! (*Sally comes to her rescue.*)

SALLY   I've got it.

CHLOE   This would have been so much quicker with a microwave. So where is Sam the Man?

SALLY   He's under the house.

CHLOE   What's he doing under the house? Your neighbors are very, very attractive.

SALLY   He's snooping.

SAM (*From below.*)   I'm not snooping, I'm exploring!

JOHN   Don't start with the neighbors, Chloe.

CHLOE   Do I look like I'm starting?

JOHN   You always look like you're starting.

CHLOE   I like people. I love you. (*She kisses John on the top of the head.*) That was wonderful last night. I'm still glowing. "Gigue." 4 Down is "gigue."

JOHN   You know I hate it when you do that.

CHLOE   "So sue me. Sue me. Shoot bullets through me." (*She is almost singing it by now.*) "I love you." God, I love that show, it's a classic. (*She waves.*) Good morning!

JOHN   Chloe!

CHLOE   He waved at me first. Who are you anyway? Bluebeard? Henry the Eighth? Someone got up on the wrong side of the bed this morning! (*She joins Sally at the easel.*) I guess that's telling him. I wish I could do that.

SALLY   Why don't you try?

CHLOE   It's too deep for me. Jazz exercise is about as profound as I want to get. That and Little Theatre. Did you really like me in *A Little Night Music?*

SALLY   Yes.

CHLOE   That Sondheim is such a little devil. He writes real tongue twisters. I don't suppose people like you have ever wanted to get up on a stage and expose themselves?

SALLY   Not really.

CHLOE   Count your blessings. It's a curse. Stick with your painting. Do you ever sell anything?

SALLY   Neighbors, people at the office.

CHLOE   I envy you sometimes. A real job. John says I'm too emotional to work. That's coming along. I'm impressed.

SALLY   I'm not very happy with it. Trying to put the power of all that, the play of light, the volume, the space, onto canvas with a brush and a few colors. It's pathetic. It's arrogant almost.

CHLOE   Well it's not like you're out robbing liquor stores.

SALLY   I think I see the ocean but when I try to break it down into colors, forms, brush strokes, it all comes apart, and I don't think I'm capable of truly understanding or seeing anything at all.

CHLOE   There you go again, Sally. Deep, deep, deep. I thought you did this for fun. You make it sound like torture. That's why I won't do heavy drama. They're doing Arthur Miller next month. "No way," I told them. Listen, I even think a show like *Carousel* is pushing its luck. I love how you do that with the brush, those swirly-swirl-swirls! Does this bother you?

SALLY   Yes.

CHLOE   I'm sorry! (*Calling to Sam.*) Sam? What are you doing down there?

JOHN   Why don't I get a large rock and bash her head in?

CHLOE   Sam!

SAM (*From below.*)   What?

CHLOE   What are you going to feel like for dinner?

SAM (*From below.*)   I thought I'd throw a shark on the barbie, mate!

JOHN   Jesus, Chloe, we just had breakfast.

CHLOE   That's all that one thinks about, food! He used to drive our poor mother crazy. I don't know how you put up with him, Sally! (*To John.*) Look who wasn't hungry.

JOHN   Shove food in somebody's face and of course they'll eat it.

CHLOE   I didn't shove food in your face. I put a buttered, toasted Entenmann's bran muffin on your plate.

JOHN   You know I have no will power. You married a weak man.

CHLOE   I wish you wouldn't say things like that. It's very upsetting. It's certainly not amusing.

JOHN   It wasn't meant to be.

CHLOE   I think this whole weekend will be fraught enough for Sally without you contributing your very peculiar dark humor. I can take little barbs. After fourteen years, I'm like an archery target! But I don't think other people understand or appreciate them. 'Nuff said? God, what a glorious day! (*Music has begun from next door. The selection is Schubert's* Moments Musicale, #3 in F minor. *Chloe breathes it in.*) Listen to that! *Crème de la crème*, your neighbors, what did I tell you? I love classical music. It's so soothing. What is this piece, Sally? You know everything.

SALLY   I think it's Schubert. One of the *Moments Musicales.*

CHLOE   You're pretty smart for a girl.

SALLY   I don't know everything, Chloe.

CHLOE   Yes, you do. (*She goes back into the kitchen. We will able to watch her take things from the toaster, butter them, etc., and arrange everything on a tray.*)

JOHN   Sally, do you know a 7-letter word beginning with "t," ending with "r" that's a coin in the Gabon Republic?

SALLY   What do you think, John?

JOHN   You've never ceased to astonish me.

SALLY   There's always a first time.

JOHN   That's all right, just so long as there's never a last.

CHLOE (*From the kitchen.*)   Did somebody call me?

JOHN   They both know. They have to know. It's the way we look at each other. It's the way we don't look at each other. She knows my eyes are on her. Have been all morning. Turn around, Sally. I'm not going to hurt you. Look at me. Please.

SALLY   How many times David must have stood right here and tried to take all this in with his camera. The sea, the sky. It's too much, it's overwhelming. I feel diminished.

JOHN   "Trapkur!"

SALLY   Diminished. That was his word. At Dad's funeral when David was trying to comfort Mom and she said he couldn't really understand her loss, or know what she was feeling, that the love between a man and a woman was different, I should have stood up for David because when Mom said that, he couldn't stand up for himself. I just looked away. Instead of feeling comforted, he told me, he felt rejected and diminished by us both. What a terrible word. Diminished.

JOHN   "Trapkur!"

SALLY   What?

JOHN   It's "trapkur," the word is "trapkur."

SALLY   If you say so!

JOHN   I made it up.

SALLY   Isn't that cheating?

JOHN   I just wanted you to turn around. I had a feeling a word like "trapkur" would do the trick. Hi, Sally, remember me?

SALLY   Yes, John.

CHLOE (*From the kitchen.*)   Sally, may I have a word with you?

SALLY   I'd like to finish this before the light—

CHLOE (*At the sliding glass door.*)   This could be serious.

SALLY   What, Chloe?

CHLOE   I don't see any Kahlua.

SALLY   We'll manage.

CHLOE   Maybe we'll manage but we won't be having any Black Russians after supper. I'm doing a total inventory in there for you.

SALLY   That's all right.

CHLOE   I don't mind.

SALLY   I wish you wouldn't.

CHLOE   I have no emotional investment in this house. I only met David once. Is he still down there? Sam?

SAM (*From below.*)   What? They've got a lot of nice things down here!

CHLOE   First call for alcohol. Do you want something?

SAM (*From below.*)   You mean like a drink?

SALLY   Sam!

CHLOE   No, I mean like an enema! Drove her stark, raving mad!

SAM (*From below.*)   What is everyone else having?

JOHN   I'll have a Bloody Mary. Very, very hot.

CHLOE   John's having a Blood Mary.

SAM (*From below.*)   That sounds great. But not too hot.

CHLOE   I know how you like it. Do I know how he likes it. Sally?

SALLY   Nothing for me. Sam!

SAM (*From below.*)   What?

SALLY   It's only—

SAM (*From below.*)   What!

SALLY   Nothing.

SAM (*From below.*)   Jesus Christ!

CHLOE   What happened?

SAM (*From below.*)   I just saw a big fucking snake down here.

CHLOE   Well, leave it there? *Je n'aime pas les serpents.*

SALLY   I told you to be careful.

CHLOE   Did he ever put a snake in your bed when you were trying to read a book and it crawled up your leg?

SALLY   Not that I remember, Chloe.

CHLOE   Count your blessings. When we were kids he used to do it all the time. No snakes up here, Sam! Got that?

SAM (*From below.*)   John! Come down and look at this snake!

JOHN   Leave me out of this.

CHLOE   God, it's so beautiful out here I could ry. *Bonjour, tristesse!*

SALLY   Chloe, why do you always sprinkle your conversations with French?

CHLOE   Because I'm bored with English. (*Singing.*) *Non, rien de rien. Non, je ne regrette rien.* (*She goes into the kitchen and begins making drinks.*)

JOHN   I'm married to Edith Piaf.

SALLY   She's a very nice woman.

JOHN   I know. Believe me, I know.

SAM (*From below.*)   I think it's a copperhead.

JOHN   Have you thought about what happened?

SALLY   Of course I have.

JOHN   You haven't even looked at me.

SALLY   That's not true.

JOHN   You said you would call.

SALLY   She's right inside.

CHLOE (*From the kitchen.*)   Did you say something, darling?

JOHN   Are you going to be like this all weekend?

SALLY   I knew this would happen.

SAM (*From below.*)   It's too big for a coral snake.

CHLOE (*From the kitchen.*)   There's no Smirnoff. They've got Stoly and Absolut.

SAM (*From below.*)   I'm going to kill it. (*We hear the sounds of a spade striking the sand from under the house. It will continue for maybe 30 seconds while the actions on the deck continues.*) Ugh! (*John has kissed Sally. She slaps him.*)

CHLOE (*From the kitchen.*)   John? The Stoly or the Absolut?

JOHN   The Stoly.

CHLOE (*From the kitchen.*)   What about Sam?

JOHN   The Stoly. We'll all drink Russian vodka and get very Chekhovian.

CHLOE   That sounds like a terrible idea.

SALLY   We'll talk.

JOHN   When?

SALLY   I promise.

JOHN   He follows you around like a dog.

SALLY   That's not true.

JOHN   I've got an erection.

SALLY   Don't say things like that.

CHLOE (*From the kitchen.*)   It's very hard to hear you in there!

SAM (*From below.*)   This is gross! It's all over the shovel.

JOHN   I want you so much. Just let me hold you.

SALLY   I can't.

JOHN   Please.

SALLY   No. (*Chloe appears at the sliding glass door with a tray of drinks.*)

CHLOE   *Voilà les beverages!*

JOHN   Hold it. (*He goes quickly to the door and opens it for her.*)

CHLOE   I don't believe it. This is one doll you can knock over with a feather. I made Sally a Diet Pepsi, just in case. Sally, I made you a Diet Pepsi, just in case. Sam! If he brings a snake up here! How's your puzzle?

JOHN   Impossible. It's got a theme. I hate theme puzzles.

CHLOE   I can't believe I know someone who can do the *New York Times* crossword in ink without cheating! And that I'm married to him? I'm very impressed with myself.

JOHN   What are you talking about? You got "gigue."

CHLOE   It's a dance term. I've had training. Ask me who wrote *Gone with the Wind* and I draw a blank. (*Sam comes back onto the deck from the stairs below. He is carrying a file and a hammer in an open gardener's basket.*) Do you have that snake with you?

SAM   Sis, I am a grown man with my own business, two mortgages and a hernia operation next month. I don't have time to play with snakes.

CHLOE   This is just what he used to do: all innocence.

SAM   Where would I have a snake? In here? (*He pulls something out that looks very like a dead snake. Chloe screams.*) It's a piece of hose for Christ's sake! Do you believe this?

CHLOE   I fall for it every time.

SAM   Here's the snake. (*He pulls out the real dead snake and dangles it in front of Chloe who screams and runs into the house. Then he dangles it in front of Sally who doesn't flinch.*) You're pretty brave for a girl.

SALLY   Married to you I'd have to be. Now get rid of it. (*He dangles the snake in front of John who looks at it calmly.*)

SAM   John's not scared of snakes. John was in the Peace Corps in darkest Africa.

JOHN   That looks like a pith viper.

SAM   What the hell is a pitch viper?

CHLOE (*From within.*)   Is it gone? I'm not coming out of here until it's gone!

JOHN   *Pith* viper. We had them in Chad. I'm glad you killed it. They're fatal.

SAM   Yeah?

JOHN   You didn't get any venom on you? It can eat right through the skin.

SAM   What do you know? Learn something every day. Fucking Fire Island. They ought to have signs up. Beware of snakes.

CHLOE (*From within.*)   Don't even think about lunch as long as that snake is out there! (*Sam throws the snake into the beach grass on the side of the house.*)

SALLY   Sam!

SAM   What?

SALLY   That's the neighbor's property!

SAM   It's not my snake. We don't own it. It's not like I threw a beer can in their yard. It probably came from under their house anyway. It heard unfamiliar voices and came over to check us out.

SALLY   And got its head bashed in for its trouble.

SAM   Whose side are you on? The snake's?

SALLY   I don't know why you have to kill everything.

SAM   I don't kill everything. That's a lousy thing to say. I don't kill everything. (*He goes into their room to wash his hands.*)

SALLY   I didn't mean that. He gets me so—

JOHN   I know. (*Calling off.*) It's okay, Petal!

SALLY   What's the word I want? (*Chloe comes out on the deck.*)

CHLOE   Is the coast clear?

SALLY   Angry.

JOHN   I know. All clear!

SALLY   I'm sorry, Chloe.

CHLOE   Don't. It's brother-sister stuff. If he'd done it to you or John it would have been hostile. Where is the son of a bitch?

SALLY   I think he's inside washing his hands.

SAM (*From within.*)   I'm washing my hands! (*Music begins from the house on the left of them. Billie Holiday singing "You've Changed" cut from her* Lady in Satin *album.*)

JOHN   Oh, great! Now we've got stereo. Are you okay, Petal?

CHLOE   I'm fine. How are you? (*Sam comes out of the their room, drying his hands.*)

SAM   I'm sorry, sis. It was just a joke.

CHLOE   Remind me to laugh when I get home from Bellevue after I've had a complete nervous breakdown. (*A blast of Joan Sutherland from the house on the right.*)

SAM   That's a real toe-tapper.

JOHN   I thought people went to the beach for peace and quiet. I hope those are renters, Sally. You don't want permanent neighbors like that.

SAM   You want me to go over and say something to them, honey? You know, tell them who we are. The new owners.

SALLY   I think they know.

JOHN (*Calling off.*)   Excuse me! Excuse me! Gentlemen! Would you mind turning that down, thank you!

CHLOE   Party pooper!

JOHN (*Low.*)   Goddamn fairies.

CHLOE   We didn't hear that. (*To others.*) He doesn't mean it. We have three gay men and one lesbian in administration at Sturman. God only knows how many on faculty. One of the men in admissions right under John has AIDS. John has been terrific about it.

JOHN   Shut up, Chloe.

SAM   John.

CHLOE   It's all right. I need it. I want it, in fact. I tend to run on. John keeps me in line. (*She kisses John on the top of the head.*) He's my knight in shining armor!

JOHN   Chloe, you know I hate it when you do that.

CHLOE   So spank me, daddy. Spank me right out here in total daylight. (*To Sam and Sally.*) You know, I'm not usually like this. You know what it is? It's being without the kids. It's grown-up time. We can behave like grown-ups! Fuck, fuck, fuck. Shit, shit, shit. Piss, piss, piss. Cunt, cunt, cunt. Dick, dick, dick.

SAM   Have you taken your medication, Chloe?

CHLOE   One day people are going to believe you when you say things like that. I'm not on medication, Sally. I hope nobody minds if I shut up for a while. I'm gonna get some sun. (*Chloe puts down a blanket and applies lotion to her legs. Sam pushes the locked box aside and comes over to where Sally is painting.*)

SAM   I'm losing my touch. I was famous where I grew up for picking locks. I could hot-wire any car in thirty seconds flat, even a Mercedes. I seriously considered a life of crime but then I met you and I went straight. I like that.

SALLY   Thank you.

SAM   I really like that.

SALLY   This is the part I hate most about painting: people looking at it. They're not looking, they're judging and it's never as good as I want it to be but it's always better than anyone thinks it is. Humble-slash-arrogant. That's me.

SAM   My brain has become a collision course of random thoughts. Some trivial, but some well worth the wonder. Sometimes I think I'm losing my mind. I'm not sure of anything anymore. It's the same anxiety I have when I think I've forgotten how to tie my tie or tie my shoelaces or I've forgotten how to swallow food and I'm going to choke on it. Three days ago I was standing in front of our bathroom mirror in terror because I couldn't knot my tie. I wanted to say "Sally, please come in here and help me." But I couldn't. What would she have thought? Last night I spit a piece of steak into my napkin, rather than risk swallowing it because I was afraid I would choke. Maybe it's trivial and that's why no one wants to talk about it, so I'm talking to myself. No one wants to listen to who we really are. Know somebody, really. Know you leave shit stains in your underwear and pick your nose. Tell a woman you've forgotten how to swallow your food and she's in her car and out of your life before you can say "Wait, there's more. Sometimes I have to think about someone else when I'm with you because I'm afraid I won't stay hard if I don't. Or how much I want to fuck the teenage daughter of the couple that lives three doors down. How my father takes all the air out of the room and I can't breathe when I'm with him. How if I could tear my breast open and rip out my heart and feed it to these seagulls in little raw pieces, that pain would be nothing to the one I already feel, the pain of your betrayal! How most afraid I am of losing you." How can I tell you these things and there be love?

SALLY   —slash–arrogant. That's me.

SAM   Well, I really like it. (*Sally has seen something on the beach below and in front of the deck.*)

SALLY   Hey! Hey! I see you! I see what you're doing!

SAM   What's happening?

SALLY   That's not his robe. He's taking that guy's robe. That's not your robe! I know who it belongs to!

CHLOE   John! Trouble! (*John gets out of the chaise.*)

SALLY   We have witnesses! We all see you!

SAM   He can't hear you.

SALLY   I'm going to tell him.

SAM   Stay out of it, Sally.

CHLOE   I don't know what the world is coming to.

SALLY   Once upon a time I would have run down there and wrestled someone for doing that. I would have won, too. God, every single day for the rest of my life, with Your help, I want to renew my membership in the human race. Amen. Thank you. (*John returns to his place on the chaise and reads. Sam takes a hard swing at the lock with the hammer. It falls open but it's broken. He won't be able to relock it.*)

SAM   Shit!

SALLY   What happened?

SAM   I broke the lock.

SALLY   What are you going to find in there?

SAM   I don't know. What are you so afraid of? Now what have we got here?

CHLOE   Sally?

SALLY   What?

CHLOE   Do you see what I see?

SALLY   Where?

CHLOE   There, on the beach, in the blue thong bikini. Joan Rivers was right about those things. It does look like he's flossing his ass. He's looking right up here. Wave. (*She waves wildly.*)

SALLY   Chloe!

CHLOE   All right, don't wave. (*Calling.*) You are so fucking hot, honey! (*She watches the man disappear.*) You compare that or your brother or your neighbors next door with the hi-fi to our two and you have to ask yourself something: don't straight men think we have eyes? Don't they occasionally look at themselves in the mirror? God knows, they expect us to. (*To John.*) Give me twenty push-ups. Let's go. The party's over. (*To Sally.*) Sally, can I say something, just woman to woman.

SALLY   Chloe, I don't think I can take any more of your bombshells.

CHLOE   My what?

SALLY   I'm very fragile this weekend. I'm sorry. I adore you, Chloe.

CHLOE   Really?

SALLY   You know I do.

CHLOE   Then say it again. Ever since I turned 30 I've become very needy.

SAM   You were just 40.

CHLOE   I know. Now I'm out of control. If my husband doesn't make love to me this weekend, my own brother isn't safe.

JOHN   We made love last night.

CHLOE   You know what I mean, big love! Last night was *petit*. I'm talking *l'amour grand!* Get out the whips and chains, handcuff me to the bed, let me take a dildo to you and you see what it feels like.

SALLY   This is just what I was talking about.

CHLOE   You and Sam don't have a dildo?

SALLY No, and even if we did, it's none of your business. I don't enjoy standing on a sun deck in broad daylight on the Fourth of July taking about dildos. I don't think this is what Thomas Jefferson had in mind.

CHLOE I used to be like that.

SALLY Like what?

CHLOE Uptight. Honey, this is Fire Island, not Palm Beach. (*Music from the house on the left. The overture to* Gypsy.) Wait! Stop! Hold everything! We did this show. I know it. It's on the tip of my brain.

JOHN I come to the shore to hear the ocean, not this noise.

CHLOE It's not noise, it's theatre music. Come on, John, help me. Name Broadway musicals. Sally!

SAM You stay out of this. Did I tell you what she hit me with last week? *What's Up Baby Joan!*

SALLY I still don't see what's wrong with it.

SAM There's no such movie. It's *What Ever Happened to Baby Jane? What's Up, Doc?* Joan has nothing to do with it.

JOHN I'm going inside if this keeps up.

CHLOE I've got it. *Annie.* It's the overture to *Annie.* No wonder I didn't recognize it. I wasn't in *Annie.* I was in Bridgeport General having Megan when we did *Annie.*

SAM Oh my God, that *Annie.* I cried my eyes out. All those orphans. What a movie.

CHLOE I didn't see the film version. I generally don't. I'm sure they made many changes unfaithful to the stage production. Hollywood will do that. (*John gets up and goes into his room. We will be able to see him lie down on the bed and read.*) John, where are you going? We're sorry. We'll stop. (*Calling across to the house on the right.*) Excuse me! My husband isn't feeling well—. Thank you. No, you don't have to turn it all the way off. (*The volume of the music from the house of the left is lowered before she can call over.*) Thank you! You read our minds! (*She heads towards their room.*) Darling, they're turning it down. Did you take your—?

JOHN Yes, mother.

CHLOE   Would you like a massage? (*She goes into their room. We can see them sitting on the bed together. After a while we will see Chloe giving John a massage.*)

SAM   I'm sorry. It was a bad idea. We shouldn't have done this. I just didn't think we wanted to spend a long weekend together in a strange beach house. I didn't know what we'd be getting into out here.

SALLY   They could have brought the children.

SAM   Any place but this and they probably would have. They're going through a patch. I should talk! We're going through a patch. Every marriage does. As long as there's no one else, we'll work it out. (*Pause.*) I said, as long as there's no one else, we'll work it out.

SALLY   I heard you.

SAM   Is there someone else?

SALLY   (*After another pause.*)   No.

SAM   Then we'll work it out. Weren't you going to see Sugarman this week? (*Sally nods.*) What did he say?

SALLY   No.

SAM   Have you been—?

SALLY   Yes, everything he tells me to do.

SAM   I'm not—

SALLY   I didn't say you were.

SAM   It's nobody's fault.

SALLY   Yes, it is. (*There is a pause. Sam continues to look in the safety-deposit box.*)

SAM   I found the Certificate of Occupancy the lawyer asked for.

SALLY   I'm leaving all that up to you.

SAM   You act like you're angry David left you this place. Angry or guilty.

SALLY   Sometimes I think I'm a little of both.

SAM   Here's some old photos. This must be when David bought this place. See? There's no pool yet. Here's one of your father standing in front of that stupid old Pontiac he loved.

SALLY   That was just before Dad died.

SAM   What else? Some letters, documents, jewelry, cuff links, a ring . . . oops! (*The ring rolls into the pool.*)

SALLY   Sam!

SAM   I'll get it. (*Sally looks into the pool.*)

SALLY   It's his ring.

SAM   Where's it going to go? I said I'll get it.

SALLY   I don't see it. (*Music has begun during this from the house on the left. "Che puro ciel" from Gluck's* Orfeo. *John comes out onto the deck.*)

JOHN   Your sister has magic fingers, Sam. She's all yours.

SAM   No, thanks.

JOHN   It's getting hot out here. This is a little more like it. This is beautiful. Do you know what it is, Sally?

SALLY   I think it's by Gluck.

CHLOE (*From within.*)   John?

JOHN   It's very soothing. I feel like I'm floating on a cloud.

SALLY   You should be. It's a description of Paradise. Where the Happy Shades go.

JOHN   Well that's us. (*He stretches out on the chaise again.*)

CHLOE (*From within.*)   Are you coming back, John?

JOHN   Gluck, you say?

SALLY   I'm pretty sure.

SAM   Gluck? Gluck who? Who's Gluck? Where do you know about Gluck from?

JOHN   That's what I want to be. A happy Happy Shade!

SALLY   That's the man I slept with. There! Right there! For just an instant I caught a glimpse of him again. (*Chloe comes out on the deck.*)

CHLOE   I'll do refills. (*She goes into the kitchen.*)

SAM (*He starts to read from a postcard.*)   Here's a postcard from Aaron. "Dear David, Having a terrible time, wish *I* wasn't here." Houston? I don't blame him.

JOHN   Sam?

SAM   What?

JOHN   Sssshhh. We're blissing out.

SAM   Speak for yourself. I'm too sensitive, that's my problem. (*Sally stands and looks out to the ocean.*)

SALLY   I think I see—! There! Please, God, let it be him! (*She stares at the horizon line, not moving now. Sam continues to read, his lips still moving. Chloe is the only one still animated. She is at the sliding screen door with her tray of drinks.*)

CHLOE (*From within.*)   Don't worry everybody. I can manage this time. (*She struggles to open the door with her foot.*) Oh!! (*She drops the tray. Everything shatters. She is still behind the sliding screen door. She calls out to the others on the deck.*) It's all right. Don't get up. I'll handle it. (*She begins to clean up. As she works, her movements become slower and slower until she is still. Lights fade down except for special lamps on our four characters. They are isolated by them. They do not move. The Gluck continues to the end of the piece. There is a brief pause. We hear the ocean, maybe a gull. The lights snap off.*)

END OF ACT ONE

ACT TWO

Noon. The sun is beating down on the deck full-strength.

There is music coming from the two houses off. From the stage left house, we hear the 1st movement of the Brahms Piano Concerto, No. 1. *From the stage right house, some Zydeco.*

Sally sits on the edge of the pool, dangling her feet in the water. Her easel stands where she left it. Chloe is cooking hamburgers on the grill. The necessary garnishes are on the picnic table. She has changed into another attractive ensemble.

John is flying a kite, which involves a lot of footwork and bobbing back and forth. Sam has found an astronomical telescope in the locked room and is checking it out.

SALLY We should do something.

JOHN Like what?

SALLY Report it.

JOHN What are we going to report? Some stranger went swimming and we didn't see him come back?

CHLOE How does everyone like their burgers?

SALLY I know he's still out there.

JOHN If he is, he's drowned and he'll wash up miles from here. Have you ever seen a drowned person? You don't want to. Let it go, Sally.

CHLOE Sally?

SALLY Medium rare. This is going to bother me all weekend.

CHLOE Sam?

SAM Rare. Very, very rare. (*Fiddling with telescope.*) This is fantastic. Wait until tonight. Does anybody remember if there's a moon?

CHLOE John? There was a moon last night, almost full.

JOHN   Medium rare. Fly, baby, fly! All right! (*He's like one of his students.*)

SAM   There was a moon last night?

SALLY   Only that big!

SAM   I'm a city boy. Nature kind of rolls off my back. Really, really rare, sis. Bloody.

CHLOE   I know. I've only been cooking burgers for him since he was that high. I'd say "Everybody into that glorious pool," except we're about to eat.

SALLY   Maybe we should call the Coast Guard.

SAM   John's right, Sally. If the guy is drowned, he's drowned. There's nothing we can do about it. *Que sera, sera.*

SALLY   Am I crazy?

SAM   Yes, you're crazy.

JOHN   Look, it's a speck now.

CHLOE   Of all things to be allergic to! And I love to swim. John calls me a human porpoise.

JOHN   It wasn't a compliment.

CHLOE   I'm taking it as one. I feel about ten years old in the water. The years just come tumbling off and I'm a little girl again. John says he's never seen me happier than that week we went to the islands. Where were we, honey, what island?

JOHN   I don't remember.

SAM   St. Bart's. You sent us a card.

CHLOE   Well wherever it was—

SAM   It was St. Bart's! Jesus.

CHLOE   Yours truly was in the water from sunup to sundown and then some. We did some skinny-dipping right in front of the hotel.

SAM   At night?

CHLOE   No, in broad daylight! Talk about romantic! I remembered why I married this crazy lug. We started making love right then and there. The moon and stars were shining. The water looked and felt like black velvet.

SALLY Shut up, please, shut up, all of you.

CHLOE Yachts were floating, bobbing all around us.

SALLY Why do people have to speak to one another? Why can't we just be?

CHLOE Unfortunately, just as you-know-who was getting ready to climax . . . (*She nods with her head toward John flying his kite.*)

SALLY David, are you laughing somewhere? I hope so.

CHLOE . . . we sort of floated, bobbed ourselves into another couple who were doing exactly the same thing. I wish you could have heard the yell this one let out. The hotel lit up like that.

JOHN She exaggerates.

CHLOE People came out of the hotel and onto the boat pier to see what was happening.

JOHN One person.

CHLOE We hid behind a little dinghy. *Petal*. I'll always remember its name, *Petal*.

SAM "Petal," so that's where he gets it from. I'll say one thing for John. When he wants to, he can be wonderful with her. "Petal." I like that, "Petal." I don't have a name for Sally. Sally doesn't have a name for me.

CHLOE Funny, the things we remember; the things we don't. Forget the name of the island, remember the name of the boat!

SAM St. Bart's, for Christ's sake.

CHLOE How did you say you wanted your burger, Sally?

SALLY Medium's fine.

SAM Very rare for me.

JOHN Medium rare. Look, look at that crazy gull! He's attacking the kite! (*Sam and Chloe look up at the kite high above them. Sally just dangles her legs in the water.*)

SAM   I wish somebody would tell me why we can't eat seagulls. We eat everything else. They're big, they're plentiful. How bad could they be? You could feed a lot of poor people with seagulls. Same with pigeons. There's a lot of meat on your city pigeon.

CHLOE   Just don't go vegetarian on me.

SAM   She knows. She brings one bean sprout into that house and I'm out of there.

CHLOE   Pammie Bernstein went vegetarian and completely lost her singing voice. You're going to lose that kite.

SAM   Pammie Bernstein? I don't think we know her.

CHLOE   Sure you do. *The Pajama Game.* "Steam Heat." She had dink! dink! steam heat. Shea had dink! dink! steam heat.

SAM   That one? She was terrific. She lost her voice?

CHLOE   Can't get above middle "G" now. She doesn't think it's from going vegetarian but I know it is. What else could it be?

JOHN   Hah! Did you see that maneuver? The Red Baron flies again!

SAM   Can I try it awhile?

JOHN   No.

SAM   No?

JOHN   Get your own kite.

SAM   That was the only one in there.

JOHN   Then you should have put it up.

SAM   I didn't know it would be so much fun.

JOHN   Monkey see, monkey do.

SAM   Just for a few minutes.

JOHN   No!

SAM   Please?

JOHN   When I'm done.

SAM   When will that be?

JOHN   When I'm done. Jesus!

SAM   Pig. Kite hog!

SALLY   Sam! (*She motions him to join her sitting at the edge of the pool.*)

CHLOE   If you decide to keep this place, may I make one more teeny-tiny suggestion?

SAM (*To Sally.*)   This is their first and last weekend. (*He sits at pool's edge next to Sally.*)

SALLY   Are you burning? Let me see. (*She looks at his neck.*)

SAM   Ouch! Jesus Christ!

SALLY   Does it hurt?

SAM   It does now. It was fine until you—!

CHLOE   I would landscape like crazy. I don't care who your neighbors are—Nelson Rockefeller or Nelson Mandela—you don't want them looking at you all day. People stare. It's human nature. Don't get too lovey-dovey comfy down there, you two. We're about to eat.

JOHN   I don't want mine if it's too done.

CHLOE   Go fly a kite! (*She breaks herself up.*) Well, I thought it was funny.

SALLY   I told you to put sunblock on the back of your neck.

SAM   I hate him.

SALLY   This is what happened in Florida. (*She will apply a sun lotion to the back of his neck.*)

SAM   He thinks he's such hot shit because he's the director of admissions at a swanky prep school and they're members of a fucking country club! Ow, I said!

SALLY   I didn't get it all!

SAM   I know you've slept with him.

SALLY   Sam!

SAM   I do.

CHLOE   Come and get it!

SAM Do you deny it?

CHLOE *Allons enfants de la patrie. À table!*

SAM What's the pause for?

SALLY That you'd even think such a thing.

CHLOE Sally? Sam? Earth to Mars. Come in Mars.

SAM Then you deny it?

SALLY Yes.

SAM Liar. (*He gets up from edge of pool and starts putting fixings on his hamburger.*)

CHLOE Well I'm glad someone heard me. (*To John.*) You want to bring that in, Captain Lindbergh?

JOHN Honey, I can eat and—

CHLOE No!

JOHN —do this at the same time.

CHLOE No! Sometimes I have to put my foot down and this is one of them. We are eating at the table like civilized people.

JOHN Yes, mother. (*He will tie the kite string to his end of the picnic table.*)

CHLOE Treat them like adults and you might as well be talking to yourself. But treat them like little boys and *voilà!* Am I right, Sally? Sally knows I'm right. Married to you, she'd have to be. (*John and Sam are sitting at the picnic table. Sally is still sitting by the edge of the pool. Chloe is bustling about serving.*)

SALLY It's gone, that moment to speak to the truth. He'll ask again, I'll lie again. The truth is, I don't want him to know.

CHLOE Are you all going to be staring at that string all through lunch?

JOHN Don't let it bother you.

CHLOE What I do for love! Beautiful song. It should be my anthem. You didn't see it when we did *A Chorus Line?*

SAM I don't remember.

CHLOE   That's all right, I wasn't in it. Sally, *à table, s'il vous plaît? Merci.*
They brought in some director from the city who said she wanted real
dancers, whatever that means. Gloria Munster cracked on the high
note in that song every single performance, every one. I know. I was
ushering. And to show her legs in public on a stage gives new meaning
to an old Jewish expression: *Chutzpah.*

JOHN   Chloe.

CHLOE   I know: shut up. Sometimes I can read his mind. Sometimes?!
(*She kisses the top of his head and hugs him from behind.*) I can imagine only
one thing worse than being married to this man and that is not being
married to this man! (*She waves to someone on the deck of the next house.*)
Hi! (*Sam and John turn to see whom she is talking to.*) What? . . . Well, let's
hope it *is* good. You can't eat looks! . . . I said, you can't eat looks!

JOHN   Sit down, Chloe.

CHLOE (*Continuing.*)   No, no, no! I'm just a friend of the family. *This* is
David's sister. (*Sally waves.*) This is her husband, Sam. (*Sam waves.*)

SAM   Why are you doing this?

CHLOE (*Continuing.*)   I'm the overbearing sister-in-law and this is my
husband, John.

SAM   Just sit down. Jesus, she's got a whole deckful of them looking at
us now.

CHLOE (*Continuing.*)   Who? Aaron? I don't know. (*To Sally.*) Is Aaron
coming out? (*Sally shakes her head.*) No! . . . Thank you . . . You enjoy
yours. Nice talking to you . . . What's your name? . . . Nice talking to
you, Mr. Beckenstein . . . Harry! *Ciao!* (*She sits.*) He said to enjoy our
lunch.

SAM   Why did you do that?

CHLOE   Do what?

SAM   They're going to think we want to be friends. They'll be over
here all the time now. Drinks, barbeques, before you know it, you-
know-what.

CHLOE   Because you're such an *homme fatal!*

SAM   What's an *homme fatal?* Something insulting, I bet.

CHLOE   The opposite of a *femme fatale*.

SAM   That's Sally over there.

CHLOE   Sally, it's getting cold.

SALLY   Okay. (*She gets up and joins them at the picnic table.*)

CHLOE   Another teeninetsy suggestion, Sal. Get a gas grill. No more struggling with charcoal, you can control the heat, fabulous!

JOHN   What *are* you thinking about the house?

SALLY   I don't know. It's so far for us. I don't know how much we'd use it. Part of me thinks I should just give it to Aaron.

SAM   The insane-menopausal-crazy-woman part! Minimum, *minimum*, this place is worth eight.

CHLOE   8,000 dollars?

SAM   800,000 dollars.

CHLOE   That's what I thought. You can't get a closet for 8,000 dollars anymore.

JOHN   Chloe. Why would you give something worth maybe close to a million dollars to a total stranger?

SALLY   He's not a total stranger.

SAM   He's black, y'know.

SALLY   He was wonderful to David. He took extraordinary care of him. Never left his side, slept in the hospital, everything one person can possibly do for another.

SAM   Did you both know he was black? Black, black. Very African, that kind of black. Nothing white about him.

SALLY   There should be some way to acknowledge that kind of devotion.

SAM   I agree. Thank you. Thank you very much. You want the TV set? The books, the records. Take what you want. But an 800,000-dollar beach house. I'm sorry.

SALLY   I keep thinking David would want me to give it to Aaron.

SAM   Then why did he leave it to you?

SALLY   I don't know. I really don't know.

SAM   He got the apartment for Christ's sake.

SALLY   I don't think we'd ever feel really comfortable here.

CHLOE   John? (*She motions that he's got catsup on his chin.*)

SALLY   I don't think I have anything against gay men. I just don't want to be the only nongay people here.

CHLOE   You don't want to be a token anything. I hear you. Who wants to feel like everyone's staring at them?

JOHN   You want my advice? Hang on to it. Property like this is only going to go up in value. There's no shoreline left, from Maine to Florida. It's all been developed. There's no more where this came from. Ten years from now it will be worth two million.

CHLOE   John has a real nose for real estate.

JOHN   If you're really uncomfortable here, rent. But hold on to it.

CHLOE   I'm totally comfortable here but then of course I'm in the theatre. Lesbians make me a little nervous but I've never had a problem with the men.

JOHN   Chloe. (*To Sally.*) As far as his friend goes, I wouldn't confuse sentimentality with common sense. I don't know what your finances are like—

SAM   We're doing fine! We're doing fine.

JOHN   —but I can't imagine anyone in this day and age blithely turning their back on 800,000 dollars.

SAM   No one's blithely doing anything, John.

SALLY   Can we not talk about this?

JOHN   I'm sorry I brought it up.

SALLY   Thank you for the advice. Catsup?

CHLOE   Cal and Rhea Kaufman have a place in Vermont and they're always complaining they never get up there. Distance *is* a factor.

SALLY   May I have the catsup, John?

CHLOE   This place would be a hop, skip and a jump for us—we just ferried right across the Sound—

SALLY   Thank you. Relish.

CHLOE   —but for you two! You can have that New Jersey Turnpike. Nothing but trailer trucks! And those signs everywhere: Welcome to the Garden State. What garden? I never saw any garden. I saw refineries and some very unattractive people waiting in line to use the ladies' room at Howard Johnson's.

JOHN   Chloe.

CHLOE   I know. "Shut up." He loves me!

JOHN   This is more than shut up. This is more like a total ban on all sounds emanating from your throat for the next six hours. Let's see. It is 1:30 p.m. I don't want to hear so much as a peep out of you until 7:30.

SALLY   I'm really not enjoying this, you two.

CHLOE   Oh! It's just us!

SALLY   Well it's very depressing.

CHLOE   Not everyone has your perfect marriage, Sally.

SALLY   I never said it was perfect.

SAM   Try to take it easy, John. She is my sister.

JOHN   Stay out of this.

CHLOE   He's right, Sam. But before I go into my 6-hour exile (joyfully! I'll get the second act down pat,) I think you should know something about me. All of you. I think it is precisely the small things I run on about and that seem to annoy you so, the little day-to-day details, the nuances, that give our lives some zip and some meaning. I care about cooking the burgers so each of you get exactly what you ask for. I worry about who's driving the children's car pool that particular week. I notice what's going on around me, every detail. I don't miss a thing. I've got all your numbers. I talk too much probably because it's too horrible to think about what's really going on. You should try it, Miss Broody-Woody, Miss High Falutin! You think you're so superior. Well maybe you are. But to whom? Me? Honey, just about anyone is superior to me. You're going to have to do a lot better than that if you want to keep that attitude up. I'll try to think of something lofty to say at dinner. (*She starts to go to her room, then turns back.*) You know, I'm not mad at any of you. Really. I think we're all pathetic. Sally, will you clean up? We'll have bugs galore. Pussy Galore! Remember her? (*She goes into her room and lies down on the bed.*)

SAM   One of us should go in there.

JOHN   Why?

SAM   To find out what's wrong.

JOHN   She just told us.

SAM   When did you two get like this?

JOHN   We're fine. We're copacetic, which is the word I'm looking for, 47 Down. Thank you, Sam. (*He takes up the puzzle.*)

SAM   I don't think you're so fine.

SALLY   Sam, you heard Chloe. It's none of your business.

SAM   She's my sister.

JOHN   And I'm her husband.

SAM   I love it when you get macho. Especially in that outfit. I start wetting my pants.

JOHN   I'm not going to sit here and exchange puerile insults with my brother-in-law.

SAM   "Puerile?" What's "puerile?"

JOHN   How you're behaving. Look at you!

SAM   I'll show you puerile. Come on, you miserable son of a bitch. You want puerile? You got puerile. (*He puts his fists up and starts bobbing back and forth on his feet.*)

JOHN   Sally, can't you control him?

SALLY   Sam, stop it. I think you're both impossible.

SAM   He wants puerile. Okay, here's some puerile. (*He punches John on the arm.*) You want more puerile? Okay, here's more puerile. (*He keeps punching John on the arm. John slowly stands, which makes Sam dance a little away but still within range. John is clearly making ready to fight.*)

SALLY   Chloe! Will you come out here?

CHLOE (*From within.*)   There's more beef patties in the refrigerator!

SALLY   Now, Chloe!

JOHN   Look, you little jerk!

SAM   I'm trembling, I'm quaking!

SALLY   Stop it, both of you! Chloe, will you stop them before they hurt one another? (*Chloe has come to the door of her room.*)

CHLOE   Stop them? Honey, I want the cable rights to this. (*Sally grabs hold of Sam's arm. He pulls violently away, the force of his gesture sending her reeling.*)

SAM   I'm going to fucking kill you.

CHLOE   All right, that's enough. Break it up. Both of you!

JOHN   You miserable little asshole. (*By now we should realize the men are deadly serious.*)

CHLOE   John, people are looking from the other deck. (*She waves.*) Will you gentleman please tell them how silly they look? (*John and Sam keep circling each other, dukes up. Punches have been thrown, but none landed.*)

JOHN   Come on, big shot. You started something, now let's finish it. (*John swings at Sam and misses. Sam swings at John and misses.*)

SALLY   Sam, you're going to hurt yourself.

SAM   I'll kill the bastard.

CHLOE   Don't rip his shirt, Sam. I just bought it—

JOHN   Fight fair. (*Sally picks up Chloe's large glass container for making sun tea.*)

SALLY   Okay, that's it. (*Sally throws the container of tea at them. It drenches both men but instead of parting them, they leap at each other and start grappling.*)

SAM   Ow! (*John twists Sam's arm behind him in a hammerlock. Now both women rush at them and try to pull them apart.*)

JOHN   You give up?

SAM   No!

SALLY You're hurting him, John!

JOHN You give up?

SAM No!

JOHN You give up?

SAM Yes.

SALLY Now let him go.

JOHN "I give up, John."

CHLOE That's enough, John.

JOHN "I give up, John!!"

SAM I give up, John.

SALLY Now let him go. (*She pulls at John.*)

JOHN "And I admit I'm a stupid piece of shit!"

CHLOE John, stop it! (*Both women are pulling at John now, trying to get him off Sam.*)

JOHN "And I'd admit I'm a stupid piece of shit!"

SAM No.

JOHN "And I admit I'm a stupid piece of shit."

SAM No.

JOHN Say it, goddamnit.

SAM No, I said!

JOHN Say it!

SAM No!

JOHN Say it!!

SAM No!! Break my fucking arm! (*John is suddenly aware of how far his passions have carried him. It is a moment of terrible humiliation for both men. John is now very ashamed of himself.*)

JOHN I'm sorry, Sam. I don't know what else to say. I'm sorry. Excuse me. (*He goes quickly to his bedroom and throws himself on the bed, his back to the door. Sally and Chloe are helping Sam.*)

SALLY   Honey, here, lean on me.

CHLOE   Careful.

SAM   I'm fine.

SALLY   Take his other arm.

SAM   Ow!

SALLY   Not that arm.

CHLOE   This arm?

SAM   Ow! Jesus, what are you two? Nurses of pain? I'm fine. Just let go of me.

SALLY   Sit. No, lie down on the chaise. Chloe, get him some ice tea.

SAM   I don't want iced tea.

CHLOE   Good, 'cause there is none. She drenched you in it.

SALLY   What happened? One minute you're horsing around and the next you're trying to kill one another?

CHLOE   Are they still looking over here? I'm too embarrassed to look.

SALLY   You want to lie back? You want to lean forward? Yes? No?

SAM   You're married to a goddamn maniac.

SALLY   Where does it hurt? Tell me.

CHLOE   (Calling off.)   They were just fooling around. Rehearsing for a play . . . What? What play? (To Sally.) Quick, give me the name of a play, someone.

SALLY   Not now, Chloe.

CHLOE   (Trying to think.)   Something with violence. Fucking Alzheimer's! All I can think of is Bells Are Ringing and Bye Bye Birdie. (She's got it.) Westside Story! They were rehearsing for West Side Story! (Under her breath.) "Sure they were," they're all going. "Sure they were." I'm so embarrassed!

SALLY   Chloe, believe it or not, but this is not about you and how you feel.

CHLOE   I know that! I was concerned for you. They're your neighbors. You're going to have to live with them. I can stand anything but being misunderstood. (*She bursts into tears and goes into her room and throws herself on the other bed.*) Why does she hate me? Why does everybody hate me?

SALLY   How do you feel?

SAM   Great. I could bowl ten frames.

SALLY   What happened?

SAM   What do you think? You were right there. He insulted my sister, he insulted me. He's so superior in his pink slacks, his little polo player shirt and his faggy white shoes. He looks like one of them. He fits right in. You know, we could drive a bigger car, too. We just don't need one. I don't need a BMW to make me feel like I'm somebody. You know what kind of mileage they must get? And I'll tell you something else: I wouldn't want to join any country club that would let him be a member. (*Sally gives him a big hug.*) What was that for?

SALLY   I love you.

SAM   Thank you. I still hate him.

SALLY   Ssshhh!

SAM   And have you noticed how he holds his fork? Watch him next time. I'm not saying my sister married a fruitcake but she didn't marry any Pete Rose either.

SALLY   Listen to the waves.

SAM   I hate waves. I hate the beach. I hate nature. I like New Jersey.

SALLY   Listen, will you? (*We hear music from the first house. Jussi Bjorling is singing "O Paradiso" from Meyerbeer's L'Africaine.*) It's beautiful.

SAM   Tell me something, what have these people got against Tony Bennett?

SALLY   Every time you say "these people" or "fag" or—you know all the words—I feel I'm holding a stranger.

SAM   I'm sorry, you're right.

SALLY   I don't think they have anything against Tony Bennett. I don't think anybody does. It's all just music. (*During this last exchange between Sally and Sam, ever since we became aware of the music, John has gotten up,* *come out of the bedroom, and walked across the deck, to stand at the apron of the stage facing us. Chloe is still lying on the other bed, Sally and Sam remain rapt in themselves.)*

JOHN   The weekend's ruined. The four of us can never look at each other the same way again. I hate what happened back there. I overpowered another man, fairly, and I had reason, but it wasn't enough. I wanted to humiliate him in front of his wife. I wanted him to feel small about himself in front of me. I could feel the bone in his arm about to snap like a dry, brittle wishbone. "Break the fucking arm." When he looked at me and said "Break the fucking arm" I didn't know who he was talking to. "Break the fucking arm." Jesus. Where was I? Whose arm was it? That could have been Chloe or one of the kids or one of them. In my head, I do it all the time. Cut ahead of me in traffic. Check your bank balance and start paying bills on the quick cash machine when there's a line. Say "Hunh?" with an accent when I ask you a question in perfectly good English. Fucking nigger, dumb cunt, idiot faggot. I kill a couple of hundred of them a day in my impotent fashion.

CHLOE *(From within.)*   John!

JOHN   In a minute! When I turned 40, my mother gave me a baby picture of myself. Everyone cooed and aahed but I took it as a reproach. There I am, golden curls, laughing, chipped front tooth, holding an apple. And now look at me. I've become a stranger to the very woman who bore me. I just wish I knew the precise moment I stopped being that laughing child with apple and turned into this. I would go back there again and again until I understood it. I know the precise moment I almost broke my brother-in-law's arm.

CHLOE *(From within.)*   John!

JOHN   I'm on my way! Sally will never let me fuck her again. That pisses me off as much as it saddens me. We gave each other great pleasure. We can never talk about these things the way they really happened and what they really meant. There's no apology deep enough to undo what I did to Sam. None. I will say "I'm sorry" and he will accept my apology but they will be just words and lies to get us through the business of living.

SALLY   You could have really hurt him.

SAM   It isn't that bad.

JOHN I'm sorry. Really, I . . .

SAM Let's not ruin the girls' weekend because of us.

CHLOE (*Standing at the door.*) Did you hear me?

SALLY Maybe you should . . .

JOHN Leave?

SAM No.

CHLOE Have you seen my lens case?

JOHN You plugged it in the kitchen, by the toaster.

CHLOE I'd lose my head if I didn't have it screwed on tight! (*We will see her enter the kitchen from inside and get her contact lenses. She comes outside and proceeds to put them in.*)

JOHN Maybe we should.

SAM No, I said.

JOHN If this is going to be awkward for everyone . . . !

SAM It's not going to be awkward for me, you son of a bitch.

JOHN We'll go. I'm sorry, Sally.

SAM Why let my bad mood spoil everyone else's weekend? Three against one. The Good Mood-ers have it! The subject of premature departure is closed. Premature ejaculation I'm up for!

JOHN (*To Sally.*) What do you think?

SALLY No one's in a good mood, Sam. (*To John.*) Stay. Go. I don't care. Stay.

SAM God, I'd like to jump in that pool.

SALLY Why don't you?

SAM We just ate. You have to wait an hour.

SALLY You don't believe that!

SAM I certainly do. Didn't your mother raise you that way? Ours did. Didn't she, sis?

CHLOE Didn't who what?

SAM   Mom. Raise us to wait a full hour before going back in the water.

CHLOE   She certainly did. To the minute. There was a big clock at the municipal pool and if we had swallowed our last bit of hot dog and Coke at 12:39 we weren't allowed back in the water until the sweep hand hit 1:39 exactly. Not a moment sooner. Sam and I would be poised at the edge of the pool like Esther Williams and Johnny Weismuller ready to dive back in the moment the hour was up.

SAM   I still can't.

CHLOE   It's a terrible legacy to carry around with you the rest of your life. I pray we haven't scarred Little John, Megan and Benjamin like that. As soon as they eat, I throw them back into the pool. "Eat the wiener and swim, you kids!" I'm kidding, I'm kidding. Jesus! Who would throw children in a swimming pool?

SALLY   My father did. That's how I learned to swim. He threw David and me off the end of a pier.

CHLOE   What was he thinking?

SALLY   I don't think he was. All of a sudden we heard him saying "All children can swim, it's a natural instinct" and the next think we knew he was picking us up and dropping us off the end. Plop, plop!

CHLOE   How old were you?

SALLY   Six or seven. David was two years younger.

CHLOE   Your father dropped a four-year-old child off the end of a pier?

SALLY   Maybe he was five. I don't remember exactly.

JOHN   What happened?

SALLY   I guess I instinctively knew what to do. I started paddling like a little dog but David when right to the bottom like a stone.

CHLOE   Did he drown? I mean, did he start to drown?

SALLY   He would have. My father dove right in and brought him up.

JOHN   That was big of him.

CHLOE   John hates his father.

JOHN   I do not.

CHLOE   Yes, you do, darling. Don't interrupt.

SALLY   He just ignored David, like it never happened and went back to drinking with his friends, but you could see he was disappointed in his son. Poor David. He looked so sad.

CHLOE   I wonder why. That's a terrible story. It sounds like your brother never had a chance.

SALLY   At what?

CHLOE   I know I'm not supposed to say "normal." "Straight" is the word I'm supposed to use. I hate it. It sounds like a ruler. And heterosexual is just plain ugh-y! I hate all those "O" words.

SALLY   I think the causes of our sexuality run a little deeper and are a hell of a lot more mysterious than being thrown off a pier.

CHLOE   It's entirely the parents' fault. If any of our three turned out that way, I would feel like killing myself. I probably wouldn't do it, actually it is a mortal sin, after all, for those of us who still practice the faith of our fathers—

SAM   Don't start, Chloe.

CHLOE   —but I would feel like doing it. It's such a rejection! Can we change the subject? This is very depressing.

JOHN   You brought it up, Chloe.

CHLOE   I dredge everything up sooner or later. I'm a walking nerve end. I think these are very difficult times to be a parent in.

SALLY   I think these are very difficult times to be anything in.

JOHN   I'll drink to that.

SAM   This used to be a wonderful country.

JOHN   It still could be.

CHLOE   It still is. I mean, look at Russia.

SALLY   Now it's my turn: can we change the subject?

CHLOE   Second!

JOHN   Is there a movie theatre anywhere on the island?

SAM   No! No bowling alley either. I don't know how people are supposed to entertain themselves.

CHLOE   I guess you've noticed, Sally, I've decided to let bygones be bygones. I don't believe in holding grudges.

SALLY   Neither do I. I'm sorry we keep getting off on the wrong foot.

CHLOE   Sally, may I make one teeny, teeny, teeny, teeny, tiny suggestion?

SALLY   Of course you may.

CHLOE   The next time you tell that story about your father and the swimming lesson, don't refer to yourself as a paddling like a dog. It's a real put-down.

SALLY   Really? Thank you.

CHLOE   Thank *you*. (*Takes a deep breath.*) This ocean air is so calming! I'm sorry I took those pills. (*To Sam.*) Where are you going?

SAM   I feel a little sticky. I want to get this tea off me.

CHLOE   Why don't you just jump into the pool?

SAM   We've been through that.

SALLY   Be careful of the hot water. It's very hot. Scalding almost. (*Sam will use the outdoor shower during the following.*)

CHLOE   Does anyone mind if I practice out here?

JOHN   That depends on what you're going to practice.

CHLOE (*To Sally.*)   Ignore him. He's such a clown.

JOHN   We don't want any Voodoo or Black Magic this weekend, Chloe. None of your Witchcraft.

CHLOE   I left it all in Connecticut. This is strictly Mr. Frank Loesser, *Guys and Dolls,* A Musical Fable of Broadway, opening September 5 through October 10. (*Goes inside.*)

SAM   Ow!

SALLY   I warned you!

JOHN (*To someone next door.*)   Excuse me?

SAM   There's no soap!

SALLY   Yes, there is!

CHLOE (*From within.*)   Is there an outlet out there?

JOHN (*To someone next door.*)   let me ask Mrs. Trumann . . . Mrs. Trumann, David's sister. (*To Sally.*) We've been asked next door to watch the fireworks tonight.

CHLOE (*From within.*)   Did you say something?

SALLY   I don't know. What do you think?

JOHN   I don't know.

SALLY   Can't we think about it?

JOHN   What is there to think about?

SALLY   Is it just going to be men?

JOHN   I didn't ask him. Hurry up. They're all looking over here. (*Chloe comes out of her room with a portable cassette player.*)

CHLOE   I don't need an outlet. I've got batteries. Dumb, dumb, dumb!

SALLY (*To someone next door.*)   Hello, I'm Sally Trumann, David's—! . . . You were there? . . . It *was* beautiful . . . My brother-in-law told me. That's very kind of you. Unfortunately, we have other plans.

CHLOE   Who is she talking to?

JOHN   The neighbors.

CHLOE   What plans? What's happening?

SAM   Ow! Did someone flush the toilet?

SALLY (*To someone next door.*)   It sounds wonderful. I wish we'd known.

SAM   Who are you talking to? Who is she talking to?

CHLOE   Your neighbors.

SAM   What about?

CHLOE   What do I look like? Swami Lou, the Mind Reader?

SALLY (*To someone next door.*)   Not since the lawyer's. Have you been in touch with him? . . . Bridgehampton? That's out on Long Island? . . . Oh, I hope so. Well, nice shouting across a deck with you.

JOHN (*To Chloe.*)   See the guy in the yellow shirt?

CHLOE   Where?

JOHN   Don't just turn around and look. He'll see you.

SALLY (*To someone next door.*)   Oh, excuse me, but have you heard anything about a drowning?

CHLOE   Bright yellow?

JOHN   There's only one yellow.

SALLY (*To someone next door.*)   A drowning!

SAM   There's a big next of something up there.

CHLOE   What about him?

SALLY (*To someone next door.*)   No, I don't *know* that there's been a drowning—!

JOHN   I've seen him in our neck of the woods.

SAM   What is that? Hornets, wasps, what?

SALLY (*To someone next door.*)   I saw someone swim out and I didn't see him swim back!

CHLOE   Oooooooh.

JOHN   Oooooh? What does that mean, oooooooh?

CHLOE   He's cute.

SALLY (*To someone next door.*)   I'm sure you're right. I've always been a little frightened of the ocean.

CHLOE (*To someone next door.*)   With good reason. Her father threw her off a pier!

SAM   Ow!! Goddamnit, someone's flushing a toilet!

SALLY   No one's flushing a toilet. Chloe, please!

CHLOE (*To someone next door.*)   I hope you boys don't mind a little show.

JOHN   Leave them alone, Chloe.

SALLY   Don't call them boys, Chloe.

CHLOE (*To someone next door.*)   If you like what you see, send money. If you don't, I don't want to know. I have very thin skin.

SALLY   Chloe, they were only asking us over for drinks tonight. They weren't requesting a floor show.

CHLOE   Drinks? That's so nice of them! (*To someone next door.*) I'll bring some dip!

SAM   Will someone bring me a towel?

SALLY   I just got through telling them no.

JOHN   That word isn't in her vocabulary.

CHLOE   That's not true. (*To Sally.*) So we're not going over?

SAM   A towel, someone!

SALLY   I think it's best.

CHLOE   It's your house. (*To someone next door.*) I'll still send some dip over!

SAM   Would somebody please bring me a towel? (*John crosses to the bedroom to get a towel for Sam.*) Thank you.

JOHN   How was it?

SAM   Great, except the water keeps getting red hot.

JOHN   Your neck is red. You've got a real line where your shirt was. I've got something that takes the sting out pretty good. (*John hands Sam a towel.*)

SAM   Thank you.

JOHN   You've been losing weight.

SAM   Who? Me?

JOHN   God knows, I'm not. It's all that goddamn ice cream Chloe keeps bringing into the house.

CHLOE (*To Sally.*)   Look! The menfolk.

SALLY   I see them.

CHLOE   Knock on wood. (*She knocks on her head. Sally goes into her room. Chloe sets up her portable cassette player. John is still talking to Sam who is toweling off in the outdoor shower.*)

JOHN   I guess you heard. They wanted us for drinks next door, the port side. We said no. Have you always had that mole there?

SAM   Would you mind . . . ?

JOHN   I'm sorry.

SAM   I'm not real good at this locker room stuff. I never was. If you'd just let me dry off and get some clothes on.

JOHN   I'm terribly sorry.

SAM   It's nothing personal.

JOHN   I don't take it as such.

SAM   Sally!

JOHN   She's in the house. What do you need?

SAM   A pair of shorts, *under*shorts! There's clean polo shirts in the drawer, I've got some blue slacks in the closet.

JOHN   Any particular color polo shirt?

SAM   It's doesn't matter. Red, the red one.

JOHN   Anything else?

SAM   That's it, I think. Oh, a comb. In the bathroom.

JOHN   I'll be right back. (*He goes into Sam and Sally's room. He gathers Sam's clothing. Chloe walks over to the shower.*)

CHLOE   I'm so glad to see you two getting along or should I be waiting for the other shoe to drop?

SAM   Your husband turns on a dime. Prick, nice, prick, nice. I wish he'd make up his mind. (*Chloe starts the cassette player. We hear clumsy piano playing.*) What the hell is that music?

CHLOE   It's Megan playing the chords to my number. I know it doesn't sound like much.

SAM   Jesus!

CHLOE   It's just chords for Christ's sake. Give the kid a break. Vladimir Horo-what's-his-hoosie couldn't do much with just chords.

SAM   What are you doing?

CHLOE   I want to see your dick.

SAM   What? No! Are you nuts?

CHLOE   Oh come on, I'm your big sister. Let me see it.

SAM   No.

CHLOE   I let you see my thing when I was in high school and you were still some little squirt in the fifth grade. You and your friend, Claude Barbizon, came into my bedroom. I didn't make *you* beg.

SAM   What drugs did you take? What cult have you joined?

CHLOE   When did you become such a prude?

SAM   I'm not a prude and I resent you saying that. I resent it very much.

CHLOE   It's not like I asked to see your bank balance.

SAM   I don't believe this.

CHLOE   Come on, let me see it. For old time's sake. I'll never ask you again. It's a one time proposition.

SAM   There. Are you satisfied?

CHLOE   It's very nice.

SAM   Thank you.

CHLOE   I'm impressed.

SAM   Thank you.

CHLOE   And I'll tell you something. It's much bigger than you-know-who's, certainly in that state of flaccidity. Is that a word? I think I just made it up. You tell him I said that and I'll deny every word of it. My compliments to our parents. (*We see John and Sally laughing and talking within the house.*)

SAM   What are they doing in there?

CHLOE   Talking.

SAM   I hear laughing.

CHLOE   All right, they're laughing.

SAM   Would you please see what your husband is doing with my wife?

CHLOE   Right now it looks like he's got her legs over her head in some Kama Sutra position we learned at Club Med. (*Sam emerges from the shower with a towel around his waist and crosses to Chloe.*)

SAM   That's not funny.

CHLOE   I know.

SAM   Then you know?

CHLOE   I only know what I read in the paper.

SAM   He's fucking her.

CHLOE   He fucked her. It's over.

SAM   How do you know?

CHLOE   He told me.

SAM   And you believe him?

CHLOE   Yes.

SAM   Why?

CHLOE   I want to.

SAM   That's a wonderful reason.

CHLOE   You got a better one.

SAM   The truth.

CHLOE   That word has gotten more people into more trouble than all the lies that were ever told. Fuck the truth. It's more trouble than it's worth. (*She goes back to her cassette and rewinds it to the beginning.*) If I don't believe the son of a bitch, I've only got one option as I see it.

SAM   What's that?

CHLOE   Wait till he's sound asleep, take a hammer and bludgeon him to death. (*Sam moves away and stubs his foot on the deck.*)

SAM   Ow!

CHLOE   What's the matter?

SAM I got a splinter. Sally! Sally! (*Sally comes out onto the deck, John following.*)

SALLY What happened?

SAM I got a splinter in my foot.

SALLY Do we have tweezers?

JOHN I do. (*He crosses the deck to his and Chloe's room.*)

SALLY Get off it! Let me see! (*Sally helps Sam to sit.*)

SAM I can't look! It's big! It's huge. It's in there about six inches.

SALLY Let me look at it.

JOHN (*From within.*) Honey, where's my dop kit?

CHLOE I knew he was going to ask me that! (*To John.*) Try the bathroom. (*To Sally.*) I never know where anything is when we travel.

JOHN (*From within.*) Got it!

CHLOE Thank You! (*She crosses herself.*)

SAM Is there a hospital on the island?

SALLY You're not going to need a hospital—! (*John comes onto the deck.*) I can't deal with this! It's a lulu.

SAM What? What? It's a what? What's a lulu?

JOHN Let me see.

SAM I don't want you doing it—! I want Sally to! (*Chloe has started her tape cassette going. She will begin to practice a song from a musical she is rehearsing. It will be a while before the others notice this going on while they deal with Sam's foot.*)

JOHN Keep your foot still.

SAM I am!

JOHN Sally, hold his foot.

SAM Do we have to make *The Song of Bernadette* out of this?

JOHN Okay. Got it! (*He yanks something out of Sam's foot.*)

SAM (*Erupting.*)   Jesus Christ. You fucking bastard! (*John holds up a sliver that is almost two inches long.*)

JOHN   Look at that!

SALLY   Do you want to keep that down, Chloe?

CHLOE   Don't mind me! I'm just doing my thing. I can't deal with any kind of puncture of the human flesh.

JOHN   I'm going to sterilize a pin with a match and then I want to probe for any small slivers left in there.

SAM   The hell you are!

JOHN   It's the slivers that cause the infections.

SALLY   He's right.

SAM   Since when do you know so much about it?

JOHN   We need iodine.

SAM   No iodine.

SALLY   Try our medicine cabinet. (*John goes into Sally and Sam's room.*)

SAM   I don't want him rummaging around in the medicine cabinet.

SALLY   It's going to be fine.

SAM   I have put some extremely personal things in there. I don't want some stranger knowing certain things about me.

SALLY   He's just getting the iodine.

JOHN (*From within.*)   Got it!

SALLY   You're both impossible.

SAM   He's not probing around in my foot with a sterilized safety pin and that's that. (*John returns with the iodine.*)

JOHN   I found a pin on your dresser.

SAM (*To Sally.*)   You see? You see?

JOHN   Hold this. (*He hands pin to Sally and lights a match.*) Do you want to knock that off, Petal?

CHLOE I'll keep it low. (*Indeed, we will barely be able to hear her as she mouths the words and does her steps.*)

SAM She's really very talented for a housewife. I actually preferred her *Mame* to Lucille Ball's. (*John finishes sterilizing the pin.*)

JOHN Hold his foot again.

SAM I want Sally to do that.

JOHN Okay. (*He hands pin to Sally and steps aside.*)

SALLY Now don't move. I don't want to hurt you.

SAM I'll be brave, mama. (*She works on his foot. Chloe is still singing sotto voice and dancing to the clumsy piano accompaniment playing on the cassette. John moves apart from the others. He looks at Chloe practicing her number.*)

JOHN You're looking good, Petal.

CHLOE Give me five more weeks! Can we call the kids tonight? I gave Mima the number here but you know how cheap she is.

JOHN I'll tell mother you said so. Yes, we'll call! Hey! I love you.

CHLOE What?

JOHN You heard me. (*He goes to the edge of the deck and looks out to the ocean.*)

SALLY When did your feet get so callused and bunioned and corny?

SAM Those are bunions. Old people have bunions. Stick to the splinter. Ow!

SALLY I'm sorry!

SAM Ow!!

SALLY I said I was sorry!

SAM That's enough. (*Sam takes the pin away from Sally and begins to work on his own foot. The lights are coming down on Chloe silently singing and dancing, John watching her, and Sam bent over his foot. Sally stands and looks out to sea. Very strong special on Sally. Her eyes tell us that she has seen something on the shore.*)

SALLY Oh my God. Drowned. (*The light snaps off.*)

END OF ACT TWO

ACT THREE

Night. There is a full moon and many, many stars. The main source of light is the pool. There is an ultraviolet bug lamp which we will hear zapping insects throughout the act.

There are two noisy parties going on in the two next-door houses. The Beach Boys are heard coming from one party, stage right. Ella Fitzgerald from the other house, stage left.

The wind has stopped blowing. It is warm and muggy, a perfect night for a midnight dip.

Sam is playing with the telescope, Sally is washing dishes in the kitchen, John is on a cordless telephone, Chloe is in her room dressing.

SAM This is fabulous! The clarity! You can see everything! John, have you—?

JOHN (*On the phone.*) I don't think you want to do that, son.

SAM (*Calling off.*) Sally! Come out here!

JOHN (*On the phone.*) What does your grandmother say? (*Calling off.*) Chloe! (*On the phone.*) Well where is she? (*Calling off.*) Chloe! Goddamnit! (*Sam goes to the sliding screen door and speaks to Sally who is still working in the kitchen.*)

SAM Honey, come on, you gotta see this. It's like being in a planetarium. You've never seen so many stars. It will get your mind off what happened this afternoon.

JOHN (*Covering phone, to Sam.*) They want to go on a hayride in the rain. Their grandmother is at her Weight Watchers' meeting. Count your blessings. (*Sees limp kite string.*) My kite's down. Shit! When did this happen?

SAM (*To John.*) You really ought to take a look through this.

JOHN When did my kite come down?

SAM I assume it was when the wind stopped. (*Under his breath.*) You don't have to be Isaac Newton to figure that one out.

JOHN I was trying to break a record.

CHLOE (*From within.*) Did somebody say something?

JOHN (*On the phone.*) Have Mima call us the minute she gets back. Your uncle Sam wants to talk to you. He's pulling the phone right out of my hand. Stop it, Sam! I don't think your uncle Sam thinks it's a good idea to go hayriding in the rain either. (*Hands phone to Sam.*) Tell them they can't go hayriding in the goddamn rain for Christ's sake, will you?

SAM (*Into phone.*) Hello? (*John goes to door of his room and speaks to Chloe.*)

JOHN They want to go for a hayride in a rainstorm. Mrs. Dietrich says it's all right. My mother's at a goddamn Weight Watchers' meeting! She's at the wrong meeting! She should be at AA. Why didn't somebody tell me my kite had come down? (*He will start reeling in the string.*)

SAM (*On the phone.*) I'm sorry Megan, I thought you were Little John. (*To John.*) Which one did you give me?

JOHN I don't know. They're all on there. Different extensions. (*To Sally, within.*) They want to go for a hayride in a rainstorm. (*To Sam.*) Tell them they could be electrocuted!

SAM You could get electrocuted!

JOHN You know, struck by lightning! (*To Sally, within.*) I was just telling Sam: count your blessings.

CHLOE (*From within.*) John, did you see my—? Never mind, I've got it! (*Sally comes out onto the deck drying a large pasta pot.*)

SAM (*Into phone.*) All right, everybody shut up! Listen, kids, your aunt Sally is dying to talk to you. She's grabbing the phone from me. (*He hands the phone to Sally.*) They want to go for a hayride in the rain. Maybe they'll listen to their aunt. Chloe! (*He crosses to the screen door outside Chloe's room.*)

SALLY (*Into phone.*) Hello? Children? This is your aunt Sally. Now just a minute—!

SAM (*To Chloe.*) They want to go for a hayride in a lightning storm!

CHLOE (*From within.*) Do you think this top matches this bottom?

SAM   What do I know? You're the clotheshorse.

CHLOE (*From within.*)   Sammy!

SAM   You're asking the wrong person. I think you always look great. Is that the new *Life* magazine? Can I take a—?

SALLY (*Into phone.*)   All right, now it's my turn. The reason your father doesn't want you to go for a hayride in the rain is that he loves you and he doesn't want anything to happen to you while he's away and unable to protect you. You could catch a cold. You could be struck by lightning. What else could happen to you if you go for a hayride in the rain? That should be enough, Benjamin.

JOHN   It won't be.

SALLY (*To John.*)   Who is Mrs. Dietrich?

JOHN   A neighbor.

SALLY   That's what parents do: love their children and protect them from the dangers of the world. If I had children, they would be so safe. They would never be alone. I would never let them go. (*John puts his hand on her arm.*) Don't touch me.

JOHN   I'm sorry.

SALLY (*Into phone.*)   I'm feeling very sad and angry and un-listened to right now. That's why it's so important you understand me. I saw a terrible thing this afternoon. I saw what happens when we're not loved and protected and we feel so alone.

JOHN   You're not alone, Sally.

SALLY (*Into phone.*)   I saw a man who drowned in the ocean.

JOHN   Jesus, Sally, don't—

SALLY (*Into phone.*)   He was very young. Even though his features were swollen from the water, he was very handsome. Nobody wanted to look at him like this, but I made myself.

JOHN   We all told you not to go down there.

SALLY (*Into phone.*)   I wanted to see what death looks like and not be afraid of it.

JOHN   What kind of thing is that to say to a child?

SALLY (*Into phone.*)   Oh, he could swim all right, Megan. He could swim too well too far. I saw him swim out this morning. I knew he wouldn't come back and I didn't do anything.

JOHN   Jesus, Sally, you're scaring them. (*John takes the phone from her.*)

SALLY   Our eyes met.

JOHN   Children, this is your father again.

SALLY   His wave did acknowledge me.

JOHN   Now settle down.

SALLY   I let him swim out never to return.

JOHN   Aunt Sally's still upset by what happened. We all are. (*He continues but we don't hear him.*)

SALLY   My eyes didn't say "Stay, life is worth living." They said "Go, God speed, God bless." My wave didn't say "Hurry back, young man, happiness awaits you ashore." It said "Goodbye, I know where you're going. I've wanted to go there too." I knew his secret, and he knew mine. Even from a great distance we know so much about each other but spend our lives pretending we don't. He wanted to die and I helped him. Oh children, children, such perils await you, such pain and no one to protect us. (*She touches her stomach.*) Don't you leave me. Stick around this time.

JOHN   Aunt Sally's still upset by what happened. We all are. (*Chloe opens the screen door with a flourish. She has changed into a snappy resort-wear ensemble.*)

CHLOE   Ta-da! How do I look?

JOHN (*Into phone.*)   Your mother wants to talk to you. She's tearing the phone out of my hand.

CHLOE   Don't tell them that. They're spoiled enough. Do I match?

JOHN (*Holding the phone to Chloe.*)   They want to go on a hayride in the rain.

CHLOE   You mean that hasn't been settled yet? I swear, sometimes I don't know what fathers are for. The mothers do everything. (*She takes the phone from John and speaks into it.*) Hello, this is Mommy. No. N-o. Nada. Rien. Forget the hayride. The hayride is out. Got that? (*To Sally.*)

You just have to be firm with them. Don't be intimidated by them, like they were something special. They're just little people. That's all you have to remember about them.

JOHN (*To Sally.*)   Does Sam know you get like this?

CHLOE (*Into phone.*)   Is that all settled now? Is everything under control?

JOHN   Does he?

SALLY   I hope not.

JOHN   I mean . . . why? What's wrong?

SALLY   I don't know.

CHLOE (*Into phone.*)   The next time you go to Mima's we'll be sure there's a Nintendo there. We'll give her one for Christmas.

JOHN (*To Sally.*)   Your brother?

SALLY   I don't know.

JOHN   Is it you and Sam?

SALLY   No.

JOHN   Was it us?

SALLY   I said I don't know. (*She moves away from him.*) Sam, what are you doing in there?

SAM (*From within.*)   There's an incredible article in here on jellyfish.

JOHN   Why won't you talk to me?

SALLY   There's nothing to say.

SAM (*From within.*)   You can die from them! The pictures are disgusting.

CHLOE (*Into phone.*)   I'm sure Aunt Sally didn't mean to frighten you.

JOHN   Please, Sally, don't be like this.

SAM (*From within.*)   Look at this guy's face from them.

SALLY   I don't know how else to be.

SAM (*From within.*)   His chest, his arms!

JOHN   It's not fair.

SALLY   I'm sorry.

CHLOE (*Into phone.*)   She was upset. We all were. It was a terrible thing. You should see me, I'm a wreck. I hope you children never, ever see anything so dreadful. (*Sam comes back onto the deck with a copy of* Life *magazine.*)

SAM   You want to see something to turn your stomach? And this is supposed to be a family magazine! (*He will show a picture in the magazine to* John.) Imagine if those things got wrapped around your dick.

JOHN   I'd rather not.

SAM (*To Sally.*)   Honey, take a look at this. They're called Portuguese Man O' Wars. I'd rather swim in this pool than risk my tender gonads to one of those suckers. And all you were worried about was sharks!

CHLOE (*Into phone.*)   Aunt's Sally's sorry if she upset you.

SALLY   That's not true, Chloe.

CHLOE (*Holding phone to Sally.*)   Tell them you're sorry, Sally.

SALLY   But I'm not.

CHLOE   It doesn't matter. Tell them anyway.

SALLY   Why?

CHLOE   For me.

SALLY   What about for me?

CHLOE   They're children. It's not fair.

JOHN   Leave Sally alone, Chloe.

SAM   What did she do?

CHLOE   Upset my children. (*Into phone.*) Hold on.

SAM   Your children are always upset. What did you say, honey?

SALLY   I told them to be careful. To be very, very careful.

SAM   What's wrong with that?

CHLOE   You told them you'd seen the face of death and that there was no one to protect them.

SALLY   Not them, us. All of us.

CHLOE   Be that as it may—!

SALLY   There isn't, Chloe.

SAM   What are you talking about?

JOHN   I've tried. Maybe she'll tell you.

CHLOE   Well it scared them!

SALLY   Good. I want to scare everyone tonight.

JOHN   She told them how alone she was.

SAM   Alone? With all of us here? Honey, that's nuts!

CHLOE   Please! Tell them something comforting.

SALLY   I don't know how to talk to children. I don't know what they want to hear.

CHLOE   The same thing we all do. That they're loved. That they're safe.

SALLY   But we're not.

CHLOE   That's your opinion.

SALLY   Then you tell them, Chloe.

CHLOE   They have to hear it from you.

SALLY   I'm sorry. I can't. (*She sits at the edge of the pool and dangles her feet in the water.*) Has anyone been in the pool yet?

CHLOE (*Into phone.*)   Aunt Sally is very sorry if she said anything to upset you. She doesn't have children of her own so she says things she doesn't mean. Your father wants to talk to you.

JOHN   I've already spoken to them—

CHLOE   He's grabbing the phone from me. (*She gives the phone to John and heads for her room.*) That really wasn't very nice of you, Sally.

SALLY   I'm tired of being nice. (*Sam sits by her side at the edge of the pool. Chloe will change into another outfit.*)

JOHN (*Into phone.*)   Mom, thank God you're back. We can't deal with this hayride thing long distance. Will you talk some sense into them—?

SAM   What's the matter, honey? Tell me.

JOHN (*Into phone.*)   Thank you. What magic sway do grandparents have over their children their real parents don't? Oh, something they thought their aunt said they completely misunderstood. Wait a minute, I'm losing you! (*He fusses with the antenna on the cordless phone and wanders to another part of the deck that is out of sight to us.*)

SAM   You want to talk about it? (*Sally shakes her head.*)

JOHN (*Off.*)   So how was Weight Watchers? It's a racket, like everything else. How much have you lost? That's great. We're going to have to get you a bikini for Mother's Day. Wonderful weekend. Beautiful house. Clear as a bell. There's a full moon, stars. We could use a little breeze. It's very still. Muggy almost. Everything is soggy. The sheets, the towels. Hello? There you go again? Hello?

SAM   Okay. (*They both sit, dangling their feet in the pool. The sound of the bug lamp is very "heard." The party sounds have pretty much become second-nature to us now, i.e., we are scarcely aware of them, unless there is a particularly loud outburst of laughter.*) Look, I think we all feel terrible about what happened this afternoon. It's put a damper on everything. I don't know how those guys can act like nothing happened. Was he a friend of David's? Did you find out?

SALLY   Nobody seemed to know who he was.

SAM   He must have come from somewhere.

SALLY   They checked every house. (*John reappears with the cordless phone in his hand.*)

JOHN   They haven't perfected these things yet. Not that we were talking about anything important. Where's Chloe?

SAM   Inside.

JOHN   Am I interrupting anything?

SAM   I wish you were.

JOHN   Mind if I join you? Chloe! (*He sits at the edge of the pool and dangles his feet in the water.*) That feels good!

SAM   Why don't you go in?

JOHN   Maybe later. Why don't you and Sally?

SAM I still feel that steak and baked potato and corn on the cob and strawberry shortcake with real whipped cream right here. I'd sink like a rock.

SALLY None of us are ever going to go into that pool so can we just stop talking about it?

CHLOE (*From within.*) Did somebody say something?

SALLY We all think it's infected. We all think it's polluted. We all think we'll get AIDS and die if we go in.

JOHN That's not quite true, Sally.

SALLY One drop of water in your mouth or on an open sore and we'll be infected with my brother and his black lover and God knows who else was in here. Pissing, ejaculating. I think we're very brave to dangle our feet like this. They may fall off.

CHLOE (*From within.*) If you have something to say to me, John, come in here and say it. I cannot hear through walls or screens or whatever they are! Partitions!

JOHN When did you develop this uncanny ability of yours to say absolutely the most inappropriate thing you could think of?

SALLY Everybody's thinking them. I've merely decided to say them. (*She splashes John.*)

JOHN Stop that!

SALLY Close your mouth!

JOHN Sally, stop it. I said!

SAM Sally!

SALLY You afraid of the water? (*She splashes him, too.*) Everybody's afraid of dying around here.

JOHN If you can't control your wife, Sam!

SALLY I can't believe I heard that. Have some more water, Mr. Haddock!

SAM Sally!!

SALLY Come on, Sam, you heard the man. Control me! Your wife is out of control. Do something. (*She splashes him.*) It's your last chance to be a man! (*She stops splashing him and scoops up water from the pool in the palm of her hand and drinks it.*) Then let's all get AIDS and die! (*Sam knocks her hands away from her mouth. He grabs and holds her right wrist. She pulls him to her with her other hand and kisses him very hard and long on the mouth.*) I love you.

SAM   Jesus, Sally, what's gotten into you?

SALLY   Thank you for not being a man. Thank you for not controlling your wife. (*She kisses him again. He pulls away from her and tries to clear his mouth. Clearly, he is not comfortable with the thought of the taste of her mouth in his. He gets up from the edge of the pool.*)

SAM   Stop that! I don't want to kiss you. I'm sorry your brother died but it's not my fault. I didn't kill him. I don't know about pools and AIDS and homosexuals. I don't want to. It frightens me, all right? All of this! I'm sorry, I can't help it, it's who I am. Excuse me. (*He goes quickly into their room and exits into the bathroom beyond.*)

JOHN   That was ugly, Sally.

SALLY   That's your opinion.

JOHN   Ugly to watch, ugly to listen to.

SALLY   I don't think so. I don't want to be married to a man who thinks he can control his wife. Or wants to. Or needs to. Or thinks he has a right to. I would hate being married to you. Sam doesn't do anything. That's why I married him. (*Sam is heard gargling Listerine off.*)

JOHN   That's charming.

SALLY   I needed you very badly that weekend.

JOHN   So did I. I won't pretend I wasn't hoping it would happen again.

SALLY   I'm sorry. You may not believe this but you are almost the only other man I've been with but Sam.

JOHN   I figured as much.

SALLY   How come?

JOHN   Something about you. Passionate but not promiscuous. Maybe you could help me. Was it my breath?

SALLY   Your breath was very sweet. I wanted the parts you don't give to anyone else. Your secrets, your fears. Not the parts of you that connect us, the parts that separate.

JOHN   No one gets them, Sally.

SALLY   Not even Chloe?

JOHN   Especially Chloe.

SALLY   Don't you want everything from another person?

JOHN   No. I respect the distance between people. I rather like it, in fact.

SALLY   Why?

JOHN   To know me is not necessarily to like me. I'm afraid to run that risk.

SALLY   Right now I feel much closer to you than I ever did when we were making love. You're not even pretending to let me in.

JOHN   What you want from a man, you can never have.

SALLY   That will never stop me wanting it.

JOHN   Look, there's a ring down there.

SALLY   It's my brother's.

JOHN   Would you like me to get it for you?

SALLY   You're not afraid of the pool?

JOHN   Not everyone is dying from AIDS, Sally. There are other malevolent forces at work on God's miraculous planet.

SALLY   What's that supposed to mean? (*Chloe comes back onto the deck. She is wearing a different outfit.*)

CHLOE   I don't care what anybody says: I didn't match! *This* matches. Where's Sam? I've decided not to let you get my goat, Sally.

SALLY   That's a very good decision, Chloe. (*John has started retrieving the ring.*)

CHLOE   John, are you sure you want to do that?

JOHN   I'm sure. (*He splashes some pool water on her.*)

CHLOE   Stop that! Are you insane?

JOHN Sally thinks we're all afraid of getting AIDS! Are we, Chloe? Come on, let's show her we're not.

CHLOE That's very, very, very funny. Sam!

JOHN She's figured out why no one's using her brother's beautiful pool.

CHLOE Including her, I noticed.

JOHN Sally's not afraid. She drank the water. She scooped it up and drank it. I think Sally was right. I think we should all get AIDS and die.

CHLOE What are you doing?

JOHN I don't know, Chloe. (*He plunges his head into the pool and blows out his breath there, making the water bubble.*)

CHLOE Stop that! John! I said stop! This is all your fault. You've been morbid and disruptive ever since we got here. Sam! Sam!! (*Sam comes out on the deck.*) You're frightening me, John!

SAM What's he doing?

CHLOE Make him stop it, Sam.

SALLY That's enough, John.

SAM Come on, John, enough's enough. (*No on moves. They all watch John. John stops moving. He stops blowing out air. His head and shoulders float motionless on the water's surface. There is an enormous burst of laughter from one of the parties on either side. Sam grabs John by the shoulders and lifts his head out of the pool and lets his body roll heavily on his back on the deck. John looks like he's dead. Sam turns away from him. Chloe bends over his body. John spurts a stream of pool water in her face. Chloe doesn't flinch.*)

JOHN Now we're all infected.

CHLOE Just so long as you're all right. You're my life. (*John takes one of her hands and begins to kiss the fingers.*) I should take my hand away. I don't want to.

JOHN Thank God for these dear, familiar fingers.

CHLOE My hand is paralyzed. He needs it so much right now, to heal his shame.

SALLY   When I was at the hospital with David and he'd lost his sight, he would put his fingers on my face "to remember me," as he put it. "To remember me."

SAM   I am watching two men make love in the bushes next to the house. It's probably poison ivy but they don't care. They are in the throes of passion.

JOHN   Fingers that have stroked and held me. Prepared our food. Diapered our children.

CHLOE   It would be like taking a teat away from a child. Even if I wanted to, I couldn't. I want him to need me like this.

SALLY   He would touch my eyes, my mouth. His hands would trace my profile over and over.

SAM   Is that what we look like when we make love? I see huffing and puffing and biting and licking and kissing and hugging and grunting and groaning but I don't hear anyone say "I love you."

JOHN   See! The first faint tracings of a liver spot. She will grow old without me.

CHLOE   I'm as close to love as he's ever going to get and that suffices. It shouldn't but it does.

SALLY   I hated his fingers on my face. I hated the smells of his room. I hated him being gay. And yet I loved him. Who he'd been. Not what he'd become.

SAM   Now one man throws his head back, utters a cry, his body shudders and he lies still. Now the other: head jerking back, oh!, shudder, shudder, shudder, still.

JOHN   Familiar, pedestrian, banal fingers of a woman who was foolish enough to want to share her life with me. I feel such guilt before such uncomplicated goodness.

CHLOE   You are my life. I don't know what I'm going to do.

SALLY   I thought he was my best friend. And then there was Aaron. No warning, no indication. Just a matter-of-fact "Sis, this is Aaron." You don't put people out of your heart so quickly, not if you love them.

SAM   They still don't move. They lie in each other's arms on the sand, in the poison ivy, under a full July moon, the sounds of the Atlantic

Ocean and Ella Fitzgerald wondering "How High the Moon." And now I hear it. I hear "I love you." (*There is a burst of color in the night sky above them. The Fourth of July fireworks have begun. Each new display will be greeted with a chorus of "oohs" and "aahs" from the houses on either side of theirs.*)

CHLOE   Look! Fireworks! A full moon! The ocean! The Fourth of July. Sally, if you don't keep this house you should have your head examined. (*To John.*) Darling, why don't you go inside and change? You'll catch cold.

JOHN   I'm fine. Look at that, will you?

CHLOE   At least let me get you a towel. (*She will go into their room and bring out a towel and dry John's hair for him.*)

SALLY   This is like that scene in that movie with Cary Grant and Ava Gardner.

SAM   Here we go again! What movie, Sally?

SALLY   *Catching a Thief.*

SAM   Thank God for small arms control!

JOHN   Leave her alone, Sam.

SAM   People like you don't deserve the movies. (*Chloe comes out of her room with a towel and begins to dry John's hair as he sits and watches the fireworks.*)

JOHN   Ow!

CHLOE   What's wrong?

JOHN   You're toweling too hard.

CHLOE   You want me to get you a dry shirt?

JOHN   I'm fine.

SAM   There we go! The best one yet. (*Calling next door.*) Aren't these fabulous? Makes you proud to be an American. I hope you had your hot dogs and hamburgers and apple pie for today!

JOHN (*Calling off.*)   Excuse me? Are you talking to—? Thank you. The same to you. Do we have any what? (*To others on deck.*) Do we have any flags to wave?

SAM   What are you getting us into?

JOHN (*Calling off.*)   We left all our flags in Connecticut! That's all right, you don't have to do that—! The fireworks will be over before you know it—! (*A packet of small American flags held together with a rubber band is tossed onto the deck. John catches them and will distribute them. Calling off.*) Thank you. (*Red, white and blue streamers and confetti are being tossed down onto the deck from the taller houses on each side.*)

SAM (*Calling off.*)   Thank you. Thank you. (*To others on deck.*) They gonna come over here tomorrow and clean this mess up?

CHLOE   Don't be so ungracious. It's the Fourth of July.

SAM   I know. Just don't make it sound like Christmas Eve and we're the Cratchits. (*The fireworks are reaching a noisy, colorful climax. Lots of different colors are exploding in the sky. The noise is deafening at the very end of this final barrage. John has given everyone a small American flag to wave.*)

CHLOE   Happy Fourth everyone! *Vive les États-Unis* and the republic for which it stands!

SAM   What are we supposed to do?

JOHN   Just wave your flag.

SAM   I feel like an idiot. (*They are watching the fireworks explode above them and waving their flags.*)

CHLOE   John, remind me to remind Little Theatre we haven't done *The Music Man* in ages. (*She starts to sing "America the Beautiful." John and Sam join in lustily. Sally sings, too, but more quietly. She is crying. Halfway through their singing their voices will be drowned out by the barrage of fireworks. In the first silence after the fireworks, the bug lamp will seem very loud again.*)

JOHN   I guess that's it.

SAM   There's usually one last— (*There is a final, thunderous report.*) There it is. (*Calling off.*) Happy Fourth to you too. Thank you.

CHLOE   *À bientôt. À demain. Ciao.* (*To others.*) Quick, quick, quick. How do you say it in Jewish—? (*She's got it.*) *Shalom! Bonsoir! Gute Nacht!* (*To others on the deck.*) There's something about the ocean. I feel so fucking liberated by it. Now who wants what? Sally, a white wine spritzer, *n'est-ce pas?* (*She will start making a round of drinks for everyone.*)

SALLY   That's all right.

CHLOE   The night is young, the stars are clear. I'm making you a sprizter. I know what you two lushes want. I've having a Diet Pepsi. I have to be thin, thin, thin for Miss Adelaide. That costume designer has me practically naked. (*Sam comes up to Sally who has moved away since the singing and who is still quietly crying. At the same time, John goes in to his and Chloe's room and draws the drapes. Perhaps we can see his silhouette against them.*)

SAM   Are you all right?

SALLY (*Nodding.*)   I'm fine. It's a stirring song.

CHLOE (*Calling over to them.*)   Chablis or Soave, Sally—? Oh, you two are talking! *Fermez la bouche*, Chloe. John? Now where's he gone to?

SALLY   I didn't think I'd feel David so strongly this weekend. Sometimes I feel I can't breathe.

SAM   We don't have to decide about the house tonight.

SALLY   What did we tell that lawyer?

SAM   That we'd be in touch. That's all. That we'd be in touch. You know, we could keep it and rent it.

SALLY   Look, they're dancing up there. Both houses.

SAM   That's not all some of them are doing.

SALLY   I wish I had a better opinion about all this.

SAM   I know. It's hard.

SALLY   Seeing them touching sort of sickens me. I can't help it. I was glad I never saw my brother dancing with another man and now I never will. (*She breaks down and cries. Sam comforts her.*)

SAM   I'm right here.

SALLY   And yet if we had a child and they grew up that way, I know I would love them all the same. I know I would, I know it. But my love stops right there. It can't go any further.

SAM   It's okay, nobody's judging you.

SALLY   I'm judging myself.

SAM   If we had a child, he wouldn't grow up that way. I know it, I just know it. We would do everything right, so he wouldn't, and then even if he did, or her, you're right, we would love them all the same. But it won't happen. I'd be willing to bet my life on it.

CHLOE Soup's on! Come and get it!

SAM Come on, a little drink will do you good. (*Calling to Chloe.*) I'll get John.

SALLY There's something I want to tell you before the weekend is over.

SAM Okay. There's something I want to tell you. (*To Chloe.*) I'll raise his highness! (*He pulls back the drape of John's room.*) John? (*He goes into their room.*)

SALLY Do you need any help?

CHLOE Why thank you, Sally! Where's Sam?

SALLY He's in with John. (*Sam comes out of John's room.*)

SAM (*Over his shoulder, to John.*)   I'm sorry.

SALLY What's wrong?

SAM I'm not sure. (*Chloe comes forward with a tray of drinks.*)

CHLOE *Voilà les caps du nuit!* Nightcaps! John, don't hibernate in there. We're going to finish trouncing these two in charades.

SAM He'll be right out. Sis, what's up? I've never seen so many pills as he's got in there. I didn't knock, I'm sorry. From the look on his face, you'd think I caught him shooting up.

CHLOE John was diagnosed with cancer of the esophagus six weeks ago. We don't talk about it. We're going to fight it. They don't think they can operate. The pills are aggressive therapy. Don't ask me what that means. We're going to fight and hope. Hope and fight.

SALLY Chloe, I'm so sorry.

CHLOE You're not supposed to know. Either of you. He'll kill me.

SAM You're my sister.

CHLOE John sees the world as everyone else and him. We're all against him. A director said to me last month, "Why I believe those are real tears you're crying, Mrs. Haddock! Where did they come from? It's only *Oklahoma!*" "I guess I'm one of those Method actresses you read about,

Jan," I told him. Just one of those Method actresses." (*She begins to cry. Sam takes the tray from her. Sally puts her arms around her. John comes out of the bedroom.*) There he is. There's my man. Now I'm holding you all to your promise. Sally, you go first. It was your turn. You were in last place.

SALLY   We don't have to play anymore—!

CHLOE   I insist. I've been looking forward to it all evening.

SAM   I'm sorry, John, I should have knocked.

JOHN   She hadn't told you?

SAM   Not a word. If there's anything I can—?

JOHN   There is, actually. You can die for me.

SAM   That's not funny.

JOHN   Well then don't ask, my friend.

CHLOE   Come on, Sally, choose a title or a phrase or a—.

SAM   Not a title, for God's sake, don't encourage her.

JOHN   What's happening?

CHLOE   Sshh! No talking. We're beginning. It's Sally's turn. I'm timing her. Ready, set, go! Well go, Sally, don't just stand there. The clock is running. (*Sally is not very good at playing charades. It's an ordeal for her, from beginning to end, but she's trying to be a good sport. Each word costs her great effort and is very painful.*) What are you doing?

SALLY   I don't know.

CHLOE   Have you chosen your category?

SALLY   No.

CHLOE   Sally!

SALLY   I have to choose a category?

CHLOE   You know you do. What were you doing all afternoon? I'm stopping the clock. Now choose a category.

SAM   Honey, if you don't want to play charades—

SALLY   I've got one.

CHLOE You're sure? It's something we've all heard of? I hate *recherché* charades. I'm starting the clock. (*Sally acts out her category.*) A book? A play? A movie?

JOHN A famous disease?

SAM A song title?

SALLY Yes!

CHLOE No, dear, you can't talk, remember? Put your finger on your nose when we guess it. Now how many words in your song title? (*Sally counts on her fingers.*) They say it's going to be nice tomorrow.

SAM This is torture for her.

CHLOE Torture for her?

JOHN I love avoidance!

CHLOE You invented it.

SALLY I think "eight."

SAM What do you mean you "think" eight? Just count them.

SALLY Some are, you know, squished together—I don't know if they're one word or two.

SAM Just make a choice!

SALLY All right, seven!

SAM Seven now!

CHLOE She's not supposed to be talking. I'm sorry but I think there should be a penalty for that.

JOHN I do, too. One multiple sclerosis for Sally.

CHLOE Ignore him, First word.

SALLY I can't do the first word.

CHLOE Then do the second word. (*Sally shakes her head.*) Why not?

SALLY I'm doing the second word. It's "no."

SAM Do the third word, honey.

SALLY I can't. It's too hard.

SAM   Then do the fourth. (*To Chloe.*) I could kill you right now.

CHLOE   All right, we'll play teams. Help her. But hurry up, I'm not stopping the clock. (*Sam goes to Sally. She whispers in his ear.*) Can I get you anything?

JOHN   They know.

CHLOE   I had to tell someone. He's my brother. She's his wife.

SAM (*To Sally.*)   What? Say it again?

SALLY   "There's no business like—"

SAM   Not out loud! That's it. We give up! Forfeit! Let's have another drink! John? Another drink?

CHLOE   What was it, Sally, your song title?

SALLY   "There's no business like the show business."

SAM   There's no "the" in it. It's "There's No Business Like Show Business" period.

CHLOE   That doesn't sound right.

SAM   Of course it doesn't sound right. It's wrong.

CHLOE   No, "There's No Business Like Show Business." There's a word missing. Sally's right, there is a "the" there. "There's No Business Like The Show Business."

JOHN   "There's No Business Like The Show Business." It doesn't make sense without the "the." You don't say "Auto Industry." You say "the" Auto Industry, "the" garment industry.

SALLY   I thought I was right.

SAM   I'm losing my mind! Sing it! "There's no business—"

CHLOE   "—like the show business."

SAM (*Calling to the next house.*)   Let's go to the experts. Excuse me! Yoo-hoo! Fellas!

SALLY   He hates to be wrong.

JOHN   You owe your wife an apology, Sam.

SAM (*Turning away from the next house.*)   They don't hear me. They're all doing the Twist or something.

CHLOE   I doubt if they're doing the Twist. Does that date you! The Twist, Sally!

JOHN   We all agree. You're wrong. Just say it.

SAM   "There's no business like the show business."

CHLOE   Well, if you say it like that—mockingly.

SAM   "There's no business like the show business."

JOHN   Right!

SAM   "There's No Business Like Show Business."

CHLOE   Wrong!

SAM   Yeah? I could have sworn . . .! Are you sure? "There's No Business Like The Show Business." It sounds right now.

JOHN   It *is* right. Talk about stubborn!

SALLY   That's why he grinds his teeth in his sleep. He sets himself against the tide and won't go with it.

CHLOE   When did you start grinding your teeth in your sleep?

SAM   I don't know that I do. This is her opinion.

CHLOE   John grinds his teeth in his sleep.

JOHN   I do not.

CHLOE   I think all men grind their teeth in their sleep. It's their brutal nature expressing itself.

SALLY   If he keeps it up, Dr. Roston says he's not going to have any teeth left. They're getting all worn down. Show her.

SAM   No!

CHLOE   Let me see. Sam! I'm your sister. (*She takes his face in her hands. Sam opens his mouth while Chloe looks in. John looks over her should to see, too.*) Oh my God, you're right. I see what you mean. Like stubs, some of them are. Hold still! What's that?

SALLY (*Looks into Sam's mouth.*)   I don't know what that is. I never saw that before. Sam, when did you get that?

JOHN   It looks like an abscess. (*Sam succeeds in pulling away from Chloe.*)

SAM   Why don't you charge admission and sell tickets! I don't have an abscess. Fuck you!

CHLOE   Keep grinding and you're not going to have any teeth left. You either, Mr. Haddock.

JOHN   I don't grind my teeth.

SAM   Neither do I. I clench my jaws sometimes maybe but I don't get down there and grind.

SALLY   It's a horrible sound. I can't sleep. Tell John how Dr. Roston is treating you.

SAM   No. It's stupid.

SALLY   He wants him to fall asleep saying "Lips together, teeth apart" over and over again to himself.

JOHN   "Lips together, teeth apart"?

SAM   It's very romantic. "What did you say, darling?" "Nothing, dearest, lips together, teeth apart. Do you want to make love tonight? Lips together, teeth apart."

CHLOE   Does it work?

SAM   I don't grind my teeth.

SALLY   He won't even try it. I'm the one who falls asleep saying it for him. "Lips together, teeth apart."

JOHN   I believe you do. That sounds very loving. I'm jealous.

CHLOE   Do you want to fall asleep with me saying that? "Lips together, teeth apart?" I'll do it, lover. I guess this means it's the end of charades?

SALLY   Please, Chloe. We're all dreadful at them.

SAM   Speak for yourself.

JOHN   Look, I don't want my health to be an issue this weekend or any other. With or without cancer I'm still the same person, so there's no reason to change your opinion of me. I mean, riddled with the stuff, I'm still going to be the same rotten son of a bitch. I wish I could change. I really, really, really do. Profoundly. I can't. I just can't. I apologize to all of you. I think maybe you, Sam, the most.

SAM   Why me? Why most of all me?

JOHN   You seem the least defended of all of us.

SAM   I've got Sally.

SALLY   You certainly do.

CHLOE   Look at that moon! I could look at a full moon forever. I mean, next to that, all this is pretty small potatoes.

JOHN   Look next door. Everybody's dancing.

CHLOE   Thank God they still can.

SAM   You want to, honey . . . ?

SALLY   No, thanks, I'll just listen. You go ahead. Dance with Chloe.

SAM   Come on, sis, let's borrow this music. We used to cut a mean rug. May I, John?

JOHN   She's all yours.

SAM   She always has been. (*Sam and Chloe begin to dance. They're very, very good. John comes over and sits by Sally.*)

JOHN   May I?

SALLY   It's a free country. That's what we're celebrating today.

JOHN   They're nice together. I like watching them.

SALLY   The doctors think I'm pregnant again.

JOHN   That's wonderful. It's what you want. What does Sam say?

SALLY   I haven't told him yet. I've disappointed him so many times.

JOHN   It's his?

SALLY   Of course.

JOHN   I'm sorry. I shouldn't have asked that. He'll be very happy.

SALLY   I hope so.

JOHN   Sure he will.

SAM I'm going to dip you now.

CHLOE I've had three children. Don't you dare! (*He dips her.*)

SALLY He knows.

JOHN So does Chloe.

CHLOE John, when we get home I want to get one of those bug lamps. I don't care what Betty Thompson and her ecological goon squads say, I am sick of being eaten to death by mosquitoes.

SAM Sis, you wouldn't!

CHLOE What has a mosquito ever done for me? Zap 'em! "Shut up and dance." That's from *Gypsy*. God, I wanna do that show one day!

SALLY I used to hate that sound.

JOHN The zapping? Me, too.

SALLY Now I find it very comforting.

JOHN Me, too.

SALLY Zap. It's all over. Zap. Peace. Zap. No more pain.

JOHN The end. *La commedia è finita.*

SALLY I can hear our neighbors' even when I'm in bed. They leave it on all night. No mosquitoes on their property! We're swarming with 'em of course. I think they can see the property line. Sam's grinding his teeth, the neighbors' bug lamp is zapping the mosquitoes, God's in His Heaven, or at least our neck of New Jersey, and all's right with the world. I helped David to die. Sam doesn't know that. I don't want him to ever.

JOHN You've got it.

SALLY How sick are you?

JOHN Very.

SALLY I'm sorry.

JOHN Zap.

SALLY Zap. (*They sit quietly and look out to sea. Sam and Chloe are dancing a slow foxtrot now.*)

SAM Sis, I don't want to have children. Don't say anything. I know that's hard for you but just listen: I'm scared they won't love me. I'm scared I won't know how to raise them. Two little eyes looking up at me! Needing me, trusting me. I don't want that responsibility. I don't believe in enough to be a father. I don't have anything to give or teach. I'm empty. I'm just coasting. You don't love "empty." Please, I don't want you to say anything. This isn't about answers.

CHLOE They would love you. You would be a wonderful father.

SAM I wish I could believe that. How am I going to tell Sally?

CHLOE I hope you never will. (*They stop dancing.*)

JOHN Zap.

SALLY Zap.

SAM Maybe you're right, honey. Maybe we should get one of these lamps.

SALLY Zap.

JOHN Zap.

SAM Zap. (*Chloe sees a shooting star on the horizon.*)

CHLOE Look! A shooting star!

SAM Where?

CHLOE There!

SAM Oh!

SALLY Oh!

JOHN Oh! (*They freeze. The opening music, the trio from Mozart's* Così Fan Tutte *is heard again, only this time it comes from all over the theatre. It begins slowly but will get louder and louder. As it gets louder, both the stage lights and the house lights will come up to full intensity. The actors still have not moved. Their eyes are fixed on that distant star, their fingers pointing to it. The stage and the theatre are blazing. Audience and actors are in the same bright light. The music reaches a climax. All the lights snap off.*)

END OF PLAY.

A PERFECT GANESH (1993)

The most beautiful physical realization a play of mine has received is the premiere production of *A Perfect Ganesh* at the Manhattan Theatre Club. In asking designers to take the audience to India—from a room at the Taj Palace Hotel in Bombay to the primordial chaos and serenity of the Ganges at Varanasi to the Taj Mahal itself—I was asking the impossible.

Ming Cho Lee, the set designer; Santo Loquasto, the costume designer and Stephen Strawbridge, the lighting designer, delivered it. So did Carmen de Lavallade and her movement direction.

I considered them collaborators. I had a large vision for this play—the physical journey to India itself and the interior spiritual journey of the two fractured hearts who had gone there to heal, even if they didn't know that at first—and I found the designers who could realize it.

It is one thing for a playwright to type "A small boat on the Ganges River, predawn. It is chilly and foggy. Ganesh is the boatman." I believe it is their job (and their delight) to dream those sorts of big dreams for their plays. But it is quite another to find the fellow theatre artists who can actually realize the writer's vision in the no-nonsense reality of a workable set, affordable costumes and artificial light.

In Shakespeare's theatre, the physical world was entirely defined by the language of the play. The scenery *was* the language. The lighting was the sun. Though they were standing in the pit of the Globe Theatre on the South-bank of London on a hot afternoon, the audience was instead transported to the cool night gardens of Verona as Romeo wooed his Juliet and swore his eternal love by a moon and stars the audience could only see in their mind's eye—but see it they could, as we still do, because of the splendor of the language. The audience designed the set as the tumult of Shakespeare's extraordinary words filled their ears with sights for their mind's eye.

Modern audiences are not so generous with their imagination. They want to see sets and lights that tell them where they are and what time of day it is. With electricity, Edison changed the very nature of theatre and made it "modern" every bit as much as Chekhov did with his revolutions of plot, form and characterization. Today's audience doesn't have to work as hard to "see" a play as Shakespeare's: sets are detailed and multiple, lighting effects are stunning and complex, the actors' voices are often amplified. The audience doesn't lean forward to experience a play; they can lean back in their seats and let the play come to them. In fact, they rather insist on it. An active experience has become a passive one.

A new play in its first production is only as strong as its weakest link. Too often that weakness is an uninspired production design. "A bare stage" is a meaningless stage direction. The audience is always looking at *something* and if what they are looking at is wrong for the play, the play—especially a new one—is compromised.

The excuse is usually financial constraint but the true poverty in most cases is artistic, not economic. I am not against helicopters and falling chandeliers in the theatre. I am for design that is a metaphor for meaning. It can be done for millions of dollars, of course, but it can also be done for thousands, hundreds even. The trouble is it's not done often enough. Spending money isn't the answer. Good design begins with theatre artists with a vision equal to the playwright's. Good designers can take us anywhere in the world (or in the playwright's imagination) on a not-for-profit theatre's budget. I had great designers for *Ganesh* and in Ming Cho Lee I had my first experience of working with an authentic genius. He works in a dimension I don't pretend to understand or could even begin to articulate. Of this I am certain: his work is as perfect as it is inevitable. Once seen, there is no other way but his. And he does it with artistry, not dollars.

I try to work with people I think are smarter than me. It's the only way I'm going to learn something. I don't like being the smartest person in the rehearsal room—it usually brings out the worst in me—and I generally make sure I'm not.

That said, the most mysterious collaboration in the theatre is the one between the playwright and the director. To be honest, I still don't know what directors do. And yet I've learned something from every director I've worked with—and I've worked with many with whom the adjective "great" is commonly invoked. Even if I don't know what these men and women are doing while they're doing it, I know what they've done after they've done it and I'm always grateful and just a little bit mystified by it all.

I know, of course, good directors tell you they like your play and want to direct it. They have "notes." Everyone in the theatre has "notes." That's the least of what a director does for your play. They help you find wonderful actors who will embody in speech and behavior the characters you labored so long to capture in words. They will choose the right design team to support your vision for your play. They will block the play with clarity and elegance. They will run the rehearsal room like a tight ship. They will attend the numerous production meetings to which the playwright is never invited. They will strive to keep everyone focused. They will deal with actors' neuroses. They will not roll their eyes when in the middle of a fraught dress rehearsal with the set falling down and the leading actor not knowing his lines, the actress with the least consequential part asks whether she should wear the blue shoes in the first scene and the red shoes in the second or maybe it should be the reverse? They will be the first to arrive at rehearsals and the last to leave. Directors sort of do everything. Once a play is in rehearsal, they are the ones in charge, which is as it should be.

Eventually, the play will open, and hit or miss, the director will disappear into someone else's play and it's as if they were never there and it's just you and the actors and the text again.

All this I know but I still don't know what directors really *do*. How do they make that unmistakable difference between disaster and success? When do they make the one suggestion that changes everything? What secrets do they whisper to the actors that transform a performance from wrong and tentative to right and confident?

What do they know about my play that I don't?

Anyone who thinks that playwrights know everything about their play is mistaken. We write them; that doesn't mean we understand them. That's not even our job. Elaine May, the first great director I worked with, kept telling me all she cared about was what the characters in *Next* were *doing*, not what they were saying. The dialogue *per se* did not interest her, only the behavior of the characters. That was a tough pill to swallow for a young playwright who flattered himself on how naturally he wrote dialogue. The theatre, she would mutter to herself (but within my earshot), is not about what we say to one another but what we do to each other. Of course she was right but I had to learn that for myself. It's taken years and years and I'm still working on it. Every time I get "stuck" in a scene I think of Elaine and the creative log jam is broken every time.

Frank Galati's production of *Ragtime* stretched my imagination into another dimension of theatrical time and the infinite possibilities of storytelling. Joe Mantello is a harsh taskmaster when it comes to telling the truth. Joe believes you get away with nothing in the theatre and even the smallest dishonesty on the page will eventually come back to bite you in the ass. Hal Prince believes God is in the details and finds Him at every turn. Jack O'Brien understands the continuum that extends from the new American play he is directing on West 42nd St. all the way back to the Theatre of Dionysus in 4th-century BC Athens and doesn't let anyone in the rehearsal room forget it. John Doyle embraces clarity, simplicity and the power of movement to convey the deepest feelings. His "less is more" is enormous.

A Perfect Ganesh was the last time I worked with John Tillinger, a director who had championed so much of my early work and had given play after play of mine successful and honest productions. Joey, as we called him, "got" me and I was both lucky and grateful to have him at my side for most of my years at MTC. We were a team.

To this day, I don't know why I never offered him another play to direct after *Ganesh.* We never quarreled, we certainly never had a disaster. I think the answer might lie in my uncertain understanding of what I expect, let alone can reasonably demand, of a director. Would another director challenge me more? Make me a better playwright? Our familiarity bred no contempt but it wasn't pushing us in new directions either. We were both too much in our comfort zones. Maybe I thought we could never top or better what we had created together with *Ganesh.*

When I offered *Love! Valour! Compassion!* to Joe Mantello, a young actor whose work as a director I had been admiring in the Circle Rep's directors' lab, instead of Joey, I knew it would be a serious, perhaps permanent, rupture in our relationship. I had worked longer and more successfully with Joey than I ever had with anyone else. I am proud of our work together but I think it's a truth that all directors eventually disappoint their playwrights and we decamp before we disappoint *them.* They disappoint us precisely because we can't specifically define what we want from them. We expect them to be benevolent dictators who love us and our plays to death, and wave their magic wands to make all our plays' warts diminish, if not completely disappear. We want a hit, the gorilla in the rehearsal room, whether we can admit that or not.

Joey delivered a definitive production of *Ganesh.* It was his idea to engage Ming Cho Lee to design it and they worked in wonderful tandem to transform the unforgiving basement that was MTC at City Center in those years into boundless and rapturous vistas in which space became time and time became space. We were in a dream of India buffered by the rude world of mortals but tempered by the benevolent, unconditional love of the gentle Hindu god Ganesh.

It was my first chance to work with Zoe Caldwell, who had been my unsuspecting muse for all those years since I first saw her at Stratford while I was a student. I did not write the part "for" Zoe but I knew she would be remarkable in it. She was but I realized in rehearsal I had not written the role she deserved from me. That would come with *Master Class.* Zoe is emphatically not one of us, i.e., a mere mortal. She is a creature of the theatre, a monster, an apparition, a time traveler from Aeschylus to Shakespeare to Chekhov to Merman to Stratford on Avon. *Ganesh,* if nothing else, taught me how to write for Zoe Caldwell.

Frances Sternhagen, who has been described by more than one of her peers as a "perfect" actress, was her costar. I see no reason to qualify my friend's appraisal of her gifts. I would happily cast Frannie in any part she was right for but I wouldn't know how to write a part "for" her.

Fisher Stevens played multiple roles, all of them perfectly. I love actors who aren't shy about "acting" and meet the challenge of being many different people with enthusiasm. I'm not saving money when I write multiple roles for an actor; I'm giving him or her the opportunity to strut their stuff. Fisher strutted magnificently.

And yet the evening finally belonged to our Ganesh, Dominic Cuskern, who—though not a young man—was making his professional debut in this august company of actors. Dominic had moved to New York from London, where we had begun a relationship while I was working on the film of *The Ritz*. Dom was a social worker and a very good one. I had never suspected he wanted to try his hand at acting. When he did, I realized that he had seen the immense satisfaction that a life in the theatre had given me. A life in the theatre is its own reward. You either get that or you don't. Dominic got it. I wrote the part of Ganesh for him, never imagining that he would be cast in it. Instead, his simple honesty made every "experienced" contender for the role seem artificial by comparison. After a preliminary reading of the play, I remember Zoe announcing she didn't know if she wanted to do the play without him.

My favorite memory of the production is Jessica Tandy coming backstage and asking to be introduced to the actor who had played Ganesh. She was wearing a lovely pale rose silk suit. When she went to hug Dominic, he backed away, fearing his elaborate makeup and the grime of his costume would soil her delicate outfit.

"I don't care, I want to hug you," she said and threw her arms around him. When they parted, the suit was definitely stained. She didn't care. She had just hugged a god.

People often tell me *A Perfect Ganesh* is their favorite play of mine. Right now, remembering Jessica Tandy and her hug, it's mine, too. The play is the landscape of my soul. I'm only surprised it took me so long as a playwright to be in touch with my spiritual side. I was too busy writing about the flesh to contemplate the spirit. A trip to India five years earlier led me to thinking about people like *Frankie and Johnny in the Clair de Lune*. By the time of *Ganesh*, *Corpus Christi* was just beginning to stir in my heart and mind. I begin to write a play when I feel it in my gut. After *Ganesh*, that play was *Love! Valour! Compassion!*

A Perfect Ganesh

for Don Roos

A PERFECT GANESH was originally produced by the Manhattan Theatre Club (Lynne Meadow, Artistic Director; Barry Grove, Managing Director) in New York City, June 27, 1993. It was directed by John Tillinger; the set design was by Ming Cho Lee; the costume design was by Santo Loquasto; the lighting design was by Stephen Strawbridge; the sound design was by Scott Lehrer; the movement direction was by Carmen de Lavallade and the production stage manager was Pamela Singer. The cast was as follows:

GANESHA   Dominic Cuskern

MAN   Fisher Stevens

MARGARET CIVIL   Frances Sternhagen

KATHERINE BRYNNE   Zoe Caldwell

CHARACTERS

MARGARET CIVIL
Handsome, good bearing, not noisy.

KATHERINE BRYNNE
Vivid-looking, forthright, an enthusiast.

MAN
Someone else in each scene.

GANESHA
A Hindu god. He has an elephant's head. His body is covered in gilt.

SCENERY

The play takes place during two weeks in India—getting there and coming home, too.

TIME

Now. Or very recently.

ACT ONE

Silence. The lights come up slowly on a stage which has been painted a blinding white. Ganesha is there. He is eating fruit and vegetables his followers have left him as offerings. He looks at us.

GANESHA   I am happy. Consider. I am a son of Shiva. My mother was Parvati. I am a god. My name is Ganesha. I am also called Vighneshwara, the queller of obstacles, but I prefer Ganesha. To this day, before any venture is undertaken, it is Ganesha who is invoked and whose blessings are sought. Once asked, always granted. I am a good god. Cheerful, giving, often smiling, seldom sad. I am everywhere. (*Music. Ganesha begins to gently dance.*) I am in your mind and in thoughts you think, in your heart, whether full or broken, in your face and in the very air you breathe. Inhale, *c'est moi*, Ganesha. Exhale, *yo soy*, Ganesha. *Ich bin; io sono. Toujours,* Ganesha! I am in what you eat and what you evacuate. I am sunlight, moonlight, dawn, and dusk. I am stool. I am in your kiss. I am in your cancer. I am in the smallest insect that crawls across your picnic blanket towards the potato salad. I am in your hand that squashes it. I am everywhere. I am happy. I am Ganesha. They're coming! (*Music stops. Ganesha stops dancing.*) I can see them. I can see everything. They're just outside the International Departures terminal, struggling out of Alan's sensible, metallic blue Volvo station wagon. Not a Sky Cap in sight. George is at home in Stamford watching a desultory quarter-finals match in the Virginia Slims Tournament coming live from Tampa on the Sports Channel. George doesn't particularly like women's tennis but he is paralyzed this evening. He didn't even get up when his wife left. Katharine kissed the top of his head while he let his head roll to his right shoulder so that it connected with, lay against, her right hand resting there. But their eyes didn't meet. "Well, I'm off." He'll miss her, he knows that already, but he doesn't know how much. "You sure you have enough money?" He is always asking her that. (*Lights up on Man. He is George.*)

MAN   You sure you have enough money?

GANESHA   Alan and Margaret tooted once from their driveway. (*An automobile horn sounds off.*) "More than enough. Don't forget to water the ficus." She decided not to say anything about the children. "I'll miss you."

MAN   I'll miss you, too.

GANESHA   Two toots this time. (*The automobile horn sounds again, twice this time: short, staccato toots.*) The Civils aren't the sort of people you like to keep waiting. "I love you. Bye." And she was gone. (*Lights go down on Man.*) She was on her way to India. He would never see her again. (*Lights up on Man. He is an Airlines Ticket Agent now.*)

MAN   Air India announces the departure of Flight 87, direct service to Bombay, with an intermediate stop in London. Now boarding, Gate 10.

GANESHA   You have to imagine the terminal more bustling. (*He lightly claps his hands twice. At once, we hear the hubbub of excited travelers' voices.*) Every seat is taken this evening. A Boeing 747 filled to capacity. It has been for months. It's the feat of Hali where I come from. (Even gods who are everywhere have to come from somewhere!) Entire families are going home for it. Men, women, children. Lots and lots of children. This is Air India, after all! (*He claps his hands again: we at once hear children crying, yelling, laughing, playing.*) Listen to them! How could I not be? Happy, that is. Is there a more joyful sound than children? A more lovely sight than their precious smiles? A sweeter smell than their soiled diapers? *There's* a place to bury one's face and know bliss! But I digress. They're here. (*Margaret enters. She has two large pieces of matched luggage. The bags are on wheels and she has no trouble pulling them along behind her. She also has a small, matching flight bag, and a sturdy, ample purse.*)

MARGARET   Good evening. We're on your flight to Bombay this evening. There's two of us. Business Class. Maharani Class, I think you call it. I believe we already have our boarding passes and seat assignments. (*She hands him the tickets.*) I think we have adjoining seats. Mrs. Brynne has a window seat and I'm on the aisle. 15A and 15B. At least that's what we asked for and the travel agent assured us we had. I can't sit anywhere but an aisle seat. I'm claustrophobic. Actually, I hate to fly. No offense. I'm a terrible flier, but I do it. This *is* the 20th century. Too bad there's not a nice boat to India . . . Oops! Ship, ship, ship; I always do that! . . . to India. That should be 15A and 15B in Business Class. Maharani Class! That's really very sexist. Shame on you. Shame on Air India. Is there a problem?

MAN (*Head never up from his computer keyboard.*)   There shouldn't be. What is the name of the party you're traveling with?

MARGARET   A Mrs. Brynne. Mrs. George Brynne. Katharine Brynne. B–R–Y–N–N–E. I left her at the passenger drop-off with my husband. One of her bags flew open. But she's definitely here. We both are.

MAN   Let me try something. (*He types furiously.*)

MARGARET   Is the flight very full?

MAN   Not a seat.

MARGARET   That's what I was dreading. And lots of lots of children, all screaming and running up and down the aisles all night! When I was their age I was left at home. I wasn't whizzing about from continent to continent, I can tell you that! The 20th century! Isn't it grand, though! From here to India in what? How long is this flight? Something like 18 hours, yes?

MAN   It's closer to 48 hours, actually.

MARGARET   What? 48 hours! They told me it was 18!

MAN   Just a little joke.

MARGARET   Well it wasn't very funny.

MAN   Eighteen swift hours.

MARGARET   That's what I thought.

MAN   Unless of course.

MARGARET   Unless of course what?

MAN   Unless of course nothing! I'm sorry. You looked like someone I could have a few laughs with. I'm sorry. I don't exactly have the most exciting job or life of anyone who ever lived. A few laughs on the way to the graveyard, I suppose that's asking too much in this, the *Götterdämmerung* of American Civilization.

MARGARET   Is there a problem or not?

MAN   Let's hope not.

MARGARET   If you can't give us aisle seats, I'm not going.

MAN   Who made these arrangements?

MARGARET   Our travel agent. Wanderlust Holidays. They're in the Town and Country Mall in Greenwich. A Mrs. Cairn made the booking, Edith Cairn, like the terrier. (*Katharine enters. She has two large, ill-matched suitcases and an alarming amount of "carry-ons": flight bags, a portable computer, a camera and a VCR, and a portable music system.*

KATHARINE   "O for a Muse of fire." If I said it once, I've said it a million times and I'll say it again: "O for a muse of fire" to describe all this. Words fail me. The entire English language fails me. If I feel this way in the terminal can you imagine what I'm going to be like when we actually hit India? I'm sorry, but this all too much for a white woman.

MARGARET   Will you keep your voice down?

KATHARINE   So what's up, doc? What's the story?

MARGARET   We're lost in the computer. Leave it to Edith Cairn. She's your friend. I never liked the woman. Look at me: I'm a wreck. I told this nice young man if I can't have an aisle seat, I'm not going.

KATHARINE   I'm sure we'll be fine, Maggie.

MAN   I've got you on standby, just in case!

KATHARINE   *Gracias. Muchas gracias.*

MAN   *De nada.* Let's try another routing. (*Ganesha has come up behind the ladies and now waits patiently in line behind them. He is wearing a bowler hat and carried a briefcase and* Times *of London.*)

MARGARET   I knew this would happen. A wonderful start to a trip. Tallyho and bon voyage. (*To Ganesha.*)

KATHARINE   We're going to India for two weeks. I told my husband, "Enjoy TNT, AMC and canned tuna fish. I'm out of here."

GANESHA (*Presenting his boarding pass.*)   Excuse me, but am I in order here?

MAN (*After a quick glance.*)   Yes, you're fine. Go right aboard. Have a nice flight, Mr. Smith.

GANESHA   Thank you very much. (*Ganesha departs.*)

MARGARET   This is ridiculous. We booked this flight months ago.

MAN   That was your first mistake. Excuse me. (*He makes another public announcement.*) Air India announces the departure of Flight 87, direct service to Bombay, with an intermediate stop in London. Now boarding, Gate 10.

MARGARET   Look at you: you're exhausted already. I told you not to take so much.

KATHARINE   I'm not exhausted.

MARGARET   None of that is going under my seat. I'm not going all the way to Bombay with my knees up to my chin because you insisted on bringing all that crap with you. I'm sorry, it's not crap. But I'm not going to be your porter, Kitty. You read all the books: travel light. If they had one common theme, one simple message, it was "travel light."

KATHARINE   Let's not fight, Margaret.

MARGARET   We're not fighting. Do you have your passport?

KATHARINE   It's right here.

MARGARET   He's going to want to see your passport. Get it out. (*Katharine starts looking for her passport in one of her travel bags.*) Can I give you one travel tip, Kitty? You should always be ready to show your passport. Keep it someplace where you can get to it quickly, without holding everyone up.

KATHARINE   I'm not holding anybody up, Maggie.

MARGARET   I didn't say you were. It was just a tip. (*To Man.*) How are we doing?

MAN   Have you ever been to Zimbabwe? Just a little joke. We're fine.

MARGARET   That's not your passport, Katharine. That's your international driver's license. *That's* your passport.

KATHARINE   What do I do with it?

MARGARET   Hold on to it.

MAN   Would these reservations be under any other name?

MARGARET   Of course not.

KATHARINE   My maiden name is Mitchell, if that's any help.

MARGARET   Why would I make our reservations under our maiden names, Kitty?

KATHARINE   Hers is Bennett.

MAN (*Making another announcement.*)   This is your final call for Air India's Flight 87, final call. Final boarding, Gate 10. All aboard, please.

MARGARET   Now what exactly is going on here?

MAN   I'm afraid you two ladies have vanished without a trace into the vast nether world of our computer system.

MARGARET   Is that supposed to be funny, too?

KATHARINE   It's not his fault, Margaret. He didn't do it on purpose.

MARGARET   I want those two seats.

MAN   I can't. They're being occupied by a Mr. and Mrs. D.M. Chandra of Hyderabad.

MARGARET   They're our seats. We booked them months ago. Mr. and Mrs. D.M. Whatever will just have to catch the next flight. Or put them in the back of the plane in Tourist Class.

MAN   We don't call it that. We call it Leper Class. All right, all right, Mrs. Civil! I'll tell you what I will do.

MARGARET   No, I will tell you what I will do if you don't give us those seats.

KATHARINE   Give him a chance, Margaret.

MARGARET   No one is sticking me back in Tourist Class with a lot of noisy children and natives. Some of them looked like peasants. Shepherds. I wouldn't be surprised if there were a few goats on board.

MAN   That's honest.

MARGARET   I want to see India my way, from a comfortable seat, somewhat at a distance.

KATHARINE   That's terrible, Margaret.

MARGARET   So, in the inimitable words of my traveling companion, Mrs. Brynne here, what's up doc? What's the story, Air India?

MAN   I'm afraid Business Class is completely full. So is Tourist.

MARGARET   This is outrageous. I'm going to call that travel agent.

MAN   All I have are two seats in First Class, sleeperettes.

KATHARINE   We couldn't possibly afford that.

MAN   It's a complimentary upgrade, Mrs. Brynne. It's our error. Would that be satisfactory?

KATHARINE   Satisfactory? It's fabulous. Thank you. First Class! What's your name?

MAN   Lennie. Leonard Tuck.

KATHARINE   I'm going to write a letter telling them how wonderful you were to us. Tuck. Leonard Tuck. Like Friar Tuck.

MAN   *Gracias.*

MAN   Will First Class be satisfactory, Mrs. Civil?

MARGARET   Of course it will. But I could have been perfectly happy in our own seats.

KATHARINE   What a beginning! What luck! First Class! "O for a Muse of you know what!"

MAN   Abracadabra! (*The computer whirs. Tickets and boarding passes emerge.*) See how easy that was, Mrs. Civil? (*Making another announcement.*) Final call. Air India, Flight 87, direct service to Bombay. Final call, please.

MARGARET   Come on, Katharine. (*She goes.*)

KATHARINE   Goodbye, America. Goodbye, husband and children. Goodbye, Greenwich, Connecticut. Goodbye, Air India terminal. Goodbye, Leonard Tuck.

MAN   Bon voyage, Mrs. Brynne. (*Katharine goes. She leaves one of her flight bags behind. Man closes down quickly and is gone. Ganesha reappears.*)

GANESHA   They're on their way. Well, almost! (*Katharine rushes back on.*)

KATHARINE   My flight bag! I had a flight bag.

GANESHA   She doesn't see it.

KATHARINE   Did anyone see a flight bag?

GANESHA   Or me. I have that power.

KATHARINE   Hello? (*She rushes off at the sound of jets revving up. The sounds will grow.*)

GANESHA   It begins. Well, it all began long ago. World without end, amen, and all that. This particular adventure, I was meaning. These two little, insignificant, magnificent lives. (*He is shouting to be heard over the roar of the jet engines.*) Can you hear me? Did you hear me? I said, these two little, insignificant, magnificent lives! I'll see you aboard at 36,000 feet. Wait for me! (*Sounds reach a deafening volume as Ganesha hurries aboard. The stage is bare except for Katherine's flight bag. Man enters. He is a Thief. He picks up the flight bag and rifles through it as he exits through the audience, scattering things he doesn't want in the aisles. Sounds and lights reach maximum intensity, then quickly level off: the lights to the level of an airplane in the middle of the night; the sounds to the gentle, steady thrust of jet engines at cruising speed.*)

SCENE 2

Margaret and Katharine are seated in the first-class cabin. They both have headsets on. Margaret is watching the movie. Katherine is listening to a cassette.

MOVIE SOUNDTRACK   "I don't think you know what love is. Not real love. Love that enriches, love that lifts up, love that ennobles. I'm talking about love in its profoundest sense. Love as everything."

CASSETTE TAPE   "All right, now that you've visualized your 10 Personal Power Goals, I want you to *choose* them. It's not I *want* to lose weight or I *want* to make a million dollars but I *choose* to meet the perfect mate, I *choose* to drive a Lexus Infinity. Ready? Take a deep breath. Hold it." (*Katharine inhales.*)

MOVIE SOUNDTRACK   "I think you understand obsession. I think you understand control. I think you understand passion. God knows, you know how to pleasure a person with your body. There's a word for people like you—the French have one, every language does—*fatale*."

CASSETTE TAPE   "These are vocal affirmations. I want to hear you. Don't be shy. That's right, I'm talking to *you!* All right, go. I choose—!"

KATHARINE   I choose to be happy.

MARGARET   After all that they're still going to make love!

KATHARINE   I choose to be healthy.

MARGARET   The movies think that's the solution to everything! A lot they know!

KATHARINE   I choose to be good.

MARGARET   I'm very surprised at Air India for showing such a film. I wonder what an Indian thinks when they see—!

KATHARINE   I choose to be—! (*The plane heaves.*)

MARGARET   What was that?

KATHARINE   What was what?

MARGARET   The plane, it jiggled.

KATHARINE   It didn't jiggle.

MARGARET   Well it did something it shouldn't. There it goes again!

KATHARINE   That's just a little turbulence. "I choose—" Now I've forgotten what I choose. "I choose to be happy." I already said that.

MARGARET   I hate this. I hate it, I hate it.

KATHARINE   Just think of it as a bumpy road.

MARGARET   What?

KATHARINE   It will be over soon.

MARGARET   How soon?

KATHARINE   I don't know. Soon. Soon soon.

MARGARET   We should have gone TWA.

KATHARINE   TWA is for sissies. Anyone can go TWA. Air India is an adventure. I feel like we're already there. (*Man appears. He is a Steward.*)

MAN   Ladies! Ssshh! Please. Your headsets, you're too loud. People are sleeping.

KATHARINE   Will you tell my friend we're not going to crash?

MAN   We're not going to crash. That's the good news. The bad news is we'll be starting dinner service just as soon as we're out of this. That was a joke.

MARGARET   I'm quite aware of that. Tell me, does everyone connected with Air India think they're a comedian?

MAN   People think Indians are humorless. They think we're funny but they think we're humorless.

MARGARET   You're not funny and you're not Indian.

MAN   On my mother's side. Her father was born in Calcutta. I was born on Teller Avenue in the Bronx. Whoa! Ride 'em cowboy! That was a good one. It's always a little dicey over the Atlantic this time of the year. (*The plane heaves.*) I better get back to my seat. The pilot has the Fasten Seat Belt sign on for the crew now, too. Excuse me. I shall return with your pickled herring and hot towels. The towels are tastier. (*He goes.*)

KATHARINE   Does he remind you of Walter?

MARGARET   The steward? Not in the least.

KATHARINE I didn't know you were afraid of flying.

MARGARET I've flown over this part of the Atlantic this time of year at least 15 times and it was never like this.

KATHARINE Actually, I like a little turbulence.

MARGARET You're the type who would.

KATHARINE It lets me know we're really up there. If it gets to quiet and still, I worry the engines have stopped and we're just going to plummet to the earth.

MARGARET Can we talk about something else?

KATHARINE Do you want to hold my hand?

MARGARET Of course not.

KATHARINE Do you want some gum?

MARGARET Is it the kind that sticks to your crowns?

KATHARINE I don't know.

MARGARET If it is the kind that sticks I don't want it.

KATHARINE You're out of luck. It must have been in the bag I left in the terminal.

MARGARET What's that?

KATHARINE A whistle. George made me take it. In case we get into any sort of trouble in India, I'm supposed to blow it so help will come. "Who?" I aksed him. "Sabu on an elephant?"

MARGARET Will you keep your voice down? (*The plane heaves, extra-mightily this time.*)

KATHARINE This is ridiculous. Give me your hand.

MARGARET We're all going to die.

KATHARINE Just shut up and say a "Hail Mary."

MARGARET Methodists don't' say "Hail Mary."

KATHARINE We're going to be all right.

MARGARET Ow! That's too tight. (*The turbulence subsides.*)

KATHARINE See?

MARGARET I can bear anything as long as I know it's going to end.

KATHARINE Remember the last year we went to St. Kitts?

MARGARET The men got sick from eating crayfish.

KATHARINE They were *langouste*.

MARGARET They looked like crayfish.

KATHARINE That's not the reason I never wanted to go back there.

MARGARET Alan nearly died. Besides, it was time for a new island.

KATHARINE It was the incident with that little plane.

MARGARET What incident? I don't remember.

KATHARINE Yes, you do! We were swimming in front of the hotel. A small, single-engine plane had taken off from the airport. The engine kept stalling. No one moved. It was terrifying. That little plane just floating there. No sound. No sound at all. Like a kite without a string. I don't think I've ever felt so helpless.

MARGARET I remember.

KATHARINE Finally, I guess the pilot made the necessary adjustments, the engine caught and stayed caught and the little plane flew away, as if nothing had happened, and we finished swimming and played tennis and after lunch you bought that Lalique vase I could still kick myself for letting you have.

MARGARET You've envied me that piece of Lalique all these years? It's yours.

KATHARINE I don't want it.

MARGARET Really, I insist, Kitty. I think I only bought it because I knew you wanted it. That, and I was mad at Alan for some crack about how I looked in my new bathing suit. The plane's stopped jiggling. Smooth as glass now.

KATHARINE I've thought about that little plane a lot. Maybe we were helpless. Maybe we weren't responsible. Maybe it wasn't our fault. But what kept that plane up there? God? A God? Some Benevolence? Prayer? Our prayers? I think everyone on that beach was praying that morning in their particular way. So maybe we aren't so helpless. Maybe we are responsible. Maybe it is our fault what happens. Maybe, maybe, maybe.

MARGARET   Do you want to give me my hand back?

KATHARINE   I'm sorry. Thank you. Did I do that? I *was* holding tight! I'm sorry. (*She kisses Margaret's hand.*) What happened to your liver spots? You used to have great big liver spots.

MARGARET   Will you keep your voice down? I keep begging you to come with me. The man's a genius. And it's paradise there.

KATHARINE   And it costs 3000 dollars a week. I'd rather go to India for my soul than some spa in Orange Country for the backs of my hands.

MARGARET   Happily, you can afford both.

KATHARINE   I keep thinking about Walter.

MARGARET   Why would you do that to yourself?

KATHARINE   I can't help it.

MARGARET   Well, stop. Stop right now. Think about something else. Think about the Taj Mahal. Think about India.

KATHARINE   They say it's like a dream, the Taj Mahal.

MARGARET   I hope it's not like the Eiffel Tower. All your life you look at pictures of the Eiffel Tower and then when you actually see it, it looks just like the pictures of it. There's no resonance when you look at the Eiffel Tower. I'm expecting some resonance from the Taj Mahal. I'll be terribly disappointed if there isn't any. You're humming again, Kitty.

KATHARINE   I'm sorry.

MARGARET   Well you aekd me to tell you.

KATHARINE   All of a sudden, I can't remember when it was built.

MARGARET   It was begun in 1632 and completed in 1654.

KATHARINE   All that reading up on it and for what!?

MARGARET   Do you remember who it was built for?

KATHARINE   Of course I do. Someone's wife.

MARGARET   Everyone knows that, Kitty. What was her name?

KATHARINE   I knew you were going to ask me that. Marilyn? Betty? Betty Mahal? I know who built it. Shah Jahan.

MARGARET   The favorite wife was Mumtaz Muhal.

KATHARINE   Mumtaz, of course! It was on the tip of my tongue.

MARGARET   It took 22 years and 20 thousand workers to build.

KATHARINE   Is this going to be some sort of pop quiz?

MARGARET   I was trying to get your mind off Walter.

KATHARINE   Nothing will ever get my mind off Walter.

MARGARET   This is a wonderful start to a trip!

KATHARINE   I'm sorry. (*She hums a little.*)

MARGARET   Kitty, sshh!, you're doing it. It's nobody's fault. (*Katharine begins to read from a travel brochure she has taken out of her purse.*)

KATHARINE   Now listen to this. (*She reads.*) "Don't drink the water, which means absolutely no ice in your drinks or eating of washed fruit and vegetables." Sounds charming. "Above all be patient. Accept, allow, be."

MARGARET   That's what I've telling you. (*A light comes up on Ganesha. He is sitting on the wing. He wears a leather flight jacket and an aviator's white silk scarf which blows wildly in the rushing wind we can suddenly hear. He waves to Katharine.*)

KATHARINE (*Suddenly.*)   What's out there?

MARGARET   Oh, my God! Out where?

KATHARINE   Out there, On the wing!

MARGARET   I don't want to know.

KATHARINE   Margaret, look!

MARGARET   I don't want to look.

KATHARINE   There's nothing wrong. There's something wonderful. He's beautiful. Just look. (*Man appears. He is an Aging Hippy. He leans over Margaret to look out the window.*)

MAN   What's happening? We on fire? Oh wow!

MARGARET   Do you mind?

KATHARINE   Do you see what I see?

MAN   We don't get shit like this on the back of the plane.

KATHARINE   It looks like an angel. Do you believe in angels?

MAN   Lady, I believe in everything.

MARGARET   If you'd like me to get up, so you two can continue this—

MAN   I was just on my way to the head. You want to see some real fucking angels, pardon the expression, check out the caves in Ajanta. Angels and red monkeys. I didn't believe in shit till I checked out Ajanta.

KATHARINE   Ajanta? Is that on our itinerary, Margaret?

MARGARET   You know it is. Thank you.

MAN   Okay, okay lady. You made your point. I'm going to Peasant Class.

MARGARET   I didn't say a word.

MAN   You didn't have to. It was in the eyes. It's always in the eyes. You have cruel eyes. They're filled with hate. I mean that nicely. I mean that sincerely.

KATHARINE   Now just a minute.

MAN   Your friend needs a good purge in the Ganges. I don't think she's ready for Katmandu yet. There's not enough dope in the Himalayas to mellow that dude out. (*He goes.*)

MARGARET   I hate it when they do that. The first class bathrooms should be for the first class passengers.

KATHARINE   Do you want me to make a citizen's arrest? Relax, Margaret.

MARGARET   When did you get so serene?

KATHARINE   I took a pill.

MARGARET   I don't know why they bother to have classes if they're not going to enforce them.

KATHARINE   You don't have cruel eyes.

MARGARET   Thank you.

KATHARINE   You have beautiful eyes. Don't cry.

MARGARET   I'm not crying. Does it look like I'm crying? (*She puts her headset back on.*)

KATHARINE   People like that don't know what they're saying half the time. That, or they speak before they think. Don't mind them. I've always liked your eyes.

MARGARET   I'm fine, Kitty, I'm trying to watch the movie! (*Katharine watches her a moment, then puts her own headset back on. Ganesha shakes his head and looks up from his newspaper.*)

GANESHA   Lord, Lord, Lord! Little Puck said it best: "Shiva, what fools these mortals be!" Such thoughtless, needless cruelty. Down there on earth, up here at 41,000 feet. (We went high to avoid the turbulence while you weren't looking.) We are the ones who are powerless. We can only sigh and shake our heads. There's serenity in being a god but very little real power. We gave it all to you.

KATHARINE   "I choose to be happy. I choose to be loving. I choose to be good." (*She will repeat this over and over. Tears are running down Margaret's cheeks as she watches the movie. Man appears on the wing of the plane. He is Walter. His clothes are bloodied; his features are battered from the beating which killed him.*)

GANESHA   Hello, Walter.

MAN   Mind if I join you out here?

GANESHA   I'd be honored.

MAN   I really have to draw the line at bad curry and movies about unrepentant heterosexuals.

GANESHA   Heterosexuals aren't so bad. Where would we be without them? Please. (*Man sits on the wing at Ganesha's feet.*)

MAN   What are you?

GANESHA   I take whatever I can get. I'm speaking about affection. Physical love was never my strong suit. I'm not that sort of god. Fag? (*He offers Man a cigarette.*) I'm sorry. The day is over but the melody lingers on! The Hindi word for tobacco is *nanded*.

MAN   *Nanded,* that's a nice word. Well, nicer than "fag." (*They will smoke.*)

GANESHA   I thought that you when we were boarding.

MAN   Where my mother goes, can this one be far behind? Listen, India has got to beat another annual, same old 2 weeks in the Caribbean with the Civils.

GANESHA   Mrs. Civil is inconsolable. You must have heard what happened.

MAN   It served her right.

GANESHA   Look at her. I hate to see a woman cry.

MAN   I don't like Mrs. Civil. Mrs. Civil didn't like me. Let her cry her stone-cold heart out. Mrs. Civil was a bitch. Is. Is a bitch. I'm the was.

GANESHA   Your words are like daggers, Walter. They cause me such pain.

MAN   Different people sing from different charts, old man.

GANESHA   Not half so old and hard as you.

KATHARINE   "I choose to be happy. I choose to be loving. I choose to be good."

GANESHA   Your mother's been thinking about you again.

MAN   I'd like her to stop. I'd like her to forget all about me.

GANESHA   There will never come that day. She loves you. You're her son.

MAN   That's not love. It's guilt that's become a curse. She should have loved me not just for falling down and scraping my knee when I was a little boy but for standing tall when I was a young man and telling her I loved other men. She should have loved me when my heart was breaking for the love of them. She should have loved me when I wanted to tell her my heart was finally, forever full with someone—Jonathan!—but I didn't dare. She should have loved me the most when he was gone, that terrible day when my life was over. (*Katharine has taken off her headset but she will be drawn into the scene.*)

KATHARINE   "I choose to be happy. I choose to be loving. I choose to be good."

MAN   Instead you waited. You waited until late one night, I was coming home, no! to our "apartment" as you always put it; "Two men can't have a 'home,' Walter"; maybe I had a little too much to drink, certainly a lot too much pain and anger to bear—

KATHARINE   I didn't know.

MAN   A car whizzes by. Voices, young voices, scream the obligatory epithets: "Fag. Queer. Cocksucker. Dead from AIDS queer meat."

GANESHA   Oh dear, oh dear!

MAN   I make the obligatory Gay Ninetiess gesture back. (*He gives the finger.*) Die from my cum, you assholes!

GANESHA   Oh dear, oh dear.

MAN   The car stops. The street is empty. Suddenly this art seems obligatory, too. Six young men pile out.

KATHARINE   Black! All of them black!

MAN   No, mother! All of them you!

MARGARET   (*Loudly, because of the headset.*)   I think we saw this movie at Watch Hill!

MAN   Six young men with chains and bats. One had a putter.

KATHARINE   Six young black men! Hoodlums! Two of them had records!

GANESHA   Oh dear! Oh dear! All of you!

MAN   I stood there. It seemed like it took them forever to get to where I was standing. There was a funny silence. Probably because I wasn't scared. I said "Hello." I don't know why. I hated them. I hated everything about them. I hated what they were going to do to me. I knew it would hurt. I wanted it to be quick. So I said "Hello" again. The one with the putter swung first. You could hear the sound. *Whoosh!* Ungh! against the side of my head. I could feel the skull cracking. He'd landed a good one. They all started swinging and beating and kicking. I stayed on my feet a remarkably long time. I was sort of proud of me. Finally I went down and they kept on swinging and beating and kicking, only know it wasn't hurting so much. It was more abstract. I could *watch* the pain, corroborate it. Finally, they got back in their car, not speaking anymore. They weren't having such a good time either anymore, I guess. None of us were. I was just lying there, couldn't move, couldn't speak, when I could hear their car screeching a U-turn and it coming towards me, real fast, just swerving at the last minute, only missing my head by about this much. What I figure is this: they were gonna run me over but at the last second one of them grabbed the wheel. So they weren't 100% animal. One of them had a little humanity. Just a touch. Maybe. If my theory's right, that is. But that's when you waited to love me, mama.

KATHARINE   I always loved you.

MAN   That's when you waited to know it.

KATHARINE   Why are you doing this?

MAN   Let me go. Let us both go.

KATHARINE   I can't. You're my firstborn.

MAN   There's pop. There's Jerry. There's sis and the kids.

KATHARINE   You were my favorite.

MAN   You were mine. We killed each other.

KATHARINE   Where's your scarf? You'll catch a chill without your scarf.

MAN   You sound like Jonathan.

KATHARINE   Give me a kiss.

MAN   No, I don't want to kiss you.

KATHARINE   You will. (*She puts her headset back on.*)

MAN   Pop! I never called dad "pop" in my entire life! It must be the altitude. (*He goes. Margaret takes off her headset in disgust with the movie. She has stopped crying.*)

MARGARET   And they all lived happily ever after. Sure they did. (*She sees that Katharine is crying now. She takes her hand soothingly.*) It's all right. It's all right.

KATHARINE   "I choose to be happy. I choose to be loving. I choose to be good." (*Lights begin to fade on the two women.*)

GANESHA   Oh dear, oh dear! Let's go to India! (*He claps his hands twice. Music. The sound of jet engines will fade away and all we will hear* *are the delicate sounds of a wooden flute. Ganesha has pulled down a map of the subcontinent.*) India, a republic in South Asia; comprises most of former British India and the semi–independent Indian states and agencies; became a dominion in 1947; became fully independent on January 26, 1950, with membership in the British Commonwealth of Nations. Population as of the last census, 813 million. Area: 1,246,880 square miles. Principal language: Hindi. I was born right here. Kerala. The most beautiful part of India. The beaches alone. The temples at Tiruchirappalli (trust me, but don't ask me to spell it). How I was born is a very interesting story. Some say I was created out of a mother's loneliness. Some say I was the expression of a woman's deepest need. I say: I don't know. What child does?

Scene 3

Man appears. He is a porter at the Bombay airport. He has Katharine's and Margaret's luggage on a dolly.

KATHARINE   Wait! Stop! Stop right there! Come back with those!

GANESHA   Excuse me. They've landed and things are getting quite out of hand at the Bombay airport.

KATHARINE   I had eight pieces. Something is missing. One, two, three . . . !

MARGARET   Where's the guide? They said he'd be waiting with a sign with our names on it.

KATHARINE   There's only seven now. I know I had eight.

MARGARET   When we got off the plane, they said he'll meet you at customs. At customs, they said he'll met you just outside customs and there's not even someone to tell us the next place he's not going to meet us!

KATHARINE   I know what's missing: my cassette player with all my tapes. All my Frank Sinatra and Mozart and Cole Porter. This is terrible. Do you speak English, young man? Do you understand? He doesn't speak English. (*Ganesha steps forward to greet them. He is wearing a blazer.*) Mrs. Alan Civil? Mrs. George Brynne?

MARGARET   Thank God!

GANESHA   You're welcome, Mrs. Civil. Just a little joke.

KATHARINE   And you are?

GANESHA   Your representative from Red Carpet Tours. I have a car and driver waiting for you at the curb. Your suite at the Taj Palace is in order. You have a most excellent view of the harbor and the Gate of India. Come.

KATHARINE   I'm missing something. A cassette player and all my tapes.

GANESHA   Did you take her cassette player?

MAN   What do you think?

GANESHA   I think you should give it back to her.

MAN   Get lost, pop.

GANESHA   Is this the impression you want our country to make?

MAN   Well it's a little more honest than yours. "You have a most excellent view of the harbor and the Gate of India." I'll show the ladies a most excellent view of my ass.

KATHARINE   What are they saying?

MARGARET   I don't speak Hindi, Kitty.

KATHARINE   Why are you snapping at me?

MARGARET   I've been up for a day and a half on plane. I'd like to get to our hotel.

KATHARINE   So would I.

MARGARET   I don't know why this should call for a big discussion. What's he saying?

GANESHA   He says he will check the lost and found and bring your player to the hotel if it is returned.

KATHARINE   Returned? That means someone took it!

GANESHA   I meant "found." I translated badly. (*Man starts wheeling the luggage off on his dolly.*)

KATHARINE   Where's he going?

GANESHA   Not to worry. I told him to start loading the boot.

KATHARINE   That's it for the cassette player? Don't I get a receipt, a claim check or something?

GANESHA   Leave everything to me.

MARGARET   What do you want him to do, Katharine? Mrs. Brynne is a loser. I mean she loses things. That came out badly in translation, too.

GANESHA   Come. India and a soft bed await you.

KATHARINE   Just a minute. I want to take all this in.

MARGARET   What is there to take in, Kitty? It's an airport. (*Katharine doesn't budge. Margaret sighs audibly.*) Hurry up if you're going to do that. (*To Ganesha.*) Mrs. Brynne is also something of an enthusiast. (*Margaret and Ganesha start walking off. Katharine will remain.*)

GANESHA   What would like to know about Bombay?

MARGARET   Nearly everything but not right now. I'm too tired.

GANESHA   It's very big, Bombay.

MARGARET   So was China. (*They are gone.*)

KATHARINE   "O for a muse of fire!" I'm not going to let a missing cassette player spoil this. The world is filled with ill–manufactured cassette players from Taiwan but only one me, Katharine Brynne, *née* Mitchell, born too many years ago in a ridiculous place when I consider where I've come, experiencing this one particular and special moment. Look. Attack things with your eyes. See them fiercely. Listen. Hear everything, ignore nothing. Smell. Breathe deeper than you've ever dared. Experience. Be. But above all, remember. Carve adamantine letters in your brain: "This I have seen and done and know." Amen. No, above all, *feel!* Take my heart and do with it what you will. (*She takes a long look at the terminal.*) Yes. (*Lights change to make transition to next scene but Katharine stays where she is. Music. Ganesha appears.*)

GANESHA   There are three people you must know about in my story. (*He pulls down a chart with the appropriate pictures.*) My mother, Parvati (isn't she lovely?), my father, Shiva and me. One day, before I was born, my mother Parvati, was sitting in her bath. She told an attendant to let no one enter, not even Shiva, her lord and master. But Shiva is everyone's lord and master and no one dare stop him from entering his wife's bath. Parvati covered herself in shame, she had no prestige now, but she was angry, too. Some say she decided then and there she must have a gana of her own. A gana is someone obedient to our will and our will alone. No woman had ever had a gana of her own. This is what happened: my mother Parvati gathered the saffron paste from her own body and with her own hand created a boy, her firstborn, her gana, me! Oh how lovely it is to be born! We were so happy! (*Lights have changed. We are in a hotel room.*)

SCENE 4

A hotel room with an overhead fan and a balcony. Margaret is reading from a guide book. Katharine is listening to Ganesha.

MARGARET   I'm a little worried how we're going to handle your poverty, Mr. Vitankar.

KATHARINE   Maggie, please, we're right in the middle of something important.

MARGARET   I thought he was finished.

KATHARINE   I'm sorry, Mr. Vitankar.

GANESHA   It's quite all right. I'm sure you'll be handling it very well indeed, Mrs. Civil. Your poverty is angry. Ours is not. In India, poverty is not an emotion. It's a fact.

MARGARET   What about the status of women in India?

GANESHA   The lot of women in India is very, very dismal. We set you on fire when you don't obey and expect you to set yourselves on fire to show proper mourning when we die. Does that answer your question?

MARGARET   I think so.

KATHARINE   That's dreadful.

GANESHA   But we're a democracy now. That's the main thing to know about us. The largest democracy in the world. So maybe there's hope for you ladies yet. Change things. Vote. Tell us men where to go. You're very tired. We'll continue the story of Lord Ganesh tomorrow.

KATHARINE   You have so many gods! Keeping them straight! Vishnu, Parvati, Ganesh! He sounds like a Jewish food.

GANESHA   No offense, but Lord Ganesha is better than a bagel.

KATHARINE   We're not offended. We're not Jewish.

GANESHA   Tomorrow morning then? Eight o'clock. (*Man is now a Waiter. He carries a tray with two Coca-Colas.*) The ladies asked for Diet Pepsi.

MARGARET   That's all right.

MAN   The ladies are very fortunate to get anything at this hour.

GANESHA You are a very rude waiter, young man.

MAN We're a union now. I don't have to be polite anymore.

GANESHA He said the hotel is out of Diet Pepsi and a million apologies.

MARGARET It's a wonderful language. It almost sounds like Japanese.

MAN What is she saying?

GANESHA She agrees. You're a very rude waiter, young man. Shame on you.

MAN Shame on me? Shame on you. These are Jew Christian old whores with white saggy skin. Their shit is on your tongue from all the ass licking. You are no Indian. You are no one. Tell them in your perfect English that I'm waiting for my tip. For another 20 rupees I will fuck them.

MARGARET See what I mean, Kitty? It's more the rhythm than the sound of Japanese. (*Ganesha gives Man a tip.*)

MAN Thank you, Papa India. Thank you, *babu*. I smile at the ladies. I exit the room backwards and bowing. I wish the old bags a good night. (*He smiles and is gone.*)

MARGARET Thank you.

KATHARINE *Muchas gracias!*

MARGARET That smile! Those wonderful teeth against that wonderful dark skin! It's like ebony. No, mahogany! Are all Indian men such heartbreakers, Mr . . . .I'm sorry.

GANESHA Mr. Vitanker. (*The telephone rings.*)

KATHARINE (*She answers phone.*) Hello? Hello?

MARGARET Till tomorrow then, Mr. Vitanker. Good night.

GANESHA (*Taking his leave.*) Mrs. Civil, Mrs. Brynne.

KATHARINE (*Still into phone.*) Hello? (*To Ganesha.*) Good-bye! *Gracias! Muchas gracias!*

GANESHA *De nada.*

KATHARINE (*Back into phone.*) Hello? There's no one there.

GANESHA   Now you're truly in India. (*He bows, backs himself out of the room, much as the Man/Porter did.*)

MARGARET   Really, Katharine!

KATHARINE   What?

MARGARET   That is so patronizing!

KATHARINE   What is?

MARGARET   Speaking Spanish to an Indian. What is that? Your generic Third World "thank you?"

KATHARINE   I'm sorry, but I didn't know the word for "thank you" in Hindi.

MARGARET   Well, it isn't *gracias*!

KATHARINE   He knew what I meant.

MARGARET   He would have known what you mean in your native language. *Gracias* reduces him to the level of a peon and you to that of a horrid tourist.

KATHARINE   My intention was to thank him, Margaret. On that level I think *gracias* was highly effective. Now which bed would you like?

MARGARET   It's really of no interest to me.

KATHARINE   I wish you would adopt such a generous attitude towards me. I'll take this one then. I hope you remembered the alarm clock. That was your responsibility! (*They have begun to unpack.*)

MARGARET   I'm sorry, but if we're going to travel together you've got to understand something about me. I'm very sensitive to the feelings of others.

KATHARINE   You could have fooled me.

MARGARET   Frankly, you've said and done several things that have offended me since we got on the plane. No, "offended" is too strong a word. Let's say "embarrassed." There! I've said it and I'm glad. The air is cleared.

KATHARINE   Don't stop now, Margaret, I'm all ears.

MARGARET   You're sure?

KATHARINE   Absolutely! If we're going to "travel together" for the next two weeks, let's have absolute candor. I hate that outfit.

MARGARET   Be serious! That remark about Jewish food just now. I could have died. Comparing one of their gods to a bagel.

KATHARINE   He compared him to a bagel. I only said he sounded like something Jewish you ate.

MARGARET   Will you keep your voice down?

KATHARINE   No! And stop staying that. I'm sick and tired of being told keep my voice down when I am not in the wrong. And even if I were in the wrong, you have no business telling me to keep my voice down. I am not your cowed daughter or your catatonic husband and I am not about to become your cowed and catatonic traveling companion. I'm me. You're you. Respect the difference or go home. I came to India to have an adventure. This is not an adventure. This is the same old Shinola.

MARGARET   Well it's nice to know what your best friend really thinks of you. And your family.

KATHARINE   I didn't mean that. I'm very fond of Joy. And Alan's just quiet around us. I'm sure he's quite talkative when you two are alone.

MARGARET   Not especially.

KATHARINE   I'll give you "O for a muse of fire." I probably do it just to annoy you, like you and the Lalique.

MARGARET   Every time you say it, I say to myself "O for someone who didn't say 'O for a muse of fire' at the drop of a hat."

KATHARINE   It wouldn't bother me if you did.

MARGARET   Well that's the difference between us.

KATHARINE   If you can't respect it, at least observe it.

MARGARET   You've changed. Ever since you went to those lectures in Bridgeport. Nurturing your Inner Child! You know what I say? Stifle him! If we all nurtured our inner child, Katharine, this planet would come to a grinding halt while we all had a good cry.

KATHARINE   Well maybe it should. (*There is a pause. They are each lost in their own particular thoughts. When they take a breath and sigh, it will be together.*)

MARGARET   "O for a muse of fire" is right! Bartender, one fiery muse, a decent analyst and an extra-dry gin martini.

KATHARINE   Don't' say that. I think it's wonderful what you've done. I couldn't have done it.

MARGARET   I finally know what the skin of your teeth means. It's a layer you don't want to be involved with. Anyway, I'm sorry I let it get under my skin. Not you, "it."

KATHARINE   It's Shakespeare. "Muse of fire."

MARGARET   I know that. That is so patronizing to tell me it's Shakespeare!

KATHARINE   I didn't know until they showed it on Public Television. It's the first line of *Henry V.* How hard it is to really describe anything. And I have trouble, don't you?

MARGARET   I don't know. Probably.

KATHARINE   "Muse of Fire" is my talisman. It's my way of telling myself "Savor this moment, Katharine Brynne *née* Mitchell. Relish it. It is important. You'll never be here or feel this way again."

MARGARET   This is what I mean. Those lectures in Bridgeport.

KATHARINE   That's not nurturing my Inner Child. It's Shakespeare. Telling you you can be a pain in the ass is nurturing my Inner Child.

MARGARET   Now I'm a pain in the ass! (*They have finished unpacking and will now begin to make ready for bed.*)

KATHARINE   I didn't say you were a pain in the ass. I said you could be a pain in the ass. I'm hoping the next two weeks you won't be. (*The phone begins to ring. This time Margaret will answer it.*)

MARGARET   I have never been a pain in the ass for two entire weeks. Have I? (*Into phone.*) Hello?

KATHARINE   That's right, we were only in Barbados for 11 days.

MARGARET   Blame that trip on Barbados, not me! Hello?

KATHARINE   Everyone's toilet was broken.

MARGARET   Seven years later she throws Barbados in my face! Hello? (*She hangs up.*) There's no one there.

KATHARINE   I hope you haven't come to India for their telephones *or* the plumbing!

MARGARET   There you go again! Patronizing! I've come to India for personal reasons. Just as you've come for yours.

KATHARINE   I thought we came to India for a vacation.

MARGARET   I adore you, Kitty, even when you're impossible.

KATHARINE   No, you don't. I don't think we are best friends. I don't think we know each other at all.

MARGARET   I'm sorry you feel that way. I feel very warmly towards you.

KATHARINE   I know. Me, too.

MARGARET   It's going to be fine. From this moment on, we're going to get along famously and become the very best of friends.

KATHARINE   Who says?

MARGARET   My Inner Child. Do you mind if I nip in the loo first?

KATHARINE   Where do you think we are, luv, the Dorchester? (*Margaret goes into the bathroom area of their hotel room.*) We have a balcony. Did you know we had a balcony? We have two of them! (*She steps forward onto the balcony.*)

MARGARET   How does the rest of it go? Do you know? "O, for a muse of fire" *what*? (*Katharine stands looking at the harbor in front of the hotel. She is overwhelmed by what she sees.*)

KATHARINE   "O, for a muse of fire, that would ascend The brightest heaven of invention!" (*Margaret screams in the bathroom.*)

MARGARET   Don't mind me. It's only a water bug the size of a standard poodle.

KATHARINE   "A kingdom for a stage, princes to act, And monarchs to behold the swelling scene!" Well something like that. (*The Man has appeared on the adjoining balcony. He is Harry, a young man.*)

MAN   Very good.

KATHARINE   Hello.

MAN   Hi. Fairly spectacular, isn't it? Especially this time of almost-morning, not-quite-dawn. We couldn't sleep.

KATHARINE   We just got in.

MAN   "Then should the warlike Harry, like himself, Assume the port of Mars; and at his heels, Leashed in like hounds, should famine, sword, and fire Crouch for employment."

KATHARINE   Very good yourself!

MAN   I have no idea what it means: "Crouch for employment?"

KATHARINE   I like the sound of it.

MAN   I did that part! I wore red tights and everyone said I had terrific legs. No one mentioned my performance.

KATHARINE   You're an actor?

MAN   For one brief shining hour in college. I'm a doctor. Or I was. I'm sick now. A physician who cannot heal himself.

KATHARINE   I'm sorry.

MAN   "But pardon, gentles all
    The flat unraised spirits that hath dared
    On this unworthy scaffold to bring forth
    So great an object." Deedle-diddle-dee.
    You've got to help me here.

KATHARINE   "Can this cockpit hold
    The vastly fields of France? Or may we cram
    Within this wooden O" . . .
    That's my favorite part.

MAN   Me, too. "This wooden O!"

KATHARINE   "Within this wooden O the very casques"—

MAN (*Very loud and heroic.*)   "That did affright the air at Agincourt?" (*His last words ring in the night air.*)

MARGARET   Kitty? What's going on out there?

MAN (*Over his shoulder.*)   Okay, we'll keep it down, Ben. Sorry. (*To Katharine.*) He's got his hands full with this one.

KATHARINE   So does Mrs. Civil.

MAN   You're traveling with someone you call Mrs. Civil? This is very Tennessee Williams or very Dickensian, I can't decide which.

KATHARINE   Well I don't call her Mrs. Civil. Her name is Margaret. I'm Katharine, Kate, Kitty, I've been called everything. I prefer Katharine.

MAN   Hello, Katharine, I'm Harry.

KATHARINE   Katharine Brynne.

MAN   Harold Walter Strong.

KATHARINE   I had a son named Walter.

MAN   I'm sorry.

KATHARINE   Me, too.

MAN   How long has it been?

KATHARINE   Three years, feels like yesterday. Is that the Gate of India?

MAN   It was built for Queen Victoria's Jubilee Visit to her prize colony. She never came. I guess she had something better to do. The British have a real attitude problem when it comes to anyone else, especially wogs. (Their not-so-nice word for people of a certain color.) God knows, they loathe us. (I'm assuming you're a Yank.) All that "luv" and "darling" and "Ta-ta, duckie" and they hate our guts. Ask me how I know all this? Did I spend a term at Oxford? No. Did I rent rooms for the season in Belgravia? No. I'm talking off the top of my head. It's just a feeling I have. I'll shut up and watch the sun rise over Bombay Harbor with you. (*By now we should be aware that Katharine is humming again.*) What's that you're humming?

KATHARINE   Oh, nothing, I'm sorry.

MAN   "Blow the Wind Southerly," right?

KATHARINE   I don't know.

MAN   It is. I love that song. (*He begins to sing it.*)

KATHARINE   Please. Don't. I couldn't bear it. It was my son's favorite song.

MAN   I understand. I'll tell him he had good taste in music and mothers.

KATHARINE   Don't talk like that. (*Ganesha comes out on the terrace with Man.*)

GANESHA   You're barefoot. Where are your slippers? And your robe! You're drenched. Jesus! You're soaking wet.

MAN   This is Ben, Katharine. He worries about me. That's all right, I worry about him. We're neither of us terribly well.

GANESHA   Hello, Katharine, Excuse me. You're burning up.

MAN   I'm freezing actually! (*Margaret comes out of the bathroom area of their room. She is brushing her teeth.*)

MARGARET   It's all yours, Kitty! (*She will go out onto another balcony off their hotel room.*)

GANESHA   I'll get your robe.

MAN   I can do it. (*They exit, Ganesha supporting Man.*)

MARGARET   I said it's all yours. I picked up Crest gel instead of their toothpaste. I'm always doing that. I think they make the boxes almost identical to confuse people. I hate gel. It sticks to my fingers. I guess that's the Gate of India, Bombay Harbor, and the Indian Ocean beyond. I guess we're here. We're really, really here. What is all that down there, Kitty? In the square, the plaza, in front of the hotel and around the Gate? It's like something moving.

KATHARINE   It's people sleeping.

MARGARET   It's too dense for people.

KATHARINE   It's people.

MARGARET   Then it's all people. There's no place we're seeing the pavement then. Wall-to-wall people.

KATHARINE   I think it's beautiful.

MARGARET   I'm sure they don't. Excuse me, I've got to spit again. (*She goes back to bathroom area.*)

KATHARINE (*Singing softly to herself.*)
"Blow the wind southerly, southerly, southerly
Blow the wind south o'er the bonny blue sea.
Blow the wind southerly, southerly, southerly
Blow bonny breeze my lover to me.

(*She has trouble continuing. Ganesha has appeared on an adjoining balcony.*)

They told me last night there were ships in the offing
And I hurried down to the deep rolling sea.
But my eye could not see it, wherever might be it
The bark that is bearing my lover to me."

GANESHA   Don't stop.

KATHARINE   I'm sorry. I should have realized. Everyone's doors are open.

GANESHA   My wife said, "Listen, Toshiro. Listen, an angel is singing."

KATHARINE   I'm hardly an angel, I have the voice of a frog and truly, I didn't mean to wake you.

GANESHA   Why are you crying, Mrs. Brynne?

KATHARINE   I'm not crying.

GANESHA   May I assuage your tears?

KATHARINE   I said, I'm not crying.

GANESHA   I would like to help you.

KATHARINE   How do you know my name?

GANESHA   We were going through customs. I see I made very little impression. Permit me to introduce myself again. Toshiro Watanabe of Nagasaki. My wife is Yuriko.

KATHARINE   If you say so.

GANESHA   Be care of India, Mrs. Brynne. Be careful here. If you're not, you may find yourself here.

KATHARINE   You sound like someone in a very bad novel or movie or play about India.

GANESHA   Lord knows we've had our fill of them.

KATHARINE   I came to India because I didn't want to go to some mindless resort in the Caribbean with our two husbands for the 90th year in a row and the children and the in-laws and the cats and the dogs and the turtles are all out of the house or dead or married and no one is especially depending on me right now. This is my turn.

GANESHA   Why India?

KATHARINE   Why not?

GANESHA   Why not the Grand Canyon? Why not Niagara Falls? What not Disneyland? Why India?

KATHARINE   I heard it could heal. And now I sound like someone in a very bad novel or movie.

GANESHA   What part of you needs healing, Mrs. Brynne?

KATHARINE   I thought you Japanese were very circumspect. You go right for the jugular, Mr. . . .

GANESHA   Watanabe. I am one singular Nipponese, Mrs. Brynne! (*Man is heard calling off to Ganesha.*)

MAN   Toshiro!

GANESHA (*Over his shoulder.*)   I'm coming, Buttercup. I'm coming! (*To Katharine.*) You think it is only your heart that is broken. May I be so bold as to suggest it is your soul that is crying out in this Indian dawn. Hearts can be mended. Time can heal them. But souls . . . ! Tricky, tricky business, souls. I wish you well. You've come to the right place. *Ciao*, Mrs. Brynne, *sayonara*. (*He goes. Margaret returns. She is in a nightgown. She goes to "her" adjoining balcony.*)

MARGARET   Sorry I took so long. I . . .

KATHARINE   What?

MARGARET   Never mind. It's all yours now.

KATHARINE   This view is extraordinary. See? They are people. Thousands and thousands and thousands of people.

MARGARET   It's more like hundreds, Kitty. Dreadful! Well, don't say they didn't warn us. We were warned!

KATHARINE   Extraordinary!

MARGARET   I thought I heard voices out here. Were you talking to someone?

KATHARINE   Our neighbor, one very outspoken Jap.

MARGARET   Oh my God, I hope you didn't call him that, Kitty! To his face!

KATHARINE   I don't remember.

MARGARET   They're not Japs, you don't call them Japs anymore, the war is over! They're Japanese. You're going to start an international incident.

KATHARINE   I think I called him an Oriental.

MARGARET   That's just as bad. It's worse. Oriental conjures up flying carpets, Sheherazade and chop suey.

KATHARINE   Whatever I called him, he didn't seem to mind.

MARGARET   Then he was being polite. Everyone minds being called something.

KATHARINE   Can we just enjoy this?

MARGARET   We should be sleeping.

KATHARINE   I'm too excited to sleep. Let's go down there.

MARGARET   What? Are you mad? Do you know what time it is?

KATHARINE   I just want to walk among them. Experience them.

MARGARET   You can experience them from up here.

KATHARINE   Don't you feel drawn to be a part of all that?

MARGARET   No.

KATHARINE   Come with me. Before it gets light. They won't know we're tourists.

MARGARET   I'm not dressed.

KATHARINE   I'm scared to do it alone.

MARGARET   I'm scared to do it with an army. You can't just throw yourself into a mob of homeless, dirty, disease-ridden beggars your first hour here, Kitty.

KATHARINE   Who says?

MARGARET   What if there are lepers down there?

KATHARINE   I hope there are. Yes or no?

MARGARET   No.

KATHARINE   I'll wave up at you. (*She goes.*)

MARGARET   Katharine! (*Almost at once the phone begins to ring.*) Hello? Hello? (*She hangs the phone up. She goes back onto the balcony. Ganesha has come back onto an adjoining balcony. He is wearing a colorful silk kimono.*)

GANESHA   My husband said you were upset. May I be of help?

MARGARET   Your husband was talking to my traveling companion, Mrs. Brynne.

GANESHA   Ah! And you? What about you?

MARGARET   I'm fine. No I'm not. That's a beautiful wrap.

GANESHA   What's wrong?

MARGARET   I'm not very good at keeping an eye on people. They rush out into danger and I'm helpless to save them. I've just lost Mrs. Brynne in that still sleeping, just stirring crowd down there.

GANESHA   Your friend is in no physical danger.

MARGARET   Is there any other kind?

GANESHA   Yes. I heard you cry out in the bathroom. I'm sorry, but the air vents, I couldn't help but hear.

MARGARET   Oh, that! An enormous insect. I'm terrified of bugs. I'm sure the entire hotel heard me.

GANESHA   Twice you cried out. The second time was very soft. "Oh!" you went, just "oh!"

MARGARET   There's a lump in my breast. I keep hoping it will go away. From time to time I touch it and it's always larger.

GANESHA   May I? (*Margaret allows Ganesha to touch her.*)

MARGARET   My first night in India and I'm allowing a strange woman in a gorgeous silk kimono that I covet—it's the other one—to touch my right breast. There you are. Home base. Feel it?

GANESHA   Oh!

MARGARET   You don't have to say anything.

GANESHA   Does your friend know?

MARGARET   She has enough troubles. We both do.

GANESHA   You're a very sad woman, Mrs. Civil. I'm so sorry.

MARGARET   Everyone thinks I'm a bossy bitch.

GANESHA   It's a clever defense.

MARGARET   I even fool Alan. Kitty's the one everyone loves. People like Kitty just have to be born to be loved. I've always had to work at it. I had my big chance and blew it. A son, my firstborn. His name was Gabriel. Such a beautiful name. Such a beautiful child. Gabriel. Never Gabe. Alan chose it. I used to love just saying it. Gabriel. Gabriel.

GANESHA   What happened?

MARGARET   I don't want to tell you. Where's Kitty? I don't see Kitty. We were in a park, Abigdon Square, Greenwich Village, in New York City. You wouldn't know it.

GANESHA   Where Bleecker and Hudson and 8th Avenue all converge just above Bank Street. Go on.

MARGARET   I'd just bought him a Good Humor bar. Maybe you know them, too?

GANESHA   Oh, yes; oh, yes! They're "sclumptious!"

MARGARET   His little face was covered with chocolate. I took a handkerchief out of my purse and wetted it with my tongue to clean his face. He pulled away from me. "No!" I pulled him back. "Yes!" Our eyes met. He looked at me with such hate . . . no! anger! . . . and pulled away again, this time hurting me. I rose to chase him but he was off the curb and into the street and under the wheels of a car before I could save him. Isn't that what mothers are supposed to do? Save their children. His head was crushed. He was dead when I picked him up. I knew. I wouldn't let anyone else hold him. They said I carried him all the way to the hospital a few blocks away. I don't remember.

GANESHA   St. Vincent's. It's very famous. Dylan Thomas and Billie Holiday died there. I'm sorry.

MARGARET   He was four years old. Gorgeous blond curls I kept long— you could then. I think he would have grown up to be a prince among men.

GANESHA   All mothers do.

MARGARET   Do you have children?

GANESHA   No, and sometimes it is a great sadness to me. But only sometimes.

MARGARET   I don't know why I told you this. Strangers in the night. Scooby-dooby-do.

GANESHA   No, new friends in the Indian dawn.

MARGARET   I've never told anyone about Gabriel. His brother and sister who came after. What would be the point? Alan and I never talk about it. This was years and years and years ago. We moved, we started a new family. I have another life. I wish I saw Kitty down there. The woman who drove the car was a black woman. We called them Negroes then. It wasn't her fault. She was devastated. I felt so sorry for her. During the service, Episcopalian, Alan's side of the family insisted, we're simply Methodist, we all heard a strange sound. Very faint at first. (*Ganesha has begun to hum the spiritual, "Swing low, sweet chariot."*) We weren't sure what we were hearing or if we were hearing anything at all. I thought it was the organ but we hadn't asked for one. It was the Negro woman whose car struck my son. She'd come to the funeral. I don't know how she heard about it. She was sitting by herself. She was sitting by herself in a pew at the back. She was just humming but the sound was so rich, so full, no wonder I'd thought it was the organ. The minister tried to continue but eventually he stopped and we all just turned and listened to her. Her eyes were closed. Tears were streaming down her cheeks. Such a vibrant, comforting sound it was! Her voice rose, higher and higher, loud now, magnificent, like a bright shining sword. And then the words came. (*She sings in a voice not at all like the one she just described.*)

> "Swing low, sweet chariot,
> Comin' for to carry me home.
> Swing low, sweet chariot,
> Comin' for to carry me home."

(*Ganesha joins her.*)

> "Swing low, sweet chariot,
> Comin' for to carry me home.
> Swing low, sweet chariot,
> Comin' for to carry me home."

GANESHA   You're shivering. Here. Put this on. Lovely! It's yours! (*He puts the kimono over her shoulders.*)

MARGARET   I couldn't.

GANESHA   Please, I insist.

MARGARET   It's not wanrranted, such kindness. (*Lights come up on Katharine and Man in a different part of the stage. They are "walking" down the street as they talk. A turntable would be useful to accomplish this effect of walking and talking.*) There she is!

KATHARINE   This is wonderful. Even more wonderful than I'd imagined. Sshh! We don't want to wake them. The light will do that soon enough. We have all this just to ourselves for a little while longer and then we'll disappear into it. Are you scared?

MAN   No. Am I nervous? Yes. Am I ready to run like hell back up to my room and Ben? You bet. Careful!

KATHARINE   I thought it was a—

MAN   It's a person.

KATHARINE   We must hold hands and we must never let go of each other.

MAN   It's a deal. Are you always so adventurous?

KATHARINE   Almost never. It's India.

GANESHA   That young man is going to die soon. So is his gentleman friend.

MARGARET   Must they?

GANESHA   Yes.

KATHARINE   Is this too fast for you?

MAN   Well maybe a tad, Mrs. Brynne.

KATHARINE   You must call me Katharine and we shall be great friends forever and ever.

MAN   It's going to be a scorcher.

KATHARINE   Have you done Elephanta Island yet?

MAN   On our first day. Frankly, I was disappointed. They're Buddhist. I came to India for the Hindu stuff. Ben adored them. Of course, I fell, which didn't exactly help the festivities. Be careful getting off the ferry.

KATHARINE   Thank you. We will.

MARGARET (*To Ganesha.*)   Why must they die?

GANESHA (*With the slightest of shrugs.*)   Why not?

MAN   I'm afraid my Ben is going to be rather annoyed with you when he finds out I joined you down here in the madding crowd. He prefers to stay far from it. I've been dying to do this all week. (*He looks up and see Margaret and Ganesha on the balconies looking down at them.*) Look up there! We're being watched. (*He calls up to Ganesha.*) Good morning! Thank your husband for the cough syrup. It was very helpful.

KATHARINE   She can't hear you.

MARGARET   Kitty! Up here!

GANESHA   She can't hear you. Excuse me. I'm wanted elsewhere.

MARGARET   I can't accept this. You must let me give you something.

GANESHA   There's no need.

MARGARET   Do you smoke? I brought scads of cigarettes.

GANESHA   *Sayonara*, Mrs. Civil.

MARGARET   Goodbye. (*He goes. Margaret remains on the balcony. During the following, although the stage is almost bare, we will hear the sounds of many, many people. Dogs barking. Vendors. Intense crowds. India. Katharine and Man have reappeared on the street below Margaret's balcony.*)

KATHARINE   I don't believe it, Harry! Almost the first thing I see in India and it's a cliché. I asked for a Muse of Fire and I get a bloody snake charmer!

MAN   Since when is a man in rags squatting on the pavement playing a wooden flute making a cobra coil out of a straw basket such a cliché for a lady from Connecticut? Can we stop a minute?

KATHARINE   I'm sorry. People probably think I'm your mother.

MAN   I'm sure my own mother wishes you were.

KATHARINE   What do you mean?

MAN   We don't get on. Let's keep walking. They're starting to wake up. You'll be getting the good ol' rope trick next!

KATHARINE   It serves me right. Thinking I would find India, experience it, my first morning here. But you see, Harry, I have a dream of this place, a dream of India.

MAN   I think we all do who come here, Katharine. Mine's easy. I want Ben and I to get well. If there's a choice, me first. I'm petty.

KATHARINE   No, you're not. My dream of India is this: that I am engulfed by it. That I am lost in a vast crowd such as this and become a part of it. That I'm devoured by it somehow, Harry.

MAN   I understand.

KATHARINE   It's a terrifying dream but I have to walk through it. It's a dream of death, but purgation and renewal, too. (*A light has come up on Ganesha sitting on the ground in a beggar's attitude. As Katharine moves towards him, the Man will recede as she leaves him behind.*) Look! (*Ganesha takes off his elephant's head. It is the first time we have seen his face. He is a leper. He is hideous.*) When I was a very young woman I wrote something in my diary that I've never wanted anyone to know until now. This was before George. Before Walter. Before any of them. This is what I wrote, Harry. (*Harry is gone by now.*) "Before I die, I want to kiss a leper fully on the mouth and not feel revulsion. I want to cradle an oozing, ulcerous fellow human against my breast and feel love." Katharine Mitchell. (*Ganesha has opened his arm to her, half-begging, half-inviting her to come to him.*) That's why I've come to India. I don't think I can do it, Harry. (*She turns for support. He isn't there.*) Harry? Harry?

MARGARET (*Waving wildly.*)   Kitty, come up now! It's getting light!

KATHARINE   Harry, where are you? Of God, if he's fallen somewhere in this crowd. Harry! (*The sounds of India are getting louder and louder. It is the roar of a vast multitude, the tumult of humanity. It's more like a vibration than a sound. Ideally, we will all feel it as well as hear it.*)

MARGARET   Kitty! Look up here! I'm calling you!

KATHARINE   Harry! Please! Don't do this! Where are you! Margaret!

MARGARET   She can't hear me. Something's wrong. Just come up now! (*Katharine begins to blow on the whistle George gave her.*)

MARGARET   Kitty! Kitty! Kitty!

KATHARINE   Please, someone, help!

MARGARET   I can't hear you . . . Kitty, Kitty . . .

KATHARINE   I've lost someone, a young man, he's not well, he may have fallen. (*She blows and blows the whistle, as Margaret continues to call down from the balcony. The roaring is almost unendurable. Ganesha claps his hands together once and all sounds stop. Twice and the others all freeze. The third time and all the lights snap off.*)

END OF ACT ONE

ACT TWO

SCENE I

Another hotel room. The telephone is ringing wanly. We can also hear the sound of Margaret being sick in the bathroom off. Ganesha is working a carpet sweeper over a patch of very old, very thin rug. As he works, he watches a Hindi soap opera on the television set. The Man enters, using a passkey. He is carrying a tray of fresh fruit. He is the Hotel Manager.

MAN Knock, knock.

GANESHA Who's there?

MAN Mahatma.

GANESHA Mahatma who?

MAN Mahatma Gandhi! (*They roar with laughter.*)

GANESHA Very good, Mr. Biswas, very droll! (*To us.*) Humor does not travel well. Especially Indian humor. "You had to be there" is, I believe, your word for it. Well, five words actually. You have to be here, I'm afraid.

MAN What are you watching?

GANESHA *The Ramayana.* It's very sad. Valmiki's wife is dying. She sent for their firstborn to bless him before she dies. My husband says I cry at everything.

MAN The actress playing her has fine breasts. Do you know what they call them in Boston? Jugs. The actress playing her has very fine jugs. (*Phone stops ringing but Man picks it up anyway.*) Hello? Hello? (*He hangs up.*) Bloody phone system. Bloody Third World. Bloody India. Why is it so dark in here? Are they here?

GANESHA The nice one.

MAN Mrs. Brynne?

GANESHA Mrs. Civil.

MAN (*Calling out.*)   Hello? *Bonjour? Guten Tag*, Mrs. Civil!

GANESHA   She's in the bathroom being sick.

MAN   That's how most of them see India. Staring at the bottom of a toilet bowl. Tell me, Mrs. Jog, would you fly halfway around the world and spend all your husband's money, just to heave your guts up for a fortnight in a country you have no way of understanding? I've seen this episode. It's a bloody rerun.

MARGARET (*Off.*)   Yes? Is someone out there? Kitty? Is that you?

MAN   Some fruit, madam, compliments of the Lake Palace Hotel. Welcome to Udaipur!

MARGARET (*Off.*)   What? I can't hear!

MAN   Let me open your shutters. You have a wonderful view here. (*He throws open the shutters. Enormous light change. The gauze backdrop begins to sway in a delicious breeze coming in from the lake.*) Lord, but it takes my breath away every time, Mrs. Jog! You can bloody this and bloody that, Mr. Victor Biswas, but you can never say bloody *that*. (*Margaret comes into the room. She is in a robe and looks very pale.*)

MARGARET   Yes? Can I help you?

MAN (*Singing, but not well.*)   "There she is, Miss America!" Welcome to the lake city of Udaipur, known as the City of the Sunrise, a cool oasis in the dry heart of Rajasthan, scene of a delightful episode in *Jewel in the Crown* and the exciting submarine/helicopter chase sequence in the most excellent James Bond motion picture *You Only Live Once*. Mr. Sean Connery himself occupied this very room.

MARGARET   Really?

GANESHA   *Twice. You Only Live Twice.*

MAN   Shut up. (*To Margaret.*) The maid wants to know if she can get you anything?

MARGARET   No, thank you. I just want to be still for a little while. I'm a bit weak. It's so bright in here.

MAN   The way the sun hits the water. The Mughals used to tie their prisoners to stakes and sew their eyelids open and make them look at the water until they went blind or mad or both.

MARGARET   How horrible!

MAN   We were conquered by a very cruel people. I hope you will find that very little of that cruelty remains. (*To Ganesha.*) What are you looking at?

GANESHA   I like hearing you speak English, Mr. Biswas. I am in awe of people who can speak with other people in a language not their own. That is a God-like thing to be able to do.

MAN (*To Margaret.*)   The maid is saying she likes to hear me speak English. (*To Ganesha.*) Why? You don't understand. If you did, you would know I am telling this rich American lady what a lazy, worthless worker you are and that you are this close to being made redundant. Now clean room 617. Mr. Thomas had an accident on the sheets last night.

GANESHA   Please, don't make me redundant, Mr. Biswas. I need this job.

MAN   Then don't ever correct me again. Especially in front of a woman. (*To Margaret.*) She's saying she hopes you enjoy your stay with us. Her name is Queenie.

MARGARET   Thank you, Queenie. (*Ganesha heads for the door just as Katharine returns. Katharine has been shopping. She has packages. She is out of breath, but very excited.*)

KATHARINE   Offamof! Off-a-mof! Is that our view? (*She stands by the open window.*)

MAN   This is our very finest accommodation.

KATHARINE   Well, sir, as my grandchildren would say: OFF-A-FUCKING-MOFF! The things I've seen and done this morning! You people have Bombay knocked into a cocked hat! (*To Margaret.*) How are you feeling?

MARGARET   Much better.

KATHARINE   You sure? You had me worried. Poor baby.

MARGARET   This is Mr. Biswas. The hotel manager.

MAN   Victor Biswas. At your service, madam.

KATHARINE   Hello. I can see some color in her cheeks. Thank God! We have a train to catch this evening. (*She makes a quick Sign of the Cross.*) Whew! I've been shopping my tits off, Margaret. (*She finally sits.*)

MAN   Tits? Are they like jugs, Mrs. Brynne?

KATHARINE   I think they're a little more contemporary than jugs, Mr. Biswas.

MAN   I am also puzzling over your curious expression "off-a-mof." The adjective you embellished it with I understood most clearly.

KATHARINE   It's short for "O for a Muse of fire," which is Shakespeare and which I say when I get excited and can't describe things, and since I'm excited a lot lately, Mrs. Civil can't stand me saying it all the time and out of deference to her I shortened it to "offamof."

MAN   I see.

KATHARINE   "Thank you, Kitty." "*De nada*, Margaret." I didn't buy that much. It just looks like it. I spent fifty dollars, tops.

MAN   I hope you find everything you are looking for in our country, including good bargains. I come home burdened down with VCRs and Calvin Klein underwear whenever I visit yours. Excuse me. We have a busload of Japs arriving. (*He goes.*)

KATHARINE   Did you hear that? He said "Japs."

MARGARET   He doesn't know better. Besides, it's not his first language.

KATHARINE (*To Ganesha.*)   Queenie, did you wash and iron my blouse?

GANESHA   Yes, Mrs. Brynne.

KATHARINE   Ladesh. (*To Margaret.*) That's Hindi for "thank you." (*To Ganesha.*) Ladesh, Queenie, *ladesh*.

GANESHA   *De nada*, Mrs. Brynne. (*He goes.*)

KATHARINE   Did you hear that, too, Margaret?

MARGARET   I heard it, Kitty. (*Katharine sticks her tongue out at her.*)

KATHARINE   I'm sorry. I couldn't resist. I'll shut up. It's the heat, I'm delirious, all this talk about Calvin Klein underwear! Do you want to see what I bought? (*She will show her purchases to Margaret during the following.*)

MARGARET   Kitty, what do you think a man like Mr. Biswas thinks when you say something like "shop your tits off"?

KATHARINE   I don't know. I don't care. I'm in India. I'm just your basic white trash, Margaret. You like these?

MARGARET   Don't be ridiculous.

KATHARINE   It's true. You are traveling with a woman whose father was a postal clerk and whose mother did ironing. I thought this blue bag would be for Linda Nagle.

MARGARET   Your father worked in a post office?

KATHARINE   For twenty-two years. He dropped dead selling Mrs. Feigen a three-cent stamp. Remember them? I was still in school. I did a little ironing myself after that. I think these are absolutely stunning, don't you? Only two dollars!

MARGARET   I had no idea, Kitty. Not that it matters.

KATHARINE   Oh, it matters, Margaret. Eventually, it matters. I have no class.

MARGARET   Don't say things like that.

KATHARINE   It's true.

MARGARET   Don't even think them. You and George have a wonderful life.

KATHARINE   I suppose we do, but it's not what I'm talking about. I think these will make darling luncheon napkins. You know how I met him? I crashed a dance at the Westchester Country Club. My best friend and I, Flo Sullivan, we made ourselves fancy evening dresses and hiked our skirts across the wet grass on the golf course and snuck into the party through the terrace. The ballroom was so beautiful! Roses everywhere. Real ones. A mirror ball. Guy Lombardo was playing. Himself, no substitute but the real thing. This was a class affair, right down the line. Guy Lombardo and His Royal Canadians. "Begin the Beguine." I knew right away this was where I wanted to be and I would do everything I could to stay there. I would scratch, I would fight, I would bite. Barbara Stanwyck was my role model. George was in a white tie and tails, if you can imagine him in such a thing. He had a silver cigarette case and was tapping one end of his cigarette against it to get the tobacco down. I thought it was the most elegant gesture I'd ever seen a man make. (*Lights up on Man. He is George, dressed in white tie and tails and tapping a cigarette against a silver case. He will dance to the music Katharine has described.*) We hit it off right away. I was a wonderful dancer. I'd made sure of that. I knew how to let the man think he was leading. With George I didn't have to. I knew he was going to ask me where I went to college. What I didn't know was what I was going to answer. When he did, it was during a Lindy. I closed my eyes, held my breath and jumped. "I graduated Port Chester High School and I'm working in the city as a dental assistant." "Great," he said. "I was afraid you were going to say you went to Vassar!" and laughed and lifted me up by the waist over his head for this incredibly long second, like we were two colored kids jitterbugging in Harlem and I felt a blaze of happiness, like I've never felt before or since! After two hours, I said "Let me wear your class ring. For fun. We'll pretend." It was a Yale ring. I showed it to Flo in the ladies' room during a band break. She couldn't believe it. She asked if she could try it on. I was washing my hands and it slipped out of my fingers and it disappeared down the drain. What do you tell a man you just met two hours ago at a dance you crashed when you've lost his senior ring? You don't tell him very much, Maggie. You sleep with him on the first date and you say "I do," after you make sure he asks you to bury him on the third. I mean, marry him. I can't believe I said that. Bury him. This is my favorite. (*She is holding a small carved figure.*)

MARGARET   What an extraordinary story. You never told me that.

KATHARINE   "Hi, I'm Katharine Brynne. I met my husband crashing a dance at the Westchester Country Club." I don't think so, Margaret. Do you know who that is? It's Ganesha. (*Margaret examines the carving. Lights up on Man. He is Walter. he is unbloodied.*)

MAN   May I have this dance, Miss Stanwyck? Oh, come on, it's only me. It's a slow fox-trot. Your favorite kind. (*He holds his arms out to her.*)

KATHARINE   Since when do you like to dance with women?

MAN   I don't. I'll suffer. (*She joins him.*) Besides, you're not a woman. You're my mother. (*They begin to dance. There is music.*)

KATHARINE   Go ahead. Say it. Criticize. Everything I do is wrong.

MAN   How could you tell that story to a total stranger and not your own son?

KATHARINE   She's not a total stranger. Besides, you wouldn't have understood.

MAN   No, I would have understood. That's what you were afraid of. That's the kind of story that makes you like someone. We might have become friends over a story like that.

MARGARET   He—I guess it's a he; in this day and age, I better watch what I say—he/she/it's got the head of an elephant.

KATHARINE   You wouldn't have approved, Walter.

MAN   You think Mrs. Civil does? (*He laughs.*) God, I was a judgmental little shit where you and Dad were concerned.

KATHARINE   Serves us right. We, me certainly. So am I still your best girl? Your *numero uno*?

MAN   I don't think we're supposed to say things like that.

KATHARINE   So sue me. That's from *Guys and Dolls*.

MAN   "Shut up and dance." That's from *Gypsy*.

MARGARET   it looks like he's got four arms. I'm sure it's a he. Six arms? No, four. Definitely four.

MAN   This is a long song.

KATHARINE   We can stop.

MAN   I'm too much of a gentleman.

MARGARET   What's that around his waist? A snake! A cobra. And one of his tusks is broken. (*Lights up on Ganesha. He is on a platform and holds his broken tusk in his right hand.*)

GANESHA   I broke it off one night and threw it at the moon because she made me angry by laughing at me.

KATHARINE   You still don't know how to hold a woman.

MAN   You mean, like this? (*He pulls her to him hard and close.*) Is this how you mean? (*She slaps him.*)

KATHARINE   I'm sorry. I'm sorry.

MAN   No, you're not. (*Margaret approaches him.*)

MARGARET   May I cut in?

MAN   Thank you. (*They begin to dance.*) Do I know you?

MARGARET   No, Gabriel.

KATHARINE   Break her heart, the way you did mine. I hate you. I hate both of you!

MAN   Who are you?

MARGARET   Never mind. I just want to dance with you. I have always wanted to dance with you.

GANESHA (*To Katharine.*)   Join me. With worshippers at my feet I dance my swaying dance. Come, join us!

KATHARINE   Who are you?

GANESHA   I am Ganesha, a very important god in India. Don't laugh. Just because I'm fat and have the head of an elephant doesn't mean that I'm not a god of great influence and popularity. They call me "The Lord of Obstacles." I am good at overcoming problems and bringing success to people. I am also known as a god of wisdom and wealth.

MARGARET   You're a wonderful dancer.

MAN   Thank you.

MARGARET   I'm not. You don't have to say anything.

MAN   I wasn't going to. Hang on! (*This time he will whirl her wildly.*)

MARGARET   Oh, Gabriel! (*They are gone.*)

KATHARINE   I think you're darling, Ganesh!

GANESHA   Or Ganesha. It's all the same to me.

KATHARINE   I like Ganesh. Tell me more. I want to know everything about you.

GANESHA   Because I'm a god, I don't have to look or do things the way ordinary people do. For instance, as you can plainly see, I have an elephant's head. You don't. You travel by Ford Escort or on foot. I ride a rat. It may seem strange for a big fellow like me to have such a small vehicle, but I find him very helpful for getting out of tight situations. He's almost always with me but sometimes hard to find. Look for him carefully.

KATHARINE   I see him! I see the rat!

GANESHA   This demonstrates the concept—so important to me!—that opposites—an elephant and a mouse—can live together happily. That love of good food (I am always eating) and profound spiritual knowledge can go together. That a fat, rotund person can still be a supreme connoisseur of dance and music. In fact, I prove that the world is full opposites which exist peacefully side by side.

KATHARINE   You can stop right there. I'm sold. Do you come any smaller? I couldn't possibly lug you back to Connecticut like that.

GANESHA   Let me check for you. (*Lights fade off Ganesha as Margaret and Man appear again, still dancing. Katharine watches them. Man whispers something in Margaret's ear. She throws her head back and laughs.*)

KATHARINE   May I cut in?

MARGARET   No.

MAN   I'm sorry. (*They dance away from her.*)

MARGARET   Was that terrible of us?

MAN   Terribly! You're very beautiful.

MARGARET   Thank you.

MAN   For your years.

MARGARET   Did you have to say that?

MAN   Are you happy? (*He stops dancing.*)

MARGARET (*Wanting to resume.*)   Yes. No. I don't know. Does it matter? Are you? Please, don't look at me like that. (*He kisses her.*)

MAN   You should be happy.

MARGARET   I can't be.

MAN   I never knew what hit me. (*He snaps his fingers.*) Like that. (*He goes. Lights up on Ganesha. He approaches Katharine with a small carving of himself.*)

GANESHA   Is this small enough, excellent lady? (*He hands it to Katharine.*) I come key-ring and necklace pendant–size, too, but when I get that small I only come in plastic and you lose all the detail.

KATHARINE   Excuse me, did you say "I?" "I only come in plastic?"

GANESHA   Oh, Lordy, no! That would be blasphemy.

KATHARINE   This one is perfect. What's it made of?

GANESHA   I believe that's amethyst but let me check. Solar! My wife has all the answers. Solar!

KATHARINE   How much?

GANESHA   Fifty rupees?

KATHARINE   I'll take two. My friend, Mrs. Civil, is back in our hotel room writhing in agony. Her stomach. Montezuma's Revenge they call it in Mexico. What do you call it here?

GANESHA   Just dysentery. We have no sense of humor when it comes to the bowels.

KATHARINE   Margaret would say, "That's something!"

GANESHA   You must not drink our water. Or eat our fruit. No matter how tempting.

KATHARINE   She didn't.

GANESHA   That's what you all say.

KATHARINE   But she didn't!

GANESHA   Solar! (*He goes.*)

KATHARINE   I'm hoping this will cheer her up! (*She looks down at the carving in her hand. So does Margaret. They're back in the hotel room now.*) Isn't he darling? Maybe he'll help me get back that camera I lost in Jodhpur. George is going to kill me.

MARGARET (*Reading.*)   "I'm happy and I want people to be happy, too." Thank you, Kitty.

KATHARINE   I'm just glad you're better. You're going to miss India at this rate. The Towers of Silence were the highlight of Bombay and you completely missed them.

MARGARET   I thought you couldn't see them.

KATHARINE   No, I said you just couldn't see the vultures actually eating the flesh of his bones, if that's what you're talking about. You have to be a Parsi. But you could stand outside looking up at the towers and see the vultures swooping down on the bodies on top. That was quite enough for this cookie, thank you very much. Talk about feeling mortal. That could have been me up there! One day it will be. When I go, that's what I want done, Margaret. Just leave me out on the pier at the Greenwich Yacht Club and let the seagulls go to work. (*The telephone begins to ring wanly again.*) I'm not even going to answer it anymore. I'm glad you like him. I thought you would. (*The sounds of a train have gotten quite loud.*)

MARGARET   I just want to know why he has a head for an elephant?

KATHARINE   What?

MARGARET   I mean, why has he an elephant's head?

KATHARINE   What? I can't hear you! (*Transition as sounds level out.*)

SCENE 2

The Palace on Wheels, India's legendary luxury train. Teatime. Margaret, Katharine, and the Man. The Man is an Authority. He is examining a figure of Ganesha.

MARGARET   I wish they kept these windows cleaner. How are we supposed to see anything! How's your side?

KATHARINE *(Miserably.)*   The same.

MARGARET   I told you to take Pepto-Bismol.

MAN *(Returning the Ganesh.)*   It's soapstone.

KATHARINE   They said it was amethyst.

MAN   I'm surprised he didn't tell you it was marble. That's their usual ploy, God love 'em! No, it's soapstone. I'm afraid they saw you coming, Mrs. Brynne.

MARGARET   That's what I told her. Maybe she'll listen to you.

KATHARINE   I don't care what he's made of. I love him.

MARGARET   Kitty's become besotted with this Ganesh/Ganesha person.

KATHARINE   He's a person. He's a god. And I'm not besotted with him.

MARGARET   I'm just hoping someone will tell us how he got his elephant's head.

MAN   It's a dreadful story. I don't think Mrs. Brynne wants to hear it on that stomach of hers.

KATHARINE   I'm fine.

MAN   Let's get some tea first. *(He rings.)* So you two ladies have fallen under the spell of Ganesha, too? Most travelers to India do. My first trip I couldn't get enough of him. I started developing this lump in the middle of my forehead. A sort of psychosomatic trunk.

KATHARINE   He's kidding, Margaret.

MARGARET   I know that. I knew that.

KATHARINE   I'm not besotted. I'm curious. I don't think Mrs. Civil is enjoying India.

MARGARET   That's not true.

KATHARINE   I adore it, of course.

MAN   Hindu mythology is so violent. It gives me the creeps. I'll settle for a hammer and nails, your basic wooden cross and a nice Jewish boy any day of the week. I hope I haven't offended anyone.

KATHARINE   Just about everyone.

MAN   You two are a trip. I'm so glad I ran into you.

KATHARINE   Why thank you, kind sir! You should see me when my guts don't feel like someone has got their hands in there and is tying them in knots.

MARGARET   She'd be dancing on the table.

MAN (*To Katharine.*)   You know, you remind me of someone: my mother.

KATHARINE   Ow! Such cramps. Out of the blue. Just when you think they've—! Ow! Ow! Ow!

MARGARET   I told her: don't eat that papaya.

KATHARINE   It wasn't a papaya! I thought peeling it would make it safe. (*Ganesh appears. He carries a tray.*)

MAN   Tea for three, please. Understand? Tea for three.

KATHARINE (*As Ganesh hurries off.*)   Ladesh.

MARGARET (*Anticipating what Katharine will say.*)   "That's Hindi for 'thank you.'"

KATHARINE (*To man.*)   That's Hindi for "thank you."

MARGARET   What did I tell you?

MAN   My wife would get such a kick out of you two!

KATHARINE   I can't believe she just flew home without you.

MAN   She couldn't take India. A lot of people can't. Too much poverty, too much disease.

KATHARINE   Too much everything. The colors, the smells, the sounds. My head is whirling, when my stomach isn't heaving.

MARGARET   Our husbands wouldn't even consider coming with us. "No way, Jose" was how Alan put it.

MAN   Actually, we had an incident in Benares. Are you going there?

KATHARINE   Absolutely. Benares is one of the reasons I most wanted to come to India.

MARGARET   You never told me that.

KATHARINE   What happened?

MAN   I don't want to upset you or anything and I'm sure this won't happen to you, but we were down at the ghats where they burn the bodies. I've always been terrified of death and I thought maybe looking at it would help. Hundreds of dead bodies being burned like so many logs. Who knew? Maybe it *would* help and besides, people like us, we don't go to Benares without seeing the burning ghats, am I right?

KATHARINE   Go on.

MAN   They were burning the body of an old woman. I wish I could say I thought it was beautiful or spiritual but I thought it was horrible and it scared the shit out of me. Kelly was holding my hand so tight I thought she would puncture my flesh with her nails. "I hate this, you bastard," she kept saying. Suddenly, someone called out behind us. A harsh, ugly sound. We turned and this wretched figure in rags on the ground was pointing at us and yelling. We started to run but Kelly tripped, I lost my grip on her, and she fell on top of him. When their bodies hit, he somehow seemed to throw his arms around her, hug her almost, and they rolled over and over in the mud. I couldn't pull them apart. Kelly was screaming but he wouldn't let go. Finally, it seemed like forever, two policemen appeared and they pulled him off her and apologized and then hit the old man with their truncheons and escorted us back to our hotel.

MARGARET   You're not going to the burning ghats!

MAN   I don't know if he was a leper, Kelly says he was, but she did say "I will never, ever be clean again. I know it." She took shower after shower after shower but nothing would convince her that she was rid of him: his smell, his dirt, his essence, I supposed. I haven't heard from her since she got back to Boston. Poor baby. Let's hope.

KATHARINE   You didn't think of going back with her?

MAN   We don't have that sort of marriage. No children and we're very independent.

KATHARINE   But still . . .

MAN   I don't expect other people to understand. Besides, being in India is rather a solo project anyway. It's finally just you and it. (*Ganesha has returned with the tea.*) Thank you. (*To Katharine.*) What was that word?

KATHARINE   *Ladesh.* (*The compartment suddenly goes dark. The train has entered a tunnel.*)

MARGARET   What happened!

KATHARINE   It's just a tunnel.

MAN   A long one, ladies. You haven't read your guide books. The Chittaurgahr Pass. The longest tunnel in India. Nearly 42 kilometers.

MARGARET   What is that in miles?

MAN   I don't know. Thirty-five miles or so.

KATHARINE   If this were a movie, one of us would have a dagger in his back when he came out of it!

MAN   Or been kissed or pinched or both.

KATHARINE   You have a romantic imagination.

MAN   And you have a morbid one!

KATHARINE   You were going to tell us how Ganesh got his elephant's head.

MAN   All right, but I warned you.

MARGARET   Are we really going to be in a dark tunnel for the next hour?

KATHARINE   We're fine, Margaret. Nothing's going to happen.

MARGARET   Palace on Wheels! Dungeon on Wheels is more like it.

KATHARINE   Ignore her. Go ahead.

MARGARET   There was a dead spider in my bed last night.

MAN   Where was I?

MARGARET   I won't even go into the food!

MAN   Oh, Ganesha's head!

MARGARET   Oh! That wasn't funny.

KATHARINE   What?

MARGARET   Whoever did that, I didn't appreciate it. (*Ganesh strikes a match and lights a kerosene lamp for them.*)

MAN   *Ladesh. Ladesh.*

KATHARINE   What's the matter, Margaret?

MARGARET   Someone . . . I distinctly felt a hand . . .

KATHARINE   What?

MARGARET   On my breast. Someone . . . touched it . . .

KATHARINE   Margaret.

MARGARET   I'm sure of it.

KATHARINE   Was it a friendly hand?

MARGARET   I'm serious.

KATHARINE   I'm sure whatever it was—if it was anything—just felt like a hand.

MARGARET   I guess I still know what a hand on my breasts feels like, Katharine, even if you don't remember.

KATHARINE   What is that supposed to mean?

MARGARET   I think you know.

GANESHA   Is there something wrong? The lady seems agitated.

MARGARET   What's he saying?

GANESHA   The tea was not good? I shall bring more candles?

MARGARET   I didn't accuse him. I don't know what he's babbling about. (*Ganesh is in a dither.*)

KATHARINE   Well, who else were you accusing?

MAN   I can assure you, Mrs. Civil, grabbing women's breasts in dark railway tunnels is not my thing.

MARGARET   I didn't say it was.

MAN   And I doubt it was our porter. He's gay as a goose, can't you tell?

GANESHA (*With a napkin.*)   Crumbs on the lady! Here, let me—! (*He moves to brush off her chest with his serving napkin. Margaret pushes him away.*)

MARGARET   No!

GANESHA   I have done something wrong? I have given offense?

MAN   Fine. Everything is fine!

MARGARET   Everything is not fine.

KATHARINE   Now who's the Ugly American?

MARGARET   This isn't about that, Kitty.

KATHARINE   And I won't forget that remark about George.

MARGARET   What remark?

KATHARINE   He touches me just fine! What would you know about it?

MAN   Ladies, please!

GANESHA   The lady is frightened of the tunnel? Tell the lady there is nothing to fear. See? I laugh at the tunnel. Ha ha ha!

MAN   Go! Go back to where you came from!

GANESHA   Ganesha loves you. Ganesha will protect you.

KATHARINE   Wait! He said something about Ganesha. Did you say Ganesha?

GANESHA (*Joyfully.*)   Ganesha, yes, Ganesha!

KATHARINE   There, hear that? He said Ganesha.

MARGARET   I suppose Ganesha fondled my breast!

GANESHA   Ganesha! Ganesha!

KATHARINE   Now it's "fondled." First it was just "touched." Next we'll be having the Marabar Caves incident.

GANESHA (*Fearfully.*)   Marabar! No, no! No, Marabar!

KATHARINE   I'm not accusing you!

GANESHA   No, Marabar! Bad, Marabar! You wrong! No, Marabar! I am going to my supervisor and tell him the truth before you ladies lie and have Anant made redundant. Marabar, no! (*He goes.*)

KATHARINE   What did I say? Rather, what did he think I said?

MAN   The one porter in all Rajasthan who's read *A Passage to India*.

MARGARET   I'm glad you find this so amusing.

KATHARINE   No one finds it amusing, Margaret, but we can't go around accusing people because we feel superior to them.

MARGARET   I don't feel superior to that person.

KATHARINE   Yes, you do. So do I. And by our standards, we are. That's the terrible thing.

MARGARET   Spare us, Kitty.

MAN   If you ladies will excuse me but I've already done this part with Kelly.

KATHARINE   We're sorry.

MAN   I saw a three-month-old copy of the *Village Voice* with a review of Bob Dylan at the Garden in the library. Or what Indian Rail calls the library. Bob Dylan! God, we're all getting so old! (*He goes.*)

MARGARET   No, he doesn't remind me of Walter either.

KATHARINE   I wasn't going to say that.

MARGARET   There is evil in the world, Katharine.

KATHARINE   I know that.

MARGARET   And I was just subjected to some of it.

KATHARINE   So was my son.

MARGARET   Do you want to cut the trip short?

KATHARINE   No. Do you?

MARGARET   No. (*Long pause. The sound of the train gets louder and louder.*) I'm sorry.

KATHARINE   It's all right. So am I. So am I. (*Suddenly the train comes out of the tunnel and the light will seem very bright.*) I thought he said we'd be in there for an hour.

MARGARET   That type thinks they know everything.

KATHARINE   I thought you liked him.

MARGARET   I did, for fifteen minutes. Look, there's some nice scenery coming up. (*They look out the window on different sides of the compartment.*) I like everyone for fifteen minutes.

KATHARINE   Thank you.

MARGARET   Don't be ridiculous. You're my oldest friend.

KATHARINE   We hardly know each other.

MARGARET   That's not true. We know each other. We love each other. We just don't especially like each other. I've got water buffaloes on my side. What do you have?

KATHARINE   Camels.

MARGARET   I would imagine people had this same view thousands of years ago, before electricity, before television and atomic bombs, before we all got so neurotic. You were born, you grew up, you worked in a field like those, you got married, you had children, you got old, you died and with a little luck, somebody remembered you kindly for at least one generation.

KATHARINE   I don't feel like I'm in India. I see sky and hills and horizons and trees. What makes it India and not Danbury? We travel, but we don't go anywhere. I'm stuck right here. The earth spins but I don't. (*Ganesha appears in the compartment. He is the Supervisor.*)

GANESHA   Excuse me, ladies, I understand there was some disturbance here? Some confusion?

MARGARET   No, nothing, we're fine. We're both fine.

KATHARINE   Yes, thank you.

GANESHA   But I was told—

MARGARET   Really, it's quite forgotten. When are we getting to Jaipur?

GANESHA   At exactly 23:30. In time for the fireworks and the great Hali Festival.

KATHARINE   I have a feeling we won't be three for dinner this evening.

GANESHA   Ah, yes, the gentleman already explained that. Goodbye then. (*He goes.*)

MARGARET   I wish I could be a better friend to you, Kitty, and vice versa. I don't know what stops me.

KATHARINE   Thank you for not making an issue about your breast.

MARGARET   It's all that good Yankee breeding, don't you know. It's all in the genes and we all have these marvelous cheekbones and talk like Katharine Hepburn. We're both the same age and we're from the same background—

KATHARINE   Or so you thought!

MARGARET   Our husbands make approximately the same living. We're both mothers.

KATHARINE   You've never lost a child.

MARGARET   Well, that's true.

KATHARINE   Nothing compares to losing a child. No, nothing compares to losing that particular child. Why couldn't it have been his brother or Nan or one of her kids or George even? Do you think God will strike me dead for saying something like that?

MARGARET   Of course not.

KATHARINE   I think maybe he should. Every time the phone rang I dreaded it being him and him saying, "Mom, I've got it. I've got AIDS."

MARGARET   You want to talk about it?

KATHARINE   What else is there to say? Who are you to tell me there's evil in the world? You think some little brown man touched your tit in a tunnel. I'm surprised the earth didn't spin off its axis! I know what 1,2,3,4,5,6—count 'em: six!—African Americans did to my son at two-thirty in the morning at the corner of Barrow and Greenwich. They get off (Walter was a faggot after all!) and I don't even get to say nigger! I know there's evil. I'm not so sure there's any justice.

MARGARET   I wish I could comfort you.

KATHARINE   I wish you could, too. Now I've got the water buffaloes.

MARGARET   May I put my arm around you?

KATHARINE   I'd rather you wouldn't. (*Margaret puts her arm around her.*)

MARGARET   You don't have to say anything. Sshh! Sshh! I'm not going to say anything.

KATHARINE   Thank you for that, at least.

MARGARET   You're not alone, Kitty. I'm here. Another person, another woman is here. Right here. Breathing the same air. Riding the same train. Looking out the window at the same timeless landscape. You are not alone. Even in your agony.

KATHARINE   Thank you.

MARGARET   I love you. I love you very much. "Offamof."

KATHARINE   What?

MARGARET   "Offamof."

KATHARINE   Oh, yeah. "Offamof!" (*Lights up on Ganesha. He comes down to us as the sounds of the train come up and the lights dim on Margaret and Katharine.*)

GANESHA   And so it happened that while Margaret Civil and Katharine Brynne stared with heavy, sad, sad, eyes at what Mr. Ray of India injudiciously called the most beautiful scenery in India, some 8,345 miles away, at 11:20 p.m. their time, George Brynne, Katharine Brynne's husband, Caucasian male, aged 62, lost control of his car on a patch of something called glare ice on his way home from a movie Katharine had refused to see because of its purported violence (she was right! an appalling motion picture it was, too!), went into a skid and slammed into a 300-year-old oak tree. He died instantly. Mrs. Brynne will not learn of her loss until she gets home. Since her children cannot reach her by phone (the ladies are off their itinerary and frequently without reservations; in Khajuraho they slept on two cots in the garden of a sympathetic postmaster), her children decide it is better to meet her at the airport when she and Mrs. Civil return. (*Lights are coming up on Margaret and Katharine. The sounds of the train have faded. We hear the periodic ringing of a temple bell.*)

MARGARET   I can't believe you've actually lost your guidebook, Kitty.

KATHARINE   Sooner or later I lose everything.

MARGARET   How are you going to know what you're looking at?

KATHARINE   I am putting myself completely in the hands of our guide, Mr. Kamlesh Tandu of Jodhpur.

GANESHA (*To us.*)   I think Mrs. Brynne has a slight "thing" for me, I believe you call them. It's very curious but not uncommon. In her own country she wouldn't give me the time of day.

MARGARET   Well don't come running to me when we leave Mr. Tandu in Jaiselmir and you want to know what something is. I'm not going to tell you.

KATHARINE   As Rudyard Kipling said, "Oh, bugger off, Margaret!"

MARGARET   I'm sure Rudyard Kipling never said "Bugger off, Margaret." Somerset Maugham maybe.

GANESHA (*Stepping forward.*)   Welcome to my humble village, ladies. No television, no electricity. Puppet shows and traveling players are our windows on the world. It's lovely.

KATHARINE   You said you had a treat for us, Mr. Tandu.

GANESHA   No, for you, Mrs. Brynne. That is if you don't mind, Mrs. Civil.

MARGARET   Not in the least.

KATHARINE   Why just for me?

GANESHA   Why not? (*He claps his hands.*) Puppets, please!

SCENE 3

A village square. Dusk. A puppet show is in progress. The Man is a Puppeteer. There are three camp stools for Margaret, Katharine and Ganesha.

GANESHA   Once again, lovely ladies, "How Lovely Lord Ganesha Got His Lovely Elephant's Head." Puppets please. (*He has handed her a small book.*)

KATHARINE   What's this?

GANESHA   Your part. In India we participate in theatre. We don't sit back, arms folded and say "Show me." (*Margaret has been sitting exactly like that.*)

MARGARET   I'm sorry.

KATHARINE   "Still in a fury that his wife would not see him, Shiva sent his forces to kill the boy who barred his way."

GANESHA   Very good.

KATHARINE   "But Parvati created two shatkis to defend her son against her husband, Kali and Durga."

MAN (*Showing the puppets.*)   Kali and Durga!

MARGARET   What's a shatki, Mr. Tandu?

GANESHA   I believe you call them She-Devils, Mrs. Civil.

KATHARINE   No, we say bitches. Don't interrupt, Margaret. This is my big moment. "To his amazement, Shiva forces were completely routed by the valiant youth. He knew what he must do."

MAN   "I will have to kill the boy with my own hands. Let it never be said that a man was subservient to his wife!"

MARGARET   That sounds familiar.

KATHARINE   "Shiva charged the boy with his silver-shining trident but the boy swung his iron club and sent him sprawling." Good for the boy!

MAN   "That should teach you a lesson, old man, pop." (*Katharine looks up from the book.*)

KATHARINE   What?

MAN (*To Katharine.*)   "Mother, see how I serve you." (*From this point, Katharine will not be able to take her eyes off the puppets and the Man. She will let the playbook lie open in her lap.*)

GANESHA   And the boy laughed. Oh, how he laughed!

MAN   Ha ha ha! Ha ha ha!

GANESHA   Ha ha ha! Ha ha ha! This is charming.

GANESHA   And while the boy laughed, Shiva came up from behind him and with one swift stroke of his sword, cut off Walter's head.

MAN   Woosh. Ung.

GANESHA   He could hear the sound against the side of his head.

MAN   Woosh. Ung.

GANESHA   Shiva had landed a good one. You're not looking, Mrs. Brynne.

MAN   I stayed on my feet a remarkably long time, Mama. I was sort of proud of me.

KATHARINE (*Looking back to the book.*)   Where does it say that?

MAN   "Mother, see how I serve you."

KATHARINE   He's not following the script.

GANESHA   And down he fell.

KATHARINE   Why me, Mr. Tandu?

GANESHA   Again, why not you, Mrs. Brynne? As the boy lay dying, Shiva realized what he had done.

KATHARINE   Shiva, not I! (*She abruptly stands up.*)

MARGARET   Where are you going?

GANESHA   You must hear the story to its end, Mrs. Brynne.

KATHARINE   I know how it ends. In a New York hospital. Twenty minutes before I got there.

GANESHA   No, it ends in reconciliation, renewal, and rebirth.

KATHARINE   Tell it to Mrs. Civil. (*She hands the playbook to Margaret and goes.*)

MARGARET   I think your story upset Mrs. Brynne.

GANESHA   Perhaps she needed some upsetting, Mrs. Civil. May we continue? It is very bad form to abandon Lord Ganesha in midstream. Shiva went to his wife and begged forgiveness for what he had done.

MAN   "O, great goddess, wife and mother, forgive me."

GANESHA   Parvati faced him with great dignity. That's you, Mrs. Civil.

MARGARET   "I will forgive you. But my son must regain his life, and he must have an honorable status among you."

GANESHA   Lord Shiva responded with great humility.

MAN   "Your will shall be done. Vishnu, go north. Bring the head of the first creature that crosses your path. Fit that head to the boy's body and it will come to life."

MARGARET   And the first creature they saw was an elephant! With a single tusk!

GANESHA   Vishnu threw his golden discus and killed him.

MARGARET   And they cut off his head and fitted it to the body of her little boy.

GANESHA   The boy sat up.

MARGARET   He was reborn.

MAN   Then Shiva placed his hand on the boy's head and pronounced these solemn and healing words.

GANESHA   "Even as a mere boy you showed great valor. You shall be Ganesha, the presiding officer of all my ganas. You shall be worthy of worship forever."

MAN   Mighty is the Lord Shiva, great is his compassion.

GANESHA   Here ends the story of how Lord Ganesha got his lovely head.

MARGARET   Thank you.

GANESHA   There are many others, Mrs. Civil, if the ladies are so inclined.

MARGARET   I don't think so. I'm worried about my friend.

GANESHA   I said something wrong perhaps?

MARGARET   It almost seemed deliberate.

GANESHA   It's only a legend. You Christians take everything so literally.

MARGARET   She had a son who . . .

GANESHA   Whose head was cut off? My, my, my! This New York City of yours must be a fearful place.

MARGARET   Don't be ridiculous. His head wasn't cut off. He was murdered.

MAN   I heard of a man who went there and they ate his toes they were so hungry.

MARGARET   Don't believe such stories. I assure you, it hasn't come to that.

MAN (*To Ganesha, unconvinced.*)   They sold his eyeballs for drug money.

MARGARET   You have a horrible imagination.

MAN   Thanking you very much.

MARGARET   Work on your English. It wasn't a compliment. (*She starts walking in the opposite direction Katharine took.*) Katharine! Kitty!

GANESHA   Tonight they ride elephants to a banquet in a maharajah's palace and dine by torchlight. Oh, lordy, look at me! I have to dress. *Sayonara. Ciao.* (*Lights fade on Man and Ganesha while Margaret and Katharine walk. Again, a turntable would be useful.*)

MARGARET   Kitty! Kitty!

KATHARINE   God, leave me alone, woman. All of you. No more guides or puppets. No more India. I want to go home and forget I ever came here. I'm sick of your mythology. It's as false as ours. My son was not reborn. He died twenty minutes before I got to the hospital. His murderers never asked my forgiveness. You had it easy, Parvati. No honor has ever been made to me. I have my anger and nothing more. No love. No love at all.

MARGARET   Katharine! Kitty! Now where is she gone to? She'd lose herself and not just the train tickets if I didn't keep an eye on her. I'm ashamed to admit it but I never realized how dependent we are on the men. She won't admit that but it's true. This may be the last time I go anywhere with anyone. I'm not a fellow traveler. I almost told her about Gabriel. It would have been such a tiny leap across that void between two people. "I lost a son too, Kitty." Six little words and I couldn't do it. "I lost a son too, Kitty." Kitty! (*Katharine has started walking with Ganesha.*)

KATHARINE   How old are you? Do you speak any English? Seven years old? Eight? How old are you? (*Margaret has started walking with the Man. He is a Foreign Tourist.*)

MARGARET   Dutch? We've been to Holland. Twice. You have wonderful museums there. The Rembrandt Museum, only it's in London at the National Gallery.

MAN   London, yes?

KATHARINE   You have the dearest face! Oh God, I wish I knew your name. When I get back to America I would send you the biggest box of anything you wanted.

GANESHA   Are you from America? How old are you? Are you rich? Is there really a Rocky? Who is your leader there now?

KATHARINE   Slow down, slow down! I don't understand a word you're saying. I do not speak Hindi.

GANESHA   I like you.

KATHARINE   Where are we going? I'm letting you take me.

MARGARET   It's called *Woman Bathing*.

MAN   Yes?

MARGARET   Well, in English it's called *Woman Bathing*. I don't know what it's called in Dutch. Do you know it?

MAN   Yes, *Woman Bathing*.

MARGARET   It's just a woman wading in a river. She has her shift pulled up to her thighs. She's looking at herself in the reflection of the water. She's very pensive but very powerful, too. It's a dark painting, most Rembrandt is, but there's strength. I'm terrible talking about art. Are you good at it?

MAN   Yes? (*A bolt of blue fabric is rolled across the white floor of the stage. It is a river. Katharine and Margaret will find themselves on different sides of it.*)

MARGARET   Oh, look, there's a river here. Can we sit and bathe our feet?

MAN   Very nice. (*They sit.*)

KATHARINE   So this is where you were leading me? What's this river called?

MARGARET   Kitty, hello? Kitty! There's my friend on the other side of the river.

KATHARINE   Hello! That's Mrs. Civil. She is my friend.

MARGARET   She can't hear us. Who's your little friend?

KATHARINE   Behave yourself, you two! What is she doing? (*Margaret has started wading in the river.*)

MARGARET   *Woman Bathing* by Rembrandt!

MAN   *Woman Bathing*, ah, yes! Ha ha ha.

KATHARINE   You're a happy little person, aren't you? What's your secret? Everyone in India seems so content. I'm sure that's not true but you seem to possess some inner calm or confidence that we don't. I bet if I put even one finger on your belly you'll fall over giggling like a little doughboy! (*She touches Ganesha in the stomach and he falls over giggling. She will continue to tickle him awhile. He is enjoying himself enormously.*)

MARGARET   Every time I go to London I visit it. But the last time I looked at it something strange and rather awful happened. Two museum guards were talking as if I weren't there. One was a man, more or less my age, talking to a much younger woman, whom I assume was Indian or from Pakistan. You know what he said to her? Right in front of me, as if I were invisible! "No one wants me anymore. I've had my day. It's gone now." I wish people wouldn't say such deeply personal things in public. It stayed with me our entire trip. It almost ruined my Rembrandt. This was 5 or 6 years ago. It just came back to me.

MAN   London. Father's sister, London.

MARGARET   "No one wants me anymore. I've had my day. It's gone now." Isn't that a terrible thing to say with a total stranger listening?

KATHARINE   They're going back. (*She waves and calls across to them.*) I'll see you in the room.

MARGARET (*Waving and calling.*)   Five o'clock! Drinks with the manager! (*Margaret and Man withdraw. Light change suggests the passage of time. Ganesha's head is lying in Katharine's lap.*)

KATHARINE   My little brown *bambino*. My nutmeg *Gesù*. What color is your skin? Coffee? That's not right either. What color is mine? Not white? Where do words come from? What do they mean?

GANESHA   Walter.

KATHARINE   What? I thought you said, "Walter."

GANESHA   Walter.

KATHARINE   You did! You did say Walter!

GANESHA   Walter.

KATHARINE   Walter must be a word in Hindi then! Yes? Tell me, what does it mean, Walter?

GANESHA (*Laughing merrily.*)   Walter! Walter! (*He suddenly throws his arms around her and holds her tight.*)

KATHARINE   Does it mean laughter? It means something joyful! Something good! It must! Walter! Walter! (*She puts her hands to her mouth and calls across the lake.*) Walter! Walter!! (*Ganesha imitates her.*)

GANESHA   Walter! Walter! (*There is an echo. "Walter! Walter!" There is a silence as the echo dies away.*)

KATHARINE   It's gone.

GANESHA   Why have you stopped smiling? (*She kisses him fiercely.*)

KATHARINE   Stay this way forever. When you grow up, I won't like you. I will hate you and fear you because of the color of your skin—just as I hated and feared my son because he loved men. I won't tell you this to your face but you will know it, just as he did and it will sicken and diminish us both.

GANESHA   Why are you looking at me so intently? What do you want to see?

KATHARINE I came here to heal but I can't forgive myself. Maybe if I shout out the names of my fear and hatred of you across the holy river they will vanish, too, just as "Walter" did. Faggot. Queer. The words keep sticking.

GANESHA (*Trying to imitate her, like before.*)   Faggot? Queer?

KATHARINE A small boy says it better than you.

GANESHA Faggot? Queer?

KATHARINE Again.

GANESHA (*Happily, for her approval.*)   Faggot! Queer!

KATHARINE Again!

GANESHA (*Bigger.*)   Faggot! Queer!

KATHARINE Louder!

GANESHA Faggot! Faggot! Queer! Queer!

KATHARINE No, with hatred! Like they did: Fag! Queer! Cocksucker! Dead from AIDS queer meat!

GANESHA Oh dear, oh dear!

KATHARINE FAGGOT! FAGGOT! QUEER! QUEER! NIGGER! (*Katharine begins to break down. In the silence, we hear only her sobs. "Echo: Faggot, faggot! Queer, queer! Walter, Walter!"*) Walter. Forgive me. (*Ganesha cradles Katharine at the bank of the river. Man has appeared as Walter. He waves to Katharine, blows her a kiss and disappears.*)

GANESHA Foolish woman. You were holding a god in your arms. (*Lights change. Katharine stays where she is. Ganesha picks up a long pole. He is a Boatman. Sounds of water lapping.*)

MARGARET We're coming! We're coming. (*Margaret enters, hair covered by a scarf. The Man is with her. He is a Guide.*)

SCENE 4

On the Ganges River in Varanasi. Margaret, Katharine and Man sit in a small skiff, piloted by Ganesha. It is early morning and very misty.

MARGARET   Look what you left in the room! We wouldn't have seen a thing. Thank God I went back for a scarf. (*She has a pair of binoculars.*) Is someone going to give me a hand? (*Ganesha puts his hand out to her as she steps aboard the skiff. It threatens to capsize.*) Oh my God! Is this safe? Are we all going to drown in the Ganges?

MAN   Not if you sit down, Mrs. Civil!

MARGARET   I can't sit down until it stops rocking.

GANESHA   She's going to make us capsize.

MAN   Grab the sides and sit! (*Margaret steadies herself and sits. Ganesha will help Man board the skiff and then guide it out into the river.*)

MARGARET   This is madness. I'm never going to see Pumpkin Fields Lane again. I hate you for doing this. I hate myself for coming.

MAN (*To Ganesh.*)   Thank you.

MARGARET (*To Ganesha.*)   Oh, yes, thank you! (*Then.*) Who would think to bring Dramamine to India? Dramamine is for when we take the QE2. Where's your scarf? Mr. Tennyson warned us about this damp morning air. You just got over dysentery. Next stop, pneumonia. Then on to God knows what!

KATHARINE   Margaret, please, sshh!

MARGARET   You're right, I'm sorry. I'll practice what they taught us at the yoga institute in Delhi. Om! It's not working. Don't mind me, everyone. They're not. That's what's so pathetic!

MAN   Benares, now called Varanasi, the "eternal city," is one of the most important pilgrimage sites in India and also a major tourist attraction.

MARGARET   Oh my God, look at that: a dead rat floating by.

MAN   For the pious Hindu, the city has always has a special meaning. Besides being a pilgrimage center, it is considered especially auspicious to die here, insuring an instant routing to heaven.

MARGARET   Oh my God, what's that?

GANESHA Cow!

MARGARET What's he saying?

GANESHA Cow!

MARGARET It looks like a cow.

MAN I think it is.

GANESHA Cow!

MARGARET What's the Hindi word for "cow"?

MAN I don't know.

MARGARET I'm going to be sick.

KATHARINE Tell us about the ghats, Mr. Tennyson.

MAN Ghats are the steps which lead down to the river, from which the pilgrims make their sin-cleansing dip in the Ganges. Dawn is the best time to visit them.

MARGARET Oh my God, Kitty, look! It's a body.

KATHARINE I see it, Margaret.

MAN The pilgrims will be there for their early morning dip, the city will just be coming to life, the light is magical.

MARGARET We're going to bump right into it. (*We hear the thud of the body against the skiff.*)

MAN There are 100 ghats in all, of which—

KATHARINE Tell us about the burning ghats.

MAN There are two principal ones, the Marnikarnika ghat and the Charanpaduka ghat. There, you can just see the fires. This is where bodies are cremated after making the final journey to the holy Ganges— the men swathed in white cloth, the women in red—and carried on a bamboo stretcher—or even the roof of a taxi.

GANESHA Baby!

MARGARET Oh my God, don't look, Kitty. It's a child.

GANESHA Baby!

MARGARET   We're going to hit again! (*Again we hear the sound of the body hitting against the side of the skiff.*) Oh, that sound! (*Ganesha takes the skiff pole and pokes at the body.*)

GANESHA   Boy baby!

KATHARINE   It's a little boy.

MARGARET   How can you look even!?

MAN   Perhaps we should go back. Mrs. Civil doesn't seem to be able to handle this.

MARGARET   You're right, she's not. Please, Kitty, I've had enough.

MAN (*To Ganesha.*)   Back! Take us back! (*Ganesha takes the pole from the body and resumes navigating the skiff. In so doing, he splashes some water on Margaret.*)

MARGARET   Oh! Be careful! (*Margaret is brushing at the water on her clothes.*) He was poking the body with that pole! I feel slimy now.

KATHARINE   What brought you here, Mr. Tennyson?

MAN   It's Norman, please! I was looking for something I couldn't find in Wilkes-Barre, Pennsylvania. I forget what it was now but for a couple minutes back there in my youth, I thought I'd found it. Maybe it was just extra-good grass. (*The sound of another body against the skiff.*)

MARGARET   Please, can we get home?

KATHARINE   I thought I would be more appalled by all this.

MAN   Thought or hoped? Some people come to Varanasi to find their hearts have completely hardened. It's a terrible realization.

MARGARET   What are we supposed to do? I can't accept all this. My heart and mind would break if I did. And yet I must. I know it.

KATHARINE   Everything in and on this river seems inevitable and right. Something dead, floating there.

MARGARET   It's a dog.

KATHARINE   That old woman with sagging breasts bathing herself is oblivious to us.

MARGARET   She is lovely.

KATHARINE   Even us in our Burberry raincoats. We all have a place here. Nothing is right, nothing is wrong. Allow. Accept. Be.

MARGARET   Yes. (*Ganesha brings skiff to shore. Man leaps off and helps the others to disembark.*)

MAN   Home again. I think you'll find the shopping here a little more to your liking. Varanasi is famous all over India for its silk brocade.

KATHARINE   I'm still looking for a figure of Ganesh.

MARGARET   You've already bought almost a dozen.

KATHARINE   I'm looking for a perfect Ganesh.

MAN   Is there such a thing?

KATHARINE   I'm sure of it.

MAN   Let's get a move on, ladies. We have Sarnath before lunch.

MARGARET   What's in Sarnath?

MAN   Buddha! (*They walk away from Ganesha, who looks after them, brings his hands together and bows.*)

GANESHA   You're welcome. You're welcome. You're welcome. (*He has Margaret's binoculars, Katharine's first Ganesh figure and the Man's Marlboros. Lights are changing.*)

SCENE 5

A hotel room. There are louvered doors leading to a balcony fronting on a street.

KATHARINE   May I? (*Margaret stands with her back to us. She holds her blouse open to Katharine who is sitting in front of her. A dog is barking off. It stops. In the silence.*) Oh! (*Margaret closes her blouse and begins to button it.*)

MARGARET   I don't know what annoys me more about this country: the heat, the music, or the barking dogs.

KATHARINE   How long have you known?

MARGARET   I wasn't sure until that first night in Bombay.

KATHARINE   We'll go back at once.

MARGARET   No, we've come this far, I want to see the Taj Mahal. It's just a few more days.

KATHARINE   But you promise you'll—?

MARGARET   Of course.

KATHARINE   Just as soon as we get back!

MARGARET   Absolutely.

KATHARINE   I'm so sorry, Margaret.

MARGARET   Well. And that's about as philosophical as I'm going to get. I don't want anyone else to know; unless I have to, of course.

KATHARINE   Of course not. Thank you for confiding in me. It means a good deal to me. More than you could know. I need a friend. That sounds ridiculous at my age. But you're going to tell Alan, of course?

MARGARET   I don't know. Not if I don't have to. It would give him one more reason to work late. He's had one reason for almost 7 years. Her name is DeKennesey. She must be divorced. I know she's got two kids. I've seen them. She's only 10 years younger than me. He's got her in one of those condos by the club.

KATHARINE   I had no idea.

MARGARET   We're not supposed to.

KATHARINE   I'm so sorry.

MARGARET   You've got to stop saying that. What happens to women? Who are we? What are we supposed to do? What are we supposed to be? Men still have all the marbles. All we have are our children and sooner or later we lose them. (*She goes to the louvered doors, opens them and goes out. Lights up on the Man. He is a leper, as hideous as the first one.*) Your friend is back down there.

KATHARINE   You think I'm crazy, don't you?

MARGARET   Yes. (*Katharine has joined Margaret on the balcony looking down at the Man.*)

KATHARINE   I couldn't do it. Yesterday, while you were resting, I went down to the lobby and ordered a tea and just sat and stared at him out there. I felt so drawn to him, Margaret, yet so repulsed. I had to go out to him. (*She moves out of the room and to the Man. Margaret just stays on the balcony watching them.*)

MARGARET   I was up here. I wanted to call out to you but I didn't. I guess I wanted you to do it for the both of us.

KATHARINE   Why are you diseased and hideous? What can I do to change that?

MAN   Love me. (*Lights up on Ganesha, again with his elephant's head.*)

GANESHA   Love me, the man said and smiled at the lovely American.

KATHARINE   Here, in the warmth and light of India, I want to hold you in my arms, as I could not hold my son while he lay dying on a dark city street.

MAN   Love me.

GANESHA   Love me, the man said and smiled again.

KATHARINE   Now, in the moment when we are so close but so alone, I want to kiss you on the lips, as I could never kiss my son for fear of terrifying him how much I loved him.

MAN   Love me.

GANESHA   Love me, the man said again but this time he did not smile.

KATHARINE   You frighten me. You disgust me.

MAN   Love me.

KATHARINE I cannot do it.

GANESHA And Mrs. Katharine Brynne reached into her purse and gave the man 50 rupees and one of her perfect Ganeshas. She did not sleep well that night. She worried about her soul. The man, however, had the finest meal of his entire, miserable life. (*Katharine comes back to Margaret on the balcony. Again they look down at the Man just sitting there.*)

MARGARET I couldn't do it either.

KATHARINE The whole trip was a failure then.

MARGARET You're too hard on yourself. You can't save the world.

KATHARINE I can't even save myself. Here. (*She hands Margaret another of her Ganeshas.*)

MARGARET That's one of your favorites.

KATHARINE There's plenty more where it came from. I've got more than a dozen of them now. I still haven't found the perfect one.

GANESHA They're all perfect, Katharine. (*With a gesture he reveals a dazzling array of all sorts of Ganeshas: stone, clay, ivory, etc.*)

KATHARINE I know. I wish I could believe that. I can't. I just can't. (*To Margaret.*) It's for good luck with—

MARGARET You're a kind woman. (*They just look at each other a moment. It would be hard to say who opens her arms to the other first. They embrace. They kiss.*)

KATHARINE The Taj Mahal, then home.

MARGARET The Taj Mahal! (*Light change. Blinding light. It should be hard to look at the stage. Music.*)

SCENE 6

The Taj Mahal. We sit through Margaret and Katharine's eyes. They are transfixed.

GANESHA   What does one say before such beauty? If one is wise, very, very little. (*The Man appears. He is another American Tourist reading from a guidebook.*)

MAN   If there's a building which evokes a country—like the Eiffel tower does for France, the Sydney Opera House for Australia—it has to be the Taj Mahal for India.

MARGARET   Do you mind? We're trying to appreciate all this.

MAN   It's a free country.

KATHARINE   No, that's America. This is India. (*He withdraws. The two women are in rapture.*)

MARGARET   I've stopped breathing.

KATHARINE   My heart is pounding.

MARGARET   This has been worth everything.

KATHARINE   It's the most beautiful thing I've ever seen.

MARGARET   I'm not going to cry. I refuse to cry.

KATHARINE   Go right ahead. I just may join you.

MARGARET   I think it's better if we don't.

KATHARINE   I want you to see what I'm seeing. Look, over there!

MARGARET   I see it, I see it. And over there, Kitty, have you ever . . . ?

KATHARINE   We're in paradise. This is a dream. It isn't true.

MARGARET   But it is true. And we're here. And we will have this forever.

KATHARINE   Look!

MARGARET   Look! (*Ganesha draws a filmy gauze drape across the stage. It is the first time the stage has been "closed" the entire evening.*)

GANESHA   Two days later, they were back in Connecticut, met at the airport by a solemn delegation of Alan Civil and various Brynnes bearing the mournful news of Katharine's husband, the glare ice and the oak tree. Vacations can end abruptly like this. Trips have a way of going on. Mrs. Civil and Mrs. Brynne's visit to India was of the second variety. (*He pulls back the gauze curtain. To one side is a king-size bed. Katharine is undressing to get into it. On the other side, there are twin beds. Margaret is getting ready to get into one of them. The Man is already in his bed. He is Alan.*)

MARGARET   What's this postcard? (*She picks up a postcard on the pillow.*)

MAN   It came yesterday. It was addressed to the two of you. What were you two doing over there? Picking up strange men? That was a joke, Margaret. (*Margaret sits on the end of the bed and begins to read the card.*) I'll never know if I did the right thing. But who knows where to find you? It's a big country. I said to their kids, go to the Taj Mahal, hang out, sooner or later, they'll turn up. Good night, Maggie, I'm glad you're home. I missed you. (*He turns out the light. Margaret picks up the phone and dials a number. Katharine is sitting on the edge of her bed. She is humming/ singing "Blow the Wind Southerly." The telephone rings.*)

KATHARINE   Yes.

MARGARET   Are you okay?

KATHARINE   Better than expected.

MARGARET   We got a postcard from Harry and Ben.

KATHARINE   I'm sorry, I don't—

MARGARET   Yes, you do! The two young men, next door, our first day in Bombay. They were both sick.

KATHARINE   I remember.

MARGARET   "Dear Girls, (all right, *ladies!*), welcome home! Hope you had a wonderful trip and didn't have to use that police whistle again. Did you see the Taj Mahal? Didn't you just die a little? Thanks for all your kindness. Harry is still in the hospital here but doing well. We're both hanging in there. What else are you gonna do? Love, Ben." Guess who the postcard's of? Your favorite, Ganesha. A perfect Ganesh. I'll bring it over tomorrow. Are you sure you're okay?

KATHARINE   I'm fine.

MARGARET   I love you.

KATHARINE   Thank you.

MARGARET   You're supposed to say, "I love you, too."

KATHARINE   I love you, too, Margaret.

MARGARET   Good night, Kitty.

KATHARINE   Good night. (*They hang up. They each are sitting on the edge of their beds. Katharine begins to sing/hum "Blow the Wind Southerly." The Man has begun to snore. Margaret looks at him, then at the postcard and begins to sing/hum "Swing Low Sweet Chariot." At exactly the same time i.e., simultaneously, the two women get into bed and under the covers. Ganesha appears between them. He takes off his elephant's head. His face is gilded and he is revealed as a handsome man. He bends over Margaret and kisses her. She stops singing and sleeps. Then he bends over Katharine and kisses her. She, too, stops singing and sleeps. The Man is still snoring.*)

GANESHA (*Singing.*)
   "Good night, ladies
   Good night, ladies
   Good night, ladies
   The milkman's on his way."

(*He pulls the drape across the stage. He looks at us. He puts his finger to his lips.*) Good night. (*He disappears through the curtain. The Man is still snoring.*)

END OF PLAY.

LOVE! VALOUR! COMPASSION! (1994)

The first time I went to the Tony Awards was in 1993. I had been nominated for my book *Kiss of the Spider Woman*. I won; our show won Best Musical. I remember Bruce Wasserstein, a powerful investment banker, saying to his sister Wendy, the playwright, when her play *The Sisters Rosensweig* lost the Best Play Award to *Angels in America: Millennium Approaches* the same evening, "What do these people have against normal people?"

The time has come to speak about gay theatre. Fortunately, that's a phrase you don't hear much anymore. Unfortunately, there was a time when that's pretty much all that was said about a play if the characters and/or the playwright were out. Theatrical excellence or originality of mind were not held up for critical scrutiny if the play and its author could be labeled as gay. Rather, these plays and their playwrights were swept into a collective dust heap and marginalized as theatre written *by* a minority *for* a minority. No wonder these plays weren't being done on Broadway. Stanley Kauffmann, the New York Times' drama critic for a mercifully brief period of time after he succeeded the legendary Brooks Atkinson, was the Gaybuster with the largest audience.

At the time, more blatant homophobes such as John Simon were confined to ranting in more obscure publications. Even so, a "friend" asked me if I had read Simon's review of my first play, *And Things That Go Bump in the Night* in *The Sewanee Review*. Naturally, I hadn't. It took a trip to the Jefferson Market Library on 6th Avenue to track one down. Simon's review was entitled "Come back, Albertine"—an allusion to Proust, whom it was okay to call a homo. He had been dead since 1922 and there was no danger of a libel suit. I should have stopped at the headline. Instead, I ploughed on. "Wilde's love that dared not speak its name, now won't shut up." I burst into tears. It was the first time I'd cried since the opening and the last time I ever sought out a review in an obscure literary magazine.

So instead of *John Loves John* or *When Rachel Met Roberta*, gay and lesbian playwrights kept gay plot lines and characters off the stage and their sexuality to themselves. It must be remembered this was a time, even in the theatre, traditionally the most welcoming venue for gay men and women, when it was good to be married, especially if a playwright—anyone in the arts for that matter—wanted a major career. Institutions like the Metropolitan Opera and the New York Philharmonic did not want unmarried men (let alone women!) running them. The classical arts in this country were suspect enough without opening *that* can of worms. The theatre wasn't much better. Of course there were rumors about writers like Wilder and Williams and Inge and McCullers and Albee but they were never addressed by the subject of these rumors themselves. Don't Ask, Don't Tell indeed. It was an elaborate game and both sides of the fence were very good at playing it.

There were a few snarky critics who implied they knew what was going on with these playwrights and their plays. Williams's women weren't "real" women; *Virginia Woolf* was, if the truth be told, about four men. It was William Inge who lusted for hunky drifters, not the love-starved women in his plays. As for Carson McCullers, she wanted to be a boy. Fortunately for him, Thornton Wilder had already ascended to Great Man of American Letters status, which made him an icon beyond suspicion. More importantly, sex is pretty much a no-show in his plays. In *Our Town,* two teenagers standing on separate ladders doing their homework in the New Hampshire moonlight is about as carnal as it gets.

While it wasn't libelous to describe a play as homosexual, these critics knew to stop short of branding its playwright as gay. Mr. Showmanship himself, Liberace, sued for libel and won when a British newspaper outed him. Even my beloved Nana, who adored "Lee," put on her best Sunday dress and poured herself a glass of sherry and lit a candle to watch his weekly telecast probably thought deep inside that her favorite entertainer was gay but as long as no one openly acknowledged his sexuality, especially Liberace himself, she was content to convince herself he was "normal." In that respect, she was much more innocent and forgiving than Wendy's brother.

By 1993 the situation and the perception of these plays and playwrights had begun to change. Wendy's brother was on the wrong side of history but he didn't know that then. People on the wrong side of history are usually the last to know.

A lot of things had happened to change the situation in the twenty-eight years between the Broadway opening of my first play, *And Things That Go Bump in the Night*, in 1965 and that evening at the Tony Awards in 1993. Stonewall had happened. AIDS had happened. They were each a call to arms and an urgent, painful wake-up to reality. The cocoon of the theatre was no longer enough to either spare or delude us. For the first time since *Death of a Salesman*, it felt as if the theatre and real life in America were in conversation again. The theatre stopped being a place to hide and became a place again where we began to examine, probe and heal the very things that were tearing us apart.

I still remember the relief and pride I felt when Jane Chambers's *Last Summer at Bluefish Cove* was reviewed as a play about lesbians and not as a lesbian play. The easygoing naturalness with which a significant gay relationship was treated in Lanford Wilson's *Fifth of July* was a huge step forward—so huge no one seemed to notice. I sure did.

The AIDS plays that were certain artists' responses to the crisis were as inevitable as they were powerful. They opened the eyes of audiences that had only read of the suffering and not experienced it so viscerally as in the theatre at a performance of *As Is* or *The Normal Heart*. Some plays change minds *and* hearts. *Angels in America* was perhaps the culmination of our sorrow and rage.

A lot more was to happen after 1993 as well. We were preparing a reading of *Kiss of the Spider Woman* in the spring of 2012 when my husband, the producer Tom Kirdahy, burst into the rehearsal room with the news that the Supreme Court had struck down the Defense of Marriage Act.

No wonder you don't hear the catch-phrase Gay Theatre anymore. A play needs a lot more than cute young men in their tighty-whities to attract an audience—not at today's ticket prices. Today's buff young men had better be in a well-written, meaningful play as well. LGBT artists can no longer count on the support of their own kind just because they're gay. Gone are the days when I ate terrible meal after terrible meal at the Fedora on West 4th St. but kept coming back because it was gay-owned and -operated and as a gay man I had to support it.

I always felt that certain playwrights' displeasure at the designation "gay playwright" was just another exercise in semantics for playwrights who were *au fond* uncomfortable with their sexuality. "I'm a gay man who writes plays but I'm not a gay playwright," these men, who generally looked miserable about it, would insist, while accepting an award for their play or musical about Medieval tapestry weavers.

I was more angry at the failure of certain theatre icons to even come out, let alone acknowledge that there was something terrible going on and doing something about it. I still am, especially when these same men are regularly awarded and happily accept "gay" awards for their past achievements. AIDS separated the men from the boys, that's for sure.

L!V!C! is about eight gay men spending the three seminal weekends of a summer together—Memorial Day, the Fourth of July, and Labor Day—at a comfortable farmhouse on a lake in upstate New York. I have never been to upstate New York in my life but Shakespeare had never been to Venice,

Athens or the New World either. Playwriting is an act of imagining. I could imagine Gregory's country house; I knew these eight men. They were me divided into eight; I was all of them. I knew their secrets because they were my secrets. It is probably the least autobiographical of my plays but it is definitely the most personal.

I wanted to write about how extraordinary the very ordinariness of these eight lives was. In that sense, *L!V!C!* represents the first stirrings in my soulgut that were to lead to *Corpus Christi* four years later. Gay men were no longer a topic of my plays; gay lives in all their matter-of-fact routine were. AIDS was a given. So were jokes about Barbra and arguments about politics, the arts and who was going to do the dishes. Gay intimacy, it turns out, is no more or less complicated than anyone else's. When a Broadway audience watched Perry trim the hair in Arthur's ears, I knew we had come a long way together as a society since the time when Sigfrid and Clarence had sex in *And Things That Go Bump in the Night* and so many critical and audience hackles were raised. If anything makes *L!V!C!* special, it is its ordinariness. Gay men and women don't spend much time sitting around talking about being gay. It's the given in their lives. The question isn't why we're gay, it's how we are going to lead fulfilled lives that include deep relationships and useful, satisfying careers.

L!V!C! doesn't say it's okay to be gay or it's good to be gay. *L!V!C!* says it's everything to be gay. It's a big play thematically and a long one by the clock. Our two six-minute intermissions at the Walter Kerr Theatre were not popular with the audience or the actors, who had to get used to people finding their way back to their seats at the tops of the second and third acts.

I didn't want to write about AIDS when I began the play but of course there was no way I could avoid it. It was what was happening to us. But I also wanted to write about what else we were doing while so much of our world seemed to be burning. Life went on for us, not just death. We became each other's families. Night after night, I could feel a sense of community spreading through the theatre: we were in this nightmare together. The play and the audience were in mutual embrace of shared emotion. Something special was happening. We all felt it. This was more than the play being a hit. The theatre became a place of healing.

The original ensemble of actors was beyond all expectation. They all deserved Tony Awards (not just John Glover who won one for his *tour de force* as the identical twins, John and James), both individually and as an ensemble. So did Joe Mantello, the director, whose work was unsentimental and pitch-perfect. He and Loy Arcenas, the designer, solved the "impossible" stage directions I had so blithely described in the script: an onstage game of tennis doubles; two canoes at a great distance; a choreographer at work creating a new ballet. Dream big, young playwrights. There are fellow theatre artists out there who will realize your dreams for you. That's their job. Yours is to imagine a universe.

I have always written to music. The comic first act of *The Lisbon Traviata* was written with Rossini overtures playing softly behind me; the brutal second act was informed by Mascagni's *verismo* masterpiece, *Cavalleria rusticana* (the Callas recording, of course), though at a higher volume.

And when music isn't playing while I am working, I am often remembering music that touches me. I owe the end of the first act of *L!V!C!* to Samuel Barber's masterpiece, *Knoxville: Summer of 1915,* as sung by the great American soprano Eleanor Steber. (Be warned: there is no other version.) Edward Albee introduced me to this miraculous, perfect masterpiece about what it means to be young and spread blankets on the lawn and look up at the stars. When I hear this music, I always think of Edward and his great example and influence on all of us of my generation and I guess I subconsciously wanted to thank him for that in my play. At the same time, I think of Barber's influence on Edward and I feel the great connection between artists that is as comforting as it is thrilling.

I don't know what Bruce's response was when *L!V!C!* took the Tony Award for Best Play in 1995. Wendy's was pretty great. But artists are generally more accepting of their fellow artists than brothers or bankers are.

I know I was very glad I didn't hear a single comment about "normal people" that evening. In fact, I don't think I've heard that phrase—like Gay Theatre—since 1993.

The last time I went to the Tonys was in 2014. *Mothers and Sons* was nominated for Best Play. It didn't win; it should have. If it had been nominated for Best Gay Play it would have won in a landslide. I'm very glad it wasn't. I'd rather be a loser than marginalized.

Time doesn't heal all wounds, but it does march on.

Love! Valour! Compassion!

for Nathan Lane

LOVE! VALOUR! COMPASSION! was originally produced by the Manhattan Theatre Club (Lynne Meadow, Artistic Director; Barry Groves, Managing Director), in New York City, on October 11, 1994, with funds provided by AT&T: On Stage. It was directed by Joe Mantello; the set design was by Loy Arcenas; the costume design was by Jesse Goldstein; the lighting design was by Brian MacDevitt; the sound design was by John Kilgore; the choreography was by John Carrafa; the production stage manager was William Joseph Barnes and the stage manager was Ira Mont. The cast was as follows:

GREGORY MITCHELL   Stephen Bogardus

ARTHUR PAPE   John Benjamin Hickey

PERRY SELLARS   Stephen Spinella

JOHN JECKYLL/JAMES JECKYLL   John Glover

BUZZ HAUSER   Nathan Lane

BOBBY BRAHAMS   Justin Kirk

RAMON FARNOS   Randy Becker

The production subsequently transferred to Broadway as a Manhattan Theatre Club presentation, by special arrangement with Jujamcyn Theaters. It opened at the Walter Kerr Theatre on January 20, 1995. The only cast replacement was Anthony Heald in the role of Perry Sellars.

THE PLAYERS

BOBBY BRAHAMS
early twenties

RAMON FORNOS
early twenties

BUZZ HAUSER
mid–thirties

JOHN JECKYLL
late forties

JAMES JECKYLL
his twin

GREGORY MITCHELL
early forties

ARTHUR PAPE
late thirties, early forties

PERRY SELLARS
late thirties, early forties

THE SETTING

A remote house and wooded grounds by a lake in Dutchess County, two hours north of New York City.

THE TIME

The present. Memorial Day, Fourth of July, and Labor Day weekends, respectively.

ACT ONE

Bare stage.

There are invisible doors and traps in the walls and floors.

Lights up.

The seven actors are singing "Beautiful Dreamer" by Stephen Foster to a piano accompaniment.

Gregory turns out and addresses us.

GREGORY   Um. I love my. Um. House. Everybody does. I like to fill it with my friends. Um. And walk around the grounds at night and watch them. Um. Through the lighted windows. It makes me happy to see them inside. Um. Our home. Mine. Um. And Bobby's. Um. I'm sorry. Um. I don't do this. Um. On purpose. Um.

ARTHUR   It's okay, Gregory.

GREGORY   It was built in 1915 and still has most of the. Um. Original roof. The wallpaper in the dining room. Um. Is original, too. So is. Um. A lot of the cabinet work. You'd have to be a fool. Um. To change it. This sofa is my pride. Um. And joy. It came with the house. It's genuine. Um. Horsehair. It's itchy but I don't care. I love it.

PERRY   Tell them about the sled.

GREGORY   Jerome Robbins gave me this sled.

PERRY   Mutual admiration, he said. One master choreographer to another.

GREGORY   It's flat here, I said. No hills. Um. What am I going to do with a sled? It's not a sled, Gregory, he told me. It's an antique.

JOHN   It's not an antique, Gregory. It's a piece of junk.

GREGORY   I hope you. Um. Appreciate detail. That. Um. Wainscoting there. The finial here. The main stairs. Um. Have a very gentle rise. Everyone comments how easy it is to. Um. Climb them.

BUZZ   I love your stairs, Gregory. They're so easy.

ARTHUR   Don't tease him like that.

BUZZ   Who's teasing? I'm not teasing!

GREGORY   They don't build houses like this anymore. Um. The golden age. Um. Of American house building.

BUZZ   If this is going to be Pick On Buzz weekend...!

GREGORY   Not architecture, mind you, but house building. This house. Um. Was meant. Um. To stand. Welcome. Make yourself at home. (*As the men begin to break apart and drift to their various bedrooms, we see that two of them are kissing furiously: Bobby and Ramon.*)

BOBBY   No. No. No. (*They continue. Now it is Perry who turns to us.*)

PERRY   Anyway. Bobby has gone downstairs for cookies, Pepperidge Farm Brussels, and a glass of milk. Whether Ramon had followed him or was waiting from him, quiet like a cat, bare feet cold on the bare wood floors, I don't know. I was upstairs, asleep with my Arthur.

BUZZ   I was upstairs, asleep with myself. All this I heard later that summer—when everything changed, for good and bad but forever—but I wouldn't have been surprised.

BOBBY   Don't. Stop. Please. (*They continue.*)

PERRY   Anyway. I prefer the latter: the waiting. It implies certainty. That Bobby would wake up and steal from Gregory's bed and make his way down to their country kitchen—

BUZZ   Which actually was in the country. You're in Dutchess County, two hours north of the city.

PERRY   —and feel unfamiliar arms surround his bare chest from behind, raking his nipples, and in his surprise drop the milk bottle and break it—(*Sound of a bottle of milk breaking.*)

GREGORY   Bobby?

PERRY   —splattering milk and shards of glass everywhere—(*A pool of spilt milk is forming around them.*)

ARTHUR   What was that?

PERRY   —pinning them to that spot where they found themselves in the dull light of the still-open Frigidaire door. (*John sits up in bed.*)

JOHN   Ramon?

BOBBY   Just tell me, who is this? (*Ramon whispers in his ear.*)

PERRY   What name did Ramon whisper in Bobby's ear that first night? His? One of the others'? Mine? (*One by one the other four men resume singing.*) Anyway. They stood like this for quite some time and achieved some sort of satisfaction. After he'd come, Ramon whispered more words of love and passion into Bobby's ear, and stole quietly back up the stairs and into the bed he was sharing with John.

JOHN   Where were you?

RAMON   I couldn't sleep.

PERRY   Bobby cleaned up the mess on the kitchen floor, the whole time wondering what an episode like this meant, if, indeed, it meant anything at all. (*Arthur has come into the kitchen area.*)

ARTHUR   What happened?

BOBBY   Perry?

ARTHUR   It's Arthur.

PERRY   Arthur's my lover. We're often—

ARTHUR   What happened?

PERRY   It's very annoying.

BOBBY   Be careful. There might be broken glass.

ARTHUR   I'm okay, I'm wearing slippers.

PERRY   Arthur is always wearing slippers.

BOBBY   I think I got it all. Did I?

ARTHUR   I can't tell.

PERRY   Bobby is blind.

ARTHUR   Do you mind if I turn the light on? I'm sorry.

BOBBY   It's all right.

PERRY   People are always saying things like that to him. Me, too, and I've known him since he and Gregory got together. Bobby doesn't seem to mind. He has a remarkably loving nature.

ARTHUR   You know the refrigerator door is open.

BOBBY   Thanks. I was just going up. That's all we needed: a refrigerator filled with spoiled food and a house full of guests.

PERRY   See what I mean? Never puts himself first. I don't understand people like that.

ARTHUR   You're not going anywhere. Sit.

BOBBY   What's the matter?

ARTHUR   You cut yourself. Hang on, I'll be right back.

BOBBY   I'm fine.

ARTHUR   Sit. (*Arthur turns his back to Bobby. We hear running water and the sound of a piece of cloth being torn to make a bandage.*) I read an article that said most blind people hated to be helped.

BOBBY   We love to be helped. We hate to be patronized. It's people assuming we want help that pisses us off. I'm standing at a corner waiting for the light to change and some jerk grabs my elbow and says, "Don't worry, I've got you," It happens all the time. People think blindness is the most awful thing that can happen to a person. Hey, I've got news for everybody: it's not.

PERRY   I'm not in this conversation. I'm upstairs sleeping in the spoon position with my Arthur. Well, thinking I'm sleeping in the spoon position with my Arthur. Arthur's down in the kitchen expressing his remarkably loving nature to Bobby. (*Perry goes to his and Arthur's bed. He hugs a pillow and tries to sleep.*)

BOBBY   "Really, I'm fine," I said.

PERRY   I would have taken him at his word. When someone tells me he's fine, I believe him. But now we're getting Arthur's Mother Teresa.

GREGORY   Don't make yourself sound so cynical, Perry.

PERRY   That's Gregory expressing his remarkably loving nature. Shut up and go back to sleep. It was nothing. (*Gregory rolls over.*)

JOHN   Americans confuse sentimentality with love.

PERRY   That's John, expressing his fundamentally hateful one. (*John is standing with his back to us. We hear the sound of him relieving himself as he turns over his shoulder and addresses Perry, who is trying to sleep.*)

JOHN   It's true, duck. (*Arthur turns around.*)

ARTHUR   I'll try not to hurt. (*He kneels and begins to dress Bobby's foot. Arthur is attracted to Bobby.*)

BOBBY   Ow!

ARTHUR   Sorry.

PERRY   John is sour. He wrote a musical once. No one liked it. There or here. I don't know why they brought it over.

JOHN   Retaliation for losing the War of Independence. (*He follows Ramon.*)

PERRY   He's usually funnier than that.

JOHN   I missed you. I said I missed you.

RAMON   I heard you. Ssshh. Go back to sleep.

JOHN   *Te quiero, Ramon Fornas. Te quiero.*

PERRY   Does everyone know what that means? "I love you, Ramon Fornos. I love you." Anyway, the show closed, John stayed.

JOHN   Some people liked it. Some people rather liked it a lot, in fact. Not many, but some. The good people.

RAMON   Hey, c'mon, it's late!

PERRY   He's Gregory's rehearsal pianist now. When he's not pounding out *The Rite of Spring* for Gregory's dancers, he's working on a new musical-theatre project for himself.

JOHN   The life of Houdini. It's got endless possibilities. I've written thirteen songs.

PERRY   John is always working on a new musical-theatre project, I should hasten to add.

JOHN   What do you mean, you "should hasten to add"? Is that a crack?

RAMON   I'm going to find another bed if you keep this up.

PERRY   Anyway!

BUZZ (*Stirring.*) Did somebody say something about musicals? I distinctly heard something about musicals. Somebody somewhere is talking about musicals. (*He sits up with a start. Perry holds him.*) I was having a musical comedy nightmare. They were going to revive *The King and I* for Tommy Tune and Elaine Stritch. We've got to stop them!

PERRY Buzz liked John's musical.

BUZZ It had a lot of good things in it.

PERRY Buzz likes musicals, period.

BUZZ I'm just a Gershwin with a Romberg rising in the house of Kern.

PERRY (*To us.*) He's off.

BUZZ I was conceived after a performance of *Wildcat* with Lucille Ball. I don't just love Lucy, I owe my very existence to her. For those of you who care but don't know, *Wildcat* was a musical by Cy Coleman and Carolyn Leigh with a book by N. Richard Nash. It opened December 16, 1960, at the Alvin Theatre and played for 172 performances. Two of its most-remembered songs are "Hey, Look Me Over!" and "Give a Little Whistle." For those of you who care but know all that, I'm sorry. For those of you who don't know and don't care, I'm really sorry. You're going to have a lot of trouble with me. So what's up, Doc?

PERRY Buzz, you weren't awake for this.

BUZZ If I was, I don't remember it.

PERRY You weren't.

BUZZ Okay. (*He rolls over and goes back to sleep.*)

PERRY If it isn't about musicals, Buzz has the attention span of a very small moth. That wasn't fair. Buzz isn't well. He makes costumes for Gregory's company and does volunteer work at an AIDS clinic in Chelsea. He says he's going to find the cure for this disease all by himself and save the world for love and laughter.

BUZZ It sounds ridiculous when you say it like that!

PERRY I know. I'm sorry. (*He kisses Buzz on the head, goes back to his own bed, picks up a pillow, and hugs it close to him.*) None of us was awake for this. (*Gentle snoring begins—or humming, maybe. Arthur has stopped bandaging Bobby's foot. He is just looking at him now. His hand goes out and would touch Bobby's bare chest or arms or legs, but doesn't.*)

BOBBY   What are you doing?

ARTHUR   I guess you should know: there's a rather obvious stain on your pajamas.

BOBBY   Thanks.

ARTHUR   I didn't know I could still blush at my age.

BOBBY   That's okay. Your secret is safe with me.

ARTHUR   So is yours.

BOBBY   I'm the one who should be blushing, only blind men don't blush.

ARTHUR   That sounds like the title of one of Perry's detective novels.

BOBBY   I had sort of an accident.

ARTHUR   What you had was a mortal sin. I hope you both did. You know what we used to call them back in Catholic boys' school? Nocturnal emissions. It's so much nicer than "wet dream." It always made me think of Chopin. Nocturnal Emission in C-sharp Minor.

BOBBY   I don't want Greg to know.

ARTHUR   I swear to God, I only came down here for a glass of milk.

BOBBY   I swear to God, I did, too.

ARTHUR   We don't have to have this conversation at three a.m. We don't have to have this conversation ever.

BOBBY   Okay.

ARTHUR   We can talk about you and Greg. We can talk about me and Perry. We can talk about John and his new friend. We could even go back to bed.

BOBBY   It was Ramon.

ARTHUR   I figured.

BOBBY   Why?

ARTHUR   Who else would it be?

BOBBY   I shouldn't have. I'm not very strong that way.

ARTHUR   Most people aren't. (*They start walking up the stairs to their bedrooms.*)

BOBBY Is he attractive?

ARTHUR I'm not supposed to notice things like that. I'm in a relationship.

BOBBY So am I. Is he?

ARTHUR I think the word is "hot," Bobby. Okay? I love these stairs. They're so easy.

BOBBY Everyone says that. Have you ever . . . ? On Perry . . . ?

ARTHUR Yes. I don't recommend it.

BOBBY Did he find out?

ARTHUR No, I told him and it's never been the same. It's terrific, but it's not the same. Here we are. End of the line. (*He looks at Bobby.*) Don't fuck up. You are so . . . (*He hugs Bobby.*) He's not that hot, Bobby. No one is.

BOBBY I know. Thanks. Good night. (*He goes into Gregory's room. Gregory is awake. Arthur joins Perry in their room. Perry is still clutching his pillow.*)

GREGORY Are you all right?

BOBBY Ssshh. Go to sleep.

ARTHUR Sorry. (*He lies next to Perry.*)

GREGORY Where were you?

ARTHUR Bobby cut himself.

BOBBY Downstairs.

ARTHUR He dropped a milk bottle.

BOBBY I cut myself.

ARTHUR Remember milk bottles?

BOBBY I dropped a milk bottle. (*He lies next to Gregory.*)

ARTHUR Only Gregory would have milk bottles.

GREGORY Are you—?

BOBBY I'm fine. Arthur took care of me. Go to sleep.

ARTHUR   Are you awake?

GREGORY   I missed you. (*Bobby snuggles against Gregory.*)

BOBBY   Sshh. (*Arthur rolls over, his back to Perry now. Buzz and Ramon are snoring.*)

ARTHUR   He's so young, Perry!

GREGORY   I had a dream. We were in Aspen. The company. We were doing *Wesendonck Lieder*.

ARTHUR   I wanted to hold him.

GREGORY   The record got stuck during "Der Engel." (*Music starts.*) I had to do it over and over and over.

ARTHUR   Desire is a terrible thing. I'm sorry we're not young anymore. (*Gregory begins to sing: very softly, not well, and never fully awake.*)

GREGORY   In der Kindheit frühen Tagen.
  Hört'ich oft von Engeln sagen,

(*John sits up, while Ramon sleeps beside him, and listens. Gregory is beginning to drift off. At the same time we will hear a soprano singing the same words, her voice gently accompanying his.*)

die des Himmels hehre Wonne,
tauschen mit der Erdensonne . . .

(*Gregory sleeps. He and Bobby roll over in each other's arms. John has left Ramon and come out of their room. The soprano continues. All the men are snoring now.*)

JOHN   I am that merry wanderer of the night. Curiosity, a strange house, an unfaithful bedfellow drive me. Oh, there are other distractions, too, of course. A dog barking in the distance. Bed springs creaking; perhaps love in being made on the premises. The drip of the toilet on the third floor. Can they not hear it? But it's mainly the curiosity. I am obsessed with who people really are. They don't tell us, so I must know their secrets. (*Buzz moans in his sleep.*) I see things I shouldn't: Buzz is sleeping in a pool of sweat. They've increased his medication again. And for what? He's dead. (*He puts his hand on Buzz's shoulder, then moves to where Perry and Arthur are sleeping.*) Arthur has begun to sleep with his back to Perry, who clutches a pillow instead. I overhear what was better left unsaid: Arthur's sad confession of inappropriate desire. I read words I often wish were never written. Words that other eyes were never meant to see. (*He moves to where Gregory and Bobby are sleeping, takes up a journal, and reads.*) "Memorial Day Weekend. Manderley. Out here alone to work on the new piece. We've invited a full house and they're predicting rain. We'll see if Fred Avens has fixed that leak on the north side porch this time. Thought he would never get around to taking down the storm windows and putting up the screens. The garden is late. Only the cukes will be ready. Everything else will have to come from the A&P." This isn't quite what I had in mind. (*Buzz appears. He is carrying a knapsack.*)

BUZZ Where is everybody?

JOHN Did you know Gregory has only three places he feels safe? His work, in Bobby's arms, and in his journal.

BUZZ That's disgusting.

JOHN What is? The weather? Or the startling unoriginality of naming your house Manderley, after a kitsch-classic movie?

BUZZ Reading someone's journal.

JOHN Did you just get here?

BUZZ Yes. Where's Gregory?

JOHN Down by the lake. Are you alone?

BUZZ No, I have Michael J. Fox in here. Are you?

JOHN No. "I've rounded up. Um. The usual suspects. Um."

BUZZ That's not funny. You're a guest in his home.

JOHN "I think I'll make my special ginger soy vegetable loaf Sunday night." You see why I do this? Gregory's cooking. There's still time to buy steaks.

BUZZ If I thought you'd ever read anything I wrote when we were together, I'd kill you. I mean it.

JOHN "I'm stuck on the new piece. Maybe the Webern was a bad choice of music."

BUZZ I hate what you're doing. (*He grabs the journal from John.*)

JOHN I'm puzzled. What kind of statement about his work do you think a choreographer is making by living with a blind person?

BUZZ I don't know and I don't care. It's not a statement. It's a relationship. Remember them?

JOHN Nevertheless, the one can't see what the other does. Gregory's work is the deepest expression of who he is—or so one would hope—and Bobby's never seen it.

BUZZ That's their business. At least they've got someone.

JOHN Speak for yourself.

BUZZ So you got lucky this weekend. Don't rub it in. Who is he? Anyone I know?

JOHN I doubt it.

BUZZ Is he cute?

JOHN Yes.

BUZZ I hate you. I really hate you. What does he do?

JOHN He's a dancer.

BUZZ How long have you been seeing him?

JOHN Three weeks.

BUZZ Is it serious?

JOHN In three weeks?

BUZZ I get serious in about three seconds. People say "What's your rush?" I say, "What's your delay?"

JOHN What happened to you and—?

BUZZ I got too intense for him. That's my problem with people. I'm too intense for them. I need someone like Dennis Hopper. A cute, young, gay Dennis Hopper. In the meantime, I'm through with love and all it meant to me.

JOHN Are you going to be holding that when they come back? (*Buzz hasn't resisted stealing a glance at Gregory's journal.*)

BUZZ Perry's work for Greg is *pro bono*?

JOHN   Arts advocacy is very in.

BUZZ   He does the clinic, too.

JOHN   So is AIDS. I'm sorry.

BUZZ   That's five dollars. Anyone who mentions AIDS this summer, it'll cost them.

JOHN   Who made this rule up?

BUZZ   I did. It's for the kitty. Cough it up. (*John holds his hand out for the journal.*)

BUZZ   Did you?

JOHN   Did I what?

BUZZ   Ever read anything I wrote?

JOHN   I don't know. Probably. I don't remember. If you left if out, yes.

BUZZ   I would hardly call a journal left on someone's desk in their own room in their own home while they took the other guests swimming "out." (*He returns the journal.*)

JOHN   People who keep journals—thank you—expect them to be read by people like me. They just pretend they don't. Freud was on to them like that! (*He snaps his fingers while continuing to skim the pages of the journal. We hear thunder. It will increase.*)

BUZZ   Shit, it's going to rain.

JOHN   Here's something about you.

BUZZ   I don't want to hear it.

JOHN   "It's Buzz's birthday. We got him an out-of-print recording of an obscure musical called *Seventeen*."

BUZZ   I have *Seventeen*.

JOHN   "They assured us he wouldn't have it."

BUZZ   Don't worry, I'll act surprised.

JOHN   "It cost seventy-five dollars." You better act more than surprised.

BUZZ   I just paid a hundred and a quarter for it. They said it was the last copy.

JOHN   Calm down. You can exchange it.

BUZZ   For what? *Call Me Madam?* I mean, how many copies of a forgotten musical that opened in 1951 and ran 182 performances at the Broadhurst Theatre are they going to sell in one week? Do you know what the odds are against this sort of thing? This is like the time Tim Sheahan and Claude Meade both got me *Whoop-Up!* (*John has resumed reading in the journal, but Buzz continues, speaking to us.*) You may wonder why I fill my head with such trivial-seeming information. First of all, it isn't trivial to me, and second, I can contain the world of the Broadway musical. Get my hands around it, so to speak. Be the master of one little universe. Besides, when I'm alone, it gives me great pleasure to sing and dance around the apartment. I especially like "Big Spender" from *Sweet Charity* and "I'm Going Back Where I Can Be Me" from *Bells Are Ringing.* I could never do this with anyone watching, of course. Even a boyfriend, if I had one, which I don't. I'd be too inhibited.

So, when I'm not at the clinic thinking I am single-handedly going to find the cure for this fucking scourge (it doesn't sound ridiculous when I say it, not to me!), I am to be found at my place in Chelsea doing "Rose's Turn" from *Gypsy.* I can't think of the last time I didn't cry myself to sleep. Hey, it's no skin off your nose.

I think that's so loathsome of you, John.

Gregory and Ramon return from swimming.

GREGORY   Hello! We're back! Where is. Um. Everybody?

JOHN   I'd better return this.

BUZZ   We're up here.

GREGORY   John?

JOHN   Coming.

GREGORY   You don't know. Um. What you're missing. The lake. Um. Wonderful.

RAMON   Don't believe him. It's freezing! (*He drops his towel.*) ¡Ay! ¡Coño! ¡Madre de Dios!

GREGORY   Did. Um. The others get here?

JOHN   Just Buzz!

BUZZ   Hello.

GREGORY   Buzz!

RAMON   My nuts. Where are they? I have no nuts. They're gone.

GREGORY   They're not gone. Um. They're just. Um. Hiding. (*John and Buzz have returned.*)

RAMON   I had enormous nuts. I was famous for my nuts. Where are my fabulous nuts?

JOHN   I warned you, sweetheart. They got so cold in Gregory's lake they fell off and one of those goddamn snapping turtles is eating them as we speak.

GREGORY   My turtles don't. Um. Snap, Ramon. This is Buzz.

RAMON   Hi, Buzz. I had balls. He doesn't believe me. Tell him about my balls, John.

JOHN   Ramon had legendary balls up until twenty minutes ago.

BUZZ   I know. I've been following them for the last two seasons. From a tiny performance space in the East Village all the way to the Opera House at BAM. The three of you have come a long way, baby.

JOHN   Do you believe this man and I were an item?

BUZZ   A wee item, Ramon.

JOHN   You don't want to go there, Buzz.

BUZZ   But seriously (and don't you hate people who begin sentences with "But seriously"?), are you guys going to be back at the Joyce? That last piece was sensational.

GREGORY   You mean *Verläkte Nacht?*

BUZZ   Speak English! The man can barely get a whole sentence out and then he hits us with *Verläkte Nacht!* (*Then to Ramon:*) I don't suppose you want to get married?

RAMON   No, but thank you.

BUZZ   Just thought I'd get it out there. Anyway, *Verlächte Schmatta*, whatever it is, was a thrilling piece. It blew me away. And you were fantastic.

RAMON   Thank you.

BUZZ   Your balls weren't bad, either. I stood.

GREGORY   It was wonderful work. Wonderful. Um. Energy.

RAMON   You saw us, Mr. Mitchell?

GREGORY   I wanted to know. Um. What all the. Um. Shouting was about.

RAMON   I would have freaked if I'd known you were out there, Mr. Mitchell.

GREGORY   It's Gregory, please. You're making me feel. Um. Like. Um. An old man with "Mr. Mitchell." It was great. You reminded me. Um. Of me. Um. At your age.

BUZZ   "So what's next for you guys?" he asked in a casual, bantering voice, though his heart was beating so hard he was sure everyone could hear it.

RAMON   Right now we're all just hoping there will be a next season. We're broke.

GREGORY   Every company is, Ramon.

RAMON   Not yours, surely.

BUZZ   It's "Gregory." He doesn't like "Shirley." I'm sorry. Ignore me.

JOHN   He is.

BUZZ   What you need is a Diaghilev.

RAMON   What's a Diaghilev?

BUZZ   A rich older man who in return for certain favors funds an entire ballet company.

RAMON   Where is this rich older dude? I'm all his.

JOHN   Don't you want to know what these favors are first?

RAMON   I'm a big boy. I have a pretty good idea.

GREGORY   I'm in line first for him, Ramon.

BUZZ   Gregory, your dancers love you. We all do. We'd work for you for free.

GREGORY   I won't let you. Artists should be paid.

RAMON   Right on. The only thing an artist should do for free is make love.

JOHN   Now you tell me. Now he tells me! This is getting entirely too artsy-fartsy/idealistic/intellectual for me. Can we go upstairs and fuck?

GREGORY   I'm going to start. Um. Dinner. They should be here soon. I thought. Um. I'd make my special. Um. *Penne Primavera.* (*He goes.*)

BUZZ   I brought those sketches you wanted. I've got everyone in Lycra. Lots and lots of Lycra. I'm entering my Lycra period. You still know how to clear a room, John. (*He goes.*)

RAMON   I didn't appreciate that fucking remark in front of your friends.

JOHN   I don't appreciate you flapping your dick in everybody's face, okay? Are you coming upstairs?

RAMON   Maybe. (*John heads upstairs. Gregory looks at his watch and begins to chop onions. Buzz covers his eyes with some computer printouts and rests. John waits upstairs while Ramon sits downstairs. Arthur, Perry, and Bobby come into view. They are driving in heavy traffic.*)

PERRY   Cunt! Goddamn cunt. Fuck you and your ultimate driving machine!

ARTHUR   Perry!

PERRY   Well, they *are* when they drive like that.

ARTHUR   Don't use that word.

PERRY   Men are cunts when they drive like that. Did you see how she just cut right in front of me?

BOBBY   Are you talking to me? Sorry, I was reading the life of Ray Charles. What happened?

PERRY   Some asshole-whore-cunt-bitch-dyke with New Jersey license plates and Republican candidates on her bumper practically took my fender off at seventy miles an hour.

BOBBY   It sounds like an extremely cunt-like maneuver, Batman.

PERRY   You see? Boy Wonder agrees with Bruce.

ARTHUR   I think you're both disgusting. If I had any convictions I'd ask you to let me out right here.

PERRY   You have too many convictions. That's your trouble.

ARTHUR   Maybe you have too few and that's yours.

PERRY   They're just words. They don't mean anything.

ARTHUR   Can I quote him, Batboy?

PERRY   I was mad. Words only mean something if you say them when you're not mad and mean them. I agree: "Nancy Reagan is a cunt" is an offensive remark.

BOBBY   I wouldn't go that far, Bruce.

PERRY   But "Cunt!" when she grabs a cab in front of you after you've been waiting twenty minutes on a rainy night and she just pops out from Lutèce is a justifiable emotional response to an enormous social injustice.

BOBBY   You're right. He's right. Let's all kill ourselves.

ARTHUR   All I'm saying is, it's never right to use words to hurt another person.

PERRY   How did I hurt her? She didn't hear me. She's halfway to Poughkeepsie by now, the bitch. Don't get me started again. I was just calming down.

ARTHUR   We hurt ourselves when we use them. We're all diminished.

PERRY   You're right. I don't agree with you, but you're right.

ARTHUR   Of course I'm right, you big fairy. And what are you laughing at back there, you visual gimp? There's no really good insulting word for a blind person, is there?

BOBBY   I think you people decided nature had done enough to us and declared a moratorium.

PERRY   Do you ever wonder what Gregory looks like?

ARTHUR   Perry!

BOBBY   It's all right. I don't mind. I know what he looks like.

PERRY   No, I mean, what he really looks like.

BOBBY   I know what he really looks like. He's handsome. His eyes shine. He has wonderful blond hair.

PERRY   But you've never seen blond hair. You have no concept of it.

BOBBY   In my mind's eye, I do, Horatio.

ARTHUR   That shut you up.

BOBBY   That wasn't my intention. In my mind's eye, I see very clearly the same things you and Perry take for granted. Gregory's heart is beautiful.

PERRY   What do we look like?

ARTHUR   Perry!

BOBBY   Like bookends.

PERRY   Is that a compliment?

BOBBY   I think you've come to look more and more like each other over the years.

PERRY   You haven't known us that long.

ARTHUR   That's not what he's saying.

BOBBY   I think you love each other very much. I think you'll stick it out, whatever. I think right now you're holding hands—that when Perry has to take his hand from yours, Arthur, to steer in traffic, he puts it back in yours as soon as he can. I think this is how you always drive. I think this is how you go through life.

ARTHUR   Don't stop.

BOBBY   I think you're both wearing light blue Calvin Klein shirts and chinos.

PERRY   Wrong!

ARTHUR   Look out for that car—!

PERRY   I see it, I see it! What color is my hair?

BOBBY   What hair? You're totally bald.

PERRY   Wrong again. What color?

BOBBY   I wanted to be wrong. I don't like this game. It's making me afraid.

RAMON   Okay. (*He stands up.*)

JOHN   He's coming. (*Ramon starts up to John's room.*)

PERRY   I'm sorry. I didn't . . . (*They drive in silence. Ramon comes into the bedroom. John is sitting on the bed.*)

JOHN   Hello.

RAMON   Hi.

JOHN   I'm sorry.

RAMON   Look, I'm sort of out of my element this weekend. He's Gregory Mitchell, for Christ's sake. Do you know what that means? You're all old friends. You work together. You have a company. I'm just somebody you brought with you. I'd appreciate a little more respect, okay? I'm being honest.

JOHN   Okay.

RAMON   Thank you. What's wrong with your neck?

JOHN   Would you be an angel and massage my shoulders?

RAMON   Sure. Just show me where. (*Ramon works on John.*)

BOBBY   Now it's my turn. I want you to tell me what someone looks like.

PERRY   Don't tell me, let me guess: Tom Cruise, Willard Scott. I give up, who?

BOBBY   John.

ARTHUR   John Jeckyll?

BOBBY   What does he look like? Describe him. After all this time, I still can't get a picture.

PERRY   Can you visualize Satan, Bobby?

ARTHUR   Don't start.

PERRY   Do you have a concept of evil?

BOBBY   A very good one, actually.

ARTHUR   Not everyone shares your opinion, Perry. Perry has a problem with John, Bobby.

PERRY   I don't have a problem with him. I can't stand him and I wish he were dead.

JOHN   Don't stop.

PERRY   Beware him, Bobby. People like you are too good for this world, so people like John Jeckyll have to destroy them.

ARTHUR   You can't say these things, Perry.

PERRY   Yes, I can. He doesn't have to believe them.

BOBBY   I'm not so good. If anything, this world is too good for us.

PERRY   What do you care what John Jeckyll looks like anyway?

BOBBY   I just wondered. People like that intrigue me.

PERRY   What? Shits?

ARTHUR   It's going to be a wonderful weekend.

PERRY   What does that mean?

ARTHUR   John had nowhere to go, so Gregory invited him.

BOBBY   Didn't Gregory tell you?

PERRY   No, he did not. Probably because he knew I wouldn't come if he did. Shit! Why would Greg do this to me?

ARTHUR   He didn't. He told me. I elected not to tell you.

PERRY   Why?

ARTHUR   "Why?"!

PERRY   I assume he's coming alone.

ARTHUR   Why would you assume that?

PERRY   Who would willingly spend Memorial Day weekend at a wonderful big house in the country on a gorgeous lake with John Jeckyll when they could be suffocating in the city all by themselves?

BOBBY   He's bringing someone.

ARTHUR   A new boyfriend?

PERRY   One of the Menendez brothers.

BOBBY   A dancer.

ARTHUR   Someone from the company?

BOBBY   No. I think Greg said his name was Ramon. Ramon Something.

ARTHUR   Sounds Latino.

PERRY   "Something" sounds Latino? Since when?

BOBBY   He's Puerto Rican.

PERRY   A Third World boyfriend. So John Jeckyll has gone PC.

ARTHUR   I don't think Puerto Rico qualifies as Third World.

PERRY   This is like Adolf Hitler shtupping Anne Frank.

ARTHUR   You are really over the top this afternoon!

PERRY   Wait till the weekend's over! Here's the driveway. You're home, Bobby. (*Sounds of the car approaching. Everyone in the house reacts to the sound of it.*)

GREGORY   They're here! Buzz, John! They're here! I hear the car!

PERRY   Any other surprises for us, Bobby?

JOHN   I guess they're here. Perry and Arthur are lovers. Bobby is Greg's.

RAMON   I'm terrible with names.

GREGORY   Buzz, wake up, they're here!

BUZZ   I was dreaming about a vacuum cleaner. I need to get laid. (*Gregory, Buzz, John and Ramon go to greet the others, who are carrying bags.*)

GREGORY   I was beginning to. Um. Worry. How was the. Um. Traffic?

PERRY   Terrible. Especially before Hawthorne Circle.

ARTHUR   I told him to take the Thruway, but no!

BUZZ   The train was horrendous. I should have waited for you. But guess who I saw? Tony Leigh and Kyle. Together again. A handshake? What is this shit? I want a hug, Martha.

GREGORY Where's my. Um. Angel?

BOBBY Hi. Have you been working?

GREGORY I didn't leave. Um. The studio. Um. All week.

BOBBY How did it go?

GREGORY Great. Don't ask. Terrible. (*They embrace and withdraw a little.*)

JOHN Hello, Perry. Arthur. You both look terrific. Don't you two put on weight? Ever? Anywhere?

ARTHUR Look who's talking! I'd love to see the portrait in his closet.

JOHN No, you wouldn't. Ramon, Arthur and Perry.

PERRY He's Arthur, I'm Perry. He's nice, I'm not. Hi.

ARTHUR We're both nice. Don't listen to him.

BUZZ So what are you driving now, boys? A Ford Taurus?

PERRY What do you care, you big fruit? I don't know. I just get in, turn the key, and go. When they stop, I get a new one.

JOHN You should see the wreck we rented.

ARTHUR It's a Mazda 626, Buzz.

PERRY He's so butch.

ARTHUR Someone had to do it. That's why he married me. Can you change a tire?

PERRY No.

ARTHUR Neither can I.

BUZZ That's from *Annie Get Your Gun.* "Can you bake a pie?" "No." "Neither can I." Ethel Merman was gay, you know. So was Irving Berlin. I don't think English is Ramon's first language.

GREGORY I missed you.

BOBBY It's so good to be here. The city is awful. You can't breathe. They still haven't fixed the dryer. Flor was in hysterics. Here. I've got your mail in my backpack.

GREGORY What's this?

BOBBY   The CDs you wanted. And I got your sheet music from Patelson's.

GREGORY   You didn't have to.

BOBBY   I wanted to.

GREGORY   John, look, the Elliott Carter!

RAMON (*To Bobby.*)   Hi, I'm Ramon.

GREGORY   I'm sorry! (*Ramon puts his hand out to Bobby.*) Bobby doesn't. Um. See, Ramon.

RAMON   I'm sorry, I didn't—

BOBBY   Don't be sorry. Just come here! (*He hugs Ramon.*) Welcome. Ramon, is it?

RAMON   Right.

BOBBY   Latino?

RAMON   Yes.

BOBBY   *Mi casa es su casa.* I bet you were wishing I wasn't going to say that.

BUZZ   We all were, Bobby.

PERRY, ARTHUR, AND BUZZ   We all were!

RAMON   Listen, that's about as much Spanish as I speak.

BOBBY   You're kidding.

RAMON   Sorry to disappoint you. The Commonwealth of Puerto Rico is a territory of U.S. imperialism.

JOHN   No speeches, please, Ramon. No one's interested.

RAMON   We speak American. We think American. We dress American. The only thing we don't do is move or make love American.

BOBBY   I've been like his since birth, Ramon. Gregory and I have been together four years. I get around fine. It'll surprise you. Any more questions?

RAMON (*Off guard.*)   No. (*They separate.*)

GREGORY   Let me. Um. Show you. Um. To your room.

ARTHUR After all these years, I think we know, Gregory. If those walls could talk!

BUZZ They don't have to. We've all heard you.

ARTHUR What room are you in?

BUZZ That little horror under the eaves. I call it the Patty Hearst Memorial Closet.

ARTHUR Give me a hand with these, will you, Perry?

PERRY I told you not to take so much.

ARTHUR It's my hair dryer.

PERRY You don't have enough hair to justify an appliance that size.

ARTHUR Has it ever occurred to you that I stopped listening to you at least ten years ago.

RAMON Here, let me.

ARTHUR Thank you. (*They will start moving to the house.*)

GREGORY We're having. Um. *Salade Niçoise.* Um. For Lunch.

BUZZ You know I'm allergic to anchovies.

GREGORY We just. Um. Swam the float out. Me. Um. And Ramon.

BUZZ He knows I'm allergic to anchovies.

PERRY I'm not going in that lake until you get it heated.

GREGORY I hope you brought. Um. Your swimsuits.

ARTHUR No one is wearing swimsuits. We're all going skinny-dipping after lunch. What are we? Men or wimps?

BUZZ You just want to see everyone's dick.

ARTHUR I've seen everyone's dick. Answer the question.

BUZZ Sometimes we're men and sometimes we're wimps. You haven't seen Ramon's dick.

ARTHUR You're a troublemaker.

BUZZ   I'm not a troublemaker. I'm an imp. A gay imp. (*He goes. The new arrivals are beginning to settle in. Perry and John remain for the following until indicated.*)

PERRY   Anyway. Gregory knew he'd left Bobby downstairs and outside the house.

GREGORY   Does everyone. Um. Have towels?

PERRY   It was their ritual. Whenever they arrived at the house from the city, Bobby liked to be alone outside for a while, even in winter. Gregory never asked what he did.

BOBBY   Hello, house.

ARTHUR   Greg! We need some towels.

PERRY   No, we don't. We brought our own. Remember?

BOBBY   Hello, trees.

ARTHUR   Never mind! That's right, we hate his towels.

BOBBY   Hello, lake.

GREGORY   Who said they needed towels?

PERRY   Greg's house is very large.

ARTHUR   Too large. I get sick of shouting. We're fine! Forget the towels!

BOBBY   I bless you all.

PERRY   None of us saw Ramon when he returned to the driveway, the parked cars, and Bobby. Arthur and I were settling in. (*Ramon has returned to where Bobby is standing. He watches him.*)

JOHN   I was on the phone to London with my brother, James.

PERRY   I didn't know you had a brother.

JOHN   A twin brother. We're like *that*. (*He opens his arms wide.*) He's not well.

PERRY   I'm sorry.

JOHN   This is about them. (*He nods toward Bobby and Ramon.*)

PERRY   Minutes passed. Gregory fussed. Buzz washed salad greens in his hosts' pricey balsamic vinegar. He's very diligent about germs. He has to be. Ramon looked at Bobby.

BOBBY   Thank you, God.

RAMON   Excuse me?

BOBBY   Who's that?

RAMON   I'm sorry.

BOBBY   You startled me.

RAMON   It's Ramon. I'm sorry. I thought you said something.

BOBBY   I was thanking God for all this. The trees, the lake, the sweet, sweet air. For being here. For all of us together in Gregory's house.

RAMON   I didn't mean to interrupt or anything.

BOBBY   I'm not crazy. I'm happy.

RAMON   I understand.

GREGORY   Here are the towels you asked for.

ARTHUR   Thank you.

GREGORY   Anything else?

ARTHUR   We're fine.

GREGORY   Perry?

PERRY   We're fine.

GREGORY   Um. I'm glad. Um. You're both here.

RAMON   Do you need a hand with anything?

BOBBY   No, thanks.

BUZZ   Pssst! Gregory!

GREGORY   What?

BUZZ   John is on the phone with his brother in London. I didn't hear him use a credit card or reverse the charges.

GREGORY   Um. I'm sure he'll. Um. Tell me.

BUZZ   Don't you ever believe the worst about anyone?

GREGORY   No. (*Ramon hasn't moved. He scarcely breathes. He has not taken his eyes off Bobby.*)

BOBBY   You're still there, aren't you? What are you doing? What do you want? Don't be afraid. Tell me. All right. Don't. Stay there. I'll come to you. Just tell me, should I fall (which I don't plan to), what color are my trousers? I think I put on white. I hope so. It's Memorial Day.

PERRY   I don't know why, but I'm finding this very painful.

BOBBY   Children play at this and call it Blindman's Bluff. Imagine your whole life being a children's birthday-party game!

JOHN   Painful, erotic, and absurd.

BOBBY   I can feel you. I can hear you. I'm getting warm. I'm getting close. I like this game. I'm very good at it. I'm going to win. You haven't got a chance.

PERRY   Bobby didn't see the rake. (*Bobby trips and falls. He hurts himself. There will be a gash on his forehead.*)

RAMON   Oh!

BOBBY   He speaks! The cat has let go his tongue. I wouldn't say no to a hand. (*Ramon goes. Bobby calls after him.*) At least tell me, what color are my trousers?

PERRY (*Moved.*)   White. White.

BOBBY   Sometimes I get tired of behaving like a grown-up. Ow! Gregory! (*At once, everyone converges on the scene and surrounds him.*)

GREGORY   What happened?

BOBBY   I'm okay. Just—

GREGORY   The rake! You tripped. It's my fault. Um.

PERRY   Take his other arm.

BOBBY   I'm fine. I want Gregory to do it.

BUZZ   Who would leave a rake out like that?

ARTHUR   Shut up, will you?

JOHN   He's cut.

BOBBY   I'm not cut.

JOHN   His forehead.

BOBBY   What color are my trousers?

GREGORY   White.

BOBBY   Are there grass stains on them?

BUZZ   Bobby, you are the only fairy in America who still wears white pants on the first holiday of the summer.

PERRY   White pants were before my time, even, and I'm pushing forty.

BUZZ   Not. You pushed forty when *Chorus Line* was still running.

PERRY   That's not true. I was born in 19—

ARTHUR   We have an injured person here. (*Ramon returns.*)

BOBBY   I'm not injured.

JOHN   Where have you been?

RAMON   Down by the lake. What happened?

BOBBY   Nothing happened. Who's that?

BUZZ   The new kid on the block.

RAMON   Is he all right?

BOBBY   I fell. Big deal. I do it all the time.

GREGORY   No, you don't. No, he doesn't.

BOBBY   Now everyone back off. Everyone but Gregory. I can feel you all crowding around me.

GREGORY   One!

BOBBY   What are you doing?

BUZZ   Rhett picks up Scarlett and carries her up the stairs.

GREGORY   Two!

BOBBY   No, I don't want you to.

GREGORY   Three! (*He tries to pick Bobby up but can't. He staggers with the weight, then sets him down. The others look away in embarrassment.*) I couldn't get a good. Um. Grip.

BOBBY   It's not you. It's all that ice cream I've been eating.

GREGORY   That's never happened. Usually I—I feel so—

BOBBY   It's okay, it's okay. (*Bobby and Gregory go into the house. The others hang behind somewhat sheepishly.*)

BUZZ (*Singing.*)   "Just a weekend in the country."

RAMON   Is that a joke?

BUZZ   Come on, I need you in the kitchen. I'll explain the entire Sondheim oeuvre to you while we peel potatoes. I'm borrowing your humpy boyfriend, John. I love the way I said that. Oeuvre. I'm quite impressed. Oeuvre. Say it with me. Oeuvre. (*Buzz and Ramon go.*)

ARTHUR   Don't ever try to pick me up.

PERRY   It's lucky for you I did.

JOHN   I'd rung off from my brother feeling a rage and desolation I didn't know how to cope with. "Didn't I?" I never have.

ARTHUR   What's the matter?

JOHN   My twin brother. The National Theatre seamstress. He wants me to come over. He's not well. He needs me and I don't like him.

ARTHUR   That's a tough order. I don't envy you. Perry, I'm going to take a canoe out. You want to come?

PERRY   I promised Greg I'd go over some company business with him.

ARTHUR   It's your last chance to get rid of me.

PERRY   No, it's not. (*Arthur goes. Only Perry and John remain.*) I work with quite a few AIDS organizations.

JOHN   Thank you.

PERRY   They can help him find a doctor.

JOHN   Thank you.

PERRY   It never ends.

JOHN   No.

PERRY   How does Buzz look to you?

JOHN   I don't know. How does he look to you?

PERRY   I can't tell anymore.

JOHN   He wouldn't tell me if things were worse.

PERRY   I can't look at him sometimes.

JOHN   Anyway.

PERRY (*Pleasantly.*)   You got that from me, you know.

JOHN   Got what?

PERRY   The "anyway."

JOHN   It's a word in the dictionary. Page 249. You can't copyright the English language, duck.

PERRY   Hey, I'm trying! Fuck you. (*He goes.*)

JOHN   Anyway. *En tout cas!* The weekend had begun. Everyone was in place. Old wounds reopened. New alliances forged. For fifteen minutes, while I helped Arthur wash their car, he was my best friend in the entire world. Later that afternoon, after too much picnic, when I came upon him and Perry all cozy in a hammock on the porch, he barely gave me the time of day. The hours until dinner seemed endless. (*The other men are reassembling for after-dinner after a very big meal.*)

PERRY   No, Gregory. It's out of the question. Jesus, I hope this isn't why you invited us out here for the weekend.

GREGORY   I've. Um. Committed us.

PERRY   Well, *un*commit us!

GREGORY   It's too late.

PERRY   Leave it to me. I'll get you out of it.

GREGORY   No, I want to. Um. Do it. It's for a good cause.

PERRY   I don't care if it's the greatest cause in the history of Western civilization, which it's not, you are not going to find six men, nondancers all, to put on tutus and do *Swan Lake* for another AIDS benefit at Carnegie Hall. You're going to find one man!

BUZZ   Speak for yourself, Perry.

PERRY   Well, *you!* The love child of Judy Garland and Liberace.

ARTHUR   When is it, Greg?

GREGORY   Um. It's. Um. Early September, right after Labor Day.

PERRY   Bobby, tell your lover he is not going to find six men to make fools of themselves like that.

BOBBY   How would they be making fools of themselves?

PERRY   By dressing like women. Men in drag turn my stomach.

RAMON   Why?

ARTHUR   Don't start, Perry.

BUZZ   You wouldn't be in drag. I'd have you in tulle, lots and lots of tulle. A vision of hairy legs in a tutu and toe shoes.

PERRY   This will go over big at the NEA, Gregory. That's all we need. A picture of you looking like some flaming fairy in the Arts and Leisure section.

GREGORY   I. Um. I am a flaming fairy. I thought we all were.

PERRY   You know what I'm talking about.

BOBBY   Don't yell at him. It was my idea. I thought it would be funny.

PERRY   What do you know about funny? I'm sorry, Bobby, but sometimes boyfriends should stay boyfriends.

GREGORY   Sometimes. Um. Lawyers should stay. Um. Lawyers.

PERRY   You've done enough for AIDS. We all have.

GREGORY   Nobody's done enough. Um. For AIDS.

BOBBY   It's okay, Gregory.

GREGORY   Never mind, Perry. I'll ask someone else. Now who wants what?

ARTHUR   We're all fine.

PERRY   No, we're not.

JOHN   People are bloody sick of benefits, Gregory.

PERRY   That's the truth.

BUZZ   Not the people they're being given for.

GREGORY   *Basta*, Buzz. The subject is closed.

ARTHUR   Dinner was delicious. The mashed potatoes were fabulous, Gregory.

BUZZ   The mashed potatoes were mine. (*He signs from* The King and I.) I don't know why I've bothered to perfect flawless imitation of Gertrude Lawrence when none of you cretins has even heard of her!

JOHN   We've heard, luv. We don't care.

BOBBY   Who's Gertrude Lawrence?

PERRY   A British actress.

GREGORY   She was. Um. Gay, you know.

BUZZ   That's not funny. Julie Andrews made a rotten film about her.

ARTHUR   Isn't Julie Andrews gay?

BUZZ   I don't know. She never fucked me. Don't interrupt. Gertrude Lawrence wasn't an actress. She was a star. Hence, the rotten film, *Star!*, but don't get me started on movies. Movies are for people who have to eat popcorn while they're being entertained. Next question? Yes, you, at the end of the table with the lindenberry sorbet all over his face.

RAMON   Who's Julie Andrews?

BUZZ   I should have seen that one coming. I was born in the wrong decade, that's my problem.

RAMON   I was kidding. I was *Mary Poppins*. But who's Liberace?

BOBBY   Who's Judy Garland? Who are any of these people? (*Bobby and Ramon laugh together.*)

ARTHUR   You want me to clean up, Gregory?

BUZZ   Who's Ethel Merman? Who's Mary Martin? Who's Beatrice Lillie? Who's anybody? We're all going to be dead and forgotten anyway.

BOBBY   Gregory's not.

BUZZ   I'm talking about mattering!

PERRY   I just don't want to be dead and forgotten in my own lifetime.

ARTHUR   Nattering?

BUZZ   Mattering! Really mattering.

ARTHUR   Oh, I thought you said "nattering"!

JOHN   You admit people like Gertrude Lawrence don't really matter?

ARTHUR   I thought he said "nattering."

BUZZ   I cannot believe a subject of the U.K. could make a remark like that. Gertrude Lawrence brought pleasure to hundreds of thousands of people. You wrote a musical that ran for eleven performances.

JOHN   I have United States citizenship.

RAMON   I know who Barbra Streisand is.

BUZZ   She'll be very pleased to hear that.

BOBBY   I don't know who most of those people are, either.

PERRY   When did you take out U.S. citizenship?

JOHN   Nine years ago, October 25.

BUZZ   Barbara Cook's birthday. "Who's Barbara Cook?" No one. Nobody. Forget it. Die listening to your Madonna albums. I long for the day when people ask "Who's Madonna?" I apologize to the teenagers at the table, but the state of the American musical has me very upset.

PERRY   The state of America is what should get you upset.

BUZZ   It does. It's a metaphor, you asshole!

PERRY   Now just a minute!

BUZZ   I have a picture of a starving child in Somalia over my desk at the clinic. He's covered in dust.

JOHN   We all know the picture.

PERRY   It doesn't justify you calling me an asshole.

BUZZ   The child has fallen forward on his haunches, he's so weak from hunger, he can barely lift his head.

PERRY   Buzz, we know the picture. It was in every magazine and paper.

BUZZ   Clearly, the kid is dying. He's got what? Five minutes? Ten? Five feet away a vulture sits. Sits and waits. He's not even looking at the kid. He's that confident where his next meal is coming from. There's no way this kid is going to jump and launch into a number from *Oliver!* or *Porgy and Bess.*

PERRY   We've all seen the picture!

BOBBY (*Quietly.*)   I haven't. (*Gregory takes his hand.*)

PERRY   What's your point?

BUZZ   Point? I don't have a point. Why does everything have to have a point? To make it comfortable? I look at that picture every day and I get sick to my stomach and some days I even cry a little. The newspaper has already yellowed, but the nausea and the occasional tears keep coming. But so what? So fucking what? That kid is dead meat by now.

JOHN   That's disgusting.

BUZZ   You bet it is.

JOHN   Your language.

BUZZ   So sue me. That's from *Guys and Dolls,* for you kiddies.

RAMON   Happy Memorial Day.

PERRY   I think the point is, we're all sitting around here talking about something, pretending to care.

ARTHUR   No one's pretending.

PERRY   Pretending to care, when the truth is there's nothing we can do about it. It would hurt too much to really care. You wouldn't have a stomachache, you'd be dead from the dry heaves from throwing your guts up for the rest of your life. That kid is a picture in a newspaper who makes us feel bad for having it so good. But feed him, brush him off, and in ten years he's just another nigger to scare the shit out of us. Apologies tendered, but that's how I see it.

ARTHUR   Apologies not accepted.

GREGORY   Don't, you two.

ARTHUR   I hate it when you talk like that.

PERRY   You'd rather I dissembled, sirrah? (I wasn't an English major at Williams for nothing!)

ARTHUR   Yes. I'd rather you would. Rather the man I shared my life with and loved with all my heart, rather he dissembled than let me see the hate and bile there.

PERRY   The hate and bile aren't for you, love.

ARTHUR   That's not good enough, Perry. After a while, the hate and bile are for everyone. It all comes around. (*He starts clearing the table.*)

PERRY   Anyway.

ARTHUR   I hate that word. You use it to get yourself out of every tight corner you've ever found yourself in. Shall I load the washer?

GREGORY   Just rinse and stack. Thank you, Arthur.

RAMON   Do you need a hand?

ARTHUR   No, thank you. (*He goes.*)

PERRY   The younger generation hasn't put in their two cents, I notice.

RAMON   As a person of color, I think you're full of shit. As a gay man, I think—

JOHN   No one cares what you think as a gay man, duck. That wasn't the question. What do you think as a member of the human race?

RAMON   As a gay man, I think you're full of shit. (*We hear a door slam. Arthur isn't back. Everyone reacts.*) I think the problem begins right here, the way we relate to one another as gay men.

JOHN   This is tired, Ramon. Very, very tired.

RAMON   I don't think it is. We don't love one another because we don't love ourselves.

JOHN   Clichés! Clichés!

RAMON   Where is the love at this table? I want to see the love at this table.

BOBBY   I love Gregory.

GREGORY   I love Bobby.

PERRY   I love Arthur. I love Gregory. I love Bobby. I love Buzz. Right now I love you, your righteous anger.

BUZZ   I sure as hell don't love anyone at this table right now. All right, Bobby and Greg. A little bit, but only because they're our hosts.

JOHN   I love the Queen; she's been through hell lately. My Aunt Olivia in Brighton in a pensioners' villa—an old-age home, you call them? My Welsh Corgi, Dylan, even though he's been dead lo these eleven years (I'm surprised his name came up!). And my job.

GREGORY   Thank you.

RAMON   Everything you love is dead or old or inanimal. Don't you love anything that's alive and new?

JOHN   Of course I do, but I choose not to share them around a dinner table. And you mean "inanimate."

PERRY   That's honest.

JOHN   I thought that's what we were all being. Otherwise, what's the point? Are you satisfied, Ramon?

RAMON   None of you said yourself.

PERRY   Maybe it goes without saying.

JOHN   We were waiting for you, Ramon. How do you love yourself? Let us count the ways.

RAMON   I love myself. I love myself when I dance.

JOHN   That's one.

RAMON   I love myself when I'm dancing. When I feel the music right here. When I'm moving in time and space. Gregory knows what I'm talking about.

GREGORY   Yes, yes, I do.

RAMON   When I dance I become all the best things I can be.

JOHN   Ramon loves himself when he dances. That's still only one, Chiquita. One and counting.

RAMON   I love myself when I'm making love with a really hot man. I love myself when I'm eating really good food. I love myself when I'm swimming naked.

JOHN   That's four.

RAMON   The rest of the time I just feel okay.

PERRY   I'm jealous. We don't reach such an apotheosis at the law firm of Cohen, Mendelssohn and Leibowitz.

RAMON   But most of all I love myself when I'm dancing well and no one can touch me.

JOHN   Is this as a gay dancer, luv?

RAMON   Fuck you, John.

BUZZ   You tell him, sweetheart. That's right: Fuck you, John.

JOHN   Americans use that expression entirely too often.

BUZZ   Everybody!

ALL BUT JOHN   Fuck you, John!

JOHN   In England we think it nearly as often as you do, but we don't actually say it to someone's face. It would be too rude. Half the people who are being knighted at the Palace every year are thinking "Fuck you" as they're being tapped with that little sword, but they don't come right out and say it, the way an American would, which is why we don't knight Americans, the only reason—you're too uncouth.

ALL BUT JOHN   Fuck you.

JOHN   What do you mean when you tell another person "Fuck you"?

RAMON   Fuck you, John. And don't you ever call me Chiquita again.

BUZZ   This is good.

JOHN   I think you mean several things. Mixed signals, I believe they're called in therapeutic circles. "I hate you. Get out of my life." At least, "I hate you, get out of my life for the moment."

RAMON   Fuck you.

JOHN   "I love you, but you don't love me. I want to kill you but I can't so I will hurt you instead. I want to make you feel small and insignificant, the way you've made me feel. I want to make you feel every terrible thing my entire life right up until this moment has me feel." Ah, there's the link! I knew we'd find it. The common bond uniting this limey and the Yanks. The resolution of our fraternal theme.

RAMON   I said "Fuck you."

JOHN   But until we recognize and accept this mutual "Fuck you" in each of us, with every last fiber of my fading British being, every last ounce of my tobaccoed English breath, I say "Fuck you" right back. Fuck you, Ramon. Fuck you, Buzz. Fuck you, Perry. Fuck you, Gregory. Fuck you, Bobby. Fuck all of you. Well, I think I've said my piece. (*He moves away from the others, who remain at the table.*) I feel like playing, Gregory. Did you have your mighty Bechstein tuned in honor of our royal visit?

GREGORY   The man. Um. Was just here.

JOHN   What would you like to hear?

PERRY   I don't think anyone much cares.

JOHN   I'll play very softly.

BUZZ   I don't suppose you know *Subways Are for Sleeping*?

JOHN   Would anyone say no to a little Chopin?

RAMON   I would.

JOHN   One of the nocturnes. (*He goes into the next room.*)

RAMON   I'm still saying "Fuck you," John!

BUZZ   What brought that on?

PERRY   His brother?

BUZZ   That's no excuse. Play something gay. We want gay music written by a gay composer.

PERRY   There's no such thing as gay music, Buzz.

BUZZ   Well, maybe there should be. I'm sick of straight people. Tell the truth, aren't you? There's too goddamn many of them. I was in the bank yesterday. They were everywhere. Writing checks, making deposits. Two of them were applying for a mortgage. It was disgusting. They're taking over. No one wants to talk about it, but it's true. (*John starts playing the piano, off.*)

JOHN (*Off.*)   This is for you, Buzz. It's by Tchaikovsky. Peter Ilitch. One of us. Can't you tell? All these dominant triads are so, so gay! Who did he think he was fooling, writing music like this? (*Melancholy music fills the room. They listen.*)

BUZZ   I like this. It's not Jerry Herman, but it's got a beat. (*Perry gets up.*)

GREGORY   Where? Um . . . ?

PERRY   I'd better find Arthur. (*He goes.*)

JOHN (*Off.*)   This is depressing. How's this, Gregory? (*He starts playing the* Dance of the Little Swans *from* Swan Lake.)

BUZZ   That's more like it.

GREGORY   That's the. Um. Music. *Swan Lake.* The benefit. The *Pas des Cygnes.* Thank you, John. (*Gregory stands up from the table. He begins to dance the* Pas des Cygnes *from* Swan Lake. *He is an entirely different person when he moves: free, spontaneous, as physically fluent as he is verbally inhibited.*)

BUZZ   What are you doing?

GREGORY   The *Pas des Cygnes.*

BUZZ   I don't do *Pas des Cygnes.* What is it?

GREGORY   The *Dance of the Swans.* Come on. I can't do it alone. Ramon!

RAMON   No, thanks.

GREGORY   Come on, Buzz.

BUZZ   Why are you holding your arms like that? (*Indeed as Gregory dances he holds his arms crossed in front of him, each hand on its opposite side, ready to link hands with another person and form a chain.*)

GREGORY   I'm waiting for you to take my hand.

JOHN (*Off.*)   What are you doing in there?

GREGORY   We're dancing! Don't stop! Take my hand, Buzz. (*Buzz tentatively takes his hand and will try to follow Gregory's steps.*)

BOBBY   What are they doing?

RAMON   Now they're both dancing.

BOBBY   How do they look?

BUZZ   Ridiculous. What do you think?

BOBBY   You see? I knew it would be funny. (*Ramon and Bobby begin to laugh. Gregory and Buzz continue to dance while John plays piano from another room.*)

GREGORY   That's it, Buzz, that's it.

BUZZ   My admiration for Chita Rivera has just become boundless!

RAMON   You should see this.

BOBBY   I can imagine.

JOHN   Can I stop?

THE OTHERS   NO!!

GREGORY   Now you've got it!

BUZZ   Eat your heart out, Donna McKechnie! (*Their arms linked, Gregory and Buzz dance themselves out of the house and out onto the grounds.*)

BOBBY   What happened?

RAMON   They're gone. They danced themselves right out onto the lawn. (*Perry has joined Arthur down by the lake.*)

PERRY   Listen to them up there. We're missing all the fun.

ARTHUR   We better talk.

PERRY   Okay. I bought you a sweater.

ARTHUR   Thank you.

PERRY   And one of their blankets. I thought we could spread it and look at the sky. The stars are incredible. Thick as . . . whatever stars are thick as. "Molasses" doesn't sound right.

ARTHUR   Thieves? No. Diamonds! Thick as diamonds on a jeweler's black felt!

PERRY   I love you.

ARTHUR   I know. Me, too.

PERRY   I'm sorry we don't always understand each other. I hate it when we're not in sync. I hate what I said at the table.

ARTHUR   I hated it, too.

PERRY   I just get so frightened sometimes, so angry.

ARTHUR   It's all right, Perry, we all do.

PERRY   Don't give up on me.

ARTHUR   No. I thought you were coming down here with me. It's spectacular. I can see Orion's Belt and both Dippers.

PERRY   That's not the Dipper. That's the Dipper. (*The piano music stops. John comes back into the room where Bobby and Ramon are.*)

JOHN   Where is everyone?

BOBBY   They were last sighted heading for the boathouse. Gregory was very pleased with himself.

JOHN   You see, I'm good for something. I'm not entirely bad!

BOBBY   No one is, John.

JOHN   Thank you. I can't tell you how good that makes me feel. I was a shit tonight and I'm not even drunk. I'm sorry, Ramon. Am I forgiven?

BOBBY   Ramon?

JOHN   "Am I forgiven?" I said.

RAMON   Yes.

JOHN   Thank you. Forgiveness is good. We all need it from time to time. It's this business with my brother. (*He goes back into the adjoining room and begins to play a Beethoven sonata.*)

BOBBY   Are you still there?

RAMON   Yes.

BOBBY   What are you doing?

RAMON   Nothing.

JOHN (*Off.*)   This one is for me.

ARTHUR   He plays beautifully, the son of a bitch. The devil's fingers.

PERRY   So many stars, so many stars! Say a prayer for Buzz.

BUZZ   Arthur and Perry lay on blankets and looked at the heavens and talked things out. Gregory danced on by a couple of times. John played a melancholy piano until the wee small hours of the morning. Bobby and Ramon sat quietly talking across the deserted dining table, empty glasses, soiled napkins between them. All in all, there was a lot of love in Gregory and Bobby's house that first night of the first holiday weekend of the summer. It didn't start raining till the next morning. It didn't stop until the drive back home on Monday night. It rained all weekend.

BOBBY   It was raining when Buzz started crying in the middle of a movie on AMC and couldn't stop.

RAMON   It was raining when Gregory sat alone in his studio for six hours listening to a piece of music and didn't move from his chair.

BUZZ   It was raining when Ramon waited for Bobby by the refrigerator and he dropped the bottle.

ARTHUR   It was raining when John wanted Ramon to fuck him the next afternoon anyway.

PERRY   Anyway! There's that word again. And he's wrong, this one. I don't say "anyway" when I'm cornered. I say it when I'm overcome. I love you, Arthur Pape. (*He kisses Arthur on the lips. Gregory and Buzz will dance by again. They are having a wonderful time. Bobby and Ramon remain at the dining table. John is playing a Chopin nocturne. The lights fade. The music swells.*)

ACT TWO

Lakeside. Blaze of noon.

The men are singing "In the Good Old Summertime."

As they move apart, they reveal Ramon sprawled naked on an old-fashioned wooden float at a distance offshore.

One by one, they stop singing, turn around, and take a long look back at Ramon splayed on the raft.

Even Bobby.

Finally, only John and Ramon remain.

JOHN Anyway. (*He turns away from Ramon and takes out Gregory's journal and begins to read.*) "Fourth of July weekend. Manderley. Promise of good weather. After Memorial Day we deserve it. John Jeckyll is arriving with his twin brother, James. Perry has already dubbed them James the Fair and John the Foul. John will also have Ramon Fornos, a superb young dancer, in two. I thought they were over. Chances of finishing the first section of the new piece before they all descend on us looking slim. Bobby says he will stand sentry outside the studio while I work. I tried to tell him our guests aren't the reason I—Too late. They're here." (*Lights up on Perry, Arthur, Gregory, and Buzz making ready to play tennis doubles. Arthur and Gregory are partners. So are Buzz and Perry. John is free to walk among them as he reads.*)

BUZZ Which end of the racquet do I hold?

PERRY That's it! Change partners. You show him, Gregory! (*He crosses to Arthur.*)

BUZZ Good teachers are patient. (*Arthur is looking off to Ramon.*)

PERRY What are you looking at out there?

ARTHUR Nothing. (*Gregory has his arms around Buzz in the classic "teacher's" position.*)

GREGORY   Here, Buzz. Make a. Um. V with your thumb. Um. And forefinger.

BUZZ   Thank you. See how I respond to human kindness?

GREGORY   You bring your arm back like this, step into the ball, and pow! (*They continue.*)

JOHN   "Buzz arrived alone again. We were hoping he'd bring someone. He looks thinner."

PERRY   Try to keep your eye on this ball, not those.

JOHN   "Perry and Arthur asked if they could celebrate their anniversary with us. I warned them John would be here."

ARTHUR   That wasn't called for.

JOHN   "Poor John. People don't like him." (*He closes the journal and becomes "visible" to the others.*)

PERRY   I don't want to fight. I want to beat them in tennis.

JOHN   Who's winning?

BUZZ   We are. We're killing them.

JOHN   I can't believe it.

PERRY   You can't believe it?

BUZZ   Look who I have for a coach and partner. Why can't you have a twin brother?

ARTHUR   Don't make Gregory blush!

JOHN   What's wrong with mine?

BUZZ   He looks too much like you and acts too much like me. Where are all the men? There are no eligible men!

PERRY   Will you keep your voice down?

BUZZ   For what? We're in the middle of nowhere! Will I keep my voice down! You're a martyr, Arthur, a genuine martyr. I would have pushed him off your tasteful lower Fifth Avenue balcony ten years ago.

JOHN   Ramon is eligible, gentlemen.

BUZZ   I don't date dancers. I've made it a rule. It's very simple. Dancers don't want to date me. So fuck 'em.

JOHN   In Ramon's case, you don't know what you're missing. Does anyone want anything from the house?

GREGORY   There's tea in the. Um. Fridge.

JOHN   I'll send James down with it. (*He goes.*)

PERRY   I've got another: the Princes of Light and Darkness.

ARTHUR   Could we concentrate on winning this set?

BUZZ   So what's the score? A thousand to one? I'm really getting into this.

PERRY (*Annoyed.*)   Love-forty! (*He cranks up for a serve.*)

BUZZ   Getting ready to serve now, the ever-lonely Dr. Renee Richards. (*Perry flubs.*)

GREGORY   Double fault. Game! Change sides.

PERRY   Fuck you, Buzz.

BUZZ   What did I do? Who won?

GREGORY   We did.

BUZZ   We did? We didn't do anything. I love tennis. (*They change sides.*)

PERRY   You heard John: he's eligible!

ARTHUR   Perry.

PERRY   Lighten up. Your serve, Martina. (*The game continues. John is heard playing the piano, off. Ramon raises up and looks around. He shields his eyes with his hand, scans the horizon, and lies back down. Bobby appears. He is wearing a robe. He will advance to the stage apron.*)

BOBBY   When Gregory told me he thought John and Ramon were over and was surprised that John would be bringing him again, I didn't tell him that they were and that Ramon was coming with him because of me. I didn't tell him that when the phone rang Monday night, and then again Thursday, and there was no one there, and he kept saying "Hello? Hello? Who is this?" I didn't tell him it was Ramon on the other end. (*He falls off the stage.*) Don't anyone touch me. I don't want help. (*He climbs back onto the stage.*) And I didn't tell him what Ramon's mouth felt like against my own. I didn't tell him the last time we made love I thought of it. I didn't tell him Ramon whispered to me this morning. He would be waiting for me on the raft when I swam out there. (*He drops his robe and goes out to the lake. James appears, wheeling a serving cart with iced tea and potato chips.*)

JAMES   It's not who you think. I'm the other one. When John stops playing the piano, you can start getting nervous again.

PERRY   Ball!

JAMES   My brother gave me the most extraordinary book. *Outing America: From A to Z*. I'm absolutely riveted.

PERRY   Ball, please!

JAMES   It gives the names of all the gay men and lesbians in this country in alphabetical order, from the pre-Revolutionary period (Pocahantas, I think her name was) right up to now, someone called Dan Rather.

PERRY   Ball, please!

ARTHUR   Which one of them is it?

BUZZ   It must be James. The grass isn't turning brown.

ARTHUR   I think he's attractive, Buzz.

BUZZ   Yeah?

PERRY   Goddamnit! (*Perry retrieves the tennis ball.*) Thanks for nothing.

JAMES   I'm sorry?

PERRY   Just wait till you say, "Ball, please!"

JAMES   I haven't the vaguest notion what you're talking about, luv.

PERRY   Skip it. (*He goes.*)

JAMES   I must say, and I hope you take this in the best possible way, for a young country, you've turned out an awful lot of poufters. In two and a half centuries you've done almost as well as we have in twenty. John Foster Dulles. Who is that? Is it a juicy one? Benjamin Franklin. Him we've heard of. Very into kites. Knute Rockne. Lady Bird Johnson. Americans have the most extraordinary names! Booker T. Washington.

Babe Ruth. Buzz Hauser. (*He settles himself to read as Perry rejoins the others.*)

BUZZ   Whose serve is it?

PERRY   Still yours. Don't patronize us.

ARTHUR   We can always stop.

PERRY   No!

BUZZ   What's the matter? Are you okay?

GREGORY   I'm fine. (*He's not. He's tired.*)

BUZZ   Are you sure?

GREGORY   I'm fine!

BUZZ   What's wrong?

GREGORY   I don't. Um. See Bobby.

PERRY   Are we playing or what?

BUZZ   Time. Is that legal? Can I call time?

GREGORY   I saw him go into the lake. Um. He doesn't like me to. Um. Watch him swim. It's an honor. Um. System. And I'm not. Um. Very honorable.

BUZZ   Ramon's out there. He'll be fine.

PERRY   What's the problem, people?

GREGORY   There he is! (*Bobby appears at the side of the raft. He is winded from the swim and just hangs there.*)

BOBBY   Hello? Anyone aboard? (*Ramon doesn't move.*) Ramon? (*Ramon still doesn't move.*)

RAMON   This time I would let him find me. I waited, not daring to breathe, while his hands searched for me on the raft. I prayed to our Holy Blessed Mother I wouldn't get a hard-on.

BOBBY   Ramon?

RAMON   My prayers weren't being answered. I thought I would explode.

BOBBY   Ow! (*He's gotten a splinter from the raft.*)

GREGORY   Ow! (*He's twisted something running for a ball and falls heavily to the ground.*)

BUZZ   Are you hurt?

GREGORY   No. Yes. Ow! (*Buzz, Perry, and Arthur help him to his feet.*) Get some ice.

BUZZ   What is it? Your ankle?

GREGORY   My ankle, my knee, everything.

BUZZ   Careful with him.

PERRY   Take his other arm.

ARTHUR   I've got you. Get him to the house. (*They are helping him off.*)

GREGORY   No, the studio. I've got ice packs there. (*They help him off in another direction. Buzz looks out across the lake to the raft.*)

BUZZ   Bobby! (*Bobby is still hanging on to the raft with one arm. He works on the splinter with his teeth Ramon sits up and gently takes hold of Bobby's wrist.*)

BOBBY   Oh! Who's that? (*Ramon takes Bobby's finger, puts it in his mouth, sucks out the splinter, and spits it out.*)

BUZZ   Bobby! Come in! It's Gregory! He's hurt!

BOBBY   They're calling me.

RAMON   I waited for you last night. I thought you'd come down. Meet me somewhere tonight.

BOBBY   I can't.

RAMON   I'll be in the garden after supper.

BOBBY   Not in the garden. The boathouse. (*Bobby kisses Ramon this time, passionately, and then disappears back into the lake. Ramon watches him disappear. After a while, he will lie back down and sleep. Buzz joins James in the shaded area.*)

JAMES   No! I won't even say it. It's not possible. Do you think? Dare we dream?

BUZZ   What?

JAMES   This book says John F. Kennedy, Jr., is gay.

BUZZ   That explains it. (*He has seen the rolling tray of refreshments.*) Is that for us? (*He goes to it.*)

JAMES   That explains what?

BUZZ   I've seen him in the Spike. It's a leather bar in Chelsea. He comes in with friends. Daryl Hannah, the Schlossbergs, Willi Smith.

JAMES   I don't believe it.

BUZZ   I'm the wrong person to ask. I think everyone is gay, and if they're not, they should be. (*He calls off to the raft.*) Ramon! Noon! Teatime! (*Ramon doesn't react.*) He doesn't hear me. He's going to burn to a crisp. Ramon! If that was my boyfriend, I would swim out there and drag him in by the hair.

JAMES   If he were my boyfriend, he could do anything he wanted.

BUZZ   I know what you mean. Maybe that's why I don't have a boyfriend. I'm too caring. (*They are both looking out across the lake to Ramon.*)

JAMES   My brother has always had a good-looking man in his life.

BUZZ   Thank you.

JAMES   I beg your pardon.

BUZZ   He didn't tell you? It was when he first came to this country. Short and sweet. Six months, tops.

JAMES   I'm sorry. What happened?

BUZZ   We were both very young. I was too needy. He wasn't needy enough.

JAMES   I don't think John can love anyone.

BUZZ   Now you tell me!

JAMES   Perhaps one of us had better go out there and tell Ramon.

BUZZ   I'll let you break it to him. I don't think I'm his type.

JAMES   I don't think either of us is. (*They are both still staring out across the lake to Ramon on the raft.*) I enjoy looking, though. (*Buzz and James sigh.*)

BUZZ   Is there a British equivalent for "machismo?"

JAMES   No. None at all. Maybe Glenda Jackson.

BUZZ Do you have a boyfriend over there?

JAMES Not anymore. What about you?

BUZZ (*Shaking his head.*) When the going gets tough, weak boyfriends get going. Or something like that.

JAMES I can't honestly say I'm minding. Last acts are depressing and generally one long solo.

BUZZ They don't have to be. (*Buzz finally looks at James.*) How sick are you?

JAMES I think I'm in pretty good nick, but my reports read like something out of Nostradamus. (*He looks at Buzz.*) I should have died six months ago.

BUZZ Try eighteen. Do you have any lesions?

JAMES Only one, and I've had it for nearly a year.

BUZZ Where is it?

JAMES In a very inconvenient spot.

BUZZ They're all inconvenient. May I see it?

JAMES It's—All right. (*He pulls up his shirt and lets Buzz see the lesion.*) I have a lesbian friend in London who's the only other person who's ever asked to see it. I was quite astonished when she did. Touched, actually. Mortified, too, of course. But mainly touched. Somebody loves me, even if it's not the someone I've dreamed of. A little love from a woman who works in the box office at the Lyric Hammersmith is better than none. Are you through? (*Buzz kisses the lesion.*) Gwyneth didn't go that far. It doesn't disgust you?

BUZZ It's going to be me.

JAMES You don't know that.

BUZZ Yes, I do.

JAMES You learn to make friends with them. Hello, little lesion. Not people you like especially, but people you've made your peace with.

BUZZ You're very nice, you know.

JAMES Frankly, I don't see how I can afford not to be.

BUZZ   No, I mean it.

JAMES   So are you.

BUZZ   I didn't mean to interrupt your reading.

JAMES   It was getting too intense. They just outed George and Ira Gershwin.

BUZZ   Wait till they get to Comden and Green. Would you like me to bring you a real drink down? I know where they hide the good liquor.

JAMES   An ice-cold martini. Very dry. With a twist.

BUZZ   Is that going to be good for you?

JAMES   Of course not.

BUZZ   Does this make me an enabler?

JAMES   No, but it makes me your slave for life. I'll snitch a frock out of National Theatre storage for you. Something of Dame Edith Evans'.

BUZZ   What's the matter?

JAMES   I'm waiting for you to tell me she was gay.

BUZZ   She wasn't, actually. One of the two British actresses who isn't. I think Deborah Kerr is the other one. But all the rest—galloping lezzies! (*He goes. James looks after him and does not resume reading for quite some time. Gregory's leg is being tended to by Arthur. Perry watches squeamishly. Bobby is with them.*)

ARTHUR   How's that?

GREGORY   Ow!

PERRY   Jesus, Gregory! I never really looked at your body before. I mean, except when you're on stage in a costume and lights and I'm in the fifth row.

GREGORY   Well, don't start now.

PERRY   It's amazing.

GREGORY   It's just old. Um. And very used.

PERRY   Your legs are like knots. And your feet. I can't even look at them. Does everything hurt?

GREGORY   Yes. They have for years.

PERRY   Why do you do it?

GREGORY   I don't know. I just know I don't know what I'd do if I didn't.

ARTHUR   What do you practice, law?

PERRY   Law doesn't do that to me.

BOBBY   Gregory says a dancer's body is the scars of his dancing.

GREGORY   Bobby.

BOBBY   Isn't that what you say?

GREGORY   To you. Now it sounds pretentious.

ARTHUR   It's not pretentious, Greg.

BOBBY   The dances are gone, but his body's effort to do them isn't. Show them, Gregory.

GREGORY   Here's the Philip Glass.

ARTHUR   Look, Perry.

PERRY   I can't.

GREGORY   Here's the Bach-Schoenberg. Here's the Ravel. The Sam Barber. Here's the best one of all: the David Diamond. (*Buzz enters.*)

BUZZ   I can't leave you kids alone for a second! Bobby bwana, you be having a phone call in the Big House.

BOBBY   Thanks, Buzz. Show them *Webern Pieces.*

GREGORY   There are no. Um. *Webern Pieces* yet.

BOBBY   There will be.

PERRY   There better be. We've signed the contracts.

BUZZ   I can understand not having a phone down here, but what has he got against an intercom? (*Buzz and Bobby go.*)

PERRY   While Arthur tended Gregory and I gaped at his life's wounds (his body didn't look old; it looked exhausted, spent—like that barren soil of Africa that can't produce anymore), and while James waited with more anticipation than he realized for Buzz to return, and while Ramon bronzed his already bronzed body even bronzer, Bobby was learning via a very iffy connection with a not very forthcoming sub-attaché at the American consulate in Jaipur that his sister, two years his senior, was dead. Valerie, I think her name was. Just like that.

BOBBY   What? I can't hear you. You'll have to speak up.

PERRY   It was a freak accident.

BOBBY   What?

PERRY   Something to do with a faulty installed ride at a fun fair at a religious festival celebrating the god Shiva.

BOBBY   How? (*Gregory will join Bobby and put his arms around him from behind while he talks on the phone.*)

PERRY   A sort of swing you sat in that spun around a sort of maypole. (*Arthur joins him.*)

ARTHUR   We never got the full story. (*He rests his head on Perry's shoulder. James stops reading. Buzz comes out of the kitchen, mixing bowl in hand. Ramon sits up on the raft.*)

BOBBY   Thank you for calling. (*He lets the phone drop.*)

GREGORY   Oh, honey, I'm so sorry.

PERRY   No one knew whether to stay or go. There is nothing quite like the vulnerability of weekend guests.

BOBBY   It's all so fucking fragile. So fucking arbitrary.

GREGORY   I know, I know.

ARTHUR   It's not what we want. It's what Bobby wants.

BOBBY   I want you to stay.

RAMON   We stayed.

BOBBY   Let's go upstairs. (*Bobby and Gregory leave. There is a silence. From the house Bobby is heard howling his grief: a wild, uncontainable animal sound.*)

JAMES   Poor lamb. I'm afraid those martinis have made me quite, quite maudlin. I'm all teary. (*John is heard playing the piano, off: the* Pas des Cygnes *from* Swan Lake.)

PERRY   *Swan Lake.* My blood just ran cold. Gregory is serious about that goddamn benefit.

JAMES   So many costumes, so little time.

PERRY   (*Calling off.*)   Give it a rest, will you, John? (*He gives up.*)

JAMES   Gregory says you're a good sport and you'll do it in the end.

PERRY   Gregory is wrong.

ARTHUR   I'm working on him, James.

PERRY   And you're not getting up in any goddamn tutu and toe shoes either.

ARTHUR   My lord and master here. Do you want to go for a swim?

PERRY   I want to get some sun.

ARTHUR   We can swim and sun.

PERRY   You just want to visit your boyfriend on the raft.

ARTHUR   You want to talk about giving something a rest? (*James buries himself in his book and begins to read aloud.*)

JAMES   "No one who had ever seen Catherine Morland in her infancy would have supposed her born to be a heroine." (*Buzz has entered with more refreshments. He is wearing an apron, heels, and little else.*)

BUZZ   They said the same thing about me.

PERRY   Jesus Christ, Buzz.

BUZZ   What?

PERRY   You know goddamn well what.

BUZZ   No What? This? (*He flashes Perry.*)

PERRY   Put some clothes on. Nobody wants to look at that.

BUZZ   That? You are calling my body "that"?

PERRY   You're not at a nudist colony. There are other people present.

BUZZ   I thought I was among friends.

PERRY   I'm sure James here is just as uncomfortable as we are, only he's just too polite to say so.

JAMES   James here is still reeling from the news about the Kennedy boy. You could all be starkers and I wouldn't bat an eye.

PERRY   Tell him, Arthur.

ARTHUR   It's not bothering me.

BUZZ   Thank you, Arthur. I'm glad Isadora Duncan and Sally Kirkland did not live entirely in vain.

PERRY   Please, Buzz.

BUZZ   No. Close your eyes. Take a walk. Drop dead.

PERRY   What brought this on?

BUZZ   Nothing brought it on. Some people do things spontaneously. It's a beautiful day. The sun feels good. I may not be around next summer. Okay? This is what I look like, Perry. Sorry it's not better. It's the best I can do. Love me, love my love handles.

ARTHUR   That's what I keep telling him!

PERRY   None of us may be around next summer. (*Arthur starts undressing.*) What do you think you're doing?

ARTHUR   Come on, I'll race you out to the raft.

PERRY   Go to hell.

ARTHUR   I can't believe you actually lived through the sixties, Perry. We only read about them in Kansas, and I'm less uptight than you.

PERRY   You know, I could walk around like that, too, if I wanted to.

BUZZ   Who's stopping you?

PERRY   I just don't want to.

BUZZ   I think she's got it. By George, she's got it! (*Buzz and Arthur do a little celebratory twirl before he braves the lake waters.*)

PERRY   I give up. I hope your dick gets a sunburn.

ARTHUR   Yadda, yadda, yadda.

BUZZ   That's the spirit. The world loves a good sport. (*Arthur goes into the lake and starts to swim out to the float.*)

PERRY   Both your dicks!

BUZZ   I forgot my sunblock!

PERRY   Would you bring mine? It's on our dresser. The lip balm should be right with it.

BUZZ   I thought you were mad at me. I see! Get me waiting on you hand and foot and all is forgiven.

PERRY   Oh, and the Walkman. There's a Bob Dylan tape with it.

BUZZ   Bob Dylan? You sure you don't want Rosa Ponselle? Get a life, Perry. They've invented penicillin. You can actually pick up a phone and talk to someone in New Jersey now.

PERRY   I still like Bob Dylan—and don't tell me he's gay.

BUZZ   For his sake, I hope he's not. Would you date him?

PERRY   That's cruel.

BUZZ   I know. So's dating. (*He goes. Arthur has reached the raft. He is winded from the swim.*)

RAMON   I'll race you back in!

ARTHUR   What? No. I just got here.

RAMON   Aw, c'mon.

ARTHUR   No, I said. Give me a hand. (*Ramon helps Arthur onto the raft.*)

RAMON   I'll let you catch your breath. Then we'll race.

ARTHUR   My breath is fine. We're not racing. (*He flops on the raft. Ramon stays in a sitting up position.*)

RAMON   I hate the country. I fucking hate it. There's no cabs to get you fucking out of it. I like mass transportation. I like the fucking pavement under my feet. I like places that sell food that stay open all night. I fucking hate it.

PERRY   Should I be trusting my lover skinny-dipping with a horny Puerto Rican modern dancer?

JAMES   It depends on what makes you suspicious. Horny, Puerto Rican, modern, or dancer?

PERRY   All of them.

JAMES   How long have you two been together?

PERRY   Fourteen years. We're role models. It's very stressful.

JAMES   Two or three years was the most I ever managed. Mutual lack of attention span. (*Buzz returns.*)

BUZZ   Here's your desperate attempt to stay young, Mr. Sellars. *Blood on the Tracks*. Wasn't this originally released on 78s?

PERRY   Bob Dylan will go down in history as one of the great American songwriters. (*He puts on the headset and lies back.*)

BUZZ   He's no Lerner and Loewe! (*He is getting ready to settle down, too.*) Wake me if I doze off. I have a VCR alert for AMC. *Damn Yankees* at one-thirty. Gwen Verdon is hosting. Poor James, you don't have a clue what I'm talking about.

JAMES   I seldom know what any American is talking about. (*Reading:*) "No one who had ever seen Catherine Morland in her infancy would have supposed her born to be a heroine."

BUZZ   I love being read to. I feel five years old. (*Perry sings along with his Dylan tablet. James reads to Buzz. John is playing the piano. Ramon smacks Arthur on his bare ass.*)

ARTHUR   Ow!

RAMON   You had a fly on you. You know, you got a nice ass for someone your age.

ARTHUR   Thank you.

RAMON   You both do.

ARTHUR   Thank you.

RAMON   I really hate it. (*Gregory and Bobby are in their room.*)

GREGORY   When is the body—?

BOBBY   Not until Tuesday.

GREGORY   So long?

BOBBY   Red tape. She always said there was nothing worse than Indian red tape. We're meeting it in Dallas. I'll fly down Monday.

GREGORY   I think we should both fly down tonight.

BOBBY   No. You stay here and work. I want you to finish the piece. It's more important.

GREGORY   It's all important. Why don't you want to go down there tonight?

BOBBY   We've got a houseful.

GREGORY   I'll manage.

BOBBY   We'll see. Do you know what this music is?

GREGORY   No. But it's Russian. It's definitely Russian. There are times I wish you could see me.

BOBBY   I see you, Gregory.

GREGORY   See me looking at you. The love there. I'm not—

BOBBY   I know.

GREGORY   It only happens when I'm alone with you. It's like a little present. I know this is a terrible thing to say right now, but I am so happy, Bobby. Thank you, God, for him.

BOBBY   You know how we tell each other everything, even when it's hard?

GREGORY   Yes.

BOBBY   I'd like to make this one of those times.

GREGORY   All right.

BOBBY   Memorial Day weekend.

GREGORY   Yes.

BOBBY   Something happened.

GREGORY   Why do I have a feeling I don't want to hear this?

BOBBY   Ramon and I.

GREGORY   Don't, Bobby. Don't.

BOBBY   We made love. I didn't want it to happen, but it did.

GREGORY   Is there more?

BOBBY   No. I'm sorry.

GREGORY   So am I.

BOBBY   This was better than not telling you, Gregory. (*Gregory is starting to have difficulty speaking again.*)

GREGORY   It's Scriabin. Um. The music, it's. Um. It's definitely Scriabin.

BOBBY   Talk to me, Gregory.

GREGORY   Have you. Did you. Do you. Want to. Again?

BOBBY   No, I'm with you.

GREGORY   You're. Um. Very lucky you. Um. Can't. Um. See right now, Robert. Go to Texas tonight. I don't want you in our house.

BOBBY   Where are you going?

GREGORY   Down to the lake. Don't. Um. Come. Um. With me. Um. It's back. That was brief. (*He goes. Bobby comes forward to us.*)

BOBBY   Do you believe in God? Don't worry, I'm not going to fall off this time! Do you? I think we all believe in God in our way. Or want to. Or need to. Only so many of us are afraid to. Unconditional love is pretty terrifying. We don't think we deserve it. It's human nature to run. But He always finds us. He never gives up. I used to think that's what other people were for. Lovers, friends, family. I had it all wrong. Other people are as imperfect and as frightened as we are. We love, but not unconditionally. Only God is unconditional love, and we don't even have to love Him back. He's very big about it. I have a lot of reservations about God. What intelligent, caring person doesn't lately? But the way I see it, he doesn't have any reservations about me. It's very one-sided. It's unconditional. Besides, He's God. I'm not. (*He goes. Arthur stirs on the raft.*)

ARTHUR   Sun like this makes you want to never move again. I feel nailed to this raft. Crucified on it.

RAMON   Sun like this makes me horny.

ARTHUR   Well . . .

RAMON   I bet I can hold my breath underwater longer than you.

ARTHUR   I bet you can, too.

RAMON   Come on, you want to see?

ARTHUR   No! If you're so bored . . .

RAMON   Come on!

ARTHUR   I don't want to. Play with someone else.

RAMON   Come on! *Venga*, baby, *venga!*

ARTHUR   I'm resting. It's a national holiday.

RAMON   Come on! You know you want to! Don't be an old fart! Who knows? We get down there together, who knows what might happen? Yeah? (*He jumps off the raft and goes under the water.*)

ARTHUR   Damn it. You got me all—Shit. I was nice and dry. I'm not going in there. I don't care how long you stay under. You can drown, Ramon. I hope you can hear me down there. You're not getting me in. All right, Ramon. That's enough. Come on. Stop. (*Gregory appears at the side of the raft. He hangs there.*)

PERRY   I remember when Gregory bought this place. I was dead against it. "It's in the middle of nowhere. What are you going to do for fun?" Now it seems like bliss. No one for miles and miles. We could be the last eight people on earth.

BUZZ   That's a frightening thought.

JAMES   Not if you're with the right eight people. Who's that out there on the raft?

BUZZ   It looks like Gregory.

PERRY   Where's Arthur? He was out there.

BUZZ   You're looking good, Gregory!

PERRY   Arthur? Arthur? He was with Ramon.

BUZZ   We'd better put a stop to that. Arthur! Your mother wants you. Arthur! The *MacNeil/Lehrer Report* is on. Arthur! (*To Perry and James.*) Help me. One, two, three.

BUZZ, PERRY, AND JAMES   Arthur!! (*Buzz starts coughing. He can't stop.*)

JAMES   Are you all right?

BUZZ   Ooooo!

JAMES   Here.

BUZZ   Thank you.

JAMES   Just get your breath. Lean on me. There you go.

BUZZ   Look at Gregory out there. He's lucky. He is so lucky.

JAMES   So are we.

BUZZ   Not like that. Not like that. (*In the silence, we will begin to notice the throbbing, humming sounds of summer's high noon. The figure of Gregory on the raft glows, shimmers, irradiates in the bright light. Nothing moves.*)

JAMES   Listen. What's that sound?

PERRY   Nature.

JAMES   It's fearful.

PERRY   It's life.

BUZZ   It's so loud.

PERRY   Because we're listening to it. Ssshh.

BUZZ   I never—

JAMES   Ssshh.

PERRY   Arthur and I were in Alaska once. We flew out to a glacier. When the pilot cut the engine, it was so quiet you could hear the universe throbbing. I didn't know it did that. It was thrilling. (*Tableau. The three men do not move. James has his arms around Buzz. Gregory is sitting on the raft with his knees pulled up to his chin. He is crying. There is a distant but ominous roll of thunder.*) Five minutes later, it was raining buckets. Thunder, lightning, wind. Everybody scattered. James, take the hammock in. Gregory! Come in! Lightning!

BUZZ   Auntie Em! Auntie Em!

PERRY   Buzz, run the flag down. Where is my Arthur? Arthur!! (*Arthur appears, fully dressed and dry. He will join Perry.*)

ARTHUR   Your Arthur was gasping for breath on the other side of the lake. (*Ramon appears; he is not dressed and he is still wet. He is laughing and playful.*)

RAMON   I knew I'd get you in!

ARTHUR   You scared me. I thought something had happened to you.

RAMON   I wanted to stay down there forever. I wished I was a fish.

ARTHUR   He was sitting on the bottom of the lake. When I swam to him he pulled me towards him and kissed me on the mouth.

RAMON   I was goofing.

ARTHUR   Than he swam away.

PERRY   In all the excitement, the tragedy of Bobby's sister was quite forgotten. Where were you?

ARTHUR   Nowhere. I was swimming. Their door is still closed. You were right, Perry, we should have left.

PERRY   Don't do that.

ARTHUR   Do what?

PERRY   Disappear.

RAMON (*Holding a magazine.*)   Okay, here he is, I found him. Gather round, gentlemen.

BUZZ   It was after lunch and Ramon was having a hard time convincing us of an adventure he claimed to have had on the island of Mykonos.

RAMON   That's him. I swear on my mother's life.

BUZZ   And I had sex with the ghost of Troy Donahue.

PERRY   First you said he was the model for Calvin Klein's Obsession. Now he's the model for—

RAMON   I can't keep all those names straight, but I don't forget a face and a body like that.

BUZZ   You all know the picture.

ARTHUR   And you found this person in the same position sleeping adrift in a fishing boat?

RAMON   Yes. You ever been to Greece? There are a lot of fishing boats. Why won't you believe he was in one of them?

PERRY   And you made love to him?

RAMON   Not in the fishing boat. It started raining. We went ashore. We found sort of a cave.

JAMES   This is very Dido and Aeneas. I'm calling Barbara Cartland. (*He goes.*)

RAMON   Why would I make up a story like that? It's too incredible.

PERRY   You're right, it is.

RAMON   Fuck you, all of you. I don't care. But the next time you see his picture or you're tossing in your beds thinking about him, just remember: somebody had him and it wasn't you. I know how that must burn your asses.

BUZZ   Go to your room! (*He goes. The others stay with the magazine.*)

ARTHUR   Do you think he's telling the truth?

BUZZ   No, do you?

PERRY   The thought of Ramon and his possible encounter with the Obsession Man hung over the house like a shroud. We all wanted him and never would—

BUZZ   I bet he's got a rotten personality.

PERRY   Anyway. There is nothing like the steady drumming of a summer rain on wooden shingles to turn even this pedantic mind into a devil's workshop. I've got an idea. (*He whispers to Arthur and Buzz, who surround him. Ramon and John are seen in their room.*)

RAMON   I don't know people like you and your friends. I don't know what you're talking about half the time. Who the fuck are Dido and Aeneas? We used to beat up people like you where I grew up.

JOHN   Come here.

RAMON   Do you believe me?

JOHN   Do you want me to believe you?

RAMON   Maybe.

JOHN   So come here. (*Ramon will take his time coming over to where John is.*)

PERRY   Unfortunately, John and Ramon were not alone. Buzz and I had hidden in their closet. Our plan was to leap out at the moment of maximum inopportunity and embarrassment and then regale the rest of the household with what we'd seen and heard.

BUZZ It'll serve John right.

PERRY What does that mean?

BUZZ Never mind. Squeeze!

RAMON What? (*John kisses Ramon.*)

PERRY It was a terrible idea. Arthur would have no part of it.

ARTHUR Happy anniversary to you, too, Perry! (*He goes.*)

PERRY Is today the—I'm sorry, Arthur. Oh, shit.

JOHN What's the matter?

RAMON I thought I heard something.

PERRY That was our last chance. We should have taken it.

JOHN Sit down.

RAMON You want to? Now?

JOHN Sit.

RAMON I'm a little sunburned.

JOHN Sit.

RAMON Aren't you going to lock the door?

JOHN It's locked. Sit. (*Ramon sits in a straight-back chair.*) Put your hands behind your back. Feet apart. Head down. Ready for interrogation. My beautiful bound prisoner. Look at me. You look so beautiful like that. I think I could come without even touching you.

BUZZ Oh!

RAMON I think I could, too. Let me go.

JOHN No.

RAMON Please. The rope. It's too tight. My wrists, the circulation.

JOHN Go on, struggle.

RAMON I can't get loose.

JOHN Look at me. Don't take your eyes from mine. Who do you see?

RAMON No one. You! Let me touch you.

JOHN Not yet. Who do you see? Who do you wish I were?

RAMON No, I won't tell you.

JOHN Yes, you will. Who? Look at me. Look at me! Who? Who do you wish I were?

RAMON Kiss me. Gag me with your mouth. (*John kisses him.*)

PERRY We knew what they were doing. We didn't have to see.

BUZZ I was singing "Ninety-nine Bottles of Beer on the Wall" silently to myself. It's a very hard song to sing silently to yourself.

RAMON Who do you see? Who do you want in this chair?

JOHN I don't know.

RAMON Yes, you do. Everybody does. Who do you see? Who do you want here like this? Tell me, it's okay, John.

JOHN I can't.

RAMON Who? Come on, baby, who?

JOHN Don't make me.

RAMON I can't make you do anything. I'm your fucking prisoner, man. You got me tied up here. Gagged. Mmmm. Mmmm.

JOHN His name was Padraic. The Irish spelling.

RAMON Fuck the spelling!

JOHN Padraic Boyle. He was seventeen years old. I was nineteen.

RAMON I hear you. Seventeen and nineteen.

JOHN He will always be seventeen years old and I will always be nineteen. Neither of us grows old in this story.

RAMON What did he look like, this hot fucking stud Irishman?

JOHN He was a fierce-looking ginger Irishman with big powerful shoulders and arms with muscles with big veins in them. You could see them blue through the white skin of his biceps. Always in hip boots and a vest.

RAMON A vest? He was wearing a fucking vest?

JOHN I'm sorry—undershirts, you call them.

RAMON   That's more like it. Fucking Fruit of the Looms, fucking BVDs, fucking Calvins.

JOHN   He worked for us. So did his father. We owned a fleet of coaches. Padraic and his father washed them. But that didn't matter. We were friends. He liked me. I know he liked me.

RAMON   Cut to the chase.

JOHN   Cut to what chase? There wasn't any chase.

RAMON   It's a movie expression. Get to the good part.

JOHN   It's all good part.

RAMON   Get to the sex. One night . . . !

JOHN   One day we started wrestling. It was summer. He was washing a coach (that's a bus), and—

RAMON   I know what a coach is. I've been to London.

JOHN   And Padraic squirted me with a hose and I got him with a bucket of water and then we started fooling around, and one thing led to another and we started wrestling, we were in the garage now, and suddenly Padraic put his hand down there and he could feel I was hard and he said, "What is this? What the bloody hell is this, mate?"

RAMON   What did you do?

JOHN   I put my hand on him down there and he was hard and I said, "And what the bloody hell is that, mate?" and we both laughed, but we didn't move.

PERRY   Even from the closet, we were beginning to share Ramon's impatience.

PERRY AND BUZZ   Cut to the fucking chase!

JOHN   He stopped laughing. "Do you know what we're doing?" I had no idea, so I nodded yes. He took off my belt and wrapped it around my wrists. He raised my arms over my head and hung them to a hook along the wall. I probably could have freed myself. I didn't try. He took out a handkerchief and gagged me with it. Then, and this frightened me, he ripped open my shirt. Then he unfastened my trousers and let them drop to my ankles. Then he undressed himself and took a chair, very like this one, and sat in it, maybe five feet away from me. He had some rope. He wrapped it around his wrists like he was tied to the chair. He gagged himself, too, with his own knickers. He looked right at me. He didn't move. Not even the slightest undulation on hips, and then he came and all he'd let out was this one, soft "oh." After a while, he opened his eyes, asked me how I was doing and cleaned himself up. Then he stood up and kissed me lightly on the lips. No man had ever kissed me on the lips before. I wanted to kiss him back, but I didn't dare. He moved to whisper something in my ear. My heart stopped beating. He was going to tell me he loved me! Instead, he said, "I've doused this place in petrol. I'm lighting a match. You have three minutes to get out alive. Good luck, 007." And then he laughed and walked out whistling. He never wanted to play again. The last time I saw him he was overweight, the father of four and still washing our coaches. But that's who I still see there. Every time. And that's why we hate the bloody Irish!

PERRY   Clearly the mood was broken. I felt a certain relief. (*Gregory appears outside their door.*)

GREGORY   Knock, knock!

JOHN   Yes.

GREGORY   Can I. Um. Get in there a sec?

JOHN   Sure.

RAMON (*Playfully.*)   Maybe Greg can rescue me. (*He puts his arms behind him, struggles again.*) Mmmmm. Mmmmm. Help.

JOHN   Stop that. (*Gregory comes into the room.*)

GREGORY   Sorry. I need to. Um. Get a suitcase. Um. For Bobby.

RAMON (*Playfully.*)   Mmmmmm! Mmmmmm!

JOHN   Ignore him. (*Gregory opens the closet and sees Perry and Buzz.*)

PERRY (*To Gregory.*)   Ssshh. Please. I'll explain.

JOHN   Was it in there?

GREGORY   No, wrong closet.

RAMON   Help! Mmmmm. (*Gregory goes. Buzz manages to exit with him without being seen by John and Ramon.*) It sounds like Bobby's leaving. I want to say goodbye. Do you mind if we don't—

JOHN   Suit yourself.

RAMON I'm not Padraic.

JOHN And I'm not Bobby. *C'est la vie.*

RAMON I don't know what you're talking about. (*He goes.*)

JOHN Wait up. I'll go with you.

PERRY I suppose the next few moments could be called out of the closet and into the fire. John had forgotten his wallet. People like John don't feel fully dressed unless they're carrying their wallets, even on Fourth of July weekends on forty-plus acres.

JOHN You son of a bitch.

PERRY I'm sorry.

JOHN You miserable son of a bitch.

PERRY It was a joke. It was supposed to be funny.

JOHN You scum. You lump. You piece of shit. How dare you?

PERRY I wasn't thinking. I'm sorry, John. I have never been sorrier about anything in my entire life.

JOHN How fucking dare you?

PERRY I will get down on my knees to you to ask your forgiveness.

JOHN What did you hear?

PERRY Nothing.

JOHN What did you hear?

PERRY I won't tell anyone. Not even Arthur. I swear on my mother's life, I won't. (*John spits in Perry's face.*)

JOHN I hope you get what my brother has. I hope you die from it. When I read or hear that you have, then, then, Perry, will I forgive you. (*He goes.*)

PERRY I don't know which was worse. His words or his saliva. Right now I can't think of anything more annihilating than being spat upon. I could feel his hate running down my face. So much for the unsafe exchange of body fluids. (*Arthur is trimming the hair in Perry's ears.*)

ARTHUR I'm glad you're getting your sense of humor back. I'd like to flatten that limey motherfucker. I'm tired of "limey." Aren't there any other hateful words for those cocksucking, ass-licking, motherfucking, shit-eating descendants of Shakespeare, Shelley, and Keats?

PERRY   Come on, honey. Let's drop it.

ARTHUR   I don't go around hitting people or using words like "motherfucker," but that's how mad I am.

PERRY   Let it go. I love my bracelet. Thank you.

ARTHUR   Happy anniversary.

PERRY   I'm sorry I forgot. What do you want?

ARTHUR   Towels.

PERRY   Towels? That's not very romantic.

ARTHUR   The last time your mother stayed with us I could see she thought the towels were my responsibility. It's one thing for her son to be gay just so long as he's not the one who's doing the cooking. Towels and a Mixmaster!

PERRY   Who wound you up?

ARTHUR   That asshole did. Don't get me started again. He's just lucky I'm a big queen.

PERRY   Don't forget the left ear.

ARTHUR   And you're really lucky I'm a big queen.

PERRY   One thing you're not, Arthur, and never will be is a big queen.

ARTHUR   I know. I'm butch. One of the lucky ones. I can catch a ball. I genuinely like both my parents. I hate opera. I don't know why I bother being gay.

PERRY   I was so sure you weren't the first time I saw you. I came this close to not saying hello. (*Perry suddenly kisses one of Arthur's hands.*)

ARTHUR   Where did that come from?

PERRY   Are we okay?

ARTHUR   We're fine. Don't rock de boat. It don't need no rocking. Fourteen years! Make you feel old?

PERRY   No, lucky.

ARTHUR   My first time in New York. You had your own apartment in "Green-wich Village." Exposed brick. I was so impressed.

PERRY   It's pronounced Greenwich. You're lucky you were so cute.

ARTHUR   The Mark Spitz poster right out where anyone could see it. (*Buzz crosses the room.*)

BUZZ   He's gay, you know.

ARTHUR   He is?

BUZZ   They're all gay. The entire Olympics.

PERRY   This is my roommate, Buzz. Buzz, this is—I'm sorry—

ARTHUR   Arthur.

PERRY   Oh come on, I didn't—

ARTHUR   You did.

PERRY   Why are we whispering?

BUZZ   I've got someone in my room. He's a Brit. I'm getting him tea. (*Now John crosses the room.*)

JOHN   Don't mind me, ducks. Just nipping through. Is that the loo? (*He goes.*)

BUZZ   Don't say anything, Perry. I think he's cute. He's written a musical. I think I'm in love.

PERRY   Take it easy this time, will you?

BUZZ   Perry likes it rough, Arthur—really, really rough. (*He goes.*)

ARTHUR   He was right—you did.

PERRY   Look who's talking! Do you want me to do your ears now?

ARTHUR   That was John? I'd completely forgotten. He and Buzz met the same night we did. We lasted, they didn't.

PERRY   I thought you were the most wonderful-looking man I'd ever seen.

ARTHUR   Did you? Did you really think that?

PERRY   Unh-hunh.

ARTHUR   Ow!

PERRY   Sorry. When was the last time I did this?

ARTHUR   Don't make a face.

PERRY   I'm not making a face.

ARTHUR   I can hear it in your voice.

PERRY   I wouldn't do this for anyone but you.

ARTHUR   You know, if you really think about it, this is what it all come downs to.

PERRY   What? Trimming the hair in your boyfriend's ears? Oh God, I hope not. (*Buzz and James appear. They are ready for a tutu fitting. James motions Arthur and Perry to come close.*)

ARTHUR   That and helping your best friends out by putting on a tutu for five minutes in front of three thousand people in Carnegie Hall. (*Buzz and James have put a tape measure around Perry's waist. Buzz drapes him in tulle.*)

PERRY   You're wasting your time, Buzz, I'm not going to do it. (*Buzz writes down the measurements.*)

BUZZ   She's a classic *Gisselle* size, I should have guessed. Thirty-six! Whose measurements are these?

JAMES   Yours, luv.

ARTHUR   Is that good or bad?

JAMES   For a tutu it's a little big. For a gay man it's a disaster.

BUZZ   I'm not thirty-six! What metric system are you on? Let me see that. What are you laughing at? You're next. (*Buzz and James pursue Arthur off.*)

PERRY   Anyway. The heavens cleared. The sunset was spectacular. The next day would be glorious. We would have a fabulous Fifth of July, sodden fireworks and strained relationships notwithstanding. Only the evening lay ahead. (*The sound of crickets. Bobby is waiting in the yard with his suitcase. It is night. Ramon appears.*)

RAMON   Hi.

BOBBY   Hi. Betty's Taxi is living up to their reputation. "We're on our way, Mr. Brahms." Five minutes, she promised and that was twenty minutes ago.

RAMON   I have a sister, too. I love her very much. I'm sorry.

BOBBY   Thank you, Ramon.

RAMON   Where's your cowboy boots? They told me home for you was Texas. I thought you'd be in boots and a Stetson.

BOBBY   Home for me is right here. My folks are in Texas. Paris, Texas.

RAMON   Aw, c'mon. There's no such place.

BOBBY   French is my second language.

RAMON   You're kidding.

BOBBY   I'm kidding. The settlers had delusions of grandeur. (*Ramon takes Bobby's hand.*) Don't.

RAMON   I'm sorry. (*He lets go of Bobby's hand.*)

BOBBY   A part of me is, too. I can't.

RAMON   Does Gregory—?

BOBBY   No.

RAMON   That night by the refrigerator . . . ?

BOBBY   Any of it. (*Gregory appears outside the house.*)

GREGORY   You're still here?

BOBBY   They're on their way.

RAMON   Safe trip, amigo. I'm really sorry. (*He goes back into the house.*)

GREGORY   I would have driven you. Um. In. Um.

BOBBY   We've got guests.

GREGORY   We both need time to think.

BOBBY   I don't. I'm sorry. I love you.

GREGORY   (*He is angry.*)   Are any of you. Um. Gardeners? I'm especially. Um. Proud of what I've done here. Um. It's a. Um. Seasonal garden. Always something blooming. Um. Just as another dies. That's a.

Um. Bobby knows the names of everything. *Dianthus barbatus.* That's the Latin name. Um. I can't think of the. Um. Common one.

BOBBY   Sweet William. It's Sweet William. And this one is rue. Bitter. Very bitter. Buzz says I would make a great Ophelia if I wouldn't fall off the stage.

GREGORY   He shouldn't. Um. Say things like that. Um. To you. (*He is crying.*)

BOBBY   And this is. Wait. Don't tell me.

GREGORY   It's a rose.

BOBBY   I know it's a rose. Connecticut Pride Morning Rose.

GREGORY   I'll never understand it. The will to know the names of things you'll never see.

BOBBY   It's one way of feeling closer to you. (*Gregory embraces Bobby, but they don't kiss.*)

GREGORY   Hurry back to me. (*He goes back into the house. Bobby will stay in the yard until the cab comes. The other men have gathered in the living room. The TV is on.*)

BUZZ   It's not my turn to clear up. I'm waiting for the musical remake of *Lost Horizon.* I never miss a chance to watch Liv Ullman sing and dance.

JAMES   May I join you? (*He sits next to Buzz.*)

ARTHUR   What's this?

PERRY   Open it.

ARTHUR   You didn't forget. You had me fooled.

JAMES   What are we watching?

BUZZ   The *Dinah Shore Classic.* Dykes playing golf in the desert.

PERRY   Do you like it?

ARTHUR   I love it. Look, guys. A solar-powered calculator.

PERRY   For your work. Arthur's an accountant.

RAMON   Very nice.

BUZZ   Switching channels! (*We hear Bobby's cab tooting off. Bobby takes up his suitcase and goes to it. Gregory watches him through a window.*) Oh, look, the President's on MTV! He's made a video.

PERRY   Only in America!

BUZZ   He's gay, you know.

PERRY   Dream on, Buzz.

BUZZ   Why not? We could have a gay president.

PERRY   It'll never happen.

BUZZ   We're going to have a gay president in this country, you'll see.

PERRY   It's the Fourth of July, Buzz, no gay rights stuff, please. (*Ramon gives the appointed "signal."*)

RAMON   Are we having dessert or what?

BUZZ   No dessert. You're too fat. We're all too fat.

RAMON   My friend in the fishing boat didn't think I was too fat.

BUZZ   Stay out of the kitchen. We're all on diets. (*Buzz, James, and Ramon go into the kitchen.*)

ARTHUR   Go to CNN.

PERRY   Not a moment too soon. I'd like to know what's going on in the world. (*Gregory is apart from the others.*)

ARTHUR   Cheer up, Gregory. He's coming back.

GREGORY   Thanks, Arthur.

ARTHUR   That looks like Gore.

PERRY   It's a gay demonstration in Seattle. The Vice-President is out there speaking up for endangered species. I don't think we were included. Jesus! Did you see that? He whacked that guy with his nightstick right against the head. Motherfucker!

GREGORY   What's happening? (*He joins them in front of the TV set.*)

PERRY   Why do they have to him them like that? Jesus! (*They watch in silence. Appalling sounds of violence are coming from the television.*)

ARTHUR   I can't watch this.

GREGORY   Um. Um. Um.

ARTHUR   It's okay, Greg, it's okay. Turn that off, will you?

PERRY   What is wrong with this country? They hate us. They fucking hate us. They've always hated us. It never ends, the fucking hatred. (*The lights in the room go off. Buzz, James, and Ramon bring in a cake with blazing candles.*)

BUZZ, JAMES, RAMON, AND GREGORY (*Singing.*)
Happy anniversary to you,
Happy anniversary to you,
Happy anniversary, Arthur and Perry,
Happy anniversary to you.
Make a wish. Speech, speech.

PERRY   I'm married to the best man in the world, even if he doesn't put the toothpaste cap back on and squeezes the tube in the middle. I wish him long life, much love, and as much happiness as he's brought me.

ARTHUR   Ditto.

PERRY   Ditto? That's it? Ditto? (*They begin a slow dance together.*)

JAMES   That's nice.

BUZZ   You don't have to go all Goody Two Shoes on us.

ARTHUR   Everybody dance. All lovers dance.

BUZZ   What about us single girls? (*To James:*) You know you're dying to ask me. (*He starts dancing with James. There are two couples dancing now.*)

PERRY   So what was your wish? (*Arthur whispers something in his ear.*) No fucking way, José. He still thinks you're going to get me into one of those fucking tutus. (*Perry now leads Arthur. They dance very well together. Buzz and James are dancing closer and closer in a smaller and smaller space. Pretty soon they're just standing, holding on to each other, their arms around each other. Gregory sits apart. Ramon watches them all.*) Arthur, look.

ARTHUR   What?

PERRY   Answered prayers. (*The two couples dance. Ramon and Gregory sit staring at each other. The lights fade swiftly. The music continues until the house lights are up.*)

ACT THREE

Dawn. Gregory is alone in his studio. Perry is sleeping with Arthur. James and Buzz are walking by the lake. Ramon and Bobby are both awake.

PERRY Gregory was always stuck. He had been since the beginning of summer. And here it was Labor Day weekend. You'd think he'd move on, but Gregory is stubborn. I don't know if I admire that. (*Ramon steals from his bed.*)

RAMON Bobby?

PERRY So was Ramon.

RAMON Bobby?

PERRY I don't know if I admire that, either.

ARTHUR You're taking all the covers.

RAMON Bobby, it's me.

PERRY You hear that? They are up to something.

ARTHUR Mind your own business.

RAMON He's out in the studio. I can see the lights. I won't do anything. I just want to . . . Fuck it. I'll be downstairs making coffee. (*He goes.*)

PERRY I wonder if Gregory had counted on Ramon showing up with John. I remembered the time Arthur had been unfaithful and how badly I'd handled it. I don't know what to say anymore and I certainly don't know what to do. "Don't ask, don't tell." No, that's something else. I prayed for good weather, took a Unisom, and wrapped myself around my Arthur. (*He rolls overs and sleeps with Arthur.*)

ARTHUR No funny stuff. Go back to sleep. (*Gregory puts on the* Webern Opus 27 *and plays the same passage over and over.*)

BOBBY Gregory's not stubborn. He's scared. He's started telling people the new piece is nearly done when the truth is there's nothing there.

I want to tell him to just stay in the moment, not to think in finished dances. That it doesn't have to be about everything. Just to let it come from here. But when I do he says, "What do you know about it? You're blind. You betrayed me." It hasn't been easy since I got back from Texas.

GREGORY   Shit.

BOBBY   I wish it were just the two of us this weekend. (*John appears with Gregory's journal.*)

JOHN   The lawns were brown now, the gardens wilted. The autumnal chill in the air was telling us this would be our last weekend. Soon it would be "back to school." Manderley had changed once again, but I hadn't. Still hung up on Ramon and our rituals. Still reading what other eyes were never meant to see. (*Reading from the journal.*) "James Jeckyll has decided to stay in this country. Buzz says he will get much better care here. He will also get Buzz. They are in love. I'm glad it happened here. Who could not love James? We have all taken him to our hearts. It will be a sad day when the light goes out."

GREGORY   Shit, shit, shit, shit, shit!!! (*He stops dancing in a rage of utter frustration. He picks up a chair and smashes it again and again until it is in pieces. He falls to his knees and begins to cry.*)

PERRY   I can't sleep. You didn't hear that?

ARTHUR   Will you leave them alone?

PERRY   Who?

ARTHUR   Other people. All of them. You're as bad as John. And stop taking all the covers.

PERRY   I'm not as bad John. No one is as bad as John. I smell coffee. Do you smell coffee?

ARTHUR   That's it! I want a divorce.

PERRY   Are you awake now?

ARTHUR   Thanks to you.

PERRY   I'll bring you up some. How do you want it?

ARTHUR   Black with eleven sugars. How do I want it?

PERRY   You take it with milk, with Equal.

ARTHUR   Why is he torturing me? (*Perry rolls out of bed.*)

PERRY   It looks like rain. (*He goes.*)

JAMES   I'm so cold, I'm so cold.

BUZZ   I'm right here.

JAMES   Two hours ago I was drenched in sweat.

BUZZ   Tonight'll be my turn.

JAMES   We're a fine pair.

BUZZ   We're loverly. I wouldn't have it any other way.

JAMES   I left England for this?

BUZZ   How are you feeling?

JAMES   Not sexy.

BUZZ   How are you feeling, really?

JAMES   "We defy augury."

BUZZ   What does that mean?

JAMES   I don't know. It's from a Shakespearean play we did at the National. The actor who played it always tossed his head and put his hand on his hip when he said it. I think he was being brave in the face of adversity.

BUZZ   Would this have been Lady Derek Jacobi or Dame Ian McKellen?

JAMES   I believe I have the floor! So, whenever I don't like what's coming down, I toss my head, put my hand on my hip, and say "We defy augury."

BUZZ   Shakespeare was gay, you know.

JAMES   You're going too far now.

BUZZ   Do you think a straight man would write a line like "We defy augury"? Get real, James. My three-year-old gay niece knows Shakespeare was gay. So was Anne Hathaway. So was her cottage. So was Julius Caesar. So was Romeo and Juliet. So was Hamlet. So was King Lear. Every character Shakespeare wrote was gay. Except for Titus Andronicus. Titus was straight. Go figure.

JAMES   People are awake.

BUZZ   I'll get us some coffee. (*He goes to the upstairs bathroom, where Perry is standing with his back to us. Ramon is making coffee and singing a Diana Ross song. Gregory comes into the kitchen.*)

RAMON   Good morning, Gregory. The coffee's brewing. I woke up in my diva mode and there is no greater diva than Diana Ross. (*Sings Diana Ross song.*) I figured you were working out there. I saw the lights. I didn't want to disturb you. How's it going. Don't ask, hunh? (*He sings a Diana Ross song and undulates. He's terrific.*) These are the exact movements that won me my high school talent contest. My big competition was a girl in glasses—Julia Cordoba—who played "Carnival in Venice" on the trumpet. Next to "You Can't Hurry Love" she didn't have a chance. But just in case anybody thought I was too good as Diana, I went into my tribute to Elvis, the title song from *Jailhouse Rock*. (*He sings from the title song from* Jailhouse Rock *and dances. He's electric. He remembers the choreography from the movie perfectly.*) I was turning the whole school on. Girls, boys, faculty. I loved it. If I ever get famous like you, Greg, and they ask me when I decided I wanted to be a dancer—no, a great dancer, like you were—I am going to answer, "I remember the exact moment when. It was the stage of the Immaculate Conception Catholic High School in Ponce in the Commonwealth of Puerto Rico when—" (*He slows down but keeps dancing.*) What's the matter? What are you looking at? You're making me feel weird. Come on, don't. You know me, I'm goofing. "Great dancer you *are*." I didn't mean it, okay? (*He dances slower and slower, but he has too much machismo to completely stop.*) Fuck you then. I'm sorry your work isn't going well. Bobby told me. But don't take it out on me. I'm just having fun. Sometimes I wonder why we bother, you know? Great art! I mean, who needs it? Who fucking needs it? We got Diana. We got Elvis. (*He has practically danced himself into Gregory and is about to dance away from him at his original full, exuberant tempo when Gregory grabs his wrist.*) Hey! (*Gregory leads him to the sink.*) What are you doing? Let go. (*Gregory throws a switch. We hear the low rumble of the disposal.*) What are you doing? I said. I don't like this. (*Gregory turns off the disposal. He grabs Ramon's other arm and twists it behind his back. At the same time he lets go of his wrist.*) Ow!

GREGORY   Put your. Um. Hand down the drain.

RAMON   Fuck you, no!

GREGORY   Do it.

RAMON   No, I said. Ow! Ow!

GREGORY   I said, do it!

RAMON   What for?

GREGORY   You know what for.

RAMON   I don't.

GREGORY   You know.

RAMON   Because of Bobby.

GREGORY   Because of Bobby? Did you say "Because of Bobby"? What, because of Bobby?

RAMON   Nothing. Nothing because of Bobby.

GREGORY (*Slowly and deliberately.*)   Put your hand down the drain.

RAMON   No. Ow!

GREGORY   Do it or I'll break it fucking off.

RAMON   You're crazy. You're fucking crazy. (*Perry enters the kitchen area. Buzz is right behind him.*)

PERRY   Jesus, Gregory. What are you—?

RAMON   He wants me to put my fucking hand down the drain.

GREGORY   Tell them why.

RAMON   I don't know.

GREGORY   Tell them why.

RAMON   He thinks me and Bobby . . .

GREGORY   That's why.

PERRY   Somebody's gonna get hurt fooling around like this.

BUZZ   Let him go, Greg.

RAMON   Ow!

GREGORY   I'll break it.

RAMON   All right, all right. I'll do it, I'll do it. (*Ramon puts his hand down the drain.*) Go ahead, turn it on, cut my fucking fingers off. (*Gregory lets go of Ramon's arm.*)

GREGORY   Is that coffee. Um. Ready yet?

BUZZ   That wasn't funny, Greg.

PERRY   Are you all right?

RAMON   That wasn't about me and Bobby. That was about me and you.

GREGORY   Coffee, Perry?

PERRY   Thank you.

RAMON   You're old and you're scared and you don't know what to do about it.

GREGORY   Buzz?

BUZZ   Sure.

RAMON   I'm young and I'm not scared and I'm coming after you.

GREGORY   Ramon?

RAMON   That's what it was about. Yes, please, with milk.

GREGORY   One *café con leche* for Ramon.

RAMON   Thank you.

PERRY   Anyway. My stomach is up in my throat.

RAMON   I knew he wouldn't do it. I knew you wouldn't do it.

BUZZ   Macho man herself here.

RAMON   He's just lucky I didn't pop him one. (*Gregory turns on the disposal. Everyone jumps a little.*)

GREGORY   Sorry. Coffee grounds.

BUZZ   You're not supposed to put them down there.

GREGORY   Live dangerously. That's my. Um. Motto.

PERRY   Anyway. The incident was never mentioned again. Funny, the things we sit on, stuff down. The simplest exchanges take on an entirely different meaning.

GREGORY   Ramon. Would you. Um. Take this up to. Um. Bobby. Thank you.

PERRY   No, not funny. Amazing. (*Gregory returns to the studio, puts the music on, and goes back to work.*) Anyway. We spent all day in bed. We napped, we cuddled. Arthur read the life of Donald Trump. Don't ask. We listened to the rain.

ARTHUR   It's stopped.

PERRY   Of course it's stopped. The day is shot. We'll all go out and get a good moonburn tonight.

ARTHUR   It's not shot. Come on, we're going canoeing.

PERRY   It's dusk. It's practically dark, Artie. No. Absolutely not. We went canoeing. (*They begin to paddle.*)

ARTHUR   I don't believe the rain this summer. First Memorial Day, then the Fourth.

PERRY   It's simple. God doesn't want you to beat me in tennis anymore.

ARTHUR   It's not what it means. It means he doesn't want us to develop skin cancer from overzealous exposure to His sun in our overzealous pursuit of looking drop-dead good to one another. Look out for that log.

PERRY   That's big of Him. I see it.

ARTHUR   After AIDS, he figures we deserve a break.

PERRY   That's five dollars.

ARTHUR   I think we've stopped playing that game.

PERRY   Who won?

ARTHUR   Not Buzz and James.

PERRY   How did we manage?

ARTHUR   Depends on who you slept with.

PERRY   Fourteen years. I haven't been perfect. Just lucky.

ARTHUR   I've been perfect.

PERRY   Sure you have!

ARTHUR   Do you ever feel guilty?

PERRY   No, grateful. Why, do you?

ARTHUR   It used to be nearly all the time. No, first I was just scared. Then the guilt. Massive at first. Why not me? That lingers, more than the fear. We've never really talked about this. Paddle.

PERRY   I'm paddling.

ARTHUR   Every time I look at Buzz, even when he's driving me crazy, or now James, I have to think, I have to say to myself. "Sooner or later, that man, that human being, is not going to be standing there washing the dishes or tying his shoelace."

PERRY   None of us is. Are. Is. Are?

ARTHUR   I don't know. Are. You're right. It's no comfort, but you're right.

PERRY   Will be. None of us said will be.

ARTHUR   Paddle, I said.

PERRY   Why not, not you?

ARTHUR   That's a good question. I wish I could answer it. (*James and Buzz come into view in a canoe. Buzz is doing the paddling. James is up front.*)

PERRY   Can we drift for a while? Look, there's Buzz and James. Hello!

ARTHUR   Can we finish something for a change?

JAMES   I feel guilty. You're doing all the paddling.

BUZZ   Good, I want you to. Look at the turtle!

JAMES   I'm going to miss all this.

BUZZ   Ssshh. Don't say that. Sshh. Don't even think it.

JAMES   There's Perry and Arthur.

BUZZ   I don't want to talk to anyone. Just us.

ARTHUR   I think we're back to zero with this thing, but I'm willing to bend my shoulder and start all over again. What else am I going to do with my time? But the fellow next to me with his shoulder to the same wheel isn't so lucky. He gets sick, I don't. Why is that? I think we should both go together. Is that gay solidarity or a death wish?

PERRY   Don't talk like that.

ARTHUR   I will always feel guilty in some private part of me that I don't let anyone see but you, and not even you all of it; I will always feel like a bystander at the genocide of who we are.

PERRY   You're not a bystander.

ARTHUR   If you didn't save the human race you're a bystander.

PERRY   That's crazy. You sound like Buzz.

ARTHUR   That's how I feel.

PERRY   You're not a bystander.

JAMES   Buzz, could we go back now?

BUZZ   Sure, honey.

JAMES   Right away. I'm not feeling terribly well.

BUZZ   You're there.

ARTHUR   Hello! They see us.

BUZZ   We'll see you at dinner!

PERRY (*To Buzz and James.*)   You want to race?

ARTHUR   Perry!

BUZZ   What?

ARTHUR   Jesus.

PERRY   I'm sorry. I wasn't thinking.

BUZZ (*To Perry.*)   What did you say?

PERRY   Nothing! It's all right!

ARTHUR   Let's go in. (*They paddle.*)

PERRY   You're not a bystander.

BUZZ   Grace. I thought he said something about grace.

JAMES   I think I soiled myself.

BUZZ   We're almost there. (*He paddles.*)

PERRY   Anyway. Anyway. That evening. I'm sorry. (*He can't continue.*)

JAMES   That evening it rained harder than ever. I'll do it. (I hate making someone cry.) There was talk of tar-and-feathering the weatherman.

PERRY   I'm sorry.

JAMES   A slight case of the runs, Perry. I'm fine now. My bum is as clean as a baby's. The best is yet to come. The real horror.

BUZZ   We don't know that.

JAMES   Yes, you do.

PERRY   I don't know what came over me.

ARTHUR   It's all right, come on, Perry. (*They go.*)

JAMES   I thought I put it very politely. I mean, I could have said, "I shit myself."

BUZZ   We're all walking on eggshells. I'll draw your bath, luv.

JAMES   Was that "luv" or "love," luv?

BUZZ   For people who insist on spelling "valor" with a *u* and using words like "lorry" and "lift," you're lucky we have a lenient immigration. (*He goes.*)

JAMES   Anyway. (If I'm going to fill in for Perry here, I might as well try to sound like him. Bloody unlikely!) After my bath, Buzz (and I never remotely thought in my wildest imaginings that I would be making love to someone called Buzz and saying things like "I love you, Buzz," or "How do you take your tea, Buzz?"), this same, wonderful Buzz wrapped me in the biggest, toastiest bath sheet imaginable and tucked me safely into that lovely big chair by the window in the corner of our room. I fell asleep listening to my brother play Rachmaninoff downstairs. I would wake up to one of the most unsettling, yet strangely satisfying, conversations of my long/short life. And I will scarcely say a word. (*He closes his eyes. The piano music stops. He stands up and looks down at the chair. He is John.*)

JOHN   There's no point in pretending this isn't happening. You're dying aren't you? There are so many things I've never said to you, things we've never spoken about. I don't want to wait until it's too late to say them. I've spend my life waiting for the appropriate moment to tell you the truth. I resent you. I resent everything about you. You had Mum and

Dad's unconditional love and now you have the world's. How can I not envy that? I wish I could say it was because you're so much better than me. No, the real pain is that it's something so much harder to bear. You got the good soul. I got the bad one. Think about leaving me yours.

They have names for us, behind our back. I bet you didn't know that, did you? James the Good and John the Bad, the Princes of Charm and Ugly. Gregory keeps a journal. We're all in it. I don't come off very well in there, either. So what's your secret? The secret of unconditional love? I'm not going to let you die with it.

My brother smiled wanly and shook his head, suggesting he didn't know, dear spectators. And just then a tear started to fall from the corner of one eye. This tear told me my brother knew something of the pain I felt of never, ever, not once, being loved. Another tear. The other eye this time. And then I felt his hand on mine. Not only did I feel as if I were looking at myself, eyes half-open, deep in a winged-back chair, a blanket almost to my chin, in the twilight of a summer that had never come, and talking to myself, who else could this mirror image be but me?, both cheeks wet with tears now, but now I was touching myself. The hand taking mine was my own. I could trace the same sinews, follow the same veins. But no! It brought it to other lips and began to kiss it, his kisses mingling with his tears. He was forgiving me. My brother was forgiving me. But wait!—and I tried to pull my hand away. I hated you. He holds tighter. I. More kisses. I. New tears. I wished you were dead. He presses his head against my hand now and cries and cries and cries as I try to tell him every wrong I have done him, but he just shakes his head and bathes my hand with his tears and lips. There have never been so many kisses, not in all the world, as when I told my brother all the wrongs I had done him and he forgave me. Nor so many tears. Finally we stopped. We looked at each other in the silence. We could look at each other at last. We weren't the same person. I just wanted to be the one they loved, I told him. (*John sits in the chair.*)

JAMES   And now you will be. (*Lights up on Gregory dancing in the studio. Perry returns to the stage.*)

PERRY   Gregory was working! The lights in his studio had been burning all that night and now well into the next day. Bobby shuttled food and refreshments from the main house while keeping the rest of us at bay. None of us had ever seen Gregory at work. He'd always kept the studio curtains closed. But this time it was as if he wanted us to watch.

ARTHUR   We shouldn't be doing this.

RAMON   Hey, c'mon, quit crowding me.

ARTHUR   I'm sorry.

RAMON   Watch Gregory. He is so good. He is so fucking good. I'd give my left nut to work with him.

PERRY   Ouch.

ARTHUR   Did you ever tell him that?

RAMON   I'm in a company.

ARTHUR   Not his. And I think the expression is "right arm," Ramon. He told Perry he thinks you're a magnificent dancer.

RAMON   He never told me.

ARTHUR   What are you two having? A withholding contest? Duck! He'll see us.

RAMON   I think he knows we're out here.

BOBBY   Someone's out there, Gregory.

ARTHUR   He's going to kill you. (*He goes. Gregory finishes the dance. He is exhausted.*)

PERRY   When Gregory finished, he knew he had made something good, something he was proud of.

GREGORY   It's done, Bobby. It's finished.

BOBBY   The whole thing? Beginning, middle, and end?

GREGORY   Yes! It's even got an epilogue. Give me a hug, for Christ's sake! No, give me a chair. You got an old boyfriend, honey.

PERRY   He also knew he would never be able to dance it. Not the way he wanted it to be danced.

BOBBY   What's the matter?

GREGORY   I can't do this anymore.

BOBBY   Your legs just cramped. Here, let me. (*He massages Gregory's legs.*)

PERRY   It wasn't just his legs. It was everything. Gregory had begun to hurt too much nearly all the time now. He knew he'd never make it through a whole performance.

GREGORY Ramon!

BOBBY You let him watch?

GREGORY I wanted him to watch. Ramon! (*Ramon comes into the studio.*)

RAMON I'm sorry, Gregory, I couldn't help myself. But Jesus, where does stuff like that come from? I would give my life to dance something like that solo one day.

PERRY Ramon had obviously reconsidered his priorities.

BOBBY What are you doing, Gregory?

PERRY Gregory was suddenly a forty-three-year-old man whose body had begun to quit in places he'd never dreamed of, looking at a twenty-two-year-old dancer who had his whole career ahead of him.

GREGORY You're good, Ramon. You're very good. You're better than I was at your age, but that's not good enough, you should be better.

RAMON Don't you think I know that?

PERRY What Gregory next said surprised everyone, but no one more than himself.

RAMON You mean your solo? In rehearsal? So you can see how it looks?

GREGORY It would be your solo at the premiere. New York. Early December.

RAMON I don't know what to say.

PERRY I can't believe people really say things like that. I mean, all your life you wait for the Great Opportunity and you suddenly don't know what to say. It reminds me of the time I—

RAMON Where are you going to be?

GREGORY Out front. Watching you.

RAMON What about . . . ? (*He motions toward Bobby.*)

PERRY Someone had to bring it up. It wasn't going to be any of us.

BOBBY What about what?

GREGORY   Ask him.

BOBBY   What's happening? Don't do this to me.

RAMON   I'm asking you.

GREGORY   I'm fine, Ramon. Are you?

BOBBY   What's happening?

RAMON   When do we start?

GREGORY   The fifteenth. Ten a.m.

RAMON   I'll be there on the first.

GREGORY   You won't be paid.

RAMON   Is this a secret? I mean, can I tell people? I want to call my mother. Is that okay? She'll shit. She won't know what I'm talking about, but she'll shit. (*His enthusiasm is spontaneous and infectious. He runs off yelling.*) Eeeeeoww! ¡Dios mio!

GREGORY   We always said I would stop when it's time.

BOBBY   Time. I hate that word, "time."

GREGORY   It's time, Bobby.

PERRY   You should have seen this man ten years ago, even five. No one could touch him. He's always been sort of a god to me.

GREGORY   I just want to stay like this, my eyes closed, and feel you next to me, our hands touching. Two blind mice now. I didn't know I was going to do this, honey.

PERRY   Ever since I'd known Gregory, he'd been a dancer. I didn't think I would mind this moment so much.

BOBBY   You did the right thing. (*They stay as Gregory has described them. John appears and stands very close to them.*)

JOHN   This is what Gregory wrote in his journal that day. "Bobby and I made love. We kissed so hard we each had hickeys afterwards. I don't think I'll tell him. When I feel his young body against my own, I feel lucky and happy and safe. I am loved."

GREGORY   Okay.

BOBBY   You ready? (*Bobby and Gregory get up and slowly leave the stage. John stops reading, closes the book, and looks in the direction Bobby and Gregory have gone.*)

JOHN   "And I am all alone." That's from a song. What song? Anyway. (*He sits and stares straight ahead.*)

PERRY   Anyway. (*Buzz has returned.*) How's James?

BUZZ   Don't ask. Like ice. I'm running his tub.

PERRY   Poor guy. How are you?

BUZZ   Weary and wonderful. (*Gregory appears.*)

GREGORY   Who's using all that hot water?

BUZZ   We are, Gregory, I'm sorry.

GREGORY   That's all right, that's all right. I'll shower later. Really, Buzz, it's fine. (*He goes.*)

BUZZ   If this were a musical, that would be a great cue for "Steam Heat." "Really, Buzz, it's fine." "I've got ding! ding! steam heat!" Of course, if this were a musical, there would be plenty of hot water, and it would have a happy ending. Life and Gregory's plumbing should be more like a musical: Today's Deep Thought from Buzz Hauser.

PERRY   Musicals don't always have happy endings, either.

BUZZ   Yes, they do. That's why I like them, even the sad ones. The orchestra plays, the characters die, the audience cries, the curtain falls, the actors get up off the floor, the audience puts on their coats, and everybody goes home feeling better. That's a happy ending, Perry. Once, just once, I want to see a *West Side Story* where Tony really gets it, where they all die, the Sharks and the Jets, and Maria while we're at it, and Office Krupke, what's he doing sneaking out of the theatre?—get back here and die with everybody else, you son of a bitch! Or a *King and I* where Yul Brynner doesn't get up from that little Siamese bed for a curtain call. I want to see a *Sound of Music* where the entire von Trapp family dies in an authentic Alpine avalanche. A *Kiss Me Kate* where's she got a big cold sore on her mouth. A *Funny Thing Happened on the Way to the Forum* where the only thing that happens is nothing and it's not funny and they all do down waiting—waiting for what? Waiting for nothing, waiting for death, like everyone I know and care about is, including me. That's the musical I want to see, Perry, but they don't write musicals like that anymore. In the meantime, gangway, world, get off my runway!

PERRY   You're my oldest friend in the world and next to Arthur, my best.

BUZZ   It's not enough sometimes, Perry. You're not sick. You two are going to end up on Golden Pond in matching white wicker rockers. "The loons are coming, Arthur. They're shitting on our annuities."

PERRY   That's not fair. We can't help that.

BUZZ   I can't afford to be fair. Fair's a luxury. Fair is for healthy people with healthy lovers in nice apartments with lots of health insurance, which, of course, they don't need, but God forbid someone like me or James should have it.

PERRY   Are you through?

BUZZ   I'm scared I won't be there for James when he needs me and angry he won't be there for me when I need him.

PERRY (*Confronting him.*)   I know, I know.

BUZZ   I said I wasn't going to do this again. I wasn't going to lose anyone else. I was going to stay healthy, work hard for the clinic, and finish cataloging my original cast albums. They're worth something to someone, some nut like me somewhere. That was all I thought I could handle. And now this.

PERRY   I know, I know. But it's wonderful what's happened. You know it's wonderful.

BUZZ   Who's gonna be there for me when it's my turn?

PERRY   We all will. Every one of us.

BUZZ   I wish I could believe that.

JAMES (*Off.*)   Buzz, the tub!

BUZZ   Can you promise me you'll be holding my hand when I let go. That the last face I see will be yours?

PERRY   Yes.

BUZZ   I believe you.

PERRY   Mine and Arthur's.

BUZZ   Arthur's is negotiable. I can't tell you how this matters to me. I'm a very petty person.

PERRY   No, you're not.

BUZZ   I've always had better luck with roommates than lovers.

PERRY   I think this time you got lucky with both.

JAMES (*Off.*)   Buzz, it's running over.

BUZZ   I adore him. What am I going to do? (*The other men are assembling in the living room.*)

GREGORY   All right, everyone. This is your five-minute call. This is a dress. (*Buzz, Bobby, Arthur, Ramon, and Gregory will get ready to rehearse the* Swan Lake Pas des Cygnes. *This time they will put on tutus and toe shoes. They will help each other dress. Think of a happy, giggly group of coeds. Perry watches from the side.*) John? Are you ready in there?

JOHN (*Off.*)   All set. (*He starts playing.*)

GREGORY   Not yet! Not yet!

RAMON   Okay, let's do it!

GREGORY   Lord, but you. Um. Have big feet, Bobby.

BUZZ   You're heartless. Picking on the handicapped.

BOBBY   I'm not handicapped. Not anymore. I'm visually challenged.

BUZZ   I'm sorry, doll.

BOBBY   That's all right, doll. It took me forever.

GREGORY   John, are you still ready?

JOHN (*Off.*)   Yes, Gregory.

GREGORY   Tuck it in, Arthur.

ARTHUR   I beg your pardon.

PERRY   You see? That's what I keep telling him.

ARTHUR   If you're just going to sit on the sidelines and be a kibitz.

RAMON   Kibitz? What's a kibitz?

BUZZ   It's a place where very old gay Jewish couples go. (*Gregory claps his hands with a choreographer's authority.*)

GREGORY   All right, gentlemen. Line up. From the top.

BUZZ   We're in big trouble.

GREGORY   John? Are you ready?

JOHN (*Off.*)   Yes, for the eighty-fifth time! (*Gregory claps his hands again.*)

GREGORY   Okay, everybody. This is a take. All set, John. (*John begins to play offstage and they begin to dance. They have improved since they started rehearsing.*) Very good. Very good.

RAMON   Ow! Buzz kicked me.

BUZZ   Tattletale. Shut up and dance.

ARTHUR   That's from *Gypsy*.

BUZZ   That's amazing from an accountant.

BOBBY   How are we looking?

PERRY   Actually, you look like you're having fun.

BOBBY   Well, come on then! (*James enters. He has put on his tutu.*)

JAMES   You started without me.

BUZZ   We thought you were resting.

JAMES   Don't stop. Let me in. (*He links arms with Bobby and joins in the dance. The others are apprehensive about his participation but try not to show it.*) Left! I always want to go right on that step.

BUZZ   If you do and I hear about it . . . ! That was the punchline to a politically incorrect joke nobody dares tell anymore.

ARTHUR   But you will.

BUZZ   Absolutely. Hervé Villechaize, the deceased midget, was talking to Faye Dunaway.

ALL   She's gay, you know.

BUZZ   Keep trying, guys. One of these days you'll get it. Anyway. Hervé and Faye.

PERRY   Anyway. While my friends rehearsed and laughed and I watched and felt envious of their freedom (I couldn't believe that was my Arthur with them! My button-down, plodding Arthur!) something else was happening, too. Something awful. James collapsed. (*Everyone stops as James falters. John keeps playing the piano, off.*)

JAMES   I'm fine. I said, I'm fine. Everybody, please. Back off. I just want to lie down a little.

BUZZ   I'll—

JAMES   No, I'm fine. Don't stop. Go on. You need all the rehearsal you can get. (*He goes.*)

GREGORY   John, will you stop. John, goddamnit! (*The music continues.*)

RAMON   I'll tell him. (*He goes.*)

ARTHUR   Buzz, maybe you should go with him.

BUZZ   Maybe you should mind your own business.

ARTHUR   I'm sorry. (*Ramon returns.*)

RAMON   John's gone up to him.

BUZZ   Put on the record. That's how we're going to perform it anyway. The piano is for stop-and-start. We're beyond stop-and-start.

ARTHUR   We're one short again.

BUZZ   We'll live. (*He starts taking charge, his way of being in denial about James's condition.*) Let's go. Places, ladies. From the top.

RAMON   You're being replaced, Gregory.

BUZZ   Did anyone object to me calling them ladies? Speak now or forever hold your peace.

PERRY   I object.

BUZZ   You're not in this piece. (*He claps his hands. This time we hear the Tchaikovsky in the full orchestral arrangement. They begin the dance again. The dance continues.*)

PERRY   I wanted to join them. I couldn't. I just couldn't. I was a dancer once. I was a good dancer. What happened?

GREGORY   Come on. Um. Perry. We need. Um. You. It's a. Um. *Pas de six.*

BUZZ   That sounds dirty. I wish it were. (*As the dance proceeds, one by one the men will stop dancing, step forward, and speak to us.*)

PERRY   I have twenty-seven years, eight months, six days, three hours, thirty-one minutes, and eleven seconds left. I will be watching *Gone with the Wind* of all things again on television. Arthur will be in the other room fixing me hot cocoa and arguing with his brother on the phone. He won't even hear me go.

ARTHUR   You insisted on keeping the TV on so loud. Wouldn't buy a hearing supplement.

PERRY   I hate that word, "supplement." They're aids. Hearing aids. They're for old men.

ARTHUR   Three years later, it's my turn. One the bus. The M-9. Quietly. Very quietly. Just like my life. Without him, I won't much mind.

GREGORY   You're getting behind, Arthur, catch up!

BUZZ   I don't want to think about it. Soon. Sooner than I thought, even. Let's just say I died happy. They'd reissued *Happy Hunting* on CD and I'd met Gwen Verdon at a benefit. She was very nice and I don't think it was because she knew I was sick. Perry and Arthur said, "You know what Ethel Merman was going to do to you, telling everyone she was a big dyke?"

GREGORY   On the beat, Buzz, on the beat. (*James appears.*)

JAMES   I wasn't brave. I took pills. I went back home to Battersea and took pills. I'm sorry, Buzz. (*He goes.*)

RAMON   I don't die. I'm fucking immortal. I live forever. Until I take a small plane to Pittsfield, Massachusetts. I was late for a concert. Nobody else from my company was on it. Just me and a pilot I didn't bother to look at twice.

BOBBY   I don't know.

GREGORY   You—

BOBBY   I don't want to—

GREGORY   You won't be with me.

BOBBY   I'm sorry.

GREGORY   What was his name?

BOBBY   Luke.

GREGORY   That's right, Luke.

BOBBY   You knew that. He knew that. He does that just to . . . what about you?

GREGORY   There was no one else. Not even close. You were the last.

BOBBY   I'm sorry, Gregory.

GREGORY   It was my age.

BOBBY   No.

GREGORY   It was my age.

BOBBY   Yes.

GREGORY   You—

BOBBY   I said I don't want to know.

GREGORY   Don't be afraid.

BOBBY   I'm not.

GREGORY   It will seem like forever.

BOBBY   I'm sorry. I couldn't stay with you.

GREGORY   I. Um. Bury every one of you. Um. It got. Um. Awfully lonely out here. (*John appears.*)

JOHN   I didn't change. And I tried. At least I think I tried. I couldn't. I just couldn't. No one mourned me. Not one tear was shed. (*Long pause. No one moves. Finally:*)

PERRY   Anyway. (*The dance resumes and the Tchaikovsky is heard again. By this final reprise of the dance their precision and coordination is as good as it's going to get.*) It was just about now when the lights went out. (*The music stops and the lights go off abruptly.*) Violent thunderstorms are taken for granted in this neck of the woods. So are power failures when you live as remotely as Gregory. (*Already matches are being struck and candles lit.*) The benefit rehearsal would have to wait.

BUZZ There will be no performance of *Ze Red Shoes* tonight. (*More and more candles are being lit.*) When do you expect the power back?

BOBBY Are the lights still out? Aaaww! It could be forever.

BUZZ You don't have to sound so cheerful. (*The stage is ablaze with lit candles by now.*)

ARTHUR You know what's going to happen, don't you? We'll all be sound asleep and the lights will come back on the music will start playing and we'll all be scared to death. Why is it that when the lights go off the telephones usually still work? Hunh?

BUZZ Gay people aren't expected to answer questions like that.

PERRY Speak for yourself.

BUZZ I was. I usually do. Whose turn is it do the dishes?

BOBBY I'll start.

PERRY You cooked.

ARTHUR Hey, no fair.

BOBBY Who said life was fair? It certainly wasn't a blind person. (*John enters.*)

BUZZ How is he?

JOHN He's been sleeping but he's better. He's a little better. You've all been so . . . There aren't words enough. Can I give anyone a hand? I want you to like me. (*John exits.*)

ARTHUR Look out there. It's clearing up. There's a full moon.

PERRY This is why people have places in the country.

BUZZ Even gay people, Perry.

ARTHUR Drop it, you two.

RAMON You could practically read by that moonlight. The dishes can wait. Come on, Bobby.

BOBBY It's wasted on me. Go on down to the lake. All of you. Make them, Greg. I'll join you.

BUZZ   He's a saint. He's gorgeous and he's a saint.

GREGORY   John? We're all going down to the lake.

PERRY   What's the weather supposed to be tomorrow?

ARTHUR   More rain. (*Perry, Ramon, Arthur, Buzz, and Gregory move to the rear of the stage, where they sit with their back to us looking at the moonlight on the lake. Arthur begins to sing "Shine On, Harvest Moon." The others will join in. Bobby is clearing up. James enters. He is wearing a robe. He watches Bobby.*)

BOBBY   Who's there? Somebody's there.

JAMES   It's me. Forgive me for staring. You looked very handsome in the moonlight. Very handsome and very graceful. You took my breath away. I'm going to remember you like that. It's James.

BOBBY   I know. Are you supposed to be down here?

JAMES   No. And neither are you. There's a full moon and everyone's down by the lake. I saw them from my window. Come on. I'll go with you. (*He takes Bobby by the arm.*) I have a confession to make. I've never been skinny-dipping in the moonlight with a blind American. You only live once.

BOBBY   If you're lucky. Some people don't live at all. I thought you were scared of that snapping turtle.

JAMES   I'm terrified of him. I'm counting on you.

BOBBY   Let's go then.

JAMES   I have another confession to make. I'm English. I've never been skinny-dipping in the moonlight with anyone.

BOBBY   I knew that. (*They leave. The front of the stage and main playing area are bare. Everyone is taking off his clothes to go swimming now. One by one we see the men at the rear of the stage undress and go into the lake. As they go into the water and swim out, the sound of their voices will fade away. Silence. Empty stage. John enters. He looks back at the lake. He looks up at the sound of a plane overhead. He looks out to us.*)

JOHN   Anyway. (*He looks straight ahead. He doesn't move. The lights fade. Blackout.*)

END OF PLAY.

MASTER CLASS (1995)

I love sounds. My plays are filled with stage directions asking for different sounds: a barking dog, a jetliner high in the sky above, people in the next room making love, specific pieces of music. These sounds are as integral to the meaning of my plays as the mysterious and diverse sounds that Chekhov asks for in *The Seagull* or *The Cherry Orchard*. I am always disappointed when directors ignore these sounds. It is as if a character had gone missing from my play or crucial lines of dialogue had been cut.

Not only do I love sounds but I fall in love with them, and the sound I most love is the human voice. No two of them are alike. Our voice is ours and no one else's. We don't sound like anyone else when we speak. It's ironic then that so many writers have trouble finding their own voice when they sit down to write. When I teach playwriting—*try* to teach playwriting, rather—I am happy at the end of a term if even one of my students has begun to write in his or her own voice.

Our voices are unmistakable and unique when we speak. They are our audible identity, as special to us as our fingerprints.

Whether I wanted to or not, I grew up listening to my father's favorite singer, Edith Piaf. He could listen to *La vie en rose* or *Les Trois Cloches* for hours on end. I didn't know what she was singing about but the urgency, the drama in her every song made a lasting impression. A "pretty" voice soon becomes uninteresting after the metallic, often strident, vinegary timbres of a Piaf. Patti Page and Doris Day were okay for a couple of weeks on the Hit Parade but Piaf is permanent.

It is not surprising then that I fell in love with the voice of Maria Meneghini Callas. Like Piaf's, it is a voice that once heard can never be confused with anyone else's. You hear the first sung "*Non*" and you know it is Piaf. That's all it takes: one word, one note. It's the same with Callas. "*Ah*" and you know at once you are listening to *La Divina*. There is no confusion, no ambiguity. This is the kind of voice you can live with for the rest of your life. If there is indeed love at first sight (and I believe there is; the wedding band on my left hand is proof of it), then there is also love at first listen.

So it was with Callas. Knowledgeable people still say they have "trouble" with her voice, as if it were a sound that had to be understood rather than experienced. It's a complex sound, to be sure. "Pretty" or "beautiful" are not adjectives that come to mind when describing it. Instead, from the first listening to her recording of *Lucia di Lammermoor*, I heard an urgency to communicate deep emotions to her audience. It was as if she were speaking to us, not singing an aria. To this day, Callas is the only opera singer I know who doesn't sound like an opera singer. She sounds like a person in a dramatic situation who uses her voice to express the emotions that situation is evoking in her. A familiar aria like "*Vissi d'arte*" from *Tosca* sounds like a brand new piece of music, as if Tosca were making it up in response to her desperate situation. When is the last time you heard an actor make "To be or not to be" words you had never heard before and were drawn into Hamlet's dilemma instead of silently repeating to yourself the all too familiar words of his distress as the actor on stage dutifully recited them? Simon Russell Beale accomplished that extraordinary feat for me in a recent National Theatre production of *Hamlet*. It doesn't happen very often.

Callas sings as if her life depended on it. She sings as if she might never sing again. Every performance had the tension of a last performance. No wonder her career was so brief by any reasonable measure. The vocal experts say she gave too much too soon. Still, I loved Beverly Sills even more than I already did when she said she'd rather sing like Callas for ten years than sing like anyone else for forty.

Writing a play about Maria Callas was the furthest thing from my mind when I wrote *The Lisbon Traviata* in 1989. That play is about people who worship certain artists because they fill an emotional void in their lives. Mendy and Stephen appreciate Callas as a musician but they need the sound of her voice to take them to a place where they feel protected from the harsh realities of an outside world that does not understand or accept them. They need it perpetually. They are condemned to it. Callas is their Judy Garland, their Barbra Streisand, their Lady Gaga. She is the voice they need to hear telling them that all is right with the world. If that voice were silenced, the consequences for them would be as unimaginable as they are unfathomable.

When I was done with *The Lisbon Traviata*, I thought I was done as a writer with Callas. Six years later, I was in a theatre enjoying a collection of very good actors performing brief excerpts from my plays. My mother was my date. There is no better event to take a mother to than when her child is being feted. Zoe Caldwell did a speech from *A Perfect Ganesh* and I was reminded how I still had not written the right role for her unique abilities as a great stage actress. I was still fretting about that when Nathan Lane followed her on stage with Mendy's monologue about what Callas "meant" to him from *The Lisbon Traviata*. He was barely ten seconds into it when the thunderbolt that all creative people hunger for but seldom experience hit me full force: Of course! Zoe Caldwell as Maria Callas teaching a master class. The first line is "No applause." and the last is "Well, that's that." All I have to do is write the play that connects them and I'm home free.

At that point, I was jotting the two lines down on my program when my mother punched me on the arm. "Pay attention! They're honoring you. That's very rude." I didn't care, I had my next play.

The actual seeds for *Master Class* had been sowed several years earlier when John Guare and I were leading the inaugural playwright's program at Juilliard. After one particularly frustrating session, I felt more than ever that I did not have the patience or true generosity to make a good teacher. I wondered if the playwrights were as disappointed, if not angry, with me as I was with myself.

In the elevator, a small announcement had been taped above the floor buttons: "Master Class with Leontyne Price, Juilliard Theatre, 4 p.m."

That sounded a lot more appealing than taking the number 1 train back to the Village. I flashed my Faculty I.D. and went in.

The moment Mme Price entered, I thought what a theatrical situation it was. One of the most famous singers in the world was insisting that she was there to teach and that we should forget all about who she was. Our focus should be on the student singer, not the *prima donna*. We did our best to comply but since the teacher insisted on breaking the fourth wall and talking to us, it was hard to focus on the singer and her song. All pretensions at the game we were playing completely disappeared when Mme Price, after listening to a young soprano struggle with a phrase from "*Come scoglio*," from Mozart's *Così fan tutte*, an aria that Mme Price had sung to thunderous ovations when she was still performing, said to the floundering young woman something like, "Darling, it's so hard to explain but when I did it, I did it something like this." With that she sang the last bars of the aria, including the formidable cadenza with its exposed high note—and sang it with the voice that had conquered the world. For that one brief moment, Leontyne Price was again the greatest soprano in the world.

Her reward was a thunderous ovation: bravos, cheers, feet stamping the floor. For that we were scolded: "You shouldn't have done that. This isn't about me. It's about her." At that point, I doubt Mme Price knew the young woman's name any more than we did.

"Next student," Price called in her most preemptory diva voice, lowering both the temperature and the expectations in the theatre.

And then, while the next singer got ready, she couldn't resist a good one-liner: "If I'd known I was still going to be able to sing like that, I wouldn't have retired three years ago."

Another ovation but this time no admonitions from the teacher for our enthusiasm. Instead, a big happy smile from someone who—if only for a moment—was center stage, reborn again.

Nothing could have been more theatrical than that afternoon with "Lee" as we fans called her (behind her back, of course). I filed it away somewhere and forgot all about it, I guess, until that moment at another theatre with Zoe and Nathan when it all came thrillingly back and told me I had a play to write.

I don't think any play of mine has undergone fewer rewrites than *Master Class*. I don't remember a single one. Of course I told myself I had lived this play. I had been writing it since first hearing The Voice at my best friend at Ray High School Rand Carter's house in Corpus Christi in 1954. I had been writing it since I stood in line outside the Metropolitan Opera House for twenty-four hours to get standing room tickets in the Family Circle to be at Callas's debut in *Norma* in 1956. It would be the first time I had seen or heard her live, and my very first time inside the Met. I had been writing it since attending some of the actual Callas master classes at Juilliard, several years before Price's. I had been writing it since the evening I spent in her apartment at the Plaza Hotel and listened in overwhelming disappointment as she rattled on about the price of things, television sitcoms she was enjoying and how annoyed she was that she had been asked to sing at a colleague's memorial. "For free!" She sounded incredulous. I went home and put on *La Sonnambula*. I never met her again. The expectations we put on our idols are unreasonable beyond all measure. To know her would have been unfair to her.

The trouble with the play, everyone assured me, was that only a few thousand people in the world, Callas fanatics, all of them, would be even remotely interested in seeing it. The play's chances for popular success were deemed nonexistent.

I was invited to Big Fork, Montana, to participate in a series of staged readings of new plays for a local audience. I thought to myself "If *Master Class* can hold an audience in Big Fork, Montana, maybe, just maybe, it has a chance in a slightly bigger and more sophisticated venue."

To my intense amazement, Zoe Caldwell, whom I had written the play for, agreed to make the journey with me and the director, Leonard Foglia. I think she was too embarrassed to tell me she and her husband, the producer Robert Whitehead, thought the play had no commercial possibilities and the least she owed me for my efforts in writing it on her behalf, was this one performance in Big Fork.

We arrived at the beginning of spring. Everything was thawing. The ground was like walking on a sponge. The hotel had been closed for the season. Re-opened for us, it reeked of mildew. We rehearsed in the back of a bookstore with an out-of-tune piano and a man who could not even pretend to have the high notes for the tenor's aria in the second act. Everyone had trouble pronouncing the names and the Italian words in the text, Zoe most of all.

After two days of this, and only two days before the "performance," I found Zoe in the parking lot throwing a suitcase into her car. "I'm too old, too rich, and too famous for this," she said in her best Medea voice. I think "this" referred to absolutely everything in Big Fork, including the fact that I hadn't finished the second act. She was going home.

I don't remember who or what changed her mind. Maybe there is a certain truth to "The show must go on," and Zoe stayed to honor the tradition, not her playwright.

The performance was wonderful. Playwrights don't need a critic to tell them when a play works. The audience does. They breathe as one. You feel them collectively holding their breath, then all together releasing it. The playwright who can hear a pin drop during a performance, I promise you, is a happy one. While an audience's laughter is balm, its silence is even better.

When the reading was over, I agreed to do a talkback with the audience. I wanted to hear their comments or, if any, their confusions. I already could tell they "liked" the play from my standing place at the back of the theatre.

One man asked me if Maria Callas was a real person. When I assured him she was, he said audibly to his wife and with not a little satisfaction in his voice, "I told you she was real." An appreciative woman complimented Zoe's performance and then asked if she were a professional actress. When Zoe modestly assured her she was, the woman nodded encouragingly, "You're very talented, you know." "Thank you," Zoe said.

As the song says, if we could make it in Big Fork, we could make it anywhere. We had a play that worked for more than just Callas fanatics. There would be other productions and many awards. In fact, *Master Class* is one of my most performed plays, both here and internationally.

Years later, at a chance meeting at the Kennedy Center, when I told Mme Price that she, not Callas, was the real inspiration for *Master Class* she asked me why she hadn't received any royalties. I told her I owed her quite a bit of money at this point. She asked me why I hadn't written a play about her. I told her I wouldn't know how to. Her look seemed to suggest that she agreed I couldn't. I then told her about a friend of mine who had invited the great Italian soprano Renata Tebaldi to attend a performance of *Master Class* with him. "Why would I want to see a play about *her*?" was *La voce d'un angelo*'s withering refusal.

"I can understand that," Mme Price said.

Master Class is my most autobiographical play. While most of the facts about Callas's professional and personal life are accurate, many of the feelings she expresses about the need for the arts in our lives are my own. Callas's valedictory remarks to her students is the closest I have come to putting my own artistic manifesto into words.

Without self-pity, I can say the sacrifices an artist makes on the altar of a career are many and genuine. They wouldn't have it any other way. But so are the rewards. I have never stood center stage at La Scala and received a Callas-like ovation. But I have felt the profound connection between me and another human being when one of my plays has *mattered* to them. I have been heard. *Master Class* is about making myself heard.

Thank you, Anna Maria Sofia Cecilia Kalogeropoulous.

Master Class

for Elaine Steinbeck

MASTER CLASS was originally commissioned by Circle Repertory Company, and received its premiere at Philadelphia Theatre Company (Sara Garonzik, Producing Artistic Director) at the Plays and Players Theater, in Philadelphia, Pennsylvania, on March 1, 1995. The production subsequently traveled to the Mark Taper Forum (Gordon Davidson, Artistic Director) in Los Angeles, California; the Eisenhower Theater at the Kennedy Center in Washington, D.C.; and to Broadway at the John Golden Theatre (Robert Whitehead, Lewis Allen and Spring Sirkin, Producers) where it opened on November 5, 1995. It was directed by Leonard Foglia; the set design was by Michael McGarty; the lighting design was by Brian MacDevitt; the costume design was by Jane Greenwood; the sound design was by Jon Gottlieb; the production stage manager was Dianne Trulock; the stage manager was Linda Barnes and the assistant to Mr. McNally and Mr. Foglia was Thomas Caruso. The cast was as follows:

MARIA CALLAS Zoe Caldwell

FIRST SOPRANO (SOPHIE) Karen Kay Cody

SECOND SOPRANO (SHARON) Audra McDonald

TENOR (TONY) Jay Hunter Morris

ACCOMPANIST (MANNY) David Loud

STAGEHAND Michael Friel

MASTER CLASS was subsequently presented on Broadway at the Manhattan Theatre Club, opening on July 7, 2011. Lynne Meadow was the Artistic Director and Barry Grove, the executive producer. The production was directed by Stephen Wadsworth; the set design was by Martin Pakledinaz; the sound design was by Jon Gottlieb; production stage manager was Susie Cordon and the stage manager was Allison Sommers. The cast was as follows:

MARIA CALLAS Tyne Daly

FIRST SOPRANO (SOPHIE) Alexandera Silber

SECOND SOPRANO (SHARON) Sierra Boggess

TENOR (TONY) Garrett Sorenson

ACCOMPANIST (MANNY) Jeremy Cohen

STAGEHAND Clinton Brandhagen

CHARACTERS

MARIA CALLAS

FIRST SOPRANO (SOPHIE)

SECOND SOPRANO (SHARON)

TENOR (TONY)

ACCOMPANIST (MANNY)

STAGEHAND

ACT ONE

The house lights are still up when the Accompanist takes his place at the piano. He adjusts his seat. He checks his music. He waves at friends in the audience— if he has any.

Maria enters. She is dressed in an expensive pantsuit, accessorized with a Hermès scarf. She wears expensive Italian shoes and carries a largish Chanel bag. She walks briskly to the stage apron.

MARIA   No applause. We're here to work. You're not in a theatre. This is a classroom. No folderol. This is a master class. Singing is serious business. We're going to roll up our sleeves and work. I appreciate your welcome but enough is enough. *Basta. Fini.* Eh? So. How is everyone? Can you hear me? I don't believe in microphones. Singing is first of all about projection. So is speech. People are forgetting how to listen. They want everything blasted at them. Listening takes concentration. If you can't hear me, it's your fault. You're not concentrating. I don't get any louder than this. So come down closer or leave. No takers? What? You're all scared of me? Eh? Is that it? I don't bite. I promise you. I bark, I bark quite a bit actually, but I don't bite. I don't know what you're expecting. What did they tell you? I hope you're not expecting me to sing. Well, we shall see what we shall see. *Allora,* so, let's begin.

Where is the first student? Who is the first student? Are they here? When I was a student, I never missed a lesson. Never. Not once. I was never late for one either. In fact, I was usually early. I never wanted to leave the conservatory. I lived, ate and slept music. Music is a discipline. Too many of you are looking for the easy way out. Short cuts. No. If you want to have a career, as I did, and I'm not boasting now, I am not one to boast, you must be willing to subjugate yourself... is that a word? ... subjugate yourself to the music. Always the music. You are its servant. You are here to serve the composer. The composer is God. In Athens, and this was during the war, I often went to bed hungry but I walked to the conservatory and back every day, six days a week, and sometimes my feet were bleeding because I had no proper shoes. I don't tell you this to melodramatize. Oh no. I tell you to show you who I am.

Discipline. Courage. Here. Right here. From the guts. These lights.
Who is in charge of these lights? Is someone in charge of these lights?
May we have the lights in the auditorium off, please? This is really
terrible. We can't work under these conditions. I'm not going to ask a
student to come out here until these lights are taken care of. This is what
I was talking about. Attention must be paid to every detail. The lights.
Your wig. The amount of stage dust. A career in the theatre demands
total concentration. 100 percent detail. You think I'm joking. I'm not
joking. You wait, you'll see. If you're ever so lucky to sing in one of the
great theatres. I mean La Scala. I mean Covent Garden. I mean L'Opéra.
I mean Vienna. I mean the Metropolitan. You think it's easy? A great
career? Hah! That's all I have to say to you. Hah! Is this my chair? I don't
see a cushion. I asked for a cushion. Thank you. (*To the Accompanist.*)

Hello. You don't look familiar. Have I seen you before? Where?
When? Speak up, I can't hear you if you mumble.

ACCOMPANIST   We worked on *Don Carlos.*

MARIA   I can't hear him. Can you hear him? No one can hear you.

ACCOMPANIST   Yesterday morning, we worked on *Don Carlos* together.
Eboli's aria *"O don fatale."*

MARIA   Was that you? You look different. You were wearing a red
sweater. Where is it? It's important to have a look. A signature. Be
someone. So people will remember you. You all think you're so special.
You're a dime a dozen. There are hundreds, no, thousands of you out
there, studying, auditioning, going here, there, hither and yon. You
expect people to remember you if you don't have a look? *Po po po!* I was
never arrogant that way. I knew I needed a look and I got one. You. Yes,
you. And don't take this personally. You don't have a look. You look
very nice, I'm sure you are. You look very clean, very *comme il faut* but
you don't have a look. Get one. As quickly as possible. It's much easier
than practicing your scales. Or maybe it's not. When you weight 500
kilos—like some singers I could mention but I won't—a look is a little
more difficult. What are you smirking about. Yes, you, right behind this
person without a look. You don't have a look either. In fact, I don't see
anyone out there with what I consider a look. If you do, and I haven't
seen you, and I don't have the best vision in the world (we'll speak more
on that later!), if you do, I salute you. If you don't, get one. (*The house
lights are turned down.*)

There. *Bravo!* Now we have the atmosphere for some serious work. Isn't that much better? Thank you. We must have some rules here. Otherwise, chaos. This is not a circus, I really must insist on no applause or picture takers or autograph seekers. All it takes is one troublemaker to spoil the concentration. You are here to observe the students. Not me. Forget all about me. Poof! I'm invisible.

What's your name?

ACCOMPANIST   Me?

MARIA   Unless you want me to refer to you as The Person Who Was Wearing A Red Sweater Yesterday Morning.

ACCOMPANIST   Manny.

MARIA   Manny?

ACCOMPANIST   Short for Emmanuel.

MARIA   Emmanuel. That's a Jewish name I would imagine.

ACCOMPANIST   Yes.

MARIA   And you are Jewish.

ACCOMPANIST   Yes.

MARIA   I don't think there's a person in this auditorium who doesn't know that Eboli's aria is *"O don fatale."* Eh? So. Your little . . . how shall we say? . . . dig? reminder? . . . was quite unnecessary. Have I made myself clear? Eh?

ACCOMPANIST   Yes. I only—

MARIA   I accept your apology. How was I?

ACCOMPANIST   Pardon?

MARIA   When we worked on the *Don Carlos,* how was I? Don't answer that. This isn't about me. Now. Our first victim. Where is she?

ACCOMPANIST   You were wonderful.

MARIA   Thank you. It's a glorious bit of music. But really, you shouldn't have said that. This isn't about me. I'm quite cross with you, Manny. Is it all right if I call you Manny?

ACCOMPANIST   Please, I insist.

MARIA   And you must call me Madame. That was a little joke. So was "victim." Sooner or later you'll catch on to my sense of humor. Or you won't. Some people don't think I have one. Tenors. See? I can be witty. Only let's get down to the serious business at hand. We'll save the jokes for out there. The real world. Whatever that means. Brutal expression. Brutal place. At least in here we know where we are. We know where we stand. *Allora*. Is it me or it is warm in here? Can someone do something about the temperature? I won't have my singers sweating like pigs. It's hard enough supporting a tone with our diaphragms without dealing with overheating. Of course in Athens during the war there was no heat at all but that's another story. We froze but did we complain? Not a word. We were just grateful to be alive. Elvira de Hidalgo, a great soprano and my only teacher, Madame de Hidalgo used to say to me, "Maria, I have never seen anyone suffer so much in silence." Be that as it may. I guess I was made of sterner stuff. I had to be. Nobody cares the troubles you've seen. It's our work that matters. Our only work. Well, I'm ready. Are you? Has the heat been taken care of? I might as well be talking to myself.

ACCOMPANIST   They're working on it.

MARIA   And I am the grand duchess Anastasia Romanov and the check is in the mail. Is the first singer ready?
  Don't just stand there. *Avanti*, darling, *avanti*. (*The First Soprano comes onto the stage.*)
  We'll be right with you.
  And while you're fixing the heat and getting the cushion I requested at least three times before coming out here, the last being only an hour ago, would you see if you could find a little footrest for me? You see, my feet aren't going to quite reach the ground when I sit on such an uncommonly high chair as the one you've provided me with. Thank you. I'm sure that's the last we'll see of those people! *Coraggio!*
  I'm sorry.

FIRST SOPRANO   That's all right.

MARIA   Close your ears, child. You're just what I was talking about. I said close your ears. I don't want you to hear this. Are they closed?

FIRST SOPRANO   Yes.

MARIA   This is just what I was talking about. She doesn't have a look, poor thing. I'm not talking about her face, her figure. She can't help them.

I'm talking about flair, style, *élan*. Even the most wretched of us can do something about them. All right, you can open them. Did you hear that?

FIRST SOPRANO   No.

MARIA   Good. Well, hello, welcome. Are you nervous?

FIRST SOPRANO   Yes, a little.

MARIA   Only a little? You should be nervous a lot! All these people looking at you, waiting to hear what you sound like, all ready to judge you? I'd be terrified.

FIRST SOPRANO   I am, I am.

MARIA   Well stop it. You can't sing if you're nervous. You can't do anything if you're nervous. Nerves have destroyed more singers than a bad teacher ever did. All nerves mean is a lack of confidence. A lack of preparation. Do I make you nervous?

FIRST SOPRANO   Yes.

MARIA   Good. I take this seriously and so should you.

FIRST SOPRANO   I do.

MARIA   Eh?

FIRST SOPRANO   I do take this seriously.

MARIA   What's your name? Eh? You'll have to speak up, darling. You're on a stage now. People are listening. Hundreds and hundreds of people. They want to know who you are. Don't disappoint them. God gave you a voice. Use it.

FIRST SOPRANO   Sophie De Palma.

MARIA   *Brava!* See how easy that was! Sophie De Palma. It's not an ideal name for a career but it's good enough. I can see it outside a theatre. Sophie De Palma as . . . what? . . . Sophie De Palma as Frasquita in *Carmen*. Sophie De Palma as The Third Norn in *Götterdämmerung*. Italian?

FIRST SOPRANO   Greek/Italian.

MARIA   *Po po po!*

FIRST SOPRANO   My teacher says that accounts for my temperament. I'm very fiery.

MARIA   Are you?

FIRST SOPRANO   That's what my teacher says. I was making a little joke. I don't believe you can be a great artist without temperament. Neither does he. We're working on it. Everyone said you had. I mean have. Great temperament. I'm hoping to get some from you, frankly. Am I saying the wrong thing?

MARIA   Do something fiery.

FIRST SOPRANO   I can't. Not just like that. No one can.

MARIA   WHERE IS MY FOOTSTOOL?

FIRST SOPRANO   Well, I guess some people can.

MARIA   You thought that was fiery? Wait. Just wait. My fire comes from here, Sophie. It's mine. It's not for sale. It's not for me to give away. And even if I could, I wouldn't. It's who I am. Find out who you are. That's what this is all about. Eh? This isn't a freak show. I'm not a performing seal. "I'm hoping to get some from you, frankly!"

FIRST SOPRANO   I'm sorry.

MARIA   So. What are you going to sing for us? Sophie De Palma?

FIRST SOPRANO   *Sonnambula? "Ah, mon credea mirarti."*

MARIA   *Brava!*

FIRST SOPRANO   Is that all right?

MARIA   Into the lion's den, eh? I salute your courage. Be our guest. One of the most beautiful *bel canto* arias, if not the most difficult.

FIRST SOPRANO   They say you were unsurpassed in the role. I have your recording, of course. Even Sutherland.

MARIA   Stop right there. This is important. For all of us. I won't hear anything against any of my colleagues. And neither should you. She did her best. That's all any of us can do. Joan was . . . Well, that's a whole other story. Like her looks, it wasn't her fault. A twelve-foot Lucia de Lammermoor. Whoever heard of such a thing? But what was she to do? Stoop her way through the role? I don't want this class to disintegrate into a discussion of personalities. I won't let it happen.
    What?

ACCOMPANIST   Me?

MARIA   Yes, you. Who else? You've been trying to get a word in. I saw you back there. I have eyes in the back of my head. You have to if you want a career in the theatre. Someone somewhere is always behind you plotting your downfall. That's a fact. Always. If you don't develop eyes in the back of your head, you'll soon end up with a dagger in your back. Look what they did to me. The envy. The malice. But that's another story. So? What? Speak. We're wasting valuable time.

ACCOMPANIST   The footstool. It's here.

MARIA   Well bring it out. Do I have to do everything myself?

ACCOMPANIST   They didn't want to interrupt.

MARIA   What would you call this? Do you understand now what I go through? All I'm trying to do is hold a simple master class. (*A Stagehand brings out a footstool. He wears jeans and a T-shirt.*)

STAGEHAND   Where do you want it?

MARIA   There.

STAGEHAND   Here?

MARIA   That's where the chair is. (*He puts the footstool down in front of Maria's chair.*) *Bravo!* Well done.

STAGEHAND   Hunh?

MARIA   See how simple that was? Tell your supervisor we can begin now. Thank you.

STAGEHAND   I don't have a supervisor. You're welcome. (*He goes.*)

MARIA   People like that have absolutely no interest in what we're doing here. It's very humbling. We bare our hearts and they say "Hunh?" I always thought our art reached everyone. Well, I used to think a lot of things I don't anymore. Eh? So. Carmen De Palma. Are you ready? Straighten up. Head high. We're not hiding anything.

FIRST SOPRANO   It's Sophie. Sophie De Palma. You said Carmen.

MARIA   I can't be expected to keep everyone's name straight. I'm focused on the music now. And so should you be. Manny? Are you ready? Did I get that right at least? You are Manny?

ACCOMPANIST   Yes.

MARIA   Well, I'm good for something. I'm going to sit down now. Ignore me. Forget all about me. Poof! I'm invisible. I asked for a cushion, too. You see? You see? Never mind now. It's too late. We're working. All right. Now I want total silence and complete concentration. Sophie De Palma. Amina's aria. *La Sonnambula.* Good luck. (*She makes herself comfortable.*) You see why I asked for this stool? I have short legs. I always looked tall in the theatre but I always had short legs. When Zeffirelli dressed me in *Norma.* But that's another story. Are you waiting for me? Begin. (*Accompanist begins to play.*) Posture, posture. Not yours. Hers! (*She listens to the introduction to the* scena *and recitative.*)

FIRST SOPRANO   "Oh!"

MARIA   Stop right there. I'm sorry to do this to you but what's the point of going on with it if it's all wrong? Eh? You're not listening to the music.

FIRST SOPRANO   I wasn't?

MARIA   Let it fill you up. It's so simple. Listen. It's all there. Who she is. You don't have to do anything but listen. A simple country girl. An innocent victim. He's broken her heart. Have you ever had your heart broken?

FIRST SOPRANO   Yes.

MARIA   You could have fooled me. This is the theatre, darling. We wear our hearts on our sleeves here.

FIRST SOPRANO   But she's sleepwalking. She's a sleepwalker.

MARIA   She's not a sleepwalker. That's the artifice. Something some writer made up so there could be a silly story. Find the truth of her situation. A broken heart. Anyone can walk in their sleep. Very few people can weep in song. Again, Manny. I am so sorry to interrupt so quickly before you've scarcely sung a note but I get so impatient when I see a singer who doesn't listen to the music. I'll be very good this time. I promise. (*Accompanist begins to play again.*)
   Better, better. You're listening. I'm seeing Bellini on your face. *Attenzione!* Now I'm seeing terror. Now I'm seeing Sophie. Do you mind if I do it?

FIRST SOPRANO   Please. I wish you would.

MARIA   I don't want you to imitate me. I never want any of you to imitate me. I only want to show you how I did it. It's so hard to say what I mean. So much easier to show you. All right, now at La Scala when I worked with Luchino, Visconti, Luchino Visconti, the *régisseur*, the *metteur en scene*, you know him in this country, eh? Luchino had me appear high above the stage. One false step and I would have fallen to my death. A fate that would have not distressed some of my colleagues who were sitting out front. Colleagues? Enemies, I should say. So. There I am. Sleepwalking. My heart broken. Unaware that death is but one false step away. I'm ready. (*She nods to Accompanist. He plays the introduction. Maria stands and listens to its end, then:*)
Well, something like that. No applause.

FIRST SOPRANO   That was wonderful.

MARIA   See how easy that was?

FIRST SOPRANO   I'll try.

MARIA   Just listen. Everything is in the music. (*She sits and listens as Accompanist plays again.*)

FIRST SOPRANO   "Oh!"

MARIA   You know I'm going to interrupt you again, don't you?

FIRST SOPRANO   Yes. But I was listening that time, wasn't I? I really thought I was listening.

MARIA   You can listen till the cows come home. Is that the expression? Listening is beyond the point. We're singing now. I want to talk about your "Oh!"

FIRST SOPRANO   I sang it, didn't I?

MARIA   That's just it. You sang it. You didn't feel it. It's not a note we're after here. It's a stab of pain. The pain of loss. Surely you understand loss.

FIRST SOPRANO   I'm always losing my umbrella. You mean a person.

MARIA   It's not just a question of singing. Anyone can get the notes out. Well, that's not true actually. Scotto has no business singing this music. Know your limitations. That's important. So, what are we talking about here, eh? Feeling, feeling, feeling.
"Oh!" You hear the difference?

FIRST SOPRANO   Yes.

MARIA   I want to hear everything in that one sound. "Oh!" Can you give me that?

FIRST SOPRANO   I'll try.

MARIA   Try isn't good enough. Do. The theatre isn't about trying. People don't leave their homes to watch us try. They come to see us do.
    All right, you can come out now. Excuse me, Sophie. (*Stagehand appears with a cushion for Maria.*)
    Avanti, avanti! The theatre isn't for people who like to be in their ivory towers either.

STAGEHAND   Is this what you wanted?

MARIA   It's fine. Interruptions every moment.

STAGEHAND   You said you wanted this.

MARIA   I did. This is a class. I'm making a point. You're singing an aria and they're building scenery in the wings.

STAGEHAND   I wasn't building scenery.

MARIA   You see? You see?

STAGEHAND   Anything else?

MARIA   No. Let's give him a hand. (*Watching him go.*)
    Couldn't care less!
    Allora. Where were we? Ah, yes, "oh!" I'm not going to stop you this time, *cara.* Now, I may speak to you while you sing but I'm not going to stop you.

ACCOMPANIST   From the top?

MARIA   Yes from the top. This is music, not piece work. (*Accompanist begins. First Soprano begins again. This time Maria looks for something in her purse while Accompanist and First Soprano continue.*)
    Go ahead. I'm listening. There it is! I thought I'd lost it. Continue.

FIRST SOPRANO   *"Oh! Se una volta sola."*

MARIA   Diction, Diction. *Volta.* Bite into those consonants. I want to hear them. There's an "L" in *volta*, there's a "T."

FIRST SOPRANO   *"Volta sola,*
        Rivederlo io potessi"

MARIA   *Rivederlo!* Where's your "R" in *rivederlo?*

FIRST SOPRANO   *"Rivederlo io potessi*
Anzi che all'ara altra sposa
Ei guidasse! . . ."

MARIA   I'm not hearing any consonants. You're singing in Sanskrit. I'm only getting vowels. Words mean something. Vowels are in the inarticulate sounds our hearts make. "Oh." Consonants give them specific meaning. *"Oh! Se una volta sola."* Hear the difference? I just made that up. Vowels, consonants. But I think I'm on to something. Eh? You. I like you. You nod and smile at everything I say. (*To Sophie.*) What are you saying?

FIRST SOPRANO   You mean.

MARIA   The words.

FIRST SOPRANO   I'm saying.

MARIA   Translate them.

FIRST SOPRANO   "Oh!" Obviously, "Oh!" means "Oh!" "If one time alone. Or more. If one more time. See him again, I could." No, wait. "If only I could see him one more time again." Something like that.

MARIA   *"Oh! se una volta sola"*—"One more time!" That's all she wants. *"Rivederlo io potessi."* She's never going to see this man again. *"Anzi che all'ara altra sposa ei guidasse!"*—Before he takes another bride to the altar. *"Vana speranza"*—what a terrible expression. "Vain hope." Her life is over. *"Io sento suonar la sacra squilla"*—She hears the wedding bells. They don't ring for her. *"Al tempio ei muove"*—They're on their way to the church! *"Io l'ho perduto"*—I've lost him. *"E pur"*—this is important.—*"E pur"*—and yet, and yet. *"Rea non son io."* I am not guilty. I wasn't.

FIRST SOPRANO   This is hard.

MARIA   Of course it's hard. That's why it's so important we do it right. "This is hard." Where am I? I thought I was somewhere where people were serious. This is not a film studio where anyone can get up there and act. I hate that word. Act. No! Feel. Be. That's what we're doing here. "This is hard." I'll tell you what's hard. What's hard is listening to you make a mockery of this work of art. "Mockery" is too strong a word. So is "travesty." I'm not getting any juice from you, Sophie. I want juice. I want passion. I want you.

FIRST SOPRANO   I'm not that sort of singer.

MARIA   Well try. Just once in your life, try.

FIRST SOPRANO   I'm not that sort of person either.

MARIA   What sort of person are you then?

FIRST SOPRANO   I just want to sing.

MARIA   Am I stopping you?

FIRST SOPRANO   No. You're.

MARIA   We don't have to finish this. If you're unhappy.

FIRST SOPRANO   I don't know what you're talking about.

MARIA   Yes, you do. You don't want to do it. Everyone understood what I was talking about when I was singing. They simply didn't want to listen. Too difficult. Too painful. Too controversial. At my final performance at La Scala in *Pirata* in the Mad Scene when I came to the words *"il palco funesto"*—"the fatal scaffold"—I pointed to the general manager in his box, the same man who has said my services in his theatre were no longer necessary, and hurled the words right at him. I don't know what came over me, I was possessed, like a Fury, and I went right to the stage apron, just meters from where he was sitting, and I sang *"il palco funesto."* The audience gasped. Ghiringhelli reeled from the force of it. They say it was the greatest ovation in the history of La Scala. He ordered them to ring down the fire curtain to stop my applause. Why deal with someone like me when you can get Tebaldi or Sutherland or Sills. I don't blame them. I did but I don't now. They said they didn't like my sound. That wasn't it. They didn't like my soul. Too. What? Too. Something. You have a lovely voice, you know. A charming sound.

FIRST SOPRANO   Thank you.

MARIA   Much lovelier than mine ever was. And no one ever accused me or my voice of charm. That was my sister. She was the charming one. The pretty one. The one the boys. Wanted. Anyway. *En tout cas.* All that got her wherever she is, I don't know, we don't speak, and got me where I am, sometimes I think the whole world knows where that is, or was, and which is right now up here with you talking to you about your voice, your sound. Who you are. Who are you? Sophie De Palma, you've told us your name but who are you? Tears will get you nowhere, darling. Not in the theatre, not in real life. Certainly not with me. No one cares how many nights I cried myself to sleep. I sang *Norma* better than anyone had in years and I interpolated a high F at the end of the first act. That's all people cared about. When you're fat and ugly (and I'm not saying that you are either of those things) you had better have a couple of high F's you can interpolate into your life. No one cares about your damp pillow. Why should I? Did you care about mine? Did anyone? But that's another story. I can cry all I want now (don't worry, I won't. Tears come hard when you're me) but you can't, Sophie De Palma. You've got to sing for your supper. Sing for your salvation. Shall we try again? (*First Soprano nods. Maria gives her a tissue and glances at her wristwatch.*)

Did you know one of my baptismal Greek Orthodox names was Sophie?

FIRST SOPRANO   No.

MARIA   Anna Maria Sofia Cecilia Kalogeropoulous. December 2, 19——. But that was another life. *Allora. Cominciamo. Ricominciamo.*

FIRST SOPRANO   From "*Gran Dio*"?

MARIA   *Va Bene.*

If you're not enjoying this, you can leave. No one's keeping you.

We have someone going through his diary in the third row, Sophie, I told him if he wasn't enjoying our work here, he's free to leave.

Are we ready? (*First Soprano and the Accompanist nod.*)

Do you call them that in this country? Diaries? Agendas? Never mind. Sshh! Before we start, what is the orchestra playing here, darling?

FIRST SOPRANO   Nothing?

MARIA   And why do you think that is? What is Bellini up to?

FIRST SOPRANO   I don't know.

MARIA   He wants us to concentrate on the sound of the human voice. The most expressive instrument there is to reveal human emotion. Bellini wants us to hear you in all your glory in the *recitativo*. When you can no longer bear to speak, when the words aren't enough, that's when he asks you to sing. Not a moment before.

FIRST SOPRANO   But recitative is singing, surely.

MARIA   Of course it's singing. It's sung. But it's the equivalent of speech. Eh? Again.

FIRST SOPRANO   Again? I haven't. Once. I'm sorry.

MARIA   Remember to use the words. From *"Gran Dio."*

FIRST SOPRANO   *"Gran Dio"*

MARIA   What are you doing?

FIRST SOPRANO   I'm sorry?

MARIA   What does it say on the score?

FIRST SOPRANO   I begin on the C above middle C and—

MARIA   I'm not talking about the notes. There's a direction from the composer.

FIRST SOPRANO   There is? (*First Soprano goes to piano and looks at music Accompanist is playing from.*)

MARIA   This is what I've been talking about the entire time. This lack of detail. This sense of nothing matters.

FIRST SOPRANO   You mean, *"inginocchiandosi."* (*She has difficulty with the word.*)

MARIA   I mean, *"inginocchiandosi."* (*First Soprano doesn't understand.*)

FIRST SOPRANO   It's important?

MARIA   It's life and death, like everything we do here.

FIRST SOPRANO   I don't know what it means.

MARIA   We can see that.

FIRST SOPRANO   It's a reflexive verb, I know that much. It means I do something to myself.

MARIA   Don't tempt me to tell you what that might be. Kneel.

FIRST SOPRANO   Kneel?

MARIA   It means, kneel. *Così!* (*She drops to her knees and opens her arms wide.*)
   "Gran dio!" This is how we speak to God. On our knees, *a terra,* our arms open to Him.
   "Non mirar il mio pianto." Do not heed these tears I shed.
   "Io gliel perdono." I forgive him them. The orchestra is sounding like an organ here. A church organ. What is Bellini up to?

"Quanto infelice io sono, felice ei sia." Let him be as happy as I am unhappy.
"Questa d'u cor che more e l'ultima prehgiera." This is the last prayer of the heart that is dying. That explains the organ. It's all in the music. *"Ah, si!"* She says it again. She has to. *"Questa d'un che muore è l'ultima prehgiera."*

FIRST SOPRANO   I see what you mean now.

MARIA   What do you do now? What does the score say?

FIRST SOPRANO (*Haltingly.*)   *"Guardandosi la mano"*—

MARIA (*Impatiently.*)   *"Guardandosi la mano come cercando l'anello."*
    She's looking for the ring that isn't there, Sophie. (*She looks at her left hand for the ring.*)
    "L'anello mio."

FIRST SOPRANO   My ring!

MARIA   *"L'anello."*

FIRST SOPRANO   The ring.

MARIA   *"El me l'ha tolto."*

FIRST SOPRANO   He took it from me.

MARIA   *"Ma non può rapirmi l'immagin sua . . ."*

FIRST SOPRANO   But he cannot from me take image his. His image.

MARIA   *"Sculta ella è qui . . ."*

FIRST SOPRANO   Sculptured it is here.

MARIA   "Here!" *"Qui . . . nel petto."*

FIRST SOPRANO (*Soprano reads from the score.*)   "Amina takes Elvino's faded flowers from her bosom." (*Accompanist begins playing the introduction to the aria proper.*)

MARIA   Just listen to the music and think about what the words mean. It's all there, Sophie. These composers knew the human heart. All we have to do is listen.
    *"Ah! non credea mirarti
    Si presto estinto, o fiore,
    Passasti al par d'amore,*

Che un giorno solo, che un giorno sol durò.
Che un giorno solo, ah, sol durò.

Potria novel vigore
Il pianto, il pianto mio recarti . . .
Ma ravvivar l'amore
Il pianto mio, ah no, no, non può,
Ah, non credea,
Passasti al par d'amor . . ."

No words now, just our voices, weeping in song. Rising, rising, then falling.

"d'amor"

No applause. Something like that, Sophie. Eh? You see what I mean now?

FIRST SOPRANO   I think so. Thank you.

MARIA   You think you can do that?

FIRST SOPRANO   I'll. Yes.

MARIA   Did you mark your score? Those phrases I pointed out.

FIRST SOPRANO   No.

MARIA   Why not?

FIRST SOPRANO   I don't have a pencil.

MARIA   Then how do you expect to remember what you've learned? Five, maybe ten years from now, you'll be singing this role in some little theatre somewhere and you'll be saying to yourself, "What did she tell me? What did she say?" Does anyone have a pencil for a student who doesn't have one? If you can imagine such a thing.

FIRST SOPRANO   I didn't think we'd be—

ACCOMPANIST   I have one.

MARIA   Thank you.

FIRST SOPRANO   Thank you.

MARIA   At the conservatory Madame de Hidalgo never once had to ask me if I had a pencil. And this was during the war, when a pencil wasn't something you just picked up at the five and ten. Oh no, no, no, no. A pencil meant something. It was a choice over something else. You either had a pencil or an orange. I always had a pencil. I never had an orange. And I love oranges. I knew one day I would have all the oranges I could want but that didn't make the wanting them any less.

Have you ever been hungry?

FIRST SOPRANO Not like that.

MARIA It's. It's something you remember. Always. In some part of you.

You should see my scores. They're covered with pencil marks. You can hardly see the music. I wrote down everything. Every hint, every trick, every suggestion. Like a sponge I was. You have to be like a sponge. Absorb, absorb. These are centuries of opera we're talking about here, eh? We don't make this music up. The notes, the phrasing. We're talking about tradition.

Do you know who created Amina?

FIRST SOPRANO You mean who.

MARIA The same soprano who created Norma.

FIRST SOPRANO They did?

MARIA Pasta. Giuditta Pasta.

FIRST SOPRANO I've heard of her.

MARIA She'll be happy to hear that. When you sing this music I want to hear all the links that take you back to her. I want to hear Callas, I want to hear Ponselle, I want to hear Lehmann, I want to hear Pasta.

FIRST SOPRANO Do you want to hear Sutherland? I'm sorry.

MARIA I want to hear you. A straight line. From you through me to Pasta. Eh? How can you sing this music and not know who Pasta was? Shame, Sophie, shame.

All right. Let's hear it again. With a broken heart this time.

I hate to say it but you should wear longer skirts or slacks. During daytime it's all right. But you must remember, I'm sorry I'm bringing this up, but the public that looks at you from down there sees a little more of you than you might want. Eh? It's no use now. You should have thought of it before. Forgive me, eh? No laughing. This is a serious matter. Maestro. (*Accompanist begins to play again.*)

I want you to imagine you are Amina. This is opera, Sophie. You're alone on a great stage. Make us feel what you feel. Show us *that* truth. (*First Soprano begins the recitative again as lights fade on her and Accompanist and come up strong on Maria who is hearing her performance of the same music. So are we.)*

How quickly it all comes back. The great nights. (*She listens.*)

Ma, Luchino, perchè? Why do you have me wearing jewels? I am supposed to be a poor Swiss village girl. "You are not a village girl. You are Maria Callas playing a village girl." *Ah, capisco, capisco!* I understood. (*She listens.*)

This was the terrifying moment. The beginning. In the utter, utter silence, my voice filling the void of that vast, darkened auditorium. I felt so alone, so unprotected. *Coraggio.* It's begun. (*She listens.*)

What were they expecting? (*She listens.*)

Ari always said, They're not coming to hear you, no one comes to hear Callas anymore. They've come to look at you. You're not a singer. You're a freak. I'm a freak. We're both freaks. They've come to see us. You're a *monstre sacré* now. We are both *monstres sacrés.* And we are fucking.

I don't like that word, Ari.

Fuck you, you don't like that word.

This phrase. Lovely. And I did it well.

Did you hear what I aid? Before you were just a singer.

A canary who sang for her supper. A fat, ugly canary. And now you are a beautiful woman who fucks Aristotle Onassis.

Ari.

This is how I talk. This is how I have always talked. This is who I am. I'm coarse. I'm crude. I'm vulgar. Unlike some people, I remember from whence I came.

I remember, I remember too well.

They listen to you sing this boring shit music and clap and yell Brava! Brava La Divina! but what they all want to know is what we do in bed. The two Greeks. The two sweaty, piggy, beneath-them Greeks. The richest-man-in-the-world Greek and the most-famous-singer-in-the-world Greek. Together we rule the world. I have people by the balls and I squeeze. I squeeze very hard and without pity. I have you by the balls, Anna Maria Sofia Cecilia Kalogeropoulous. Everyone is for sale and I bought you.

This part. "She sang Anima's great lament in a voice suffused with tears."

You give me class. I give you my big thick uncircumcised Greek dick and you give me class. I give you my wealth and you give me respect where I never had any. I give you safety from your terror of the theatre, you don't have to go there anymore. I give you everything you want and need but love. I'm lucky. I don't need love. I have class now. (*"He" laughs.*)

Everyone needs love, Ari. I'm proud. I'm very proud but when it comes to this, to love, to you, to us, I am not.

I don't give love to anyone but my children. Have a child of mine and I will love him. Yes?

Yes, Ari.

Hey, canary, chin up. Look at me. You don't need love either. You have theirs. The snobs and the fags. They adore you. The snobs all want to take you to dinner at Lutèce and the fags all want to be you. Frankly, I'm not threatened. You hate it when I call you canary, don't you? It's affectionate. Can't you hear the affection in canary?

I was good tonight. I was very good.

Why don't you give all this up. It's *caca, skata* anyway. Eh? You know it, I know it. You live on the boat. You can go anywhere you want, stay as long as you want, buy anything you want, within reason. Always within reason. I hate a woman who tries to bleed a man dry. Of course she would have to be some woman to bleed this motherfucker dry. Do you know how much I'm worth? Do you have any idea of just how much money I have? I breathe money, I sweat money, I shit money.

I don't have to sing anymore? I won't if you don't want me.

Okay, so you don't sing anymore. You don't retire, you stop. There's a difference. Retiring is depressing. Stopping is class. They beg you. You're adamant. No means no, you tell them. I bet you didn't know I had that word in me, did you? Adamant. It means unshakable or immovable, especially in opposition. Hard. Like diamonds. That's us, baby.

That's us, Ari. A matched pair.

But when I want you to sing, you sing. You sing for me. I have you under the most fucking exclusive contract anybody ever had. And when I ask you to sing, you know what you're going to sing for me, baby? None of that opera *skata*. That song I taught you about the whore from Piraeus who took it five different ways at the same time. I had to tell you what four of those ways were.

I don't like that song, Ari.

Where have you been all your life, canary? Don't they fuck in the opera house?

I don't like that song.

Sing it anyway. (*The aria proper has ended. We hear the audience applaud.*)

I never heard their applause here. I was too deep in a dream. Like Amina, I'd been sleepwalking. But there I was on the stage of La Scala. I was beautifully dressed, heavy with diamonds, real diamonds, my hair in a tight chignon bound with real white roses flown to Milan the day of the performance from the south of France. "The ghost of Maria Taglioni," one critic wrote. I was beautiful at last. (*The music continues directly into the cabaletta conclusion of the scene and opera itself. We hear Maria's voice singing* "Ah, non giunge.")

I keep thinking of a pretty, slim blond girl back at the conservatory in Athens. Madame de Hidalgo gave her the part of Amina at the student recital. I was so heartbroken but I wanted to scratch her face with my nails at the same time, too. I was cast as a nun in *Suor Angelica* instead. But I want to sing Amina in *Sonnambula*, Madame de Hidalgo. With your voice and figure you're better off as a nun, my child. Look at me now, Madame de Hidalgo. Listen to me now. Sometimes I think every performance I sing is for that pretty, slim, blond girl taking all those bows at the Conservatory. Whatever happened to her with her freshly laundered blouses and bags full of oranges? My sister was another slim pretty blonde. They're not up here, either one of them. I'm up here. The fat ugly greasy one with the thick glasses and bad skin is up here and she's dressed by Piero Tosi and she's wearing so many diamonds she can scarcely move her arms and she is the absolute center of the universe right now.

I know they're not all out there in the dark. My enemies. My mother. My sister. The other singers. Smiling. Waiting for me to fail. The daredevil stuff is coming up. The hullabaloo. I'm not afraid. I welcome it. Reckless. You bet, I'm reckless! Someone said I'd rather sing like Callas for one year than like anyone else for twenty! Now the embellishments. The second time around. Never do it the same way twice. Flick your voice here. Lighten it. Shade it. Trill. Astonish. (*She listens. Slowly the rear of the stage will become the magnificent interior of La Scala.*)

Now the genius part of the production. Visconti has the house lights in the auditorium begin to come up while I'm still singing. Slowly, slowly. We're both waking up from a dream, the audience and me. The effect is unheard of. There's never been a night like this is in the history of La Scala. The theatre is garlanded with fresh roses hung form the boxes. The audience is magnificently dressed. It's the biggest *prima* of the season. There's Tebaldi. There's Lollobrigida. Magnani. The Rainiers. They're all here. And here I am. Dead center-stage at the greatest theatre in Europe singing roulades in full voice. Hurling notes like thunderbolts.

Daring anyone to challenge me. They can all see me but now I can see them. We are in the same room together at last. I have everyone where I want them. They're not smiling now. With each phrase, I come closer to the footlights. The auditorium grows brighter and brighter as my voice goes higher and higher. People have stopped breathing. My revenge, my triumph are complete. The applause is washing over me. I only have one note left to sing. Ah, yes, it's over. I've won again! (*Maria stands listening to the ovation. It is tremendous. When it fades to silence, the lights have faded back up to the level of the master class. Both the First Soprano and the Accompanist are waiting anxiously for her approval.*)

That was better.

FIRST SOPRANO   Thank you.

MARIA   Much better.

FIRST SOPRANO   Thank you.

MARIA   We'll take a break now. (*Maria goes to her chair, takes up her purse and leaves the stage.*)

FIRST SOPRANO (*To Maria.*)   Thank you. (*To Accompanist.*) Thank you. I thought she was going to critique me. I guess she liked me. (*To Accompanist.*) Now how do I get offstage? They should teach us that. They should teach us a lot of things they don't.

ACCOMPANIST   Your score.

FIRST SOPRANO   Thank you. (*He returns her score and they go off. The stage is bare except for the piano and Maria's chair. They house lights are fully up now.*)

END OF ACT ONE

ACT TWO

Someone has placed a bouquet of flowers on the piano.

The Accompanist enters and sits quietly at the piano. This time he ignores the audience.

The house lights are lowered.

There is a long wait.

Eventually, Maria enters. She comes to the stage apron.

MARIA   That's better. Eh? Isn't that better? With the lights like this? Eh? It's better we don't see you up here. That's how it is in the theatre. Just us and the music. Or that's how it should be. I know some singers, oh yes, who look out at the audience, if you can imagine such a thing, when they're meant to be involved in a dramatic situation. Of course, I don't consider these people serious artists. *Pas du tout, n'est-ce pas?* They're more like . . . oh, what's the word? . . . you know, help me: no arms, they swim, throw them a fish and they—seals! That's what they are: performing seals!

Did you have a good interval? I had a friend, who shall remain nameless, who used to say his favorite part of opera was the intervals. Well, people like that, we're not going to concern ourselves with them today, thank God. To think there are actually people to whom beauty, art, what we do, isn't important! Don't get me wrong: I think we should be paid for what we do and some of us are paid very well, (it's no secret I was paid more than any of my rivals, which was the newspapers' word for them, not mine. As if I had any! How can you have rivals when no one else can do what you do? So much has been written about it, so much nonsense.) The point I'm making, and it's a very simple one, is that art is beauty and you should be paid for it. Am I making myself clear? Never give anything away. There's no more where it came from. We give the audience everything and when it's gone, *c'est ça, c'est tout. Basta, finito.* We're the ones who end up empty. *"He dato tutto a te."* Medea sings that to Jason when she learns he's abandoning her for another woman. A younger woman. A woman of importance. A princess. *"Ho dato tutto a te."* "I gave everything for you. Everything." That's what we artists do for people. Where would you be without us? Eh? Think about that. (*To Accompanist.*)

Am I right?

ACCOMPANIST   I'm sorry?

MARIA   He knows I'm right.

And the friend who shall remain nameless who preferred the intervals of *Norma* to *Norma* itself was no friend. I don't know the proper word for people who are everywhere in our lives but don't wish us well at all as it turns out. Eh? Do you know what I'm talking about? She knows what I'm talking about. I know *one* word but I think the ceiling would fall down if I used it in this holy place and I do believe we are in a holy place. The stage, the theatre are sacred places, oh, yes. I lose my sense of humor the moment I walk through the stage door. I'm rambling. I had a terrible interval, actually. Well, you're not interested in my problems. Any more than I'm interested in yours. We're here to work. Put everything else behind us. Am I right?

ACCOMPANIST   Absolutely.

MARIA   Don't tell me . . . it's a Jewish name, I remember that much . . . I remember the red sweater . . . *Po, po, po!* . . . I give up.

ACCOMPANIST   Weinstock, Manny Weinstock.

MARIA   Of course it is! *Siete pronto, Signor Weinstock?*

ACCOMPANIST   *Sì.*

MARIA   *Bravo, bravo, acribravo!* You're doing very well.

ACCOMPANIST   Thank you.

MARIA   Isn't he doing well? I salute you. (*She applauds him.*) We all salute you. (*She encourages the audience to applaud him, then looks at index cards she has been carrying.*)

Who's next? Lady Macbeth, Tosca, Lucia. I must say, what these students lack in voice and technique, they make up for in self-confidence. Don't laugh. That's important. Well, we shall see what we shall see. I wish them well. Next victim! That was a joke. My last one, I promise. (*To the Accompanist.*)

And what is that folderol on the piano there, please?

ACCOMPANIST   You mean the flowers? They're for you. You have an unknown admirer. Very operatic.

MARIA   Is this a classroom or a circus? (*Second Soprano is coming out onto the stage. She is in an evening gown.*)

   That was very naughty of someone. I won't pretend I'm not flattered but I'm also not amused. Very, very naughty.

   (*To Second Soprano.*) *Avanti, avanti!* Don't linger. If you're going to enter, enter. If you don't want to be out here, go away. I'll be right with you. Are you going somewhere after this?

SECOND SOPRANO   No.

MARIA   (*She reads the card on the bouquet.*)   "*Brava, La Divina. We love you.*" "*La Divina.*" Don't make me laugh. And it's always, "We love you," never "I love you." So. Now who do we have here?

SECOND SOPRANO   Sharon Graham.

MARIA   Sharon Graham. Definitely not Greek.

SECOND SOPRANO   No.

MARIA   What's in a name, eh? I was Maria Meneghini Callas for a time. Of course, I was Signora Meneghini for a time as well. So. Sharon Graham. What are you going to sing for us?

SECOND SOPRANO   Lady Macbeth?

MARIA   Are you sure you want to do that, Sharon?

SECOND SOPRANO   I also have *Queen of the Night*, "*Die Hölle Rache*" and *Norma*, the "*Casta Diva.*"

MARIA   I think we'll stay with Lady Macbeth. The Sleepwalking Scene, I suppose.

SECOND SOPRANO   No, "*Vieni! t'affretta,*" I thought.

MARIA   Ah, the Letter Scene! Well, that's something. They usually all want to start with the Sleepwalking Scene. You're humble, like me, that's good. So. This is her entrance aria, yes?

SECOND SOPRANO   Yes.

MARIA   So what are you doing out here? Go away. We don't want to see you yet.

SECOND SOPRANO   You want me to go off and come back out?

MARIA   No, I want you to enter. You're on a stage. Use it. Own it. This is opera, not a voice recital. Anyone can stand there and sing. An artist enters and *is*.

SECOND SOPRANO   I thought this was a classroom.

MARIA   It doesn't matter. Never miss an opportunity to theatricalize. Astonish us, Sharon.

SECOND SOPRANO   How do I do that?

MARIA   You can start by not entering as Sharon Graham. Enter as Lady Macbeth. Enter as Shakespeare's Lady Macbeth. Enter as Verdi's Lady Macbeth.

SECOND SOPRANO   I'll do my best.

MARIA   And Sharon, may I say one more thing? That's a beautiful gown, obviously. We've all been admiring it. It's gorgeous. I wish I had one like it.

SECOND SOPRANO   Thank you.

MARIA   But don't ever wear anything like that before midnight at the earliest and certainly not to class. We're talking about what's appropriate. This is a master class, not some Cinderella's ball. Eh? Off you go now. And come back as her. Come back as Lady. (*Second Soprano exits.*)
Sometimes we just have to say these things, eh? Am I right? I learned the hard way. I didn't have anyone to tell me these things. I auditioned for Edward Johnson at the old Met wearing a red and white polka-dot dress, white gloves, and a blue hat with a veil and what I later learned were known as Joan Crawford "Catch me/your-F-word-me" pumps. I'm sorry, but that's what they were called. I was overweight and looked like an American flag singing *Madama Butterfly*. No wonder I wasn't engaged. She'll thank me one day.
Are we ready? (*Accompanist nods.*)
I haven't heard this music in years. Even the thought of it makes the hairs on the back of my head stand out.
I guess I'm ready. Begin. (*Accompanist begins to play Lady Macbeth's entrance aria. Maria listens hard, making sounds along with it, rather than actually singing the notes.*)
Satanic music, don't you think? We know where this music is coming from, don't we? What part of her body? Verdi knew his Shakespeare.

The curtain is flying up now. No Sharon yet. This an interesting choice for an entrance. I was onstage at this point. (*The music stops. No sign of the Second Soprano.*)

Sharon? We're all waiting. Excuse me. (*She leaves the stage and comes back a moment later.*)

No Sharon. She's gone. If her skin is that thin, she's not suited for this career. It's not like I said anything about her voice. I didn't even let her open her mouth.

This will make the papers. They'll have a fine time with this. "CALLAS HURTS STUDENT'S FEELINGS."

This is just what I was talking about: If you're going to stand up here, naked, and let people judge you, you can't afford to have feelings like Sharon's. A performance is a struggle. You have to win. The audience is the enemy. We have to bring you to your knees because we're right. If I'm worried about what you're thinking about, I can't win. I beg, I cringe for your favor instead. *"Ho dato tutto a te."* Eh? It doesn't work that way. You have to make them beg for yours. Dominate them. *"Ho dato tutto a te."* Eh? Art is domination. It's making people think that for that precise moment in time there is only one way, one voice. Yours. Eh? Anyone's feelings can be hurt. Only an artist can say *"Ho dato tutto a te"* center stage at La Scala and even Leonard Bernstein forgets he's Leonard Bernstein and listens to you. Next student, please. Is there water? I need water.

ACCOMPANIST   Right over here. Please, let me..

MARIA   There's one advantage in being this nearsighted. You don't have to follow the conductor. How can you. You can't see him. But I never made them follow me. No, we worked together. *Insieme. Tutto insieme.* Art is collaboration, too. Domination. Collaboration. *Ecco.*

If you have feelings like Sharon, hide them. It's that simple. That's what I did. Excuse me. (*She drinks as Tenor comes out onto the stage.*)

Avanti, avanti. You all lack presence. Look at me. I'm drinking water and I have presence. Stand straight. Let us see who you are. *Bravo!* You're a good-looking man. You have what the Italians call *bella figura.*

TENOR   Thank you.

MARIA   That's wasn't a compliment. It was a statement. We're talking turkey here.

A singer has to know his assets. This is a business too, after all, let's never forget that. Domination. Collaboration. Assets. What are you?

TENOR   You mean, my name?

MARIA   No, I mean your voice.

TENOR   I'm a tenor. Couldn't you tell?

MARIA   A tenor. *Gran dio*. God save us sopranos from you tenors. And that is the only tenor joke you're going to hear from me.

TENOR   People think we're stupid.

MARIA   I wonder why that is.

TENOR   I don't know.

MARIA   Actually, I love tenors. When they sing, it's our chance to go to our dressing rooms and catch our breath. But no such luck today. I'll be right over here. Are you nervous?

TENOR   No.

MARIA   Good. What's your name?

TENOR   Tony.

MARIA   Tony? Just Tony?

TENOR   You mean, when I sing! Anthony Candolino.

MARIA   I always mean, when you sing. I only mean, when you sing. This is a master class, not a psychiatrist's office. Are any of you out there undergoing psychiatry? I hope not. Tell us about yourself. Your training. Your professional experience, if any. Your hopes, your dreams.

TENOR   I have a BA in music from USC and an MFA in voice from UCLA.

MARIA   Go on.

TENOR   I've done Billy Jack Rabbit in *La Fanciulla Del West* with Opera Ohio and I'm covering Rinuccio in *Gianni Schicchi* for Opera West.

MARIA   We all have to begin somewhere. You haven't told us about your dreams.

TENOR   I want to be a great singer. Like you. I want to be rich and famous. Like you. I want it all. Like you. Move over, Richard Tucker. Here comes Tony Candolino.

MARIA   May I have more water, please? (*There is a longish pause.*)

TENOR   Are we waiting for your water?

MARIA   No, we're waiting for you.

TENOR   I've chosen *Tosca*. (*Stagehand enters with another pitcher of water.*) Cavaradossi's aria, the first act.

MARIA   I can tell you right now: if you hold the B-flat longer than the composer asks for, it's going to be off with your extremely handsome head. (*To Stagehand.*)
  Thank you. (*To Tenor.*)
  No showing off, eh?

TENOR   I'll be happy if I get the B-flat, period.

MARIA   No happier than we.

STAGEHAND   You're welcome. (*He exits. Accompanist begins to play* "Recondita armonia" *from Puccini's* Tosca.)

MARIA   Just a moment, Tony. Feelings like Sharon's: we use them, we don't give them away on some voodoo witch doctor's couch. Again. (*Accompanist plays; Tenor begins to sing.*)

TENOR   *"Dammi i colori."*

MARIA   I'm going to stop you.

TENOR   I got more out than the soprano did. You stopped her at "O."

MARIA   This is no joke. I don't know why you're smiling.

TENOR   I wasn't smiling.

MARIA   Was he smiling?

TENOR   I'm sorry.

MARIA   You're either going to flirt with the public or we're going to work. Which is it going to be?

TENOR   Work.

MARIA   Now what were you doing?

TENOR   Nothing. I was singing.

MARIA   You were right the first time. You were *just* singing, which equals nothing. Again. (*Accompanist begins again.*)

TENOR (*He sings.*)   *"Dammi i colori."*

MARIA   Where are you?

TENOR   You mean, right now? Or in the opera?

MARIA   No games, Tony.

TENOR   I'm in Rome, I'm in a church, I'm painting a picture. I just asked the old Sacristan for my paints. That's what *"Dammi i colori"* means: "Give me the paints."

MARIA   What church? Whose picture? Quick, quick. I don't have all day.

TENOR   I don't know. St. Patrick's! No, that's in. St. Peter's? St. Somebody's! Whose portrait? Some woman's obviously. Tosca's? No. The Mona Lisa, I don't know!

MARIA   So, let me get this straight. You don't know where you are, you are about to paint a portrait but you don't know of whom, and yet you are about to sing an aria. No wonder people don't like opera.

TENOR   I don't think you have to know all those things. I have a voice, I have a technique, I even have a B-flat.

MARIA   So do I. It's not enough.

TENOR   It was for Mario Lanza. I'm sorry. I love Mario Lanza. He's my hero. So kill me.

MARIA   You haven't done your homework, Tony.

TENOR   I just came out here to sing for you.

MARIA   I'm not interested in just singing.

TENOR   Sing and get your feedback.

MARIA   My what? My feedback? What an ugly word. What is feedback? He wants my feedback. I don't give feedback.

TENOR   Your response.

MARIA   I respond to what I feel. I feel nothing but anger for someone who so little treasures his art. You're not prepared, Mr. Tony Tight Pants. Go home. You're wasting our time. Next student.

TENOR   No.

MARIA   No?

TENOR   No.

MARIA   That's the first interesting thing you've said since you came out here.

TENOR   I came here to sing.

MARIA   You weren't ready.

TENOR   I'm going to sing.

MARIA   And I can't stop you?

TENOR   I need your help. I want to sing. I want to sing well. I know I have a voice and I know it's not enough. I want to be an artist. (*He sings.*)
  "*Dammi i colori.*" (*To Maria.*)
  Please. (*Maria nods to the Accompanist who begins again.*)

MARIA   You're in the church of Sant'Andrea Della Valle, just off the Corso. Do you know Rome?

TENOR   No.

MARIA   It doesn't matter. It's ten a.m. on a beautiful spring morning. You made love all night to Floria Tosca, the most beautiful woman in Rome. And now you're painting another woman, unobserved, as she prays to the Blessed Mother. They're both beautiful but it's Tosca's body against yours you feel. Now sing.

TENOR   It doesn't say anything about ten a.m. or spring or Tosca's body on the score.

MARIA   It should say it in your imagination. Otherwise you have notes, nothing but notes. Sing!

TENOR   "*Recondita armonia.*"

MARIA   On the breath, on the breath!

TENOR   "*di bellezze diverse!*"

MARIA   Don't force.

TENOR   "*È bruna Floria.*"

MARIA   Much better.

TENOR   "*l'ardente amante mia.*"

MARIA   You're singing about your mistress! Look happy.

ACCOMPANIST   *"Scherza coi fanti e lascia stare i santi!"*

TENOR   Bravo!

MARIA   Concentrate.

TENOR   *"E te, beltade ignota,*
cinta di chiome bionde,
tu azzurro hai l'occhi,
Tosca ha l'occhio nero."

MARIA (*At will, during the above.*)   That's right, open it up. Let me feel that blonde hair. Blue eyes. Tosca's black eyes now.

ACCOMPANIST   *"Scherza coi fanti e lascia stare i santi!"*

MARIA (*As before.*)   Do you know what you're singing about, Tony? (*He shakes his head while continuing to sing.*)
    Art, in all its mystery, blends these different beauties together. One woman, one ideal!

TENOR   *"L'arte nel suo mistero*
le diverse bellezze insiem confonde:"

MARIA   Here it comes. The Big Tune! Go for it!

TENOR   *"ma, nel ritrar costei*
il mio solo pensiero,
ah! il mio sol pensier sei tu,
Tosca, sei tu!"

(*Maria silently mouths the final high notes along with the Tenor. The music ends. Maria is silent.*)

MARIA   That was beautiful. I have nothing more to say. That was beautiful.

TENOR   I've also prepared *Werther* and *"Ah, sì, ben mio."*

MARIA   That won't be necessary. Are we scheduled for a break now? No? Great music always takes so much out of me. I feel quite faint. That will be all, Mr. Candolino.

TENOR   You can call me Tony.

MARIA   I wish you well on your career.

TENOR   Thank you. Don't you have any advice for me?

MARIA   Remember the springtime. Now go. (*He goes. Maria sits in the chair.*) Next student. I never really listened to that aria. I'm quite emotional. I was always backstage preparing for my entrance. "Mario, Mario"—just two words from offstage and your goose is cooked. I've seen entire audiences turn against a Tosca because they didn't like the way she sang "Mario, Mario." It's a terrible career, actually. I don't know why I bothered. I didn't say that. You didn't hear it and I didn't say it! (*The Second Soprano comes back onto the stage.*)

SECOND SOPRANO   I'm back! (*Maria looks at her blankly.*) I'd like to try again. I've been in the ladies' room throwing up. I must have eaten something. (*Maria holds up her hand to stop Second Soprano from going into further detail.*) So should I go out and come in again? (*Maria nods.*) I'll yell when I'm ready. (*Accompanist nods. Second Soprano exits.*)

MARIA   Water. I need more water.

SECOND SOPRANO (*Off.*)   I'm ready! (*Accompanist begins Lady Macbeth's entrance music again. Second Soprano enters at the appropriate moment in the text. The music stops. She begins.*)
   "*Nel dì della vittoria io le incontrai.*
   Stupito io n'era per le udite cose;"

MARIA   Where's your letter? You're meant to be reading a letter.

SECOND SOPRANO   I was pretending to hold one. Couldn't you tell?

MARIA   I don't want pretending. You're not good enough. I want truth. This is a letter. (*She seizes a piece of paper and thrusts it at Sharon.*) What are you saying?

SECOND SOPRANO   I'm saying "I met them on the day of victory. I was rapt in wonder at the things I heard. When the King's messengers hailed me as Thane of Cawdor."

MARIA   Put some wonder in your voice! Thane of Cawdor! It's what she's dreamed of.

SECOND SOPRANO   "Thane of Cawdor! 'A prediction made by those same seers who foretold a crown upon my head. Keep deep in your heart these secrets. *Addio.*'"

MARIA   Do you know this speech in Shakespeare?

SECOND SOPRANO   I've read the play, of course, but that was in high school.

MARIA   You want to sing this music without knowing your Shakespeare?

SECOND SOPRANO   I'm not an actress. I'm just a singer.

MARIA   Do you think Verdi composed it without knowing his Shakespeare? *Vergogna*, Sharon, shame. And that wasn't an entrance. You came on but it wasn't an entrance. That goes for all you, too. An entrance is everything. It's how we present ourselves to an audience. It's how we present ourselves in life. A man who would barge in on a woman in her bath is a pig. She should know from his entrance how it's to end. I'll show you an entrance. You can set the scene for our colleagues. Just read from the score. (*She quickly leaves the stage. The Second Soprano is all at sea. She sits cautiously on the edge of Maria's chair. She picks up and reads from Maria's score.*)

MARIA (*Off.*)   *Sto pronta, maestro!* (*The Accompanist begins again.*)

SECOND SOPRANO   "Scene Two. The grand hall in Macbeth's castle. There are several rooms leading off it. There is a grand staircase descending from the floor above. There are two small thrones. It is night. A violent storm is raging. Thunder. Lightning. Rain. Curtain. Lady Macbeth enters at the top of the stairs. She is magnificently arrayed. She is reading a letter. (*Maria has entered as Verdi's Lady Macbeth, reading a letter.*)

MARIA   "*Nel dì della vittoria io le incontrai*
Stupito io n'era per le udite cose;
Quando i nunzi del Re me salutaro
Sir di Caudore;
Vaticinio uscito dalle veggenti stesse che
predissero un serto al cap mio. Racchiudi in cor
questo segreto. Addio."

(*Maria begins to sing the first lines of Lady Macbeth's recitative. What comes out is a cracked and broken thing. A voice in ruins. It is a terrible moment.*)

"*Ambizioso spirito tu sei Macbetto . . .*"

Go on, you're the student here. Not I. And see how important a prop is.

SECOND SOPRANO   You hardly looked at the letter.

MARIA   She has it memorized. She's read it over and over and over. My choice. Not Verdi's. Not Shakespeare's. Callas. You think you can do that now?

SECOND SOPRANO   Not like you.

MARIA   I don't want it done like me. I want it done like Verdi.

ACCOMPANIST   With music?

MARIA   Yes, with music. This isn't a play. (*Accompanist begins to play and Second Soprano recites as Maria coaches, cajoles.*)

SECOND SOPRANO   *"Ambizioso spirito tu sei Macbetto."*

MARIA   There's two "t's" in "Macbetto." I want to hear them.

SECOND SOPRANO   *"Mac—"*

MARIA   Don't repeat, keep going!

SECOND SOPRANO   *"Alla grandezza aneli, ma sarai tu malvagio?"*

MARIA   "You would be great, but will you be wicked?" Ah, there's the question! Don't stop, don't stop!

SECOND SOPRANO   *"Pien di misfatti è il calle della potenza e mal per lui che il piede dubitoso vi pone, e retrocede!"*

MARIA   He's weak. She knows it. She must be strong for both of them!

SECOND SOPRANO   The aria?

MARIA   Yes, don't even think of stopping! You are Lady Macbeth! (*Accompanist goes directly into the introduction for the aria proper as Maria circles the Second Soprano, working with her.*)
   Use this introduction to focus yourself. Why are you moving your hand? Never move your hand unless you follow it with your heart and soul.

SECOND SOPRANO   How do I know when to move at all?

MARIA   The composer tells you. It's all in the music. Now!

SECOND SOPRANO   *"Vieni! t'affretta! accendere!*

MARIA   Bite into those words. Spit them out.

SECOND SOPRANO   *"Ti vo' quell freddo core!"*

MARIA   Let yourself go. Who are you saving it for?

SECOND SOPRANO   *"L'audace impresa a compiere*
Io ti darò valore, Io ti daro valore,
daro valore;"

MARIA   She's going to give him some balls. I'm sorry, but that's what she's saying.

SECOND SOPRANO   *"Di Scozia a te, a promettono."*

MARIA   The melody broadens here. Let it through you.

SECOND SOPRANO   *"Le profetesse il trono."*

MARIA   The throne of Scotland has been promised to him! What is he waiting for?

SECOND SOPRANO   *"Che tardi? Accetta il dono,*
Ascendivi a regnar.
Ascendivi a regnar,
Accetta, accetta il dono . . ."

MARIA   This is important to you! You make me want to shake you, Sharon!

SECOND SOPRANO   *"Ascendivi a regnar.*
Che tardi?"

MARIA   What are you waiting for? Accept the gift. Take what I'm giving you.

SECOND SOPRANO   *"Che tardi? Accetta il dono,*
Ascendi, ascendi, ascendivi a regnar."

MARIA   Rise and rule. Rise and take your place in this world.

SECOND SOPRANO   *"Che tardi? Acceta il dono,*
Ascendivi a regnar.
Che tardi? Accetta il dono,
Ascendivi a regnar.
Che tardi? Che tardi?"

MARIA   This isn't just an opera. This is your life.

SECOND SOPRANO   *"Ah! . . .*
ascendivi a regnar."

MARIA   Go on. (*Music for aria proper ends.*)

SECOND SOPRANO   The *cabaletta?*

MARIA   Yes, the *cabaletta!* Why do you want to keep stopping? This is where everything changes. The dramatic situation, the tempo. An *aria* without its *cabaletta* is like sex without an orgasm. I don't mean to speak crudely but sometimes even we artists must sink to the gutter to rise to the stars. Eh? Am I right?
So what happens here? Hurry up, you're running out of steam.

SECOND SOPRANO   Someone comes in and—

MARIA   Not someone. No one is someone.

SECOND SOPRANO   A servant.

MARIA   Now you're talking!

SECOND SOPRANO   He tells her that the King, Duncan! will be at their castle that very evening.

MARIA   Is Macbeth with him?

SECOND SOPRANO   Yes!

MARIA   And how does that make her feel?

SECOND SOPRANO   Happy?

MARIA   Don't keep looking at me for answers, Sharon. Tell me, show me. *Vite, vite!*

SECOND SOPRANO   Really happy.

MARIA   Love happy? Christmas morning happy?

SECOND SOPRANO   Murder happy!

MARIA   Ah! And what is she going to do about it?

SECOND SOPRANO   She's going to sing a *cabaletta!*

MARIA   She's going to kill the King! Do you know what that means?

SECOND SOPRANO   Yes, it's terrible.

MARIA   Not to her! Do you believe women can have balls, Sharon?

SECOND SOPRANO   Some women. Yes, I do!

MARIA   Verdi is daring you to show us yours, Sharon. Will you do it?

SECOND SOPRANO   Yes!

MARIA   *Andiamo. (Accompanist goes into the music accompanying the bridge between the aria and the cabaletta. Maria "becomes" the Servant who brings Lady Macbeth the news of King Duncan's arrival.)* The music here is ridiculous. Ignore it.

ACCOMPANIST   *"Al cader della sera il Re qui guinge."*

SECOND SOPRANO   *"Che di? Macbetto è seco?"*

ACCOMPANIST   *"Ei l'accompagna. La nuova, o donna, è certa."*

SECOND SOPRANO   *"Trovi accoglienza, quale un Re si merta."*

MARIA   Wait till he's gone. Keep the mask on. It's hard. This is what you've been waiting for. Go!

SECOND SOPRANO   *"Duncano!"*

MARIA   Use the words. *"Duncano."*

SECOND SOPRANO   I'm sorry.

MARIA   Haste makes waste. Again, please, Sharon. *(She glances at her wristwatch.)*

SECOND SOPRANO   *"Duncano sarà qui . . ."*

MARIA   She can't believe her ears.

SECOND SOPRANO   *"Qui . . ."*

MARIA   When? How soon? Before you burst with it.

SECOND SOPRANO   *"Qui la notte?"*

MARIA   Tonight! It's now or never. She's going crazy here. It's all in the music. Listen to those dissonances. Don't act, listen. It's always in the music, Sharon. Don't look at me for help. Listen to Verdi, listen to Shakespeare.

SECOND SOPRANO   *"Or tutti sorgete—ministri infernali,*
Che al sangue incorate,
spingete i mortali!
Tu, notte ne avvolgi
Di tenebra immota;"

MARIA   Is there anything you would kill for, Sharon?

SECOND SOPRANO   I don't think so.

MARIA   A man, a career.

SECOND SOPRANO   Not off the top of my head.

MARIA   You have to listen to something in yourself to sing this difficult music. When I sang Medea I could feel the stones of Epidaurus beneath the wooden floorboards at La Scala. I was standing there where Medea, Electra, Klytemnestra had stood. There was a direct line through me to the composer to Euripides to Medea herself. These people really existed. Medea, Lady Macbeth. Or don't you believe that? Eh? This is all make-believe to you?

SECOND SOPRANO   I've never really thought about it.

MARIA   That's because you're young. You will. In time. Know how much suffering there can be in store for a woman.

SECOND SOPRANO   But you were young when you first sang Lady Macbeth and Medea.

MARIA   I was never young. I couldn't afford to be. Not to get to where I was going. Anyway. Enough of that. You came back. You had *mut*. That's something. Do you know that German word? It means courage. I had to know it when I sang *Fidelio* for the Germans during the Occupation during the war. It was 18 years old. I needed lots of *mut* that day. *Mut!*

SECOND SOPRANO   *Mut.*

MARIA   It's a good word, don't you think? *Mut.* I don't like many things in German. But I do like *mut*. Again.

SECOND SOPRANO   You want me to do it again?

MARIA   Yes! Off you go now. (*Second Soprano exits.*) And this is for all of you: there are no shortcuts in art, no easy ways. This isn't life, where there are so many. There is no being at center stage as if by magic. There is always an entrance first, just as there is always an exit after. Art is about those transitions. There is only discipline, technique and *mut*. The rest is *kaka-peepee-doodoo*. I'm sorry but there it is. Eh? (*She listens to someone in the audience.*)

I was asked something about genius, inspiration. Well of course. Without them, we're nothing. We're a Milanov at best. Don't snicker. It was a great voice, but an artist? I don't think so.

Are you ready back there? (*To Accompanist.*)

What is her name?

ACCOMPANIST   Sharon.

MARIA   Are you ready back there, Sharon?

SECOND SOPRANO (*Off.*)   I think so.

MARIA   Don't think, don't hope, do. *Mut.* Sharon, *mut.* Every eye is you. (*To audience.*)

Notice I didn't say ear. (*To Second Soprano.*)

All right, Sharon. I'm not going to interrupt this time. (*To Accompanist.*)

Per piacere, maestro Manny. (*Accompanist begins introduction to Lady Macbeth's entrance aria.*)

Does anyone know what time it is? I have a beauty parlor appointment after this. I can't get a good wash and set in this city. Ssshh! You can me later. *Eccola!* (*Second Soprano enters with a prop letter and begins the scene again. It isn't long before Maria is reciting the words along with her.*) Ah, ah! Careful! That's better. Don't look at me. You're on your own now.

MARIA AND SECOND SOPRANO
> "*Nel di della vittoria io le incontrai . . .*
> *Stupito io n'era per le udite cose;*
> *Quando I nunzi del Re mi salutaro sir di Caudore;*
> *Vaticinio uscito dalle veggenti stesse*
> *Che predissero un serto al capo mio.*
> *Racchiudi in cor questo segreto, Addio.*"

SECOND SOPRANO   "*Ambizioso spirto*
> *Tu sei, Macbetto . . .*
> *Alla grandezza aneli,*
> *Ma sarai to malvagio?*"

(*Second Soprano continues but we no longer hear her. Instead, there is a light change. This time we hear an orchestra playing the turbulent introduction to Lady Macbeth's "Letter Scene." It is a live performance from 1952.*)

MARIA   This infernal music. Come, fill me with your malevolence. Let me be her. That sound of the curtain parting. The stage dust. Don't breathe it in. They see me. "Who is this fat Greek girl we never heard of making her debut in our temple of temples?" Ah! the silence. It's time. Begin. (*This time Maria reads the letter along with her own voice on the recording.*)

MARIA AND RECORDING   "*Nel dì della vittoria io le incontrai . . .*
Stupito io n'era per le udite cose;
Quando i nunzi del Re me salutaro sir di Caudore;
Vaticinio uscito dalle veggenti stesse
Che predissero un serto al capo mio.
Racchiudi in cor questo segreto, Addio."

MARIA   They're waiting for you to sing.

RECORDING   "*Ambizioso spirto*
Tu sei, Macbetto . . ."

MARIA   That's who I am! This voice.

RECORDING   "*Alla grandezza aneli,*
Ma sarai to malvogio?"

MARIA   Yes, I dare to go to the greatest heights! My whole life has led up to this moment.

RECORDING   "*Pien de misfatti è il calle della potenza,*
E mal per lui che il piede dubitoso vi pone,
E retrocede!"

MARIA   A debut at La Scala. With Maestro de Sabata, no less. Good chest note there. Now the first high C. They're impressed. Just wait. You haven't heard anything yet. (*The orchestra plays the introduction to the aria proper.*)

Ah, Verdi! Ah, Shakespeare! Ah, my own ambition. (*The aria itself has begun now. During the following, Maria will occasionally listen to it, comment on it but sometimes not even be aware of it.*)

The costume is so heavy. I can scarcely move. They've made me look so fat.

"But the *signorina* is, how shall we say? "ample." There are limits to what we can do. We're not magicians."

Hideous giggling behind little fairy hands.

"The *signorina* is *Signora Meneghini*, my wife, and you will show her courtesy and respect and you will make her another costume and send me the bill."

"Thank you, Battista."

"You are my wife, Maria. I adore you."

I can breathe now. Maybe I'll have success now!

"He's old enough to be her father."

"With a figure like that, who else would want her? She should count her blessings."

"But that voice!"

"You can't fuck a voice."

I know what they're saying. I don't care. I know what I want and after tonight I'll have it. They haven't heard anything like this since Malibran! In less than one year I've become the Queen of La Scala. That has to count for something. La Divina. Imagine being called La Divina. I am La Divina. Listen to that! I've won, Battista, I've made something of myself.

"Why can't you say you love me, Maria?"

Don't ask me that. Not now. I have a performance. Where is my eyebrow pencil? Someone's taken it. They're all jealous. They want to see me fail. They take my makeup. They tear my costumes. Where is my rouge? Everything is in disarray. Not now, Battista. I can't bear to see you in my dressing room mirror standing there behind me, always asking me if I love you. You got what you wanted. A famous wife. I got what I wanted. This night and every night that I go out there and sing. When I sing, I'm not fat. I'm not ugly. I'm not an old man's wife. I'm Callas. I'm La Divina. I'm everything I wanted to be. So don't bring up love when you look at me in my mirror like that, Battista. Love can wait.

Tell me, is the theatre full? Has the tenor apologized? He called me a cow. Have you paid the claque, Battista? We have work to do, my husband. Lady Macbeth, Norma, Lucia, Tosca. We have made as unholy a pact as Macbeth and his Lady.

I've become thin. Look at me. Another Audrey Hepburn they're all saying. I've become a beautiful woman, Battista. I like being beautiful. I had thirty-seven curtain calls at the theatre tonight. They say a student leapt from the balcony for love of me but he wasn't killed. "Then he really didn't love me," I told the reporters and I laughed for the photographers. I laughed!

I can't bear it when you look at me like that. It's worse here, when we're alone, than at the theatre. I want you to sleep in your room. You're an old man. The thought of sleeping with you repulses me. Wait! And yet I do love you. Not the way you hoped, I know. Not the way I hoped either. I thought it would suffice. Why are you looking at me like that? You know what I'm going to say. It's been in all the papers. Of course he's going to marry me. I'm sorry, Battista. I never meant you harm.

I told him, Ari. I think I broke his heart. We must be very happy together, you and I, to have caused so much pain. I realize now: all those years of singing, perfecting my voice, so that it would express everything I felt, they were for you. My song of love was for you, Ari, all those great passionate melodies, Bellini, Verdi, Donizetti, my siren songs to a man who doesn't even like opera! It's very funny when you think about it. A great ballerina dancing for a blind man.

I have news, Ari, such great and wonderful news. I'm going to have your child. No, our child, our son. I would not insult you by giving you a daughter. And we will name him Odysseus for the greatest Greek hero of them all, like you, and because he wandered the world the longest, like me, until he came home to love.

No, I don't need your child to feel like a woman. I am a woman. I don't need anything. Some people would say I don't need you. I want a child. Your child. I love you. There, I've said it.

Don't ask me to do that. Why would you ask me to do that? What do you mean, you've changed your mind? I'm not a young woman. This may be my only chance. I'll give up anything, my career even, everything I've worked for, but not this.

Then don't marry me. I won't do it. You can't make me. I won't let you make me.

Don't leave me! I've been alone all my life until now!

O child I will never see or know or nurse or say how much I love you, forgive me.

It's done, Ari.

Now what?

Sing? You're telling me to sing? Sing what? "Stormy Weather?" Sing where? In the street? I'm losing my voice! Don't you read the papers? I'm getting by on sheer nerve. I always did. That's what's going, not the voice.

They fired me at La Scala. As if I cared, I have you. (*She kneels.*)

Marry me, Ari. Your canary is asking you to marry her.

She opens her arms.

"Ho dato tutto a te."

The Macbeth aria is over. We hear the audience applauding. Second Soprano sings the last line of the aria. "No . . . no . . . no . . ."

SECOND SOPRANO Madame Callas?

MARIA Ssshh! Listen, they're applauding. Never move on your applause. It shortens it.

SECOND SOPRANO No one was applauding. You told them not to.

MARIA I would never tell anyone that, *ma chère*. The worst part about being a teacher is being misunderstood. Applause is what we live on. Sometimes it's the only thing we have. Did that feel better that time, yes?

SECOND SOPRANO I don't know. What do you think?

MARIA I think you have a lovely voice.

SECOND SOPRANO Thank you.

MARIA I think you have some spirit, too.

SECOND SOPRANO Thank you.

MARIA I wish you well.

SECOND SOPRANO Thank you.

MARIA But I think you should work on something more appropriate for your limitations. Mimi or Micaëla maybe. But Lady Macbeth, Norma. I don't think so. These roles require something else. Something. How shall I say this? Something special. Something that can't be taught or passed on or copied or even talked about. Genius. Inspiration. A gift of God. Some recompense for everything else. (*The Second Soprano bursts into tears.*)
What did I say? This is what I'm talking about. *Mut! Corragio!* It takes more than a pretty voice to build a career.

SECOND SOPRANO I wish I'd never done this. I don't like you. You can't sing anymore and you're envious of anyone younger who can. You just want us to sing like you, recklessly, and lose our voices in ten years like you did. Well, I won't do it. I don't want to. I don't want to sing like you. I hate people like you. You want to make the world dangerous for everyone just because it was for you. (*She leaves. There is an awkward silence.*)

MARIA   So. *Po po po.* I think we should stop here. Miss Graham thought I wanted her to sing like Maria Callas. No one can sing like Maria Callas. Only Anna Maria Sofia Cecilia Kalogeropoulous could sing like Maria Callas. I'm very upset. I'm hurt. As strange as it may seem to some of you, I have feelings, too. Anyway. That's another story. Et cetera, et cetera, eh? Maybe this whole business of teaching is a mistake. Thank you, Manny. That will be all. (*Accompanist exits.*)

If I have seemed harsh, it is because I have been harsh with myself. I'm not good with words, but I have tried to reach you. To communicate something of what I feel about what we do as artists, as musicians and as human beings. The sun will not fall down from the sky if there are no more *Traviata*s. The world can and will go on without us but I have to think that we have made this world a better place. That we have left it richer, wiser than had we not chosen the way of art. The older I get, the less I know but I am certain that what we do matters. If I didn't believe that.

You must know what you want to do in life, you must decide, for we cannot do everything. Do not think singing is an easy career. It is a lifetime's work; it does not stop here. Whether I continue singing or not doesn't matter. Besides, it's all there in the recordings. What matters is that you use whatever you have learned wisely. Think of the expression of words, of good diction, and of your own deep feelings. The only thanks I ask is that you sing properly and honestly. If you do this, I will feel repaid.

Well, that's that. (*She gathers her things and goes. The stage is bare. The house lights are turned up.*)

END OF PLAY

AND AWAY WE GO (2013)

John Steinbeck gave me only one piece of advice as a writer. "Don't write for the theatre. It will break your heart." This was a surprising admonition coming from the author of one of the staples of the American theatre, a writer whose name, like Hemingway's, was synonymous with American literature in the early 1960s.

He was a grand old man of letters but he would have punched anyone who told him that to his face. I was a young man who had seen a lot of theatre and was beginning to think he could write a play of his own, especially since his plans for writing the Great American Novel weren't going anywhere. "Listen up," I told myself.

But it wasn't the playwright John Steinbeck of *Of Mice and Men* (1937) speaking to me that afternoon in the study in his brownstone on East 72nd St. It was the playwright John Steinbeck of *The Moon Is Down* (1942) and *Burning Bright* (1950), his two Broadway failures that followed *Of Mice and Men*, talking to a young man, fresh out of Columbia, whom he was considering engaging to accompany him and his wife, Elaine, on a year-long trip around the world as tutor to his two sons, Tom and John.

I thought he was teasing me as part of the interview but it quickly turned out he wasn't. After his initial success as a playwright, John had found the theatre a hostile, unfathomable environment for a writer. His most recent experience on Broadway, though uncredited, had been trying to salvage Rodgers and Hammerstein's *Pipe Dream* (1955), a musical based on his novel *Sweet Thursday* and some of his other Cannery Row stories and characters.

"They turned my whore into a nun," John said, his face suddenly dark and scowling, some six years after the show's short run. If I remember correctly, he started quoting word for word some of the reviews for *Pipe Dream*. He remembered the stinging, hurtful phrases about his work written by critics who were forgotten in their own lifetime, while almost half a century after his death, Steinbeck's place in the American literary canon rests secure.

The enduring success of *Of Mice and Men* was little comfort for the subsequent attacks he had endured wearing a playwright's cap. The man I met that afternoon wanted absolutely nothing to do with the American theatre.

That's the real problem with bad reviews: people remember them. Good reviews are nice but quickly shrugged off. Besides, the praise is never as high as it ought to be. A good review is never good *enough*. It's the bad ones that stay with us—as they did with Steinbeck—seared into our consciousness and memory banks more permanently than Hester Prynne's Scarlet Letter. I only stopped reading reviews with my two most recent plays, *And Away We Go* and *Mothers and Sons*. I wish John had given me that piece of advice. But like the piece he did give, I probably wouldn't have taken it anyway. I found out for myself. Pretty much everything I know and believe in is self-taught. Some things can only be done the hard way. Theatre is one of them.

During the year John and I traveled together, I fell in love with the theatre even more than I already was after four years in New York, and he was one of the reasons why. He loved to tell me about growing up in Salinas, California, on the Monterrey Peninsula and when he talked about going to "the city," he meant San Francisco. "To this day, 'to the city' still means going to San Francisco," he told me. And what attracted him to the city were the sights to be seen there and many of them were inside a theatre.

The way he would remember seeing the great Italian actress Eleonora Duse in *Ghosts* or *The Lady from the Sea* was so clear and detailed you would have thought he had seen her the week before, not fifty years earlier. He had never forgotten the intensity of her eyes and the power of her presence on stage. But it was her hands, "so delicate, so delicate, the way she used them, Terrence, you can't imagine." He was equally transfixed by the great Russian bass, Feodor Chaliapin, in *Boris Godunov*. The Clock Scene, when the demented Tsar wanders incoherently through his palace, was for him the finest piece of acting he had ever seen and the Death Scene, the most moving. John was our Scheherazade, holding us fast in his thrall as he remembered those moments in the theatre that had changed his life. Elaine and the boys were as enraptured as I was. John was a great storyteller, obviously, and his times at the theatre as a young man were stories he never got tired of telling. No wonder he wanted to write plays. He had Duse and Chaliapin. I had Merman and Callas.

We went to the theatre often during our year overseas but I soon learned that it is not much fun to sit through a play in a language you don't understand. Molière in French at the Comédie-Française or Chekhov in Russian at the Moscow Art Theatre sounded thrilling in the anticipation (besides, I knew *The Misanthrope* and *Uncle Vanya* from my time at Columbia, surely I would be able to navigate where I was in both plays) but soon after the curtain rose on both occasions, I got restless. Language in the theatre had never seemed more paramount.

What I most remembered from the Comédie-Française was Molière's chair displayed in the lobby for generations of worship from the audience. At the Moscow Art Theatre, the tradition of applauding certain speeches in the play and bowing after each act appalled me. Did Stanislavsky's disciples at the Actors Studio on West 46th St. know about this?

The only production that transcended the barrier of a foreign language was Giorgio Strehler's production of *El nost Milan,* a play spoken in a Milanese dialect at his Piccolo Teatro di Milano. I didn't understand a word the actors were saying but I was transported by the boldness and honesty of Strehler's theatrical vision. It was realer than real: it was the reality of theatre. So it would seem there is something else in theatre as paramount as the words being spoken. I would call it the truth.

John was more enamored of the glamour of the Broadway theatre than one might think of the author of *The Grapes of Wrath* and *The Red Pony.* He had white tie and tails plus a collapsible silk top hat and a voluminous cape he wore for opening nights. A silver-knobbed walking stick served as his only accessory. When he showed up dressed like that for the premiere of *And Things That Go Bump in the Night,* I sort of cringed. No one dressed like that for the theatre in 1965 but John Steinbeck. I think you had to *be* John Steinbeck to get away with silk top hats and capes and a silver-knobbed walking stick in 1965. Somehow his out-of-date sartorial celebration of my first effort as a playwright made its critical reception even more painful to accept.

What I most remember from our travels abroad were the times when word got out that the great American writer John Steinbeck was having a meal at a local restaurant. We usually traveled incognito but somehow it was never too long before word of his arrival had spread.

And then it would begin: a steady, modest procession of people asking John to sign their copy of one of his books. Very often these editions were battered and stained from being passed from one family member to the next.

They were well used because they were well read. The people wanted to thank John for having written stories that meant something to them. It didn't matter that they were Italian or French or Greek. John's novels and stories had meant something universal to them. He had been heard. The connection between a writer and his or her audience is the deepest satisfaction that an artist can know. John won the Nobel Prize shortly after we returned to the States. For me, he had won something greater two years earlier at a *trattoria* outside Perugia: the grateful tears of an old man holding up his weathered copy of *The Grapes of Wrath* for John's autograph. He was going to give it to his great-grandson when he was old enough to read it. (It was called *Furore* in Italian; Elaine mischievously preferred it in Japanese where it was translated as *The Angry Raisins*). I have never forgotten the lesson of that afternoon. What we do matters. If I didn't believe that . . . !*

In my time I have been called stagestruck as if it were a bad thing. If a person isn't stagestruck, what are they doing working in the theatre in the first place? It's too hard and the rewards are too few and far between to sustain a life in it without the nonnegotiable belief that what happens between an audience and the stage is fundamental and necessary for the good of everyone in the community.

I've been stagestruck as long as I can remember. Even when I wanted to be a journalist and thought going to Columbia College would make going to graduate school at Columbia's School of Journalism just across the campus that much easier, I was going to the theatre or the opera or New York City Ballet every night. The IRT subway was my reading room. The lights under the top steps of Standing Room at the Old Met on 39th St. were where I read Plato and Thomas Hardy when the action on the stage four tiers below wasn't compelling enough to watch. I *heard* more operas from my place up there than I actually saw.

Standing room at the Old Met was famous for a lot of things, not all of them musical. One night, the soprano was about to sing her big aria in the second act of *Tosca* when a man's voice rang out through the theatre. "I told you: not during "*Vissi d'arte*." The entire audience heard it. So did our Tosca. And we all knew what that "not" was. I used the story in *Some Men*, my play chronicling what it was like being a young gay man in New York pre-Stonewall, pre-AIDS, pre-everything. Ordinarily, I don't like to repeat things I've heard in "real life" but this true-to-life episode was just too good to sit on, even though I waited almost half a century to use it.

And Away We Go is about my love of the theatre. I hope it's a joyful play to perform or read. I had a joyful time writing it. The title is my sly nod to Rodgers and Hammerstein's *Oklahoma*, for *Away We Go* was its original title when it premiered out of town in New Haven. It became *Oklahoma* in Boston.

My parents loved *Oklahoma*. So did I. I grew up on its tunes. Calling my play *And Away We Go* was my private way of acknowledging that. Now I'm telling you. That's why this volume is indeed a "memoir in plays."

It was commissioned by The Pearl, a theatre company in Manhattan whose mission it is to keep the classics—from the Greeks through Shaw—alive in performance for contemporary audiences. Without theatres like The Pearl, New York would be Ibsen-less for too many seasons. For that alone, I owe

---

*. Those last two lines are Maria's from *Master Class*. She stops, unable to even contemplate a life without the arts to enrich and inform it. Nor can I. As I've often said, *Master Class* is my most autobiographical play.

a lot to The Pearl and I was flattered when they asked me to create something for them. I wanted to give them a play that celebrates their passion for the classics. Pretty soon I found myself imagining what it might have been like when those classics were just being created, when it would be many years, even centuries, before their canonization. Rather than making art, the Globe and the Moscow Art were facing real life, day-to-day catastrophe and extinction instead—the same catastrophe and extinction everyone I know in the theatre faces on a regular basis in 2015. Tomorrow the Tony Award; today, paying the bills.

The play celebrates companies like The Pearl and theatres everywhere that do plays year after year after year for loyal audiences who must have theatre in their lives.

And Away We Go is dedicated to people who spell theatre, theatre. The other way is just plain wrong.

And Away We Go

to Aeschylus, William Shakespeare, Molière, Anton Chekhov,
Samuel Beckett and playwrights everywhere

AND AWAY WE GO was commissioned by The Pearl Theatre Company (J.R. Sullivan, Artistic Director; Shira Beckerman, Managing Director; Kate Farrington, Interim Artistic Director) in New York City, and received its first public performance on November 12, 2013. It was directed by Jack Cummings III; the set design was by Sandra Goldmark; the costume design was by Kathryn Rohe; the lighting design was by R. Lee Kennedy; the sound design was by Michael Rasbury; the dramaturg was Kate Farrington; the casting director was Nora Brennan; the production stage manager was Lloyd Davis Jr.; and the production manager and technical director was Gary Levinson. The cast was as follows:

RACHEL BOTCHAN Danae, May Burbage, Marie-Clarie, Maya Nabokov, Candace Delbo, Hazel May

DONNA LYNNE CHAMPLIN Helena, Gretna Burbage, Mlle Picard, Nina Kozlovsky, Mildred Lahr, Anne Tedesco-Boyle

DOMINIC CUSKERN Hector, James Burbage, Chevalier Berton, Boris Yeletsky, Archie Kelly, John Pick

SEAN MCNALL Dimitris, Richard Burbage, Jean-Louis Danton, Yuri Goldovsky, Peter Duggan, Soctt Harrington

CAROL SCHULTZ Phoebe, Lydia Burbage, Mme Frontain, Alexandra Mishkin, Lucine Gershwin, Shirley Channing

MICAH STOCK Pallas, Cuthbert Burbage, Christophe Durant, Pavel Leshmenev, Kenny Tobias, Gordon Light

THE PLAYERS

IN ATHENS:

HECTOR
a maskmaker

PHOEBE
Hector's mother

DIMITRIS
an actor

HELENA
Hector's wife

PALLAS
a member of the chorus

DANAE
Pallas's sister

IN LONDON:

JAMES BURBAGE
a retired actor

LYDIA BURBAGE
James's mother

RICHARD BURBAGE
his son

GRETNA BURBAGE
Richard's wife

CUTHBERT BURBAGE
his other son

MAY BURBAGE
James's daughter

IN VERSAILLES:

CHEVALIER BERTON
the King's censor

MME FRONTAIN
a leading lady

JEAN-LOUIS DANTON
an actor

MLLE PICARD
her understudy

CHRISTOPHE DURANT
a playwright

MARIE-CLAIRE
a seamstress

IN MOSCOW:

BORIS YELETSKY
a theatre owner

ALEXANDRA MISHKIN
a patron of the arts

YURI GOLDOVSKY
a set designer

NINA KOZLOVSKY
a cleaning woman

PAVEL LESHMENEV
a delivery boy

MAYA NABOKOV
an actress and Yuri's mistress

IN COCONUT GROVE:

ARCHIE KELLY
a stagehand

LUCINE GERSHWIN
a subscriber

PETER DUGGAN
an understudy

MILDRED LAHR
an actor's wife

KENNY TOBIAS
a concessions worker

CANDACE DELBO
a young actress

IN THE PRESENT: A THEATRE COMPANY

JOHN PICK
the oldest member of the company

SHIRLEY CHANNING
the executive director

SCOTT HARRINGTON
the artistic director

ANNE TEDESCO-BOYLE
a member of the board

GORDON LIGHT
the stage manager

HAZEL MAY
the newest member of the company

THE TIMES and SETTINGS

Athens, 458 BC, the Theatre of Dionysus, Athens

London, 1610, the Globe Theatre, South Bank London

Versailles, 1789, Royal Theatre, Versailles

Moscow, 1896, Moscow Art Theatre, Moscow

Coconut Grove, 1956, Coconut Grove Playhouse, South Florida

A resident theatre company, the present

PROLOGUE

Six actors enter in turn. One by one, they kiss the stage, then rise to speak to us.

ACTOR   My name is (. . .). I have been acting since (. . .). My favorite role was (. . .). My least favorite was (. . .). One thing you should know about me before we begin the performance is (. . .).

They join hands, laying one hand on top of the other until there are twelve. They look at each other. They murmur something but we can't hear them and bow their heads.

Music.

THE PLAY

Behind the scenes at a performance of The Orestia at the Theatre of Dionysus, Athens, Greece, 458 BC. It is high noon, the heat is fierce.

HECTOR is working on a mask for DIMITRIS, the actor who is playing Agamemnon. HELENA, his wife, is helping him. PHOEBE, his mother, is brewing something in a small pot over a fire. PALLAS, a member of the chorus, is putting on his costume. He is playing an old woman. His sister, DANAE, is helping him.

DIMITRIS   It's too hot for *The Orestia*. I feel sorry for the audience.

PALLAS   I feel sorry for the actors.

DIMITRIS   The last time we began in the late afternoon when it was cooler, a swarm of bees attacked the judges. It was the shortest performance of *Antigone* ever given.

PHOEBE   Good for the bees.

DIMITRIS   That was the year no play was declared the winner. The judges don't want that to happen again.

PHOEBE   It's not the judges, it's this war. Plays are a diversion from bad news from the Peloponnese. The priests read the entrails this morning and declared that the position of the sun has to be just right to begin the festival of Dionysus, even if it's the hottest time of day. They're clutching at straws. They don't care about actors.

DIMITRIS   I'd rather be attacked by a swarm of bees than roasted alive in this costume. The actor playing Klytemnestra—he's in a robe as light as gossamer—and you old women of Argos aren't wearing much more.

PALLAS   He who would play Agamemnon must suffer like an Agamemnon!

DIMITRIS   Wait till it's your turn to step into the *cothurni* of a leading role, a protagonist, my young friend.

PALLAS   I'm not going to be an actor, I'm going to be a poet. I'm going to write plays. Great plays. Tragedies, comedies. I'm going to write every play ever written.

DIMITRIS   In the meantime, work on your voice.

PALLAS   What's wrong with my voice?

DIMITRIS   They can't hear you in the top rows.

PALLAS   Who says?

DIMITRIS   My wife.

PALLAS   How would she know? We're speaking in unison. Your wife doesn't know what she's talking about.

DIMITRIS   It was friendly criticism, Pallas.

PALLAS   Besides, this theatre has perfect acoustics.

PHOEBE   Perfect acoustics are a myth started by people who sit in the best seats.

DIMITRIS   The other myth is that the audience understands a single word the chorus is saying.

PALLAS   Because we're speaking from behind a mask.

DIMITRIS   So am I, so am I!

PALLAS   One day, Hector, an actor is going to tear his mask off and say to the audience: "This is what human suffering looks like. I'm roasting alive in this."

DANAE   The unmasked face of man for all the world to see, yes!

PHOEBE   The heat has you all talking crazy—actors without masks.

PALLAS   Who was it who said if you've seen one Greek tragedy you've seen them all?

PHOEBE   It wasn't a Greek.

DIMITRIS   They had a point: we tell the same stories over and over.

PHOEBE   Because we need to hear them again and again.

DIMITRIS   It's only how we tell them that's different.

HECTOR   Wire, I need a piece of wire.

HELENA   How is this?

HECTOR   Perfect.

HELENA   You missed a place . . . there, see?

HECTOR   My eyes are going.

HELENA   We won't tell anyone.

HECTOR   When I'm gone, it will be *Helena* of Athens, maskmaker supreme.

HELENA   Listen to you.

HECTOR   Nobody would know the difference.

HELENA   I would. You're the master.

HECTOR   We're a good team, Helena.

DIMITRIS   How's my mask coming, Hector?

HECTOR   Tell him it's not ready.

HELENA   It's not ready, Dimitris.

DIMITRIS   What am I going to do, Hector, when Agamemnon's entrance comes and I'm still back here without it?

HECTOR   He'll have his mask.

HELENA   He says you'll have your—

DIMITRIS   I heard him, Helena.

HELENA   He's nervous, Hector, it's his first Agamemnon.

HECTOR   I'm well aware of that, Helena. The entire company is.

PHOEBE   I remember my husband's first Agamemnon. What a triumph! They carried him all the way back to Athens on their shoulders. He never acted in the chorus again. Here, drink this, Dimitris, it will bring you good luck.

DIMITRIS   I don't need luck, I need my mask.

PHOEBE   You want something fast and cheap, you don't want Hector. My son is an artist.

DIMITRIS   Everyone's an artist in this company and nothing gets done.

HECTOR   The mask will be ready.

HELENA   It always is.

DIMITRIS   Meanwhile I have to make a triumphant entrance in a chariot as Agamemnon, King of Mycenae, with Cassandra as my trophy for the sack of Troy. Without a mask that conveys his royal presence to 15 thousand spectators, some of them in the very last row, we all might as well have stayed home. People trudged up that hill to see heroes, giants—not the likes of us.

DANAE   Do you want to run your lines?

DIMITRIS   I know my lines. I want my mask. What is she doing back here anyway?

PALLAS   It's her birthday. I said she could.

DIMITRIS   Women shouldn't be allowed behind the scenes.

DANAE   Why not?

DIMITRIS   For the same reason they're not allowed on the stage.

DANAE   What is that?

DIMITRIS   I don't know, I didn't make the rules.

DANAE   Who did?

DIMITRIS   I don't remember, it was a long time ago.

PALLAS   Danae's mad about the theatre.

DIMITRIS   She can be mad about it from out there with everybody else. She'll give away our secrets.

DANAE   You have secrets?

DIMITRIS   Of course not. It was a figure of speech. You're breaking the illusion by being back here. Pallas will just be your brother saying some lines.

DANAE   Not to me. He'll be an Old Woman of Argos, head bent, body stooped. "How many moons must we wait here for the gods to wreak their wrath on this cursed House of Atreus?"

PALLAS   You'd better be up on your lines, Dimitris. Danae has the whole play memorized.

DANAE It's a good thing the playwright is dead. That actor is mauling his words this afternoon.

They listen a moment to a voice coming from the stage at a great distance. The words are not clear but they are in Ancient Greek.

DIMITRIS Alexander's getting old. He's talking about this being his last festival.

PHOEBE He's earned it.

DANAE How thrilling it must be to be an actor! To play a god or a very great mortal. To be Prometheus or Orestes or Alcestis for an afternoon. Or even the Watchman who begins this play, a common man, one of us. (*She's a good little actress.*) "For one long year, day and night, I have kept watch on the roof of Mycenae's royal palace! Crouched like a dog—"

PHOEBE Hush! It's not right for a woman to speak the words of a play. The texts are sacred.

DANAE Then I will think them in my head. I will say them when no one is listening. I will offer them to the moon and stars on the beach at night.

HELENA Why do you learn lines that you can never speak?

DANAE They say things I feel but cannot express. They tell me what I knew but didn't know I knew until I spoke them. I will be a woman who acts.

HELENA A woman who acts! There's not even a word for such a thing.

DIMITRIS All the great roles are women. I'll take one Klytemnestra to a dozen Agamemnons. Whoever plays her always takes home the acting prize, never the Agamemnon.

PALLAS I'll write you a great role for a man. Oedipus!

DIMITRIS No, not another Oedipus. I want to be alive at the end for once.

PHOEBE It's a dog's life, an actor's.

DANAE You don't mean that.

PHOEBE The heat, the cold, the terrible pay. A beast is better cared for, only a beast doesn't have the intelligence to know he's going to die in the end and that there's no getting around it.

DIMITRIS   Your mother needs a good laugh, Hector. They're doing an excellent satyr play with lots of farts and phalluses right after us, Phoebe.

PHOEBE   The comedies say the same thing as the tragedies: Life is an unavoidable disaster but we go on. We continue until we can't. The only difference is, in a comedy nobody dies. I prefer tragedy. It's more honest.

DIMITRIS   How much longer, Hector? I have to prepare for my performance.

HELENA   He's almost done.

DANAE   Can I help you with your boots?

DIMITRIS   The *cothurni* are the last to go on. I don't like towering over everyone until I have to.

PALLAS   Danae, I want you to go to the last row and tell me if you can hear me.

DANAE   Do I have to?

PALLAS   You heard Dimitris's wife.

DANAE   It's more fun back here.

PALLAS   Of course it is.

DANAE   Remember to walk with a stoop, Pallas, the way grandmother is all bent over.

PALLAS   I'm using a cane.

DANAE   You need more than a cane. Your whole body has to age.

PALLAS   I know, now go!

DANAE   It's not fair, men get to do everything. (*Danae goes.*)

DIMITRIS   I can act in front of thousands but I can't prepare with anyone watching me. I'd feel foolish. When I return I expect the mask to be ready, Hector. (*He goes.*)

PALLAS   There's my cue! What play are we doing? *The Bacchae* or *The Trojan Woman?* (*He picks up his mask and puts it on.*) I can't see! Which way is the stage? Help me, Dionysus! I'm joking. An actor's mask is his best friend. He knows it the moment he puts it on. Thank you, Hector. (*He bends over and walks with his cane. It's a spectacular transformation. He moves like an old woman. His face seems animated, even though it's masked.*) "The palace torches burn brightly. All is ready for the king's return. What welcome will our Queen Klytemnestra make her lord husband, King Agamemnon, when he returns from Troy's toppled towers, burdened with the rich spoils of ten years of siege?" (*Pallas exits.*)

HELENA   I'm glad you're not an actor.

PHOEBE   He tried to be an actor. His father was very disappointed in him.

HECTOR   My knees shook, my hands trembled, my voice quivered. Finally, my father took pity, handed me a piece of wood and a carving knife and said "If you're going to be in the theatre, at least make yourself useful."

PHOEBE   And you have. I'm very proud of you, my son.

HELENA   So am I, Hector.

HECTOR   You weren't so proud that day I handed the actor playing Medea the wrong mask. When Medea entered on her dragon chariot for the final apotheosis with her dead children at her feet, her dagger dripping blood, she had an enormous grin on her face. I'd given the actor the mask of comedy. The spectators howled with laughter – *Medea* with a happy ending.

HELENA   The priests and judges were very confused.

PHOEBE   They'd come to see a tragedy.

ALL   They wanted their catharsis.

  BOOM! The blast of a mighty cannon. Our theatre should shake.

HECTOR   What was that?

PHOEBE   I'm shaking.

HELENA   It was a cannon.

PHOEBE   What's a cannon?

HELENA   I don't know, the word just popped out.

LONDON, 1610, THE GLOBE THEATRE. A REHEARSAL IS IN PROGRESS.

BOOM! The sound of the cannon has stopped everyone in their tracks. Dimitris has become RICHARD BURBAGE and Pallas has become CUTHBERT BURBAGE.

RICHARD BURBAGE   What the bloody hell was that?

HELENA   A cannon.

RICHARD (*To Helena.*)   It was a rhetorical question, madame. The canon discharge was a mistake. There's no performance today. We are rehearsing our next production. Thank you for your early interest. The Globe Theatre appreciates your patronage. Now where were we?

CUTHBERT BURBAGE   You were conjuring the tempest with your magic stave, brother.

Helena becomes ANNE TEDESCO-BOYLE.

ANNE TEDESCO-BOYLE   That's all right, gentlemen, don't mind me, I'm a new board member, Anne Tedesco-Boyle but everyone calls me Annie. Theatre is my addiction, I'll be quiet as a mouse. Zip! (*She zippers her mouth but can't resist one final encouragement.*) "Lay on, Macduff!" (*To us.*) I love these open rehearsals when it's not about the results and it's about the process. They've drummed *that* into our dear little heads. (*To the actors.*) Really, don't mind me, I'm invisible. (*To us.*) I joined the board of this theatre to be a part of the creative process, even if that means primarily giving them money. I'm not a creative person myself and I certainly don't pretend to understand the creative process but I've been drawn to both ever since I saw my first play: *Peter Pan.* When Tinker Bell was dying and Peter asked us to save her, no one clapped louder than me. When Shirley Channing invited me to join the board, I was hoping to change my relationship with these fascinating people. So far, it hasn't. They're grateful for my support—"Thank you, Mrs. Tedesco-Boyle"—but I've never had a satisfactory answer when I asked an artist what it's like to create. It must be wonderful. Well, there's a whole new season ahead to answer that question, our forty-ninth consecutive one, I guess I can say "our" now, including my favorite play, *King Lear* with my favorite company actor, John Pick. (*At an impatient sound from Richard.*) I should know what play you're rehearsing. *The Country Wife*, of course, our first play of the season. (*To us.*) Is there anything more fun than a Restoration Comedy? Or, as Candace Delbo, our dramaturg says, is there anything more restorative? That Candace!

I don't have to remind you: these are difficult times. More than ever we need art in our lives to get us through. (*To Richard and Cuthbert.*) It's all yours, gentlemen.

CUTHBERT BURBAGE   I believe it's your line, Richard.

RICHARD   I can't rehearse with all these people here.

CUTHBERT   This is a closed rehearsal, ladies and gentlemen. Thank you.

MRS. TEDESCO-BOYLE   We just want to watch.

CUTHBERT   I'm sorry.

MRS. TEDESCO-BOYLE   I don't understand. Shirley said it would be all right. (*To us.*) This is what I was talking about. (*To Hector and Phoebe.*) Anne Tedesco-Boyle but everyone calls me Annie. How long have you been on the board?

Hector, Anne Tedesco-Boyle and Phoebe leave.

RICHARD   People just wander in off the street in the middle of a rehearsal and think we're going to welcome them with open arms. I'll give all my acting tricks away.

CUTHBERT   You don't have any tricks, brother.

RICHARD   I'm all tricks, I'm nothing but tricks.

CUTHBERT   I've never seen you so rattled.

RICHARD   The last time the cannon went off when it shouldn't, the theatre burnt to the ground. We haven't finished paying off this one yet.

CUTHBERT   I'm sure it was just an accident, brother.

RICHARD   This theatre cannot afford accidents. It certainly doesn't forgive them. We have two options: triumph or failure.

CUTHBERT   You sound like father. "There are no mistakes in the theatre, young man, only disasters." I think it's all a mistake: the good, the bad and the indifferent. Do you seriously think I know what I'm doing when I'm acting?

RICHARD   You don't?

CUTHBERT   I pray I know all my words and don't fall off the stage.

The mighty Globe Theatre cannon booms again.

RICHARD   What is going on?

CUTHBERT   Maybe there *is* a performance today. (*Hector has returned as James Burbage.*)

JAMES BURBAGE   You trying to burn this damn place down again? Once wasn't enough?

RICHARD   It was an accident, papa.

JAMES   There are no mistakes in the theatre, young man, only disasters.

CUTHBERT   Good morning, papa.

JAMES   After your fiasco yesterday, I may have to come out of early retirement and perform my solo performance piece, *Kings, Queens and Miscreants.* I could get it back up in a day if I had to.

RICHARD   Yesterday wasn't our fault. Half the audience didn't speak English and the other half were drunk.

JAMES   Never blame the audience, they're doing their best, it's not their fault. It's our fault, it's always our fault. That's why we must surpass ourselves every performance and elevate them at the same time. If you've learned nothing from your father but this I will not have strutted and fretted my hours on this stage for nothing. No one made us become actors. (*The cannon booms again.*) For a theatre that doesn't have a performance today, you're making a hell of a racket!

RICHARD   Cuthbert, see what's going on. (*Cuthbert goes.*) There's no performance until Friday. We took the new play off a week early. I told the company: there's no point in performing a comedy without a single laugh.

JAMES   Comedies are tricky; even the great ones. I never trusted them.

RICHARD   How do you mean?

JAMES   They make an actor pander to the audience. He wants more and more laughs. After a while he'll do anything for them. I took to dropping my drawers, breaking wind, pulling faces. Your mother put a stop to that. She was always my harshest critic.

RICHARD   Comedy or tragedy, you were the best.

JAMES   The trouble starts when you separate them.

RICHARD   We have the Greeks to blame for that. Separate masks for comedy and tragedy, imagine!

JAMES   I spent a lifetime trying to bring them back together.

RICHARD   What are you talking about? You're still in the flower—

JAMES   If you say "youth" I will strike you.

RICHARD   I was going to say your art.

JAMES   The lines, it all comes down to remembering your lines.

RICHARD   It's every actor's biggest fear.

JAMES   I understand the theatre next door has a success on its hands—something about Queen Boadicea, who either defeated the Romans or they defeated her. I can never remember which. British history—there's too much of it. History plays never really appealed to me. I preferred reaching men's imaginations.

RICHARD   They deserve a hit. It's a good show. It's no *King Lear* but it's a good show.

JAMES   My boy, if I've said it once, I've said it a thousand times:

BOTH   Nothing is *King Lear.*

JAMES   And it began at this company. Never forget that. If you ever find yourself on the chopping block, just before the executioner swings his axe, remember *King Lear* began at our theatre.

A young man crosses the stage. It is Pallas/Cuthbert now Kenny in the uniform of a concessions stand worker. He is carrying several cases of bottled Coca-Colas.

KENNY TOBIAS   Don't mind me, sorry, just passing through. Cool outfits. I thought the next show was *Streetcar.* (*Calling off.*) Archie, where do they want these? (*He is already gone.*)

JAMES   Who was that?

RICHARD   Never saw him before in my life.

JAMES   Can't say I liked the costume.

RICHARD   What brings you to town?

JAMES   Your grandmother wants to shop and your sister is only too eager to help her spend what's left of my money.

RICHARD   You're just looking for an excuse to get back onstage.

JAMES   Wild horses couldn't drag me. Whatever possessed my two sons to become partners in a theatre! Commerce and art do not mix. That's where I got into trouble. The Ancients had the right idea: their theatre was free, no admission.

RICHARD   You're suggesting we throw open our doors?

JAMES   Maybe you should try barter. "Here's a lamb to slaughter, give me two places for *Cymbeline*."

RICHARD   If I thought it would fill the theatre . . . !

JAMES   You should have bailed out when I did.

RICHARD   We wanted to be a company and answer to no one.

JAMES   It's ridiculous, actors being their own managers. We're not smart enough. We can sniff out a good role for ourselves, find true pathos in the most pedestrian death scene, even dig up a few laughs where none existed—at that we're brilliant. But make sound business judgments, know what plays an audience wants?

RICHARD   Business is good. We were at 80 percent Saturday.

JAMES   What about the rest of the week?

RICHARD   We are doing plays we believe in. Let the other theatres cater to the common denominator. We aim a little higher than bear-baiting.

JAMES   Keep that up and this place will be on the market before you can say *Gammer Gurton's Needle*.

RICHARD   I still say it was your finest portrayal.

JAMES   It wiped The Theatre out.

RICHARD   That was your first mistake.

JAMES   What was?

RICHARD   Calling your theatre The Theatre. Very flat, dad. People like places to have names. The Phoenix, the Globe. It was confusing, as well. "Where you headed?" "The Theatre." "What theatre?" "The

Theatre." "No, which theatre?" "The Theatre." "The theatre?" "That's what I said, The Theatre."

JAMES   Are you finished undermining your old father, sir?

RICHARD   I wasn't talking artist to artist but as one businessman to another. That's what this is, a business.

JAMES   What it's become, you mean. What are you rehearsing?

RICHARD   It's called *The Tempest*. I'm playing a deposed duke in exile on an enchanted island who dabbles in white magic and who's planning his revenge on his brother.

JAMES   Nothing personal, I hope.

RICHARD   Cuthbert and I aren't like that. You have to be true colleagues if you're going to make it in this business.

JAMES   I never collaborated with anyone. Great actors never do. We are sufficient unto ourselves.

RICHARD   Cuthbert's playing my daughter but I've got the part. I'm years too young for it. I'm sure he wrote it for you. I think he still writes everything for you. He always thought you were the best of us.

JAMES   You and your brother are good but good—

RICHARD   Isn't good enough, I know.

JAMES   Can I tell you a secret? I'm writing a play. They're very hard. I wish someone had told me before I started.

RICHARD   You thought acting was easy?

JAMES   I don't think anything about what we do is easy. Well, maybe sitting out there—or standing—arms folded and judging others isn't too demanding. It looks different empty—not half so terrifying.

Cuthbert returns.

CUTHBERT   It was that new actor you hired. I told him that cannon isn't a toy. It's how we let the public know there's a performance that day. He won't do it again. How old is he anyway? He can't be more than thirteen. I don't think he has a Cleopatra or a Lady Macbeth in him, Richard. I can't believe he'll be my understudy. Miranda is a beautiful young woman; you hired another Witch for the Scottish Play.

RICHARD   I'm not worried, you never miss.

CUTHBERT   That's not true. I missed five Phoebes last *As You Like It.*

RICHARD   That's different. You were really sick.

JAMES   I never missed a performance in my life. I played an entire season with the Black Plague. Of course, the rest of the company was dropping like flies.

RICHARD   Father, I never know when to believe you.

CUTHBERT   "Never" is a good start.

JAMES   An actor who misses a performance for any reason but death— and I mean his own, no one else's—is not fit to step on these boards. The day I pass, you are both to play. That's an order. We are men of the theatre. The extraordinary is demanded of us. We are the sons of Thespis! We are the Burbages! (*He has only succeeded in getting winded. His sons attend to him.*)

Phoebe now LYDIA BURBAGE and Helena/Anne Tedesco-Boyle now GRETNA BURBAGE enter.

LYDIA BURBAGE   What's wrong with your father?

RICHARD   He was telling us about being a Burbage.

LYDIA   That will do it! Are you trying to kill him? Get his feet up. You promised me you wouldn't set him off again, Richard. (*To James.*) "Beginners to the stage, please, beginners to the stage. *Cymbeline*, Act One. Beginners, Mr. Burbage!" (*To the others.*) That should do it. Now heal thyself, proud physician.

CUTHBERT   What's wrong, Grandmother?

LYDIA   Tell him.

GRETNA BURBAGE   We need money to pay the coach.

LYDIA   I told the man "I am Lydia Burbage, the mother of the great tragedian, James Burbage, you should be honored, sir" but he still wanted his fare. In my day, London revered its artists. Now it's nothing but money. Everybody wants their money.

CUTHBERT   I'll pay him, Grandmother. (*He goes.*)

LYDIA   "We who have lived so long and borne so much" indeed!

RICHARD (*Low, to Gretna.*)   Did you tell her, *Gretna*?

GRETNA   No, Richard.

RICHARD   Why not?

GRETNA   Your grandmother's never acknowledged me as a Burbage. I don't think she likes me.

RICHARD   Nonsense.

LYDIA   His grandmother still has excellent hearing, Mrs. Burbage.

GRETNA   I wish you'd call me Gretna.

LYDIA   Such an unpleasant name, Gretna.

GRETNA   It was my great-grandmother's. She was a mill-keeper's daughter.

LYDIA   That is irrelevant, Mrs. Burbage.

GRETNA   What shall I call you, Mother Burbage?

LYDIA   Ma'am will suffice. I'm sorry, child, it's not your fault you're not one of us.

GRETNA   I love the theatre.

LYDIA   You attend the theatre, which is something quite different. We Burbages are the theatre.

GRETNA   I never saw a play until I met Richard.

LYDIA   That would explain so much. I pity a child who isn't taken to the theatre. I consider them incomplete. My father took me often. I counted the days to the next visit.

RICHARD   Tell her, Gretna.

GRETNA   I'm going to have a baby.

LYDIA   That's the first interesting thing you've said since you married my grandson.

Cuthbert returns.

CUTHBERT   I just sold two tickets. Buy early and buy often: the Burbage family motto.

GRETNA   I'm going to have a baby, Cuthbert.

CUTHBERT   That's great, Dickie. How's dad?

RICHARD   He's coming around.

James is stirring.

JAMES   "Beginners to the stage," you heard them. What's all this standing about?

GRETNA   You're going to be a grandfather, Father Burbage.

JAMES   Am I? That's nice. Who are you?

GRETNA   Richard's wife.

LYDIA   It was in a play that I first saw your grandfather, Clarence Burbage.

JAMES   My father.

LYDIA   —the greatest Burbage of you all. That was an actor who could put the fear of God in you. His voice, his posture, his very being. A moment of silence for Clarence Burbage.

JAMES   My father was a great actor.

LYDIA   I'm happy you can acknowledge that. Your father would have been, too. His theatre made London the sweetest spot on God's earth.

JAMES   There weren't really actors before him. Or theatre. People had something they called Mystery Plays—scenes from the Bible—that they put on in front of churches at certain times of the year. Something to do with harvests and religious festivals. Amateurs wrote them. Anyone could get up there and "act"—butchers, bakers, candlestick makers. You can imagine what that must have been like.

May Burbage has entered. She is reading from a prompt script.

MAY BURBAGE   "O brave new world that has such people in it."

CUTHBERT   Is that my script?

MAY   I thought I said it rather well. "O brave new world that has such people in it."

CUTHBERT   This is why women don't belong on the stage. If a man said a line like that, the audience would be in stitches—that is, the ones who could hear you.

RICHARD   Show our sister how it should be done, Bertie. It's the new play we're rehearsing. Cuthbert is my daughter, Miranda.

CUTHBERT   With faces and gestures?

RICHARD   Yes, with faces and gestures! You see what I put up with, dad?

CUTHBERT   "O brave new world that has such people in it."

RICHARD   It's coming along. Just a little more . . . It's better I show you. (*He takes the playscript.*) "O brave new world that has such people in it." You see, brother?

CUTHBERT   Thank you, Richard.

JAMES   May I? (*He takes the playscript.*) "O brave new word that has such people in it." Hear the difference? Not that I want you to imitate me. I never want either of you to imitate me.

RICHARD (*Gently.*)   "World," father, "O brave new world."

JAMES   That's what I said.

RICHARD   No, you said "word." "O brave new word."

JAMES   Same thing. It's not the words, it's the expression you put into them. Word, world, whatever—it's what you're feeling. "O brave new . . . ?" What's the line again?

> *Thump! Thump! Thump! We hear the three resonant knockings that signify a performance is about to begin in the classic French theatre. They are coming from under the stage of the Globe, rather like the Ghost's "Swear"s from under the stage in Hamlet. The three knocks are steady and solemn. In a series of three knocks, they will come from different places under the stage, forcing the Burbages to follow them in different directions.*

RICHARD   What is that banging?

CUTHBERT   It's that new boy again. Now he's down in the trap room.

JAMES   It's not banging. They're deliberate thumps. It's coming from here.

CUTHBERT   No, they're coming from over there.

RICHARD   Here, I tell you.

JAMES   Whatever they are, make them stop.

Cuthbert and Richard run off, following the lead of the knocks.

MAY   "Give me my robe, put on my crown. I have immortal longings in me."

JAMES   That's enough out of you, young woman.

LYDIA   You'd be surprised how much she's memorized. She can recite *Hamlet*, not just the part, the entire play.

JAMES   When did this happen?

MAY   I'm halfway through *Twelfth Night.*

The thumps from under the stage have continued, only from a different place every time.

JAMES   Now they're coming from this side.

LYDIA   Over here.

MAY   Over here.

James, Lydia and May leave in search of the thumps, leaving Gretna alone on the stage. She decides to take maximum advantage of the opportunity. When Gretna acts it is with full release of all her pent-up neglect.

GRETNA   "O brave new world that has such people in it." (*She is satisfied.*) "O brave new world."

TRANSITION: *VERSAILLES, 1789, ROYAL THEATRE. INTERMISSION AT A PERFORMANCE OF A NEW PLAY.*

Dimitris/Richard Burbage becomes JEAN-LOUIS DANTON; Pallas/Cuthbert Burbage becomes CHRISTOPHE DURANT. They are standing in the wings at a performance in progress. Jean-Louis Danton has just returned from taking a bow.)

JEAN-LOUIS DANTON   My third curtain call and it's only the first act. They love me, what can I say?

CHRISTOPHE DURANT   But what about my play?

DANTON   Your play is going well, young playwright.

GRETNA   He's right, it's very strong applause. Listen to them.

DURANT   The King was snoring in his box—and when he wasn't snoring, he was eating. During the most important scene, his mistress undid the front of his breeches and was fondling the royal penis.

DANTON   That doesn't mean he wasn't listening to your play.

DURANT   The only time His Majesty seemed engaged was during your speech about the gathering storm clouds of revolution.

DANTON   It's a brave speech. I trembled as I spoke your dangerous words. We should be grateful the King was otherwise engaged.

DURANT   They hate my play, I hate them.

DANTON   Where are you going?

DURANT   I'm going to kill myself. (*He rushes off.*)

DANTON   (If this playwright is the great hope for the future of French theatre, we are all doomed.)

GRETNA   Our playwright is just like that. And he's the greatest playwright who ever lived, only he doesn't know that yet.

DANTON   The greatest playwright who ever lived has not been born yet, *Mademoiselle*. (Who is this tasty morsel! Fee-fi-fo-fum, I smell the blood of an Englishwoman.)

GRETNA   Why has your play stopped, sir?

DANTON   We haven't stopped, it's the interval between the acts.

GRETNA   What are acts?

DANTON   Breaks in the action.

GRETNA   At the Globe we just jolly well bully through until the play's over and everyone's dead.

DANTON   On the Continent, we like to take a little time off on both sides of the curtain, if you catch my *double entendre*.

GRETNA   We don't have curtains either.

DANTON   (She doesn't but I'll have her anyway.) *Voulez-vous coucher avec moi?*

GRETNA   I've already eaten. (Luckily, I speak some French.)

DANTON   *Touché.* (Cunning little strumpet.)

GRETNA   You're welcome. (He called me a strumpet, he did, this foul-breathed frog.)

DANTON   *De rien.* (Thank God for asides.)

GRETNA   The pleasure's mine. (I shall tell the Globe about this device. Very handy.)

DANTON   Who are you talking to?

GRETNA   No one.

DANTON   It's like you're speaking to an audience.

GRETNA   Impossible, the audience is there. (*She points towards the stage off.*) There's no one here. (*She points to us.*)

DANTON   You're making my head spin. French intermissions are brief, *Mademoiselle,* if you catch my meaning.

GRETNA   *Merci, Monsieur,* but I shall be faithful to my Richard.

DANTON   Your Richard?

GRETNA   Richard Burbage, the actor. He's a famous Othello.

DANTON   Jean-Louis Danton, a famous everything.

He does a deep, extravagant bow. When he comes up from it, Gretna has fled.

DANTON   My little chipmunk has gone. *Tant pis,* I couldn't make love to a woman who doesn't know what an *entr'acte* is.

Durant returns. He has been tearing at his hair and holds clumps of it.

DURANT   I shall be bald before my time. I hate being a playwright.

DANTON   What are you doing?

DURANT   I will watch His Majesty through this peephole the rest of the performance.

DANTON   Interesting story about that peephole. Molière himself made it with his penknife. This was before he was Molière and was still using his real name, Jean-Baptiste Poquelin. (Look at him! Couldn't care less. This next generation! All they care about is themselves.)

DURANT   The King looks nervous, like in that English play when they put on a play-within-a-play before the guilty king who's murdered his brother.

DANTON   *Julius Caesar.* I'd like a crack at that part.

DURANT   I wish you'd concentrate on tonight's performance. You're killing me with your mistakes.

DANTON   A word here, a line there—the audience doesn't know the difference.

DURANT   Because they've never heard it before. They think I wrote your mistakes.

DANTON   (Playwrights are so annoying.)

DURANT   (I hate actors.)

DANTON   It's not as if you've written a masterpiece—well, maybe you have; time will tell.

DURANT   My play has no chance of becoming a masterpiece if you butcher it like this.

DANTON   (He has a point.)

DURANT   A new play is only as good as the performance it's given. (I just thought of that. I think I'm on to something!)

DANTON   I became an actor to meet beautiful women—and sometimes men.

He kisses Durant on the mouth.

DURANT   You know I don't like it when you do that.

DANTON   Neither do I, it's a tradition.

Hector/James enters. He has become John Pick. He is dressed in a bathrobe and remnants of his rehearsal costume.

JOHN PICK   My fellow actors, brothers who tread these same boards, partners in this great act of human imagination we call theatre, I salute you.

He bows with a flourish.

DANTON   Do we know you?

JOHN John Pick, AEA, SAG, AFTRA, AGVA and general rabble-rouser. (*He shakes hands.*) Well done, gentlemen, well done. It's an honor to share the stage with you.

DANTON We're in the middle of a performance.

JOHN I just finished an open rehearsal of *The Man of Mode* for our subscribers. Do you know it? I'm playing Sir Fopling Flutter. Wonderful part, delightful play. I'll be brief. (*To us.*) John Pick again. You were a wonderful audience. You've been so quiet we forgot you were there. We had a few tense moments when an overly enthusiastic new board member told you you were watching a rehearsal for *The Country Wife.* I thought to myself "Are they? I've been rehearsing the wrong Restoration play for two acts!" Even our dramaturg, Candace Delbo, gets them mixed up. I don't need to remind you: these are difficult times for the arts, especially a company like ours, dedicated to the classics.

DANTON You mean, Corneille, Racine.

JOHN To each his own, gentlemen.

DURANT Molière, Marivaux, Durant.

JOHN Who?

DURANT Christophe Durant.

DANTON Who?

DURANT Me.

JOHN Five words: Never, never, never, never, never. Lear over the dead Cordelia. The same word repeated five times. The simplest language at the profoundest human moment. When we end our season with *King Lear,* it will be my responsibility to express a lifetime in those few words. It's been my dream to play Lear. I was a dangerous, sexy Edmund, believe it or not, a fair to middling Edgar and a damn good Gloucester and Kent but Lear was the part I had my eye on. I believe I'm ready now. Help us finish our forty-ninth anniversary season in fine style. As you exit the theatre, look for company members in the lobby with baskets for your donation. See you at the Dryden next month, then *The Orestia,* ending our season with *King Lear.* (*To the others.*) Thank you, gentlemen, it's all yours. (*He goes.*)

DANTON The British are all lunatics.

DURANT   I think he was American.

Phoebe/Lydia Burbage now MME FRONTAIN enters. She is still acknowledging her enormous ovation. She has an armful of flowers with rapturous notes attached. She is in a world of her own.

DANTON   Here comes your butcher, Monsieur Durant. She'd slaughter Sophocles himself. Neophytes like you don't stand a chance.

MME FRONTAIN   Too much, *messieurs*, too much.

DANTON   (And yet my loins ache for this ravishing creature. No, they don't. Why did I say that? I've been in too many plays.)

MME FRONTAIN   I am but the humble servant of the playwright. To his words, I give breath. I am an actress, nothing more, nothing less.

DURANT   An actress who doesn't know her lines.

MME FRONTAIN   I know the soul of my character, her deepest secrets. What are lines compared to the essence of the character we are playing? It took a while tonight, I won't pretend I captivated the audience with my first rhymed couplet. I had to work the old Frontain magic to charm them. I did things with my fan that surprised even me. By the end of the act, they were eating out of my hand. (Is there anyone easier to beguile than a playwright?) I accept your apology. Where is that little seamstress?

Helena/ Gretna Burbage now MLLE PICARD enters.

MLLE PICARD   Did I hear my cue?

MME FRONTAIN   Not unless you're that little seamstress and not my understudy. I'm sorry to disappoint you, Mademoiselle Picard, I am in excellent health today. (What kind of name is Picard? It belongs on a menu: *Boeuf Picard*.)

MLLE PICARD   Madame Frontain, I pray before every performance that you are in good health.

MME FRONTAIN   (Every understudy says that.)

MLLE PICARD   You are truly the first lady of the French theatre, Madame Frontain. (Of the last century!)

MME FRONTAIN   There were snickers when they spoke of my youth and virginity.

MLLE PICARD   Nonsense. (They could have heard them all the way to Paris.)

MME FRONTAIN   This was before I entered, during that tedious part of the play—what do they call it?

DURANT   The exposition. I'm considered a master of it.

MME FRONTAIN   Then master doing away with it entirely. When I finally made my entrance, half an hour later—

DURANT   Three minutes, madame, I wrote it to an egg-timer.

MME FRONTAIN   Then get a faster egg-timer! I had to reach deep into my bag of tricks tonight.

DANTON   It's your special magic, my love.

MME FRONTAIN   There's nothing magical about it. It's hard work and technique. You don't have to be 16 to play 16. You have to *embody* 16. Molière wrote his greatest female parts for me and I haven't retired a single one of them from my repertoire.

MLLE PICARD   (The thought of this crone as Célimène.)

MME FRONTAIN   Where is that little seamstress with my pom-pom for the second act?

Danae/May Burbage now MARIE-CLAIRE enters.

MARIE-CLAIRE   I am that little seamstress, madame, with your pom-pom for the second act.

DANTON   (Nay, not seamstress—goddess, rather.)

DURANT   (This is who should be playing my Philline.)

MLLE PICARD   (So this is the little slut they all want to sleep with?)

MME FRONTAIN   (If this girl could act, it would be the end of us all.)

MARIE-CLAIRE   (Why do I feel they are all talking about me?)

Hector/James Burbage now the CHEVALIER BERTON enters.

CHEVALIER BERTON   The King is not amused. I am the Chevalier Berton, the royal censor.

DURANT   No offense to His Majesty, but the King knows nothing about the theatre.

BERTON   Of course he doesn't. He goes to the theatre to be entertained.

DURANT   And get his dick sucked.

MARIE-CLAIRE   Bravely said, young playwright, bravely said. (*To BERTON.*) You put my boyfriend in the Bastille. He's a poet.

BERTON   I'll put you in the Bastille if you continue to interrupt.

MARIE-CLAIRE   If I weren't a woman . . . .!

BERTON   (This ravishing creature will come to me to save her lover.) (*To Durant.*) Monsieur Durant, your play poses as a valentine of roses for an unsuspecting audience but I see its sharp thorns of sedition.

DANTON   Are you threatening to shut us down?

BERTON   I'm asking him to delete certain seditious lines from his otherwise merely pedestrian script. (*He hands a "censored" script to Durant.*)

MME FRONTAIN   We're all on edge this evening, monsieur.

BERTON   You actors have nothing to worry about. You only say the words; the truly dangerous men write them.

   Durant has finished his quick perusal of the proposed cuts in the script.

DURANT   Tell His Majesty I will not change a word of my play. It is a call for a new social order in which a king is no better than the corn husk with which I wipe myself. No, I'll tell him myself. Are you with me, Danton?

DANTON   Of course I am but may I think about it?

DURANT   There's nothing to think about. You're either with me or you're not.

   He rushes out.

BERTON (*To Mlle Picard.*)   His Majesty will see you after the performance in the royal bedroom, mademoiselle.

MLLE PICARD   But I'm only an understudy.

BERTON   His Majesty has a role for you in a drama of his own devising. Do I make myself clear?

MLLE PICARD   Entirely. Should I go?

MME FRONTAIN   You're an actress, you don't have a choice. (*To Berton.*) Does His Majesty wish to see me after the performance?

BERTON   By then, he will have seen quite enough of you.

MARIE-CLAIRE   They're calling places.

The three women hurry off.

DANTON   Surely, monsieur, someone in the royal box has mentioned Jean-Louis Danton?

BERTON   Who?

DANTON   Me.

BERTON   I am the King's censor, not his pimp. However, there is a certain Monsieur de Sade who never misses a performance of yours.

DANTON   Monsieur de Sade is a notorious sadist.

BERTON   He is about to become a Marquis. Play your cards right and you could be sitting pretty.

DANTON   Sitting is the last thing I'd be doing. Not all actors practice the British vice, monsieur.

BERTON   Name one.

DANTON   I can't off the top of my head. The Beatles.

BERTON   They're not really actors.

Pallas/Cuthbert Burbage/Christophe Durant now PAVEL LESHMENEV, a Moscow delivery boy enters. He carries a basket of food. Everyone will descend on it. Mme Frontain and Mlle Picard come running out of the "French" wings to share in the feast.

PAVEL LESHMENEV   I have perogis, blinis, steak tartare, chicken Kiev, black bread and pumpernickel, smoked salmon and what looks like a sturgeon dumpling. Ugh!

BERTON (*Reading the address on the basket.*)   Wrong address. Where's Pushkin Street?

DANTON   Who cares? This looks delicious.

No matter. They surround Pavel and his basket. The food is soon gone.

MLLE PICARD   If you're not going to take that, I will.

DANTON   There's enough for everyone.

MME FRONTAIN   Who wants to trade what looks like a muffin for what looks like a brioche?

PAVEL   Hey! hey! Not so fast.

MLLE PICARD   We're actors: we're always hungry and we'll eat anything.

Danae/May Burbage/Marie-Claire now HAZEL MAY enters. She is checking our her bio prior to publication in the program. She is on her cell phone with someone.)

HAZEL MAY   I need your help. They only gave me 100 words for my bio in the program. "Hazel May (Watchman) is thrilled to be making her professional debut in this production of *The Orestia*. A graduate of NYU, Hazel was raised in Stockton, California. Favorite roles so far include Masha (*Three Sisters)*, Honey (Edward Albee's *Who's Afraid of Virginia Woolf?*) and Hero (*Much Ado About Nothing*). She dedicates tonight's performance to the memory of her father, Jordan May, who supported her every dream. Hazel is represented by her agent, Jack Sprat at William Morris Endeavor." You're welcome, I thought you'd like that. "Hazel has her own website at www.HazelGirl.com. Next, Cordelia in *King Lear*." I'm 2 words over. (*She listens.*) That's perfect. (*She corrects her bio.*) "Honey (*Who's Afraid of Virginia Woolf?*)." (*She is going.*) Did I get a callback from Lincoln Center? (*She is gone.*)

By now everyone has gone. Pavel is alone for a beat.

PAVEL   Hello? Hello! Anybody here?

TRANSITION: *Moscow, 1896, The first reading of The Seagull at the Art Theatre.*

Hector/James Burbage/Chevalier Burton now BORIS YELETSKY enters. He is still changing from Berton to Yeletsky.

BORIS YELETSKY   You're early and I'm running late. The reading doesn't start for another hour.

PAVEL   Someone placed an order from this address, that's all I know about anything.

BORIS   The basket's empty except for this . . . phew! . . . sturgeon dumpling.

PAVEL   You know what they say: actors are always hungry and they'll eat anything.

BORIS   Except for sturgeon dumplings.

PAVEL   I need to be paid for it or my boss will beat me.

BORIS   He beats you?

PAVEL   With his open hand.

BORIS   And you stand for it?

PAVEL   No, he puts me across his knee.

BORIS   We do terrible things to one another in the theatre but we don't beat our own. You delivery boys are no better off than serfs. Free yourself from the shackles of food delivery-hood and experience the freedom of a life in the theatre. You can start right now.

PAVEL   Don't I need an education?

BORIS   No, none, none at all. You can arrange the chairs for a reading.

PAVEL   Do I look like someone who can read?

BORIS   We're going to read a new play that's been completely revised. The playwright's either transformed it into a masterpiece or it could still be shit. History will be made, either way. Put them in a circle, so everyone can see everyone else. There are no secrets at a first reading, no tricks up our sleeves. That all comes later. It's just us and the play. Here they come.

Dimitris/Richard Burbage/Jean-Louis Danton now YURI GOLDOVSKY and Danae/May Burbage/Marie-Claire/Hazel May now MAYA NABOKOV enter. Yuri is carrying the model of a set he has designed for the next production.

YURI GOLDOVSKY   What if they don't like the set, Maya?

MAYA   I love it. It's brilliant. Scenery that frees the actor and doesn't confine him. I can soar in such a space.

YURI   If the theatre is to convince, we must make the audience feel they're really at Arkadina's summer house. They should feel the stifling humidity. The lake shimmering in the moonlight. They should feel the mosquitoes.

MAYA NABOKOV   The mosquitoes are my job, darling. I've been practicing the mosquitoes since I read the script. (*She demonstrates swatting mosquitoes.*) We have months of rehearsal.

YURI   Realer than real, my love, but with poetry—that's my goal.

MAYA   It's mine, too, my darling; it's every actor's.

YURI   Together we will create a theatre of truth: what a wonderful time to be alive, Maya!

MAYA   People will remember us as the first to show life as it really is. Goodbye, Ophelia; *adieu*, Molière; I am Nina Mikhailovna Zarechnaya, a living breathing Russian woman now.

YURI   You are my seagull!

Helena/Gretna Burbage, Mlle Picard now NINA KOZLOVSKY had entered and is trying to clean the rehearsal room. Everyone will seem to be in her way.

NINA KOZLOVSKY   Coming through.

YURI   We're trying to work, Nina.

MAYA   Don't be like that, Yuri. We'll work over here, Nina.

NINA   Thank you.

MAYA   Nina is the ingénue's name in the play. I'm Nina.

PAVEL   My girlfriend is named Nina. She'll like that. Your play is called *Nina*?

MAYA   No, *The Seagull*. Nina's an actress but she's also the seagull.

PAVEL   I don't understand.

MAYA   They're symbols of each other.

PAVEL   I'm confused.

BORIS (*On the alert as a good producer should be.*)   The young man is confused. We should all be listening to him.

MAYA   He's a delivery boy.

BORIS   They go to the theatre, too.

PAVEL   No, we don't.

BORIS   Well, you should.

Phoebe/Lydia Burbage/Mme Frontain now ALEXANDRA MISHKIN enters reading from the playscript.

ALEXANDRA MISHKIN (*Doctor Dorn lowers his voice.*)   Get Irina Nikolayevna out of here, will you. The fact is Konstantin Gavrilovich has shot himself. . . . " (*She looks up from her reading.*) "Curtain." If that's not the most beautiful word in the Russian language, I don't know what is: "curtain." (*She closes her bound copy of a playscript with a theatrical gesture.*) To be even a small part of such a thrilling enterprise is a privilege I never dreamed of.

BORIS   It's a long way from a first reading to a first performance, Countess.

ALEXANDRA   Ssshh! Don't call me that. No one must know. My God, I will go mad with excitement before the first night!

BORIS   Everything must be perfect but everything that can go wrong, will.

ALEXANDRA   Of course it will. That's theatre.

NINA (*Still trying to clean, to Alexandra.*)   You want to take it over there, lady? Thank you.

BORIS   You understand this is a new kind of theatre we're creating?

YURI   Completely natural acting—you'll think you're peeking through a window at people who are completely unaware that you're there.

MAYA   I will go places as an actress I have never gone before.

YURI   Think of a high wall that has suddenly been taken down and you see people as they are in life but never on a stage.

MAYA   I'll give you another example: no asides.

ALEXANDRA   Thank God.

YURI   (Actually, I rather like asides.)

BORIS   No melodramatic plot turns.

YURI   The rich uncle doesn't die and leave them a million rubles at the end of act one.

BORIS   No student turning out to be a prince.

MAYA   No more plots.

YURI   What are plots?

MAYA   Artificial folderol.

BORIS   We are doing away with plots.

The three of them are almost dancing in celebration.

NINA   I hope there's a death scene.

BORIS   Unfortunately, yes. I tried to persuade the playwright against one.

NINA   I like a good death scene.

PAVEL   Me, too.

ALEXANDRA   I think everyone secretly likes a good old-fashioned death scene, Boris.

BORIS   This is a death scene only it isn't.

MAYA   It's a suicide. It happens offstage.

YURI   The principal characters aren't even aware of it. It ends the play.

ALEXANDRA   Brilliant. Brilliant, brilliant.

NINA (*To Pavel.*)   Say, I know you! You're Pavel, Tanya's little boy.

PAVEL   Not so little, little mother.

NINA   Your mother and I worked in the Imperial laundry.

PAVEL   That job killed her. Romanov bedsheets did my mother in.

NINA   It was the bleaches they used. We complained but do you think they listened to us?

PAVEL   How did you get out?

NINA   I ran for my life. Boris and his theatre took me in. If it hadn't been for them . . . !

PAVEL   I wish you'd taken my mother with you.

NINA   The revolution won't come soon enough.

PAVEL   You know, there's a demonstration tonight.

NINA   There's a demonstration every night.

PAVEL   This one's going to be different. I've got a bomb and I'm going to use it. The Tsar will be on his way to the theatre.

NINA   Be careful, Pavel.

PAVEL   I'm not afraid to die. (*To the others.*) I'll be back for my money. (*He goes.*)

ALEXANDRA   My husband accused me of being a *dilettante*, M. Yeletsky. He asked me if my arm wasn't tired from writing you so many checks.

BORIS (*He is kissing her hand all over.*)   You will have the last laugh, Countess. You will be hailed as a patron saint of the arts. You will have brought *The Seagull* back to life.

YURI   The first production was almost the death of our company.

BORIS   But we held firm, we stayed the course.

YURI   Thank God we had a revival of *The Tempest* we could put on in its place.

BORIS   Shakespeare to the rescue—once again.

MAYA   I can't stand Shakespeare. Whenever I open the program and it says "a play by William Shakespeare," I want to scream. His plays are completely unrealistic. Ghosts! When did you last see a ghost in Moscow? Prologues! Epilogues! Just get on with it and when it's over, let us go home. And who goes around talking to themselves? Or worse, to the audience? They call it soliloquies; I call it lazy playwriting.

BORIS   It was *The Tempest* or *The Misanthrope*, young woman.

MAYA   Molière! Another crowd-pleaser!

BORIS   There's something to be said for repertory. If *The Seagull* still doesn't work, we can get *The Orestia* back up with one rehearsal.

MAYA   *The Orestia!* Stick hot needles in my eyes rather.

(Pallas / Cuthbert / Durant / Pavel now GORDON LIGHT, the theatre company production stage manager, crosses the stage. He wears a PSM's headset.

GORDON LIGHT (*Into his headset.*)   I know the ladies' toilet is backed up, I told the company they had to share. Get an intern to mop it up, that's what they went to NYU for. (*Answering his cell phone, low.*) Gordon Light. Hey, mom, we're at a lull in tech, what's up? (*To the others.*) My mother asking for comps. (*Back into phone.*) *The Orestia*, it's a Greek tragedy, not a single laugh. You sure you want to see it? You don't have to . . . No, no word yet about next season but Shirley's looking very tense. It's pretty hard to put on a play when you don't have any money. Scott told us not to ask her anything about it. We're all walking on tiptoes. You may have your only son living at home again. That was a joke! In her bio, the new member of the company called it *Who's Afraid of Virginia Woolf*, not Edward Albee's *Who's Afraid of Virginia Woolf?* Somehow he got wind of it and we had to print all new Playbills. (*At something off.*) Gotta go. I'll comp you two for the Aeschylus . . . .He wrote the play you said you wanted to see! (*He hangs up.*) Chekhov, right? You guys are doing a Chekhov. I can tell from the samovar. We've done the entire canon twice, including the one acts and monologues. I wonder if his mother asked him for comps.

Gordon goes.

NINA   I'm done in here, Boris. What next?

BORIS   The foyer could use a going over. And then there's the dressing rooms. Thank you, little mother.

NINA   I hate that expression. I'm nobody's little mother. I'm an ill–paid cleaning woman.

BORIS   You get to see all our plays for free.

NINA   I'd rather have food on my table. The theatre is a luxury people like me can ill afford and even if we could, we'd spend our rubles elsewhere. Theatre's make-believe is strictly for Countess Mishkin.

ALEXANDRA   I've been recognized. So much for being incognito!

NINA   Everyone knows who you are. You ride in a gold carriage. You give more money to the arts in a month than I will see in a lifetime. I despise people like you.

BORIS   How dare you speak to the Countess Mishkin like that?

ALEXANDRA   It's all right, monsieur. The rich have always been misunderstood. The French Revolution was nothing but a grave misunderstanding that could have been avoided if more people had seen Beaumarchais's *The Marriage of Figaro*. The compassion for the lower classes in that play is breathtaking. Unlike the French aristocracy, I know what songs are being sung in the cafés, I read the popular press, I feel the winds of change.

Kenny Tobias enters with a wooden case of unopened Coca-Cola bottles.

KENNY TOBIAS   There's a pink and white Ford Fairlane two-door that's about to be towed by the Miami police.

MAYA   We were followed here, Yuri!

YURI   There's no law against putting on plays.

BORIS   I'll talk to them.

Alexandra, Maya, Yuri and Boris go.

NINA   People say they welcome revolution until they realize the revolution—if it's a true one—will sweep them away, too, along with everyone else. She'll change her tune when they put her in front of a firing squad.

KENNY   Are you in the next show?

NINA   Do I look like an actor? Maybe she is.

Phoebe/Lydia Burbage/Mme Frontain/ Alexandra Mishkin now SHIRLEY CHANNING steps forward.

SHIRLEY CHANNING   This year's executive director's mid-season report is going to be short and to the point. We are on the ropes. Despite generally excellent notices we did not meet projections. We've made all the cuts we can without completely undermining our artistic credibility. I am pledged to doing Shakespeare and Chekhov on a dime but not a nickel. I've let six actors go, effective now. I don't know what we're going to do without them. Certainly not a production of the caliber of our uncut *Man and Superman*. Scott and I are working with our set designer on coming up with a unit set for next season . . . if there is a next season. There is a strong possibility we will be forced to cancel it entirely. It is very hard to say those words, my wonderful board, but it would be irresponsible of me if I didn't put all my cards on the table. I'm considering a company sabbatical, a year with no productions so we can rent our space. It's an option. I am asking the remaining company members for salary cuts. It won't be easy. Some of them have given this company their lives. To meet the crisis halfway, I am recommending we cancel *King Lear*. I have already declined any salary until we're back on our feet. Don't thank me, thank Mr. Channing. I married a generous man. Could I be excused . . . ?

She exits.

Hector/James Burbage/Chevalier Burton/Boris Yeletsky, John Pick now ARCHIE KELLY enters and begins mopping the stage.

COCONUT GROVE PLAYHOUSE, 1956. IT IS JUST AFTER THE LAST PERFOR-MANCE OF WAITING FOR GODOT.

Pallas/Cuthbert Burbage/Christophe Durant/Pavel Leshmenev now KENNY TOBIAS enters with cases of unsold Cokes.

KENNY   One curtain call tonight and there was barely enough applause for that. You'd think they'd show a little sympathy for the actors at least. It was their last performance. The house manager says he's never seen so many people leave at intermission. They sure didn't buy any Cokes on their way out. What a disaster.

ARCHIE   Next week, *East Lynne*.

KENNY   I thought Tallulah Bankhead was next week in *A Streetcar Named Desire*.

ARCHIE   It's a theatrical expression, before your time.

KENNY   All that hard work so somebody can write, "You'll have more fun at the dentist than waiting for Godot. Even Bert Lahr can't save this turkey. P.S. Mr. Beckett's Godot is a No Show."

ARCHIE   An audience doesn't want to look at men all night. If they did, they'd go to a baseball game. Put some girls in it, call it *Waiting for Gidget* and you got half a chance.

KENNY   I have my own theory. The audience couldn't wrap their heads around the concept of Godot, so they got tired waiting for him. The way I see it, a play has got to be more than a concept. It's got to be a play first.

ARCHIE   That's what I'm saying.

KENNY   Then a play can be anything it wants, even a concept.

ARCHIE   Exactly. You're an interesting kid.

KENNY   I'm going to be a playwright.

ARCHIE   So that's your story.

KENNY   I'm a drama major at the University of Miami.

ARCHIE   You've had a lousy season.

KENNY   You mean our *House of Bernarda Alba*?

ARCHIE   I mean your football team.

Candace Delbo enters with a stack of unused programs.

CANDACE DELBO   Anybody want a program? There's a ton more of these in the house manager's office.

KENNY   Let me give you a hand with those.

CANDACE   At one point, I thought they were going to start throwing them at the stage. Are Coconut Grove audiences always so hostile to anything new?

KENNY   I got a lot of "My ten-year old could write a better play" than this.

CANDACE   I got a lot of "My five-year old could."

CANDACE   Are you gonna wait for me?

KENNY   Sure.

She goes to change out of her usher's uniform.

ARCHIE   A little offstage romance?

KENNY   Not really. More like a ride.

ARCHIE   You're blushing.

Dimitris/Richard Burbage/Jean-Louis Danton/Yuri Goldovsky now SCOTT HARRINGTON steps forward.

SCOTT HARRINGTON   Hello. For those of you who have been living under a rock for our past eight seasons, I'm Scott Harrington, company artistic director. Welcome. Great to see so many familiar faces. How are you enjoying our 49th consecutive season? We want to hear from you. Our subscribers are very important to us. So are our sponsors. Tonight's performance is underwritten by the Geraldine Stutz Foundation and the City Department of Cultural Affairs. Are your cell phones off? Your sentencing will be severe: an entire season of your least favorite playwrights. You know who they are. I have a few more announcements. (*He looks at his notes.*) Actually, no. (*He makes an obvious transition in his tone and manner.*) A lot of you were looking forward to our last show of the season, *King Lear.* So were we, especially our Lear, company veteran and everybody's favorite, John Pick. Well, we've had to cancel it. A play like *Lear* is a little beyond our reach in the current fiscal climate. Not our reach. As the artistic director I would never say that. Nothing has ever been beyond this company's *reach.* Our mean*s*, rather. A great play needs great resources. In *Lear's* place we will be presenting Samuel Beckett's *Happy Days.* It's a terrific play and a two–hander. The current crisis caught us short. We didn't see it coming. We were too busy making art. I don't think we *wanted* to see it coming. Anyway, you must be as tired of these speeches as I am. As my 9–year old would say, "It sucks, daddy." Enjoy the *Orestia.* Curtain up! I keep forgetting, we don't have a curtain. (*He exits.*)

ARCHIE   Why not a little romance? You're both young; you're both stagestruck.

KENNY   I'm not stagestruck, I'm a playwright. (*Candace returns.*) Archie thinks we're an item.

ARCHIE   I said you were both stagestruck.

CANDACE   It's not the same thing.

ARCHIE   I hope you two have a good union. I sure do.

KENNY   Playwrights have their own union: a fellowship all the way from Aeschylus to Miller.

CANDACE   I'm hoping to join Actor's Equity. Once I've joined Equity, everything's going to be so much easier.

ARCHIE   What's your name?

CANDACE   Candace, Candace Delbo. I'll be the only one with it, so I don't have to change it.

KENNY   Kenny. Kenny Tobias.

ARCHIE   I'll be looking for it.

KENNY   Kenneth Tobias for the marquee, I thought, actually.

CANDACE   Good rewrite. Candace Delbo in a new play by Kenneth Tobias.

Phoebe/Lydia Burbage/Mme Frontain/ Alexandra Mishkin/Shirley Channing now LUCINE GERSHWIN enters.

LUCINE GERSHWIN   I want to talk to someone.

KENNY   We're trying to close up, ma'am.

LUCINE   I need to talk to someone.

CANDACE   If it's about a refund—

LUCINE   I don't want a refund. I want the last two hours of my life back. I stayed for the second act—one of the few who did. I have nothing against new plays except that they're not very good. It would be a rash soul who would measure tonight's offering against *The Bacchae*. The minute I saw that set tonight—one wispy tree—I thought "You're in for it, Lucine." And then two men stood around waiting for someone who never came for two acts until someone merciful decided it was over and the lights came up. That's when I said, "That's it, Lucine, no more suffering in silence. Somebody's got to speak up for the audience. It might as well be you." God knows we need the arts in this godforsaken warm peninsula. Our hearts have grown arid. Our souls are parched. I'm talking about great theatre. I mean Ibsen, Chekhov, Shakespeare, the Greeks. We need plays that shake their fist at God and dare us to climb the heights of human existence with them. Is that asking too much at $3.50 a ticket—up a dollar from last season, need I point out?

CANDACE   At first, no one liked or understood Chekhov. His plays were ahead of their time.

LUCINE   This playwright is no Anton Chekhov.

KENNY   No, he's Samuel Beckett. We need new plays. Classics aren't the answer.

LUCINE   In the meantime, give me Prometheus bound to a rock, his punishment for giving man the gift of fire, his liver devoured by an eagle.

ARCHIE   Another box office sensation.

CANDACE   I wonder how many worthy plays vanish without a trace after a failure like this?

KENNY   The sad thing is we'll never know.

Dimitris/Richard Burbage/Jean-Louis Danton/Yuri Goldovsky/ Scott Harrington now PETER DUGGAN enters. He has his makeup kit packed to go.

PETER DUGGAN   Please, no autographs, I'm too depressed.

LUCINE   I don't remember you in the show.

PETER   I was the understudy who never went on.

LUCINE   For which part?

PETER   All of them. They were on a very tight budget. Can you imagine me going on for Bert Lahr? (*He does his best Bert Lahr imitation.*) I spent three weeks learning lines for a play that will never be performed again.

CANDACE   You don't know that.

PETER   Yes, I do. Understudies know everything.

CANDACE   What's it like, being in a play that no one likes?

PETER   It's wonderful, there's nothing like it.

CANDACE   I'm sorry, that was very insensitive of me.

PETER   I should join a resident acting company and get out of this rat race. Instead, I wanted to be on Broadway.

CANDACE   Every actor wants to be on Broadway.

KENNY   Anyone who says they don't is lying through their teeth.

LUCINE   There's a lot of crap on Broadway, pardon my French.

CANDACE   There's a lot of crap everywhere.

Helena/Anne Tedesco-Boyle/Gretna Burbage/Mlle Picard/Nina Kozlovsky now MILDRED LAHR enters.

MILDRED LAHR   It's going to be another late night, Archie. Mr. Lahr is in no hurry. It could be midnight. He took this one hard. (*To Kenny.*) I'll take one of those Cokes with rum. It might lighten my mood.

KENNY   No rum and they're twenty-five cents.

MILDRED   After all we've been through with this train wreck, you begrudge an old chorus girl a complimentary cocktail? Screw you, too, junior, and I don't mean that affectionately.

ARCHIE   It's on me, Mrs. Lahr.

MILDRED   Thank you, Archie. "And don't be stingy, baby."

KENNY   That's from *Anna Christie.*

MILDRED   What are you? A subscriber? You look like a subscriber.

LUCINE   Lifetime theatregoer.

MILDRED   God bless you anyway.

KENNY   I was hoping for Mr. Lahr's autograph.

MILDRED   It's going to be a long wait.

KENNY   I don't mind.

MILDRED   Longer then waiting for you know who.

KENNY   He never came.

MILDRED   My point exactly. I never understood why people want autographs, Archie. A signature on a check, I get—but an actor's autograph?

KENNY   It's not for me.

MILDRED   That's what you all say. Who the hell is it for then? Liberace? Here, I'll sign for him. I do it all the time. What did they expect—promoting this show as "the laugh riot of two continents"? This continent isn't one of them. (*She hands Kenny his signed program.*) Here you go.

KENNY   "Follow the Yellow Brick Road." Thank you.

MILDRED   We were ducks in a barrel after that. "Sensation at the Grove: Sensational Flop." C. Martin! The son of a bitch was afraid to use his full name.

LUCINE   C. Martin is a woman. Cassandra Martin.

MILDRED   Women are reviewing plays now? Oh brother.

CANDACE   Women are writing plays now, too.

MILDRED   Women can't write plays and men aren't much better at it. (*To Archie who has brought her a drink.*) Thanks, Archie. It's a dying profession.

ARCHIE   What does Mr. Lahr think went wrong?

MILDRED   Bert blames himself. He always does. He never thinks he's good enough. He thinks a good play is always better than the actors who perform it. But I say it's the script. When a genius like Bert Lahr can't make a play work, look no further than to the rear of the house. That's where the playwright hangs out, pacing, wearing holes in the carpet, blaming the actors, never himself, for the disaster unfolding in front of him. Playwrights are miserable sons of bitches.

PETER   It's been a privilege working with your husband, Mrs. Lahr.

MILDRED   Who the hell are you?

PETER   Peter, Peter Duggan. Mr. Lahr's understudy.

MILDRED   One of the lucky ones: you never had to go on.

CANDACE   We're studying to be in the theatre.

MILDRED   Just what the world needs: two more perfectly healthy unemployed human beings.

KENNY   I'm going to write plays. Candace is going to be an actress.

MILDRED   Save your parents the money. They can feed a starving child in China. Theatre is a sinking ship and the lifeboats are full.

KENNY   I'll remember the encouragement when I take my bow on opening night of my first play.

MILDRED   My husband thought he'd found a great play with a great part for himself. He wanted to show the world there was more to Bert Lahr than the Cowardly Lion. The man I love's heart has been broken for the last time. I say to hell with Coconut Grove and to hell with the Coconut Grove Playhouse. (*Impatiently calling off.*) Bert? You can't stay in there forever. The next Best Play Tony Award winner wants your autograph. (*She goes.*)

LUCINE   Somewhere out there is a young person who will write the great American play and I think it will be because someone kept the light on for Ibsen and Chekhov.

She starts to go.

ARCHIE   I'll go with you. There was a mugging in the parking lot last week.

LUCINE   That's very kind. They need better lights out there.

ARCHIE   No one wants to underwrite a parking lot.

LUCINE   Maybe if they named it for them they would?

Archie goes with Lucine.

CANDACE   Kenny? You coming? I have an early rehearsal tomorrow.

KENNY   You go on. I've still got stuff to do.

CANDACE   I can wait a few minutes.

KENNY   It's okay.

CANDACE   All right.

She goes.

KENNY   I'm sorry you didn't get to go on.

PETER   Me, too. I think I would have been good. This whole experience has been sad and brutal and I'm proud to have been a part of it.

KENNY   I watched you the whole run, standing at the back of the house, silently saying your lines along with the actors.

PETER   Were you spying on me?

KENNY   I ran the concessions stand.

PETER   You were very noisy.

KENNY   I was trying to watch the play *and* set up for intermission.

PETER   Talk about casting real pearls before genuine swine.

KENNY   A lot of people said they thought the play was interesting.

PETER   That must have sold a lot of tickets.

KENNY   I thought it was funny but I didn't always know why I was laughing. That bothered me at first but then I just laughed.

PETER   I know, me, too; it was weird.

KENNY   It was also sad. He never came.

PETER   Of course he never came. I think that's the whole point.

KENNY   Who do you think Godot was?

PETER   You won't laugh?

KENNY   Of course not. (*Peter whispers in Kenny's ear.*) Wow.

PETER   What do you think?

KENNY   Yours is better.

PETER   Do you want to have a drink with me?

KENNY   Um, sure.

PETER   I don't feel like being on my own tonight.

KENNY   I don't need a reason.

PETER   What about your girlfriend?

KENNY   She's not my girlfriend.

PETER   I'm Peter.

KENNY   I know. I'm Kenny, Kenny Tobias.

PETER   I know.

KENNY   You know?

PETER   I asked someone.

KENNY   Oh.

PETER   So what kind of plays do you write, Kenny Tobias?

KENNY   I don't know. I haven't written one yet.

PETER   Just be sure there's a part for me.

Danae enters.

DANAE   Ssshhh! If I can hear you back here, so can the audience. I shouldn't have to remind you about the perfect acoustics in this theatre.

KENNY   Sorry! I hate pushy ushers. Do you know her?

PETER   Never saw her before in my life.

They go as Hector enters.

DANAE   Is that Agamemnon's mask?

HECTOR   When I'm done, it will be Agamemnon himself.

DANAE   May I hold it?

HECTOR   No.

DANAE   I won't put it on.

HECTOR   No.

DANAE   One day, when you're not looking, Hector, I'll put them all on! Ajax, Heracles, Helen of Troy.

HECTOR   Don't let me catch you.

DANAE   They're just masks.

HECTOR   They're all an actor has. He can't be anyone but himself without one.

Danton enters, dragging his sword. He is not the same man we have seen before. He is an actor who has just seen his career end.

DANTON   I knew I was taking a chance on a new play by a young hothead.

HECTOR   Are you all right, citizen?

DANTON   I was booed tonight.

HECTOR   Booed?

DANTON   Booed.

HECTOR   What's a boo?

DANTON   Boo!

HECTOR   Oh, a boo.

DANTON   What are you, an echo?

DANAE   May I hold that?

Danton lets Danae take his blade.

HECTOR   You'll have to excuse her. She's just discovered the joys of your theatre. Greek tragedy seems old hat to her.

Danae is an amazing and skillful mimic. She has mastered Danton's style and movements as if to the manner born.)

DANAE   Die, villain! Die unmasked!

HECTOR   You see what you've started?

DANTON   It was at the end of the third act. I had fallen to my knees after a magnificent soliloquy—a heartfelt cry for justice. (*He falls to his knees.*) "*Liberté! Égalité! Fraternité!* I don't think an audience knows the pain an actor is in when he is kneeling.

HECTOR   You're right, they don't, but go on.

DANTON   There was a profound silence. I dared not breathe even. And then it began: a boo here, a boo there, here a boo, there a boo, everywhere a boo boo.

HECTOR   We never boo our actors.

DANAE   We revere them, ever since Thespis.

DANTON   Thespis? Who is that?

DANAE   The first actor.

HECTOR   He was the first of you to step forward from out of the chorus and speak in the voice of a character. Before him, theatre was only choral speaking.

DANTON   That wouldn't have appealed to me.

DANAE   Hector saw him once.

HECTOR   He was magnificent. Every word was crystal clear and as loud in the last row as in the first.

DANAE   His body movements told the audience everything his character was feeling.

DANTON   The critic for *Paris Matin* said the same thing about me.

HECTOR Each member of the audience felt he was speaking to them personally.

DANTON I've always strived for that kind of intimacy.

HECTOR People stopped eating.

DANTON People ate during a performance?

HECTOR Ate and drank. They're long plays.

DANAE No one ate when Thespis took the stage.

DANTON Did he win the prize?

HECTOR Not that day.

DANTON Some show-off with half his range did, I wager. The show-off always takes the palm. I believe in simplicity. Less is more, less is more, less is more.

HECTOR No, for all his magnificence, Thespis never won the prize.

DANTON He's in very good company. Angela Lansbury never won an Emmy Award. (*They listen to the play off a while.*) I don't think I know this play.

Phoebe has entered with a drink of something cool for Danton.

HECTOR It's the mother of them all. The fall of the House of Atreus. One forbidden act changed everything.

DANTON You mean like the Garden of Eden.

PHOEBE *The Orestia* is about all mankind, not just Agamemnon and his unlucky brood. A poet speaks the truth, which means he speaks to all men for all time.

HECTOR Ours do. We've been very lucky.

PHOEBE As a child, I thought a poet—a man with the power to write something that could change lives—such a man would be more like a god than a mortal. And then Hector's grandfather introduced me to one. What I saw was an old man with terrible scars whose hands trembled and bad breath kept me at a distance. I couldn't believe he had written this play. He told me that Dionysus himself told him to write plays. He was sleeping under a fig tree when Dionysus appeared to him in a blaze of lightning. "Aeschylus of Eleusis, I command you to write plays. Put aside your arms (he was a soldier, you see) and write plays to tame the savageness of men and make gentle the life of this world."

HECTOR   And he did. And people came. After a while they came in such great numbers they needed a special place to accommodate them.

RICHARD   You mean theatres?

HECTOR   And then actors and food sellers and mask makers and wardrobe keepers and judges and prizes and—

PHOEBE   We ruined it. We're human. We ruin everything.

Nina enters.

NINA   Are you the actor Danton, comrade?

DANTON   I still answer proudly to that name.

NINA   They're calling places for the fourth act.

DANTON (*To Hector.*)   Thank you, friends. Your words have given me courage. I will show the audience that Jean-Louis Danton is afraid of nothing, least of all their disapproval. (*He takes his sword back from Danae.*) For God, for France, for Thespis!

He rushes off. Danae wants to follow him.

DANAE   Please.

HECTOR   Be careful.

Danae rushes off after Danton.

Durant has entered in much agitation.

DURANT   No, no, no and once again, no!

HECTOR   There's a performance in progress.

DURANT   I will not make changes in my text because they offend His Majesty. Censorship offends *my* majesty, the sovereign state of playwriting.

HECTOR   The text of a play is sacred.

DURANT   Tell that to that Bourbon imbecile in his royal box with his penis dangling from his britches.

HECTOR   You're going to stand firm, of course.

DURANT   You insult me, monsieur, I am an artist.

HECTOR   Good! Then we will support you.

NINA   Courage, comrade, courage.

DURANT   Actually, there are a few lines that could go.

HECTOR   If they stifle you, even one word, it's all over, and they've won.

The Globe cannon booms.

DURANT (*To Nina.*)   But it's better they hear my voice even slightly lowered than they don't hear me at all, don't you think, mademoiselle?

NINA   No! When Pavel throws his bomb at the Tsar's coach tonight Comrade Romanov will hear him loud and clear.

The Globe cannon booms again. Richard Burbage enters. May Burbage enters with him.

RICHARD   That damn cannon! There's a mob outside demanding to see a play.

HECTOR   *The Orestia?*

RICHARD   Any play. They don't care, they're in a frenzy. They will not be denied.

MAY   The Globe cannot afford to disappoint them.

DURANT   You can do mine on one condition. You won't change a word of it.

RICHARD   You insult me, sir, I am an Englishman.

DURANT   She's perfect for it. Are you a quick study?

MAY   The quickest.

DURANT   I'll be right back with it. It's called *L'Oeuf, The Egg.* Which comes first: art or revolution?

Durant rushes off.

NINA   Our play is very modern, no aristocrats, just ordinary Russians struggling with day-to-day life. There's never been anything like it. Much better than theirs. Don't move!

Nina rushes off.

HECTOR   Everyone thinks he can write a play!

RICHARD   My father is writing a play. I can't wait until he realizes how hard it is.

HECTOR   "I know, I think I'll write a play today."

RICHARD   "I think I'll carve a mask."

HECTOR   "I think I'll take my own appendix out."

RICHARD   "I think I'll defeat the Spanish Armada." (*They laugh together. They understand each other.*)

Pavel enters. He is bleeding.

PAVEL   Have they come with my money yet?

PHOEBE   Look at you, my God!

PAVEL   I'm all right.

MAY   You're bleeding. He's bleeding.

PAVEL   We were protesting outside the Ministry of Justice when a policeman gave the order to knock a few heads.

PHOEBE   Setting upon poor innocent, unarmed children!

PAVEL   We're not children, little mother. Nor am I so innocent. (*He produces a small revolver.*) I am only poor—but not in spirit or in courage.

MAY (*Aside.*)   "I am poor but not in spirit or in courage." I love this young man.

PHOEBE   Here, drink this, all the way from Athens.

PAVEL   They'll beat me if I'm not paid for my deliveries.

PHOEBE   You've been beaten quite enough for one day. I'll take that for you.

Pavel eagerly drinks from the bowl Phoebe has offered him as she takes the small revolver away from him.

MAY   I'll bandage your head.

MLLE PICARD   I'll do it.

*May is in love with Pavel. Mlle Picard wants to sleep with him. With a
dramatic gesture, she tears a strip from her skirt to bandage Pavel with.*

MAY (*Looking rapturously at Pavel.*)   "O brave new world" indeed!

RICHARD   You're beginning to sound like you know what you're
talking about, which is half the secret of acting.

HECTOR   She doesn't hear you. We've lost her, Burbage.

MAY   I love you, Pavel.

Pavel is just as much in love with May as she is in love with him.)

PAVEL   I love you, too, comrade. I'm going to kill the Tsar this
evening.

May's eyes never leave Pavel.

MLLE PICARD   I can't bandage you if you don't stay still.

PAVEL   Yes, little mother.

*He sighs and lets Mlle Picard bandage his head while he looks all moony-eyed
at May. Phoebe joins Hector and Richard. She is fingering Pavel's small firearm.*

PHOEBE   Do you know what this is?

PAVEL   Be careful with that.

PHOEBE   What do you do with it?

RICHARD   Kill someone.

PHOEBE   Really?

RICHARD   In a play, no; in a dark London alley, yes.

HECTOR   So it's a prop!

RICHARD   In a play, yes; in a dark London alley, no.

PAVEL   In the play they're rehearsing, when Constantine Gavrilovich's
gun goes off, everyone jumps at the sound. It's a big surprise. In the first
version, everyone knew he had a gun; there was no surprise. It's much
better this way. It was the director's idea.

HECTOR   You used a strange word: director.

PAVEL   That's the man who tells the actors where to go.

RICHARD   I'd tell him where to go soon enough.

MLLE PICARD   If an actress needs a director, there's something wrong with her.

HECTOR   This nice boy just up and kills himself? That's how your play ends?

PAVEL   There's a curtain line. "Get Arkadina out of here. Her son has just killed himself."

PHOEBE   Greek boys don't kill themselves. The gods tell us when it's our time to die, it's not up to us. (*She has been fiddling with Pavel's revolver. It goes off.*) Oh, I see.

PAVEL   Point and pull, little mother.

PHOEBE   Point and pull. (*She fires again.*)

HECTOR   May I see that?

RICHARD   Careful with it.

PAVEL   It's all right, in a play they don't use real bullets. (*Hector fires. This time the bullet does some visible damage: a vase shatters, for example.*) I forgot, that's my gun. Sorry.

RICHARD   My turn, Hector. (*Richard fires at random.*) What's that? (*He points up.*)

HECTOR   That's an eagle, the bird most sacred to Zeus. (*Richard fires again. The eagle falls to their feet.*)

PHOEBE   Is it a real eagle or a prop?

HECTOR   It was a live eagle until he killed it.

RICHARD   And now it's a prop.

HECTOR   Now you've done it. The gods will demand retribution for your wanton cruelty.

RICHARD   Your gods are superstitions our plays have made superfluous by giving them a human face. Who you call Aphrodite, we call Cleopatra; Orestes, Hamlet. Old man, forget about your gods and celebrate man in all his glory.

PAVEL   May I have my derringer back? (*Richard gives Pavel his firearm back.*) Thank you. I can't start the revolution without it.

PHOEBE (*To Hector.*) Dimitris will be wanting his mask.

HECTOR It all comes down to our work.

PHOEBE It's all we have. Birth, work, death.

RICHARD (*As he picks up the dead eagle.*) Bird, prop, symbol.

The three of them go.

MLLE PICARD Are you hungry for some champagne and *côq au vin*, my young hero? And after, the sweet delights of love.

PAVEL Don't you hear the sounds of the coming storm?

MAY I hear them, Pavel.

MLLE PICARD We're all so busy at the theatre, the world could be coming to an end and I wouldn't know it.

PAVEL Your world is coming to an end.

MLLE PICARD They've been saying that since Marivaux.

PAVEL You and your plays are the very last gasp of it.

MLLE PICARD What you dismiss so recklessly is centuries of progress towards an aesthetic ideal that you with your basketful of pierogis can never imagine. For a few minutes you were a handsome young man who needed tenderness. As I wound your bandages, I was your mother, I was your lover. I see now the anarchist you've become.

PAVEL No, the anarchist I always was.

MLLE PICARD Bandage yourself.

Mlle Picard goes. Pavel goes to May.

PAVEL The world will be bathed in the light of justice and brotherhood. Every man and woman will be reborn in an eternity of love and laughter and bellies that are always and forever full.

MAY How I have longed for a savior who would say such things to me.

PAVEL You are the beloved I have waited for.

Pavel and May kiss passionately. Berton enters.

BERTON You're on, little seamstress.

MAY I'm nobody's little seamstress.

BERTON   Nevertheless, you're on.

MAY   I don't understand.

BERTON   Madame Frontain was standing in the wings, when a rogue bullet pierced her right wrist. She cannot act without that wrist. It is her fanning wrist. I turned to her understudy, Mademoiselle Picard, but the same bullet had pierced her left wrist. It's up to you or we're done for.

MAY   It's a tempting proposal.

BERTON   It's now or never, Mademoiselle.

PAVEL   I thought you loved me.

MAY   I do but all my life I have waited for this moment! To be an actor! I'm ready, Monsieur Berton!

BERTON   Come, glory awaits you.

MAY   I'm sorry, Pavel.

Berton and May leave.

PAVEL   There's no point in living now. When she hears the gun go off, it will be too late. If someone doesn't stop me by the count of three, it's farewell, life. One, two, three.

Danton enters.

DANTON   You there, boy, with the pistol at your head, you can have my coach brought round after the performance. Listen to them, they're delirious!

He rushes off.

PAVEL   How have people like that been allowed to live so long? (*Pavel takes his gun and puts the barrel of it in his mouth. Mildred enters.*) One, two, three—

MILDRED   Give me that. (*She puts the gun in her bag.*) I found another one almost as crazy as you, Bert. Now come out before I drag you out. (*She goes.*)

PAVEL   There are other ways to kill oneself.

He takes off his belt and begins to wrap it around his neck. Mlle Picard enters. Her arm is in a sling.

MLLE PICARD   Who is this May Burbage? Understudies don't have understudies. Just like that, this English nobody appears out of nowhere ready to go on, fanning herself with my fan.

She goes.

PAVEL   Didn't she see me trying to strangle myself with my own belt?

Gretna enters. She is nursing a baby.

GRETNA   I am married into a theatre family and I am invisible to them. They talk theatre, think theatre, sleep theatre. They shit theatre. I had a baby, it wasn't enough for them. Now we're *both* invisible.

Gretna goes.

PAVEL   That woman looked very familiar.

Helena enters.

HELENA   Have you seen Hector the maskmaker? Our Agamemnon is in a rage about his mask not being ready. Hector! Hector Kalagoropoulos!

She goes.

PAVEL   I'm in a crazy house.

Nina enters.

NINA   Oof! I'm exhausted. I hope you have a cigarette, comrade.

PAVEL   I don't smoke, comrade.

NINA   You're no fun, comrade.

PAVEL   These are awful people. There's no other word for them.

NINA   I'm crazy about them.

PAVEL   Me too.

NINA   You're a theatre person.

PAVEL   I'm not a theatre person.

NINA   You are now. It brushes off on you like lint and sticks like cat hair.

PAVEL   I'm not a theatre person.

NINA   All you anarchists say that.

Boris, Yuri, Alexandra and May enter.)

BORIS   It's a bad omen, the playwright and director being late for the first reading.

MAYA   They should have left before the demonstrations.

ALEXANDRA   I was almost late myself.

PAVEL   Have you got my money, comrade?

BORIS   Comrade? Aren't you putting the cart before the horse, young man? It's still Monsieur Yeletsky to you.

PAVEL   When are you going to wake up, old man?

ALEXANDRA   Where is my playwright? I cannot start my revolution without him.

YURI   You're more of an idealist than the boy is.

ALEXANDRA   Change will come through the arts, not in the streets with ruffians at the barricades. Throwing stones at officers of the law is a futile and finally irrelevant gesture.

PAVEL   Then so was bloodying my head.

ALEXANDRA   They brought my son home wounded by a terrorist. His crime? Riding in a carriage with our crest. He died in my arms. What did his murder accomplish? Nothing. What did his assassin's execution accomplish? Even less. But the dancing of Pavlova and Karsavina at the Imperial Ballet is already a part of a new order. At the Bolshoi we finally have Russian opera because Russian composers are writing Russian music. Only the drama has lagged behind. It's theatre's turn to lead the way.

From off there is the sound of an enormous explosion. The theatre should shake.

BORIS   My God, they're attacking my theatre.

MAYA   The revolution loves the arts.

ALEXANDRA   If a single theatre is damaged, I will move to Paris. Not one stone of the Comédie-Française was harmed in 1789.

BORIS   The windows from the Green Room overlook Peter's Square. We can assess the situation.

Boris, Alexandra, Nina and Maya rush out of the room.

YURI   I think we're beyond calling it "the situation." It's the end of one world, the beginning of a better one.

PAVEL   You hide your progressive tendencies well, comrade.

YURI   I put them in my work, comrade. I'm Yuri.

PAVEL   Pavel. What will happen to you when all the changes come? Think there'll be a place for you in the new order?

YURI   I'm certain of it. Things change, people don't. I'll be there. I was always there, I always will be. You know we've met before, don't you, Pallas?

PAVEL   You feel it, too, Dimitris?

YURI   I'm certain of it, Pallas. And after this, whatever happens, we'll meet again.

PAVEL   Coconut Grove, Florida.

YURI   You made that up, there's no such place.

PAVEL   It's in the United States. My uncle Lev lives there. I'm going to visit him one day. I know you. I have always known you. We are people of the theatre.

YURI   Creatures, rather, beasts.

PAVEL   There's a connection between us, comrade.

He leans in to kiss him. Yuri gently resists.

YURI   I'm sorry.

PAVEL   No, I'm sorry.

YURI   If I . . .

PAVEL   It's all right.

YURI   I just felt this . . . but not . . . I'm sorry if I . . .

PAVEL   I told you: Coconut Grove.

YURI   There's no such place. (*He suddenly stops and holds on to something for support.*)

PAVEL   What is it?

YURI   Something is happening to me. I'm scared.

PAVEL   Lean on me.

Pavel becomes KENNY. He is taking care of Yuri, who has become PETER and is dying.

KENNY   I spoke to your parents.

PETER   Did you tell them everything?

KENNY   I didn't want to alarm them.

PETER   They should be alarmed. I'm dying.

KENNY   You're not dying, Peter. You're sick . . .

PETER   I'm very sick.

KENNY   You're very sick, but you're not dying.

PETER   There are some things you don't know, Kenneth Tobias.

KENNY   Stop. You know I don't like it when you call me by my full name.

PETER   I'm too young for this. I mean, I haven't played Hamlet yet or Constantine or anything by Molière. I haven't done Shaw or Ibsen or O'Neill, even. You don't become an actor not to do them. They were why.

KENNY   You were a wonderful Tom in *The Glass Menagerie.*

PETER   Everyone is wonderful in that part. If they're not, they should get out of the business.

KENNY   And I know you don't agree but you were pretty damn wonderful in my play.

PETER   No offense but it was no *King Lear.*

KENNY   Nothing is *King Lear.*

PETER   It wasn't even close.

KENNY   Agreed, but you don't have to rub it in.

PETER   You'll do better after I'm gone.

KENNY   What's wrong with you today?

PETER   You'll start writing for yourself and not just a good part for your lover.

KENNY   I'm not going to feel like writing much of anything.

PETER   Now who's talking stupid.

KENNY   You'll be back on tour before you know it.

PETER   If whatever's wrong with me doesn't kill me, that goddamn play I'm in will. It's terrible, it's a piece of crap.

KENNY   Fortunately, the audiences don't think so.

PETER   In my obituary I want you to list the playwright's name as principal cause of death.

KENNY   Now that's funny.

PETER   The only great play I was ever in, everyone thought it was terrible. Now everyone thinks it's his masterpiece. I was the understudy, I knew all the parts, but I never got to go on. Why am I telling you all this?

KENNY   Why don't you get some rest?

PETER   Now I can't think of a single line from it.

KENNY   I remember quite a few: "I can't go on. I will go on."

PETER   You're paraphrasing. I hate that.

KENNY   I hate it, too.

PETER   Our play was a smash by comparison. We ran a whole month.

KENNY   That's the first time you ever said "our" play.

PETER   I would still be waiting for Bert Lahr's autograph if you hadn't asked me for a drink.

KENNY   You asked me.

PETER   Are you sure?

KENNY   Positive. And I was the one waiting for his autograph. You think autographs are stupid.

PETER   They are.

KENNY   That time I asked you to get Jason Robards's for me!

PETER   I was being a prick.

KENNY   You're not a prick.

PETER   Then what am I?

KENNY   You're someone who doesn't like autographs.

PETER   Maybe I was angry nobody wanted mine.

May enters.

MAY   Are we receiving or are we being misanthropic?

PETER   We're sleeping.

KENNY   Be nice. You have a visitor, all the way from London.

MAY   Peter was the best scene partner I ever had—and you name it, I acted with it. All I had to do was look into his eyes eight shows a week.

KENNY   I know, May.

MAY   I was in love with him.

KENNY   I know, May.

MAY   I was very jealous.

KENNY   I know, May.

MAY   He was a great actor.

PETER   Can we get off this particular merry-go-round and stop talking about me in the third person past tense? Thank you.

MAY   Then stop pretending you're asleep. Thank *you.*

KENNY   I'll leave you two alone.

PETER & MAY   Don't!

PETER   How are things at the Globe?

MAY   We keep burning down then rising up from the flames.

PETER   Good for you, good for you.

MAY   We should change our name to The Phoenix.

PETER   How long have I known you?

MAY   Does it matter?

PETER   Forever, I think.

Mildred enters.

MILDRED   MGM wants to remake *The Wizard of Oz*. Over my dead body!

KENNY   Thank you for coming.

MILDRED   I brought you a signed photograph of Bert, guaranteed genuine this time. Unfortunately it's signed to someone else.

PETER   Thank you.

MILDRED   You could at least look at it.

PETER   I don't have to. "Follow the yellow brick road."

KENNY   Actually, I was the one who wanted Mr. Lahr's autograph. Peter agrees with you about their ridiculousness.

MILDRED   So did my husband.

MAY   What does it say?

KENNY   "For Comrade Lev Ulanov. What the hell are people like us and Sam Beckett doing in Coconut Grove?"

PETER   It's a good question.

KENNY   "Glad you liked the show. That makes two of us." He was wrong, Mrs. Lahr. There were at least four of us.

Phoebe enters.

PHOEBE   Hello? I'm not too late? I brought my very special brew, all the way from Athens. (*To May.*) How is he?

PETER   I'm fine, Phoebe.

KENNY   Is Hector with you?

PHOEBE   He's making another mask, what else? (*To Peter.*) Here, I brought you something. I'm always bringing him something. It will calm you.

PETER   I don't need calming.

PHOEBE   Everyone needs calming. Take this. He's burning up.

PETER   Kenny knows that, Phoebe.

PHOEBE   You're burning up.

MILDRED   I'll cool him.

Mildred fans Peter with the feather she used as Mlle Picard while the others watch.

MAY   That's from *The Way of the World*.

MILDRED (*Correcting her.*)   No, *Tartuffe*.

PETER   I took it along with my snuff box. I took lots of props.

PHOEBE   It must be twenty past the hour—the angel of silence is passing.

MILDRED (*Working the fan over Peter.*)   Her wings are beating very, very slowly. Is that better?

PETER   Yes. Thank you.

PHOEBE   "Make gentle the life of this world."

MAY   "That has such people in it."

KENNY   May? Phoebe? Sssshhh.

MAY   Is he going?

PETER   He's gone.

Peter becomes DIMITRIS. The others do not move from where they were.

DIMITRIS   I hear my cue and I'm not ready. Damn you, Hector.

Hector appears. He holds the completed mask.

HECTOR   Dimitris.

Dimitris goes to Hector and takes the mask from him.

DIMITRIS   I can be Agamemnon now.

HECTOR   That's why it had to be perfect.

DIMITRIS   It's beautiful.

HECTOR   Your boots, don't forget your boots.

DIMITRIS   I put them on last. I don't like towering over everyone else unless it's onstage. (*He goes.*)

HECTOR   My work is done. (*He goes.*)

PHOEBE   Would you like to be alone with him?

KENNY   Please.

The others go. Kenny sits staring at the empty place where Peter was.

KENNY   You were right about that scene in the play—the scene everyone jumped on—but I'm glad I didn't change it. Sometimes you have to stand by what you say, no matter what. You taught me that.

Dimitris enters. He is wearing the mask of Agamemnon and the tall boots (cothurni) *that are a feature of Greek tragedy. He towers above the stage. Kenny looks up at him, expectantly.*

DIMITRIS   It's too hot for *The Orestia*. I feel sorry for the audience.

KENNY   Have a great show.

Dimitris makes his stately, majestic entrance onto the stage of the Theatre of Dionysus. Hector returns as Archie. He turns on a ghost light.

ARCHIE   Unless you want to be the only one left in the theatre?

KENNY   I'm coming, Mr. Kelly.

ARCHIE   You're not afraid of ghosts?

KENNY   Not your kind.

ARCHIE   Lock the door when you go. (*He goes.*)

THE PRESENT. BACKSTAGE. A THEATRE COMPANY IS GATHERED IN THE WINGS.

Scott Harrington, Gordon Light, Hazel May and John Pick are getting ready to give a performance of The Orestia. *John Pick is wearing a long, one-piece tunic for the chorus. Hazel is costumed for the Watchman.*

JOHN   Exactly 42 years ago I began on this same stage in your part. And now I'm saying goodbye as a member of the chorus. In between there's been Aegisthus, Orestes and Agamemnon.

GORDON LIGHT   Of course the part he really wanted to play was Klytemnestra.

JOHN   I don't think a man has had a crack at her since the Theatre of Dionysus in the fifth century BC.

HAZEL   Good!

JOHN   It's not fair.

GORDON LIGHT   Fifteen minutes. We're at fifteen minutes. The last performance does not mean self-indulgence. I'll be timing you.

HAZEL   They didn't teach us about nights like this at school!

SCOTT HARRINGTON   This is it, John, old buddy. Forty-nine years wasn't such a bad run. I would have preferred fifty. Why are you laughing?

JOHN   I'm remembering the review of my Falstaff. "Mr. Pick takes an unusual approach to Shakespeare's iconic clown: he isn't funny."

SCOTT   He missed the whole point of my production. Of course he's not funny: Falstaff is the Devil.

JOHN   Now you tell me. Do you know what's next for you?

HAZEL   A Lizard in Edward Albee's *Seascape*. I hope he doesn't find out.

SCOTT   I'm directing *The Gin Game* in Austin.

GORDON   That's in Texas.

SCOTT   I know. Don't make a face.

GORDON   Need a good stage manager?

SCOTT   I always do.

JOHN   I will never have the pleasure of being Lear to your Cordelia, young lady.

SCOTT   You don't know that, John.

JOHN   Yes, I do. It's time.

HAZEL   Gordon, get a picture of me with John, the newest company member and the oldest. (*GORDON takes pictures of them with his iPhone.*) Send it to me, Gordon.

GORDON   I will, Hazel.

HAZEL   That's what you always say.

SCOTT   What we had was something very special: a safe place for some of the greatest plays ever written—and maybe some that maybe weren't so great.

JOHN   The *commedia dell'arte* season.

SCOTT   Don't look at me.

HAZEL   I love *commedia dell'arte*.

JOHN   If that didn't sink us, I didn't think anything could.

GORDON   I love what we do. Damn the torpedoes, full speed ahead. Five minutes, we are at five minutes!

Shirley Channing enters with Anne Tedesco-Boyle in tow.

SHIRLEY   And this is backstage.

MRS. TEDESCO-BOYLE   Oh!

SHIRLEY   And this is our company, some of it. John Pick, our oldest member, and our newest, Hazel May, who's playing the Watchman.

HAZEL   But I'm playing him Gender Neutral.

MRS. TEDESCO-BOYLE   Good for you.

SHIRLEY   This is Anne Tedesco-Boyle from our board.

MRS. TEDESCO-BOYLE   I want everyone to call me Annie.

GORDON   Okay, that's it, places! We are at places!

SHIRLEY   Wait, Gordon, I have an announcement.

GORDON   We're at places, Shirley.

SHIRLEY   Scott has an announcement.

SCOTT   What are you talking about?

SHIRLEY   Next season.

SCOTT   There isn't going to be one.

SHIRLEY   Yes, there is. (*They all stop and look at her.*) Thanks to Mrs. Tedesco-Boyle. (*She hands Scott a check.*)

MRS. TEDESCO-BOYLE   It's "Annie," everyone, please!

Gasps, cheers, applause as the reality of what is happening becomes apparent to one and all.

GORDON   Ssssh! The house is open, the audience will hear you. Voices down. (*He gives up trying to silence them.*) Fuck the audience. (*His voice on the public address.*) Tonight's performance of *The Orestia* will begin in a few moments. (*He joins in the spontaneous celebration.*)

GORDON   Places! Night Watchman! Chorus to the wings!

HAZEL   Thank you.

JOHN   Thank you.

SCOTT   Yes, thank you.

JOHN   I've loved being an actor. It's all I ever wanted to do.

He goes to the stage, hand in hand with Hazel.

SHIRLEY (*To Mrs. Tedesco-Boyle.*)   I put you next to Warren Wilson. He's rich as Rockefeller, he loves us but we're in danger of losing him to the Philharmonic.

MRS. TEDESCO-BOYLE   I'll give him a hand job.

SHIRLEY   Mrs. Tedsesco-Boyle!

MRS. TEDESCO-BOYLE   Call me Annie, I said!

They go.

Scott has put his face in his hands.

GORDON   What's the matter?

SCOTT (*Shaking his head in his hands.*)   Nothing. Everything.

GORDON   There's going to be a next season, sir.

SCOTT   Yes.

GORDON   That should make you happy, sir.

SCOTT   I wanted to be in theatre so no one would ever call me sir, Gordon. That's a terrible name for someone your age. I re-baptize you: Ariel.

GORDON   Ariel, I like that, sir: Ariel.

SCOTT   Now get the curtain up. That's right, we don't have a curtain. And away we go. (*He goes.*)

GORDON   House to half, go. House out, go. Cue music, go. Lights up, go.

The stage is bare. Archie's ghost light grows brighter and brighter until it shatters.

The stage lights snap off just as the house lights come up. There should be no slow fade.

END OF PLAY

MOTHERS AND SONS (2013)

My best friend is a screenwriter, a wonderful one. His name is Don Roos. His best-known film, which he also directed, is probably *The Opposite of Sex*. It's a beautifully observed and written film about looking for love in all the wrong places.

No one had seen anything like it before. Don's voice is entirely his own. There *is* such a thing as a "Screenplay by Don Roos." It doesn't sound like anyone else's screenplay, though people try to emulate it. This is the crux of what I want to convey to a young writer who asks for my advice. "We have plays by David Mamet. Don't spin your wheels trying to write another one. Tell us who *you* are."

Alas, the innate human desire to please (and maybe to repeat someone else's success) can make lemmings of us all, even people who would call themselves artists when they are behaving like rug merchants and it's anything for a sale.

An argument can be made that theatre sold it's soul to the devil when it started charging admission. What had begun as a free, communal experience became an elitist experience for the few. Commercial theatre depends on success at the box office and is often reluctant to engage in issues that make an audience uncomfortable. A lot of playwrights can play this game and some of them are very good at it. An artist, however, challenges the tried and the true, avoids the familiar, and asks the questions no one else will. Commercial producers are necessarily wary. No wonder the O'Neills, the Williamses, the Millers and the Albees are few and far between. Wilde's dictum has become a challenge instead of common sense.

Maybe some of this explains why Don doesn't even especially like the theatre, which he describes as "people sitting around talking." Like many younger people (I am seventeen years his senior), Don would describe himself as a "movie" person. I like the movies, too, but I don't dream in them.

When I first met Don in Los Angeles, I was working on a television project for Norman Lear that CBS would pass on before Norman and I hit the parking lot, just minutes after we delivered it. It was the quickest response I've ever had to anything I've written.

As a screenwriter, Don was used to such cursory treatment. He was a gun for hire. A playwright is the sole proprietor of his or her work. There was no doubt in my mind which writer had the advantage. There was none in Don's either. It was a friendly draw. Don didn't want to write plays; I didn't want to write movies.

In fact, Don told me he'd never *seen* a play, unless you counted *The Sound of Music*. To this day, I'm not sure if he was kidding. I seized the advantage. *The Lisbon Traviata* was in production at the Mark Taper Forum at the Los Angeles Music Center. I think he felt trapped when I invited him to see it.

Nathan Lane and Richard Thomas were having a great success in the West Coast premiere of my play. Don was rightly impressed by their performances and said all the right things to each of us. But it was still people sitting around talking. It's a definition of theatre that's pretty hard to argue with. I hadn't changed his *idea* of theatre and what it could accomplish. Theatre is the oldest way we have of trying to tell the truth about who we are. We can compete with anything. We have the English language. We have our own voice. He would argue that humanity now has something better: modern technology to tell our stories. He likened being a playwright to being the village blacksmith in the age of the automobile.

Nevertheless, our friendship has deepened over the years and Don has seen most of my plays and even enjoyed quite a few of them. That's not the point. I have come to realize that theatre is like everything else in life, it's not for everyone. I wish I would stop banging my head against the wall when I meet someone like Don. They're not stagestruck and never will be. They grew up watching television and movies. I grew up dreaming of the next time the lights would go down, red velvet curtains would part and something magical, something realer than real, would happen all over again but as if for the very first time.

A movie is always the same; only our response to it changes. Plays change with every performance, sometimes for the worse, but just as often for the better. Movies don't do that. They can't. "There goes my performance," Michelle Pfeiffer said ruefully as she watched the cans of exposed film being taken from the *Frankie and Johnny* set to the processing lab. "I'm at the mercy of the film editor." Stage actors own their performances, every moment of them. They are at no one's mercy but their own. A Writers Guild screenwriter envies a Dramatists Guild playwright's complete autonomy when it comes to the script. No one can make a playwright change a word of his or her text. A playwright owns a play lock, stock and barrel. Screenwriters are routinely fired from their own films but then screenwriters are paid for what they write, even if the film is never made.

Playwrights, on the other hand, go for broke. For us, it's all or nothing. We write on speculation and in hope of a production. In return, we work on a contract that is the envy of everyone in the creative arts. I retain full copyright of what I have written. A screenplay is the property of the studio it was written for. My play is mine, not the producer's. But since we're not a union, we can work for free. When my play is struggling to stay open, I am asked to waive any royalty claims. I have helped subsidize more of my productions that way than I care to remember.

It's a trade-off, I'm always telling Don: artistic freedom but uncertain financial returns on the initial investment. That's why we should write every play as if it were our last one. When we first met and I told him I was a playwright, he confessed his first thought was "Shit, he's going to want to borrow money."

Maybe *Mothers and Sons* is my last play. I don't think so but at 76 there is always that possibility. I have lived hard, played the same and worked all the while. I've been ecstatically partnered, now married, since 2001 to Tom Kirdahy, a wonderful, wonderful man, and a very good lawyer turned very good producer. I'm a lung cancer survivor since six months after I met him. When I told him on one of our first dates they'd found a malignant tumor on my right lung (both lungs as it turned out after they'd opened me up), he said he'd "be there for me if I'd like." I told him I thought I'd like that very much. He chose not to run but gave *me* the option whether he should stay.

Much of our courtship happened at Memorial Sloane Kettering Cancer Center. He met some of my best friends, like Don Roos, in my hospital room. Given the circumstances, our romance cut to the chase. We were both too old to play games with one another. And when cancer is involved, time is not something you squander.

Like me, our dog, a heartbreaker of a fourteen-year old female Yorkshire Terrier named Terry, is getting older, too. To say our empathetic bond is strong is putting it mildly. Tom had just gotten Terry when I met him. He insists I tell people this, lest they think I named a dog for myself. He's right, they do. I'm setting the record straight for once and for all.

I always tell people that a life in the theatre is its own reward. It's not about celebrity or rewards. It's about doing something that can matter. It's about making yourself heard. Everything else is the cherry on the icing on the cake.

Every play of mine is who I am. I am everywhere in them but you will never find me there. That's because I am every contradictory, inconsistent thing about them: the good, the bad, the indecent, the boring, the trivial, the hopeful, the nihilistic, the contented, the demented, the unassuming, the control freak, the 8-year old demanding "Mommy, look at me," the 76-year-old man wondering if his third act is going to be as interesting as the first two were. I will always be all of them.

I'm sorry the three-act play has fallen so far out of favor. Shakespeare gave us the Seven Ages of Man; the Classic French theatre whittled that down to five acts, then four, then three. Still, there was a beginning, a middle and an end. We had time to tell our stories.

Suddenly, the two-act play became the norm. No one asked me. No one asked anyone I know. Life doesn't conveniently fold in half like that. Some stories do but not fully-lived-out lives. I coped (*Master Class*) but returned to the three-act structure whenever I could (*Lips Together, Teeth Apart; Love! Valour! Compassion!*).

The one-act, no-intermission play is the recent development in the New York theatre. Ticket takers tell me the question they are asked most is whether or not there is an intermission. They say the relief is palpable when the ticket holders are told there is none. I don't know why that is. I wish I did. I wish I knew a lot of things about theatre but I'm usually so engrossed in a first-draft or rehearsals that there's never the opportunity to look for the big picture. Maybe there isn't one. Maybe theatre, like God, is in the details and if I knew everything I wouldn't be writing plays, since writing is the only way I have of knowing who I really am and trying to answer all the questions I still have about this art form that so effortlessly drew me to it more than half a century ago. As long as I'm still making theatre, it seems untoward to theorize about it.

Mothers and Sons is my first one-act since the beginning of my career at a time when one-acts were very popular, mainly because of the extraordinary success of the double-bill of Samuel Beckett's *Krapp's Last Tape* and Albee's *The Zoo Story*. Audiences couldn't get enough of the "new" playwrights in the '60s and '70s and evenings of one-act plays by different playwrights were a popular way to find out who we were. *Morning, Noon and Night* by, respectively, Israel Horowitz, myself and Leonard Melfi even made it to Broadway.

I didn't know *Mothers and Sons* would be in one-act when I sat down to write it. A playwright instinctively feels a natural break in the action. I soon realized there was none here. *Mothers and Sons* is a play about a woman taking her coat off. That's how I tracked in Katharine's behavior: when would she allow Cal to take her coat? The dialogue all flowed from that central situation: a self-defended, angry woman from Dallas in her mink coat in a probably overheated New York apartment confronting her dead-from-AIDS son's lover who has moved on with his life while she hasn't. Her coat is her armor. If she takes it off, it means she is going to stay awhile and for Katharine, to stay there and begin to talk and listen is to begin to heal. The tragedy of Katharine Gerard is that she doesn't want to change. She has become comfortable in her agony.

Many of my plays are written for or dedicated to actors. *Lips Together, Teeth Apart* was written for Nathan Lane after we'd worked together on *The Lisbon Traviata*. I wrote *Mothers and Sons* for Tyne Daly after she starred in a revival of *Master Class*. A dedication is my way of saying "Thank you" to an actor for their sometimes profound contribution to my plays. Indeed, I often wonder if *Master Class* would have enjoyed the same success and been a play anyone *wanted* to revive some 20 years later if Zoe Caldwell had not created the role of Maria in the first place.

I want the Marias and the Katharine Gerards to come to know who their ancestors were.

Great actors inspire playwrights. You don't write parts like Hamlet and King Lear if you don't have the actors to play them. The Globe must have been an extraordinary company of actors to write for. Shakespeare had Will Kemp. Chekhov had Olga Knipper. I have Nathan Lane and Zoe Caldwell. Playwrights learn from good actors. Harold Pinter began as one. I can't think of better training for a playwright than standing on a stage as an actor. A good actor lives in the moment. So does a good playwright. While a play can be literature, it is also by necessity a diagram, a blueprint of an actual experience happening in real time. Theatre is a full-body contact sport. It is not created by people living in ivory towers. From the Ancient Greeks to New York City 2015, it never has been.

Bette Davis told us "Old age isn't for sissies." When I was a young, young man I didn't know what she was talking about.

I can tell you now, "Neither is theatre."

But at my next opening I will deny I ever wrote that. I will be a young, young man all over again. I will be hopeful that this time we got it really and truly right. That I have been heard. That what I have done with my life mattered.

As Maria says at the end of *Master Class*, "Well, that's that."

Mothers and Sons

for Tyne Daly

The world premiere of MOTHERS AND SONS was originally produced at the Bucks County Playhouse (Jed Bernstein, Producing Director) in June 2013. It was directed by Sheryl Kaller; the set design was by Wilson Chin; the costume design was by Jess Goldstein; the lighting design was by Travis McHale; and the sound design was by John Gromada. The cast was as follows:

KATHARINE GERARD   Tyne Daly

CAL PORTER   Manoel Felciano

WILL OGDEN   Bobby Steggert

BUD OGDEN-PORTER   Grayson Taylor

MOTHERS AND SONS was presented on Broadway at the John Golden The-atre in New York City, opening on March 24, 2014. It was produced by Tom Kirdahy, Roy Furman, Paula Wagner & Debbie Bisno, Barbara Freitag & Loraine Alterman Boyle, Hunter Arnold, Paul Boskind, Ken Davenport, Lams Productions, Mark Lee & Ed Filipowski, Roberta Pereira/Brunish Trinchero, Sanford Robertson, Tom Smedes & Peter Stern, and Jack Thomas/ Susan Dietz. It was directed by Sheryl Kaller; the set design was by John Lee Beatty; the costume design was by Jess Goldstein; the lighting design was by Jeff Croiter; the sound design was by Nevin Steinberg; and the production stage manager was James Harker. The cast was as follows:

KATHARINE GERARD   Tyne Daly

CAL PORTER   Frederick Weller

WILL OGDEN   Bobby Steggert

BUD OGDEN-PORTER   Grayson Taylor

CHARACTERS

KATHARINE GERARD
Andre Gerard's mother.

CAL PORTER
Andre's lover.

WILL OGDEN
Cal's husband.

BUD OGDEN-PORTER
6 years old.

THE TIME

The present. A blustery and very cold winter's day. The shortest day of the year. It will be dark soon. The change from pale winter light coming through the apartment windows when the play begins to the evolving warmth of the interior as and when the living room lamps are turned on during the play should be marked.

THE SETTING

A desirable apartment on Manhattan's Central Park West with a maximum view of the park. It belongs to Cal and Will.

It is a warm and very livable space. It is tended with care but well-used. Evidence of a child: a bicycle or a skateboard maybe.

Doors and hallways lead off to bedrooms, a kitchen and bathrooms.

It is important it doesn't look "decorated" but someone at *Architectural Digest* would love to get their hands on it. The possibilities are boundless; they just haven't been realized yet.

KATHARINE and CAL are taking in the view of the park below them. She still has her coat on.

CAL   That's the reservoir . . . see? People jog around it, even in this weather, *crazy* people! I should know: I'm one of them. Christmas Day, hurricanes, monsoons, we're out there. Will thinks we're all insane. He says he watches us through that telescope and laughs and laughs. I can see his point. From up here we look like obsessive insects making our appointed rounds, except that's all they are is *rounds*. We're not going anywhere in the circle of fitness that other people aren't. We all end up in the same place. Will would say that's a metaphor and why he laughs. Will's a writer. Are you sure I can't take your coat, Mrs. Gerard?

KATHARINE   I'm not staying. (*But she doesn't move from her place at the window.*)

CAL   That view is pretty mesmerizing. I still pinch myself at least twice a day. The greatest city in the world and it's right there. I don't have to do anything but look. It's mine for the taking. Andre would have loved this view. As they say about London, the man who would grow tired of this is a man tired of life. Can I get you anything?

KATHARINE   I'm fine, thank you.

CAL   Oh, this will amuse you. Interest you, anyway. Directly across the park from us, there's a legendary apartment house, 1040 Fifth Avenue, just by the museum. See the obelisk? That's Cleopatra's Needle, well, not *really* but it's what they call it. Just beside it, that's the Metropolitan Museum of Art, the Met, the *other* Met. To a Westsider, and you are on the Westside, the Met means the Metropolitan Opera; to an Eastsider it means the Metropolitan Museum. If you don't know this, an out-of-towner can end up looking at a Rembrandt instead of listening to *Turandot*. Anyway, I'm getting all tangled up in Manhattan arcana here: we have a very good view of 1040 Fifth Avenue. That's where Jackie lived. Jackie O. Mrs. Onassis. Mrs. Kennedy.

KATHARINE   I know who you're talking about.

CAL   Andre would have loved having it for a view. He worshipped her.

KATHARINE   Didn't we all?

CAL   Can't you see him waking up every morning and bounding to that window and waving across the park to her, *"Bonjour, Jackie, ça va aujourd'hui?"*? It would have been a ritual. I thought that might amuse you.

KATHARINE   Very little amuses me, Mr. Porter.

CAL   It was an unfortunate word choice, I'm sorry. And please, it's Cal.

KATHARINE   Who lives there now?

CAL   I don't know, rich Republicans, I suspect. Since Mrs. Kennedy died, I don't think anyone knows or cares who lives at 1040 Fifth.

KATHARINE   I'm sure the people who live there do. How long have you had this place?

CAL   It's getting on to nine years.

KATHARINE   The last address I had for you was on Perry Street.

CAL   85, 85 Perry. That was a century ago. It was one room in the basement that had the building's only access to the furnace which was always breaking down. We got quite friendly with the super that first winter. Things got better after Perry Street but not much. We were young, poor, and ready to take this city on. We were ready for anything. Well, we thought we were ready for anything. You're sure you won't take your coat off?

KATHARINE   I'm fine. I'll let you know when I'm not. I just stopped by on the chance you might be here.

CAL   Somebody usually is. As I said, Will's a writer and on weekends we're both sort of homebodies.

KATHARINE   I got the address from your sister.

CAL   Penny? You've kept in touch?

KATHARINE   Not really, Christmas cards. She gave me your unlisted phone number as well, but if you went to the trouble of having an unlisted telephone number, I'm sure it was to avoid calls from people like me.

CAL   No, never, no! I'm very glad to see you. Unlisted numbers are a New York fetish. Everyone has one. The woman who cleans for us, our doorman, the super. One winter night Andre and I had locked ourselves out and we couldn't call anyone who might have a key. None of them had a listed number. We were frozen by the time we got in.

Katherine is still looking down at the park.

KATHARINE   Growing up, I used to daydream about a view like this.

CAL   Where was that?

KATHARINE   Rye.

CAL   Rye, New York?

KATHARINE   It's a small town, more of an enclave really, in Westchester.

CAL   I know Rye. It's next to Port Chester, which is definitely not an enclave. I even know Rye Brook. I dated someone from Rye Brook. He never let me forget it. You know Mrs. Kennedy and I know Rye. Are you sure I can't get you something? In this weather, something to warm you up?

KATHARINE   Before it's too dark, where's the place we . . . ? Where we had the . . . ?

CAL   You mean the memorial?

KATHARINE   Can you see it from here?

CAL   See the little bridge? That's the Bow Bridge and just to the right of it, there's a lovely smallish lawn area—well, a lovely smallish lawn area 9 months of the year but this isn't one of them—It leads down to a duck pond. See it?

KATHARINE   I remember the ducks. They had a lot to say for themselves that day.

CAL   You would have thought it was too cold to quack. It was 12 degrees, the coldest day in years.

KATHARINE   I've never been so cold.

CAL   We all stood there in a circle and spoke.

KATHARINE   I was the only one who didn't.

CAL   I'm sure you weren't.

KATHARINE   It didn't matter. Your friends said everything that could possibly be said. They were very impressive. I didn't know Andre had so many friends and how eloquent they were. Some of them were quite funny.

CAL   We were attracted to people with a sense of humor.

KATHARINE   I personally thought the story about the two of you in the swimming pool in Mexico was a little risqué . . . .at least for my taste it was. Blue humor and funerals are not something I'm accustomed to.

CAL   It wasn't a funeral, Mrs. Gerard.

KATHARINE   You know what I meant. The music at the church had set such a serious and thoughtful tone, almost spiritual, I wasn't prepared for the transition to naked men in a swimming pool filled with gardenias.

CAL   It was pretty funny.

KATHARINE   I guess you had to be there.

CAL   In this case, I'm very glad you weren't.

KATHARINE   I couldn't get that one piece of music out of my head. The one the young woman sang at the church. I even went to a record shop and tried humming it to the clerk. *Nada.* He looked at me like I was crazy.

CAL   You should have asked. It was one of our favorites. It's by Mozart, a little known opera of his, *Il Re Pastore, The Shepherd King, "L'amerò saro costante."* "I will be constant in my love for him." I'll write it down for you. That same young woman is singing at the Met now and quite successfully. Andre always predicted a big future for her. "That, Cal," he would say, "is a star."

KATHARINE   If there are perfect moments, that was one of them. Naturally I was disappointed to see the rest of the service descend to jokes.

CAL   It wasn't a service either, Mrs. Gerard. It was a remembrance of someone we all loved and would miss. We still do.

KATHARINE   Except for the Mozart maybe it was all a little too gay for my taste.

CAL   There was some Shakespeare, too. I read "Fear no more the heat o' the sun" from *Cymbeline*. But except for them and a little Bach and my sister and my father and you and our dentist (our jury was still out on him. It's come in since then: gay as a goose.), I guess it was pretty gay.

KATHARINE   I never understood that expression, gay as a goose.

CAL   Neither did I.

KATHARINE   Is that . . . ?

CAL   What? Where?

KATHARINE   It looks like some sort of amphitheatre.

CAL   It's called the Delacorte Theatre, free Shakespeare in the Park. With the windows open in summer, we can hear them.

KATHARINE   Is that where Andre . . . ?

CAL   Yes. Where he played Horatio, the summer of 80 . . . what? Eight? Nine?

KATHARINE   I didn't come up that summer. His father wasn't well.

CAL   It was the same summer he played Hamlet himself at another outdoor theatre in Washington, D.C. They were almost back-to-back. (*He starts off.*)

KATHARINE   Where are you going?

CAL   The poster's in the hallway, I'll check.

KATHARINE   That's all right, there's no need.

Cal goes.

It gets dark so early this time of year. And so fast. There's no dusk. It goes from day to night before you realize it. There's no transition.

Cal returns with a large, framed poster.

I was just saying, I almost missed this wonderful view of the park.

CAL   I'm glad you didn't. (*Reading from the poster.*) "1989, August 7 through September 3." There is no place on earth hotter than an outdoor theatre in Washington, D.C. in late summer.

KATHARINE   Yes, there is, Dallas, Texas.

Cal turns the poster towards her.

CAL   It's starting to show its age. They didn't print this on the best stock.

Visibly affected, Katherine turns away from the image on the poster.

I'm sorry.

KATHARINE   You might have warned me.

CAL   You want to sit down?

KATHARINE   That's not necessary.

CAL   I think you should.

KATHARINE   Thank you.

Cal leads her to a place to sit.

CAL   I should have realized.

KATHARINE   What were you thinking?

CAL   I wasn't, I wasn't thinking.

KATHARINE   We were talking and then all of a sudden, just like that, there he was.

CAL   I'm sorry. I'm sorry.

KATHARINE   It's all right.

CAL   I'd forgotten how much I love this poster. Pictures in a hallway don't really get looked at that often—everyone's on their way somewhere else. They're sort of non-places that way. There was a time it made me happy every time I looked at it. Of course there was a time it made me very sad as well. I used to think maybe you should have it but I never got around to sending it. I was being selfish. It captures so much about him. His passion, for sure, his vitality. He was a very urgent person.

KATHARINE   Yes. Yes, he was.

CAL   There was no stopping him. He's still the best Hamlet I've ever seen. We were both sorry you missed it.

KATHARINE   All right, I'm ready now.

CAL   You sure?

KATHARINE   We'll see.

CAL   We don't have to do this.

KATHARINE   I know. (*Cal turns the poster to where they both can see it.*) It's him all right.

CAL   It was taken when Hamlet is crying "Vengeance!"—it was his favorite moment in the play. "Vengeance!" Sword in hand. The photographer caught him in full Andre splendor. Talk about eyes that blaze. He's not too hard to look at either. I believe the expression is "one handsome devil." Our boy asked me once "Is that a old-time pirate?" I said "No, honey, that was a wonderful Hamlet on his way to becoming a great one," which was more information than any four-year-old needs or cares for.

KATHARINE   Your boy?

CAL   We have a son. My sister didn't tell you? That's okay, she didn't tell me you'd been in touch all these years either. I don't think he's looked at it once ever since. When we first met, I thought Will might have a problem with it but he's fine.

KATHARINE   Will?

CAL   My husband.

KATHARINE   Of course, you told me that.

CAL   Our son is 6, his name is Bud. That's his real name, it isn't a nickname for anything. I always loved Bud for a boy. Now it's got a little gravitas: it's on his birth certificate: Bud Ogden-Porter.

KATHARINE   Ogden-Porter?

CAL   My husband's last name is Ogden. Will Ogden.

KATHARINE   How easily you say that word, husband.

CAL   Not always. The first couple of times I tried to use it, nothing came out. I'd say, "This is my h-hu-hus . . . ." "Your *who*?" "My hu-hu-hu-." I'd gotten so used to "boyfriend" or "partner" all those years when marriage wasn't even a thought, let alone a possibility, that it took me a while to realize we'd won and that our relationship was as legitimate as everyone else's. Andre would have said it was internalized homophobia.

KATHARINE   I'll pretend I know what that means.

CAL   It means you've become so accustomed to being unloved because of who you are that you've become adept at not loving yourself because of who you are.

KATHARINE   I'll still pretend.

CAL   Andre and I were what people called boyfriends then. Or partners. Lovers was another word people used. We didn't like any of them. Boyfriends sounded like teenagers, partners sounded like a law firm and lovers sounded illicit. They all seemed insubstantial, inadequate. Then along came the new- but-old-and-obvious name for it. It'd been there all along: husband. Who would have thought! I've come to like husband. I actually sort of love it. Spouse still makes me a little queasy. It's too gender neutral and I think sounds either dishonest or somewhat embarrassed about the whole marriage thing. Husband cuts to the chase. "Have you met my husband?" "My husband and I are interested in a season subscription." "The reservations are in my husband's name."

KATHARINE   This has been very informative, Mr. Porter.

CAL   You do understand that husband wasn't a possibility then? Your son called me Cal and I called him Andre.

KATHARINE   I would hope so. It was his name, chosen with great care.

CAL   I might have gotten in a honey or two over the years.

KATHARINE   I don't like nicknames. Andre is a challenge to people who insist on them.

CAL   You succeeded. He was always Andre.

KATHARINE   I did something right then.

CAL   Andre was a wonderful person, Mrs. Gerard, everyone liked him.

KATHARINE   This Mr . . . your . . .

CAL   Ogden, Will Ogden.

KATHARINE   Are you going to tell him our little secret?

CAL   I didn't know we had one.

KATHARINE This visit.

CAL Of course I'll tell him. We don't have secrets.

KATHARINE Everyone has secrets.

CAL We don't.

KATHARINE That's wonderful.

CAL Why would this be a secret in the first place?

KATHARINE I was giving you an option.

CAL An option not needed. We're always off to a bad start.

KATHARINE Will you tell him I'm sorry I missed him?

CAL They're in the park. They'll be here any minute. I'd like you to meet them.

KATHARINE It's getting late.

CAL The days are short, you said so yourself. It's only half-past—

KATHARINE I'm glad you didn't send me the poster.

CAL You are?

KATHARINE Rage and anger are not how a mother wishes to remember her son. I had enough of them without a poster to remind me.

CAL He's playing a part in that picture. It's him but it's not him. It's him as someone else.

KATHARINE We all play parts. Some of them we play so long, so well we become the part. I'm Andre's mother. You won't let me be anyone else. You can't. I can't either. You're Andre's friend, you always will be.

CAL We've gotten very good at playing those parts.

KATHARINE I was still a young woman when Andre died.

CAL I realize that now.

KATHARINE Now?

CAL I'm about the same age you were when Andre died. I was cruel about age then, most young people are. I judged you harshly, too harshly no doubt. We're still not the same age but closer. Closer.

KATHARINE   Thank you for not saying, "You and Mr. Gerard have your golden years ahead." Mr. Gerard passed at Easter.

CAL   I didn't know that.

KATHARINE   You didn't ask and there's no reason you would.

CAL   I'm very sorry to hear it.

KATHARINE   Everyone dies, sooner or later, even 29-year old, perfectly healthy, beautiful young men.

CAL   They shouldn't.

KATHARINE   Maybe I'll find another husband, too, and pick up where I left off and adopt a child and start a new family.

CAL   It was eight years before I met Will, Mrs. Gerard.

KATHARINE   Or maybe I'll just get it over with and jump out the window. I live in the tallest condominium in Dallas. That should do the trick. Thank you for asking, Mr. Porter, but Andre's mother is doing just fine.

CAL   I'm so sorry, Mrs. Gerard, how could I have known? Penny should have told me.

KATHARINE   Penny didn't know. The morning paper said "Mr. Gerard died after a long struggle with illness." I would have said "after perpetual disappointment with life. He is survived by his wife, Katharine, a Yankee humdinger who never fit. A son, Andre, died at age 29 after a short struggle with a pesky summer cough."

CAL   That's what we all thought at first.

KATHARINE   I never felt at home in Texas.

CAL   I don't think Andre did either.

KATHARINE   I don't like gratuitous familiarity. "How y'all doing today, darlin'?" "Y'all hurry back now, sugar, you hear?" I never got accustomed to being addressed as "sugar" by the checkout girl, black or white. Well, that's neither here nor there. How long have you and . . . .?

CAL   Will.

KATHARINE   I'm sorry. Will.

CAL   Will Ogden.

KATHARINE   How long have you and Mr. Ogden been together?

CAL   It will be 11 years this summer.

KATHARINE   You and Andre . . . .?

CAL   We had 6 years together.

KATHARINE   That many?

CAL   I wouldn't call 6 years many—not when you plan to spend the rest of your life with someone. I think you should have the poster, Mrs. Gerard.

KATHARINE   I wouldn't know what to do with it, Mr. Porter. I'm downsizing. My things, my life, everything.

CAL   My dad downsized when his lady friend passed.

KATHARINE   His lady friend?

CAL   My mom passed when we were very little. I never knew her. Our dad raised Penny and me. Then he met someone, a widow. Neither of them saw the point of getting married. It rocked Bethel, New Hampshire. Anything would rock Bethel, New Hampshire. Andre and I sure did the times we visited.

KATHARINE   Your father seemed like a nice man.

CAL   He still is. He's 75 and not going anywhere in the foreseeable future. His father made it to 91. He died tapping maple syrup.

KATHARINE   I thought maple syrup was Vermont.

CAL   Everyone does. Maple syrup doesn't recognize state lines. Ours is better.

KATHARINE   And what about your sister?

CAL   Penny's in SoHo trying to start a family. She and her husband are having difficulties getting her pregnant.

KATHARINE   The Christmas cards didn't mention that.

CAL   He's a Danish architect with a fairly unpronounceable name. Bjorn Bjerkenfjord.

KATHARINE   Isn't anybody *from* New York anymore? In my day, everybody *in* New York was *from* New York. It's become a city of out-of-towners. My mistake was letting Mr. Gerard sweep me off to Texas. He told me there were nice, cultured people there. He was wrong on both counts.

CAL   I like Austin and San Antonio. My work used to take me there.

KATHARINE   I never understood what you did.

CAL   Neither did Andre. I'm a money manager.

KATHARINE   That much I knew.

CAL   Other people's money. I can explain it to you but it's very boring, trust me.

KATHARINE   Thank you, I will.

CAL   When my own brief fling as an actor was all too apparently going to end in perpetual unemployment, I shocked myself and Andre and became a yuppie and surprised both of us how good I was at it. But since Bud I don't travel. That was nonnegotiable. I had a lot of clients on the West Coast.

KATHARINE   You've done well, from the look of things. You've come a long way from Perry Street.

CAL   Will's mother helped us when the building went co-op.

KATHARINE   Very generous of her.

CAL   That was Jean. We never got to pay her back. She died three months later.

KATHARINE   I always told Andre the house in Dallas was his when his father and I were gone. He'd say, "Great! Now can you wrap it up and send it up East?" He could be very sarcastic.

CAL   I know.

KATHARINE   He liked to tell people he went directly from his high school graduation to the Trailways bus station to New York City on his savings, which is ridiculous. He flew to New York on Braniff Airlines, remember Braniff? One of their last flights. And guess who paid for it? Sarcastic and a little uncomfortable with the truth.

CAL   Dramatic exaggeration he called it. It was never for a mean or malicious end.

KATHARINE   We had theatre in Dallas. He was very disdainful of it.

CAL   He could be a terrible snob, too.

KATHARINE   He was barely 18 when he left Texas. That's too young to come to a city like New York.

CAL   As a young gay man he didn't feel comfortable where he was.

KATHARINE   Andre wasn't gay when he came to New York.

CAL   Okay.

KATHARINE   He came to New York to be an actor. That's a beautiful fire.

CAL   It's a gas fireplace. The logs are some sort of ceramic material.

KATHARINE   It's very realistic.

CAL   It doesn't give off much heat.

KATHARINE   I can feel it.

CAL   If you're interested, I can—

KATHARINE   No, thank you.

CAL   I guess air-conditioning is more of a necessity where you are.

KATHARINE   We have our cold spells. We call them Northers, Blue Northers. They sweep down from the Great Plains. Some of them are merciless.

CAL   I wish you'd call me Cal.

KATHARINE   If you like, all right, Cal.

CAL   Thank you—and I'd like to call you Katharine.

KATHARINE   It's my name.

CAL   Well, that's settled.

KATHARINE   It's only taken 20 years. Is it warm in here or . . . .? I really came by just to give it to you.

CAL   Let me take your coat.

KATHARINE   What time is it? I'm supposed to . . . all right, if you insist . . . (*Cal helps her off with her coat and hangs it up.*) Don't let the label

624 MOTHERS AND SONS

fool you. It says Neiman-Marcus but it came from a secondhand fur shop. My husband had a heart attack when he saw it. I had to show him the receipt to prove I hadn't bankrupted him. He was such a Scrooge about money. I hope Andre kept his sense of humor about money. He got it from me.

CAL He always said he was more like you than Mr. Gerard.

KATHARINE He was but he would have been furious if I had told him that. I always thought one of the tragedies of Andre's life was that he and his father were never close.

CAL One of the tragedies?

KATHARINE Maybe he'd still be alive.

CAL I didn't kill Andre, Mrs. Gerard.

KATHARINE I'm not saying that, Mr. Porter.

CAL I didn't give him AIDS.

KATHARINE The way he chose to live his life did.

CAL It wasn't a choice.

KATHARINE Everything is a choice.

CAL I didn't make him gay either.

KATHARINE Someone did. I hate that word. It used to mean something nice, something joyful. A good time was had by all. We lost that battle, too.

CAL I'd say you lost every battle.

KATHARINE But one. I don't have to approve.

CAL I suppose you don't. Excuse me.

KATHARINE Now where are you going? No more surprises.

CAL There's something else you should look at. (*He goes.*)

KATHARINE Were you always this stubborn? You met your match in Andre. He'd get an idea to do something and wouldn't let go of it. Before acting, he was going to be a dancer. We took him to a musical when he was a child, *Pal Joey.* He couldn't possibly have understood what it was about but for the next year he was tapping and jetee-ing all over Dallas. (*Cal returns with a large cardboard box filled with photographs and clippings.*)

CAL   I've had this box of odds and ends for years. We threw everything in here. Photos, notes, clippings.

KATHARINE   Oh God, I'm supposed to go through all that?

CAL   I'm sure there's something you'll want.

KATHARINE   I knew coming here would be a mistake. I'm trying to get rid of things, not add to the heap. New buildings are merciless when it comes to closet space.

The apartment intercom rings.

CAL   Excuse me, we're not expecting anyone.

KATHARINE   You weren't expecting me either. Maybe it's your sister. I liked her the one time we met.

Cal answers the house phone.

CAL   Yes, Lewis, what is it? I've got company. If it's a delivery you can give it to Will when they . . .Will, what's wrong? Again? I'll be right down. (*He hangs up.*) Will left without his keys and the doorman's on a break. I'll be right back.

KATHARINE   I won't steal anything.

Cal leaves the apartment. Katharine opens the box of photographs and begins to look at them.

KATHARINE   Hampton Beach, New Hampshire. It's still there. Of course it's still there, Katharine, it's a beach. Beaches don't go anywhere . . . . . . My God, a man in a bathing suit like that in Dallas would be arrested . . . How beautiful he was! . . . .A woman. How did you get in here, sweetie? . . . Here's another one. Oh my God, it's me. You weren't too bad-looking, Katharine . . . I must have been pregnant with him in this one. Who knew he had these? (*She is still looking at the pictures when Bud bursts into the apartment, still energized from his time in the park. Will and Cal will follow a few moments later.*)

KATHARINE   Hello.

BUD   Who are you?

KATHARINE   I'm Andre's mother. Who are you?

BUD   I'm Bud, I live here. Who's Andre?

KATHARINE   An old friend of your father's.

BUD   Pop-pop?

KATHARINE   Mr. Porter.

BUD   Is he a friend of Pappy, too?

KATHARINE   I don't think so.

BUD   Why not?

WILL   Is Bud giving you the third degree, Mrs. Gerard? I'm sorry, he's very inquisitive. There's never been a question he hasn't asked. Hi, I'm Will, Will Ogden.

BUD   Where is he?

WILL   Who?

BUD   Andre.

CAL   I'm afraid he's passed, honey.

BUD   Passed? What does that mean, passed?

WILL   Andre's dead.

BUD   Well why didn't you say so?

CAL   It's another way of saying it.

BUD   Dead's better.

WILL   Excuse how we look, Mrs. Gerard. Everything's turning into mush. Our hopes for a white Christmas are fading. We may have to settle for a gray slushy one. We can't keep this one off the swings, no matter how cold it is.

CAL   We think he's got some Eskimo in him.

WILL   Bud and I know you mean Inuit, don't we, darling?

BUD   What's Eskimo?

CAL   (*to Katharine*) Sorry, it's a thing between us. (*to Will*) You're right, *mea culpa*, my bad.

WILL   Cal didn't tell us we were going to have company today.

KATHARINE   He didn't know. This is an impromptu visit. I should have called first.

WILL   You're very welcome.

CAL   You want help with your boots, honey?

BUD   That's okay. We saw one of my teachers in the park.

WILL   What brings you to New York?

KATHARINE   Nothing brings me, nothing specific.

WILL   That's all right, you don't need a reason to visit the Big Apple.

KATHARINE   I'm on my way to Europe actually. I'm going to spend Christmas Eve in Rome.

WILL   Are you Catholic?

KATHARINE   No. Do I have to be to spend Christmas Eve in Rome?

WILL   You'll love Rome at Christmas. It's magical. I spent my junior year abroad there. Trastevere is fantastic this time of year. Too many tourists miss it.

KATHARINE   Trastevere?

WILL   That's the neighborhood across the river in Rome. Trastevere. It means across the Tiber. I had an apartment there in a building built in the 14th century. No hot water, no private bath but a view of a 12th century convent. Trastevere, where I was young. Trastevere, where I would have gotten enormously fat if I'd stayed even another month. The best restaurant in the entire world is there. I'll write the name down for you before you go. Cal, you didn't serve Mrs. Gerard anything?

CAL   I offered, several times.

KATHARINE   And I declined several times.

WILL   But this time you'll have a what, Mrs. Gerard? I hope you're not a martini sort of woman because I don't have the slightest idea how to make one.

CAL   I can make one. I think we have gin.

KATHARINE   My martini days are behind me. A Scotch, neat, I wouldn't say no to.

CAL   Dewar's?

KATHARINE   That was Andre's Scotch of choice. What are you gentlemen having?

Cal will make drinks.

WILL   Cal doesn't drink.

CAL   One too many martinis of my own.

WILL   And I never did.

KATHARINE   Well, you're no fun, either one of you. Bud, you want to tie one on with an old woman?

BUD   What's your name?

KATHARINE   Katharine.

BUD   Your grown-up name.

KATHARINE   Mrs. Gerard.

BUD   Where's Mr. Gerard?

KATHARINE   He's passed, too.

BUD   He's dead, too? Like . . . ?

KATHARINE   Like Andre. He died several months ago.

BUD   What happened to him?

KATHARINE   Mr. Gerard had cancer.

BUD   What kind?

KATHARINE   Lung cancer.

BUD   My friend Albert's mother has cancer. She has tubes and talks funny.

CAL   Okay, that's enough, Bud, let Mrs. Gerard enjoy her drink.

KATHARINE   Suddenly I need it. Thank you, Mr. Osgood.

WILL   Ogden. Cheers.

KATHARINE   Cheers.

CAL   Cheers.

BUD   How did your little boy die?

KATHARINE   That's a long, complicated story.

WILL   Bud knows what AIDS is.

BUD   They told us about it at school. When did he die?

CAL   Bud! I'm sorry, Mrs. Gerard.

WILL   Don't apologize for him. He has questions.

KATHARINE   Andre died March 29, 1994.

BUD   That was a long time ago.

KATHARINE   Twenty years. He was 29. How old are you?

BUD   How old are you?

KATHARINE   Older than you.

WILL   Okay, young man, that's enough.

KATHARINE   I don't mind.

BUD   Did he die of AIDS?

KATHARINE   We're not sure.

BUD   At school we saw a documentary about the quilt on World AIDS Day.

KATHARINE   The quilt?

BUD   It has the names of everyone who died from it.

KATHARINE   On a quilt?

CAL   Andre's name is on it.

KATHARINE   His full name?

CAL   It was important to me.

KATHARINE   His first and last names?

CAL   I didn't think I needed your permission.

BUD   I'm sorry your little boy died.

KATHARINE   So am I.

BUD   I'll let you be my grandmother. I don't have one. I have lots of aunts and uncles and godfathers and godmothers but I don't have a grandmother. I have a grandfather in Vermont but he can't hear anything.

CAL   Grandpa's in New Hampshire.

KATHARINE   You don't know me well enough to be your grandmother.

BUD   I didn't know any of them before either. Families just grow. I don't even like some of them.

KATHARINE   You might not like me.

BUD   You're cool, I like you.

KATHARINE   I like you, too.

WILL   I warn you, Mrs. Gerard, he doesn't take no for an answer.

KATHARINE   Excuse me but is there a little girl's room?

CAL   Of course. Right through here. You can't miss it.

   Katharine excuses herself.

WILL   The little girl's room? Did I hear right? Does anyone still say "the little girl's room"?

CAL   We make her nervous.

WILL   She makes you nervous. Eskimo? Where did that come from?

CAL   I didn't think she'd know what Inuit meant.

WILL   She probably doesn't but that's not the point. Who did you tell her Bud and I were? Your roommates?

CAL   Very funny.

WILL   Jesus, Cal, you should've warned us.

CAL   I told you in the elevator: She just stopped by.

WILL   People live in New York so other people don't just stop by. They move here just so people don't stop by.

CAL   What was I going to do? Tell her she couldn't come up?

WILL   We have plans tonight, family plans.

CAL   That's not going to change.

WILL   All these years you've told me what a monster she was. You built her up into this Gorgon of mythological proportions and now she just drops by?

CAL   I assumed we'd never see each other again. I even wondered if she were still alive. She's the last person in the world I expected to show up on our doorstep.

WILL   What do you want me to do?

CAL   She just lost her husband. Try to be nice to her.

WILL   I can promise civil but not nice. She wouldn't even take my hand when I put it out.

BUD   Are you fighting?

WILL   No. We're expressing strong dismay at an unforeseen turn of events.

BUD   What does that mean?

CAL   We didn't know Mrs. Gerard was coming by, honey.

BUD   I like her, she's nice.

CAL   She's very nice.

WILL   Mrs. Gerard's son and Pop-pop used to live together.

BUD   The way you and Pop-pop live together?

WILL   They weren't married.

CAL   We didn't have a wonderful son like you.

BUD   Why not?

CAL   People didn't do that then.

WILL   They couldn't.

BUD   Why not?

WILL   The world wasn't ready for the three of us. We were waiting for you.

CAL   And we're very glad we did.

BUD   Okay. Are we still going to trim the tree tonight?

WILL   Absolutely. After dinner, we'll put our pajamas on and make that tree amazing together. You're in charge of icicles.

CAL   What are we having tonight?

WILL   *Spaghetti al vongole.*

BUD   Yay!!!!

CAL   How else to celebrate the holidays but with your *spaghetti al vongole?*

WILL   What is she doing in there?

CAL   It hasn't been that long.

WILL   She's going through the medicine cabinet.

CAL   Don't be ridiculous.

WILL   Of course she is. It's human nature.

BUD   What's human nature? (*Bud is going through the box of photos.*)

WILL   How people are, whether they can help it or not. Your human nature is that you're going to take a bath. Pop-pop's is that he's nice to everyone, even people who disapprove of him. And mine is that I'm naïve enough to think I might finally have heard the last of Andre.

CAL   This isn't about Andre.

WILL   I think I've dealt with a man I never met pretty goddamn well.

CAL   You have. From the very beginning.

WILL   I wasn't going to compete with a ghost.

CAL   You didn't have to.

WILL   But I didn't sign on for his mother.

CAL   What was I supposed to do?

WILL   Not let her into our space.

BUD   You're fighting.

CAL   No, we're not. That's not for you, Buster.

WILL   I know Andre was a wonderful man and that he was everything you wanted.

CAL   Yes, he was. And then I met you. Do you know how much I adore you?

WILL   Yes, but she's not staying for dinner.

CAL   Did you get a haircut?

WILL   About a week ago, don't change the subject.

CAL   I'm glad we're married. Are you?

WILL   Over the moon. The divorce is going to be spectacular.

CAL   That's not even remotely funny. I can't imagine what my life would be without you.

WILL   Me either. (*Katharine has come out of the bathroom.*)

KATHARINE   I love the wallpaper in there. Very bold. Who's the decorator?

WILL   Cal.

CAL   Will.

KATHARINE   I'm terrible at decorating.

WILL   Come on, junior, let's get you into the tub.

BUD   Will you be here when I come back?

KATHARINE   Probably not.

BUD   Goodbye.

KATHARINE   Goodbye.

WILL   It was nice meeting you, Mrs. Gerard. Say hello to Rome for me. (*Will leaves the room with Bud.*)

KATHARINE   He forgot my restaurant.

CAL   I'll get it to you.

KATHARINE   That's all right. Idle promises, if we had a dime for every one of them we make . . . !

CAL   I'll be sure he does.

KATHARINE   Your little boy is a very self-possessed young man. Intelligent, too, I daresay.

CAL   We're very lucky. He has his terrorist side, of course. It's not all fun and games. Somebody should have told us. They did, of course, but we aren't good listeners when we really want to do something.

KATHARINE   Is he a good father?

CAL   Bud couldn't ask for a better one. It comes a little more naturally to Will than me. I think it's generational. I never expected to be a father. He never expected not to be one. He made it clear very early in the relationship he wanted a family. I almost bolted.

KATHARINE   Why didn't you?

CAL   I was afraid he'd leave me. Either way, I was scared. Now, to imagine my life without them . . . ! I don't think I knew who I fully was until our son was born. I'm so much *more* than I thought I was. More generous, more interesting, more resourceful, (I can do things I didn't know I could), maybe even more less-self-centered—or maybe I'm just more self-delusional and haven't changed at all.

KATHARINE   Children aren't the answer.

CAL   This child is. Did you find anything you'd like?

KATHARINE   I haven't really looked. (*She starts to examine the contents of the box. She holds up a yellowed press clipping.*)

CAL   That's the first review he ever got. It's not very good. I don't know why he saved it.

KATHARINE   I sent it to him.

CAL   Why?

KATHARINE   I was proud of him. I didn't care what some critic thought.

CAL   That's us in Paris.

KATHARINE   American men shouldn't wear berets. It makes them look desperate.

CAL   Desperate?

KATHARINE   To be something they're not.

CAL   What would that be?

KATHARINE   French.

CAL   We grew out of our beret phase pretty quickly. They made their last appearance one Halloween when we went as Jean-Paul Sartre and Simone de Beauvoir.

KATHARINE   Interesting choice.

CAL   Too interesting. Our friends thought we were Yves Montand and Simone Signoret.

KATHARINE   Who went as Sartre?

CAL   Andre. I was Simone.

KATHARINE   I don't suppose there's a picture?

CAL   I don't know. They're all mixed up. He would just toss them in there. I told him he needed an album, a scrapbook.

KATHARINE   If I see something I like, don't tell me you're an Indian giver and will want it back. Was that politically incorrect? Indian giver?

CAL   Yes, but your secret is safe with me—just as I hope my Eskimo is safe with you.

KATHARINE   I don't understand.

CAL   I should have said Inuit but I didn't think you'd know what that meant.

KATHARINE   Living in Texas has not made me a complete Neanderthal.

CAL   Will was right to call me on it, especially in front of Bud. We've set standards for him, which means absolutely nothing unless you maintain them 24/7. I still slip on words like madam chairman. It comes so naturally to his generation. I have to work at it. I expect you do, too.

KATHARINE   Where was this one taken?

CAL   Nantucket.

KATHARINE   That's very la-ti-da.

CAL   Parts of Nantucket maybe, but definitely not that one. We rented an apartment behind a dry cleaners for two weeks.

KATHARINE   If you were raised in Port Chester, New York, all of Nantucket is extremely la–ti–da.

CAL   I thought you were from Rye.

KATHARINE   They're cheek-by-jowl. They're really interchangeable.

CAL   Andre said you told everyone in Texas you were from Rye, New York.

KATHARINE   Until just now I thought that was our little secret.

CAL   He thought it was funny. He'd say, "As if people in Texas know the difference between Port Chester and Rye, Cal!"

KATHARINE   I did. You do.

CAL   I'm sorry.

KATHARINE   I'm glad it amused you. I wonder how many of our secrets he shared with you.

CAL   I'm sure that was the only one. He was never disrespectful of you.

KATHARINE   I suppose I should be grateful for small blessings.

CAL   Even when you didn't come.

KATHARINE   Who are these people?

CAL   That's some of Will's family.

KATHARINE   There's a lot of them.

CAL   I've lost count of how many uncles and aunts and nephews and nieces and first and second cousins he has. There's hardly a month without a graduation or recital or a contribution to the Tooth Fairy. Sometimes I see the rest of my life measured by Ogden gatherings. I always wanted a big family—it was just me and my sister growing up—but I figured it wasn't meant to be. And then all at once I had an enormous one—and before I knew it, Will and I were starting one of our own. Here, I'll take them. I don't know how they got in there.

KATHARINE   We were a small family, too. Too small. I was an only child, my husband was an only child, Andre was an only child. Christmas Eve we would sit around just looking at one another. The presents were open by 10. We'd end up watching midnight mass from St. Patrick's just for something to do.

CAL   So that's why Andre always wanted to turn it on.

KATHARINE   Let me finish, Mr. Porter, please. And then one day the phone rang and it was you telling me Andre was gone. I almost didn't pick up. I think I knew. So now there were just the two of us. And then Mr. Gerard up and died and there was one. I said "up and died." No one "ups and dies." He'd been sick for years. We both knew it was coming. Still, when it does . . .

CAL   Yes.

KATHARINE   Soon enough there will be none. It's the end of the line. There's no more where the Gerards came from. It's very sad when you think about it. You and Mr. Ogden don't have to worry about that.

CAL   That's not why we chose to be a family.

KATHARINE   It's not?

CAL   I told you why.

KATHARINE   Not really. Who's this?

CAL   A friend of Andre's. His name is Jeb. He's an actor, too. They met in summer stock in the Berkshires. Will and I chose to have a family because we wanted to share the happiness we feel as a couple with a child—as well as the good fortune and privilege we enjoy.

KATHARINE   There are lots of unfortunate children out there who would enjoy the advantages of a good home and what you call your privileges and good fortune.

CAL   We didn't want to adopt.

KATHARINE   I'm not criticizing. Was he a . . . .? This Jeb? A lover?

CAL   For a summer. Andre said it was more of a fling than a relationship. It was before me, obviously. They stayed friends. I think you met him at the memorial.

KATHARINE   Then he isn't the one who gave Andre AIDS?

CAL   No.

KATHARINE   Are you sure?

CAL   Yes.

KATHARINE   Who do you think did then?

CAL   I don't know.

KATHARINE   What do you mean, you don't know?

CAL   I don't know!

KATHARINE   Didn't you ask him?

CAL   No. I thought about it. I thought about it quite a lot. I made myself sick thinking about it.

KATHARINE   I would have asked him and he would have told me.

CAL   Did it ever occur to you maybe he didn't know? It could have been any of us. We were all suspect. I had myself tested once a month, just in case.

KATHARINE   In case of what?

CAL   I don't know, just in case. I had to be sure. For me, for Andre.

KATHARINE   I would have found the person who did that to Andre and killed him.

CAL   We didn't do that.

KATHARINE   Maybe you should have.

CAL   I fantasized about it.

KATHARINE   I would have made it my business to.

CAL   I had my suspicions.

KATHARINE   Suspicions?

CAL   That's all they were. No, not even that.

KATHARINE   You never did anything about it?

CAL   I was in enough pain of my own. Andre was dying, I couldn't save him. Everyone was dying. I couldn't save any of them. Nothing could. Something was killing us. Something ugly. Everyone talked about it but no one did anything. What would killing one another have accomplished? There was so much fear and anger in the face of so much death and no one was helping us. There wasn't time to hate. We learned to help each other, help each other in ways we never had before. It was the first time I ever felt a part of something, a community. So thank you for that, I suppose. I wanted to kill the world when Andre was diagnosed, but I took care of him instead. I bathed him, I cleaned him up and told him I loved him even when he was ashamed of what this disease had done to him. He wasn't very beautiful when he died, Mrs. Gerard. Our very own plague took care of that. Andre had slept with someone other than me but I had to forgive him. He was one of the unlucky ones. I'm not saying your son was promiscuous, Mrs. Gerard.

KATHARINE   I'm sure he wasn't.

CAL   But he wasn't faithful either. Monogamous. Of course we'd never taken marriage vows. We weren't allowed to. It wasn't even a possibility. Relationships like mine and Andre's weren't supposed to last. We didn't deserve the dignity of marriage. Maybe that's why AIDS happened. (*Katharine takes up another photograph.*)

KATHARINE   I remember this place as a girl, don't tell me! Our class went on a field trip.

CAL   It's Independence Hall in Philadelphia.

KATHARINE   I asked you not to tell me. Of course it is. The Liberty Bell.

CAL   Actually, Andre put me at risk.

KATHARINE   This young man isn't wearing any clothes.

CAL   I didn't know we'd be doing this.

KATHARINE   I hope I'm not going to find my son in the altogether in here.

CAL   Did you hear what I said?

KATHARINE   Yes. They're all so young. Everyone is so young.

CAL   I'm sorry I told you. I don't think he could help himself.

KATHARINE   I'd like this picture. I always liked Andre in a tie and jacket.

CAL   Which was almost never. We must have been going somewhere fancy.

KATHARINE   Thank you. (*She takes the photo.*)

CAL   Take as many as you want. We're the only two people in the world they mean anything to.

KATHARINE   I like this one, too. I really like it. May I?

CAL   Of course.

KATHARINE   Thank you. (*She takes the second photo and closes the box. WILL comes out of the bathroom and back into the living room.*)

BUD (*off*)   Pop-pop!

WILL   Your turn. He wants you.

CAL   We have company.

BUD (*off*)   Pop-pop!

WILL   Cal's Pop-pop. I'm pappy.

KATHARINE   As in Li'l Abner.

WILL   As in who?

KATHARINE   No one remembers Li'l Abner.

CAL   I do. What's wrong?

WILL   You bought the wrong bubbles.

BUD (*off*)   Pop-pop!

CAL   Excuse me, I'll be right back.

BUD (*off*)   Pop-pop!

CAL   Him and those fucking bubbles. I'm coming, honey! (*He goes.*)

KATHARINE   I'm sorry, but I don't think that's appropriate language when a child might be present.

WILL   What? Honey? Oh, fucking! I couldn't agree more. Our one hard and fast is "not in front of the bambino." "Honey" still turns a few heads when we use it in public: "We need paper towels, honey, Aisle Seven." Of course, they're just words. The sight of two men hand in hand with a child waiting for the light to change on Central Park West rattles an occasional cage. Gay dads still merit more than passing interest even in the metropolis known as Manhattan. Let me refresh your drink.

KATHARINE   I should be getting on.

WILL   Cal will blame me if you're not here when he comes out.

KATHARINE   Have you thought about what you're going to tell the boy when he asks and he is going to ask, you can be sure of it.

WILL   The boy? You mean Bud? Asks what?

KATHARINE   Who he is. Where he came from.

WILL   We're dealing with it, little by little, a day at a time.

KATHARINE   I wonder.

WILL   Wonder what?

KATHARINE   If that's going to be enough.

WILL   We're going to be fine.

KATHARINE   You're very confident.

WILL   So are you.

KATHARINE   How did you two gentlemen meet?

WILL   First of all, thank you for not saying boys.

KATHARINE   Obviously you're not, either one of you.

WILL   I'm serious. "Do you boys have plans for the holidays? Are either of you boys going home for them?" You'd be surprised how often we hear "boys," so thank you.

KATHARINE   Clearly there's an age difference.

WILL   Fifteen years. I was born in—

KATHARINE   You can spare me the math.

WILL   You're prickly.

KATHARINE   Mr. Porter and Andre were the same age.

WILL   I never let Cal forget I'm younger than him. Keeps him on his toes. I'm waiting for the day he comes home with an earring and a tattoo. Should I alert you when I'm bantering?

KATHARINE   You have a beautiful place.

WILL   Thank you, we like it. It could use a makeover but we've decided to let Bud play his havoc with it for a couple of more years before we get serious about redecorating.

KATHARINE   I understand you're a writer. I still don't understand what Mr. Porter does for a living.

WILL   Neither do I. Something to do with money, managing other people's and lots of it. Bud and I are very well provided for. He's at a great school and I'm home all day working on my novel when I'm not doing one of the million things that parents do. That's what I am, a novelist.

KATHARINE   Would you have written a novel I might have read?

WILL   Yes, but not yet.

KATHARINE   You *are* confident.

WILL   Not really. I've published a couple of short stories. Do you read *The New Yorker*?

KATHARINE   I'm a subscriber. I like to keep up.

WILL   They published one of my short stories last summer. It was called "Diamond Head." It had nothing to do with Hawaii. It took place in Brooklyn at a 24-hour diner called Diamond Head. Everyone was very alienated. It was pretty depressing.

KATHARINE   I generally don't read their fiction. I stopped after Salinger.

WILL   Wow! That was before I was born. Anyway, the short stories are sort of a muscle-flexing for my novel. That's what my agent calls them. It will be my first.

KATHARINE   Does it have a title?

WILL   Yes but I'm not going to tell you. It's bad luck.

KATHARINE   The world loves a good novel. We're still waiting for the Great American One.

WILL   I'll give it my best shot. (*Noises from the bathroom.*) Are you guys okay in there?

KATHARINE   I thought writers needed quiet, concentration.

WILL   They do but they're in short supply with a six-year-old. Everyone said we would need a nanny for Bud, so we tried one, but it turned out we liked doing everything ourselves, so we let her go. The

Great American Novel can wait. Who knows? Maybe I'll find a way before then. Anyway, to answer your question, Cal and I met online.

KATHARINE   I don't understand.

WILL   We met on the Internet.

KATHARINE   I'm completely in the dark when it comes to internets.

WILL   It's how people meet now. You go to a website. There's something for everyone. Christian Couples, Foxy Ladies, Mormon You-Name-Its. Not very romantic but it gets the job done. I saw Cal's picture and read his profile. It said *Moby-Dick* was his favorite book. I'm a sucker for men who love Melville every time, especially men who look like Cal and their favorite singer is Ella Fitzgerald, too. Thirty minutes later we met at Gray's Papaya on Broadway and West 72nd St., a place even less romantic than ManHunt. He was eating a hotdog. Even with his back turned, I knew it was him. I went up to the counter, ordered, took a deep breath, and then turned to this perfect stranger and said "Call me Ishmael." Cal doesn't believe in love at first sight. He thinks love takes time. I think it's all in that first time you look into each other's eyes. If they're not looking back at you—it's not going to happen.

KATHARINE   Is one of you the father?

WILL   We both are.

KATHARINE   I meant the actual father.

WILL   We both are.

KATHARINE   Everything I say is inappropriate.

WILL   It's uninformed. What do you want to know?

KATHARINE   I'm only trying to determine if one of you is the biological father.

WILL   We used my sperm—we thought it would be healthier, me being younger—and the eggs of an anonymous donor. After the magic of the embryo happened in the Petrie Dish, our lesbian friend Roberta carried Bud to term—only we didn't know he was going to be a son yet. Cal didn't want to know the sex. He wanted to be surprised. I couldn't wait. I was into the whole baby thing from Day One. I loved everything about it. The doctors, the tests, the procedures, the sonograms, the waiting rooms, the other parents-to-be, straight and gay.

Completely amazing, all of it. I was a gay man and I was going to be a father. I wanted to tell everybody and I probably did: I'm a gay man and I'm going to be a father. It's just so joyful being a parent. I told Cal, it's better than crack. I look at Bud sometimes and I just start crying. Sometimes he catches me. "What's the matter, pappy?" "Nothing, honey, I'm just so happy you're here."

KATHARINE   So there's really nothing of Andre in him, is there?

WILL   Why would there be?

KATHARINE   Of course not. What a foolish thing to say. (*CAL comes out of the bathroom.*)

CAL   He's wearing his goggles and seeing how long he can hold his breath underwater. We found the right bubbles: *Étoile de Paris.*

WILL   Who sent him that stuff anyway? Which one of his fairy godfathers?

CAL   Jeremy.

WILL   We're raising Bud to be gay. That's our only expectation for him. God forbid we should let him turn out the way he wants to be.

CAL   Will's joking, of course, we're not raising him anything.

KATHARINE   Andre loved bubble baths.

WILL   There you go!

CAL   Will!

WILL   What are you doing here, Mrs. Gerard? What do you want? It is suspiciously quiet in the bathroom all of a sudden. I'm turning into my mother.

KATHARINE   I thought only women turned into their mothers.

WILL   Men have gotten very good at it. Don't let me forget to give you the name of that restaurant. (*He goes.*)

KATHARINE   My mother was a very nice woman. Everyone adored her, especially Andre.

CAL   Andre tried to communicate with you.

KATHARINE   No, he didn't. He led his secret, furtive life up here and kept his father and me in the dark. He thought he was fooling us. His father maybe but not me. I knew, I always knew.

CAL   Your disapproval frightened him and it's making me sick to my stomach, all over again. You haven't changed.

KATHARINE   People don't change. That's one of the lies we tell ourselves.

CAL   People have to want to change.

KATHARINE   Maybe that's it.

CAL   That's honest.

KATHARINE   This was a bad idea. I could just as easily have sent it back to you.

CAL   I'm not sure I even want it. He would have killed me for sending it to you. He didn't believe people kept diaries for other people to read.

And for the first time we will notice a small journal on the coffee table or somewhere else in the living room. It was Andre's journal.

KATHARINE   That is popular opinion.

CAL   He thought people needed someplace safe, safe from everyone else.

KATHARINE   I've sat with it for hours, holding it, pressing it to my heart, but never opening it.

CAL   Neither did I. When he was alive or when he was gone.

KATHARINE   You should have destroyed it.

CAL   I couldn't. I didn't have that right. I still don't. I loved him but I didn't want to know his secrets.

KATHARINE   So you sent them on to me?

CAL   I always wondered if they would somehow find their way back to me.

KATHARINE   Only if I brought them.

CAL   I thought this day might come.

KATHARINE   We both did.

CAL   I guess I've been expecting you.

KATHARINE   I almost didn't come this time either.

CAL   Either?

KATHARINE   The last time we were in New York I called. When you answered, I hung up. And I don't speak to answering machines. Another trip, someone else answered.

CAL   Will probably.

KATHARINE   But I found out what I wanted to. You weren't alone anymore.

CAL   I was alone for 8 years, 8 shitty years when all I learned was how to make money.

KATHARINE   And then there was Papaya House and *Moby-Dick*.

CAL   He told you.

KATHARINE   The gist, just the gist.

CAL   At first I was embarrassed about Will. Not his age. I worry about the difference more than he does. He knows what he's getting into. But it felt like a betrayal of Andre. Of us. Even after 8 years. How much could I have loved Andre if I can love Will the way I do now?

KATHARINE   Yes, how can you?

CAL   I don't know, I don't pretend to understand these things. I honestly think Andre sent Will to me.

KATHARINE   I wish he'd do the same for his mother.

CAL   Would you let him?

KATHARINE   I don't understand how my life turned out like this. I don't know what I'm supposed to think or feel anymore. I'm confused, I'm frightened, I'm angry about almost everything. I could let that ottoman put me in a rage. Thank God for *Jeopardy* and even that's started to annoy me. I've begun taking the bus everywhere just because it takes longer than if I drive myself. It's usually late, which makes me angrier. People like me don't take the bus in Dallas, Mr. Porter. Buses are for help. And then when I get to wherever I was going, I can't bring myself to leave wherever it is I've gone.

CAL   I've noticed that.

KATHARINE   I really have thought of taking my own life. I'm a widow. My only child predeceased me. No grandchildren. I don't like most people and I think it's a pretty safe assumption most people don't like me. I'm not a joiner. My eyes are going, so reading is hard. I never liked to cook. I always dreaded mealtime, now I detest it. I could go on. So does it really matter if I draw another breath?

CAL   That's a very poor solution, Mrs. Gerard.

KATHARINE   It's a good thing you're not a therapist. A woman on television drank a bottle of Clorox. It didn't work. They rescued her. Go to all that trouble to kill yourself and they rescue you! Well, *I* thought it was funny. It's a stupid show. They're all stupid.

CAL   Have you ever been in therapy?

KATHARINE   The whole notion of spilling your guts to a stranger and then paying him for the privilege? What? Are you going to charge me for this? I don't know why I told you any of it. Forget everything I said. "What about them Yankees?"

CAL   Andre thought of suicide when things got really bad. I'm very glad he didn't. I know that was selfish of me. We stuck it out together. Some together! They put him through hell trying to keep him alive. Some of the treatments were unbearably painful. You don't want to know. They were trying to find a cure and they didn't care how they went about it. That's not fair; they were desperate to find one but time wasn't on our side. One of our best friends was diagnosed 18 years ago, two years after Andre died. He's skiing in Park City as we speak. Today, Andre would still be alive. We probably wouldn't have a child; there might be a Tony Award on the mantel (he was good, really, really good, Mrs. Gerard, you should have come up the summer he played Hamlet); we would have just celebrated our 25th anniversary and doing our best to grow old gracefully together. I don't know what else I can tell you. I wasn't expecting this. This was going to be just another day.

KATHARINE   Do you ever worry about forgetting him?

CAL   A little bit, sure, but not the best part of him. Sometimes I panic that I can't remember the color of his eyes.

KATHARINE   Gray. (*Will returns.*)

WILL   Now he's got his snorkel on and is practicing his dead man's float. So don't have a heart attack if you go in there and find him like that. I've got the name of that restaurant, *Il Gatto Bianco*, The White Cat. It's just off the Piazza San—I'm sorry, am I interrupting?

KATHARINE   Your husband has been telling me what he thinks of me.

CAL   That's not true.

WILL   What is that?

KATHARINE   That I'm a terrible woman. Men are noble, good. Men are to be loved. Women—especially mothers—are evil, cunning, vile even. Pity the young man who has a mother such as Andre's. He was doomed to a life of AIDS.

CAL   This is unspeakable. I hoped you'd let Andre go. That some part of you had accepted our loss.

KATHARINE   It will never be "our" loss. You lost a man and quickly found other men. I lost a son.

CAL   I'm sorry, I will always be sorry.

KATHARINE   Not good enough. The two of you, this fancy apartment, a child of your own who will no doubt grow up to cure cancer and take the men's title at Wimbledon. Any mother would be proud to have a son like that. I'll order another one myself. How much do they cost? What other tangible evidence of happiness haven't you shown me yet? Why did your life get better after Andre and mine got worse? Why haven't you been punished?

CAL   I can't help you, Mrs. Gerard.

WILL   Talk to her, Cal.

CAL   Bud, Buddy, are you still in there? You'll turn into a prune! (*He goes to check on Bud.*)

WILL   I know we can't understand your loss, Mrs. Gerard, but we are trying to respect it. If anything had happened to me before my mother died! I always thought she was worried it would. So were a lot of parents. I think she was relieved when I met Cal as much as anything. Loss. It's a terrible word.

KATHARINE   I know what loss means.

WILL   Try to respect Cal's. He lost more than your son. He lost a generation. People who might have mattered. Hamlets. Nureyevs. Melvilles and Whitmans. Young men who wanted to write the Great American Novel, too.

KATHARINE   Why are you telling me this?

WILL   I think people like Cal have been punished enough, Mrs. Gerard. I try to imagine what those years were like for him and Andre but I don't get very far. Maybe I don't want to. The mind shuts down— or the capacity to care. It's one way of dealing with it.

KATHARINE   I don't have that luxury.

WILL   Of course you don't. Neither does Cal. "What Happened to Gay Men in the Final Decades of the 20th Century." First it will be a chapter in a history book, then a paragraph, then a footnote. People will shake their heads and say "What a terrible thing, how sad." It's already started to happen. I can feel it happening. All the raw edges of pain dulled, deadened, drained away.

KATHARINE   I know what I did wrong: I didn't go out and find another Andre just as soon as I could.

WILL   I'm not another Andre, Mrs. Gerard.

KATHARINE   No one knows that better than I. It's presumptuous of you to think you could ever take his place.

WILL   Cal didn't want another Andre.

KATHARINE   There is no other Andre, just mine, and he is gone forever and I will mourn him forever. I don't want peace or closure— another word I detest. I want revenge. I'm Hamlet. Take my picture. I'm my own poster. Vengeance!

WILL   You won't find it here.

KATHARINE   Then where?

WILL   I don't know but not in our home.

KATHARINE   It's not a home, it's an apartment. I hate it when people call their apartments homes.

WILL   You say "hate" a lot.

KATHARINE   I dislike imprecision. You're a writer, so should you. (*Cal returns.*)

CAL   I said he could stay in for another 5 minutes. We don't have a child, we have a fish.

KATHARINE   I still want to know what you're going to tell him when he grows out of bathtubs.

WILL   I told you.

KATHARINE   Easier said than done, Mr . . .

WILL   Ogden.

KATHARINE   Ogden. Easier said than done. (*Will has noticed Andre's diary.*)

WILL   What's this? "A.G."?

CAL   A diary Andre kept, a journal. I sent it to Mrs. Gerard quite a few years ago and now she's returning it to me.

KATHARINE   I bought it for him on his 18th birthday.

CAL   I didn't know that.

KATHARINE   He hated the initials on the cover. He thought they were tacky. I thought they were classy. "A.G." It's the very last trace of him, that he ever existed.

CAL   There isn't a day I don't think of him.

KATHARINE   How does that make Mr. Porter's second husband feel?

WILL   I'm Cal's first husband. I like precision, too.

KATHARINE   I stand corrected.

WILL   I'm happy he was in a good relationship before he met me. If you're wondering if I'm jealous, I am a little bit. Cal and I weren't young together. I never got to see him screw things up the way he sees me screw up. He was all evolved and perfect and his own man by the time I met him. I'm sure Andre had a lot to do with that.

CAL   He did. (*Will opens the diary.*) What are you doing?

WILL   Aren't you curious? Very legible handwriting. (*He reads from it.*) "Fourth of July weekend. The Pines. Parker lent us his house while he's on jury duty."

KATHARINE   What are the Pines?

CAL   A community on Fire Island.

WILL   A gay community. Who's "us"?

CAL   I don't know.

WILL   Who's Parker?

CAL   I don't know.

KATHARINE   I'm sure I'm in there somewhere. It won't be flattering.

WILL   "I told my mother I was on the Cape, as if she knew what the Pines were, let alone Fire Island. The Pines is the new Port Chester. Lord, what fools we mortals be."

KATHARINE   I told you so.

WILL   "It's a beautiful day. Enjoy it while it lasts. Rain tomorrow. Right now the ocean is blue, perfect surf. I didn't want to get out but I have to run lines. It's my first Albee, the theatre said he's coming, (all the way to Providence? Really?) and I want to be good. There's a beautiful sailboat way out on the horizon (Parker has great binoculars) probably on its way to Nantucket or Martha's Vineyard. Anyway, I'm just breathing and feeling the sun and enjoying the sea breeze and wondering why life can't always be like this. The cute guy in the house next door just came out on his deck again. To be continued." It's been more than five minutes. This is between the two of you. Coming, Buddy Bud Bud! (*He goes.*)

CAL   Bud likes one of us to dry him after his tub.

KATHARINE   Andre loved my mother drying him off after a tub. She'd stand him on top of the toilet seat and put a bath towel between his two little legs and go back and forth with it. See-saw, she'd go, see-saw. I never approved. I think it's improper to touch a child down there. I don't know why I told you that. And no, I don't think Andre turned out gay because my mother ran a towel between his legs and went "See-saw, see-saw."

CAL   I wasn't going to say that.

KATHARINE   But you thought it was what I was thinking.

CAL   Nothing made Andre gay.

KATHARINE   I didn't. (*Cal holds the journal out to her.*)

CAL   Read from anywhere.

KATHARINE   "Kansas City. We're a hit. The local cricket said I had a lot of promise . . . " He called them crickets instead of . . .

CAL   I know.

KATHARINE   " . . . .of promise and predicted a bright future." I can't.

CAL   He's your son. (*She goes to another part of the journal.*)

KATHARINE   "Cal bought a NordicTrack and is taking lots of vitamins. I think he's scared. We both know I've put him at risk but we don't talk about it. It's just there, our own elephant in the room. I'm not a bad person, just a very imperfect one. Cal deserved so much better than me." Should I stop? (*Cal is motionless.*) "One day we're certain we're going to beat this. The next, I'm dying. Cal is a rock. I am blessed. My family wouldn't be able to handle it."

CAL   I wasn't a rock but I'm glad he thought so.

Will enters with Bud, who is in a terrycloth robe. Bud's hair is wet.

WILL   Meet the cleanest young man on Central Park West. You clean up good for a little boy, Buddy Bud Bud.

BUD   I'm not a little boy. I'm almost 7. (*To Katharine.*) Do you like our apartment? At the Thanksgiving Day Parade, Spider Man is so close to our window you can almost touch him.

WILL   You're lucky you have *two* dads to keep you from falling out.

BUD   Can I have a cookie?

WILL   You know where they are.

BUD   Would you like something, Andre's mother?

KATHARINE   No, thank you. I'd like you to call me Katharine.

BUD   Pappy?

WILL   Sure. (*Bud goes. We will hear sounds from the kitchen from time to time. Doors, drawers opening and closing.*)

KATHARINE   I've stayed way too long. I'll be late.

CAL   For what? You said you didn't have any friends, especially in the big cold city.

KATHARINE   The Algonquin and I are not total strangers. The Dorothy Parker Suite and I have become very good friends.

CAL   Andre loved Dorothy Parker.

KATHARINE   Who do you think got him reading her?

WILL   Our doorman will help you get a cab. Unfortunately, this is the worst time for one. They all have their Off Duty lights on.

BUD (*Off.*)   Pappy! Pappy! (*There is the sound of crash, things breaking*) Ow! (*He begins to cry.*)

WILL   Coming, honey, pappy's there! I've got it. (*He goes.*)

CAL   You should have held me that day in the park. I'd lost Andre, too. Instead you made me feel ashamed and unwanted, just as you'd made Andre feel. We weren't strong then against people like you. You held all the cards. He wanted your love all his life, so much he had to pretend he didn't. So did I that day, God forgive me. I wanted you to love me for loving Andre. I wanted to forgive you. I don't anymore. I don't care. If you hadn't done this I wonder if I would have thought of you ever again. No offense, but I don't think news of your passing will make the *New York Times*, Mrs. Gerard. And then there truly will be none. It is sad when you think about it. But this thing isn't over. This thing that brought us all together and can still tear us apart. Young men are still falling in love but some of them are still being infected. And some of them are still dying. If anything like this happened to Bud—or Will, sure, there's that possibility, too—I would be devastated but I would not reject either one of them. I'm Will's husband, not his judge; Bud's father, not his scourge. If that were my son wasting, writhing, incoherent, incontinent in that bed in St. Vincent's, I would want him to know how much I loved him, how much I would always love him. I did what I could for Andre. I hope to this day it was enough. (*He collects himself.*) Being a parent has made me quite defenseless. It's a good thing I don't want anything from you anymore. I'll get your coat.

KATHARINE   I couldn't hold you when I should have had my son to hold. I still can't.

CAL   Jesus Christ, woman, reach out to someone, let someone in.

KATHARINE   There is so much I want to say that's not about Andre. It's about me and no one else. Me, as if I were the only person on the planet which is what I have felt all my life. There were other people: a mother, a father, a husband. It didn't matter. I was still alone. And then there was Andre and I thought everything would be fine. He was going to fix it. He didn't even come close. Maybe when he fell down and I soothed him until he stopped crying, I felt a connection. When he was in pain, I was his mother. When he needed me. Like what's going on in there. (*She means the kitchen off where Bud and Will are.*) Don't mistake that for love. It means comfort. It means concern. It doesn't mean love. I watched Andre give our dog more of himself than he gave me.

CAL   We've all felt like that. It's human nature being ridiculous.

KATHARINE   He was a dachshund turning gray. Andre tried to dye him with some of my hair coloring. It didn't work.

CAL   That sounds like Andre.

KATHARINE   I'm the only one who thought Andre was a difficult child. He was smarter than anyone else. He had secrets. I was afraid of him. He could be so remote. I didn't know where he'd go in his head. I wanted him to take me with him—away from Dallas and a husband I didn't love and never *tried* to love; he was unlovable. Some people are, you know—I've turned into one—but I would have married anyone who took me out of Port Chester, even if it was only across the railroad tracks to Rye. But Mr. Gerard wanted to go west, young man. Which is ridiculous because he wasn't a young man and Dallas isn't the west, it's Dallas. I was, I am a Yankee. I remain one. I need four seasons. I need to be around people who know what time it is. I don't suffer fools. I was a smart young woman. I thought I was going to die with that secret. My father worked in the post office. My mother spent the day ironing and baking and cleaning and we ate on a table covered with an oilcloth. With my Port Chester High diploma, I went to work for a dentist, Dr. Minnerly. Dr. Pain his patients called him. He didn't believe in Novocain. I hated him and I hated my job (you can tell your husband I know how much I use that word; he didn't score any points there.). Every week I saved my money until I had enough to buy myself an evening dress that would get me into the Rye Country Club Spring Dance where I knew I would meet my savior and I did. I got him to marry me like *that*. (*She snaps her fingers.*) And I didn't get knocked up to get him to do it, like most of my girlfriends. I turned on the charm. I can when I want to. I've given you a glimpse of it. And I always had good legs. I still do. Andre got his legs from me. He had beautiful legs for a man.

CAL   Yes, yes he did.

KATHARINE   And I thought I could be happy for a little bit. I don't know what I mean by happy anymore. I thought I did then: content, not jealous, able to stop jiggling. I'm a nervous woman. I still can't cross my legs without jiggling them. Andre once said, "Mom, you look like a woman in heat when you pump your legs like that." He could be very fresh. I wanted to slap him. Then, out of the blue, just like that, he decides he wants to be an actor. Drama club, acting lessons, singing, dancing. And I was his chauffeur for all of this. I read a lot of good books in the car, waiting for Andre, our gray dachshund happily drooling away on the seat beside me. I got thanks, I got presents, I got "I love you" but I didn't get him. I got everything else but him. He was supposed to let me love him the way I'd never been loved. I was going to make him happy the way I'd never been. And then he was off to New York City. Suddenly he had a life and it had nothing to do with me. All I was was Andre's mother: the woman who bore him. He wrote something when he wasn't much older than your boy. "God bless the Lord. God bless my mommy. She has good things in her oven."

CAL   That's lovely.

KATHARINE   I was Andre's mother to him as much as I was to any of his little friends. "Can I have a cookie, Andre's mother?" "You can if you call me Mrs. Gerard." But they never did. I wasn't a person to them either. I was Andre's mother. I got pregnant when Andre was four. I aborted it. I never told anyone. I was waiting for the right time to tell Andre. It was going to be our final secret together.

CAL   Andre loved you.

KATHARINE   We all say we love someone. Words are the bridge we build across the void that separates us, desperate to cling to something. "I love you" is the best we've come up with for pretending it isn't there.

CAL   I don't agree with you.

KATHARINE   I'm almost done. Before I knew it, he was in New York and then there was a friend, who became a roommate, who became a lover.

CAL   That would be me, Katharine.

KATHARINE   You took him from me forever.

CAL   All you had to do was open your heart to him.

KATHARINE   I couldn't, I still can't. I don't know why, I don't care why anymore. It sickens me. After all these years, it still sickens me.

CAL   Is it the sex? Two men, physically intimate? Fucking, sucking, making love? All those things people do and are never going to stop.

KATHARINE   It's everything. What kind of life is that child going to have?

CAL   A better one than Andre's. A better one than yours.

KATHARINE   There's only one thing I ever did to Andre that I'm ashamed of. If he were here I would fall to my knees and tell him how sorry I am. He'd just gone to New York. I called him. It was late, very late. I woke him up. "What's wrong, mom? Are you okay?" I was laughing, I was crying, I'd been drinking. I said, "Honey, your mother just let a man pick her up at the Adolphus Hotel and he drove me in his car to the very edge of Dallas where it was still woody and dark and he started making love to me. I couldn't do it and I asked him to take me back to town. He could have been very nasty about it but he wasn't. I think he was married, too. So what do you think of your old lady now, kiddo? Somebody still wants to fuck her." He didn't say anything. After a while one of us hung up. We never spoke of it. I won't ask if he told you that story.

CAL   Thank you.

KATHARINE   And when his father was in the hospital after the first surgery for lung cancer, (I said there was only one thing, Mr. Porter. I lied. There were two. Things that can never be taken back.) I found Andre in the visitors' lounge. He was crying. I said, "I know why you're crying. You're not crying for your father. You're crying because of what you are."

CAL   I know, Mrs. Gerard. He called me right after from a pay phone there. He was pretty devastated.

KATHARINE   Can you imagine a mother saying that to her son? Her only child?

CAL   I'll get your coat.

KATHARINE   Please. (*But she doesn't move.*)

CAL   I don't want the journal.

KATHARINE   Neither do I. (*Cal brings the coat to her. He tries to help her with it but her arms stay at her side. The coat hangs on her shoulders. Awkwardly, they hug goodbye.*) Thank you. (*Bud and Will come back into the* *room. Bud is in his pajamas. He has a Band-Aid on his forehead from where he fell. He is carrying a glass of milk and a plate of Oreo cookies for Katharine. Will is right behind him.*)

WILL   Ta-da! In lieu of martinis, Master Bud Ogden-Porter is offering milk and Oreos this evening.

KATHARINE   Evening! I really must go. What time is it?

CAL   Honey, your head! Let Pop-pop see.

BUD   Pappy fixed it.

CAL   Did he give you a kiss and make it go away?

BUD   That's for little boys.

WILL (*To Cal.*)   Of course I did.

CAL   Is he okay?

WILL   A little scratch. That chair is too wobbly to stand on, I told you this would happen.

Bud has walked over to Katharine who is still sitting where she was.

BUD   Here. I was crying, too. These will make you stop. They're Oreos.

KATHARINE   Thank you.

BUD   Do they have Oreos where you live?

KATHARINE   I think they have Oreos everywhere.

BUD   You don't have to be my grandmother if you don't want. (*Katharine still hasn't taken an Oreo or touched the milk.*) They're really good, Katharine.

CAL   That's enough, Buddy.

KATHARINE   What did you call me?

BUD   I'm sorry, you're Andre's mother.

KATHARINE   No, I'm Katharine. Thank you, Bud. (*She takes an Oreo and bites into it.*) This is an excellent Oreo. I think it might be the best Oreo ever. (*She takes another bite.*) I'm sure of it.

BUD   Aren't you going to drink your milk? (*Katharine takes up the glass of milk.*)

KATHARINE   It's ice cold, just the way it should be. (*She takes a sip of the milk.*) Excellent.

BUD   You have a milk mustache.

KATHARINE   So do you.

BUD   Do you want me to tell you a story? I know how to tell stories. But you can't cry anymore, Katharine. (*He sits next to her.*) Once upon a time, there was a boy with two fathers: Pappy and Pop-pop. They lived up high where they could see Spider Man very, very close every Thanksgiving. They were blessed. But they had no grandmother. (*Cal and Will are close together but apart from Katharine and Bud. Bud continues to spin his tale. The fireplace looks especially appropriate. Katharine still has her coat on. We hear a clear, lyric soprano singing "L'amerò, saro costante" from Mozart's IL RE PASTORE, the same music that was performed at Andre's memorial service. Katharine takes it in.*)

KATHARINE   Oh.

BUD   One day they found one. She had a milk mustache and her name was Katharine.

The four of them have stopped moving. The lights have stopped fading. Instead they are swiftly raised to a blinding white intensity. We look at them like this, motionless, until the lights snap off.

END OF PLAY

ACKNOWLEDGMENTS

I would like to thank the following people for making me who I am today: my father, Hubert Arthur McNally; my mother, Dorothy Katharine McNally (née Rapp); my maternal grandmother, Margaret Rapp; *The Lone Ranger* and *Let's Pretend;* Claude Barbizon; Burr Tilstrom and Kukla, Fran and Ollie; J.D. Salinger; Rand Carter; Maria Callas; Giuseppe Verdi; Maurine McElroy; James Dean; William Shakespeare; Jared Carter; Michael Kahn; Giotto; Tennessee Williams and Eugene O'Neill; Zoe Caldwell; Bob Dylan; Edward Albee; Robert Drivas; James Coco; Lyn Austin; John Steinbeck; Elaine Steinbeck; Henri Matisse; Elaine May; Lynne Meadow; John Tillinger; Nathan Lane; Chita Rivera; Dominic Cuskern; Lynn Ahrens; Stephen Flaherty; J.S. Bach; Raymond Frontain; Tom Kirdahy, my husband (the newest best word in the English language) and best friend (always the best word in the English language); Terry the Terrier.

We really do get by with a little help from our friends.